SHORT STORIES *for Students*

Advisors

Erik France: Adjunct Instructor of English, Macomb Community College, Warren, Michigan. B.A. and M.S.L.S. from University of North Carolina, Chapel Hill; Ph.D. from Temple University.

Kate Hamill: Grade 12 English Teacher, Catonsville High School, Catonsville, Maryland.

Joseph McGeary: English Teacher, Germantown Friends School, Philadelphia, Pennsylvania. Ph.D. in English from Duke University.

Timothy Showalter: English Department Chair, Franklin High School, Reisterstown, Maryland. Certified teacher by the Maryland State Department of Education. Member of the National Council of Teachers of English.

Amy Spade Silverman: English Department Chair, Kehillah Jewish High School, Palo Alto, California. Member of National Council of Teachers of English (NCTE), Teachers and Writers, and NCTE Opinion Panel. Exam Reader, Advanced Placement Literature and Composition. Poet, published in *North American Review, Nimrod,* and *Michigan Quarterly Review,* among other publications.

Jody Stefansson: Director of Boswell Library and Study Center and Upper School Learning Specialist, Polytechnic School, Pasadena, California. Board member, Children's Literature Council of Southern California. Member of American Library Association, Association of Independent School Librarians, and Association of Educational Therapists.

Laura Jean Waters: Certified School Library Media Specialist, Wilton High School, Wilton, Connecticut. B.A. from Fordham University; M.A. from Fairfield University.

SHORT STORIES for Students

Presenting Analysis, Context, and Criticism on Commonly Studied Short Stories

VOLUME 30

Sara Constantakis, Project Editor

Foreword by Thomas E. Barden

Detroit • New York • San Francisco • New Haven, Conn • Waterville, Maine • London

Short Stories for Students, Volume 30

Project Editor: Sara Constantakis

Rights Acquisition and Management: Jermaine Bobbitt, Margaret Chamberlain-Gaston, Aja Perales, Robyn Young

Composition: Evi Abou-El-Seoud

Manufacturing: Drew Kalasky

Imaging: John Watkins

Product Design: Pamela A. E. Galbreath, Jennifer Wahi

Content Conversion: Katrina Coach

Product Manager: Meggin Condino

Gale
27500 Drake Rd.
Farmington Hills, MI, 48331-3535

ISBN-13: 978-1-4144-6694-1
ISBN-10: 1-4144-6694-3

ISSN 1092-7735

This title is also available as an e-book.
ISBN-13: 978-1-4144-7456-4
ISBN-10: 1-4144-7456-3
Contact your Gale, a part of Cengage Learning sales representative for ordering information.

Printed in the United States of America
1 2 3 4 5 6 7 14 13 12 11 10

Table of Contents

Why Study Literature At All?

Short Stories for Students is designed to provide readers with information and discussion about a wide range of important contemporary and historical works of short fiction, and it does that job very well. However, I want to use this guest foreword to address a question that it does *not* take up. It is a fundamental question that is often ignored in high school and college English classes as well as research texts, and one that causes frustration among students at all levels, namely why study literature at all? Isn't it enough to read a story, enjoy it, and go about one's business? My answer (to be expected from a literary professional, I suppose) is no. It is not enough. It is a start; but it is not enough. Here's why.

First, literature is the only part of the educational curriculum that deals directly with the actual world of lived experience. The philosopher Edmund Husserl used the apt German term *die Lebenswelt*, "the living world," to denote this realm. All the other content areas of the modern American educational system avoid the subjective, present reality of everyday life. Science (both the natural and the social varieties) objectifies, the fine arts create and/or perform, history reconstructs. Only literary study persists in posing those questions we all asked before our schooling taught us to give up on them. Only literature gives credibility to personal perceptions, feelings, dreams, and the "stream of consciousness" that is our inner voice. Literature wonders about infinity, wonders why God permits evil, wonders what will happen to us after we die. Literature admits that we get our hearts broken, that people sometimes cheat and get away with it, that the world is a strange and probably incomprehensible place. Literature, in other words, takes on all the big and small issues of what it means to be human. So my first answer is that of the humanist we should read literature and study it and take it seriously because it enriches us as human beings. We develop our moral imagination, our capacity to sympathize with other people, and our ability to understand our existence through the experience of fiction.

My second answer is more practical. By studying literature we can learn how to explore and analyze texts. Fiction may be about *die Lebenswelt*, but it is a construct of words put together in a certain order by an artist using the medium of language. By examining and studying those constructions, we can learn about language as a medium. We can become more sophisticated about word associations and connotations, about the manipulation of symbols, and about style and atmosphere. We can grasp how ambiguous language is and how important context and texture is to meaning. In our first encounter with a work of literature, of course, we are not supposed to catch all of these things. We are spellbound, just as the writer wanted us to be. It is as serious students of the writer's art that we begin to see how the tricks are done.

Seeing the tricks, which is another way of saying "developing analytical and close reading skills," is important above and beyond its intrinsic literary educational value. These skills transfer to other fields and enhance critical thinking of any kind. Understanding how language is used to construct texts is powerful knowledge. It makes engineers better problem solvers, lawyers better advocates and courtroom practitioners, politicians better rhetoricians, marketing and advertising agents better sellers, and citizens more aware consumers as well as better participants in democracy. This last point is especially important, because rhetorical skill works both ways when we learn how language is manipulated in the making of texts the result is that we become less susceptible when language is used to manipulate us.

My third reason is related to the second. When we begin to see literature as created artifacts of language, we become more sensitive to good writing in general. We get a stronger sense of the importance of individual words, even the sounds of words and word combinations. We begin to understand Mark Twain's delicious proverb "The difference between the right word and the almost right word is the difference between lightning and a lightning bug." Getting beyond the "enjoyment only" stage of literature gets us closer to becoming makers of word art ourselves. I am not saying that studying fiction will turn every student into a Faulkner or a Shakespeare. But it will make us more adaptable and effective writers, even if our art form ends up being the office memo or the corporate annual report.

Studying short stories, then, can help students become better readers, better writers, and even better human beings. But I want to close with a warning. If your study and exploration of the craft, history, context, symbolism, or anything else about a story starts to rob it of the magic you felt when you first read it, it is time to stop. Take a break, study another subject, shoot some hoops, or go for a run. Love of reading is too important to be ruined by school. The early twentieth century writer Willa Cather, in her novel *My Antonia*, has her narrator Jack Burden tell a story that he and Antonia heard from two old Russian immigrants when they were teenagers. These immigrants, Pavel and Peter, told about an incident from their youth back in Russia that the narrator could recall in vivid detail thirty years later. It was a harrowing story of a wedding party starting home in sleds and being chased by starving wolves. Hundreds of wolves attacked the group's sleds one by one as they sped across the snow trying to reach their village. In a horrible revelation, the old Russians revealed that the groom eventually threw his own bride to the wolves to save himself. There was even a hint that one of the old immigrants might have been the groom mentioned in the story. Cather has her narrator conclude with his feelings about the story. "We did not tell Pavel's secret to anyone, but guarded it jealously as if the wolves of the Ukraine had gathered that night long ago, and the wedding party had been sacrificed, just to give us a painful and peculiar pleasure." That feeling, that painful and peculiar pleasure, is the most important thing about literature. Study and research should enhance that feeling and never be allowed to overwhelm it.

Thomas E. Barden
Professor of English and Director of Graduate English Studies,
The University of Toledo

Introduction

Purpose of the Book

The purpose of *Short Stories for Students* (*SSfS*) is to provide readers with a guide to understanding, enjoying, and studying short stories by giving them easy access to information about the work. Part of Gale's "For Students" Literature line, *SSfS* is specifically designed to meet the curricular needs of high school and undergraduate college students and their teachers, as well as the interests of general readers and researchers considering specific short fiction. While each volume contains entries on "classic" stories frequently studied in classrooms, there are also entries containing hard-to-find information on contemporary stories, including works by multicultural, international, and women writers.

The information covered in each entry includes an introduction to the story and the story's author; a plot summary, to help readers unravel and understand the events in the work; descriptions of important characters, including explanation of a given character's role in the narrative as well as discussion about that character's relationship to other characters in the story; analysis of important themes in the story; and an explanation of important literary techniques and movements as they are demonstrated in the work.

In addition to this material, which helps the readers analyze the story itself, students are also provided with important information on the literary and historical background informing each work. This includes a historical context essay, a box comparing the time or place the story was written to modern Western culture, a critical overview essay, and excerpts from critical essays on the story or author. A unique feature of *SSfS* is a specially commissioned critical essay on each story, targeted toward the student reader.

To further help today's student in studying and enjoying each story, information on audiobooks and other media adaptations is provided (if available), as well as reading suggestions for works of fiction and nonfiction on similar themes and topics. Classroom aids include ideas for research papers and lists of critical and reference sources that provide additional material on the work.

Selection Criteria

The titles for each volume of *SSfS* were selected by surveying numerous sources on teaching literature and analyzing course curricula for various school districts. Some of the sources surveyed include: literature anthologies, *Reading Lists for College-Bound Students: The Books Most Recommended by America's Top Colleges*; Teaching the Short Story: A Guide to Using Stories from around the World, by the National Council of Teachers of English (NCTE); and "A Study of High School Literature Anthologies," conducted by Arthur Applebee at the Center for the Learning and Teaching of Literature and sponsored by the National Endowment for the Arts and the Office of Educational Research and Improvement.

Input was also solicited from our advisory board, as well as educators from various areas. From these discussions, it was determined that each volume should have a mix of "classic" stories (those works commonly taught in literature classes) and contemporary stories for which information is often hard to find. Because of the interest in expanding the canon of literature, an emphasis was also placed on including works by international, multicultural, and women authors. Our advisory board members—educational professionals—helped pare down the list for each volume. Works not selected for the present volume were noted as possibilities for future volumes. As always, the editor welcomes suggestions for titles to be included in future volumes.

How Each Entry Is Organized

Each entry, or chapter, in *SSfS* focuses on one story. Each entry heading lists the title of the story, the author's name, and the date of the story's publication. The following elements are contained in each entry:

Introduction: a brief overview of the story which provides information about its first appearance, its literary standing, any controversies surrounding the work, and major conflicts or themes within the work.

Author Biography: this section includes basic facts about the author's life, and focuses on events and times in the author's life that may have inspired the story in question.

Plot Summary: a description of the events in the story. Lengthy summaries are broken down with subheads.

Characters: an alphabetical listing of the characters who appear in the story. Each character name is followed by a brief to an extensive description of the character's role in the story, as well as discussion of the character's actions, relationships, and possible motivation.

Characters are listed alphabetically by last name. If a character is unnamed—for instance, the narrator in "The Eatonville Anthology"—the character is listed as "The Narrator" and alphabetized as "Narrator." If a character's first name is the only one given, the name will appear alphabetically by that name.

Themes: a thorough overview of how the topics, themes, and issues are addressed within the story. Each theme discussed appears in a separate subhead.

Style: this section addresses important style elements of the story, such as setting, point of view, and narration; important literary devices used, such as imagery, foreshadowing, symbolism; and, if applicable, genres to which the work might have belonged, such as Gothicism or Romanticism. Literary terms are explained within the entry, but can also be found in the Glossary.

Historical Context: this section outlines the social, political, and cultural climate in which the author lived and the work was created. This section may include descriptions of related historical events, pertinent aspects of daily life in the culture, and the artistic and literary sensibilities of the time in which the work was written. If the story is historical in nature, information regarding the time in which the story is set is also included. Long sections are broken down with helpful subheads.

Critical Overview: this section provides background on the critical reputation of the author and the story, including bannings or any other public controversies surrounding the work. For older works, this section may include a history of how the story was first received and how perceptions of it may have changed over the years; for more recent works, direct quotes from early reviews may also be included.

Criticism: an essay commissioned by *SSfS* which specifically deals with the story and is written specifically for the student audience, as well as excerpts from previously published criticism on the work (if available).

Sources: an alphabetical list of critical material used in compiling the entry, with bibliographical information.

Further Reading: an alphabetical list of other critical sources which may prove useful for the student. Includes full bibliographical information and a brief annotation.

In addition, each entry contains the following highlighted sections, set apart from the main text as sidebars:

Media Adaptations: if available, a list of audiobooks and important film and television adaptations of the story, including source information. The list also includes stage adaptations, musical adaptations, etc.

Topics for Further Study: a list of potential study questions or research topics dealing with the story. This section includes questions related to other disciplines the student may be studying, such as American history, world history, science, math, government, business, geography, economics, psychology, etc.

Compare and Contrast: an "at-a-glance" comparison of the cultural and historical differences between the author's time and culture and late twentieth century or early twenty-first century Western culture. This box includes pertinent parallels between the major scientific, political, and cultural movements of the time or place the story was written, the time or place the story was set (if a historical work), and modern Western culture. Works written after 1990 may not have this box.

What Do I Read Next?: a list of works that might give a reader points of entry into a classic work (e.g., YA or multicultural titles) and/or complement the featured story or serve as a contrast to it. This includes works by the same author and others, works from various genres, YA works, and works from various cultures and eras.

Other Features

SSfS includes "Why Study Literature At All?," a foreword by Thomas E. Barden, Professor of English and Director of Graduate English Studies at the University of Toledo. This essay provides a number of very fundamental reasons for studying literature and, therefore, reasons why a book such as *SSfS*, designed to facilitate the study of literture, is useful.

A Cumulative Author/Title Index lists the authors and titles covered in each volume of the *SSfS* series.

A Cumulative Nationality/Ethnicity Index breaks down the authors and titles covered in each volume of the *SSfS* series by nationality and ethnicity.

A Subject/Theme Index, specific to each volume, provides easy reference for users who may be studying a particular subject or theme rather than a single work. Significant subjects from events to broad themes are included.

Each entry may include illustrations, including photo of the author, stills from film adaptations (if available), maps, and/or photos of key historical events.

Citing Short Stories for Students

When writing papers, students who quote directly from any volume of *SSfS* may use the following general forms to document their source. These examples are based on MLA style; teachers may request that students adhere to a different style, thus, the following examples may be adapted as needed.

When citing text from *SSfS* that is not attributed to a particular author (for example, the Themes, Style, Historical Context sections, etc.), the following format may be used:

> "The Celebrated Jumping Frog of Calavaras County." *Short Stories for Students.* Ed. Kathleen Wilson. Vol. 1. Detroit: Gale, 1997. 19–20.

When quoting the specially commissioned essay from *SSfS* (usually the first essay under the Criticism subhead), the following format may be used:

> Korb, Rena. Critical Essay on "Children of the Sea." *Short Stories for Students.* Ed. Kathleen Wilson. Vol. 1. Detroit: Gale, 1997. 39–42.

When quoting a journal or newspaper essay that is reprinted in a volume of *SSfS*, the following form may be used:

> Schmidt, Paul. "The Deadpan on Simon Wheeler." *Southwest Review* 41.3 (Summer, 1956): 270–77. Excerpted and reprinted in *Short Stories for Students.* Vol. 1. Ed. Kathleen Wilson. Detroit: Gale, 1997. 29–31.

When quoting material from a book that is reprinted in a volume of *SSfS*, the following form may be used:

> Bell-Villada, Gene H. "The Master of Short Forms." *García Márquez: The Man and His Work.* University of North Carolina Press, 1990. 119–36. Excerpted and reprinted in *Short Stories for Students.* Vol. 1. Ed. Kathleen Wilson. Detroit: Gale, 1997. 89–90.

We Welcome Your Suggestions

The editorial staff of *Short Stories for Students* welcomes your comments and ideas. Readers who wish to suggest short stories to appear in future volumes, or who have other suggestions, are cordially invited to contact the editor. You may contact the editor via E-mail at: **ForStudentsEditors@cengage.com.** Or write to the editor at:

Editor, *Short Stories for Students*
Gale
27500 Drake Road
Farmington Hills, MI 48331-3535

Literary Chronology

1821: Fyodor Mikhailovich Dostoevsky is born on November 11 in Moscow, Russia.

1837: Nathaniel Hawthorne's short story "Dr. Heidegger's Experiment" is published in *Knickerbocker* magazine.

1864: Nathaniel Hawthorne dies on May 19 in Plymouth, New Hampshire.

1867: Luigi Pirandello is born on June 28 in Agrigento, Sicily.

1876: Fyodor Mikhailovich Dostoevsky's short story "The Heavenly Christmas Tree" is first published in Russian and will be published in English in 1949.

1881: Fyodor Mikhailovich Dostoevsky dies of complications associated with emphysema and epilepsy on February 9 in Staraya Russa, Russia.

1894: Nathaniel Hawthorne is born on July 4 in Salem, Massachusetts.

1904: Isaac Bashevis Singer is born on November 21 in Leoncin, Poland.

1916: Roald Dahl is born on September 13 in Cardiff, Wales.

1916: Shirley Jackson is born on December 14 in San Francisco, California.

1919: Doris Lessing is born Doris May Tayler (some sources say Taylor) on October 22 in Kermanshah, Persia (now Iran).

1928: Eugenia Collier is born Eugenia Maceo on April 6 in Baltimore, Maryland.

1930: Chinua Achebe is born on November 16 in Ogidi, Eastern Region, Nigeria.

1934: Luigi Pirandello is awarded the Nobel Prize for Literature.

1935: W. P. Kinsella is born on May 25 in Edmonton, Alberta, Canada.

1936: Luigi Pirandello dies of heart disease on December 10 in Rome.

1936: Luigi Pirandello's short story "A Day Goes By" is first published in Italian and will be published in English in 1965.

1937: Bessie Head is born on July 6 in Pietermaritzburg, South Africa.

1937: Zhang Jie is born in Liaoning Province, China.

1945: Roald Dahl's short story "Beware of The Dog" is published in the collection *Over to You.*

1947: Stephen King is born on September 21 in Portland, Maine.

1952: Chinua Achebe's short story "Marriage Is a Private Affair" is published as "The Old Order in Conflict with the New" in the *University Herald* of University College in Nigeria.

1954: Karen Louise Erdrich is born on June 7 in Little Falls, Minnesota.

1955: Shirley Jackson's short story "One Ordinary Day, With Peanuts" is published in the *Magazine of Fantasy & Science Fiction.*

1964: Doris Lessing's short story "No Witchcraft for Sale" is published in *African Stories.*

1965: Shirley Jackson dies of heart failure on August 8 in Bennington, Vermont.

c. 1972: Eugenia Collier's short story "Sweet Potato Pie" is copyrighted.

1973: Bessie Head's short story "The Prisoner Who Wore Glasses" is published in *London* magazine.

1973: Isaac Bashevis Singer's short story "The Son from America" is published in the *New Yorker.*

1979: Zhang Jie's short story "Love Must Not Be Forgotten" is published in Chinese and will be published in English in 1986.

1984: W. P. Kinsella's short story "The Thrill of the Grass" is published in the collection *The Thrill of the Grass.*

1986: Bessie Head dies of hepatitis on April 17 in Serowe, Botswana.

1987: Stephen King's short story (written in the form of a television script) "Sorry, Right Number" is broadcast as an episode of the television series *Tales from the Darkside* and will be published in the collection *Nightmares and Dreamscapes* in 1993.

1990: Karen Louise Erdrich's short story "The Leap" is published in *Harper's* magazine.

1990: Roald Dahl dies of the rare blood disorder myelodysplastic anemia on November 23 in Oxford, England.

1991: Isaac Bashevis Singer dies on July 24 in Surfside, California.

2007: Doris Lessing is awarded the Nobel Prize for Literature.

Acknowledgments

The editors wish to thank the copyright holders of the excerpted criticism included in this volume and the permissions managers of many book and magazine publishing companies for assisting us in securing reproduction rights. We are also grateful to the staffs of the Detroit Public Library, the Library of Congress, the University of Detroit Mercy Library, Wayne State University Purdy/Kresge Library Complex, and the University of Michigan Libraries for making their resources available to us. Following is a list of the copyright holders who have granted us permission to reproduce material in this volume of *SSfS*. Every effort has been made to trace copyright, but if omissions have been made, please let us know.

COPYRIGHTED EXCERPTS IN *SSfS*, VOLUME 30, WERE REPRODUCED FROM THE FOLLOWING PERIODICALS:

American Literature, v. 9, January, 1938. Copyright, 1938, Duke University Press. All rights reserved. Used by permission of the publisher.—***Black Issues in Higher Education***, v. 14, March 20, 1997. Copyright © 1997 Cox, Matthews & Associates. Reproduced by permission.—***Booklist***, v. 93, October 1, 1996. Copyright © 1996 by the American Library Association. Reproduced by permission.—***Books in Canada***, v. 13, November, 1984 for "Three Hits and a Miss" by Lesley Choyce. Reproduced by permission of the author.—***Callaloo***, v. 21, 1998. Copyright © 1998 by The Johns Hopkins University Press. Reproduced by permission.—***Children's Literature***, v. 6, 1977. © 1977 by Francelia Butler. All rights reserved. Reproduced by permission of the Literary Estate of Francelia Butler.—***Children's Literature Association Quarterly***, v. 20, spring, 1995. © 1995 Children's Literature Association. Reproduced by permission.—***Children's Literature in Education***, v. 21, June, 1990 for "Interview with Roald Dahl" by Mark I. West. © 1990 Human Sciences Press, Inc. Reproduced by permission of the publisher and author.—***Chinese Literature: Essays, Articles, Reviews (CLEAR)***, v. 9, July, 1987. Reproduced by permission.—***Journal of the Midwest Modern Language Association***, v. 33, autumn-winter, 2000 for "Envisioning the Jewish Community in Children's Literature: Maurice Sendak and Isaac Singer" by Jill P. May. Copyright 2000 by The Midwest Modern Language Association. Reproduced by permission of the publisher and the author.—***Modern Fiction Studies***, v. 33, spring, 1987. Copyright © 1987 by Purdue Research Foundation, West Lafayette, IN 47907. All rights reserved. Reproduced by permission of The Johns Hopkins University.—***Philadelphia Inquirer***, November 12, 2006. Copyright © 2006 Philadelphia Newspapers, LLC. Reproduced by permission.—***Publishers Weekly***, v. 243, October 14, 1996. Copyright © 1996 by Reed Publishing USA. Reproduced from *Publishers Weekly*, published by the Bowker Magazine Group of Cahners Publishing Co., a division of Reed Publishing USA, by permission.—***Revue***

de Littérature Comparée, v. 219-20, July-December, 1981. Copyright © Didier Erudition 1981. Reproduced by permission.—***Scotsman***, April 17, 1999. Copyright © 1999 Johnston Publishing Ltd. Reproduced by permission.—***Times Literary Supplement***, v. 4618, October 4, 1991. Copyright © 1991 by The Times Supplements Limited. Reproduced from *The Times Literary Supplement* by permission.—***Women's Review of Books***, v. 3, July, 1986. Copyright © 1986 Old City Publishing, Inc. Reproduced by permission.

COPYRIGHTED EXCERPTS IN *SSfS*, VOLUME 30, WERE REPRODUCED FROM THE FOLLOWING BOOKS:

Brown, Coreen. From ***The Creative Vision of Bessie Head***. Fairleigh Dickinson University Press, 2003. Copyright © 2003 by Rosemont Publishing & Printing Corp. All rights reserved. Reproduced by permission.—Erdrich, Louise. From ***The Red Convertible: Selected and New Stories***. Harper Collins, 2009. Copyright © 2009 by Louise Erdrich. All rights reserved. Reprinted by permission of HarperCollins Publishers Inc.—Erdrich, Louise, and Michael Dorris. From "Louise Erdrich and Michael Dorris," in ***Conversations with American Novelists: The Best Interviews from The Missouri Review and the American Audio Prose Library***. Edited by Kay Bonetti, Greg Michalson, Speer Morgan, Jo Sapp, and Sam Showers. University of Missouri Press, 1997. Copyright © 1997 by The Curators of the University of Missouri. All rights reserved. Reproduced by permission.—Friedman, Lenemaja. From ***Shirley Jackson***. Twayne Publishers, 1975. Copyright © 1975 by G. K. Hall & Co. All rights reserved. Reproduced by permission of Gale, a part of Cengage Learning.—Jackson, Shirley, Laurence Jackson Hyman, and Sarah Hyman Stewart. From "Introduction and Author Preface: All I Can Remember," in ***Just an Ordinary Day***. Edited by Laurence Jackson Hyman and Sarah Hyman Stewart. Bantam Books, 1997. Copyright © 1997 by the Estate of Shirley Jackson. All rights reserved. Reproduced by permission of Bantam Books, a division of Random House, Inc.—MacKenzie, Craig. From ***Bessie Head***. Twayne Publishers, 1999. Copyright © 1999 by Twayne Publishers. All rights reserved. Reproduced by permission of Gale, a part of Cengage Learning.—Mansfield, Katherine. From review of "European Novelists," in ***Critical Writings of Katherine Mansfield***. Edited by Clare Hanson. Macmillan Press, 1987. Copyright © 1987 The Estate of Katherine Mansfield. All rights reserved. Reproduced with permission of Palgrave Macmillan.—Rogak, Lisa. From ***Haunted Heart: The Life and Times of Stephen King***. Thomas Dunne Books (St. Martin's Press), 2008. Copyright © 2008 by Lisa Rogak. All rights reserved. In the United States and Canada reprinted by permission of Thomas Dunne Books, an imprint of St. Martin's Press, LLC.—White, Sharon, and Glenda Burnside. From "On Native Ground: An Interview with Louise Erdrich and Michael Dorris," in ***Conversations with Louise Erdrich and Michael Dorris***. Edited by Allan Chavkin and Nancy Feyl Chavkin. University Press of Mississippi, 1994. Copyright © 1994 by University Press of Mississippi. All rights reserved. Reproduced by permission of Glenda Burnside.

Contributors

Bryan Aubrey: Aubrey holds a Ph.D. in English. Entries on "Marriage Is a Private Affair" and "The Son from America." Original essays on "Marriage Is a Private Affair" and "The Son from America."

Cynthia A. Bily: Bily is a freelance writer and editor, and an instructor of writing. Entry on "The Prisoner Who Wore Glasses." Original essay on "The Prisoner Who Wore Glasses."

Catherine Dominic: Dominic is a novelist and a freelance writer and editor. Entries on "The Heavenly Christmas Tree" and "Love Must Not Be Forgotten." Original essays on "The Heavenly Christmas Tree" and "Love Must Not Be Forgotten."

Charlotte Freeman: Freeman is a freelance writer and editor who holds a Ph.D. in English. Entry on "The Thrill of the Grass." Original essay on "The Thrill of the Grass."

David Kelly: Kelly is a writer and an instructor of creative writing and literature. Entries on "Dr. Heidegger's Experiment" and "Sorry, Right Number." Original essays on "Dr. Heidegger's Experiment" and "Sorry, Right Number."

Laura Pryor: Pryor has a B.A. from the University of Michigan and over 20 years of experience as a professional writer. Entry on "A Day Goes By." Original essay on "A Day Goes By."

Bradley Skeen: Skeen is a classics professor. Entry on "Beware of the Dog." Original essay on "Beware of the Dog."

Leah Tieger: Tieger is a freelance writer and editor. Entries on "No Witchcraft for Sale" and "Sweet Potato Pie." Original essays on "No Witchcraft for Sale" and "Sweet Potato Pie."

Carol Ullmann: Ullmann is a freelance writer and editor. Entry on "One Ordinary Day, with Peanuts." Original essay on "One Ordinary Day, with Peanuts."

Rebecca Valentine: Valentine holds a B.A. in English, with an emphasis on literary analysis. Entry on "The Leap." Original essay on "The Leap."

Beware of the Dog

ROALD DAHL

1944

Roald Dahl is one the best-selling authors in history, with more than one hundred million copies of his book in print. He is also unusual in having gained nearly equal prominence as an author of adult fiction and children's books. Dahl is best known through the popular film adaptations of his children's books, including *Willie Wonka and the Chocolate Factory* (1971) (filmed again in 2005 under its original title as *Charlie and the Chocolate Factory*), *The BFG* (1989), *The Witches* (1990), and *James and the Giant Peach* (1996). Dahl's best-known works for adults are his short stories. All of Dahl's work for both adult and juvenile audiences is marked by its sardonic black humor and its frequent use of twist endings.

Dahl's short story "Beware of the Dog" was originally published in the October 1944 issue of *Harper's* magazine and reprinted in his 1945 collection of aviation stories, *Over to You*. Although it was the basis of the 1965 film *36 Hours*, the story has been neglected by critics and editors, making it among the least commonly anthologized of Dahl's stories. (However, the text is readily available on the Internet.) In "Beware of the Dog," Dahl deals with the themes of perception and the creation of a false reality by the totalitarian forces of society, ideas that are among the most important and pressing in modern literature. Dahl anticipated and perhaps influenced such landmark twentieth-century works as Orwell's *Nineteen Eighty-four* and Patrick MacGoohan's television series *The Prisoner*.

Roald Dahl *(The Library of Congress)*

AUTHOR BIOGRAPHY

Dahl was born on September 13, 1916, in Llandaff, Wales (just outside Cardiff). His parents were Norwegian and immigrated to Great Britain specifically for the purpose of having their children attend the English educational system, which they considered the best in the world. Dahl was bilingual in Norwegian and English. He was disposed, both as a child and as an adult, to carrying out elaborate practical jokes, such as an incident in which he and his friends placed a dead mouse in a candy jar in the shop of a candy seller they loathed for the general lack of sanitation on her premises. Just as frequently, he was punished at school for such pranks by being beaten with a cane, though he was also caned for infractions he did not commit (such as cheating on exams). These facts are often pointed to as the background for the extremely violent black humor that permeates his children's books. Upon completing his schooling, Dahl became a sales agent for Shell Oil in East Africa.

In August of 1939, when World War II seemed inevitable, Dahl joined the colonial military and was put in charge of a platoon of African troops. In November, however, he transferred to the Royal Air Force (RAF) and became a fighter pilot. He saw service in the British campaigns in Libya and Greece through 1942, when his physical condition no longer permitted him to fly. He was transferred to the British embassy in Washington, DC, where he worked in the propaganda section, trying to whip up American enthusiasm to fight Germany. There he published his first piece, a brief memoir erroneously titled by its editors "Shot Down over Libya," in the *Saturday Evening Post*. This marked the beginning of Dahl's writing career, and he followed it with a series of short stories based on his experiences as an RAF pilot. These stories were collected in *Over to You*. One of them was "Beware of the Dog," which was based in part on the same experience recalled in "Shot Down over Libya." Dahl began to write stories for children as well, turning the folklore of the RAF into the children's book *The Gremlins*.

After the war, Dahl became a full-time writer, one of the most successful in history, selling more than one hundred million copies of his books and writing for both adults and children. His best-known work is his 1964 children's novel *Charlie and the Chocolate Factory*. Dahl also became well known as a film and television writer in Hollywood, producing scripts for film versions of some of his own works and for many other projects, including Ian Fleming's novels *You Only Live Twice* and *Chitty Chitty Bang Bang*. He also wrote and hosted *Way Out*, a television show that became a prototype for *The Twilight Zone*. Dahl died in Oxford, England, on November 23, 1990, from a blood disease similar to leukemia.

PLOT SUMMARY

"Beware of the Dog" begins with the description of the view from the cockpit of a plane in flight: "Down below there was only a vast white undulating sea of cloud. Above there was the sun, and the sun was white like the clouds, because it is never yellow when one looks at it from high in the air." Like much of Dahl's prose in this story, the passage is lyrical and evocative, but it is also purposefully disorienting. Dahl wants the reader never to be quite sure of what the meaning of the text is. One knows what the beginning of the

MEDIA ADAPTATIONS

- "Beware of the Dog" was the basis for the 1965 film *36 Hours*, written and directed by George Seaton. It starred James Garner and Eva Marie Saint.

passage means only when one reaches the end. It develops that the view is that of the pilot (whom we later learn is named Peter Williamson) of a Spitfire, the first-line fighter plane used by the RAF during the Battle of Britain and throughout World War II. This information goes a long way toward establishing the setting.

Williamson has been shot. His right leg is almost destroyed; "the cannon-shell had taken him on the thigh, just above the knee, and now there was nothing but a great mess and a lot of blood." The "cannon" refers to the thirty-millimeter cannons that typically armed the German Messerschmitt fighter aircraft, the ME-109 and ME-110, in contrast to the .50-caliber machine guns favored by the British. With a freely bleeding arterial wound, Williamson, since he is still conscious, must have been hit no more than a few seconds before the narrative begins. Having lost so much blood, Williamson is going into shock and becoming delirious. His mind wanders to a fantasy of landing safely at his home airfield and having the mechanic Yorky and his fellow pilots think he is joking about his wound. The effects of shock keep him from feeling any pain from his wound. He is on the verge of blacking out.

In Williamson's fantasy, his comrades think he is playing a practical joke, only pretending to have a wound. The military routine of making a report on his mission to a superior officer inserts itself in his mental wandering. Then he imagines that he is visiting Bluey, his nickname for his girlfriend or fiancée in London, and getting drunk with her. The memory of repairing an axe by resecuring the head to the shaft intrudes. This fantasy of mending something broken forms an analogy to his severed leg. Fortunately, Williamson snaps back to reality and refreshes himself by breathing oxygen from his mask. He realizes that he cannot possibly fly any farther; he has to bail out and parachute to the ground if he wants to live. He is able to do so because he relies on his training rather than having to consciously think of each step he has to go through. He is returning to England from flying a mission in France, and he thinks he will probably land in the English Channel. In his confusion, he does not know exactly where he is. As he jumps out of the plane, his body begins to spin in the fall. He becomes dizzy and blacks out.

Not knowing precisely what happened to him as he fell, Williamson slowly comes back to consciousness. Dahl describes every sensory experience as Williamson gradually returns to himself and deduces that he is now lying in a hospital bed. He recalls his wound and feels his right leg, discovering it has been amputated above the knee. Just then, a nurse enters his room. She tells Williamson that he is in Brighton, a city on the Channel coast of England, and that he parachuted into the woods just above the beach. He has been in the hospital for two days. They briefly discuss his amputation, and she tries to reassure him, telling him that he will be fitted with an artificial leg in due course. An hour later, the doctor comes in and tells him that some of his comrades from his squadron have been asking about him. They will be allowed to visit him in a few days, the doctor says, as his convalescence (recovery period) allows.

Left alone again, Williamson hears the noise of aircraft engines through his window. He recognizes their distinctive sound as belonging to the German Junkers bomber, the JU-88 (most of Dahl's own five confirmed kills as an RAF pilot were on this type of aircraft). He is certain that he is not mistaking the sound of their Jumo engines, since he heard their distinctive engine noise "every day during the Battle." This refers to the Battle of Britain, when the Germans tried to gain air superiority over southern England to threaten an invasion of the island; it took place in the summer and early fall of 1940. This helps to date the story to sometime after October 1940, since Williamson looks back on it as a past event. Williamson thinks it is odd to hear the JU-88s (German bombers), since the Germans are no longer making daylight air raids against Britain, and it is odder still not to hear air raid sirens and antiaircraft artillery firing at them. Perplexed, Williamson does the only thing he can do and calls for the nurse to ask her about the anomalous situation. She reassures him that he must have heard Lancasters or Flying Fortresses returning from missions against targets on the continent (thus making the story no earlier than 1942, when America joined the war, since Flying Fortresses are American aircraft). She agrees that German bombers "never come over in daylight any longer" and dismisses Williamson's concerns. He changes the subject and asks for a cigarette. The nurse gives him a pack of a well-known British brand.

Toward evening, Williamson hears another aircraft engine that he cannot identify at all. He begins to wonder whether he is perhaps "imagining things" or is "a little delirious." When the nurse returns, she jokes with him: "I hope you don't still think that we're being bombed." She proceeds to give him a sponge bath, being careful not to let him see the stump of his leg, and tells him that her brother is also in the RAF, on a bomber crew. Williamson mentions that he went to school in Brighton, the city where the hospital is located. As she proceeds to wash him, she mentions that it is difficult to get the soap to lather, both because the quality of soap has declined since the diversion of civilian resources toward the war effort and because the water in Brighton is so hard (that is, full of mineral salts). Williamson remembers from his school days in Brighton that he particularly enjoyed his baths because of the rich lather promoted by the soft water there. He starts to mention this contradiction to the nurse, but then thinks better of it.

After the nurse leaves, Williamson keeps himself awake worrying about the contradictions he has discovered: the water is hard when he knows it ought to be soft, and he is sure JU-88s are flying around unmolested where it makes no sense for them to be. He wonders whether he is crazy and decides to prove to himself he is not by making a speech to himself, "something complicated and intellectual," on the topic of "what to do with Germany after the war." This is perhaps an ironic comment on the British public's absolute faith in its eventual complete victory, even in the darkest days of war. This thought promptly puts him to sleep. When he awakens before dawn, his mind returns to the same contradictions and he begins to doubt. What precisely he doubts, the story does not yet say, but because of this doubt, everything that he perceives seems different from before: "The room was bare. It was no longer warm or friendly. It was not even comfortable. It was cold and empty and very quiet." He decides that he must do something to find out whether what he fears is true or not. With some difficulty, because of his lost leg, he manages to crawl over to the window of his hospital room. Looking out the window, he does not see anything very important except for a sign posted on a hedge that serves as the garden wall of a private house across the street. Because of the distance and the light, he can barely see what is written on it, but he reads, "*Garde au chien*," the French for 'Beware of the dog.' Williamson concludes from this new anomaly, on top of the JU-88s and the hard water, that he is in fact in France, a country occupied by the Nazis.

When the nurse returns later in the morning, Williamson sees her in an entirely new light:

> But there was something a little uneasy about her eyes. They were never still.... There was something about her movements also. They were too sharp and nervous to go well with the casual manner in which she spoke.

She tells Williamson that he will shortly be visited by Wing Commander Roberts to debrief him. This makes Williamson think of an early briefing he had from an RAF intelligence officer, telling him to give only his name, rank, and number (his serial number, or service number) if he were ever captured by the enemy. Roberts duly arrives and starts to ask questions for the incident report on the mission during which Williamson was shot. He asks for Williamson's squadron number, and Williamson instead responds with his name, rank, and number. The story ends there, implying that Williamson will give only these answers, believing himself to be a captive of the enemy.

CHARACTERS

Bluey

Bluey is Williamson's girlfriend, fiancée, or (less probably) wife. He visits her whenever he can get away from his military duties. As he is blacking out at the beginning of "Beware of the Dog," Williamson imagines again going to visit her with a bottle of whisky (difficult to obtain during the war). He imagines springing his lost leg on her as a surprise, and also that she will not mind very much. Williamson refers to her by a nickname, as he refers to several other characters.

This was a habit of students at English public schools of the kind attended by Williamson. This can be seen, for instance, in public figures such as Air Chief Marshall Sir H. C. T. Dowding, the officer in charge of Britain's air defenses during the Battle of Britain, who was known to his friends as "Stuffy."

Doctor

The doctor who checks on Williamson in the hospital at first receives a positive evaluation because Williamson accepts him at face value: "He was an Army doctor, a major, and he had some last war ribbons on his chest. He was bald and small, but he had a cheerful face and kind eyes." He tells Williamson that he asked some airmen from his squadron to postpone visiting him for a few days, until he is feeling stronger. Williamson meekly accepts his judgment in this matter. The doctor forms one of a pair of characters with the Wing Commander, representing Williamson's view of the authority he is under before and after he realizes where he is.

Johnny

Johnny is the intelligence officer attached to Williamson's squadron. Williamson thinks of him while he is waiting to be debriefed by an RAF Wing Commander (whom Williamson believes is actually a German intelligence officer). Williamson recalls Johnny telling him and his fellow pilots what to do in case they were captured by the Germans: "Don't forget, just your name, rank and number. Nothing else. For God's sake, say nothing else." Williamson instinctively follows this advice, as he does the rest of his military training throughout the story.

Nurse

After Williamson, the unnamed nurse who attends him in his hospital bed is the most important character in "Beware of the Dog." His perception of her changes as his understanding of his circumstances changes. She is the first person Williamson meets when he awakens after blacking out, and the one he has most contact with. His first impression of her is that "she was not good-looking, but she was large and clean. She was between thirty and forty and she had fair hair." The nurse cares for him efficiently and responds to his needs and requests. As Williamson begins to find discrepancies in the world around him against his expectations, she is able to answer all of his objections. His first doubt is when he starts to ask her about the quality of the water, but then thinks better of it and changes the subject. He clearly does not want her to know that he is questioning the reality of his circumstances.

Once Williamson sees the "*Garde au chien*" sign and becomes certain he is being deceived, he sees the nurse in an entirely different way: "Her hair was very fair. She was tall and big-boned and her face seemed pleasant." This description is similar to the first, but it subtly recasts the nurse as a Nazi, particularly in the Nazi insistence on fair or blonde hair and the emphasis on the "seemed." Williamson now interprets her actions as a sign that she is nervously playing a false part:

> But there was something a little uneasy about her eyes. They were never still. They never looked at anything for more than a moment and they moved too quickly from one place to another in the room. There was something about her movements also. They were too sharp and nervous to go well with the casual manner in which she spoke.

Williamson reinterprets her character to fit his new worldview, though there is actually no demonstrable change in her character.

Wing Commander Roberts

Roberts appears in the story only after Williamson concludes that he is being held by the Nazis in France. In this case, Roberts is a Nazi spy, illegally wearing a British military uniform. When he comes to debrief Williamson, Roberts is wearing a DFC (Distinguished Flying Cross), a medal for military valor, suggesting that he, or the character he is representing, had been in the thick of the fighting during the Battle of Britain but had perhaps been wounded, necessitating his transfer to his current administrative duties. The story ends before the reader can see Roberts's reaction to Williamson answering his question with only his name, rank, and number.

Squadron Leader Peter Williamson

The whole of "Beware of the Dog" is shaped by Williamson's character. It is a story about his changing perceptions. The first section of the story describes the drifting of his mind between reality and fantasy as he blacks out from loss of blood out of his wounded leg. Paradoxically, it is here that the reader learns the most about Williamson, since, as in dreams, the details of his everyday life are also the subject of his mental fantasies. He imagines interactions typical in their details, if fantastic in their subject, with the people most important to him in his real life: his military comrades, the mechanic who services his plane, and his lover. His habits of language reveal that he belongs to the British upper classes. His circumstances as an RAF fighter pilot and the probability that he is not married suggest that he is young. Many of his reactions in this part of the story are automatic, the result of ingrained military training. This training, together with the innate ability to react instantly with necessary actions rather than wasting time considering what to do, save his life in the crisis of being severely wounded.

Once Williamson is awake in the hospital, his character is further developed through his reactions to his new situation. He is marked by a strange blend of curiosity and lack of curiosity. He considers the possibility that his mental process has become unreliable because of the trauma he has gone through in the war, most recently losing his leg. However, he dismisses this possibility with little investigation, because he is not curious about his own condition. This perhaps derives from the British aristocratic ethos of the stiff upper lip—that is, stoicism, or bearing difficulties without showing emotion—exemplified by the way that Williamson himself, his nurse, his doctor, and even Wing Commander Roberts dismiss the loss of his leg as nothing serious. Williamson's own condition is not, therefore, important to him. To the extent he does investigate the matter, he attempts to assure himself of his own sanity through his ability to make a connected logical argument, a standard no doubt inspired by the highly rhetorical education he received in his English public school.

What Williamson is curious about is the world around him. He investigates it through the limited means available to him: listening to the sounds of the air traffic he can hear through the window of his hospital room, the quality of the water in the hospital, and finally what he can see through the window when, with great effort, he drags himself from the bed to look out of it. He always discovers discrepancies between what he finds and what he expects to find in these investigations. He comes to the startling but very sophisticated conclusion that everything he sees is an illusion created by the Nazis to deceive him and that the discrepancies are hints of the real situation. Williamson is supremely confident in his own reasoning and conclusion, and he acts decisively on them, fearlessly revealing, when he is debriefed, that he is aware that he is in Nazi hands. The reader is meant to be swept along by the confidence of Williamson's character, though other explanations of the facts presented in the story are possible.

Yorky

Yorky is the first of several characters who are mentioned only during the confused memories and fantasies that Williamson experiences as he is blacking out from shock and loss of blood. Yorky is evidently the mechanic attached to the air base of Williamson's squadron who services his plane and is the first person to meet him when he lands. (In the fantasy, at least, Yorky also works on Williamson's car.) Williamson imagines first that Yorky (like the other pilots in his squadron) will think that Williamson is joking about having had his leg shot off, but then Williamson imagines that Yorky will become physically ill seeing all the blood in the plane's cockpit. "Yorky" is a nickname and may indicate that his true name is York, or perhaps that he comes from Yorkshire, a district in northern England, and hence would have a pronounced accent quite different from the one that Williamson most likely has.

THEMES

Adventure Fiction

In adventure stories, the characters are usually broadly drawn and suggestive rather than well developed and realistic. The plots are generally a simple recitation of interesting and exciting events: adventures. A popular subset of adventure fiction is aviation stories. Frequently, such stories are aimed at teenage boys and have characters who are hypermasculine, particularly in the camaraderie, self-denial, and violence required by the military, but at the same time who have some of the same limitations as their adolescent audience: they are impulsive and free of introspection. These characters frequently inhabit a world in which women are idealized, mysterious, and above all removed from the ordinary course of life. Aviation adventure stories of this kind are exemplified by the Biggles books of W. E. Johns. Starting in 1932, the popularity of this series of short stories and novels (totaling one hundred volumes, though they were originally published in pulp magazines) about the fictional World War I Flying Ace James Bigglesworth clearly defined the adventure-laden genre of the aviation story in popular culture in Britain. During World War II, the genre was imported into the United States in the form of

TOPICS FOR FURTHER STUDY

- During World War II, the United States Army Air Corps operated a segregated all-black fighter unit, the 332nd Fighter Group, popularly known as the Tuskegee Airmen. Read a young-adult book such as Sarah de Capua's 2009 study *The Tuskegee Airmen: Journey to Freedom* as background and then write your own short story in which one of the African American pilots is shot down and wakes up in hospital. Is he in a German or an American hospital? Does he use his convalescence to consider the racial policies of Germany and of his own country? In your story, consider how the change in race and nationality might influence events.
- Use the Internet to research illustrations and historical and technical information about the various combat aircraft mentioned in "Beware of the Dog," including the Spitfire, Hurricane, Lancaster, B-17 (Flying Fortress), JU-88, and ME-109. Create a PowerPoint presentation describing and illustrating the different roles and capabilities of these aircraft and present it to your class.
- Think about the few minutes after the end of "Beware of the Dog." Consider questions such as where Williamson actually is, what will happen to him, and what special military intelligence he might have. Share these new potential endings for the short story in small group settings in your classroom.
- Write a research paper investigating the actual treatment of prisoners of war by the Nazis. Find out about issues such as German adherence to the Geneva Convention and the difference in German treatment of prisoners from Western nations and the Soviet Union. Did the Nazis actually use any exotic interrogation techniques, like those suggested by this story, to get information from captured Western pilots?

comic books in such titles as *Airboy*, *Captain Flight*, and *Wings*.

In "Beware of the Dog," Dahl subverts (that is, undercuts or goes against) the expectations of the genre, while adhering to some of its superficial features. Williamson, the main character of "Beware of the Dog," is evidently an RAF pilot who has seen extensive service in the Battle of Britain and has, moments before the story opens, been involved in air-to-air combat. However, this is not described, certainly not in any high-flown heroic fashion, and is largely irrelevant to the story. The story instead concentrates on a detailed and realistic exploration of the results of that combat, namely the loss of the main character's leg; for example, he finds it extremely difficult just to get out of bed without his leg. In fact, while he is beginning to black out due to loss of blood from his wounds, the main character experiences a sort of fantasy satirizing boys' aviation adventure stories, in which he 'manfully' denies the significance of his wound and handicap, thinking that his comrades will refuse to believe and laugh it off as a joke. He further imagines explaining it to his girlfriend: "I've got a surprise for you. I lost my leg today. But I don't mind so long as you don't. We'll go everywhere in cars. I always hated walking." Here, Dahl subverts the genre's emphasis on an unrealistic disregard of pain. At one point, the main character uses banter, the sort of coded language actually used among RAF pilots, when he refers to the English channel as "the drink." This form of speech was often imitated in aviation stories. Similar to this is Williamson's tendency to refer to people by nicknames or diminutives (Yorky, Bluey, Johnny), an affectation of the English public schools that perpetuated itself in the officer class.

Fear

Williamson, the main character of "Beware of the Dog," is marked for his fearlessness. Certainly, although he is wounded in his Spitfire, he shows no inclination to panic but rather methodically carries out the steps necessary to save his life. Later, in the hospital, he does not seem to particularly fear the prospect of facing life without his leg, nor does he seem particularly frightened by his deduction that he has been captured by the Nazis. All of these are situations that one might reasonably expect to produce fear and even panic. Part of the explanation for the first instance lies in the fact that he is going into shock and losing brain function as his blood pressure falls, so that he is literally not in his right mind; he does not realize he

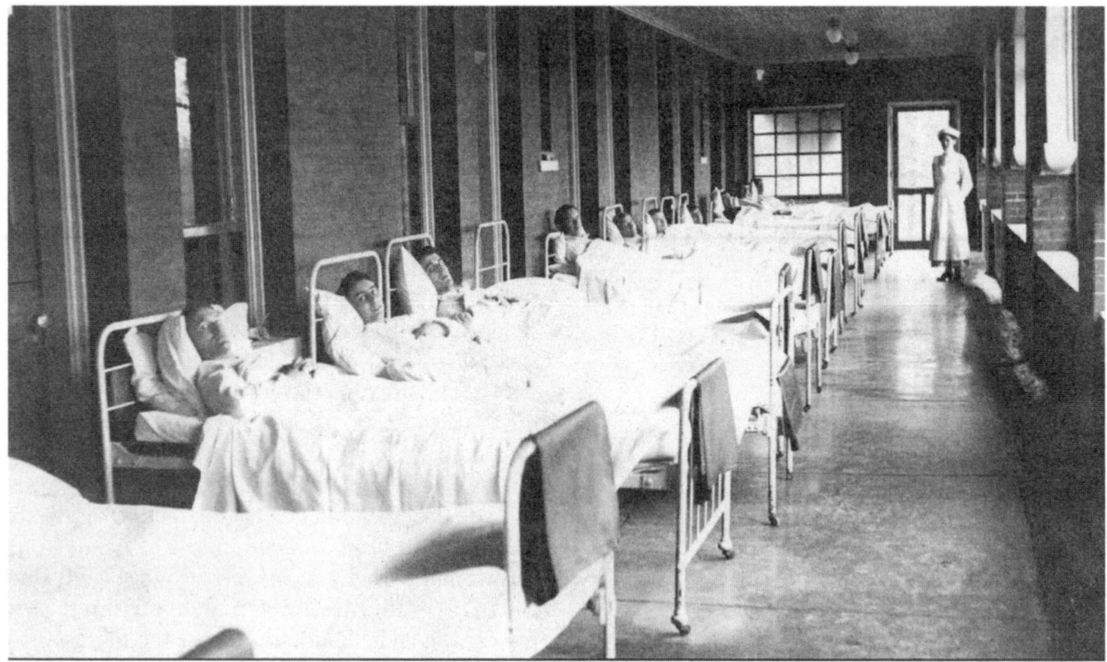

Many wounded soldiers line the halls of a hospital ward (Image copyright ChipPix, 2009. Used under license from Shutterstock.com)

ought to be afraid. For this reason, he reacts with dream-like fantasy rather than fear. However, that is far from a complete explanation. His reaction throughout the story to every crisis is to go by the book. Undoubtedly, this is because of the deep impression made on his character by his military training: "He had a moment of great clearness. His actions became orderly and precise. That is what happens with a good pilot." He is also using inner resources of curiosity and perseverance. Even once he comes to believe he is in danger, what he experiences is not ordinary fear, but rather "a light, dancing fear that warned but did not frighten; the kind of fear that one gets not because one is afraid, but because one feels there is something wrong." For the type of man that Williamson is, fear is simply irrelevant to the obstacles he has to overcome.

STYLE

Partially Omniscient Narrator

"Beware of the Dog" is told by a partially omniscient narrator. The narrative voice clearly knows facts of which Williamson is unaware, and it can tell the audience Williamson's inner thoughts and experiences, but it is nevertheless generally limited to telling the story from Williamson's viewpoint. This device provides the greatest interest to the story that is probably not immediately apparent upon first reading. Because the narrative voice is impersonal and is the only source of information about the story, the reader is inclined to trust it. However, the narrative voice concentrates on one character's viewpoint, and that viewpoint is not necessarily valid. Williamson finds various anomalies between what he would expect to exist in Brighton and what he actually finds, and he deduces from these that he is not in Brighton but in France. The first and most important piece of evidence is the supposed presence of German JU-88 bombers. At first Williamson himself rejects this evidence and explains it on the basis of his own depleted mental and physical state. Given that he has been a fighter pilot and has probably seen many of his comrades killed in action, and because he has just had his own leg shot off, he is probably suffering from what is now called combat stress reaction (which used to be called "shell shock"). One symptom of this condition is reacting to ordinary sensory stimuli as though they were threats from the enemy. This is what he means when he thinks he might be going crazy. When

Williamson eventually rejects this possibility, the reader is led to reject it too, trusting the authority of the narrative voice that takes its lead from Williamson.

In the same way, many pieces of evidence are interpreted only as confirming Williamson's theory. Other explanations are ignored, although the exploration of such alternatives might seem to follow from the plot of the story, which is essentially unraveling a mystery. For instance, Williamson's school might have gotten its water from a private well with chemical properties different from the city's water. Williamson's reading of the sign written in French is extremely uncertain since it is at the limits of his perception, and might, in any case, merely mean that a French-speaking citizen of Brighton thought it was interesting to put up such a sign. More tellingly, once Williamson has made up his mind, he begins to see everything differently, and the narrative voice presents these perceptions as facts, as if they independently confirm his conclusion, when in fact they follow from it. Thus, when his hospital room begins to seem hostile rather than friendly, nothing has changed except Williamson's judgment. The evidence that makes him suspicious of the nurse is that "her eyes . . . were never still . . . and they moved too quickly from one place to another in the room." In fact, it is normal for people's eyes to move constantly, so it generally goes unnoticed. People's eyes are still only during intense personal contact, and it is then that they are noticed. Williamson's interpretation depends on a change in his observation, not a change in the nurse's behavior. The impression that this narrative strategy creates is so strong that by the time Wing Commander Roberts enters the scene, it is unnecessary for the narrator to comment on Williamson's interpretation of the fact that his uniform is "a little shabby." The reader will draw the connection: the uniform must be shabby because it was taken from a dead or captured British officer, not because Roberts is overworked or because new uniforms are being rarely issued to soldiers off the front line. Larger issues are never addressed. What information could Williamson, a low-ranking officer unlikely to have any important military secrets, possibly give in his debriefing that would be interesting enough to the Germans for them to go to all the trouble of this deception? (This difficulty is addressed in the film adaptation *36 Hours*, where the action is transposed to the spring of 1944 and Williamson is known to be privy to the exact date and location planned for the D-Day invasion.) The fact that the reader learns nothing from the viewpoint of any other character besides Williamson and the fact that the story stops dead at the point when Roberts would respond to the charge that he is an enemy officer and before Williamson could find out the truth, one way or the other, create an elaborate confusion for the reader. Although the reader is led to believe that Williamson is a prisoner of war in German hands and the victim of an elaborate deception (as it were, the greatest of Dahl's practical jokes), there is really no way for the reader to decide the truth. This ambiguity is perhaps the greatest achievement of the story.

Twist Ending

Dahl is famous for what is generally called a twist ending. A typical story of this kind is Dahl's "Taste," which was originally published in the *Ladies' Home Journal* of March 1945 and so was probably written at about the same time as "Beware of the Dog." In "Taste," a wine connoisseur enters into a wager over whether he can identify a wine's year and vineyard simply by tasting it. He proceeds over the course of the story to lecture on the various qualities of the wine, mentally touring the vineyard through the various wine regions and chateaux of Bordeaux until he narrows in on the correct answer, only at that moment to have the maid announce that she had found the connoisseur's glasses in the study where the wine has been kept, meaning that he has been cheating all along. More or less the same pattern is followed in "Beware of the Dog," with an investigation revealing that things are the opposite of what they seem. However, Dahl had not yet perfected his technique. The solution to the problem, that Williamson is in France and the victim of an elaborate Nazi deception, though astonishing, is signaled much too soon, and the gradual investigation supports the conclusion, rather than being subverted by it.

HISTORICAL CONTEXT

Battle of Britain

Once Adolf Hitler came to power as the elected chancellor (and later the dictator) of Germany in 1933, he acted to overturn the military limitations placed on Germany by the Versailles treaty that ended World War I and to expand Germany's borders by every means short of war. In 1938, the Western powers permitted him to conquer

COMPARE & CONTRAST

- **1940s:** The health risks of smoking are not yet well understood, or at least not widely understood. Hospital patients are allowed to smoke, even in their own rooms.

  Today: Smoking is strictly forbidden in hospitals, even for staff and visitors.

- **1940s:** Dahl can rely on his readers knowing enough French to understand the phrase *Garde au chien* without explaining it.

  Today: With the vast expansion in the absolute numbers of people reading for pleasure and the simultaneous decline of foreign language enrollment in the schools, many of Dahl's modern readers are probably perplexed by the untranslated French.

- **1940s:** The Western European great powers of Great Britain, France, Germany, and Italy fight against each other in World War II, the most destructive conflict in history.

  Today: With collective military security guaranteed by the North Atlantic Treaty Organization (NATO) and all of Western Europe moving toward cooperation within the European Union, strong safeguards exist that make it unlikely that Western European countries could fight each other again.

- **1940s:** Germany follows the Geneva Convention on the treatment of prisoners of war and does not, in general, execute or torture prisoners from other signatory nations.

  Today: Since World War II, the United States and NATO fight against enemies that do not follow international law concerning the treatment of prisoners of war, including North Korea, North Vietnam, and terrorist organizations such as Al-Qaeda and the Taliban.

Czechoslovakia. This is generally counted as appeasement, the hope that Hitler would stop his aggression if he were given his way, but in fact leaders of France and Great Britain were told by their military advisors that the Western democracies would not be ready for war until 1942, so the sacrifice of Czechoslovakia could be viewed as an attempt to buy time. Nevertheless, on September 1, 1939, when Hitler's Germany attacked Poland, France and Britain declared war. France was conquered by Germany in a campaign of seven weeks during the spring of 1940 owing to Germany's advantage in the tactics of modern armored warfare, a lightning fast attack called the *Blitzkrieg*. The British army was surrounded in Northern France and Belgium; it was evacuated across the English Channel, but only at the cost of abandoning heavy equipment such as tanks and artillery pieces, which left the army in no condition to defend Britain against a German sea-borne invasion. The British Navy, however, had complete control of the seas, so the only chance the Germans had to invade Britain was to gain a victory in another new kind of warfare, air warfare. If Germany could gain air superiority over the Channel, any British warships that might attempt to repel the invasion could be destroyed by the German air force (the *Luftwaffe*).

To this end, throughout July and August of 1940, the Germans attacked the infrastructure of the RAF defenses in Britain, the radar towers that let the RAF monitor German movements in advance, and the coastal bases of the fighter aircraft (Spitfires and Hurricanes) the RAF used to attack German Bombers (JU-87 Stuka dive-bombers, JU-88s, and HE-111s). Although this effort came close to breaking the RAF, the Germans concluded after the first week of September that they had failed and began attacking British cities to create terror rather than for any military reason. After late September, German terror-bombing raids were generally confined to the nighttime hours, when British fighters could not operate. British night bombing of German cities went on throughout this period. Although

A World War II vintage P-47 Thunderbolt *(Image copyright Richard Goldberg, 2009. Used under license from Shutterstock.com)*

Dahl does not give many specifics, Williamson in "Beware of the Dog" was probably a fighter pilot during the height of the battle, which explains his close familiarity with the sound of JU-88 engines. Since the story takes place after JU-88s are no longer making daylight raids on Britain, it could be set no earlier than October or November of 1940. After that, it would be rare for JU-88s to bomb in Britain at all as the air war shifted to the Mediterranean and eventually Russia. However, its dramatic date is much later, since the nurse tells Williamson that the planes he thought were JU-88s "were probably Lancasters or Flying Fortresses." These aircraft were used in the strategic bombing campaign against Germany. The B-17 Flying Fortress, in particular, was flown by the American Army Air Corps Eighth Air Force, and so the story must take place after the United States declaration of war in 1942. However, it must be sometime before 1944, or else other factors, such as German attacks by V-weapons (primitive cruise missiles and rockets) and the D-Day landings in France would most likely have been mentioned.

World War II in the Mediterranean

In "Beware of the Dog," Williamson, during part of his mental wandering while he is blacking out from loss of blood and shock, contemplates his future with a lost leg and recalls, "I always hated walking except when I walked down the street of the coppersmiths in Baghdad." This reminiscence is doubtless based on Dahl's own military service during World War II. Enlisting in Africa at the beginning of the war in 1939, Dahl was soon sent to the gigantic Habbaniya airfield in Iraq, where he underwent his advanced training as a fighter pilot during the first half of 1940. Habbaniya was about a hundred miles from the Iraqi capital of Baghdad, where Dahl most likely visited (in transit, if not on leave). More fundamentally, however, "Beware of the Dog" is based in part on an experience of Dahl's during the war, the incident that concerned his publication of the article that initially brought him to public attention as a writer in the *Saturday Evening Post* in 1942. Dahl was posted to a fighter base supporting the front line of the desert war against the Italo-German *Afikakorps* in Libya. He became disoriented and had to land in the open desert when he ran out of fuel. Disoriented and wounded, he had to guess about the best direction to walk to try to find safety. As it happens, he had landed in the no-man's-land between the German and British lines and was lucky to walk back toward his own army. He could just as easily have walked the other direction and been killed or captured by the Germans. In the same way, Williamson in "Beware of the Dog" does not know which side of the English Channel he is on. This uncertainty is exploited in creating doubt later in the story. In the story Dahl is exploring what might have happened if he had made a different decision after he had crashed.

IN THE MODERN WORLD, EVERY PERSON IS PLACED IN THE POSITION OF WILLIAMSON, UNABLE TO TELL WHETHER THE WORLD IS AS IT SEEMS OR NOT."

CRITICAL OVERVIEW

Oddly, considering that it is among the most influential of Dahl's stories, "Beware of the Dog" has received little critical attention. It was originally published in the October 1944 issue of *Harper's* magazine and reprinted in Dahl's 1945 critically appraised short story collection *Over to You*, an anthology of seven previously published and three new stories dealing with aviators during the war. It did not, however, sell well, coming out just after the war when interest in that genre of fiction was waning. Mark I. West in the Dahl volume in the Twayne's English Author Series simply notes that the story is surreal in tone. He does, however, draw attention to a 1942 article in the *Saturday Evening Post* in which Dahl dwells on his mental confusion after his crash in the desert, his dreams before awakening in the hospital, and the shock of finding the complete destruction of his nose by his wounds, all themes of "Beware of the Dog." On the other hand, Jeremy Treglown, Dahl's biographer, is concerned mainly with "Beware of the Dog" in its role in establishing Dahl's career and later as an important source of income when his career began to take off in the early 1960s, when he sold the film rights to the story that was eventually filmed as *36 Hours.*

CRITICISM

Bradley A. Skeen

Skeen is a classics professor. In this essay, he examines Dahl's theme of totalitarian control of reality in "Beware of the Dog" in the context of George Orwell's Nineteen Eighty-Four.

Dahl uses considerable literary art to make the reader who is reading "Beware of the Dog" for the first time agree with a certain interpretation of the story that can be summarized as follows. Williamson is wounded and blacks out, losing contact with reality as he goes into shock, his mind wandering through fantasy, memory, and hallucination. When he regains consciousness, he is in an army hospital in Brighton, or so he thinks until he begins to see clues that suggest he is not in Brighton but in Nazi-occupied France. The clinching piece of evidence is a house with a "Beware of the Dog" sign written in French. He realizes he is the victim of a monstrous Nazi plot to gain military secrets from him by making him think he is in England and being debriefed by his own superior officers, when really he is to be interrogated by an enemy intelligence officer pretending to be British. Since he realizes this, when the officer starts to ask him about the incident in which he was shot down, he responds with his name, rank, and serial number, all the information he is obliged to give the enemy under the Geneva Convention on Prisoners of War. End of story.

That plot works quite well because it brings the reader along on a voyage of discovery, in which the reader penetrates along with Williamson and the narrator through veils of deception to the truth. However, there are many things wrong with the plot that do not hold up on close inspection. The film adaptation of the story, *36 Hours*, addresses many of them. For instance, how could Germans fool Williamson into thinking they were English? (In the film, Williamson is American, and his handlers are captured Americans coerced to play their parts in the deception.) What military secret could Williamson, who is not likely to know much

WHAT DO I READ NEXT?

- Dahl's 1986 autobiographical volume *Going Solo* continues his life study from the end of his education covered in *Boy: Tales of Childhood* through his service as an RAF fighter pilot during World War II.
- At the height of the Battle of Britain, the RAF decided to transfer twenty-five Indian pilots to England. They did not go in to service before the crisis of the battle was passed, but they went on to fight all over the world during the war. On November 9, 1991, the British Broadcasting Corporation interviewed the last surviving member of this group. Mahindra Singh Pujji reminisces about his wartime experiences, including racism that he faced, in the article "I Knew England was Having a Rough Time" (http://news.bbc.co.uk/2/hi/uk_news/1645374.stm).
- Dahl's 1943 young-adult novel *The Gremlins* is drawn from his wartime experiences in the RAF and presented to the public for the first time the military folklore that accidents and irregularities in aircraft maintenance are caused by mythical creatures called gremlins. Disney published the novel, but its plan to make an animated version of it never went forward. The idea of gremlins entered popular culture through a series of Warner Brothers cartoons featuring gremlins (which were not directly associated with Dahl). A facsimile of this book was published in 2006 by the comic book publisher Darkhorse.
- In 2008, after republishing Dahl's *Gremlins*, Mike Richardson, the publisher of Darkhorse Comics, published his own sequel to the book, *The Return of the Gremlins*, as a graphic novel illustrated by Dean Yeagle.
- J. M. Heimann's 2007 study, *The Airmen and the Headhunters: A True Story, of Lost Soldiers, Heroic Tribesmen, and the Unlikeliest Rescue of World War II*, gives the history of two American bombers shot down over the interior of New Guinea and how they were protected from the Japanese occupation forces by Dayak tribesman, famous in the West for their custom of headhunting. The book is based on fresh interviews with surviving airmen and also with survivors among the tribesmen who helped them. A good portion of the book is devoted to understanding Dayak culture and why its members treated the downed airmen as guests rather than enemies.
- As an author for an adult audience, Dahl is best known for his short stories. The 1960 anthology *Kiss Kiss* is one of Dahl's most important collections.
- Dahl wrote a large amount of poetry for younger readers, including his 1982 anthology *Revolting Rhymes* in which he re-envisions popular fairy tales with his characteristic twist endings.
- In 1948, Dahl published the first fictional treatment of nuclear war, *Sometimes Never: A Fable for Supermen*.

about the war except where he is ordered each morning, possibly possess that would be worth the effort of this elaborate deception? (In the film, Williamson becomes a military diplomat privy to the planning for the D-Day invasion.)

Was Dahl slipshod in his writing? By no means. He created a story that can withstand the scrutiny of repeated reading and analysis. "Beware of the Dog" also contains another story. Williamson is wounded and blacks out, losing contact with reality as he goes into shock, his mind wandering through fantasy, memory, and hallucination. When he regains consciousness, he finds his leg amputated. He has been through traumatic experiences for close to two years of war, which can have the effect of producing the temporary mental illness known at the time as shell shock. Since, as the narrator says, Williamson's leg does not hurt and he sleeps much more than eight hours a day, he is probably receiving morphine injections to control post-operative pain. All of these factors leave his state of mind unbalanced. He begins to suffer paranoid delusions, believing that everything he sees in his environment does not exist at random but is aimed directly at him and was created for the purpose of deceiving him. He finally comes to believe that he has not been rescued but has fallen into the hands of the enemy. His caretakers will be shocked when he reveals these beliefs.

There can be little doubt that Dahl wants us to read both stories, since he gives no way to choose between them. However, of course, they cannot both be true. In the second case, how could Williamson's caretakers ever persuade him of the truth? Everything they did to prove they were English would only make them seem more German. The ambiguity in the story is in one sense a practical joke played on the reader, but it has a more serious purpose as well.

Dahl is exploring in "Beware of the Dog" one of the great themes of modern literature. Starting with the Enlightenment (a period beginning in the seventeenth century in Europe, when reason became prized as a primary goal) and the Industrial Revolution (the rise of machine power, beginning in the nineteenth century), modern culture detached people from their traditional ways of life and from their traditional structures of belief. Modernity thrusts people into a new and alien world where the rhythm of life is determined not by the sun and the seasons but by a time clock, where work means the separation of the family for much of the day and means tending machines rather than producing one's food and supplies through agriculture. One hallmark of modernity is that people no longer directly experience much of their reality. Although people now know a larger reality outside of their own village, it is largely a reality presented to them through intermediaries in the mass media. People are told what is real by mass market advertising and by journalism. They must accept the report because it is what is available to them. At the same time, though, they know that a great deal that is reported to them is false. One product is much the same as another, no matter what advertisements say. Reporters parrot back now what is said by one politician and then what is said by an opponent, but they cannot get at any underlying truth. These factors and others make the reality in the modern world seem unreal.

Surrealism was a movement in art and philosophy that attempted to capture the contradictions and sense of unreality of modern life. Writing in 1942 at about the same time as Dahl, the surrealist Salvador Dalí summed up this problem this way: "The sole difference between myself and a madman is the fact that I am not mad!" The madman is mad because he believe things about the world that are different from those that everyone else believes: he does not give assent to consensus reality. Dalí also does not give assent to a consensus reality that rejects tradition and the human spirit. He does not do so because he is mad, but because he views reality as having gone mad. Williamson is in precisely the same position. Viewed objectively, his actions are those of a madman: he denies the reality of everything around him. However, the reader must at the same time recognize that in the circumstance of the war and in the persona of the Nazis modern reality has gone mad, and Williamson is acting sanely to recognize this truth. In this way Dahl dramatizes or allegorizes the problem of modernity. Williamson's life has gone wrong, his identity as a pilot is gone, and his leg has been shot off. He feels what is wrong but instead of facing it, he projects it on the world around him. He is not in England but in the hands of the Nazis. Dahl's audience may have an analogous feeling that something is wrong with modernity.

In "Beware of the Dog," a totalitarian state creates a false reality in order to deceive a prisoner of war into giving up information. This reflects a basic problem of modernity: so much of the world that one must be aware of is experienced at second hand, and modern life is so tightly controlled. A state could control its citizens by creating a false reality—it seems almost inevitable that it should. The word *propaganda* is hateful precisely because of the efforts of totalitarian states like Nazi Germany and Stalinist Russia to create an artificial reality, disseminating blatant lies as official truths, and even going so far as to alter official records such as newspapers to remove inconvenient facts or people who had fallen out of favor. Free societies have just as many false and controlling messages, however, not only in advertising but in official justifications for government policy at the highest level, such as the justification for war. The myth of the "Rape of Belgium" that the British government used to influence the public in favor of its declaration of war against Germany in 1914, as well the exaggerated or fabricated reports of United States presidents to sway the public and Congress to acquiesce in the Vietnam and Second Gulf wars show that the creation of a false reality can take place under any government. Writing only a few years after Dahl, George Orwell feared that the creation of such an artificial reality was the inevitable condition that the modern world was heading toward. He portrays one such scenario in *Nineteen Eighty-Four*.

In *Nineteen Eighty-Four*, Winston Smith has the job of rewriting old newspaper articles so that they agree with the current policies of the government of Oceania (a union of Great Britain and the United States), a state ruled by the totalitarian Party. When Smith tries to find members of a resistance movement to what he recognizes as the tyranny of the state, he is arrested by The Ministry of Love and re-educated so that he is forced, through a process of reasoned argument and torture, to agree in word and in thought with the state propaganda. His interrogator, O'Brien, begins by telling Smith that he is mad because he denies the truth and prefers to remember false things, exactly the opposite of what Smith knows to be true. He then goes on to explore the limits, or rather the lack of limits, of the state's power to control reality:

> We control matter because we control the mind. Reality is inside the skull. You will learn by degrees, Winston. There is nothing that we could not do. Invisibility, levitation—anything. I could float off this floor like a soap bubble if I wished to. I do not wish to, because the Party does not wish it. You must get rid of those nineteenth-century ideas about the laws of nature. We make the laws of nature.

Winston objects that the laws of nature are unchanging, but O'Brien simply reiterates that everything is as the Party says it is because everyone in the world accepts the Party's authority. He even insists, "The earth is the center of the universe. The sun and the stars go round it." The Party creates whatever belief it wants. The effort of creating an entire state of enthusiastic Nazis and enthusiastic Stalinists makes the problem of convincing one a man for three days that he is in England rather than France seem trivial. In the modern world, every person is placed in the position of Williamson, unable to tell whether the world is as it seems or not.

A pilot in flight (Image copyright ChipPix, 2009. Used under license from Shutterstock.com)

Source: Bradley Skeen, Critical Essay on "Beware of the Dog," in *Short Stories for Students*, Gale, Cengage Learning, 2010.

David Galef

In the following excerpt, Galef examines Dahl's various voices through his short stories and children's and adult literature.

Given the protean nature of literary genre, the question "What is a children's book?" has long been regarded as intriguing if possibly unanswerable, almost to the point of teleology: a children's book is "a book which appears on the children's list of a publisher" (Townsend 10). An equally complex but perhaps more fruitful query is "What enables an author to write both children's books and adult fiction?" Is this skill a matter of authorial personality, marketing, or a serendipitous synthesis? And what provokes the crossover?

Certainly, the list of authors who have published in both genres is long and distinguished. In *They Wrote for Children Too*, Marilyn Fain Apseloff has catalogued over a hundred "adult" writers whose works have also included children's texts (admittedly, sometimes adapted by later writers). But in fact the number of authors famous in both genres is far more limited. What links a book like Ian Fleming's *Dr. No* with his *Chitty Chitty Bang Bang?*

> "IN FACT, WHAT DAHL DOES BEST IS WRITE DAHL BOOKS, A CURIOUS MIDDLE GROUND THAT, WITH A LITTLE ALTERATION IN SUBJECT AND TONE, APPEALS TO EITHER ADULTS OR CHILDREN."

Those who write for both children and adults tend to fall into one of three categories (not including hybrids, exceptions, and bad examples). The most common category comprises writers of adult fiction who, for one reason or another, take up children's literature in mid-career. This pattern mimics the general history of publishing: an enterprise importuned by or otherwise made aware of a new audience for its goods. Unfortunately, some modern adults' authors think that all they must do to appeal to children is write pablum versions of their regular material. Those who manage the transition gracefully may have learned something about children: sometimes the impetus for a first children's book is the author's first child. Such authors may also have an intuitive grasp of children's psychology, in some cases an arrested adolescence of sorts. Another possibility in this category is an author who writes on themes appealing to readers of diverse ages. Roald Dahl is a good example of this type; so, for that matter, are such seeming opposites as Antoine de Saint-Exupéry and Fleming. But it is not an easy achievement, and each year's list of children's books are strewn with casualties, inferior works that will soon perish.

Somewhat rarer is the second type, which is simply the reverse of the first: those who start out writing for children and only later begin to write for an older audience. The obvious worry, that the original genre may constrain the new mode, seems not to apply in this direction. If anything carries over, it is the emphasis on imagination, as in Madeleine L'Engle's books for adult readers. Of course, those who achieve sufficient fame in children's literature, such as Maurice Sendak, will attract adult readers for anything they have written. But the career-arc of Russell Hoban is different; after becoming well known as both an illustrator and writer of children's books, he began to put forth adult novels of astonishing complexity and power. Perhaps accretion is in some ways easier than simplicity.

The third category, what one might term polygraphy, falls somewhere in between the first two types. Though writers such as A. A. Milne, who penned nursery rhymes and box-office hits with equal facility, are hardly a common breed, there has always been a small but recognizable subset of authors who balance an array of diverse projects and have done so since the start of their careers. Louisa May Alcott and C. S. Lewis are two good examples. Their output is generally prolific, yet marked by a high degree of craft. If some critics fault polygraphic authors for lack of depth, this quality may be attributable to speed of composition, or the tendency of popular opinion to equate prolixity with shallowness.

Perhaps the most useful way to illustrate this typology is to examine the career of one writer from each category. In selecting authors for this purpose, I seek a homogeneous group, since the variables of gender, race, class, language, and era introduce complexities that, though intriguing, are beyond the scope of this essay. Accordingly, I have restricted my discussion to three twentieth-century male English-speaking authors—Dahl, Hoban, and Milne—whose texts seem to illuminate key aspects of genre crossover.

... Dahl provides an excellent example of a latecomer to children's books, as well as to the profession of writing itself. An ex-R.A.F. pilot whose first published work was a doctored account of his plane crash in Libya, Dahl soon produced a book of stories about pilots called *Over to You* (1945). The style was tight with occasional flourishes of wit, Hemingwayesque in its spareness, yet also with Ernest Hemingway's love of technical detail. In fact, Hemingway was a friend of Dahl's, though his response to *Over to You* was curious. As Alan Warren recounts the incident: "Hemingway borrowed the volume: he returned it after two days, and when Dahl asked him how he'd like [*sic*] the stories, Hemingway, striding off along the corridor, replied: 'I didn't understand them'" (121). This kind of reader-response keeps one from defining "adult" books as those beyond children's comprehension, since they obviously confuse some adults, as well. In any event, encouraged more by Alfred A. Knopf than by Hemingway, Dahl became known as a polished short-story writer in the vein of Saki and John Collier.

A typical Dahl story, such as "Skin" or "Lamb to the Slaughter," depends on a what-if premise or a twist—what happens when a man has a masterpiece tattooed on his back? suppose the murder weapon were edible?—though the writing is not gimmicky. *Someone Like You* (1953) and *Kiss Kiss* (1959) showcase the best of these gently macabre tales, with a slight fall-off in quality when Dahl tackles the risqué in *Switch Bitch* (1974). And then one day, as Dahl puts it, "I didn't have a plot for a short story, and I decided to have a go at doing a children's book" (West, Interview 63). As further impetus, Dahl by then had a live audience, his own children. The bedtime stories he told them formed the nucleus of *James and the Giant Peach* (1961). After that, it was *Charlie and the Chocolate Factory* (1964), and Dahl was off and running. Switching genres was apparently a piece of cake, to borrow the title of Dahl's first short story.

And yet, if one looks more closely at the start of Dahl's writing career, some discrepancies emerge. First, as Jeremy Treglown chronicles in his recent biography of Dahl, switching genres was more an imperative than a lark: Dahl confessed that he had begun running out of short-story ideas, and in any event magazines such as *The New Yorker* were turning away from his brand of narrative (127). Second, Dahl had begun working on children's material well before his first published book for juveniles. *The Gremlins*, a fantasy about mythical creatures who interfere with the workings of airplanes, came out in 1943 as a picture book after being bought by Disney for possible film adaptation. Third, given the nature of Dahl's short stories, strongly plotted flights of imagination with O. Henry twists, one could argue that Dahl was always writing with a child's delight in reversals. As Mark West remarks in his book-length study of Dahl: "In almost all of Dahl's fiction—whether it be intended for children or adults—authoritarian figures, social institutions, and societal norms are ridiculed or at least undermined" (x). Treglown makes a similar point about strong maternal figures, specifically Dahl's mother, Sofie (52). Dahl depended heavily on her but also seems to have rigged events in his fiction against just such types.

Many of the plots suggest a desire for revenge on the powerful. In the short story "William and Mary," the wife sees her autocratic husband reduced to utter, bodiless dependency; in "Beware of the Dog," the shot-down pilot learns that he is not only crippled but imprisoned. The children's books showcase this incapacity. In *The Magic Finger* (1966), for instance, the duck hunters are turned into ducks, and *The Twits* (1980) is full of images of immobility: "Mrs. Twit was quite helpless now. With her feet tied to the ground and her arms pulled upward by the balloons, she was unable to move" (24).

As Freud notes in *Beyond the Pleasure Principle*, the next step after dependency and paralysis is the inorganic state, which is where Dahl often leaves his victims, sometimes literally. In "The Landlady," the new lodger finds out too late that his landlady practices human taxidermy. In "Georgy Porgy," a shy curate returns to the other end of life, birth. Afraid of eros due to a childhood memory of a rabbit eating her newborn baby, and guilty over the death of his own sexually aggressive mother, he envisions a return to the womb down the throat of a promiscuous female parishioner. He ends up engulfed—inside the woman, as he imagines, but really confined to a padded cell.

The figures due for comeuppance in Dahl's children's books are dealt with similarly: the wicked aunts in *James and the Giant Peach* are flattened, and the two odious adults in *The Twits* succumb to a fatal case of the shrinks. At first, Dahl doled out poetic justice: in *Charlie and the Chocolate Factory*, for example, Augustus Gloop falls into the Slough of Gluttony, and Mike Teavee becomes as tiny and limited as the figures he watches on television. Only in his later children's books, such as *Matilda* (1988), does Dahl settle too predictably into a back-and-forth mode of injury and vengeance. As Matilda resolves after her father insults her: "She decided that every time her father or mother was beastly to her, she would get her own back in some way or another" (29). In *Dirty Beasts* (1983), a pig decides to turn the tables on the farmer and eat him, an ant-eater eats an aunt, and so on. Revenge is sweet, but less so when it becomes systematic.

Yet as far back as the flying stories, as close to bare-bones realism as Dahl ever got till he wrote his autobiographical volumes *Boy* (1984) and *Going Solo* (1986), a sense of payback prevails, often taking an arguably childlike form. In "Madame Rosette," the pilots are like boys sassing the evil old witch, in this case the ugly madam of a brothel in Cairo. The sense of impishness is never far from even the utmost seriousness. In "A Piece of Cake," a pilot in a burning airplane crash imagines a telegraph system between the body and the brain: "Down here there is a great hotness. What shall we do? (Signed) Left Leg and Right Leg" (41). "Beware of the Dog," the penultimate story in the collection, is the stuff of childish paranoia, everyone around the protagonist seemingly kind but really an enemy—the fantasy brilliantly vindicated in the end.

... What are the implications for Dahl's voice or the writer behind it? As Dahl once said of himself: "It's a mistake to see me as two different people. I'm not" (West, "Interview" 65). In fact, what Dahl does best is write Dahl books, a curious middle ground that, with a little alteration in subject and tone, appeals to either adults or children. When he veers away from this mode, as in the sexually titillating *My Uncle Oswald*, he loses a portion of his audience. And when he writes too deliberately for children, as in *The Magic Finger* with its restricted lexicon, his narrative also suffers. In fact, Dahl has gone on record against what Jan Susina has termed "kiddie lit(e)," or "the dumbing down of children's literature" (v). In a polemic entitled "Let's Build a Skyscraper, But Let's Find a Good Book First," Dahl rails against books with limited vocabulary and "those horrible things that are called educational books" (2). More successful, from both a narrative and marketing point of view, was *Danny the Champion of the World* (1975), in which Dahl did not pare down but rather expanded on several adult stories about poaching that had appeared in *Someone Like You*.

In "Lucky Break—How I Became a Writer," Dahl lists seven qualities a fiction writer should have (*Henry Sugar* 168–69). The first is a lively imagination, but stamina, self-discipline, humor, and humility are also on the roster. In the end, the moral dimension in which Dahl places both children and adults is more complex than mere payback or turning the other cheek, since it involves luck, shrewdness, and a wit that doesn't flinch from life's ugliness. Dahl's longtime illustrator Quentin Blake, with his cartoonish but apt drawings, helps to accentuate the fun in Dahl's otherwise tendentious humor.

In these days of political correctness, Dahl has endured accusations of racism and sexism, as Jonathan Culley and others have chronicled. As for charges of sadism and vulgarity, however, Culley provides convincing analogies with folklore to show just what Dahl is about: the structures and methods of myth, with their occasional cruelty and excess. Hubris leads to a sickening fall; one foul deed is repaid with another. Hamida Bosmajian has even pointed out Rabelaisian links in an essay on Dahl's excremental vision. This kind of Lévi-Straussian analysis also explains why Dahl's appeal is so broad, since the mythic dimension knows no age limit....

Source: David Galef, "Crossing Over: Authors Who Write Both Children's and Adults' Fiction," in *Children's Literature Association Quarterly*, Vol. 20, No. 1, Spring 1995, pp. 29–31.

Frederick Raphael

In the following excerpt, Raphael discusses the commercialism in Dahl's writing career.

Roald Dahl's name alone sold both books and television series. He aroused expectations which, with renowned professionalism, he regularly satisfied. Like Alfred Hitchcock, who might have relished his calculated *frissons*, he had the gift of consistent, not to say repetitious ingenuity. "Parson's Pleasure" and "Royal Jelly" may not be sublime, but they are small masterpieces, like the best of Conan Doyle's unHolmesian tales, or the worst of Edgar Allan Poe. Whatever his lack of high art, Dahl was a classic of a kind....

Dahl addressed himself to the largest possible public. It may be that he craved critical applause, but he belonged to a tradition of self-reliant commercialism, in which the undeniable certificate of merit was top-dollar acceptance by best selling magazines. (Was it not Dorothy Parker who said that the sweetest phrase in the English language was "Cheque enclosed?")

Fastidious critics tend to assume that only trash can result from writing for a mass market. However, commercialism can develop muscles which no grant-aided aesthete will ever be able to flex. The robustness of the American short story derives not least from the journalism in which Ring Lardner, Sinclair Lewis, John O'Hara, Scott Fitzgerald and Hemingway learned to box clever and, sometimes, a little dirty. Dahl was an Englishman, of Norwegian origins, but he mixed with American editors, in the years after the war, and the "universality" of his mean myths surely owes something to their demands for the unpretentious. In vocabulary and, as they used to say, level of intent, Dahl appears to be a low-flyer: he uses fancy words only to josh his readers. His only avowed purpose is to entertain; the anecdote is paramount. He seemed to have no trouble in devising stories with delicious twists, something which only fools and fine spirits imagine is a mere trick (it may be a trick, but it is not mere).

Dahl's trademark was his mercilessness. After "William and Mary"—you remember, the one about the man whose eye and brain live on after him in a dish which his embittered wife takes home—or "The Champion of the World" (who has not relished, or even poached, that ultimate poaching story about the pram full of narcotized pheasants?), or "The Visitor" (with its sour-creamy affinities with Karen Blixen's "The Immortal Story"), it is tempting to think that one has their creator's number: he is the definitive Mr Not-Nice Guy. The same charge, on a nobler plane, was sometimes levelled against Vladimir Nabokov, of whom there are certain echoes, in the unsentimental, but luxuriant, eroticism and in the lepidopteric minutiae. It might be argued that both men concealed their vulnerability, and their wounds, behind a carapace of heartlessness.

By leading off with the stories from *Kiss, Kiss* (1960), the compilers of *The Collected Short Stories* make sure that cruel expectations are promptly met: Dahl is here in the macabre vein which turned so regularly to gold. Yet by this prompt serving of old favourites, the line of his authorial progress is distorted. His published work began, significantly, with *Over to You* (1947), in which the stories derive less from *Esquire* or the *Saturday Evening Post* than from the H. E. Bates of "Flying Officer X", or the tales of "Gun-Buster" (whose pseudonym I have yet to hear blown). The latter's stories of the desert war, in particular, chilled and thrilled my schooldays. I remember an almost unpatriotic tale of surrendering Italians being run over by one of our tanks. Perhaps inadvertently, something horribly true bled through the hit-'em-for-six optimism.

Over to You announced Dahl's Royal Air Force provenance, and intimates how, and perhaps why, he came to turn bloody experience into well-done fodder. The stories written more or less immediately after the war are only superficially of a piece with the more characteristic later pieces. In these tales of RAF life, one is conscious of the unendurable being wilfully, desperately, recycled for a readership which is both solicited and despised. If Dahl's later avoidance of naivety smacked of Smart Alec, just as his want of sentiment looked like callousness, the flying stories sometimes resemble Richard Hillary with added sugar. "They Shall Not Grow Old," for instance, tells of a young fighter ace who falls fatally in love with death. . . .

In "The Great Grammatizator", Dahl satirizes, with a rather unlight touch, the mechanical story-telling which word-processing has perhaps made imminent and which will allow editors to procure what they want by pressing the required button. His computer-operating "heroes" become filthy rich by buying up famous names and persuading them to abandon composition. Their husks are then filled with commercial corn until all individuality yields to market forces. A sour interpreter might claim that Dahl did his industrious best to impersonate just such a graceless machine, but a more sympathetic reading will detect repressed disgust (and shame perhaps) at mass culture's degradation of literature.

It may be that Dahl was not a nice man, but he seems to have been quite a nice young chap until the war introduced him, traumatically, to death. That it took him some time to come to terms with the realities behind *Over to You* is suggested by the fact that it was not until 1986, when he was seventy years old, that he published an excellent volume of autobiography entitled *Going Solo*. One cannot, of course, be sure how much of the manuscript already existed, in some form or other, nor to what degree the artful Dahl was dressing hind-sighted reminiscence in reconstituted youthfulness. Nevertheless, the metamorphosis of a nice young Shell executive in Tanganyika into a badly injured Battle of Greece veteran of twenty-five leaves one in no doubt as to the author's genuine sufferings. The ineptitude of authority, the absurdity of war, the arbitrariness of death had to be understated in order to be stated at all. Who but Dahl has pointed out that fighter pilots were often sent up without any instructions as to what to do in combat? War became a schoolboy story with death instead of half-holidays. The squeamish youth was callused into the hard case.

Dahl's misfortune was perhaps indistinguishable from his good luck: he survived (one of three out of sixteen pilots in his squadron), without much respect for those he obeyed or for whom he was said to be fighting. He remembered aces like David Coke, who died with aristocratic insouciance while cowards and time-servers went on to prosperous longevity. Living well and writing commercially were his best revenge, but the voice of Fin, hell-bent for infinity and immune to

IT'S A MISTAKE TO SEE ME AS TWO DIFFERENT PEOPLE. I'M NOT. THE MAIN THING THAT TIES ALL MY WORK TOGETHER IS A TERRIBLE FEAR OF BORING THE READER."

disillusionment, is audible behind all these artful, spun-out tales.

Source: Frederick Raphael, "Sources from the Source of Heartlessness," in *Times Literary Supplement*, Vol. 4618, October 4, 1991, p. 28.

Mark I. West

In the following interview, West asks Dahl about how Dahl began writing for children and the difficulty involved in writing for two different audiences, children and adults.

I called Roald Dahl from my hotel room in London in order to work out the final arrangements for my interview with him. He patiently explained how to catch the train to Great Missenden, a small town about thirty miles west of London, and agreed to meet me at the station. As I sat in the train, I reviewed my notes on Dahl's writing career.

I especially wanted to ask him about his early stories. I knew that he began writing during World War II while he was in the Royal Air Force but was no longer flying. I also knew that when he published his first stories, he was living in Washington, D.C., where he worked at the British Embassy. But I wanted to know more details.

Another subject I wanted to discuss with him was his ability to write for both adults and children. Many prominent adult authors try writing for children, but only a few manage to write even a single children's book that is actually read by children. Dahl, though, has achieved tremendous success in both areas. He first became famous for his macabre short stories for adults, but he is now even more famous for his bestselling children's books, including *James and the Giant Peach*, *Charlie and the Chocolate Factory*, *The BFG*, *The Witches*, and, most recently, *Matilda.*

Dahl met me at the train station and drove me to his home, which is called Gipsy House. He showed me into the living room, where we took seats on two of the beautiful antique chairs that Dahl avidly collects. What follows is a somewhat condensed version of our conversation.

Q: What was your very first published story?

A:"A Piece of Cake" was my first publication, but it was a nonfictional piece about the time my fighter plane crashed in Libya. My first fictional story was a little fantasy called "The Gremlins." I wrote it while I was in the RAF. My flying days had just ended, and I was feeling a bit nostalgic about fighting in the war, and these feelings carried over into the story. It's a story about these little creatures who make trouble for the RAF, drilling holes in the planes and so on.

Q: Did you come up with the word "gremlins"?

A: I didn't invent the word. It was being knocked about in my squadron and maybe other squadrons, too. But I think I was the first to use it in print. I invented a name for female gremlins—fifinellas, I think it was. And I called the gremlin children widgets.

Q: Was it a children's story?

A: I didn't think it was when I wrote it. The main character is not a child. But Disney bought it and started making it into a film, and everybody began thinking of it as a children's story. It was even published as a picture book. I still don't see it as a children's story; it was just a little exercise. From there I went on to write a whole series of flying stories, and none of these were for children.

Q: Why were all of your early stories published in America first?

A: I happened to be in America when I started writing, so it seemed natural to send my stories to the American magazines. And then I got an American agent in New York. From then on, Americans were always my initial publishers, that is, until quite recently. There is also a better market for short stories in America than in England. If I were a novelist I might have gone more with British publishers.

Q: Didn't you publish a novel early in your career?

A: I know what you're thinking of. It was called *Some Time Never*, and I am not proud of it. I never wanted to write it in the first place. I was pushed into it by the great Max Perkins. My short stories had come to Perkins's attention, and he sent me a note that said, "Dear

Mr. Dahl, would you come and see me." Well, I jumped high in the air, as any writer would in those days. He was, after all, editing Wolfe and Hemingway and Fitzgerald. He was the greatest editor America ever had. So I thought, oh wonderful, and I rushed to see him. He told me this delightful story about editing Wolfe's *Look Homeward, Angel*, and all of this was enthralling to a young writer. He then said, "These short stories of yours are lovely, but what interests me is a novel." To which I said, "But, Mr. Perkins, I don't think I can do a novel. I'm a short story writer." But he told me to go ahead and promised to help me. Well, I didn't know what to write about in a book of that length, so I expanded my gremlin story. It ended up being a rather silly fantasy about the end of the world. It was sort of prophetic, in a way, but it wasn't a good story. Well, I sent the first draft to Perkins, but he died before he had a chance to read it, or maybe it was my story that killed him. The book then fell into the hands of his assistant, who just published it as it was. Like I said, I'm not proud of it, but it taught me a lesson. I learned that I am not a long-distance runner. After that I wrote the stories in *Someone Like You*, and I'm still proud of that book.

Q: Who published Someone Like You?

A: Knopf. It marked the beginning of a long relationship I had with Alfred Knopf. I'll never forget my first contact with him. The phone went off in my little flat in New York, and the voice straight away said, "This is Alfred Knopf." And I thought, God, it can't be true. "Is it truly?" I asked him, and he said it was. He later told me that he never had his secretary place calls for him. He thought it was too rude. He then said, "Look, I read your short story "Taste" in the *New Yorker*. Do you have any more?" I said, "Yes, funny enough, I was just about getting a book of stories together." He said, "I'll buy it." Just like that. He was so nice and forthright.

When I got married a little later, I needed money for a honeymoon. So I went into his office and asked for a loan. I told him that I knew I didn't have much in the way of royalties yet, but I planned to give him all my other books. Well, he just stopped me and said, "How much do you need?" I told him about $5,000. "You got it," he said. That's the old-fashioned way to deal with writers. It was lovely. Nowadays they would have to go talk to their accountant and make you promise them your next five books. But there was none of that with Knopf. He was a good man. He hung out against the beastly conglomerates until finally he was ill and had to retire. Then he sold out to Random House.

Q: How did you come to write for children?

A: It's the usual story. I had been writing short stories for about fifteen years, and then I had children. I always told them stories in bed, and they started asking for some of the stories over and over. I was in New York at the time, and I didn't have a plot for a short story, so I decided to have a go at doing a children's book. I took some of these bedtime stories and turned them into *James and the Giant Peach*, I enjoyed it so much that I immediately embarked on *Charlie and the Chocolate Factory*. Well, *Charlie* took off. It was quite amazing. The hardcover sales in America went from about 7,000 in the first year to about 18,000 in the second to about 25,000 in the third. By the fifth year, *Charlie* was up to 80,000. And, of course, *James* jumped on *Charlie's* bandwagon.

Q: How did Charlie's success affect your writing career?

A: Well, of course, I kept writing children's books. I think my next was *The Magic Finger*, and then came *Fantastic Mr. Fox*. I'm especially proud of *Fox*. It's a short book, but it has a strong plot. I have always tried to come up with new stories, new plots. I despise authors who have one success and then go on repeating it endlessly, like what Lindgren has done with *Pippi Longstocking* or Bond has done with *Paddington Bear*. It shows a lack of imagination and inventiveness.

But you can't put all the blame on the author. Publishers often put a lot of pressure on authors to write sequels. This was even true back a hundred years ago when Carroll wrote *Alice*. They kept after him until he wrote *Looking Glass*, but the sequel just wasn't as good as the first. Some of the verse in *Looking Glass* is as good as anything in *Alice*, but the story doesn't measure up.

The same thing that happened to Carroll happened to me. My publishers kept screaming for another *Charlie*, and I kept saying no way, no way. I resisted for five or six years, but finally I said all right, let's do it. I tried to come up with a new plot, make it different, but it wasn't much fun writing. I'll never do it again no matter how much the publishers scream.

Q: What is the most difficult type of children's book to write?

A: All good children's books take a lot of effort, but I find it hardest to write books for the very young, books to be read by the mother or father while the child is in bed. I've only managed one, *The Enormous Crocodile*, and I'm very proud of it. I tried again with *The Giraffe and the Pelly and Me*, but I didn't quite bring it off. It's too long. It's a nice book, but it's not another *Crocodile*.

Most of the books for this age are written by illustrators. They can usually draw the pictures, but many of them can't write. This goes back to Beatrix Potter. I asked a children's book publisher what she would do if she received three or four of Potter's manuscripts without any of her illustrations, and the publisher said she would send them back. Now, if you put the pictures with it, it's a different matter. My point is that it is very difficult to come up with a plot that will hold a four-year-old's attention without the aid of illustrations.

Q: Is it easier to write for children or adults?

A: I think it's harder to write for children. It's terribly difficult to write an enduring children's book. Practically every great writer I have ever known has tried, but most have failed. The reason they try is that they know that if they hit the jackpot with just one children's book, it's an income for life. The same cannot be said for a fine adult novel. It will generate an income for several years, but then it drops off. I think the reason for this is that there are many more fine adult novels published each year than there are fine children's books. Maybe one children's book a year will endure, and if you're lucky enough to have written that one book you'll be collecting royalty checks from it for the rest of your life.

Q: Since you write for two distinct audiences, some critics tend to see you as two different writers. Do you see any connections between your adult stories and your children's books, or are they completely separate?

A: It's a mistake to see me as two different people. I'm not. The main thing that ties all my work together is a terrible fear of boring the reader. I always feel compelled to hold the reader, get him by the throat and never let go until the last page. That's why I won't indulge in two-page descriptions of sunsets. My fear of boring the reader is even stronger when I'm writing a children's book because a child doesn't have the concentration that an adult has. An adult might wade through some boring passages just because the book is famous or somebody said that it picks up toward the middle, but no child is going to do that. If the child gets bored with a book, he'll put it down and go straight away to the telly. I recognize this problem, and I won't let any page go by unless I'm pretty sure the reader is going to want to turn it over.

The problem with so much contemporary adult fiction is that it's written without any consideration for the reader. Nowadays many short story writers and novelists are too self-indulgent. Instead of writing stories with interesting plots, they write mood pieces or little vignettes. They drift around, giving their own opinions. I find it terribly boring.

Q: Do you find it more satisfying to write for children or adults?

A: It's more rewarding to write for children. When I'm writing for adults, I'm just trying to entertain them. But a good children's book does much more than entertain. It teaches children the use of words, the joy of playing with language. Above all, it helps children learn not to be frightened of books. Once they can get through a book and enjoy it, they realize that books are something that they can cope with. If they are going to amount to anything in life, they need to be able to handle books. If my books can help children become readers, then I feel I have accomplished something important.

Source: Mark I. West, "Interview with Roald Dahl," in *Children's Literature in Education*, Vol. 21, No. 2, June 1990, pp. 61–66.

SOURCES

Churchill, Winston, *Their Finest Hour*, Cassell, 1949.

Dahl, Roald, "Beware of the Dog," in *Over to You*, Reynal & Hitchcock, 1945, pp. 149–64.

———, *Boy: Tales of Childhood*, Farrar, Straus, Giroux, 1984.

———, *Charlie and the Chocolate Factory*, Alfred A. Knopf, 1967.

———, "Shot Down over Libya," in *Saturday Evening Post*, August 1, 1942, pp. 29–30.

———, *Taste*, Redpath, 1986.

Dalí, Salvador, *The Secret Life of Salvador Dalí*, translated by Haakon M. Chevalier, Dial, 1942; reprint, Dover, 1993, p. 349.

Keegan, John, *The Second World War*, Penguin, 2005, pp. 88–102.

Pearson, John, *Biggles: The Authorised Biography*, Sidgwick & Jackson, 1978.

Treglown, Jeremy, *Roald Dahl: A Biography*, Farrar, Straus, Giroux, 1994.

West, Mark I., *Roald Dahl*, Twayne's English Author Series, No. 492, Twayne Publishers, 1992, pp. 26–32.

FURTHER READING

Burdys, Algis, *Who?* Pyramid, 1958.

This novel examines a problem that is the opposite of the situation in "Beware of the Dog." Set in the 1970s (the near future at the time of writing) during a crisis in the Cold War, an American scientist is captured by the Soviets under the pretext of rescuing him from an industrial accident. He is returned after undergoing extensive reconstructive surgery. His work in military research is urgently needed, but how can the Americans be sure he is the same scientist and not a Soviet agent?

Dahl, Roald, *Collected Stories*, Random House, 2006.

This volume in the Everyman's Library, though it is not a complete collection, is the largest and most recent collection of Dahl's short stories; it includes "Beware of the Dog."

Dahl, Roald, *My Year*, Heinemann, 1991.

This is the last of Dahl's autobiographical writings. It is the diary he kept during the last year of his life, in which he reminisces about his entire life.

Fairclough, Robert, ed., *The Prisoner: The Original Scripts*, Reynolds & Hearn, 2004.

The classic 1960s television show *The Prisoner* examines many of the same themes of alienation and the manipulation of reality as "Beware of the Dog" and may have been partially inspired by Dahl's story.

A Day Goes By

LUIGI PIRANDELLO

1936

Luigi Pirandello's short story "A Day Goes By" (originally written in Italian as "Una giornata") was first published in the Italian newspaper *Corriere della sera* (*Evening Courier*) on September 24, 1936, less than three months before Pirandello's death. This short, dream-like tale of a man deposited in a train station with no memory of his past deals with themes of identity and alienation. The main character attempts to rediscover his identity, only to find that in the process of doing so, his life has passed him by. The slippery concept of identity, and how it is defined, is a common theme in Pirandello's work, as is the nature of reality: how do we truly know what is real and what is not? Throughout his life, Pirandello struggled with his own sense of alienation from the rest of the world, and even from himself. In a short biography of Pirandello that prefaces *Luigi Pirandello: Short Stories*, Frederick May writes that Pirandello claimed "he had no life outside his writing, and . . . like so many of his characters, he could sadly affirm that for himself he was nobody." Knowing of Pirandello's own estrangement, the story could be interpreted as the story of a man so detached from his own life that he has no memory of it (rather than the story of a man who has somehow lost his memories).

"A Day Goes By" is one of over two hundred short stories Pirandello wrote in his lifetime. Because it is not one of his better-known stories, it is difficult to find in print. It is included

Luigi Pirandello *(Popperfoto | Getty Images)*

in the 1987 collection, *Luigi Pirandello: Short Stories*, a Quartet Books publication, with an introduction by the translator, Frederick May.

AUTHOR BIOGRAPHY

The Italian author and playwright Pirandello was born on June 28, 1867, in Girgenti (now Agrigento), Sicily, the first son and second child of Stefano and Caterina Ricci Gramitto Pirandello. Luigi's father, Stefano, was the proprietor of a large sulfur mine. A stern man with a violent temper, Stefano insisted that young Luigi attend a technical school so that he could someday help his father with his business. Luigi, however, disliked the rigid curriculum (especially mathematics), and with his mother's support, he enrolled in the *ginnasio*, an academic junior high school, instead.

In 1880, the family moved to Palermo, the capital of Sicily, where Pirandello finished high school. He studied briefly at the University of Palermo before moving in 1887 to the University of Rome, where he began his study of philology. Two years later, he transferred to the University of Bonn, in Germany, where he wrote his dissertation on "The Phonetic Development of the Agrigento Dialect" and received his doctorate in 1891. His education completed, he returned to Italy.

Pirandello settled in Rome, where a financial allowance from his father enabled him to concentrate on his literary pursuits. He wrote poetry, short stories, and plays, unsure of which literary form he preferred. He made many friends in the literary community and sought their advice on his works in progress.

Late in 1893, he received a letter from his father requesting that he marry the daughter of his business partner, who had promised a substantial dowry. Pirandello married Antonietta Portulano on January 27, 1894. Though they barely knew each other at the time of their wedding, Pirandello and his new wife were happy in the early years of their marriage, and had three children, Stefano, Lietta, and Fausto. However, in 1903, a flood in his father's sulfur mine wiped out not only his father's fortune but also Antonietta's dowry, which had been invested in the mine. This setback precipitated the deterioration of Antonietta's mental state. She became increasingly paranoid and even violent. Despite her condition, Pirandello insisted on keeping her at home. Even when he finally committed her to an institution in 1919 (after sixteen years at home), he did so reluctantly.

After the loss of his father's fortune, Pirandello was obliged to support himself and his family on his own. To supplement his small salary as an instructor at a teacher training college, he strove to increase his output of literary work. In 1904 his novel *The Late Mattia Pascal* was published. It was not his first novel (he wrote *The Outcast* in 1893, though it was not published until 1901), but it was by far his most successful. It tells the story of a man who fakes his own death in order to live a life of complete freedom.

Pirandello gained his real fame as a playwright, but he did not focus on the theater until about 1915. This was a difficult year for Pirandello: his mother died, and not long afterward, his son Stefano, who was fighting in World War I, was captured and held prisoner by the Austrians (he would not return home until 1919). Pirandello's other son, Fausto, was called up to fight as well, but was diagnosed with tuberculosis.

When a well-known Sicilian actor requested that Pirandello write a play for the Sicilian theater, Pirandello agreed, for he needed money to pay for Fausto's medical bills. This was only the beginning: between 1916 and 1924 Pirandello wrote twenty-eight plays, including his most famous work, *Six Characters in Search of an Author*, in 1921.

With his children grown and his wife institutionalized, Pirandello could not bear to stay in the house alone; he spent the rest of his life traveling and living in hotels, attending productions of his work all over the world. His fame reached its peak during the 1920s, but his endorsement of the Fascist government of the Italian dictator Benito Mussolini earned him some harsh criticism. Some believed he only supported the Fascists to obtain government subsidization of his work. Whatever his motives, he did not overtly promote Fascist ideas in his work.

In 1934, Pirandello received the Nobel Prize for his contributions to literature. Two years later, on December 10, 1936, he died in Rome.

PLOT SUMMARY

As the story opens, the main character is on the ground in a dark, deserted train station, having been thrown off the train, though he has no memory of how or why. In fact, he cannot remember why he was on the train in the first place, or where he was going. He leaves the station and finds that it is just before dawn, and he is in an unfamiliar city. He has little memory of who he is or what he does for a living; he just remembers, "I've always worked, worked very hard, very hard indeed."

Walking down the street, he recognizes no one, although some people wave at him. In his suit pocket he finds a wallet he is sure must belong to someone else; since he does not recognize the suit he is wearing, he assumes the wallet must belong to the suit's rightful owner. Inside the wallet he finds a large, outdated banknote, and a photograph of a beautiful woman in a swimsuit, with her arms outstretched toward him. He does not recognize the woman, but he notices that the photo "is in the place where you put your fiancée's photograph."

Exhausted and hungry, he enters a restaurant, where is treated like "an honoured guest." He shows the proprietor of the restaurant the banknote he found in the wallet, and learns that this type of note is no longer in circulation, but that the bank will exchange it for him. The proprietor directs him to the bank, where he is given a large sum of money for the banknote. He returns to the restaurant, but nothing on the menu appeals to him. As he leaves, he finds a chauffeur-driven car waiting for him, which takes him to his house. He does not remember the car or the house, and feels he is "a stranger here, a kind of intruder." He begins to explore the house, and when he opens one of the doors, he discovers that it is a bedroom; waiting for him on the bed, with arms outstretched, is the beautiful woman from the photograph. He embraces her. "Is it a dream?" he wonders.

When he awakens the next morning, the woman is gone, the bed is cold, and the house has an old, musty smell it did not have the night before. When he looks in the mirror he discovers, to his horror, that he is now an old man. "So suddenly! Just like that! How is it possible?" He is still wondering how this could have happened when there is a knock at the door, and someone tells him his children have come to see him. He has no recollection of having had children. "But when?" he puzzles. "I must have had them yesterday. Yesterday I was still young." The children enter, bringing their own children with them—his grandchildren. They admonish him for having gotten out of bed: "they know perfectly well that I can't stand on my feet any longer and that I'm in a really bad way." Time continues to accelerate; the grandchildren, who were small when they entered the house, grow up before his eyes, his children now have gray hair, and he finds that he is no longer able to get up from his bed. "And with the same childlike eyes that a little while before those children had—oh, how grown-up they are now!—I sit there, looking at my old children, standing behind these new ones, and there is great compassion in my gaze." Thus the story ends, with the main character clearly at the end of his life.

CHARACTERS

Children and Grandchildren

Near the close of the story, the main character is visited by his grown children and their children, though he does not remember ever having had children ("I must have had them yesterday," he muses). When they arrive for their visit, the grandchildren are small; just minutes later, the grown children have gray hair and the grandchildren have grown up. They are affectionate and loving; it is clear they know him well, even though he does not remember them.

Fiancée

The main character first encounters his fiancée/wife when he sees her photograph in the old wallet he finds in his pocket. In the photograph, she is dressed only in a swim suit ("almost naked") and has her arms raised in greeting. Though he does not recognize her, when he looks at the photo he has "a certain feeling of pain" and he senses that he is the one to whom she is waving. Later, when he comes to his house, he finds her in person, lying on the bed in the bedroom; the next morning, she is gone.

Main Character

The nameless main character of the story knows little about himself or where he is. He is bewildered and uncertain, and he feels inadequate in the face of others' certainty and confidence: "They're without the slightest hesitancy, so naturally convinced are they that they must do what they're doing." He concludes that, because they are so confident, "*I* must be in the wrong, and the others must quite assuredly be in the right." Though he feels no such certainty, he does his best to fit in: "I must contrive to act like the others."

The character learns about himself at the same time as the reader does. He remembers that he is a hard worker ("I've always worked, worked very hard") and discovers that he has a fiancée and plenty of money. He is treated with deference and admiration at both the restaurant and the bank, indicating that he is a man of some stature in the community (the restaurant's proprietor characterizes him as "important and respectable.") A chauffeur drives him to his impressive home, where he meets his wife and children, none of whom he remembers. He is a stranger to his own life. With no knowledge of his life or the people in it, he is completely at the mercy of those around him, who seem to know much more about him than he knows of himself.

Restaurant Proprietor

At the restaurant, the main character first discovers that he is a man of some consequence in the community. The proprietor treats him with great respect, and shows him where to take his old banknote for exchange.

THEMES

Alienation

According to the Pirandello translator Frederick May, Pirandello once wrote in his private notebook, "There is somebody who's living my life. And I know nothing about him." This sense of detachment from one's life, even from oneself, is an important theme of "A Day Goes By."

From the moment the story begins, the main character knows nothing of his identity or his surroundings—he is a stranger to himself and his own life. He is also estranged from the other people he encounters when walking through the city; the words he uses to describe the others and himself are opposites. For instance, he concludes that he must be wrong, and they must be right, and while he "can't even be certain . . . that I really exist," the others are "without the slightest hesitancy, so naturally convinced are they that they must do what they're doing." Even when the others wave to him in greeting, he cannot believe that they are waving at him, and suspects "that it's this suit they're waving at and not me." This illustrates the psychoanalytic concept of persona, the image we project to the world, which is often very different from our true self. When we begin to equate the persona with our identity, we experience an alienation from our true identity, losing touch with who we really are. Here the suit represents the image the main character is projecting. The suit is just one of the trappings of his life, his image as an "important and respectable" man. It does not represent his real self; he has no knowledge of that self. Even when he sees himself in the mirror at his house, he has no recognition of himself. He refers to the image in the mirror as "this old man's face," and he is unable "to convince myself of the truth of what I'm seeing."

It is only at the very end of the story that the bleak nature of Pirandello's tale is relieved by some positive language. Though he still has no recognition of his children or grandchildren, he observes "mischievously" that his children have sprouted some gray hairs, and he regards his family with "childlike eyes," looking upon them with "great compassion." The idea that the main character feels compassion indicates that his alienation, at least in regard to his family,

TOPICS FOR FURTHER STUDY

- Despite the large number of short stories Pirandello wrote, he is known primarily as a playwright. He adapted many of his stories to the stage. Write a short play based on "A Day Goes By." What will you have to change about the story to translate it to the stage? How will you maintain the dream-like feeling of the story in a play? Remember to include descriptions of the sets and scenery you would use.
- Pirandello was criticized for supporting Italian dictator Benito Mussolini and his Fascist regime in Italy. Research the history of Mussolini's rise to power and his dictatorship, and create a PowerPoint presentation detailing these events.
- In Pirandello's written wishes for his funeral, he stated that "my death must be passed over in silence.... No one to accompany me, neither friends nor relations. The hearse, the horse, the driver—that is all." Write a short essay about why you think the Fascist regime in Italy was dismayed by this request but did abide with his wishes for a private funeral and burial.
- Read the young-adult novel *Memoirs of a Teenage Amnesiac* by Gabrielle Zevin. What difficulties does Naomi share with the main character of "A Day Goes By" in rediscovering her identity? Create a Venn diagram that illustrates the similarities and differences in the characters.
- "A Day Goes By" has a dream-like quality. Read the short book, *Demystifying Dreams: A Manual for Teens* by psychologist Marvin Rosen. If you had a dream like Pirandello's how would you interpret it? Pirandello was in his late sixties when he wrote the story. How do you think his interpretation would differ from yours? Write your own interpretation, and then write what you think Pirandello's interpretation might be.
- All of Pirandello's works were written in Italian. Find two different translations of one of Pirandello's works (*Six Characters in Search of an Author*, his most famous play, is available in several different translations). Take a few pages of each and highlight the differences in translation. What difficulty do these differences present for non-Italian readers? Discuss the differences in a small group setting within your classroom.

---

has lessened; one does not normally feel compassion for people from whom one is completely alienated.

Identity

The concept of identity, and how it is defined, is a common theme in Pirandello's work. For example, in one of his most famous plays, *Henry IV*, the main character, an actor playing the role of Henry IV, falls off his horse, and when he regains consciousness, he is convinced that he actually is Henry IV, an eleventh-century Holy Roman Emperor. "A Day Goes By" presents the reader with a list of ways by which individuals may define their identity: family, work, reputation in the community, religion (represented by the "holy picture" the main character finds in his wallet), love, financial status, appearance. It is interesting to note that the only thing the character remembers with certainty is that he has always worked, "worked very hard, very hard indeed." It is common for men (and in more modern times, women as well) to define themselves first and foremost by their work. The photo of the fiancée and the holy picture are in his wallet, a typical place to keep proofs of one's identity (such as a driver's license).

The French Marxist philosopher Louis Althusser writes of another method of defining one's identity (or subjectivity), which he calls

Pirandello's setting: an Italian town (Image copyright Jakub Pavlinec, 2009. Used under license from Shutterstock.com)

interpellation. He describes one method of interpellation as "hailing." He wrote in his 1969 essay, "Ideology and Ideological State Apparatuses," "when we recognize somebody of our (previous) acquaintance (*(re)-connaissance*) in the street, we show him that we have recognized him . . . by saying to him 'Hello, my friend,' and shaking his hand (a material ritual practice of ideological recognition in everyday life)." This recognition and response ritual confirms for us our identity as members of a society or an ideology. In Pirandello's story, the main character is "hailed" repeatedly by people on the street, who wave to him, and again by his fiancée/wife, who raises her arms to him in welcome. On the street, he fails to respond and complete the ritual; he does not choose to define himself as one of them, as a part of society. However, he does accept the embrace of his fiancée/wife when he encounters her in his house. Also, at the end, he responds to his children and grandchildren affectionately, looking on them with compassion. The main character has chosen to define himself first by his work, and secondly, by his family.

STYLE

Point of View

The use of first-person point of view in this story is critical to creating the nightmarish, surreal feeling of a man completely adrift, without identity. The reader must have access to the main character's thoughts and feelings to experience his bewilderment and horror at the strange events that occur. In addition, if Pirandello had used a viewpoint that allowed the reader access to the thoughts of the other characters, who know facts about the main character's identity that he himself cannot access, the atmosphere of chaos and uncertainty would be lost. Through the first-person viewpoint, the reader collects clues to the character's identity at the same time as the character does, thereby sharing his difficult journey.

Dialogue

Pirandello purposely avoids using direct dialogue in the story; the main character paraphrases the few conversations he has, with the restaurant proprietor and the bank staff. The one line of direct dialogue in the story occurs when the main character says to his children, "'There, that proves it's all a joke. *You've* got white hair, too.'" The rest of his conversation with his family is all paraphrased: "They immediately rush over and tell me to lean on them. Lovingly they reprove me for having got up out of bed." This gives the story the quality of a fairy tale, being recounted orally (when a person tells a tale, dialogue is usually paraphrased). It also further emphasizes the connection with his children and grandchildren; the only spoken words in the story are spoken to them, and in these few words he expresses a similarity between them (that they both have white hair). Though he is alienated from the rest of his life, at the end he finds some comfort in this connection with his children.

Allegory

An allegory is a story in which the events symbolize or represent something other than their literal meaning. For example, "The Three Little Pigs" is not meant to be a literal tale about three pigs building houses but rather a moral allegory about the value of hard work and patience, warning the reader against the temptation of the "quick fix." In Pirandello's tale, the meaning or moral is vague, but the reader can tell by the bizarre nature of the day's events that this is not meant to be the story of just one day in a man's life, but rather an allegory of a man's life from birth to death (or very near death). For instance, the opening of the story shares many features in common with birth; he is ejected from a closed-in vessel (the train) into the dark station, he has no memory of the journey, and he has nothing with him. He muses, "Am I to deduce that it's the most natural thing in the world for people to get out at this station in that particular way?" Childbirth certainly could be described as "the most natural thing in the world."

In the next part of the story, he struggles to establish an identity, to fit in with the world around him ("I must contrive to act like the others."). He is aware of being different, set apart. Still he manages to achieve financial success and the respect of the community (represented by the large banknote and the deferential treatment given him at both the restaurant and bank). He has a beautiful wife, though she is taken from him too quickly. In his concentration on work and success, time passes him by, and "overnight," he becomes an old man. He does not "discover" his family until he is too old and infirm to work any longer.

There are many parallels between the tale and Pirandello's own life. Pirandello felt throughout his life a keen sense of alienation from others, and he worked obsessively. His wife, Antonietta, was "taken" from him by mental illness after barely ten years of marriage. "A Day Goes By" was written just a few months before his death in 1936, and according to his biographer Gaspare Giudice, "In his last months Pirandello found more and more serenity with his family, especially with his grandchildren." Given these parallels, the story can be interpreted as an allegory of Pirandello's life.

HISTORICAL CONTEXT

Fascism

The Fascist Party in Italy first organized in 1919, when Benito Mussolini founded the *Fasci di Combattimento*. The word *fascio* comes from the Latin *fasces*, the name for the ceremonial bundle of rods and axe that carried in procession in ancient Rome and symbolized the unity and the power of the Roman Empire. The word came to mean group or league and had, not surprisingly, been used before by other political associations. At first, the philosophy of the Fascist Party leaned toward the liberal left. Their platform advocated giving women the right to vote and allowing workers to participate in the management of industry. Mussolini, however, was more concerned with increasing the power of the party than with adhering to any particular political ideology, and, over time, the party became more and more conservative. By the time Mussolini became prime minister in October 1922, the main support of the Fascists came from the middle class. Mussolini's government was known for strong-arm tactics and suppression of dissent, often using violence. For instance, on May 30, 1924, a young socialist leader named Giacomo Matteotti gave a speech to Parliament that accused Mussolini of fraud in the 1924 elections. Shortly afterward, Matteotti disappeared; his body was found two months later.

Pirandello was a Mussolini supporter. Though he was not active in politics (his lifelong obsession was his work, not affairs of state), he expressed his admiration for Mussolini in a 1923 interview quoted in the book *The Appeal of Fascism*, by

COMPARE & CONTRAST

- **1930s:** Italy is ruled by Fascist dictator Benito Mussolini, who has been the leader of Italy since 1922. Pirandello, to the surprise of many, supports the Fascist regime.

  Today: Italy is a democratic republic governed by a parliamentary system. As of 2009, the prime minister of Italy is Silvio Berlusconi, whose time in office is plagued by scandal and legal difficulties.

- **1930s:** Pirandello's wife Antonietta, suffering from mental illness, has been in an institution since 1919 (Pirandello tries to bring her home in 1924 but she refuses to go with him). There are few medications or effective treatments for the mentally ill. During this time, Italian psychiatrist Ugo Cerletti begins experimenting with the idea of electroconvulsive therapy (ECT, also known as shock therapy). He first tests ECT on a mentally ill patient in Milan; though the procedure is painful, the man shows improvement afterwards.

  Today: Shock therapy is still used today, though much less than in the twentieth century (drug therapies are more common). Because ECT can cause memory loss in some patients, it is generally reserved for severe cases of depression and bipolar disorder.

- **1930s:** In 1930, Pirandello's short story "In Silence" is made into the first talking picture produced in Italy; the title of the film is *The Song of Love*.

  Today: With the exception of the occasional experimental or novelty film (such as Mel Brooks's 1976 comedy *Silent Movie*, in which the only word of audible dialogue is spoken by French mime Marcel Marceau), nearly all films today are "talkies."

- **1930s:** Pirandello's last play, *No One Knows How*, is performed for the first time. The play opens shortly after Pirandello receives his Nobel Prize.

  Today: In 2006, a play titled *Kaos*, written by Martha Clarke and based on four of Pirandello's short stories, opens at the New York Theater Workshop. Pirandello's plays, especially *Six Characters in Search of an Author* and *Henry IV*, are still performed regularly.

Alastair Hamilton: "Mussolini is one of the few people who knows that reality only exists in man's power to create it, and that one creates it only through the activity of the mind."

In 1935, about a year before "A Day Goes By" was published, Mussolini's armies invaded Ethiopia. After a brutal campaign that prompted members of the League of Nations to impose economic sanctions on Italy, Ethiopia was annexed by Italy in May 1936 and Mussolini declared himself emperor. Ethiopian Emperor Haile Selassie fled and spent the next five years in exile in England, though he returned to rule Ethiopia again when Italy was ousted in 1941. Pirandello supported the invasion, and donated his Nobel Prize medal to the government as a token of his support.

Fascism in general is associated with allegiance to one powerful leader, authoritarian rule, and contempt for democracy; fascists believe that democracy is a romantic ideal that is impractical and unachievable in reality. Other examples of fascist regimes during the 1930s include Adolf Hitler's Nazi Germany and Francisco Franco's rule of Spain.

CRITICAL OVERVIEW

Luigi Pirandello is considered one of history's greatest playwrights who broke new ground in his theatrical investigations of reality and identity. *Six Characters in Search of an Author*, his best-known play, was so different from what

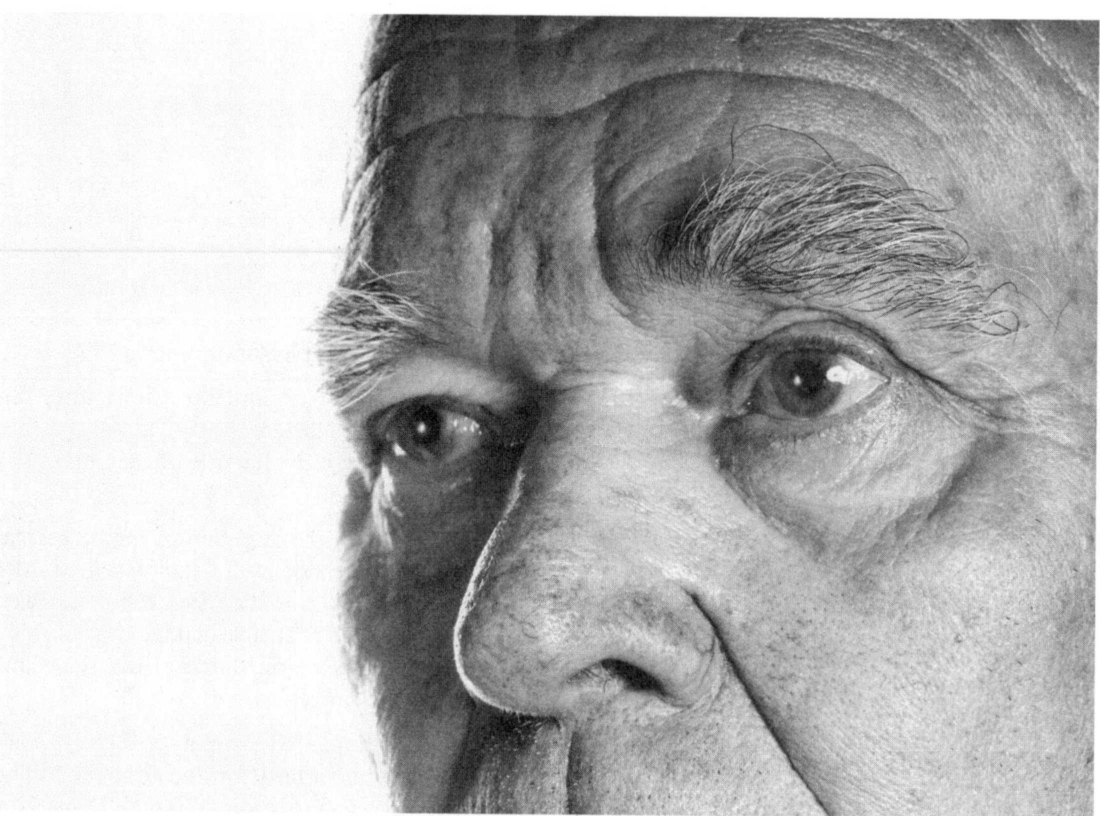

Pirandello's main character lives in a time-suspended world *(Image copyright Andrejs Pidjass, 2009. Used under license from Shutterstock.com)*

audiences were accustomed to in 1921 that at its opening in Rome, audience members shouted "Manicomio!"("Madhouse!") However, the next performance of the play, in Milan, was a great success, and the play went on to be considered one of the most important plays of the decade (possibly *the* most important). The 1920s were Pirandello's most productive period, at least in terms of his work for the theater.

Pirandello's fiction, which he wrote for years before he began concentrating on his work for the theater, is less well known, but also critically acclaimed. Literary critics often cite Pirandello's biting wit as one of the distinguishing features of his fiction. In a 1934 review of the book *Better Think Twice About It (and Twelve Other Stories)*, the reviewer Percy Hutchison writes in the *New York Times Book Review*, "That wit for which Luigi Pirandello is famous is here in abundance." Another reviewer for the same publication, in a review of Pirandello's novel *The Late Mattia Pascal*, calls Pirandello "equally philosopher and humorist," and states that it is Pirandello's "tempering of laughter with thought—and the vivification of philosophy with laughter—that makes 'The Late Mattia Pascal' a rare book." It was this humor that helped make Pirandello's sometimes bleak view of life easier for readers to accept; as a reviewer in the London *Times Literary Supplement* writes in a review of *The Naked Truth (and Eleven Other Stories)*, "Human wretchedness is rather heavily drawn upon in all these tales." In a review of the same book, Hutchison of the *New York Times Book Review* writes of one tale, "Without this healing salve of humor the story would be intolerable."

Pirandello's penchant for examining philosophical questions such as the nature of identity and reality is mentioned often by critics; while some feel that Pirandello finds new and creative ways to explore the same themes, others suggest that Pirandello should move on to new ideas. Hutchison, reviewing Pirandello's novel *One, None and a Hundred Thousand* in the *New York*

Times Book Review, a book that deals (once again) with the elusive nature of personal identity, writes, "there are indications in the novel that Pirandello has himself become a little wearied of his unanswerable thesis."

In his own time, Pirandello had his detractors; according to his biographer, Gaspare Giudice, the critic Antonio Gramsci once called one of his plays "a mere aggregate of words which create neither an image or a truth . . . a monster . . . not a play." Looking back on his entire body of work, however, many agree with Frederick May, who, in his introduction to a collection of Pirandello's short stories, called him "one of the most distinctive and characteristic voices of our age."

CRITICISM

Laura Pryor

Pryor has a B.A. from the University of Michigan and over 20 years of experience as a professional writer. In this essay, she examines the clues Pirandello gives the reader to indicate that "A Day Goes By" is an allegory of a man's lifetime.

Luigi Pirandello's short story "A Day Goes By" is considered to be an allegory of a man's life. How do we know, however, that the story is not real? Until the very end, when the main character ages overnight, nothing completely implausible occurs. And one could argue that the character has been old all along—when he sees that he is an old man, it is the first time he has looked in a mirror. It could be the tale of an actual man suffering from amnesia after falling (or being pushed) from a train. The clues to allegory in this story are much more subtle than in a fairy tale; for instance, no animals talk, no genies appear. The clues are found in the character's reactions to, and assumptions about, the people he encounters.

As the story begins, the narrator is both literally and figuratively in the dark. "Rudely awakened from sleep—perhaps by mistake—I find myself thrown out of the train at a station along the line." Not *a* train, but *the* train. Somehow, though he claims to have forgotten everything, he knows that there will not be another train for him—this is the train.

Throughout the story, there are subtle indications that the narrator does remember, that traces of his identity remain from his past. For instance, in the first sentence of the story, he allows that his awakening and exit from the train may have been a mistake. However, in the next paragraph, he says, "Nowhere on myself can I find any sign of the violence I've suffered." He does not have even "the shadow of a memory" of the incident. This, of course, prompts the question: how does he know there has been violence at all? He has made an assumption, and one cannot make an assumption without the benefit of past experience as a guide. This is one of the first clues that he knows more of his former identity than he realizes or reveals.

The narrator's perception of himself as an outcast, as inferior to the others in the town, is not necessarily based on objective observation. Several people wave to him in greeting, and he asserts that the other townspeople "all look like me, too." From this evidence he could easily conclude that he is one of them, that he belongs, even though he cannot remember this belonging. Instead he decides that they are "right" and he is "wrong." In just one paragraph he repeats this belief three times. Does his sense of separateness, of alienation, come from his lack of identity—his loss of memory—or from a pre-existing perception of himself as inferior, a past identity that still clings to him? He has no objective evidence of the scorn or judgment he attributes to the townspeople, but still he draws these conclusions: "*I* must be in the wrong. . . . Not only do they seem to know this, but they also know everything that makes them sure that they never make a mistake." This is obviously not a conclusion that can be drawn from observation alone, and the narrator never speaks to any of these people.

This raises another question that must occur to any reader of this tale: why does the narrator never ask anyone for help? He asks the restaurateur about his decrepit banknote, but only because "a scruple" obligates him—he wants to be sure he can pay for his meal. At no point does he ask anyone where he is, or if they know him, or if there is another train. And how does he get an account at the bank without a name? Surely the banker would require his name, and if the banker already knows his name, surely it would be inscribed upon the passbook the bank gives him. And yet the narrator never reveals this information to the reader.

There is an obvious answer to these questions, of course, and that is that this was never intended

WHAT DO I READ NEXT?

- *Six Characters in Search of an Author*, first performed in 1921, is Pirandello's most famous play. In the play, a group of actors are preparing to rehearse a play when six characters from another story arrive searching for their author, who has neglected to finish their tale.
- The young-adult novel *Memoirs of a Teenage Amnesiac* by Gabrielle Zevin, published in 2007, deals with a teenage girl's gradual rediscovery of her identity after a blow to the head leaves her with amnesia.
- Essays, biographies, and lectures from ten Nobel laureates from five continents are collected in the book *Nobel Laureates in Search of Identity and Integrity: Voices of Different Cultures*, edited by Anders Hallengren (2004). Countries represented include South Africa, Egypt, India, Australia, Saint Lucia, the United States, and Italy.
- *Living Masks: The Achievement of Pirandello* by Umberto Mariani, published in 2008, provides an excellent introduction to Pirandello's plays and the common themes they dramatize.
- *Pirandello: A Biography*, by Gaspare Giudice, was originally written in Italian; the English translation by Alastair Hamilton was published in 1975. The biography includes sections on Pirandello's early years in Sicily, his success as a playwright, and his involvement with Fascism.
- Pirandello's novel, *The Late Mattia Pascal*, originally published in 1923, tells the story of a man who is trapped in a miserable marriage and takes a short vacation. While on his holiday, he reads in a newspaper that a dead body, found drowned near his home, has been identified as him, Mattia Pascal. He decides not to correct the error but to establish a whole new identity and escape from his dreary home life.
- *Modern Italian Literature*, by Ann Hallamore Caesar and Michael Caesar, was published in 2007 and provides a chronological history of Italian literature, starting from the eighteenth century and progressing to literature in Italy today.
- In *Fascism: A Very Short Introduction* (published in 2002), Kevin Passmore gives readers a concise, jargon-free overview of fascism, its origins and its effects, not just in Italy but worldwide. The book is part of the "Very Short Introduction" series, published by Oxford University Press, which offers short, helpful overviews of a wide variety of subjects.

---

as a realistic story as an allegory of identity. On an intellectual level, the narrator knows perfectly well who he is, and where he is, but in a more figurative sense, he has been asleep, unconscious. Until being "rudely awakened" at the opening of the story, he has lived his life in an unconscious, detached manner, not truly experiencing the world or the people around him. He was headed towards some destination (on the train) without stopping to actually look at his life. The reader does not know what event "awakened" him. People faced with a catastrophic illness or a near-death experience often find that afterwards, their priorities are clarified, and their ability to fully appreciate life is heightened. It is useful to note that at the time Pirandello wrote this story he himself was aware of serious health problems (affecting his heart) that would lead to his death a few months later.

Still, the narrator's "awakening" does not initially seem to be increasing his appreciation or enjoyment of life. The main emotions he experiences are bewilderment and a sense of alienation. Knowledge of his respectability and financial success does little to dispel these feelings. Even when he arrives home, he feels like "a kind of intruder." Finally, he opens the bedroom door and finds his fiancée, and he is welcomed with open arms. If there is any doubt that he has found what he has been looking for, Pirandello puts a spotlight on it for us: he writes that the room is "ablaze with light."

The next morning, however, the woman is gone, as are the light and warmth. The narrator is forced to wake up all over again, this time to the realization that he is now an old man, near death (the bed is now "freezing cold, just like a tomb"). He describes the realization as "a nightmare." But when his children and grandchildren arrive, there is a marked change in the atmosphere.

Though the narrator claims no memory of his family, the rapid change in his behavior when they arrive indicates otherwise. For only the second time (his encounter with his fiancée being the first), he allows himself to be touched. His family reproves him "lovingly" for getting up, and encourages him to "lean on them." He looks upon his children, close enough to see the hairs on their heads and to watch them turn gray. His granddaughter wants to climb on him and hug him around the neck. At one point, he says, "I feel the urge to leap to my feet." There is more physicality in this one scene than in all the others combined.

The language becomes warmer and lighter in tone. He teases his family about it all being a joke they are playing on him, and he looks upon them with "compassion." This is by far the warmest and most human scene. At the beginning of the story, the narrator "wakes up" to a cold life in which he finds no friends and feels he is being judged by society. The unconscious way that he has lived his life has left him with no one, it seems, until he is reunited with his family. Family is the one connection remaining to him, and finally, with what little life he has left, he is able to appreciate it. The allegory comes full circle, from the darkness of the station, to the warmth and light of family, and back to darkness again (his impending death). It is a bittersweet story of a man who sees the light (and feels it) with hardly any time left to enjoy it.

Source: Laura Pryor, Critical Essay on "A Day Goes By," in *Short Stories for Students*, Gale, Cengage Learning, 2010.

SOURCES

Althusser, Louis, "Ideology and Ideological State Apparatuses (Notes towards an Investigation)," in *Lenin and Philosophy and Other Essays*, translated by Ben Brewster, Monthly Review Press, 1971, pp. 127–86.

Daniel, Clifton, ed., *Chronicle of the 20th Century*, Chronicle Publications, 1987, pp. 405, 415, 418, 421–22, 435, 449, 454, 456, 460.

De Grand, Alexander, *Italian Fascism: Its Origins & Development*, 3rd ed., University of Nebraska Press, 2000.

Giudice, Gaspare, *Pirandello: A Biography*, translated by Alastair Hamilton, Oxford University Press, 1975.

Hamilton, Alastair, *The Appeal of Fascism: A Study of Intellectuals and Fascism, 1919–1945*, Macmillan, 1971, p. 47.

"History of Mental Illness," in *Making the Modern World*, www.makingthemodernworld.org.uk/learning_modules/psychology/02.TU.04/?section=2 (accessed October 16, 2009).

Hutchison, Percy, Review of *Better Think Twice About It (and Twelve Other Stories)*, in *New York Times Book Review*, January 6, 1935, p. 2.

———, Review of *The Naked Truth (and Eleven Other Stories)*, in *New York Times Book Review*, September 9, 1934, pp. 2, 12.

———, Review of *One, None and a Hundred Thousand*, in *New York Times Book Review*, April 9, 1933, p. 2.

Pirandello, Luigi, "A Day Goes By," in *Luigi Pirandello: Short Stories*, edited and translated by Frederick May, Quartet Books, 1987, pp. 224–30.

Review of *The Late Mattia Pascal*, in *New York Times Book Review*, August 19, 1923, pp. 18–19.

Review of *The Naked Truth (and Eleven Other Stories)*, in *Times Literary Supplement* (London, England), March 22, 1934, p.20.

Rockwell, John, "Dance and Theater Lead the Way in the Stark Landscape of Pirandello's Sicily," in *New York Times*, www.nytimes.com/2006/12/05/theater/reviews/05kaos.html?_r=2, 2006 (accessed October 16, 2009).

Williams, Jason, "Shock Treatment Works? The Benefits of Electric Shock Therapy," in *Psychology Today*, www.psychologytoday.com/articles/200303/shock-treatment-works-the-benefits-electric-shock-therapy, 2003 (accessed October 15, 2009).

FURTHER READING

Biasin, Gian-Paolo, and Manuela Gieri, eds., *Luigi Pirandello: Contemporary Perspectives*, University of Toronto Press, 1999.

This collection of essays, written by an array of professors from universities all over the world, examines different aspects of Pirandello's work, including both his plays and his narrative fiction. The essays examine structure, meanings, and innovation in Pirandello's work.

Bosworth, R. J. B., *Mussolini's Italy: Life under the Dictatorship, 1915–1945*, Penguin, 2006.

This impressive and lengthy volume examines not just the political history of Mussolini and the Fascist regime in Italy, but also how their policies affected the everyday life of ordinary Italians.

Maggio, Teri, *The Stone Boudoir: Travels through the Hidden Villages of Sicily*, Perseus, 2002.

In this memoir of her extensive travels through Sicily, Maggio, whose grandparents were Sicilian, describes in detail many of the small villages of Sicily, where Luigi Pirandello was born and raised.

Pirandello, Luigi, *Pirandello's Love Letters to Marta Abba*, edited and translated by Benito Ortolani, Princeton University Press, 1994.

In 1925, Pirandello fell in love with a beautiful young stage actress named Marta Abba. This collection of letters written to Abba from that time until Pirandello's death in 1936 paints a portrait of Pirandello as an unhappy man, suffering from depression, insomnia, and paranoia regarding his work. Ortolani adds a detailed introduction, index, and footnotes to aid the reader.

Dr. Heidegger's Experiment

NATHANIEL HAWTHORNE

1837

Nathaniel Hawthorne's short story "Dr. Heidegger's Experiment" is a horror story in the Gothic mode. In it, a mysterious doctor invites four old acquaintances to his study and offers them a sample of water from the fabled Fountain of Youth. The contents of the doctor's study are familiar to fans of horror movies and books: Hawthorne tells of a book of magic, a talking bust, and a mirror that shows dead people. A large portrait shows the doctor's fiancée, who died the night before their wedding, fifty years earlier. There is even a real skeleton in a closet, a not-so-subtle hint that the shared history of the old people to whom Dr. Heidegger offers a second chance at life might hold the seeds of their destruction.

This story was first published anonymously under the title "The Fountain of Youth" in 1837 in *Knickerbocker* magazine. Later the same year, it was reprinted with the current title in Hawthorne's *Twice-Told Tales*, which has remained one of the most important works of the American literary tradition, just as Hawthorne has retained his place as one of the most important American writers. In the 1860 edition of that book, Hawthorne felt compelled to add a note explaining that he had not plagiarized this story from similar ideas in a novel by Alexandre Dumas, best remembered today as the author of *The Three Musketeers*. In his postscript, Hawthorne points out that the story had originally been published long before Dumas's novel, and he slyly implies that Dumas often helped himself to other writers' ideas.

Nathaniel Hawthorne *(The Library of Congress)*

Twice-Told Tales is still in print from several publishers, most notably in the 2001 Modern Library edition.

AUTHOR BIOGRAPHY

Hawthorne was born on July 4, 1804, in Salem, Massachusetts, the town his family had lived in for generations. At his birth, his last name was spelled "Hathorne"; later in life, he changed it to distance himself from an ancestor, John Hathorne, who was one of the judges at the infamous Salem witch trials. His father, a ship captain, died of yellow fever in Dutch Guiana when Nathaniel was four years old, and his mother and the two children moved in with relatives. Hawthorne broke his foot playing ball when he was nine. He spent nearly two years recuperating, during which time he read and began to write.

Hawthorne attended Bowdoin College, and after graduating in 1825 returned to Salem to work on his first novel, *Fanshawe*, about his life at Bowdoin. It was published anonymously in 1828 and earned critical approval but was not a commercial success. Over the next nine years, he published short stories in magazines; in 1837, he republished these stories in the collection *Twice-Told Tales*, which established his reputation as a rising American writer. To support himself, he went to work at the U.S. Custom House at the port of Boston from 1839 to 1841. He left there to join a utopian commune, the Brook Farm, investing all of his savings in it. In 1842, after publication of a second edition of *Twice-Told Tales*, Hawthorne married Sophia Peabody, and they moved into the "Old Manse" in Concord, a house that had been built by the grandfather of Ralph Waldo Emerson, a famous poet. By 1845, though, his money had run out, and Hawthorne, his wife, and their newborn daughter returned to Salem to live with his mother. He worked at the Custom House in Salem for the next four years. When he published his most famous work, *The Scarlet Letter*, in 1860, it included a lengthy introduction about working at the Custom House that angered his former coworkers.

Hawthorne's career as a writer was established by *The Scarlet Letter*. He followed it by publication of the novel *The House of Seven Gables* in 1851, along with several other books of short stories. That year, Herman Melville, whom he had met the year before, dedicated his masterpiece, *Moby-Dick*, to Hawthorne. In 1852, he wrote a campaign biography that helped Franklin Pierce, whom he had known since college, be elected to the presidency of the United States, and in 1853, Pierce returned the favor by appointing Hawthorne the American Consul at Liverpool, where he lived for four years. In 1858 and 1859, he returned to Europe, traveling in France and Italy. He returned to the United States in 1860. In 1864, while traveling with Pierce, Hawthorne took ill. He died in Plymouth, New Hampshire, on May 19, 1864, and was buried in Concord. Among the pallbearers at his funeral were notable authors Henry Wadsworth Longfellow, Emerson, Bronson Alcott, and Oliver Wendell Holmes, Sr.

PLOT SUMMARY

"Dr. Heidegger's Experiment" begins when Dr. Heidegger has four old acquaintances meet him in the study of his home. They are Mr. Medbourne, a once-prosperous merchant who has lost his fortune; Colonel Killigrew, who ruined his body with food and drink; Mr. Gascoigne, a former politician who has fallen into obscurity;

MEDIA ADAPTATIONS

- "Dr. Heidegger's Experiment" is one of twenty-two stories included on *Great Classic Stories*, a set of six compact discs released in 2006 by BBC Audio Books America. It is read by Nicky Henson.
- An opera that adapts Hawthorne's story, called *Dr. Heidegger's Fountain of Youth*, was released as a record album in 1979 by Sound Recording. Participants include Carol Wilcox, Judith Christin, Grayson Hirst, and Robert Shiesley. The libretto for this adaptation was by Sheldon Harnick.
- This story, along with stories by Rudyard Kipling and Oscar Wilde, is read by Jim Weiss on *Spooky Classics for Children*, a compact disc released by Greathall Productions in 1997.
- A much-altered version of this story is among several adapted for the 1963 horror movie *Nathaniel Hawthorne's Twice-told Tales*, starring Vincent Price and Sebastian Cabot. It is available on videocassette and DVD from MGM Home Entertainment's Midnight Movies series.
- A faithful adaptation was released under the name *Dr. Heidegger's Experiment* in 1969 by Clifton Fadiman. This short 16-mm film was directed by Larry Yust and was released with an instructor's guide by Encyclopaedia Britannica Educational Corp.
- Yust and Fadiman discuss the story and its literary aspects in *A Discussion of "Dr. Heidegger's Experiment,"* released in 1970 by Encyclopaedia Britannica Educational Corp.

and the Widow Wycherly, who was once a great beauty with a scandalous reputation but has lost her looks as she aged. At one time, the three men were all violently in competition with each other for Widow Wycherly's attentions. All of the people in the room—Dr. Heidegger and his four guests—are far advanced in age, and they all behave in a worried manner, which the narrator explains is normal for old people.

Dr. Heidegger's study is a strange, mystical place. Caked in dust and cobwebs, it is filled with unusual artifacts that indicate the unusual interests of its owner. There are folios (large books), of which the most striking is a leather-bound volume with silver clasps, which is rumored to be a book about magic. No one dares to open it, and rumor has it that a maid once touched it and the inanimate objects in the room moved about. There are regular-sized books, quartos, which are a quarter of the folio size, and duodecimos, a twelfth of the size of folios. There is a bust of Hippocrates, the ancient Greek philosopher who is credited with a logical, scientific approach to medicine. When he finds himself faced with difficult problems while he is pursuing his practice, the narrator says, Dr. Heidegger sometimes talks to the Hippocrates bust. A closet has its door ajar, and the people in the room can see a skeleton hanging in it. There is also a large mirror and a full-length portrait of a young lady. The narrator explains that the woman in the painting (later identified as Sylvia Ward), was engaged to be married to Dr. Heidegger more than fifty years earlier, but that she became sick with a minor illness, took some of the doctor's medicine, and died. In the mirror, the faces of former patients of Dr. Heidegger, dead now, appear when he looks at it. In the middle of the room is a table that holds a vase and four champagne glasses. Dr. Heidegger explains to his four guests that he has called them to his study to participate in one of his experiments.

The doctor takes the black folio book and opens it, but instead of reading from it, he takes out a pressed rose. It was given to him, he says, by his fiancée, to wear at their wedding. He drops the dried old flower into the vase on the table, and as it floats there, it becomes young and fresh again; its stem becomes green, and its leaves deepen in their redness. The assembled people say that it must be a trick, but Dr. Heidegger explains that a friend of his who was in Florida, searching for the fabled Fountain of Youth that brought the Spanish explorer Ponce de León to that area, actually found it, and sent him a bottle of its magical waters. His experiment is to give this youth-regenerating water to the four people he has called together. Dr. Heidegger feels that growing old was enough trouble the first time, so he himself will not drink the elixir, but will only watch them.

Just before giving his guests the water, which is effervescent like champagne or some mineral waters, Dr. Heidegger warns them: they should remember that with this second chance they should not make the same mistakes that they made the first time they were young. They find the idea that they might follow the old ways ridiculous, and they laugh and then drink the water down.

As soon as they have drunk the water, they all start looking younger. They look at each other and see the color coming back to their pale faces and the wrinkles smoothing out in their skin. The Widow Wycherly asks for more of the enchanted water. Dr. Heidegger asks everyone to be patient, but says the water is there for them to take, and so they all have another drink.

After the second drink, they seem even younger. Widow Wycherly goes to the mirror to stare at herself, while the three men act as they did when they were young. Mr. Gascoigne makes declarations about his political opinions, though they are so generalized that it is difficult to tell whether he is talking about modern politics or the political situations from fifty years ago. Colonel Killigrew, who squandered his youth with hard drinking, sings an old drinking song, clanging his glass to accompany his vocals. Mr. Medbourne thinks up a new money-making scheme that involves training whales to drag icebergs, to sell ice to the tropical islands of the East Indies. After staring at her newly young image for a while, Widow Wycherly asks for more water, and Dr. Heidegger supplies it.

With this drink, they all become even younger still. They take to mocking the old, decrepit people they had been, laughing as they walk around stiffly, amused that they are wearing the kind of clothes old people would wear. They pantomime reading with glasses, which they do not need any more, and one sits stiffly and sternly in a chair, imitating Dr. Heidegger, who is still old.

The Widow Wycherly steps up to Dr. Heidegger and asks him to dance with her, but he declines, saying that he is too old. In short succession, though, the three other men, her former suitors, come to ask her to dance with them. They all reach for her at once. One grabs her hands, one her waist, and one her head. As they tussle, the mirror shows Widow Wycherly to still be the same thin, pale, old woman she was before she drank the water.

As the three men wrestle with each other, they knock against the table, tipping over the vase holding the water: it falls to the floor and shatters. On the floor is an old, dying butterfly. Once the spilled water hits the butterfly, it rejuvenates and takes flight, landing on Dr. Heidegger's head.

The crash of the vase and the loss of the remaining water shocks them, and they turn quiet and return to their seats. Dr. Heidegger walks over to the rose that Sylvia gave him and picks it up, noting that it is already fading and aging. He says that he still loves it just as much when it is aged as he did in when it was young and fresh.

His guests notice that they are turning old again, too. They complain to the doctor about this, and he points out that the effect of the Water of Youth lasts no longer than the effect of wine would. The lesson that he has learned from watching how they behaved, Dr. Heidegger tells them, is that he would not drink the water from the Fountain of Youth even if an endless supply of it poured to his door.

The story ends by noting that the doctor's four friends learned nothing from their experience. They make a pact to go to Florida and find the Fountain of Youth.

CHARACTERS

Mr. Gascoigne

Mr. Gascoigne is one of the three former suitors of the Widow Wycherly to be summoned to Dr. Heidegger's house to participate in the doctor's experiment. When he was young, Mr. Gascoigne was a politician, but he had lost any prospects he had in politics. First, he acquired a bad reputation, though Hawthorne does not say what his bad reputation is based on or whether it is deserved. As if that were not bad enough, after his reputation was ruined, he was then forgotten, which Hawthorne implies might be an even worse fate for a person who lived to be in the public eye.

Once the Water of Youth has transformed Mr. Gascoigne, his mind goes back to the same state it once had as well. While the others are reveling in their young looks and their ability to perform physical feats that were beyond their capacity when they arrived at the doctor's study, Mr. Gascoigne stands and gives speeches on political topics. His speeches are not very focused, however, and cover only such vague but important-sounding subjects as patriotism and glory. The story specifically states that someone hearing his speech would not be able to tell whether Mr. Gascoigne was talking about the current political situation or about matters that were contemporary when he was a young, active politician.

Mr. Gascoigne joins with the other two men who participated in the experiment in fighting for the attention of the Widow Wycherly. In struggling with them to keep his hold on her, they all bump the table, knocking over the vase that holds the Water of Youth and spilling it on the floor. Like the others, though, Mr. Gascoigne does not look at his experience as a sign that he would only waste a new chance at youth. Instead, he enters into a pact with them at the end of the story to try to find the real Fountain of Youth, apparently thinking that he can control the foolishness that came out of him while under the water's influence.

Dr. Heidegger

Dr. Heidegger is the main character of this story. Hawthorne is not entirely clear about who Dr. Heidegger is. The bust of Hippocrates in his study and the fact that he prescribed medicine for his fiancée indicate that he is probably a medical doctor. However, he refers several times to bringing his friends together and giving them the alleged Water of Youth as an "experiment," indicating that his studies might also be in the field of philosophy, which at that time would have included psychology. It is suggested but not confirmed that he has an interest in the supernatural. He dwells in a creepy study with cobwebs and dust and old books, but there is nothing in the story to support the superstitious rumors about it. The big black unmarked book is said to be a book of magic, but the doctor never reads any incantations from it. Rumors say that he can see the images of dead patients when he looks in his mirror, but those are just rumors. The news that mystical things happened when a cleaning woman touched the magic book has no support beyond the word of the frightened woman herself.

What is known about Dr. Heidegger is that he is old, like the other characters in the story. Fifty-five years earlier, he was engaged to marry a woman named Sylvia Ward, but, in response to "some slight disorder," she "swallowed one of her lover's prescriptions" and died on the night before their wedding.

Dr. Heidegger gathers four old friends to his house to participate in an experiment. To prove that the water he has in the vase on the table is actually enchanted water from the Fountain of Youth, he puts a shriveled rose into it, and the rose becomes new and fresh. He warns his friends to not behave as they did the last time they were young. As his friends drink the water, Dr. Heidegger sits back and watches their behavior. His experiment is not about the powers of the water but rather about the ways that people behave when given a chance to be young again. The story is ambiguous as to whether the water actually makes them young or just makes them think they were made young.

In the end, Dr. Heidegger declares that what he has seen makes him not want to ever be young again. He says he loves Sylvia's rose as much when it is old as he did when it was young, and he feels he would, like his friends, act like a fool if given a second chance.

Colonel Killigrew

Colonel Killigrew is one of the three former suitors of the Widow Wycherly to be summoned to Dr. Heidegger's house to participate in the doctor's experiment. All are about the same age, but Colonel Killigrew seems to be in worse physical shape than the others: he "wasted his best years . . . in the pursuit of sinful pleasures." What this means is unclear, but it implies a wide range of possible afflictions, such as drug or alcohol addiction or sexually transmitted diseases. One ailment that is specifically mentioned is gout, which is a form of arthritis that is generally associated with eating rich, fatty foods.

Like the three other men who participate in Dr. Heidegger's experiment, Colonel Killigrew has a history with the Widow Wycherly, and his rivalry made him almost want to kill the others at one time. In the fifty years since he dated her, Colonel Killigrew's body has deteriorated. When Dr. Heidegger gives them the Water of Youth, Killigrew is skeptical about how it will affect their aged bodies. Like the others, though, he finds himself able to once again perform physical feats that he felt were behind him. He is the first of the men to turn his attention to Widow Wycherly once the rejuvenating formula works, noticing the change in her before the others. As they all become absorbed in their newfound youth, the Colonel reverts to the old ways that caused the wreckage of his body. He sings drinking songs, clanging the side of his glass in accompaniment, and he keeps his eye on the newly young Widow Wycherly. He is the first one to reach out to the widow, asking her to dance with him, which leads the others to reach out to her too. Their competition ends in a wrestling match that causes the table to shake, spilling the water that is left.

Colonel Killigrew does not learn from his experience. Rather than giving up the idea of regaining his youth and accepting that youthful pursuits were what wrecked him, he makes a pact with the other three subjects of the experiment to go to Florida and hunt down the fabled Fountain of Youth.

Mr. Medbourne

Mr. Medbourne is one of the three former suitors of the Widow Wycherly to be summoned to Dr. Heidegger's house to participate in the doctor's experiment. Once, long ago, Mr. Medbourne was wealthy, having made his fortune as a merchant, but he made risky investments that turned out badly. He is now very poor: "little better than a mendicant," or beggar.

When Dr. Heidegger gives his guests a drink that will make them young again, Mr. Medbourne does not raise any objection. He goes along with the others and drinks the proffered potion. As he feels younger, he, like the others, falls back to his old ways. He becomes preoccupied with adding up figures of dollars and cents in his head. Then he comes up with a new money-making scheme, calculating how much there is to be made if he were to harness a team of whales and have them tow icebergs from the polar regions to the tropics of the East Indies, to sell ice.

As the men become younger, they all, including Mr. Medbourne, become involved in a brawl for the Widow Wycherly's attention. Mr. Medbourne says that she offered him her hand in marriage a half a century earlier. When the Water of Youth is spilled, he does not realize that he behaved like a fool under its influence; instead, Mr. Medbourne joins with the others, who moments earlier had been his rivals, in a plan to go to Florida and hunt down the real Fountain of Youth.

Clara Wycherly

The Widow Wycherly is the woman who has been romantically involved with the other three people summoned to Dr. Heidegger's house to participate in his experiment. Clara Wycherly was romantically involved with Mr. Medbourne, Colonel Killigrew, and Mr. Gascoigne at one time. The story implies that all three were courting her at the same time, since they once would have killed one another over her. Their involvement was more than fifty years ago.

In the years since then, the Widow Wycherly has been living a life of seclusion; some of the townspeople are biased against her because of some unspecified scandals. When she is reunited with her three old lovers, they show little interest in her, but when they are all given the Water of Youth to drink, the Widow Wycherly moves over to the mirror, entranced to see that the beauty that had left her with age is returning. The men notice the same thing. At first they pester her for a dance, but then, as they notice that they all want her attention, a fight breaks out among them. Clara Wycherly, who once centered her life around her beauty and the admirers of that beauty, does nothing to stop their fight: she struggles against them as they all grab for her, but only slightly, allowing them all to keep a hold on her. This fight results in the Water of Youth being spilled out on the floor, giving them all a chance to see that they have been behaving like fools in the same ways that caused them to lose their good names. They pay no attention to the opportunity for a lesson, however, and the Widow Wycherly, with the others, pledges to try to find the Fountain of Youth, apparently seeing no problem with their behavior.

THEMES

Aging

The four people called to Dr. Heidegger's study have known one another for more than fifty years. Each has been successful in some field of endeavor, but their successes were long ago. Now they are failures. Colonel Killigrew, whose title indicates that he rose in the ranks of the military, is a physical wreck. Mr. Medbourne has lost the fortune he amassed, and Mr. Gascoigne is such a failure as a politician that people do not even remember his shortcomings; they do not remember him at all. Clara Wycherly was loved because of her good looks, but aging has taken those looks away, leaving her vanity unfed.

The story indicates from the beginning that these people are unhappy when they arrive at the doctor's house. When they are given the chance to

TOPICS FOR FURTHER STUDY

- Study sleight of hand magic techniques in *Kid's Magic Secrets: Simple Magic Tricks & Why They Work* or another magic book and determine a way that you can create an illusion. Perform this feat for your class. Lead a discussion with the class about how they think you performed this trick.
- Choose a photo of a house, condo, or business decorated for Halloween. Note the similarities between Halloween decorations and Hawthorne's description of Dr. Heidegger's study. Write a short story about the people who put those decorations up, revealing what each specific piece says about them.
- Although Mr. Medbourne's idea of towing icebergs to the East Indies is presented as a foolish money-making scheme, similar ideas (minus the whales) have been credibly proposed in recent years to help areas suffering from drought. Research plans to move icebergs and present a proposal that outlines conditions that would make such an action economically practical.
- The narrator of this story cannot tell whether Mr. Gascoigne's political diatribe is supposed to be about the past or the present. Study a political situation from fifty years ago or earlier and write a speech that applies equally to that event and to a current situation. Do not explain the historical situation to your class until after you have given your speech.
- Interview some people who have known each other for fifty years or more. Ask each whether the others would behave differently if given the chance to be young once more. Then write a review of this story based on how accurate you think Hawthorne has been.
- Research the uses of folios, quartos, and duodecimos in book binding of Hawthorne's time. Create a PowerPoint presentation that illustrates the differences in book binding then and now. Explain how knowing this about Dr. Hawthorne's library influences your understanding of the man.
- In groups of four, discuss what bad habits you think you will still have fifty years from now. Give the other people in your group time to discuss methods you can use to break your habit and then share information.

be young again, they are happy once more, indicating that aging results in sadness and youth is the cause of happiness. This situation does not remain stable, though: after a while of enjoying their restored youth, of dancing and joking and carousing, they end up fighting each other with such destructive intensity that the thing that is most precious to them is destroyed. Their enjoyment is tainted by the "follies of youth" that Dr. Heidegger warns them about. The result of the experiment appears to be that the troubles that are associated with aging are actually problems that come from the bad behaviors that these individuals exhibit. The story does not examine what would happen if they followed the doctor's advice and went into their second youth wisely, since none of them take that course.

Jealousy

The first thing that these four old acquaintances do when they are given back their youth is to revert back to their individual forms of foolishness. The men make proclamations about politics, commerce, and drink, while the Widow Wycherly stares at the mirror, engrossed in her own beauty, just as she was years ago. After a while, though, their separate obsessions meld into one. The men fight over the widow, and she encourages their fighting as a way of affirming her own attractiveness. They become so engrossed in their fighting, in fact, that they are willing to allow jealousy to destroy the one thing that has brought them happiness, the Water of Youth.

Dr. Heidegger could have expected these people to give in to jealousy, because that is how

An experiment at work *(Image copyright Emin Kuliyev, 2009. Used under license from Shutterstock.com)*

they behaved when they were together fifty years ago, when the men were all Clara Wycherly's lovers. It seems likely that that is actually the outcome that he intended when he contacted them. If he had not wanted jealousy to be a part of his experiment, then he could have found subjects who did not have a romantic link.

Jealous behavior is not the first reaction each man falls to upon finding himself young, a fact that seems to indicate that Hawthorne sees jealousy as more than just another foolish behavior—it is the ultimate foolish behavior. Greed, gluttony, vanity, and hunger for power are all regrettable, but they can be acted on individually until they lead these foolish people to their independent downfalls, just as they did before. Jealousy, however, is able to destroy the happiness of all involved in just a matter of minutes.

Supernatural

Hawthorne prepares readers for the appearance of a supernatural elixir that can turn back the results of time by establishing Dr. Heidegger's study as a place immersed in magic. The skeleton that is hanging in the closet, the mirror that shows the images of his former patients, the bust that allegedly talks, the book that is supposed to hold magical spells, and even the dust and the spider webs are all, even to this day, standard props in a story about mad scientists who cross the line between science and the supernatural. The sketchy story of Dr. Heidegger's ill-fated wedding adds to the atmosphere. His fiancée died on the night before their wedding, and the doctor's medicines had something to do with her death. When the mood is established, the water from the Fountain of Youth, a mysterious substance that can alter the fundamental course of time, is presented.

Although the mood is set to make a supernatural occurrence believable, Hawthorne holds back from claiming that any magic actually occurs. The weird events attributed to Dr. Heidegger's study, such as the talking bust of Hippocrates, the strange images in the mirror, and the portrait of his dead fiancée coming alive, are all presented as gossip. The restoration of youth might be nothing more than the power of suggestion. The guests' actual physical condition is carefully described in terms of how it seemed or how it looked, indicating that their youth might only be in their minds.

There are two supernatural occurrences in the story that are not easily explained away. The first is the rejuvenation of the old, withered rose when Dr. Heidegger drops it into the magic water. There seems to be no explanation for its new life other than the water's supernatural properties. Skeptical readers, however, could assume that Dr. Heidegger, who has called his old acquaintances together to participate in an experiment about what they would do if they felt young again, may have found some way to perform a conjurer's trick that is within the rules of nature. The story does not say this, though. Even more inexplicable is the dying butterfly that is touched by the Water of Youth and then flies up to settle on the doctor's head. There is no explanation for this, as there is no way that Dr. Heidegger could have known that the vase would spill onto the floor where the butterfly lay. There is much in this story to indicate that its claims to supernatural events are a sham, but this one element hints that the supernatural actually does take place in Dr. Heidegger's study.

STYLE

First-Person Narrator

This story is told with a first-person narrator who refers to himself or herself as "I" several times. This technically makes the narrator a character in the story, even though readers are never given any details about who this person might be. The narrator can, for the sake of simplicity, be identified with the author and thus referred to as "he," but this is simply a convention, and the narrator could be female.

Unlike an omniscient (all-knowing) narrator, who can give details about anything related to the story, this first-person narrator is limited in what information is available to him. He does not know, for instance, whether the doctor really conversed with the bust of Hippocrates in his study, but attributes this information to others. Similarly, the narrator does not know whether the doctor's deceased patients really appear in his mirror, saying that these reports are "fabled." Even regarding such an important matter as whether or not the four people who drank the water actually became young, the narrator has a limited perspective. He can say what they looked like, as if he is in the room with them and is hampered by the dim lighting, but he cannot say definitively whether their transformation is real or not. Although the first-person narrator is not mentioned as being a sixth person in the doctor's study that night, he relates facts as if he were. He knows local gossip, but he does not have any inside perspective on what goes on in Dr. Heidegger's mind.

Gothic

Gothic fiction is a distinctive style of writing that arose in Europe in the eighteenth century and reached the height of its popularity in the United States in the first half of the nineteenth century. Critics trace its source back to British author Horace Walpole's 1764 novel *The Castle of Otranto*, and it carried on through the works of Anne Radcliffe and Mary Wollstonecraft Shelley, whose work *Frankenstein* is considered a prime example. In the United States, Charles Brockden Brown is viewed as the earliest practitioner of the form, but Gothic fiction is invariably associated with the tales of Edgar Allan Poe.

Several characteristics are associated with Gothic literature. Stories often occur at night and include frightening elements that were as clichéd in the eighteenth century as they are in the twenty-first, such as bats, castles, skeletons, and mad scientists. The line between natural law and supernatural occurrences is often unclear, and ghosts are common. One of the most consistent elements of Gothic literature is the association of residence with resident: the unusual aspects of a house or castle (or, in the case of "Dr. Heidegger's Experiment," study) are meant to reflect the unusual elements of its owner's mind.

HISTORICAL CONTEXT

Dark Romanticism

Hawthorne came at the end of the literary movement called romanticism, when the American version had evolved in several different directions. In Hawthorne, and in his contemporary, Edgar Allan Poe, the ideals of romanticism came to manifest themselves as an offshoot that literary critics refer to as "dark romanticism."

The romantic movement developed in Europe in the late eighteenth century. Its precursor was the Enlightenment, a period of scientific curiosity and social theorizing that centered on the accomplishments of the human mind. The range of interests and accomplishments attributed to Enlightenment thinkers varied widely: philosophers John Locke, David Hume, and Immanuel Kant, for instance,

COMPARE & CONTRAST

- **1837:** Florida is a mysterious wilderness that could conceivably contain a Fountain of Youth in some hidden location.

  Today: Florida is the fourth most populous state in the United States. Most of its land has been explored or developed.

- **1837:** A doctor who is curious about the effects of a strange potion might gather some friends together to have them try it out.

  Today: The U.S. Food and Drug Administration has stringent protocols meant to ensure the safety and effectiveness of new drugs before they are tested on human subjects. Often, computer models can be run to predict results.

- **1837:** The subjects of Dr. Heidegger's experiment are thrilled about the opportunity to look years younger than they really are.

  Today: Making people look younger is a cultural obsession. Plastic surgery, hair treatments, and rejuvenating creams form a large segment of the economy.

- **1837:** Water from an underground source that bubbles like champagne appears to have magical properties.

  Today: Water with some degree of carbonation, such as Perrier, is regularly bottled from natural sources.

- **1837:** A chambermaid who has seen strange occurrences in the doctor's study, such as a moving picture or a talking bust, would tell her neighbors so that gossip would spread.

  Today: Someone with such an interesting tale to tell might report it on a Web log or perhaps try to sell it to a tabloid television show.

- **1837:** Four people who have experienced the thrill of drinking the Water of Youth from a fountain far away end up leaving the next morning for Florida, in hopes of locating the magical fountain.

  Today: After having such a thrilling experience, the people who drink the water would likely start their quest for the fountain by doing an Internet search.

---

focused their attention on abstract questions such as what knowledge actually is; scientists such as Isaac Newton looked to measuring and understanding the physical world; and social philosophers, most notably René Descartes, theorized about political and social order. Overall, the focus of intellectualism from the mid-1600s to the late 1700s was on the power of rational thought.

Romanticism is considered the backlash against that age. As with the Enlightenment, or with any literary movement, theories differ widely on what should be included in this period. One thing that makes it difficult to pin down an exact definition is the range of fields that this word is used to describe, from art to music to architecture. Rather than looking at the human mind, early romantics tended to look to the human condition as it existed before "civilized" culture existed. Writers such as William Wordsworth and Samuel Taylor Coleridge (whose introduction for their collaboration, the 1798 collection *Lyrical Ballads*, is considered by many to be the starting point of romanticism in British literature) focused on nature and humans' relationship to it, usually showing humanity as being separated from the purity of a natural life. Other themes that developed in romanticism included a fascination with the past, and in particular one's cultural history (which for most Europeans included interest in Greek and Roman mythology) and eventually the kind of sensuality that readers associate with the genre's most identifiable authors: John Keats, Percy Bysshe Shelley, and George Gordon Byron.

In the United States, romanticism took hold later, in the novels of James Fenimore Cooper. The New England transcendentalists, led by Emerson

Dr. Heidegger's study *(Image copyright Rachel L. Sellers, 2009. Used under license from Shutterstock.com)*

and Henry David Thoreau, are considered to be followers of a form of romanticism, continuing the emphasis on the natural person, untainted by society, and presenting nature as being significant as a manifestation of the individual mind.

This view of reality took an eerie turn in some of the writings of Hawthorne and Melville. While the transcendentalists viewed the human mind as mastering nature, the dark romantic vision presented nature as the manifestation of human thought that was as often as not unbalanced. Nature was controllable, but the dark romantic world view often included a place for the threat presented by supernatural occurrences that were beyond human control. Dark romanticism showed the negative ramifications likely to occur if the romantic view is true: if, instead of being pure and innocent in their natural state, humans are inclined toward evil, then the primacy of the human in this world would lead, more often than not, toward disaster.

CRITICAL OVERVIEW

By the time that *Twice-Told Tales*, the collection that includes "Dr. Heidegger's Experiment," was published, Hawthorne already had a solid literary following of people who had read the works when they were first published in magazines (which is what made them "twice told" when republished in a book) and had told others what a gifted author Hawthorne was. In a 1994 compilation called *Nathaniel Hawthorne: The Contemporary Reviews*, editors John L. Idol, Jr., and Buford Jones compiled reviews that were written when Hawthorne's works were originally published. Many reviewers believed that *Twice-Told Tales*, which came out in 1837 when Hawthorne was relatively unknown except in the smallest of literary circles, was a powerful work. Several use the word "genius" to describe Hawthorne's writing. An unsigned review in the *Daily Advertiser*, a Boston newspaper, is representative of the kind of praise that was directed at the book and the author: "Mr. Hawthorne is endowed, in no inconsiderable degree, with those elements which, when combined, make up the mysterious essence called genius." The same review goes on to note, "There is nothing, in his book, of the hackneyed commonplace of the mob of story-writers and essayists." Other reviewers compare his writing to that of respected English essayist Joseph Addison and to that of Jonathan Swift, the satirist who wrote *Gulliver's Travels*. Longfellow, who later became a good friend of Hawthorne, writes in *North American Review* of *Twice-Told Tales*.

> Every thing about it has the freshness of morning and of May. These flowers and green leaves of poetry have not the dust of the highway upon them. They have been gathered fresh from the secret places of a peaceful and gentle heart.

Later, he clarifies: "The book, though in prose, is written nevertheless by a poet."

When the second edition of *Twice-Told Tales* was published in 1842, after the book's literary reputation was established, it was reviewed by Edgar Allan Poe in *Graham's* magazine. Praising Hawthorne's tone and originality, Poe concludes, "Upon the whole we look upon him as one of the few men of indisputable genius to whom our country has as yet given birth." Poe returned in the following month's issue with a much longer review, in which he discusses individual stories. "Dr. Heidegger's Experiment," he says, is "exceedingly well imagined, and executed with surpassing ability. The artist breathes in every line of it." In the decades since then, Hawthorne has been considered one of the cornerstones of the American literary tradition.

CRITICISM

David Kelly

Kelly is a writer and an instructor of creative writing and literature. In this essay, he considers how the mystical elements of "Dr. Heidegger's Experiment" help readers understand its deeply humane message.

There are different ways to appreciate a story like Hawthorne's "Dr. Heidegger's Experiment." It is often read as a story about growing old gracefully, a message that is buoyed up by the creepy elements that make the story interesting. On the other hand, the fact that it is written by one of the great names of American literature means that the story earns itself serious consideration. In most cases, this means that critics are willing to accept the way that Hawthorne balances his story along the thin line that separates reality from fantasy, accepting that its psychological elements might be the key to a greater appreciation, even if it does seem simple. The psychological interpretation, however, often stops short, dismissing Hawthorne's achievement as a moralistic lesson about accepting the inevitable. Dr. Heidegger himself is too often treated as a wise and benevolent force who enters the lives of his friends to, for some reason, make them better people, or maybe to make humanity better with his unexplained experiment. Literary critics, who give more attention to the author's clearer allegories such as "The Minister's Black Veil," tend to treat Dr. Heidegger as just another one of the sinister trappings or background effects that Hawthorne so lavishly describes, and so they forget to look at him as a human.

To some degree, it is understandable that critics would dismiss Dr. Heidegger as being just another gothic element of the story. Hawthorne followed the romantic tradition of equating the person with his surroundings, and in doing so crossed the line that separates what can be considered symbolic and what should be considered real. Reading this as an example of Gothic romanticism, all that needs to be known about Dr. Heidegger is on display right there in the setting. The bust of Hippocrates, the reflections of his dead patients, the picture of his deceased fiancée, and the skeleton hanging in a wardrobe are not just props or hints; they are the sum of who he is. The problem with such a reading is that there is no way of confirming what is there and what is not. Hawthorne gives details about what is in the doctor's study all right, but his narrator does not claim that they are factually true, only that they are things that have been rumored by unnamed persons. Without any claim of reality, the elements that seem to be supernatural are still grounded in common reality. Dr. Heidegger's behavior, therefore, should be grounded in reality too.

> "MOST PSYCHOLOGICAL READINGS OF THIS STORY ASSUME THAT DR. HEIDEGGER IS INDEED A MAGICIAN, BUT A MAGICIAN IN THE MODERN SENSE: NOT AN OCCULTIST BUT A SHOWMAN."

In trying to understand a story like this, the first place to look is at the simplest interpretation, which is that it is just a good scare story, with a moral thrown in to justify the author's use of Gothic elements, which really are there simply to amuse. This interpretation is supported by the fact that there is no clear reason for the careful, detailed description of Dr. Heidegger's study. Readers know about the bust, the picture, the mirror, and the closet, as well as about the dust and cobwebs and books of various sizes. It is said that they all come to life when a maid touched an unmarked book, allegedly of magic, though the narrator does not claim to know that this is actually so. Without any solid confirmation, all readers really know is that the mood of Dr. Heidegger's study is eerie.

Later in the story, evidence of real magic shows up. Dr. Heidegger takes a dead rose and drops it into the liquid that he claims is water from the Fountain of Youth that Spanish explorer Ponce de León sought in Florida. The rose revivifies. He gives the water to four old friends—a drunk, a politician, a financier, and a flirt—whose lives burned out long ago from their wild ways. They come into his study old and bitter, but drinking the water makes them young again. A butterfly, lying on the floor to die, is unexpectedly splashed, and it flies with renewed energy, perching atop Dr. Heidegger's head. The effects on the rose and the people can easily be explained

WHAT DO I READ NEXT?

- Some critics accused Hawthorne of stealing the idea for this story from Alexandre Dumas's novel *Mémoires d'un Médecin* (*Memoirs of a Physician*) until Hawthorne pointed out that the 1846 novel had actually been published almost ten years after the first publication of "Dr. Heidegger's Experiment." Still, there are interesting similarities between the two tales.
- Natalie Babbitt's 1975 novel *Tuck Everlasting*, an American Library Association Notable Book, is considered an enchanting story for younger readers about a family that discovers the secret of immortality.
- The gothic touches of "Dr. Heidegger's Experiment" are often associated with the stories of Hawthorne's friend Edgar Allan Poe. Poe's 1843 story "The Tell-Tale Heart," about a man who kills an old man and continues to feel the presence of his victim, has a setting that is similar, though much more desperate. This story and others can be found in *Edgar Allan Poe: Poetry and Tales*, published in 1984 by Library of America.
- Though Hawthorne is respected for his short stories, his masterpiece is considered to be his novel *The Scarlet Letter*, which takes place in colonial Salem, Massachusetts, a setting that he wrote about often. It concerns a Puritan woman who is shunned by society for adultery. First published in 1850, it is currently available in numerous editions, including a Penguin Classic revised edition from 2002.
- Hawthorne's way of conveying psychological insight through a surreal situation is similar to that of Herman Melville, his friend and admirer, who is best known today for the novel *Moby-Dick*. Melville's story "Bartleby the Scrivener" is similar in tone to "Dr. Heidegger's Experiment." It is available in collections of Melville's works and on its own in *Bartleby, The Scrivener: A Story of Wall-Street*, published by CreateSpace in 2009.
- Hawthorne's fascinating, complex life is examined in depth in the biography *Hawthorne: A Life*, by Brenda Wineapple, published in 2004 by Random House.
- "The Fountain of Youth" is a famous Japanese fairy tale about a man and his wife who both drink the fabled regenerating water, and the lesson they learn from it. The tale was translated into English in the 1890s by Lafcadio Hearn, and it is currently available online and in *Lafcadio Hearn's Japanese Ghost Stories*, a manga written by British writer Sean Michael Wilson and illustrated by Japanese artist Haruka Miyabi. The book was published by Demented Dragon in 2007.

by the doctor's actions, while the butterfly, which is beyond his control, might just be an example of the principle that even in fiction random acts are due now and then.

Most psychological readings of this story assume that Dr. Heidegger is indeed a magician, but a magician in the modern sense: not an occultist but a showman. Reputation aside, there is nothing to show that he has any magical powers. The rose, for instance, changes its appearance just when he wants it to do so, in front of the people he has called together to witness exactly that event. Either he reverses the rose's aging process or he simply makes them think that he has. In light of what goes on later in the story, the second seems most likely. The way that he makes his four acquaintances appear to be young is easily explained without resorting to any mystical explanations. Hawthorne is fairly clear that they are not drinking a magic potion, that they are simply getting drunk and losing the inhibitions that have grown in them over the years. He uses the word "liquor" to describe the water several times (this word has other meanings and does not necessarily refer to alcohol, but it does suggest it). He gives no indication that there is any real mystical transformation of the four old people, either, qualifying nearly every statement of their change with the caveat that it only appears that way. If they are just tricked into believing that the water they drank has made them young, then it would stand to reason that the doctor's elaborate show with the dead flower is part of the trick, accomplished with some simple but unexplained sleight-of-hand.

Although it is easy to understand how Dr. Heidegger might manipulate his friends into thinking that they have turned young, finding out why he might do this requires some picking through the text. It could be that as a man of science, he is simply curious about what humans would do if they could regain their youth, and so he experiments on these four subjects in order to record their responses. It is a very unambitious experiment, though. If he wants to see the effects of the power of suggestion and a placebo, Dr. Heidegger could have chosen a wider range of subjects than four who are so similar, who have been acquainted with one another for more than half a century. His sampling base is neither broad nor varied.

Dr. Heidegger probably has more motivating him than just scientific curiosity. The key to understanding him must necessarily lie in his dead fiancée. Dr. Heidegger brings four people of dubious intelligence to his house, tells them he will make them young, shows them a flower made young, and then loosens their lips with drink. Certainly he cannot take their behavior as a surprise, or even a revelation. The experiment in "Dr. Heidegger's Experiment" is not just a matter of seeing whether he can bend others to his will. The doctor is experimenting with himself.

If the Water of Youth is the fraud it appears to be, Dr. Heidegger knows all along that he has no question about whether to choose youth or not. There is, though, a choice to be made about whether to focus on the past or on the future. In this, the antics of his test subjects, who are old but behaving childishly, offer little help. A simple interpretation of the story might hold that the doctor learns from them that youth was and always will be a time of foolishness. A closer reading reveals that his lesson, his test result, is about how ill-served one is to focus on the past. Before the story, Dr. Heidegger has surrounded himself with memories. The picture of the young woman who died fifty years ago dominates his study, and the images of dead patients that show up in his mirror must be appearing to him, if to anyone. The bust of Hippocrates does not offer advice about magic or about medicine; when disturbed, the word it says is "forbear"—that is, it commands the hearer to take no action or to show restraint.

It is naïve to think that Dr. Heidegger finds out from this experiment only that he does not want to go back to his youth. Presumably, he knows that; the past haunts him like a skeleton in his closet, like the faces of his dead patients and his lost lover. What he learns from watching three men fighting over the one woman in the room is that he loves the present. The mark of his revelation is when he says that he loves the rose Sylvia gave him. Loves—present tense. If there is no magic and he has faked the whole situation, then he has always known that he can never go back to youth, a prospect that his four gullible friends never accept. What changes for Dr. Heidegger is that he decides to stop living his life by looking to the past. It is a colossal change for a man whose study is dominated by a painting of a woman who died fifty years earlier. He does not accept age, as so many interpretations have it. He embraces it.

This story is often underestimated. Hawthorne did such a good job of blending weird and interesting details together that readers tend to finish it with a feeling of satisfaction, even if they cannot quite say what the story is about. But Hawthorne was more than a masterful storyteller. He was a writer who understood the depth of his character. Most readers would be content to think that Dr. Heidegger has somehow learned to give up a dream of going back, though such a dream is never mentioned. His shift in focus toward the future, though, is a lesson that is worth learning, a result that makes his experiment worthwhile.

Source: David Kelly, Critical Essay on "Dr. Heidegger's Experiment," in *Short Stories for Students*, Gale, Cengage Learning, 2010.

Edgar A. Poe

In the following essay, Poe describes Hawthorne as a privately admired and publicly unappreciated man of genius.

In the preface to my sketches of New York Literati, while speaking of the broad distinction between the seeming public and real private

"HE HAS THE PUREST STYLE, THE FINEST TASTE, THE MOST AVAILABLE SCHOLARSHIP, THE MOST DELICATE HUMOR, THE MOST TOUCHING PATHOS, THE MOST RADIANT IMAGINATION, THE MOST CONSUMMATE INGENUITY; AND WITH THESE VARIED GOOD QUALITIES HE HAS DONE *WELL* AS A MYSTIC."

opinion respecting our authors, I thus alluded to Nathaniel Hawthorne:—

> For example, Mr. Hawthorne, the author of *Twice-Told Tales*, is scarcely recognized by the press or by the public, and when noticed at all, is noticed merely to be damned by faint praise. Now, my own opinion of him is, that although his walk is limited and he is fairly to be charged with mannerism, treating all subjects in a similar tone of dreamy *innuendo*, yet in this walk he evinces extraordinary genius, having no rival either in America or elsewhere; and this opinion I have never heard gain-said by any one literary person in the country. That this opinion, however, is a spoken and not a written one, is referable to the facts, first, that Mr. Hawthorne *is* a poor man, and, secondly, that he *is not* an ubiquitous quack.

The reputation of the author of *Twice-Told Tales* has been confined, indeed, until very lately, to literary society; and I have not been wrong, perhaps, in citing him as *the* example, *par excellence*, in this country, of the privately-admired and publicly-unappreciated man of genius. Within the last year or two, it is true, an occasional critic has been urged, by honest indignation, into very warm approval.... These criticisms, however, seemed to have little effect on the popular taste—at least, if we are to form any idea of the popular taste by reference to its expression in the newspapers, or by the sale of the author's book. It was never the fashion (until lately) to speak of him in any summary of our best authors. The daily critics would say, on such occasions, "Is there not Irving and Cooper, and Bryant and Paulding, and—Smith?" or, "Have we not Halleck and Dana, and Longfellow and—Thompson?" or, "Can we not point triumphantly to our own Sprague, Willis, Channing, Bancroft, Prescott and—Jenkins?" but these unanswerable queries were never wound up by the name of Hawthorne.

Beyond doubt, this inappreciation of him on the part of the public arose chiefly from the two causes to which I have referred—from the facts that he is neither a man of wealth nor a quack;—but these are insufficient to account for the whole effect. No small portion of it is attributable to the very marked idiosyncrasy of Mr. Hawthorne himself. In one sense, and in great measure, to be peculiar is to be original, and than the true originality there is no higher literary virtue. This true or commendable originality, however, implies not the uniform, but the continuous peculiarity—a peculiarity springing from ever-active vigor of fancy—better still if from ever-present force of imagination, giving its own hue, its own character to everything it touches, and, especially, *self impelled to touch everything*.

It is often said, inconsiderately, that very original writers always fail in popularity—that such and such persons are too original to be comprehended by the mass. "Too peculiar," should be the phrase, "too idiosyncratic." It is, in fact, the excitable, undisciplined and child-like popular mind which most keenly feels the original. The criticism of the conservatives, of the hackneys, of the cultivated old clergymen of the *North American Review*, is precisely the criticism which condemns and alone condemns it. "It becometh not a divine," saith Lord Coke, "to be of a fiery and salamandrine spirit." Their conscience allowing them to move nothing themselves, these dignitaries have a holy horror of being moved. "Give us *quietude*," they say. Opening their mouths with proper caution, they sigh forth the word "*Repose*." And this is, indeed, the one thing they should be permitted to enjoy, if only upon the Christian principle of give and take.

The fact is, that if Mr. Hawthorne were really original, he could not fail of making himself felt by the public. But the fact is, he is *not* original in any sense. Those who speak of him as original, mean nothing more than that he differs in his manner or tone, and in his choice of subjects, from any author of their acquaintance—their acquaintance not extending to the German Tieck, whose manner, in *some* of his works, is absolutely identical with that *habitual* to Hawthorne. But it is clear that the element of the literary originality is novelty. The element of its appreciation by the reader is the reader's sense of the new. Whatever gives him a new and insomuch a pleasurable emotion, he considers original, and whoever frequently gives him such emotion, he considers an original writer. In a word, it is by the sum total of these emotions that he decides upon the writer's claim to originality. I may observe here, however, that there is clearly a point at which even novelty itself would cease to produce the legitimate originality, if we judge this originality, as we should, by the effect designed: this point is that at which *novelty becomes nothing novel*; and here the artist, *to preserve his originality*, will subside into the common-place....

These points properly understood, it will be seen that the critic (unacquainted with Tieck) who reads a single tale or essay by Hawthorne, may be justified in thinking him original; but the tone, or manner, or choice of subject, which induces in this critic the sense of the new, will—if not in a second tale, at least in a third and all subsequent ones—not only fail of inducing it, but bring about an exactly antagonistic impression. In concluding a volume, and more especially in concluding all the volumes of the author, the critic will abandon his first design of calling him "original," and content himself with styling him "peculiar."

With the vague opinion that to be original is to be unpopular, I could, indeed, agree, were I to adopt an understanding of originality which, to my surprise, I have known adopted by many who have a right to be called critical. They have limited, in a love for mere words, the literary to the metaphysical originality. They regard as original in letters, only such combinations of thought, of incident, and so forth, as are, in fact, absolutely novel. It is clear, however, not only that it is the novelty of *effect* alone which is worth consideration, but that this effect is *best* wrought, for the end of all fictitious composition, pleasure, by shunning rather than by seeking the absolute novelty of combination. Originality, thus understood, tasks and startles the intellect, and so brings into undue action the faculties to which, in the lighter literature, we least appeal. And thus understood, it cannot fail to prove unpopular with the masses, who, seeking in this literature amusement, are positively offended by instruction. But the true originality—true in respect of its purposes—is that which, in bringing out the half-formed, the reluctant, or the unexpressed fancies of mankind, or in exciting the more delicate pulses of the heart's passion, or in giving birth to some universal sentiment or instinct in embryo, thus combines with the pleasurable effect of *apparent* novelty, a real egoistic delight. The reader, in the case first supposed, (that of the absolute novelty,) is excited, but embarrassed, disturbed, in some degree even pained at his own want of perception, at his own folly in not having himself hit upon the idea. In the second case, his pleasure is doubled. He is filled with an intrinsic and extrinsic delight. He feels and intensely enjoys the seeming novelty of the thought, enjoys it as really novel, as absolutely original with the writer—*and* himself. They two, he fancies, have, alone of all men, thought thus. They two have, together, created this thing. Henceforward there is a bond of sympathy between them, a sympathy which irradiates every subsequent page of the book.

There is a species of writing which, with some difficulty, may be admitted as a lower degree of what I have called the true original. In its perusal, we say to ourselves, not "how original this is!" nor "here is an idea which I and the author have alone entertained," but "here is a charmingly obvious fancy," or sometimes even, "here is a thought which I am not sure has ever occurred to myself, but which, of course, has occurred to all the rest of the world." This kind of composition (which still appertains to a high order) is usually designated as "the natural." It has little external resemblance, but strong internal affinity to the true original, if, indeed, as I have suggested, it is not of this latter an inferior degree. It is best exemplified, among English writers, in Addison, Irving and *Hawthorne*. The "ease" which is so often spoken of as its distinguishing feature, it has been the fashion to regard as ease in appearance alone, as a point of really difficult attainment. This idea, however, must be received with some reservation. The natural style is difficult only to those who should never intermeddle with it—to the unnatural. It is but the result of writing with the understanding, or with the instinct, that the *tone*, in composition, should be that which, at any given point or upon any given topic, would be the tone of the great mass of humanity. The author who, after the manner of the North Americans, is merely at *all* times *quiet*, is, of course, upon *most* occasions, merely silly or stupid, and has no more right to be thought "easy" or "natural" than has a cockney exquisite or the sleeping beauty in the waxworks.

The "peculiarity" or sameness, or monotone of Hawthorne, would, in its mere character of "peculiarity," and without reference to what *is* the peculiarity, suffice to deprive him of all chance of popular appreciation. But at his failure to be appreciated, we can, *of course*, no longer wonder, when we find him monotonous at decidedly the worst of all possible points—at that point which, having the least concern with Nature, is the farthest removed from the popular intellect, from the popular sentiment and from the popular taste. I allude to the strain of allegory which completely overwhelms the greater number of his subjects, and which in some measure interferes with the direct conduct of absolutely all.

In defence of allegory, (however, or for whatever object, employed,) there is scarcely one respectable word to be said. Its best appeals are made to the fancy—that is to say, to our sense of adaptation, not of matters proper, but of matters improper for the purpose, of the real with the unreal; having never more of intelligible connection than has something with nothing, never half so much of effective affinity as has the substance for the shadow. The deepest emotion aroused within us by the happiest allegory, *as* allegory, is a very, very imperfectly satisfied sense of the writer's ingenuity in overcoming a difficulty we should have preferred his not having attempted to overcome. The fallacy of the idea that allegory, in any of its moods, can be made to enforce a truth—that metaphor, for example, may illustrate as well as embellish an argument—could be promptly demonstrated: the converse of the supposed fact might be shown, indeed, with very little trouble—but these are topics foreign to my present purpose. One thing is clear, that if allegory ever establishes a fact, it is by dint of overturning a fiction. Where the suggested meaning runs through the obvious one in a *very* profound under-current, so as never to interfere with the upper one without our own volition, so as never to show itself unless *called* to the surface, there only, for the proper uses of fictitious narrative, is it available at all. Under the best circumstances, it must always interfere with that unity of effect which, to the artist, is worth all the allegory in the world....

The obvious causes, however, which have prevented Mr. Hawthorne's *popularity*, do not suffice to condemn him in the eyes of the few who belong properly to books, and to whom books, perhaps, do not quite so properly belong. These few estimate an author, not as do the public, altogether by what he does, but in great measure—indeed, even in the greatest measure—by what he evinces a capability of doing. In this view, Hawthorne stands among literary people in America much in the same light as did Coleridge in England. The few, also, through a certain warping of the taste, which long pondering upon books as books merely never fails to induce, are not in condition to view the errors of a scholar as errors altogether. At any time these gentlemen are prone to think the public not right rather than an educated author wrong. But the simple truth is, that the writer who aims at impressing the people, is *always* wrong when he fails in forcing that people to receive the impression. How far Mr. Hawthorne has addressed the people at all, is, of course, not a question for me to decide. His books afford strong internal evidence of having been written to himself and his particular friends alone.

The tale proper affords the fairest field which can be afforded by the wide domains of mere prose, for the exercise of the highest genius.... History, philosophy, and other matters of that kind, we leave out of the question, of course. *Of course*, I say, and in spite of the graybeards. These graver topics, to the end of time, will be best illustrated by what a discriminating world, turning up its nose at the drab pamphlets, has agreed to understand as *talent*. The ordinary novel is objectionable, from its length, for reasons analogous to those which render length objectionable in the poem. As the novel cannot be read at one sitting, it cannot avail itself of the immense benefit of *totality*. Worldly interests, intervening during the pauses of perusal, modify, counteract and annul the impressions intended. But simple cessation in reading would, of itself, be sufficient to destroy the true unity. In the brief tale, however, the author is enabled to carry out his full design without interruption. During the hour of perusal, the soul of the reader is at the writer's control.

A skillful artist has constructed a tale. He has not fashioned his thoughts to accommodate his incidents, but having deliberately conceived a certain *single effect* to be wrought, he then invents such incidents, he then combines such events, and discusses them in such tone as may best serve him in establishing this preconceived effect. If his very first sentence tend not to the out-bringing of this effect, then in his very first step has he committed a blunder. In the whole composition there should be no word written of which the tendency, direct or indirect, is not to the one pre-established design. And by such means, with such care and skill, a picture is at length painted which leaves in the mind of him who contemplates it with a kindred art, a sense of the fullest satisfaction. The idea of the tale, its thesis, has been presented unblemished, because undisturbed—an end absolutely demanded, yet, in the novel, altogether unattainable.

Of skillfully-constructed tales—I speak now without reference to other points, some of them more important than construction—there are very few American specimens. I am acquainted with no better one, upon the whole, than the "Murder Will Out" of Mr. Simms, and this has some glaring defects. The "Tales of a Traveler," by Irving, are graceful and impressive narratives—"The Young Italian" is especially good—but there is not one of the series which can be commended as a whole.... But in general skill of construction, the tales of Willis, I think, surpass those of any American writer—with the exception of Mr. Hawthorne.

I must defer to the better opportunity of a volume now in hand, a full discussion of his individual pieces, and hasten to conclude this paper with a summary of his merits and demerits.

He is peculiar and *not* original—unless in those detailed fancies and detached thoughts which his want of general originality will deprive of the appreciation due to them, in preventing them forever reaching the *public* eye. He is infinitely too fond of allegory, and can never hope for popularity so long as he persists in it. This he will not do, for allegory is at war with the whole tone of his nature, which disports itself never so well as when escaping from the mysticism of his Goodman Browns and White Old Maids into the hearty, genial, but still Indian-summer sunshine of his Wakefields and Little Annie's Rambles. Indeed, *his* spirit of "metaphor run-mad" is clearly imbibed from the phalanx and phalanstery atmosphere in which he has been so long struggling for breath. He has not half the material for the exclusiveness of authorship that he possesses for its universality. He has the purest style, the finest taste, the most available scholarship, the most delicate humor, the most touching pathos, the most radiant imagination, the most consummate ingenuity; and with these varied good qualities he has done *well* as a mystic. But is there any one of these qualities which should prevent his doing doubly as well in a career of honest, upright, sensible, prehensible and comprehensible things? Let him mend his pen, get a bottle of visible ink, come out from the Old Manse, cut Mr. Alcott, hang (if possible) the editor of *The Dial*, and throw out of the window to the pigs all his odd numbers of *The North American Review*.

Source: Edgar A. Poe, "Tale Writing—Nathaniel Hawthorne," in *Complete Short Stories of Nathaniel Hawthorne*, Doubleday & Company, 1959, pp. 5–10.

Victor E. Gibbens

In the following essay, Gibbens explains the controversy surrounding Hawthorne and Dumas's plagiarism claims.

Apparently no one has ever been curious enough about Hawthorne's note to "Dr. Heidegger's Experiment" to investigate the facts regarding the charge and counter charge of plagiarism mentioned in it. The note runs as follows:

> NOTE: In an English review not long since, I have been accused of plagiarising the idea of this story from a chapter in one of the novels of Alexandre Dumas. There has undoubtedly been a plagiarism on one side or the other; but as my story was written a good deal more than twenty years ago, and as the novel is of considerably more recent date, I take pleasure in thinking that M. Dumas has done me the honor to appropriate one of the fanciful conceptions of my earlier days. He is heartily welcome to it; nor is it the only instance, by many, in which the great French romancer has exercised the privilege of commanding genius by confiscating the intellectual property of less famous people to his own use and behoof. *September,* 1860.

Briefly the facts are these. "Dr. Heidegger's Experiment" was published as "The Fountain of Youth" in the *Knickerbocker* for January, 1837, whereas the novel mentioned in the review—*Mémoires d'un Médecin*—was published as a serial from 1846 to 1848 inclusive, or from nine to eleven years after the short story. Both the story and a chapter in the novel treat of an elixir to restore youth to the aged, but beyond the general theme, which itself dates from classical mythology, no striking similarity exists. Of Hawthorne's main thesis that man, if restored to youth, would commit the same follies over again, there is not the slightest hint in the Dumas episode.

The inconsequent reference to Hawthorne and Dumas by the English reviewer could only by some stretch of the imagination be labelled a charge. He had written:

> In "Dr. Heidegger's Experiment" (which we fancy may have been suggested by a scene in Dumas' *Memoires d'un Medecin*), we are taught that, if we could renew our youth by some Medean draft, we should, unless altered in other respects, commit the same follies as we have now to look back to.

That Hawthorne did not rest his defense merely in exposing the patent absurdity of this suggestion of influence and that he appears not to have read the French novel before levelling his counter charge demonstrate once again that even the great are human and fallible.

Source: Victor E. Gibbens, "Hawthorne's Note to 'Dr. Heidegger's Experiment,'" in *Modern Language Notes*, Vol. 60, No. 6, June 1945, pp. 408–09.

Louise Hastings

In the following essay, Hastings examines a short story of Hawthorne's, "The First and Last Dinner," asserting that the story is the origin for "Dr. Heidegger's Experiment."

In *A Practical System of Rhetoric; or, the Principles and Rules of Style* (Portland, 1829) the author, Samuel Phillips Newman, included the following sketch, which if not written by Hawthorne, could very easily have been a source for "Dr. Heidegger's Experiment." Although the narrative contains many parallels to Hawthorne's later tales, I have confined my comparisons as much as possible to his earlier fiction. In other words, I have attempted to find an appropriate place for it somewhere between his Gothic tales and such mature pieces as "Roger Malvin's Burial" and "The Gentle Boy." Perhaps this simple, even amateurish, bit of writing will help to explain his growth, indicating that at college he did not limit his expression to the luridness of "Alice Doane's Appeal," but that he had already begun to plant the seeds for his later art.

"TRUE, THE STORY, PRAISED BY NEWMAN, IS, ON THE SURFACE, AN OBVIOUS TREATMENT OF AN OBVIOUS THEME; BUT A CLOSE COMPARISON OF IT WITH "DR. HEIDEGGER'S EXPERIMENT" HAS SHOWN ME THE PLAUSIBILITY OF ITS BEING HAWTHORNE'S OWN."

THE FIRST AND LAST DINNER

> Twelve friends, much about the same age, and fixed by their pursuits, their family connexions, and other local interests, as permanent inhabitants of the metropolis, agreed, one day when they were drinking wine at the Star and Garter at Richmond, to institute an annual dinner among themselves under the following regulations:—That they should dine alternately at each others' houses on the *first* and *last* day of the year; and the *first* bottle of wine uncorked at the *first* dinner should be recorked and put away, to be drunk by him who should be the last of their number; that they should never admit a new member; that, when one died, eleven should meet, and when another died, ten should meet, and so on; and that, when only one remained, he should, on these two days, dine by himself, and sit the usual hours at his solitary table; but the first time he had so dined, lest it should be the only one, he should then uncork the *first* bottle, and in the *first* glass, drink to the memory of all who were gone.
>
> Some thirty years had now glided away, and only ten remained; but the stealing hand of time had written sundry changes in most legible characters. Raven locks had become grizzled; two or three heads had not as many locks as may be reckoned in a walk of half a mile along the Regent's Canal—one was actually covered with a brown wig—the crow's feet were visible in the corner of the eye—good old port and warm Madeira carried it against hock, claret, red burgundy, and champagne—stews, hashes, and ragouts, grew into favour—crusts were rarely called for to relish the cheese after dinner—conversation was less boisterous, and it turned chiefly upon politics and the state of funds, or the values of landed property—apologies were made for coming in thick shoes and warm stockings—the doors and windows were more carefully provided with list and sandbags—the fire is in more request—and a quiet game of whist filled up the hours that were wont to be devoted to drinking, singing, and riotous merriment. Two rubbers, a cup of coffee, and at home by eleven o'clock, was the usual cry, when the fifth or sixth glass had gone round after the removal of the cloth. At parting, too, there was now a long ceremony in the hall, buttoning up great coats, tying on woollen comforters, fixing silk handkerchiefs over the mouth and up to the ears, and grasping sturdy walking canes to support unsteady feet.
>
> Their fiftieth anniversary came, and death had indeed been busy. Four little old men, of withered appearance and decrepit walk, with cracked voices, and dim, rayless eyes, sat down by the mercy of heaven, (as they tremulously declared,) to celebrate, for the fiftieth time, the first day of the year, to observe the frolic compact, which half a century before, they had entered into at the Star and Garter at Richmond. Eight were in their graves! The four that remained stood upon its confines. Yet they chirped cheerily over their glass, though they could scarcely carry it to their lips, if more than half full; and

> cracked their jokes, though they articulated their words with difficulty, and heard each other with still greater difficulty. They mumbled, they chattered, they laughed, (if a sort of strangled wheezing might be called a laugh,) and as the wine sent their icy blood in warmer pulses through their veins, they talked of their past as if it were but a yesterday that had slipped by them and of their future as if it were but a busy century that lay before them.
>
> At length came the *last* dinner; and the survivor of the twelve, upon whose head four score and ten winters had showered their snow, ate his solitary meal. It so chanced that it was in his house, and at his table, they celebrated the first. In his cellar, too, had remained, for eight and forty years, the bottle they had then uncorked, recorked, and which he was that day to uncork again. It stood beside him. With a feeble and reluctant grasp he took the "frail memorial" of a youthful vow; and for a moment memory was faithful to her office. She threw open the long vista of buried years; and his heart travelled through them all: Their lusty and blithesome spring—their bright and fervid summer—their ripe and temperate autumn—their chill, but not too frozen winter. He saw as in a mirror, one by one the laughing companions of that merry hour, at Richmond, had dropped into eternity. He felt the loneliness of his condition, (for he had eschewed marriage, and in the veins of no living creature ran a drop of blood whose source was in his own;) and as he drained the glass which he had filled, "to the memory of those who were gone," the tears slowly trickled down the deep furrows of his aged face.
>
> He had thus fulfilled one part of his vow, and he prepared himself to discharge the other by sitting the usual number of hours at his desolate table. With a heavy heart he resigned himself to the gloom of his own thoughts—a lethargic sleep stole over him—his head fell upon his bosom—confused images crowded into his mind—he babbled to himself—was silent—and when his servant entered the room alarmed by a noise which he heard, he found his master stretched upon the carpet at the foot of the easychair out of which he had slipped in an apoplectic fit. He never spoke again nor once opened his eyes, though the vital spark was not extinct till the following day. And this was the
>
> LAST DINNER!

The following words from this story are favorites through Hawthorne's earlier tales and many of them appear in "Dr. Heidegger's Experiment": metropolis, solitary, glided, raven locks, grizzled, withered, decrepit walk, tremulously, mumbled, chattered, wheezing, feeble, memory, fervid, merry hour, trickled, deep furrows, vow, desolate, heavy heart, gloom, bosom, babbled. Parentheses and short quotations, two other characteristic modes of expression, here appear. In fact, the diction throughout the sketch is peculiarly Hawthorne's and seems to me to be one of the best evidences that the story is his.

The tale is included among the exercises appended to Chapter One, "On Thought as the Foundation of Good Writing," to illustrate the brief discussion of "descriptive writing." Of the six selections in the group of exercises for the first chapter, this one alone is anonymous. The others are by Sir Matthew Hale, William Ellery Channing, Henry Mackenzie, James Adair, and Greenwood.

Throughout the volume there is evidence that Newman was making an especial effort to produce a rhetoric that had a real and contemporary interest. His quotations are not confined to the classic English writers, but include passages from magazines, from orations, and from American authors then living and writing. To demonstrate literary taste, Newman prints an example by Dr. Jesse Appleton, president of Bowdoin from 1807–1819, another by John T. Kirkland, president of Harvard from 1810–1828, and a third by Levi Frisbie on the occasion of his inaugural as Alford Professor at Harvard in 1817. It is of interest to note that Frisbie's father had taken Newman's father into his home and fitted him for Phillips-Exeter Academy. A number of anonymous examples appear, and that some of these might be the work of Newman's students is not inconceivable.

In 1820 Newman became Professor of Ancient Languages at Bowdoin College and in 1824 he was transferred to the new chair of Rhetoric and Oratory, which he filled until 1839. During Hawthorne's senior year (1824–1825) there was no class instruction in rhetoric, but listed among the "Exercises during the year" are "Private declamations of each class, and public Declamations of the three upper classes. Compositions in English of the two upper classes." Listed among the "Lectures" are: "On Rhetoric and Oratory delivered to the Senior class once each fortnight during the year." Hawthorne then would have listened to Newman's lectures during his senior year.

Of Hawthorne's college days George Parsons Lathrop relates:

> In writing English, too, he won a reputation, and Professor Newman was often so struck with the beauty of his work in this kind that he would read portions in the evening to his own

family. Professor Packard says: "His themes were written in the sustained, finished style that gives to his mature productions an inimitable charm. The recollection is very distinct of Hawthorne's reluctant step and averted look, when he presented himself at the professor's study and submitted a composition which no man in his class could equal."

Newman, whom Dr. Daniel Goodwin in an address to the alumni in 1873 described as "gentle," "the faithful friend, the classical scholar, the skillful and patient teacher, the accomplished Christian gentleman; beautiful, delicate," would be a man not incompatible with one side of Hawthorne's nature. Commenting upon "The First and Last Dinner" in his *Rhetoric*, Newman writes in his 1829 edition:

> In examining the passage of descriptive writing, (Ex. 6), let the student enquire 1. What is the object or scene described? 2. Are the circumstances well selected? 3. Is the scene so represented as to be brought fully and distinctly before the mind?

But in his edition of ten years later the schoolmaster becomes the literary critic in a paragraph of appreciation:

> This example of descriptive writing is justly admired. The only point to which it is designed to direct the attention of the student, is the selection of circumstances. Let any one after reading the extracts, especially the second and third paragraphs, notice with what distinctness and fulness the scene described is brought before his view—how, as it were, he is placed in the midst of the little group, and sees them and hears them and is made acquainted with their peculiarities. This, which in another part of this work is called truth to nature, is evidently effected by the skilful selection and arrangement of circumstances, and constitutes the amplification of descriptive writing. In some instances, especially where it is desirable that the description should be bold and striking, the enumeration of circumstances is less full and minute. But on this point, good sense and good taste must decide.

True, the story, praised by Newman, is, on the surface, an obvious treatment of an obvious theme; but a close comparison of it with "Dr. Heidegger's Experiment" has shown me the plausibility of its being Hawthorne's own. Similarities in the plots of the two narratives are worth noting. Friends drink together, with a host, a solitary type, officiating. Three periods of life are described, the earlier composition depicting the more easily conceived idea of decline to old age, but the pseudo-scientific tale presenting the scenes in ascending order toward youth. "Dr. Heidegger's Experiment" is an intensification of the middle period described in the first story, when four friends celebrate the fiftieth anniversary. To build a secondary series from this one period of an initial series is typical of Hawthorne's tenacious mind. He has heightened situations, adding import to them, elaborated characters, made the most of satirical possibilities, written another story; but in the original are his own fictional motifs, his own diction, and something of his methods. "The First and Last Dinner" could very well be one of those very compositions which Hawthorne brought shyly to his professor's door for criticism.

Source: Louise Hastings, "An Origin for 'Dr. Heidegger's Experiment,'" in *American Literature*, Vol. 9, No. 4, January 1938, pp. 403–10.

Bliss Perry

In the following essay, Perry discusses Hawthorne's criticism of his own works.

Hawthorne made three collections of his short stories and sketches: *Twice-Told Tales*, in *Mosses from an Old Manse*, and *The Snow Image and Other Tales*. The prefaces to these volumes express, with characteristic charm, the author's dissatisfaction with his handiwork. No critic has pointed out so clearly as Hawthorne himself the ineffectiveness of some of the *Twice-Told Tales*; he thinks that the *Mosses from an Old Manse* afford no solid basis for a literary reputation; and his comment upon the earlier and later work gathered indiscriminately into his final volume is that "the ripened autumnal fruit tastes but little better than the early windfalls."

It must be remembered that the collections were made in desultory fashion. They included some work that Hawthorne had outgrown even when the first volume was published, such as elaborate exercises in description and fanciful allegories, excellently composed but without substance. Yet side by side with these proofs of his long, weary apprenticeship are stories that reveal the consummate artist, mature in mind and heart, and with the sure hand of the master. The qualities of imagination and style that place Hawthorne easily first among American writers of fiction are as readily discernible in his best brief tales as in his romances.

"Dr. Heidegger's Experiment," with which the present volume opens, is Hawthorne's earliest treatment of the elixir of immortality theme, which haunted him throughout his life and was the subject of the unfinished romance which rested upon his coffin. He handles it daintily, poetically here, with an irony at once exquisite and profound. "The Birthmark" represents another favorite theme: the rivalry between scientific passion and human affection. It is not wholly free from the morbid fancy which Hawthorne occasionally betrays, and which allies him, on one side of his many-gifted mind, with Edgar Allan Poe; but the essential sanity of Hawthorne's moral, and the perfection of the workmanship, render "The Birthmark" worthy of its high place among modern short stories. "Ethan Brand" dates obviously from the sojourn at North Adams, Massachusetts, described in the *American Note-Book*. Fragmentary as it is, it is one of Hawthorne's most powerful pieces of writing, the Unpardonable Sin which it portrays—the development of the intellect at the expense of the heart—being one which the lonely romancer himself had had cause to dread. The motive of the humorous character sketch entitled "Wakefield" is somewhat similar: the danger of stepping aside, even for a moment, from one's allotted place. "Drowne's Wooden Image" is a charming old Boston version of the artistic miracles made possible by love. In "The Ambitious Guest," the familiar story of the Willey House, in the Notch of the White Hills, is told with singular delicacy and imaginativeness, while "The Great Stone Face," a parable after Hawthorne's own heart, is suggested by a well-known phenomenon of the same mountainous region. Hawthorne's numerous tales based upon New England history are represented by one of the briefest, "The Gray Champion," whose succinct opening and eloquent close are no less admirable than the stern passion of its dramatic climax.

Not every note of which Hawthorne's deep-toned instrument was capable is exhibited in these eight tales, but they will serve, perhaps, to show the nature of his magic. Certain characteristics of his art are everywhere in evidence: simplicity of theme and treatment, absolute clearness, verbal melody, with now and again a dusky splendor of coloring. The touch of a few other men may be as perfect, the notes they evoke more brilliant, certainly more gay, but Hawthorne's graver harmonies linger in the ear and abide in the memory. It is only after intimate acquaintance, however, that one perceives fully Hawthorne's real scope, his power to convey an idea in its totality. His art is the product of a rich personality, strong, self-contained, content to brood long over its treasures. It is seldom in the history of literature—and quite without parallel in American letters—that a nature so perfectly dowered should attain to such perfect self-expression. Here lies his supreme fortune as an artist. He was permitted to give adequate expression to a rare and beautiful genius, and for thousands of his countrymen life has been touched to finer issues because Hawthorne followed his boyish bent and became a writer of fiction.

Source: Bliss Perry, "Introduction to *Little Masterpieces*," in *Little Masterpieces*, edited by Bliss Perry, Doubleday, Page, 1906, pp. vii–x.

SOURCES

"Chronology of Hawthorne's Life," in *The Cambridge Companion to Nathaniel Hawthorne*, edited by Richard H. Millington, Cambridge University Press, 2004, pp. xiv–xviii.

Hart, James D., "Gothic Romance," in *The Oxford Companion to American Literature*, Oxford University Press, 1995.

Longfellow, Henry Wadsworth, Review of *Twice-Told Tales*, in *North American Review*, July 1837, pp. 59–93, reprint, *Nathaniel Hawthorne: The Contemporary Reviews*, edited by John L. Idol and Buford Jones, Cambridge University Press, 1994, p. 23–26.

MacAndrew, Elizabeth, *The Gothic Tradition in Fiction*, Columbia University Press, 1979, pp. 1–52.

Poe, Edgar Allan, Review of *Twice-Told Tales*, in *Graham's*, April 1842, p. 254, reprint, *Nathaniel Hawthorne: The Contemporary Reviews*, edited by John L. Idol, Jr., and Buford Jones, Cambridge University Press, 1994, p. 60.

Review of *Twice-Told Tales*, in *Daily Advertiser*, March 10, 1837, p. 2, reprint, *Nathaniel Hawthorne: The Contemporary Reviews*, edited by John L. Idol and Buford Jones, Cambridge University Press, 1994, p. 19.

———, Review of *Twice-Told Tales*, in *Graham's*, May 1842, pp. 298–300, reprint, *Nathaniel Hawthorne: The Contemporary Reviews*, edited by John L. Idol and Buford Jones, Cambridge University Press, 1994, pp. 63–68.

Thompson, G. R., "Introduction: Romanticism and the Gothic Tradition," in *Romanticism and the Gothic Tradition*, Washington State University Press, 1974, pp. 1–10.

Trimmer, Joseph F., C. Wade Jennings, and Annette Patterson, *eFictions*, Thompson Heinle, 2002, p. 443.

FURTHER READING

Easton, Allison, "Hawthorne and the Question of Women," in *The Cambridge Companion to Nathaniel Hawthorne*, Cambridge University Press, 2004, pp. 79–98.

"Dr. Heidegger's Experiment" is not examined in Easton's essay, but Hawthorne's treatment of women is relevant to a story that ends with three men pulling at a woman for her attention.

Feidelson, Charles, Jr., "Hawthorne as Symbolist," in *Hawthorne: A Collection of Critical Essays*, edited by A. N. Kaul, Prentice-Hall, 1966, pp. 64–71.

Feidelson considers Hawthorne's style weakened by its distance from reality but still powerfully effective.

Fogle, Richard Harter, "The Light and the Dark," in *Nathaniel Hawthorne: The Light and the Dark*, University of Oklahoma Press, 1952, pp. 3–14.

One of the most respected literary critics of his day looks at the moral dichotomies of Hawthorne's works, highlighting his complexity of style.

Male, Roy R., *Hawthorne's Tragic Vision*, W. W. Norton, 1957.

This book does not discuss many of the short stories in detail, but it gives a good overview of Hawthorne's frame of mind and in particular the gender divisions that controlled his way of looking at the world.

Martin, Terence, *Nathaniel Hawthorne*, Twayne Publishers, 1983.

This biography offers a good general overview of Hawthorne's life and career.

The Heavenly Christmas Tree

FYODOR DOSTOEVSKY

1876

Russian author Fyodor Dostoevsky embarked on an unusual experiment in form in the 1870s when he began writing and publishing *Dnevnik Pisatelia* (*Diary of a Writer*). What originally began as a column in the journal *Grazhdanin* (*The Citizen*) was transformed into an ongoing, self-published periodical in which Dostoevsky chronicled his thoughts, stories, and literary criticism. Eventually the works were collected and published in two volumes covering 1873 through 1881. In 1876 a short story appeared in the January issue of *Dnevnik Pisatelia.* In this story, whose title has been translated either as "The Heavenly Christmas Tree" or "The Boy at Christ's Christmas Party," a young, homeless boy freezes to death on Christmas Eve. He awakens to find himself welcomed to a celebration around Christ's Christmas tree, as he is informed by the other children, who have hugged and kissed him. As they lead him to the tree, the child finds his own mother, who died before him. The story is considered one of Dostoevsky's minor works—if it is discussed at all—in critical analyses of his writings. While Christianity is prominently featured in this story, Dostoevsky's focus on urban poverty and suffering is equally present.

Dostoevsky's short story "The Heavenly Christmas Tree" was originally translated by Boris Brasol as part of *Dnevnik Pisatelia*, which appeared in two volumes in 1949 under the title *The Diary of a Writer.* A more recent translation is Kenneth

Fyodor Dostoevsky *(The Library of Congress)*

Lanz's 1994 effort *The Diary of a Writer, Volume 1: 1873–1876*. The work is also included in a small paperback collection of Dostoevsky's short stories, *Short Stories*, published by Wildside Press in 2008.

AUTHOR BIOGRAPHY

Dostoevsky was born in Moscow, Russia, on October 30, 1821 (according to the Julian calendar) or November 11, 1821 (according to the Gregorian calendar). Both the Julian and Gregorian calendars were used in nineteenth-century Europe; they differed in the way leap years were calculated. (The Gregorian calendar is now the internationally accepted, nonreligious calendar.) The second of seven children, Dostoevsky was the son of Maria Fedorovna and Mikhail Andreevich Dostoevsky, a doctor who practiced in Moscow until 1828. During his youth, Dostoevsky attended a boarding school in Moscow. In 1828, after being granted the rank of nobleman, his father purchased a village estate in Darovoe. Following the death of Dostoevsky's mother in 1837, his father enrolled the teenager in the Military Engineering School in St. Petersburg. Two years later, his father died. After completing his education at the military academy and graduating as an officer and serving one year in the army, Dostoevsky worked for a time as a draftsman. In 1844 he quit his job in order to pursue a writing career. His first novel, published in 1846 as *Bednye lyudi* (translated into English and published in 1887 under the title *Poor Folk*). Following the critical success of *Bednye lyudi*, Dostoevsky went on to publish a number of short stories with psychological and political themes. During the next several years, Dostoevsky became involved with a group concerned with socialism, freedom of the press, and related issues concerning creative and political expression. In 1849 he was arrested for his political activities and spent eight months in prison, after which he was exiled and spent four years in a Siberian labor camp. Released in 1854, he was required to devote several years to army service in the village of Semipalatinsk. Dostoevsky continued to write during this time. In 1857 he married Maria Dmitrievna Isaeva, a widow. Dostoevsky was an epileptic, and in the years following his release from prison his epileptic attacks increased. On these medical grounds, Dostoevsky petitioned the government for an early release from his army service. He was eventually granted permission to retire from the army, and in 1859, he returned to St. Petersburg. His works were increasingly marked by themes of isolation and alienation—even paranoia. In 1864, Dostoevsky's wife and brother died. Two years later, in 1866, he published one of his best-known works, *Prestuplenie i nakazanie* (translated into English and published in 1886 under the title *Crime and Punishment*). Having taken on his brother's debts, as well as the responsibility of providing for his wife's son from her first marriage, Dostoevsky struggled financially. In 1867, he married a stenographer, Anna Grigorevna Snitkina. In the early 1870s, Dostoevsky worked for the periodical *Grazhdanin* (*The Citizen*), where he was assigned a regular column called "Dnevnik Pisatelia" ("Diary of a Writer"), in which he chronicled his own life and recorded his thoughts. Short stories, personal observations, formal criticism, biographical sketches, and the like were included. In 1874, Dostoevsky resigned from his editorial position with *Grazhdanin*, citing ill health as the reason. He subsequently began self-publishing *Dnevnik Pisatelia* as an independent journal. The works were eventually collected and published under the title *Dnevnik Pisatelia* in two volumes, which covered the years 1873 through 1881. It was in the January 1876 issue of *Dnevnik*

Pisatelia that the short story "The Heavenly Christmas Tree" first appeared. Dostoevsky's final novel *Brat'ia Karamzovy* appeared in serial form in the journal *Russkii vestnik* (*The Russian Herald*) in 1879 and 1880. The work was translated into English and published as *The Brothers Karamazov* in 1912. In the winter of 1881, Dostoevsky died of complications from emphysema and epilepsy.

PLOT SUMMARY

Dostoevsky's short story "The Heavenly Christmas Tree" opens with the narrator observing that as a writer, specifically a novelist, he has created this story, although he has the sense that it surely must have actually happened at one time somewhere. As the narrator explains, a little boy aged six years or younger wakes up one morning in a frigid cellar. He is wearing a thin dressing gown and is hungry. The boy's mother, who is thin and ill, lies nearby. The boy and his mother have recently come from another town and taken up residence here. Also in the cellar—a room rented out by a landlady who has recently been arrested—is a drunken man. In another corner is an elderly woman who, stricken with rheumatism, grumbles at the little boy to the point where he fears approaching her. The fact that it is nearly Christmas is inferred from the narrator's comments about the drunken man, who could not wait until Christmas to imbibe in alcohol to the point of extreme intoxication.

The little boy helps himself to a drink of water in another room, but he can find nothing to eat. Feeling frightened, he repeatedly considers waking his mother but decides against doing so. By dusk, no candle or lamp has been lit. The boy touches his mother's face and discovers that she is cold and lifeless. Although the boy does not comment on it, the narrator informs the reader that the woman has died; it seems her son has not yet apprehended this fact. The boy fetches his cap and leaves the cellar. He has been prevented from doing so earlier due to the constant howling of a large dog at the top of the stairs, which the boy obviously fears. Now, with no sign of the dog, the boy departs.

While walking down the street, the boy marvels at how different this new town is from the one he has recently left. In his old town, there is only one street lamp on the whole street, leaving the town quite dark. The townsfolk do not venture out at night and remain within their homes. Dogs howl all night long. There, however, he has always been warm and been given food to eat. In the new town people are out at night, the streets are lit, and the noises of horses and carriages abound. The boy is also acutely aware of the cold—and his hunger. Nevertheless he plods on. A policeman turns his head away to avoid seeing the child. Finding his way to another street—a noisy, brightly lit one where he feels certain he will be run over—the boy peers through a window, where he sees an enormous fir tree. The tree, which reaches to the ceiling, is decorated with lights, gold-colored paper ornaments, fruit, and small toys. The boy sees freshly scrubbed children, attired in their best clothing, running, laughing, and playing with one another. The little boy longingly watches the other children eat, drink, and dance. He can hear the music through the window, and he laughs a little before remembering how badly his fingers and toes ache due to the cold. He begins to cry and runs off.

At a different window he sees another Christmas tree and a table laden with all types of cakes. The boy watches as people come in from the street. The ladies sitting at the table distribute cake to everyone who comes in. The boy scrambles in from the street but is shooed away without being given any cake. One woman does give the boy a coin before ushering him back into the street. The little boy becomes frightened. His fingers are too stiff to hold the coin, which rolls away. Trying not to cry, he continues on his way, lonely and scared. The boy runs toward a crowd of people who are admiring something behind a window. He sees three little dolls, which he initially mistakes for real people. Realizing that they are only dolls, he laughs while at the same time feeling like crying as well. Someone in the crowd grabs at his smock, hits him on the head, and steals his cap after intentionally tripping him.

Terrified, the child escapes through a gate into a courtyard. Hiding behind a woodpile, the boy finds that his fear has suddenly and inexplicably been transformed into a feeling of happiness. His hands and feet grow warm. Waking with a shiver, the boy thinks that he must have fallen asleep without realizing it. Intending to retrace his steps to look at the dolls again, the boy suddenly hears his mother's singing. He tells her how nice it is to be sleeping here. The child hears a voice beckoning him to come to the Christmas tree, which he suddenly realizes is not his mother's voice. A figure bends down and holds him, but it is too dark for him to see who it is. The boy stretches out his arms toward the figure and is overcome with the brightness of a light. He then spies a Christmas tree unlike any that he has ever seen before. The child begins to wonder where he is. As he approaches the Christmas tree, he notices all the other children, whom he first mistakes for dolls. The children kiss him and he is swept up in their midst, at which point the boy does see his mother, who is smiling and laughing at him.

When the boy asks the children who they are, they reply that the tree is Christ's Christmas tree, that Christ has provided a tree for all the children who do not have one of their own. The boy discovers that all the children are like him; they have died, some as infants that froze in the baskets in which they had been abandoned. Others have been suffocated, starved, or died in various other ways. Suddenly noticing that Christ himself stands in the middle of all the children, the boy, the other children, and the "sinful mothers" all receive Christ's blessing.

In the morning a porter discovers the frozen body of the little boy on the woodpile. The mother, too, is found dead. The narrator ends the story by asserting that what happened in the cellar and by the woodpile could have happened, that he believes these events must have occurred. He also admits that he cannot say with certainty whether the appearance of Christ's Christmas tree actually took place.

CHARACTERS

The Boy

The unnamed boy is the main character of "The Heavenly Christmas Tree." The narrator describes the child as a boy of six, or perhaps even younger. It is wintertime and he is lodging in a cellar with his ailing mother. Scared, cold, and hungry, the child leaves the cellar in search of food. He wanders through the streets, in awe of the bright lights, the Christmas trees, the attractions in the shop windows. He is ejected from a shop where women are passing out cake. The boy is fascinated with the lifelike dolls he sees in another window. After being tormented by an older boy, he runs off and hides behind a woodpile in a courtyard, where he curls up and falls asleep. During the night, the child freezes to death. His lifeless body is discovered the next morning. The child's experience, however, is totally different. After falling asleep on the woodpile, he awakens to his mother's singing and has a vision of a beautifully decorated Christmas tree. Other children welcome him to what they call Christ's Christmas tree. The boy is happy and laughs along with the other children. The narrator explains toward the end of the story that his body is discovered together with that of his mother, but that mother and son "met before the Lord God in heaven." The child, whose very young age and utter poverty inspire immediate sympathy in the reader, is depicted as both innocent and brave. He falsely assumes that his mother, whose body is cold, is asleep and sets out to find something to eat. Awed and intimidated by the sights and sounds of the city, the boy is still able to laugh when he discovers the lifelike dolls in the window. After being chased by the older boy, the young boy experiences an inexplicable feeling of happiness while huddled against the woodpile, and it is in this state that he falls asleep. The joy he experiences in being reunited with his mother—in heaven, as the reader eventually discovers—does not last very long. The reality of the deaths of the boy and his mother is reiterated when the narrator describes the discovery of their bodies and again when the narrator asserts that while he believes their deaths likely resulted from a combination of the freezing weather and starvation, the salvation the story implies remains questionable. By presenting such a sad ending, Dostoevsky fashions his portrayal of poverty into a tale that is as moving as it is bleak.

The Boy's Mother

The narrator offers little information about the boy's mother. She has become ill after traveling from another town. The boy does not seem to realize that his mother has died when he approaches her lifeless body in bed in the cellar, touching her face and shoulders. She appears again at the end of the story, singing to the boy as he wakes, that is, after he finds himself in the same place where Christ's Christmas tree is located. She laughs as she watches him.

Children

The children welcome the boy to gather around Christ's Christmas tree. In their presence, the boy discovers that they are all like him, that is, they have all died, often under horrible circumstances. In the discussion of the ways in which these children died, Dostoevsky makes a number of cultural and historical references. Some of the children froze to death as infants that had been abandoned on the doorsteps of wealthy families in St. Petersburg. Others were suffocated after being "boarded out with Finnish women by the Foundling." The Foundling is likely a reference to the Foundling Hospital, an organization established in both St. Petersburg and Moscow, that rescued abandoned or orphaned children. The mention of Finnish women may be a cultural prejudice against individuals of non-Russian ethnic backgrounds. (At the time Dostoevsky wrote "The Heavenly Christmas Tree," Finland was not a sovereign nation but rather a grand duchy—essentially a territory—of the Russian Empire). Others died when their mothers starved to death. Here the narrator mentions the famine of Samara, a large city in Russia that experienced widespread famine in the early 1890s. The narrator also refers to the "foul air" of "third-class railway carriages," citing this as another cause for the deaths of many of the children. The happy children comfort their weeping mothers, begging the women not to cry.

Christ

After the boy has fallen asleep at the woodpile, he is initially awakened by his mother's singing and next hears another voice. At first he thinks it is his mother, but he immediately dismisses this notion. The gentle voice beckons the child to "come to my Christmas tree." The child feels someone embrace him in the darkness and stretch his hands out to him. He soon learns from the other children that the Christmas tree belongs to Christ. The "my" must therefore refer to Christ. After being led to Christ's tree, the boy begins to understand that he is in heaven. Christ is mentioned again as standing in the midst of the children and their mothers and blessing them. Christ and his tree convey to the child a sense of wonder and happiness as the child marvels at how "bright and shining" everything is. The joy depicted in this scene is undercut by the narrator's questioning of whether or not this portion of the story could have actually occurred.

Drunk Man

The narrator informs the reader that one of the boy's fellow lodgers in the cellar is a man who has been drunk for the past twenty-four hours.

Narrator

The narrator describes himself as a novelist. Given the fact that "The Heavenly Christmas Tree" originally appeared in *The Diary of a Writer*, he may be taken to be a substitute for Dostoevsky. The narrator acknowledges that although he is a writer of fiction and knows that he has penned this story, he nevertheless imagines that it must actually have occurred somewhere on Christmas Eve. He describes the events of the story from the little boy's point of view, doing so in such a way that his sympathies for the child are self-evident. At the end of the story, the narrator admits that the tale is "out of keeping" with a writer's diary. Yet he asserts—as he did in the story's opening—that he feels drawn to the notion that the events of the story could really have occurred. The narrator qualifies this sentiment by explaining that the mother's death in the cellar, as well as the child's death at the woodpile, could actually have happened, "but as for Christ's Christmas tree, I cannot tell you whether that could have happened or not." In this statement, the narrator calls into the question the religious salvation expressed in the story, the only instance of hope or happiness in the tale. Without it, the story remains unrelentingly bleak. By expressing doubt that this part of the story could have happened, the narrator suggests that perhaps life is as bleak as the story makes it appear.

Old Woman

The old woman is another lodger in the cellar where the boy and his mother are staying. The narrator describes the woman as being about eighty years old, a former children's nurse. Alone in the world, she is now suffering a painful death from rheumatism. The boy fears approaching her, having been previously scolded by her.

THEMES

Poverty

Throughout "The Heavenly Christmas Tree," Dostoevsky portrays the poverty of the residents in his urban Russian setting. Not only does he delineate the effects of poverty on his characters but he also comments on society's response to the poor. As the story opens, the narrator highlights the extreme conditions under which the boy and his mother exist. They are currently living in a cold, damp cellar and do not have the proper clothes or possessions to protect themselves against the elements. They have no blankets, and the boy wears a dressing gown. He is able to find water to drink but has nothing to eat. It is his hunger that motivates him. He leaves the cellar in search of food. His intense hunger is mentioned repeatedly as he explores the streets of the city. The narrator describes the way a policeman looks away so that he does not have to stare at the starving child. While peering into a shop window, he sees three young women distributing cakes to anyone who walks in from the street.

TOPICS FOR FURTHER STUDY

- Dostoevsky's *Diary of a Writer* includes a nonfiction sketch that appears just prior to "The Heavenly Christmas Tree." "The Boy with His Hand Out" is about children who are beggars. Read the nonfiction piece and then compare it with the short story. How do the works differ in tone? Do the themes of the fictional short story correspond to the general meaning of the nonfiction sketch? What do these similarities and/or differences imply about Dostoevsky's attitude toward children and poverty? Write an essay in which you compare these works. Share your essay with the class in a format accessible via the Internet (e.g., a Web page or blog).
- The poverty of the little boy and his mother in "The Heavenly Christmas Tree" is one of the main themes of the story. Using print and online sources, research the issue of poverty in Russia during the late nineteenth century. Was poverty a greater problem in urban areas or in provincial towns and villages? What political factors contributed to the levels of poverty during this time period? Were measures taken to combat poverty either by private individuals or by government groups or agencies? Compile a written report or a PowerPoint presentation on this topic. Be sure to cite all your sources.
- Aspects of the Christian religion are explored in Dostoevsky's story "The Heavenly Christmas Tree." In nineteenth-century Russia, the state religion was Russian Orthodox Catholicism. Dostoevsky was raised in a strict Russian Orthodox home. Did the czarist government allow religions other than Russian Orthodoxy to be practiced? Were there negative legal consequences for practicing other religions openly and, if so, were they practiced anyway? Research the subject of religion in nineteenth-century Russia and prepare a well-documented paper on this topic.
- In Dostoevsky's story "The Heavenly Christmas Tree," the author describes the final moments of the impoverished, homeless child's life. In Christopher Paul Curtis's award-winning young-adult novel *Bud, Not Buddy* (published by Delacorte Press in 1999), the main character is a young African American boy who is also poor and homeless. Although Curtis's novel takes place during the Depression in the 1930s, his character and Dostoevsky's share a sense of loneliness and poverty. Read Curtis's novel and compare it with Dostoevsky's short story. What else do these characters have in common? How do the authors treat the theme of poverty? Are the authors' respective tones pessimistic or hopeful? Discuss these and other questions in a book group. Be sure to also consider the differing formats (short story or novel). Does Dostoevsky's brief, stark portrait offer a more realistic view of poverty than Curtis's lengthier novelistic exploration? Prepare a group presentation in which you convey to your classmates what you consider to be the most significant differences and similarities between the two works.
- Dostoevsky's work is known for its realism. He explores human experience, both within society and within one's own mind. Consider the social and/or psychological experiences young adults face today, the personal pressures they feel, and their attempts to deal with their sense of isolation or to ascertain their own role within society. Write a short story in which you use realism (a literary term used to describe an author's presentation of the details of man's existence in a way that is true to life) to explore the subtleties of one character's attempt to deal with a social or psychological issue. Share your work by posting the story in an electronically accessible format, reading it aloud, or making an audio recording and posting it online.

Decorated Christmas tree *(Image copyright Denisenko, 2009. Used under license from Shutterstock.com)*

Yet when he attempts to enter the store he is waved off by all except one woman, who hands him a coin. Unfortunately, his fingers are so stiff from the cold that he cannot hold the coin and loses it. Ignored by the policeman and the women in the shop, the boy is next mistreated by another child. After the boy has died, the narrator describes the boy's experiences around Christ's Christmas tree and recounts the experiences of other children who have died due to poverty. Some froze to death "on the doorsteps of well-to-do Petersburg people." Abandoned and orphaned children were suffocated after being placed in the care of Finnish women. Some starved during the famine. Still others died in "third-class railway carriages." The poor, according to Dostoevsky, are ignored and abused by those who are better off, or they are killed by others or die as a result of circumstances related to their poverty. Aside from the lone woman who attempts to give the boy a coin, there are no kindhearted people in this story. In the end, their poverty kills them.

Christianity

The world in which Dostoevsky's story "The Heavenly Christmas Tree" takes place is a Christian one. All around the boy are celebrations of Christmas, the birthday of Jesus Christ, one of the holiest of Christian holidays. Christmas trees, decorations, and feasts surround the boy. Aside from the single coin offered to him by one woman, the little boy receives no charitable treatment while he is alive despite the so-called Christian environment in which he finds himself. Dostoevsky contrasts the world of people who are sufficiently well off to be able to afford celebrations with that of the boy and his mother, who are too poor to purchase a crust of bread. Furthermore, this distinction is made more obvious given the fact that it is during the Christmas season that the boy is forced to suffer extreme hunger and cold. Even at this time, when one would expect charitable feelings among faithful Christians, the boy is ignored (by the policeman) and denied food (which is free and available to everyone else). The starving boy wanders the streets in a thin dressing gown. People do not interrupt their Christmas celebrations to aid him in any way. It is only after the boy dies that he is able to celebrate Christmas with Christ himself, including all the other children who have suffered and died horrible deaths. In the end, it is grim reality that the narrator assumes to be true—represented by the freezing cellar in which the mother dies and the woodpile where the boy perishes—rather than the hopeful story of peace, according to which the boy and his mother are reunited in heaven. Throughout the story Dostoevsky appears to question the nature of those who call themselves Christians, who would ignore and abuse a young child who is starving and freezing to death. Given the fact that at the end of the story the narrator suggests that the new life in heaven with which the child and his mother are rewarded is perhaps an unlikely conclusion, it seems as though Dostoevsky is doubting the Christian belief in salvation itself.

STYLE

Realism

Dostoevsky is known for the realism he employs to describe his characters. Realism is a literary term used to describe an author's presentation of the details of man's existence in a way that is true to life. Sometimes it is used in conjunction with the term psychological. Psychological realism, a technique Dostoevsky employs in his major novels, refers to the author's attempt to portray the innermost thoughts and feelings of his characters in an accurate manner. Realism also implies a rejection of idealism, the portrayal of life as the author believes it ought to be rather than as it is. In "The Heavenly Christmas Tree," Dostoevsky presents the details of the lives, thoughts, and struggles of the boy in the story. The author describes the physical effects of the boy's poverty. The details clearly convey the child's suffering; he is freezing and starving to death. His fingers and toes ache with cold, to the point where he cannot even hold on to the coin he is handed. His hunger forces him to leave the cellar and wander through the city streets. During his wanderings, the boy is temporarily able to forget his hunger and to be distracted by the lights and sights of a city celebrating Christmas. That the boy can be entertained, however briefly, by the lifelike dolls, to take just one example, reminds us of the child's tender age. Yet his hunger drives him forward. Dostoevsky vividly conveys the enormity of the child's fear. This begins in the cellar with descriptions of the drunken man and the old woman, whose grumblings and scolding frighten the boy. The child also remains motionless, his hands resting on his dead mother's shoulders. Dostoevsky does not make plain whether or not the child knows his mother has died. This imagery heightens the reader's sense of the child's isolation and subsequent fear. Additional details underscore the terror the boy experiences: the dog at the top of the stairs; the bustle of the city, including the horses and carriages, which the boy is certain will run him over; the older boy who hits the child and trips him—all inspire understandable fear in a child too young to be alone in the world. Through his characterization and imagery, Dostoevsky creates a realistic portrait of an impoverished, homeless boy. That the hopelessness of the boy's plight is depicted in a manner so stark suggests that Dostoevsky intended to present the reader with an unvarnished portrait of the problems inherent in nineteenth-century urban Russian society.

Omniscient Narrator

The narrator Dostoevsky employs in "The Heavenly Christmas Tree" opens and closes the story with his own first-person commentary (he refers to himself as "I") and tells the tale of the boy in the third person (he refers to the boy as "he," and the boy's mother as "she"). The first-person narrator draws attention to himself by expressing his own views in the opening and closing of the story. During the story, however, the narrator makes observations that suggest he is aware of circumstances that his characters are unaware of. A narrator who shares this type of knowledge with the reader is described as an omniscient or all-knowing narrator. For example, the narrator shares such information when the boy "unconsciously" lets "his hands rest on the dead woman's shoulders," the latter being his mother. Although the narrator confirms that she is dead, the boy does not seem to realize it. The narrator also asks rhetorical questions during the story. (A rhetorical question is one in which the questioner does not expect a response; it is used to create a certain effect.) As the child discovers new sights in the city, the narrator asks "And what was this?" and "What was this again?" The effect of asking these questions and framing the story with his own first-person comments is to create a situation in which the reader feels as if he or she is being read to, or is being told a story orally. In this way, the reader is permitted to identify with the child in the story, given that the reader is experiencing the story in a manner similar to that of a child. However, the tale is not one for children, as the narrator makes clear in his closing comments when he asserts that whereas the deaths of the mother and her son "may have happened really," the rest—the heavenly resurrection following their deaths— may or may not be possible.

COMPARE & CONTRAST

- **1870s:** Much of the literature written at this time is considered realist fiction. Authors such as Fyodor Dostoevsky, Ivan Turgenev, and Nikolai Leskov write novels and stories in which the details of the characters' psychological dilemmas and the social conflicts of this time frame are explored and portrayed objectively. The idealism typical of the earlier romantic period is rejected by these writers.

  Today: Following the era of Soviet realism, during which literature is strictly censored and works are written to glorify the Soviet state, the new Russian realism harkens back to the prerevolutionary days of Tolstoy and Dostoevsky. The new Russian realism, represented by authors such as Roman Senchin, Arkady Babchenko, and Anna Starobinet, adopts a variety of approaches in exploring some of the same issues that earlier realist writers examined, including social issues, the individual's place in society, and the psychological states of characters. They are also more likely than their realist and Soviet realist counterparts to offer critical studies of Russia's past.

- **1870s:** The relationship between science and religion is one in which there is less antagonism than exists in the West. Philosophers like Vladimir Solovyov—a friend of Dostoevsky's who may have influenced the latter's views on Christianity—attempt to further integrate faith and reason in the belief that reason and faith are integral parts of a unified, organic human nature.

  Today: Revived interest in the relationship between faith and reason—specifically between religion and philosophy—begin to grow following a period of Soviet-mandated atheism. According to Russian philosopher and professor Vladimir Katasonov, writing for the online *Science and Spirit* magazine, new debates on these topics also seek to incorporate the views of both Western and Eastern philosophers, religious thinkers, and scientists.

- **1870s:** The Russian Empire is ruled by Czar Alexander II, who is—at least initially—more moderate than his predecessor and father, Nicholas I. However, from the 1870s to the end of his reign in 1881, Alexander grows intolerant of the radical political groups that gain in popularity during his moderate years. He begins to adopt his father's practices of censorship and violent repression of dissenting voices.

  Today: Russia is now an independent federation and is no longer a part of the Soviet Union, which was dissolved in 1991. It is headed by President Dimitry Medvedev and Prime Minister Vladimir Putin. Although the extreme censorship of the czarist regime no longer exists, suspicions of government censorship of the media are still common—especially in connection with Putin. During his presidency, which directly preceded Medvedev's, Putin is accused of limiting freedom of the press, the accusation being based on a 2006 *BBC News* report on a meeting in Moscow of the World Association of Newspapers.

HISTORICAL CONTEXT

Nineteenth-Century European Literary Movements

Russian realism as a literary movement flourished during the latter half of the nineteenth century, which coincided with Dostoevsky's literary career. His works and those of other prominent Russian fiction writers—including Leo Tolstoy and Ivan Turgenev—exemplified the characteristics of the realist movement. Russian realist fiction represented a reaction against the romanticism that had dominated Russian literature in the early part of the nineteenth century. Notable romantic writers included Alexander Pushkin, Mikhail Lermontov, and Nikolai Gogol. Romanticism was characterized by idealism, the drawing of inspiration from nature, and the focus on the senses and emotion over verifiable events and rational thought. It focused on the individual and ideas rather than on society and the sciences, which were the subject of the classicism of the Enlightenment period in art and literature of the late eighteenth century. Russian romanticism was also concerned with a reawakening of interest in its national history. It was further influenced by corresponding developments in works of literature by Western European contemporaries. By mid-century, however, romanticism began to yield to the new literary concerns of realism. Realists explored social and psychological realities, focusing on the darker aspects of society and of the mind. While some realists exposed social ills as part of a political agenda, others combined the romantic focus on the individual with the realist's emphasis on society. As Richard Freeborn explains in his essay on Russian realism in *The Cambridge History of Russian Literature*, when viewed within the context of Russia's turbulent history during this same period, Russian realist fiction is "concerned with the realities of individual human experience in a spirit of protest, even outrage. It was literature's duty, in pursuit of reality, to enfranchise the eccentric as well as the highest, the murderer as well as the humblest, the social outcast as well as the positive hero."

An angel carrying gifts (Image copyright ChipPix, 2009. Used under license from Shutterstock.com)

Russia during the Reign of Czar Alexander II

At the time that Dostoevsky wrote "The Heavenly Christmas Tree," the Russian Empire was headed by Czar Alexander II, who ruled from 1855 to 1881. Alexander's reign was characterized by its contrast to the reign of Alexander's father, Czar Nicholas I, who ruled from 1825 to 1855. The latter was known for his fervent belief in the supremacy of the Russian Orthodox Church and his own divine right to rule. His repressive policies led to the imprisonment of anyone—including Dostoevsky—who appeared to question the Russian government. Under Alexander II, by contrast, major reforms were implemented: the emancipation (freeing) of the serfs (peasants forced to work for landholders), the creation of provincial elected administrative assemblies (local governing bodies), and the overhaul of the judicial system. Following an 1863 uprising of Polish patriots against the Russian governing authorities, Alexander began to scale back his reforms and return to the more repressive policies instituted by his father. Censorship of the press and of political activities was reinstated; the government once again reserved the right to decide whether offenses were criminal or political, and could exile suspected radicals to Siberia. Alexander's reversal of his reformist policies was protested by intellectuals and socialists. (Nineteenth-century socialists were members of a political group that was originally formed to uphold the basic rights of all members of society, and that advocated the creation of a classless society. The more radical branch of socialism advocated the eradication, through revolution, of the oppressive Russian government and church. Another branch of socialism that was tied to Christianity supported the twin goals of democracy and brotherhood. At one time, Dostoevsky was affiliated with this type of socialism.) Alexander II's reign ended in 1881 when he was assassinated by a Russian terrorist group.

CRITICAL OVERVIEW

Dostoevsky's story "The Heavenly Christmas Tree" seldom receives direct critical attention due to its brevity, especially when considered alongside Dostoevsky's major works of fiction. His lengthy, philosophically dense novels, such as *Crime and Punishment* and *The Brothers Karamazov*, receive considerably more critical attention than the author's shorter fictional works. However, the collection in which "The Heavenly Christmas Tree" is included, *Diary of a Writer*, began as a column in a journal and subsequently appeared as an independently published journal. This work is often criticized as lacking a central focus, whereas in reality it is simply a collection of disparate, short pieces of writing. Unique in its construction, *Diary of a Writer* contains more than just first-person journal entries by the author, as one would expect of a traditional diary. Rather, it includes short fiction, biographical and autobiographical sketches, and essays of social and literary criticism. Despite being structured as a monthly periodical, it functions as a unit, a glimpse into the thought processes and creative constructs of one particular writer. According to Erik Krag in his 1962 study *Dostoevsky: The Literary Artist*, *Diary of a Writer* "was a great success, and the number of subscriptions increased rapidly, reaching as many as seven thousand the last year." Gary Saul Morson, in his introduction to the 1994 edition of an English translation of Dostoevsky's diary (translated by Kenneth Lantz and published as *A Writer's Diary*), characterizes the monthly periodical format as strange, and states that the work "is so remarkably odd, and so unlike other works, that it is hard to recognize as an integral work." Morson further observes that Dostoevsky often did not adhere to the peculiar structure of the work, further complicating the critic's efforts to analyze this "radically new structure." Unlike Morson, who explores the complications that arise when viewing *Diary of a Writer* as a unified whole, Alba Amoia, in a 1993 study of Dostoevsky's writings titled *Feodor Dostoevsky*, does not analyze Dostoevsky's short fiction as representing installments in a periodical publication. Rather, Amoia groups Dostoevsky's short fiction according to the time period in which he wrote it, noting the shared characteristics of works completed in the fiction the author wrote following his release from a Siberian prison. Amoia observes that the short stories Dostoevsky wrote during this post-Siberian period "naturally display a greater maturity of outlook and a surer mastery of literary technique than did those of his earlier efforts." Noting that "The Heavenly Christmas Tree" has been compared with the short story "The Little Match Girl," by Hans Christian Anderson (a nineteenth-century Danish author), Amoia contends that "Dostoevsky's pity for the poor and downtrodden finds ample scope in this brief account of the last hours of a little homeless boy." The critic says little else about the work, having provided a brief statement regarding the plot, and goes on to describe another, later story from *Diary of a Writer* as "more substantial," suggesting that "The Heavenly Christmas Tree" is considered one of Dostoevsky's minor writings.

CRITICISM

Catherine Dominic

Dominic is a novelist and a freelance writer and editor. In this essay, she studies the ways in which Dostoevsky conveys his philosophical interest in nihilism through the use of such symbols as the lifelike dolls that the boy in "The Heavenly Christmas Tree" glimpses through a window. She maintains that a more complete understanding of the story is possible through an exploration of the conflict between philosophy and spirituality, which is reflected in Dostoevsky's imagery.

The author of short fiction must be extremely economical in the choice of words and images. There is little space for nonessential commentary in a short story. One must therefore assume that in Dostoevsky's short story "The Heavenly Christmas Tree," there are no wasted words or images; everything is significant. Given that Dostoevsky devotes a relatively large portion of his text to a discussion of the lifelike dolls the boy glimpses in a shop window, the significance of this section of the story must be explored to fully appreciate the work as a whole. The particular aspect of the dolls that attracts the little boy is their lifelike nature. He at first thinks they are real children. When the lifelike dolls in the shop window are understood as things that appear to be other than what they actually are (they appear to be real children but are not), they may be viewed as symbolic of Dostoevsky's nihilism.

Nihilism is a complex philosophical concept that has been variously interpreted and employed for myriad political, philosophical, and literary purposes. Briefly stated, nihilism asserts that reality as humans perceive it does not exist—in other

WHAT DO I READ NEXT?

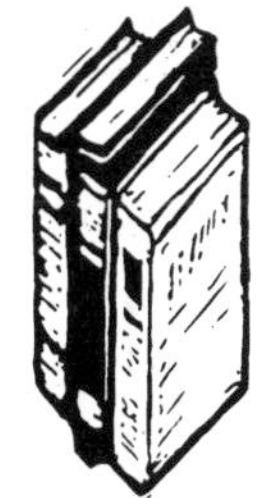

- Many of Dostoevsky's best works of short fiction are collected in *Great Short Works of Fyodor Dostoevsky*, published by Harper Perennial Modern Classics in 2004. The stories in the collection are translated from the Russian by George Bird, Constance Garnett, Nora Gottlieb, and David Magarshak. The collection includes Dostoevsky's highly acclaimed short novel *Notes from Underground.*
- Dostoevsky's novel *The Adolescent* explores a young man's attempts to find his place in the world and to work out his relationship with his father. Originally published in 1875, it is available in a 2004 edition published by Vintage (translated by Richard Pevear and Larissa Volokhonsky).
- Originally published as a periodical throughout the late 1800s, Dostoevsky's *Diary of a Writer* was published in English in 1949 as a collection that consisted of all the installments. The work—which features short stories, observations, literary and social criticism, and biographical and autobiographical sketches—is available in an abridged edition, published in 2009 by Northwestern University Press, titled *A Writer's Diary* (translated by Kenneth Lantz and edited by Gary Saul Morson).
- Dostoevsky's contemporary Leo Tolstoy, who wrote the famous novel *War and Peace*, also wrote numerous short stories. His collection of short stories, *Walk in the Light and Twenty-Three Tales*, was originally published in 1928 by Oxford University Press (translated by Louise and Alymer Maude) and is now available in a 1999 reprint by Orbis Books.
- *Ali and Nino: A Love Story*, by Kurban Said, takes place in the early years of the twentieth century, at the onset of the Russian Revolution (1917), a few decades after Dostoevsky's death. The political turmoil Dostoevsky experienced while under czarist rule was now coming to fruition as revolutionary forces sought to overthrow the czarist government. In Said's story, two Russian teenagers, one a Muslim and the other a Catholic, attempt to forge a relationship during this violent turning point in Russian history. Originally published in 1937 by Random House, the novel is available in a 2000 edition published by Anchor.
- *Anastasia: The Last Grand Duchess, Russia, 1914*, by Carolyn Meyer, takes place just prior to the Russian Revolution. Like Dostoevsky's *Diary of a Writer* this young-adult novel is written in a diary format. It describes the personal struggles of a young aristocratic girl in a world increasingly torn apart by political conflict. The work explores the demise of czarist Russia from Anastasia's perspective, while also offering glimpses into Russian life and culture during this turbulent period.
- *Rasskazy: New Fiction from a New Russia*, edited by Mikhail Lossel and Jeff Parker, includes short fiction by Russian writers who have lived the entirety of their lives in post-Soviet Russia and identify themselves with the New Realist movement. The volume was published by Tin House Books in 2009.
- *Red Azalea*, written by Anchee Min and published by Anchor in 2006, is the memoir of a young Chinese girl who grew up under a repressive Communist regime in China. Like Dostoevsky's character in "The Heavenly Christmas Tree," she suffered from extreme poverty as a child. Moreover, like Dostoevsky she lived in a country governed by those who wished to suppress and censor any and all expressions of dissent. In some ways the work parallels Dostoevsky's *Diary of a Writer* in that Min's memoir, like portions of Dostoevsky's diary, offers a first-person exploration of the author's own experiences.

"WHEN THE LIFELIKE DOLLS IN THE SHOP WINDOW ARE UNDERSTOOD AS THINGS THAT APPEAR TO BE OTHER THAN WHAT THEY ACTUALLY ARE (THEY APPEAR TO BE REAL CHILDREN BUT ARE NOT), THEY MAY BE VIEWED AS SYMBOLIC OF DOSTOEVSKY'S NIHILISM."

words, that reality is essentially unknowable. There is a moral component linked to these assertions. If reality, or truth, is unknowable, then any attempt to characterize what is perceived as "good" or "evil" is fruitless, for nothing is as it seems. Some nihilists focus their arguments on moral truth rather than the whole realm of human experience, while still making a similar argument, namely, that there is no way to objectively ascertain what is morally true. In nineteenth-century Russian philosophical thought, nihilism was closely linked with literary realism. Some believed that efforts to convey human thought and action in an accurate manner often revealed a basic absence of human morality. Evil actions could appear to be justified, while good actions might not always be as positive as they seem, or might have negative consequences. Some elements and characters in Russian realist novels convey a sense of a moral void. As Nishitani Keiji explains in *The Self-Overcoming of Nihilism* (1990), for Dostoevsky involvement in nihilism grew steadily after the publication in 1864 of his *Notes from Underground.* Keiji maintains that Dostoevsky moved toward an understanding of nihilism in which "religion, metaphysics, and morality" were negated by "science and socialism." Keiji also observes the extent to which Dostoevsky was in a state of internal conflict with respect to his nihilism, suggesting that "God, Christ, the great earth, the homeland of Russia and its peasants" are all elements that challenged his conception of nihilism. Likewise, in his 2004 work *The Dostoevsky Encyclopedia*, Kenneth Lantz emphasizes the shifting nature of Dostoevsky's views on nihilism. He explores nihilism through characters in such works as *The Devils* and *The Brothers Karamazov*, while also satirizing and criticizing them. As Lantz points out, in the year of his death (1881), Dostoevsky wrote in a notebook entry that "nihilism appeared among us because we are *all nihilists*" (emphasis in original).

Dostoevsky's nihilistic tendencies and his internal conflict over those tendencies are apparent in the short story "The Heavenly Christmas Tree" and are highlighted by Dostoevsky's incorporation into the story of the lifelike dolls. The significance of the dolls is initially underscored by the differences between the dolls and the other holiday sights the boy views through the shop windows lining the street. He first glimpses a Christmas tree around which children are merrily playing while eating and drinking. The comforts the other children are enjoying are noted by the boy, who is later reminded of his own suffering, whereupon he runs away. In another window the boy sees a variety of cakes, with three young ladies distributing cake to the people who enter the establishment. After being chased away, he runs off, crying. Peering through another window, the boy sees three dolls displayed "exactly as though they were alive." The dolls appear to be playing little violins while nodding. Upon seeing their lips move, the boy assumes they must be speaking—although he is unable to hear them since a glass window separates him from them. When he begins to comprehend that they are dolls, he laughs. "And he wanted to cry, but he felt amused, amused by the dolls." The child seems equally frightened and pleased. His response to what he sees behind this window is different from what he glimpses behind the other windows. In the other two windows, the boy is reminded of things he does not have—primarily food and secondarily companionship. The window with the dolls is different: behind it is nothing of immediate value to the boy. He seems entertained, and being distracted from his hunger is a condition not without value. However, the boy is afraid as well, and this fear diminishes his enjoyment. There is nothing for him behind this window, but it is to this window that the boy desires to return after he is chased away.

The windows themselves are significant. They form a barrier through which the boy is prevented from accessing food, shelter, and companionship, as well as experiencing the celebrations taking part around him. Viewed as nihilistic symbols, the windows exist as barriers to experiential reality and suggest that people are separated from reality—from truth—by their perceptions. The boy cannot actively experience the reality behind the window; he can only passively view reality. His perceptions, which are not informed by the truth of experience, are shaped without the benefit of the objective information derived from true experience.

The dolls also function as nihilistic symbols of the false nature of perception since they are things that are not truly what they appear to be. The dolls seem to be alive, but they are not. They represent the false reality human perceptions create. A void of meaning exists beyond the window where the boy views the dolls. The dolls appear to offer something positive—entertainment, amusement—but they frighten the boy as well. Through the boy's response to the dolls, the interplay between perception and reality parallels Dostoevsky's treatment of Christianity in "The Heavenly Christmas Tree." At the end of his short, painful life, the boy is reunited with his mother—and Christ—in heaven. Yet Dostoevsky doubts whether this resurrection in heaven could have happened. The salvation offered by Christianity appears to have a positive purpose—hope, salvation—but Dostoevsky's lack of faith in the reality of this salvation leaves the same void of meaning resulting from the contemplation of the dolls. If one cannot believe that what one is seeing is real, how can one trust what one perceives? Dostoevsky seems to be suggesting through this story that if one cannot hope for a life after death with Christ, how can one trust religion? What, then, is the meaning of the boy's life, one filled only with fear and suffering, if hope, salvation, and Christ are merely perceptions that one cannot trust? These are the nihilistic thoughts Dostoevsky explores in "The Heavenly Christmas Tree." He employs the windows as barriers to truth, with the dolls symbolizing faulty perception. By means of these symbols, Dostoevsky conveys the nihilistic notion that the reality of true experiential and spiritual meaning is inaccessible.

This questioning of the reality of spiritual—specifically Christian—meaning that the dolls underscore emphasizes the moral void in which the story takes place and to which Dostoevsky draws the reader's attention. The dolls link apparent meaning with an absence of meaning: they seem to be alive but are not; they appear to elicit a pleasurable sensation but actually frighten. Dostoevsky's use of the dolls to suggest this void of experiential meaning parallels the void of spiritual meaning that he implies at the story's end: Christianity appears to offer salvation but may not. The earlier chronology of events in the story—before the dolls, before the boy's death—is better understood within this nihilistic framework. The end of the story clearly suggests that Christianity may not be what it appears, while other, more subtle examples earlier in the story lay the groundwork for Dostoevsky's later questioning of the truth of Christian salvation. In fact, the story implies a general void of moral truth. The starving, freezing boy is offered no charity in the course of the story save for a single coin, which he accidentally loses. During the Christmas season, the child is ignored at best and physically attacked at worst. The utter lack of aid offered the child, followed by a death no one mourns and a resurrection that is called into question moments after it is described, points to Dostoevsky's attraction to a nihilistic view of the world. Yet his inability fully to embrace this view is apparent as well. Two elements of "The Heavenly Christmas Tree"—the description of a doubtful salvation and the image of a donated coin that rolls away due to the boy's frozen hands—suggest that Dostoevsky was reluctant to embrace nihilism, that he wanted to hope for the existence of moral truth rather than accept the notion of a moral void. The woman did not feed the starving child, but she did attempt to give him money. Perhaps the boy really did go to heaven after he died. Although Dostoevsky undercuts both of these hopeful elements, he at least includes them as glimmers, however dim, of hopefulness that humans are guided by moral truths, that spirituality is not without meaning.

Source: Catherine Dominic, Critical Essay on "The Heavenly Christmas Tree," in *Short Stories for Students*, Gale, Cengage Learning, 2010.

Katherine Mansfield

In the following review, Mansfield finds the author's storytelling skills enthrallingly simple.

. . . If we view it from a certain angle, it is not at all impossible to see in Dostoevsky's influence upon the English intellectuals of to-day the bones of a marvellously typical Dostoevsky novel. Supposing we select London for his small provincial town and his arrival for the agitating occurrence—could he himself exaggerate the discussions he has provoked, the expenditure of enthusiasm and vituperation, the mental running to and fro, the parties that have been given in his honour, the added confusion of several young gentlemen-writers declaring (in strict confidence) that they were the real Dostoevsky, the fascinating arguments as to whether or no he is greater than Jane Austen (what would Jane Austen have said to the bugs and the onions and the living in corners!), the sight of our

A poor child warms himself at Christmas. *(Image copyright Paul Prescott, 2009. Used under license from Shutterstock.com)*

young egoists puffing up like undismayed frogs, and of our superior inner circle who are not unwilling to admit that he has a considerable amount of crude strength before returning to their eighteenth-century muttons?

Ohé Dostoevsky! Où est Dostoevsky?
As-tu vu Dostoevsky?

Few indeed have so much as caught a glimpse of him. What would be the end of such a novel? His disappearance without doubt, leaving no trace but a feeling of, on the whole, very lively relief. For if we do not take him superficially, there is nothing for us to do but to take him terribly seriously, but to consider whether it is possible for us to go on writing our novels as if he never had been. This is not only a bitterly uncomfortable prospect; it is positively dangerous; it might very well end in the majority of our young writers finding themselves naked and shivering, without a book to clothe themselves in.

However, the danger is not a real one. There are signs that the fashion for him is on the wane. How otherwise can we interpret the avidity with which opinion seizes upon the less important, extravagant side of Dostoevsky, making much of it, making much of that and ignoring all else, than that it has had its fright, as it were, but now has been assured that the monster at the fair will not remain? But a remarkable feature of this parade of intellectual snobbishness, this laughing at the Russian giant, is that the writers appear to imagine that they laugh alone—that Dostoevsky had no idea of the exquisite humour of such a character as Stepan Trofimovitch, with his summer sickness, his breaking into French and his flight from civilization in a pair of top-boots, or that he regarded the super-absurdities of Prince K as other than quite normal characteristics. It is true that especially in some of the short stories we may find his sense of humour terribly jars on us, but that is when the humour is 'false'; it is exasperation disguised, an overwhelming nostalgia and bitterness disguised or an attempt at a sense of fun, in which never was man more wanting. Then, again, to laugh with Dostoevsky is not always a comfortable exercise for one's pride. For he has the—surely unpardonable—habit of describing at length, minutely, the infinitely preposterous state of mind of some poor wretch, not as though he were 'showing us a star', but with many a familiar nod and look in our direction, as much as to say: 'But you know yourself from your own experience what it is to feel *like this.*'

There is a story, "An Unpleasant Predicament," in this collection which is a terrible example of this. It relates how a young general, exasperated by an evening with two elder colleagues whom he suspects of treating him like a schoolboy and laughing at him because of his belief in the new ideas, in humanity and sympathy with the working classes, yields to the temptation on the way home of putting himself to the test, of proving to his Amour Propre that he really is the fine fellow she thinks him to be. Why should he do anything so dangerous? He knows in his heart that he does not believe in any of these things, and yet isn't it possible for him to impose this idea of himself on anybody he chooses? And why should he not slay reality as an offering to his goddess? The revenge that reality takes upon Ivan Ilyitch Pralinsky is wild and violent and remote enough from our experience, and yet who can read it and not be overcome by the feeling that he understands only too well. . . .

Perhaps Dostoevsky more than any other writer sets up this mysterious relationship with the reader, this sense of *sharing*. We are never conscious that he is writing at us or for us. While we read, we are like children to whom one tells a tale; we seem in some strange way to half-know what is coming and yet we do not know; to have heard it all before, and yet our amazement is none the less, and when it is over, it has become ours. This is especially true of the Dostoevsky who passes so unremarked—the childlike, candid, simple Dostoevsky who wrote 'An Honest Thief' and 'The Peasant Marly' and 'The Dream of a Queer Fellow.' These three wonderful stories have all the same quality, a stillness, a quiet that takes the breath. What have they to do with our time? They are full of the tragic candour of love. There is only one other man who could have written the death of Emelyanouska, as described by the poor little tailor:

> I saw Emelyanouska wanted to tell me something: he was trying to sit up, trying to speak, and mumbling something. He flushed red all over suddenly, looked at me . . . then I saw him turn white again, whiter and whiter, and he seemed to sink away all in a minute. His head fell back, he drew one breath and gave up his soul to God. . . .

Source: Katherine Mansfield, "Review of *An Honest Thief: and Other Stories* by Fyodor Dostoevsky," in *Critical Writings of Katherine Mansfield*, edited by Clare Hanson, Macmillan Press, 1987, pp. 77–79.

Marina T. Naumann

In the following essay, Naumann asserts that Christmas carols represent some of Dostoevsky's best writing but that they have been overshadowed by his masterpieces.

I

In Western Europe through the years authors, great and small, have written special stories to mark the birth of Christ. Each in his own, most beautiful way has tried to retell in modern terms what St. Luke did so eloquently in his sacred gospel some two thousand years ago. Annually these seasonal literary offerings, as their musical counterparts, have colorfully decked the bookstores, magazine shops, and newspaper stands, thus brightening the bleak December days. Pagan deities, roving witches, fantastic spectres, sugar-plum fairies, family ghosts, guardian angels, and even the heavenly God have been among the many actors playing their memorable and beneficent roles in blustery, wintry surroundings. Taken as a corpus these stories now comprise a distinctive genre, the literary Christmas "carol." Many tales are mere fantasies, written purely to amuse. Nikolai Leskov's Christmas stories and Nikolai Gogol's novella "Christmas Eve" are just such pieces. Others are filled with Yule jubilation, with those like O. Henry's "The Gift of Magi" extolling the gift of giving. Finally others remember the plight of the poor, sick, or dying. They inscribe their pieces with a moral or social message. For them Man's need to love and to be loved is paramount. Charles Dickens's *A Christmas Carol* is perhaps the classic of this category. The numerous Christmas stories have neither national barriers nor generational gaps. In fact, many are intended expressly for adults and children of all persuasions to share together. In addition, and as if to spotlight the birth of the Holiest Child, the best-remembered stories are those written *about* children. "Hansel and Gretel" of the Grimm brothers, "The Nutcracker and the Mouse King" of E. T. A. Hoffmann and revised by A. Dumas, "The Little Match Girl" of H. C. Andersen, *A Christmas Carol* of Dickens, and more recently "A Child's Christmas in Wales" of Dylan Thomas are now all folkloric stories which revolve around the small child at Christmastime.

II

Fedor Dostoevsky (1821–1881) also created remarkable Christmas stories. "The Christmas-Tree Party and the Wedding" and "The Boy at

> "FINALLY, I WILL ADD THAT DOSTOEVSKY, WITH A SLIGHT NUDGE FROM DICKENS AND A MUCH STRONGER ONE FROM ANDERSEN, FIRMLY ESTABLISHED THE GENRE OF THE CHRISTMAS "CAROL" IN RUSSIAN LITERATURE."

Christ's Christmas-Tree Party" stand at the beginning and the end of Dostoevsky's literary career. Clearly both stories have been overshadowed by the author's intervening masterpieces and consequently have been noted only in passing by the critics. Nevertheless these two works are special. Most remarkable is that the novelist chose a short genre and the unlikely subject of child neglect to present his two Christmas offerings. Of additional interest is that a full thirty years separated their composition. Nevertheless, a detailed comparison of these "carols" reveals many affinities.

Foremost, both tales basically concern a theme that always intrigued Dostoevsky—the soul of Man. He wrote that he sought "with full realism to find Man in Man. They call me a psychologist, that is not true. I am only a realist in the highest sense, that is, I depict all the depths of the human soul." In these Christmas stories Dostoevsky moved a step deeper. He depicted Man at his most spontaneous, impressionable, and vulnerable moment, in childhood at Christmastide.

Dostoevsky was always drawn to children. Their external features did not absorb him as much as their inner workings; "their habits, answers, words and expressions, characteristics, family life, beliefs, guilt and innocence...." And as if emphasizing their small size, he often distinguished them by their ages.

Paradoxically both Dostoevskian Christmas stories about children are compelling cameos of *unfortunate* children's lives. In "The Christmas-Tree Party and the Wedding" the evil Julian Mastakovich lecherously wins the hand of his child-bride at a Christmas party. The little heiress is thus sold into marriage while her friend, the governess's son, is forced into an indigent future. In "The Boy at Christ's Christmas-Tree Party" a pauper freezes to death at Christmas. Moreover, for Dostoevsky, all children may be subject to abuse. The privilege of wealth is not an advantage. Ironically, it is the parents who are responsible for the violation. This tragic situation is exacerbated by the Christmas setting. The author shows that these festivals which normally should be exciting for children, are grotesque nightmares. Further, the little people in fighting for their right to Christmas happiness are instead irreparably injured, even condemned. Dostoevsky sensitively portrays these tiny characters crouched in solitude, while the rest of the world makes merry around them. The sombreness of the action and tenor of the two stories is further rarefied by their brevity; they are under ten pages long, unexpectedly short for Dostoevsky. Thus their effect is directly and realistically forceful. In addition the stark contradiction between the joyful titles and the grim plots is underscored by Dostoevsky's sympathetic involvement and his serious intention in conveying his concerns to his readers.

This authorial attitude comes to the fore particularly vividly in Dostoevsky's aim in composing his second Christmas work, popularly remembered as "The Boy at Christ's Christmas-Tree Party." On 11 January 1876 Dostoevsky wrote Vsevolod Solov'ev: "Your idea of publishing some advance information about *A Writer's Diary* of course pleases me (as you may imagine), but at the present moment there is almost nothing I can tell you except in the most general terms. In the first number there will be a very short *preface* and then something about children, about children in general and in particular, about children who have fathers and fatherless children, about children's Christmas parties and children who have none, and about delinquent children... Then about *things heard and read*—everything, or some one thing, that has struck me personally during the month."

The January issue of *A Writer's Diary* appeared shortly thereafter and Chapter Two, as predicted, focused entirely on the plight of children at Christmas. Moreover, its three parts dramatically confirmed that Dostoevsky knew his lilliputian heroes and heroines firsthand and exceedingly well. Part 1, entitled "The Boy with his Hand Outstretched for Alms" [Mal'chik s ruchkoi], recorded how, early in December 1875, Dostoevsky befriended a seven-year old streetboy and how he pointedly questioned him about his miserable way of life. Part 2 grew out of the fact that on December 25 the author reportedly attended a Christmas party and a children's ball at an artist's club. His ostensible object was to study children for a projected novel on fathers and children. Dostoevsky never completed this magnum opus. Instead he left this impressive Part 2: "The Boy at Christ's Christmas-Tree Party." Part 3 bears the following cumbersome title: "A Colony of Juvenile Delinquents. Gloomy Creatures. Conversion of Vicious Souls into Innocent Ones. Measures Recognized as Most Expedient. Little and Bold Friends of Mankind." [Kolonija maloletnykh prestupnikov. Mrachnye osobi liudei. Peredelka porochnykh dush v neporochnye. Sredstva k tomu, priznannye nailuchshimi. Malen'kie i derzkie druz'ia chelovechestva.] As its title indicates, it is heavily social, philosophical, and theological in its message. Hence Part 3 in a sense matches Part 1. Both are journalistic accounts. If nowadays remembered at all, they are remembered as frames to the fine belletristic middle fragment, "The Boy at Christ's Christmas-Tree Party."

Basic to the present study is this poetic central section, "The Boy at Christ's Christmas-Tree Party." It is an unusual piece, because it downplays the expected psychological, moral, and other Dostoevskian features which so dominate his œuvre. Instead it unfolds as a straight-forward tale of how in a snowy city on Christmas Eve an orphan freezes to death and goes to heaven. The story is somewhat Dickensian in its general outlines.

Dostoevsky greatly admired the work of his English counterpart Charles Dickens (1812–1870). In the prison hospital at Omsk he read Russian translations of *David Copperfield* and *The Pickwick Papers*. These translations, he insisted, provided him with "all the nuances of the original." *Dombey and Son* and *Bleak House* were in his personal library in French translation. In addition, his letters mention these Dickens works as well as *The Old Curiosity Shop* and, most pertinently, *A Christmas Carol*. Indeed Dostoevsky was so aware of Dickens that he dubbed himself and his wife "Mr. and Mrs. Micawber." Truly Dostoevsky's preoccupations in many respects consciously or unconsciously converged with those of Dickens. Both not only shared a lifelong concern for the problems of the child, but were prolific novelists who edited prominent and popular journals or thick magazines. While Dostoevsky had *Time*, *Epoch*, and later his *A Writer's Diary*, Dickens devoted much time and energy to his *Household Words* and *All the Year Round*. In nearly every December issue Dickens included a Christmas story. Dostoevsky's "The Boy at Christ's Christmas-Tree Party," although a singular piece, of course appeared similarly, in the authorial periodical *A Writer's Diary*.

Dickens's most widely read and best-loved Christmas work is *A Christmas Carol* (1843). Its prevailing, yet subtle, moral and social tone is tempered by visions and fantasies. Marley's ghost and the three apparitions are the ministering Christmas spirits. They intercede to bring rich old Scrooge to help poor Tiny Tim and the Cratchits have a merry Christmas dinner. As many others, Dostoevsky must have been stirred by this novelette; as a writer he must have also appreciated it from the technical angle. Nonetheless, there are no distinct parallels, in either content or form, between *A Christmas Carol* and "The Boy at Christ's Christmas-Tree Party." Dickens was after all Dostoevsky's contemporary, not his master.

There is another good explanation why there was no Dickensian influence here. The Russian patterned his story on one of the charming tales of Andersen (1805–1875). Before proving this thesis I must draw attention to a few relevant points. Unlike his confreres Dickens and Dostoevsky, Andersen was not particularly fond of children. Therefore it has always been somewhat puzzling that he dedicated all of these immortal stories "for children," and that he spent so many hours reading to them. (By contrast Dickens and Dostoevsky, who also enjoyed reading their work, particularly the two aforementioned stories at Christmas, preferred adult audiences.) At first glance Andersen's work seems to be on a childish, oft-fantastic level. Much is in fact based on folklore. Nevertheless his stories generally have some deeper level which I shall explain below. Like Dickens and Dostoevsky, Andersen composed some of his most meaningful stories for the Yule season. These appeared in calendars or pamphlets; only later were they printed in book form. The most memorable of these stories are "The Fir Tree" and "The Little Match Girl." In rereading the last story, the Dostoevsky tale "The Boy at Christ's Christmas-Tree Party" acquires extraordinary new dimensions in both content and form. Before us is nothing less than a Dostoevskian paraphrase of Andersen's "The Little Match Girl."

Before turning to the striking comparisons, we must remember that this Danish story was published in December 1845, some thirty Christmases before Dostoevsky offered his fascinating Russian version. It is not clear how, when, and where

Dostoevsky came to know Andersen's fairy tale. Although in the final analysis it is of little importance, I can speculate, for the possibilities are intriguing. Dostoevsky might have known the story in one of the many early German translations. However, he would have been probably more familiar with the French translation found in the 334-page *Contes d'Andersen.* Within two years of its Parisian publication it was reviewed by Dostoevsky's literary colleague, N.A. Dobroliubov, in *The Contemporary*. The page-long criticism praised the four Andersen stories which Dobroliubov felt were the strongest and dearest pieces, "there being no fantasy in them." He included "The Little Match Girl" in this grouping. He observed: "These stories are either amusing or touching; they may well act upon the mind and heart of children, and besides that there is not the least bit of philosophizing in them.... In this precisely one sees the art and talent of the storyteller; his stories do not need a moralizing little tail (*khvostik*); they lead the children to pondering, and the stories are put into practice by the children themselves, freely and naturally, without any strain." He did note that the stories were relatively little distributed (*rasprostraneny*) in Russia. True, it would be a number of years before the tales would appear in Russian translation. In Dostoevsky's case such a time lag would be unimportant, because he was in Siberian exile between 1849 and 1859. However, in the 1860s the Russian went to live in Western Europe, visiting his old friend from his Siberian days Baron Alexander Egorovich Wrangel in October 1865. By then Wrangel was the Secretary of the Russian Embassy in Copenhagen. Possibly Wrangel spoke of Andersen and lent him a copy of the tales. This would have been natural since Wrangel had been Dostoevsky's exclusive source of books, journals, and newspapers during their Siberian time. Dostoevsky's ten-day stay could certainly have given the impressionable writer and bibliophile an ample chance to learn of the Danish tales.

The stories became available in Russian soon after, in 1863, a decade before Dostoevsky wrote his story. These stories immediately earned great popularity and were very much "in the air" thereafter. However, Dostoevsky had none of Andersen's tales in his library. Nevertheless, a copy might well have belonged to his children who were young then. Possibly he, as the doting father, or Anna Grigor'evna read them these tales. (He did read them Dickens.)

Walter Pater wrote: "Producers of great literature do not live in isolation, but catch light and heat from each other's thoughts." Andersen obviously inspired some of Dostoevsky's fellow writers. Tolstoy reworked Andersen's story "The Emperor's New Clothes" [Tsarskoe novoe plat'e] for the third of his *Alphabet Books* [Azbuka] and for *Russian Books for Reading* [Russkie knigi dlia chteniia]. Chekhov, Garshin, and later Gorky were also indebted to him for ideas. Andersen, for his part, wrote his translator on 28 August 1868: "I am very glad that my works are being read in Great Russia whose blossoming literature I know in part, beginning from Karamzin to Pushkin and right up to this time." Writers, in the nineteenth century especially, not only read one another with interest, but had many common or at least similar attitudes, concerns, and experiences. These may well have evoked comparable reactions or produced nearly identical works which at first glance might appear plagiaristic. Indeed this might well have been the case. If so, this too would be curious. But such similarities could also be instances of brilliant artists coincidentally perceiving life identically. In any event, Dostoevsky, particularly, never wrote in a vacuum. His writings contain many different and extraordinary echoes which originated far beyond Russia's cultural and linguistic boundaries.

H. C. Andersen died at the time that Dostoevsky penned "The Boy at Christ's Christmas-Tree Party." Andersen, who had also travelled in Russia, was well-known to the Russian common man. Thus it would have been natural for his death to trigger a Dostoevskian response. Certainly Dostoevsky's text speaks clearly in favor of this reaction. Dostoevsky's story assumes a new cast if read with a knowledge of Andersen's "The Little Match Girl." In fact it is as early as the first sentences that Dostoevsky's story takes on double meaning. Significantly they are voiced by the writer or, to be precise, the diarist: "But I am a novelist, and it appears I myself have composed a 'story.' Why do I write 'it appears,' after all I myself know for certain that I composed it, but still it seems to me this did happen somewhere and sometime, namely that this happened exactly on Christmas Eve in *some kind* of huge city in a terrible frost" (14). With this introductory paragraph Dostoevsky seems to hedge concerning the story's source. Conceivably someone else, somewhere else, and sometime else could have written the story; Andersen perhaps? Further, this excerpt resonates with Andersen's opening sentence: "It was so terribly cold; it snowed, and it was almost dark; it was also the last evening of the year—New Year's Eve" (153). In both stories the exact location is left unspecified; it could be St. Petersburg, Copenhagen, or any other capital of Europe. Maybe even a Dickensian London.

Dostoevsky, however, cleverly distorts his version by using the words *it appears* (*kazhetsia*) and *it seems* (*mereshchitsia*). These words in a sense undercut the writer's authority. They also remove the story from the domain of the journalistic factualism governing his Parts 1 and 3 and place it in the hallucinatory realm, so necessary for fairy tales. The fact that other such words (*budto, pochuditsia*) are used throughout the story reinforces this fantastic tone, which carries the reader through the action, bringing him to the sober concluding paragraph which in essence restates the introductory one: "And why did I compose such a story so inappropriate for a usual, rational diary, moreover that of a writer? Furthermore I promised tales for the most part about real events! But that is the trouble, it keeps appearing and seeming to me that this could all really occur; that is, that which happened in the cellar and behind the firewood, and that place about Christ's Christmas-tree party—well I don't know what to say, could it happen or not? For that reason I am a novelist, in order to invent" (18). This short concluding paragraph structurally serves as a transition back to the newspaperlike reportage given in Part 1, as it is renewed in Part 3. Conspicuously in Andersen's tale there are no comparable frames or introductory and concluding portions. It could be said that while Dostoevsky's required some explanation, Andersen's as the original required no authorial intrusion.

In the Danish and Russian stories *proper* the author, narrator, storyteller, or witness steps into the background and the central figure's point of view is taken. In both stories this is that of a very small child. Andersen's is the titular girl and Dostoevsky's correspondingly is the boy. Neither small child is named, thus acquiring the symbolic proportions of Everyman. Virtually no physical description is given. Rather it is the fact that they are very young and impoverished, inadequately clothed, and as such shivering. Their little hands, fingers, feet, and toes are red (in Andersen, red and blue) from the cold. In both stories the children are essentially rejected, and as such orphaned. To compound the agony, these little ones are good, noble souls.

In Andersen's version the father, out of desperation, has threatened to beat the child. In Dostoevsky's the father is totally absent. The feminine characters, by contrast, are loving and appropriately maternal. The little girl, who has lost her mother, readily recalls her old, loving grandmother, who has also died. Dostoevsky's boy unknowingly is present at his mother's death. The climax is built around the reunion between the children and their mothers. In Andersen it is the grandmother and in Dostoevsky, the mother. The plot lines follow one another. In both the child must go out for its destitute family, such that it is, to seek sustenance. In Andersen it is a need for shillings, while in Dostoevsky it is kopeks. It is dark and wintry when the child sets forth. The streets of the capital are snowy. Selling no matches or finding no coins, the hungry child wanders aimlessly into the night.

The setting of both is created with contrasts. In Andersen's tale this frigid evening is New Year's Eve with all its implied jubilation and optimism. Dostoevsky's takes place on Christmas Eve. (As Dostoevsky's other Christmas story is set at New Year's Eve, the difference of holidays becomes negligible.) The begging child glances forlornly through the windowpanes of the rich merchants' homes. There it sees colored lights, festively set tables, skipping children, and in the middle there is a magnificent Christmas tree colorfully decorated with small fruits, candies, and glistening papers. In both stories the description of this tree is very reminiscent of other fictional trees. In Andersen's earlier story "The Fir Tree" it is the sparrows who twitter: "We looked through the window-panes and saw them [the trees] planted in a warm room, and decked out with such beautiful things, gilded apples, honey cakes, toys, and many hundred candles" (42–43). Dostoevsky might well have also drawn on the following other excerpt from "The Fir Tree" for his description of the tree: "On some boughs they hung little bags cut out of colored paper and filled with sugarplums; gilded apples and walnuts were tied to others, so that they looked just as if they had grown there; and over a hundred red, blue, and white small candles were placed here and there among the branches. Dolls that looked human—the Tree had never seen such things before—danced to and fro among the leaves, and a large star of gold tinsel was fastened to the very top" (44). Dickens has a comparable description in his 1850 Yule piece "A Christmas Tree."

The tinseled Christmas tree is naturally a focal point in any West European Christmas celebration. By contrast, for the Russian Orthodox Christmas is not such a high holy day, Easter is the most sacred day. Nevertheless the Russian holiday merriment focuses on the Christmas tree. In fact, in Russia this tree is a Christmas symbol; the word for *Christmas tree, elka* (*fir tree* in its generic meaning), is also the word for *Christmas party* of which it is the center. Significantly Dostoevsky highlights the festive backgrounds (or is it the structural potential?) of his two stories by choosing the meaningful *elka* for the titles. He does not use the more accepted word for *Christmas* or *Nativity: Rozhdestvo*. In short Dostoevsky may have easily shaped his literary trees according to the glorious fictional predecessors of Andersen and Dickens.

The cleavage between the wealth, light, and warmth of Christmas happiness and the poverty, darkness, and cold of Christmas sorrow is emphasized by the great glass doors, shop windows, and windowpanes which pointedly divide the two worlds. Andersen's child is very mindful of the fact that "lights were shining in all the windows, and there was a tempting smell of roast goose for it was New Year's Eve" (153–154). Dostoevsky's child sees two comparable scenes through a glass pane and boyishly, even bravely, ventures into one of the homes. (In Europe it was customary for the rich to open their homes at Christmastime.) But even here the child is repulsed, kicked out of the house, and pursued by a toughie. Not unexpectedly, this last detail harkens back to the fact that the little match girl has lost her slipper to just such a bully; for this reason she is barefoot. Consequently, each child is quickly overcome by the cold and seeks warm shelter. In Andersen the child crouches "in a corner framed by two houses, one of which projected a little beyond" (154). Dostoevsky's boy hides in a courtyard behind a stack of firewood.

The children's fingers and toes are understandably the first to freeze. For warmth the little girl finally resorts to lighting the matches she should have sold. As she does this she slips into marvelous dreams; for each match flame reveals a Christmas celebration all for her. There are four wondrous scenes. Each is brought to life by the strike of a match and each vanishes with the extinguished flame. Taken together they provide a definite progression upward, toward heaven. In the first picture the child sees herself beside a large stove with brass ornaments which gives her warmth. The second shows a spread holiday table full of delicious food. The roast goose comes alive and approaches her. The third provides her with a beautiful Christmas tree in lavish surroundings. The decorations and many toys are not stressed here. Instead it is the glowing candles, which are nothing more than giant matches, which attract her: "Hundreds of wax tapers lit up the green branches and tiny painted figures such as she had seen in shop windows, looked down from the tree" (154). They give warmth and light, a true radiance which then easily provides an emotional and physical ascent. The candles then rise into the sky until they become stars. In the fourth and final scene the beloved grandmother appears. To preserve her the child lights her entire matchbox. Grandmother is dazzling and bright as she takes the child "high, so high" to where "there is no cold, nor hunger, nor sorrow" for they "are with God." All the child's wants and needs have been met from Above.

Dostoevsky's story, which I find less imaginative, follows Andersen's closely. In the boy's death trance he is gently roused from his nook; gradually we learn it has been by Christ, a slight twist from Andersen. He takes him heavenward to his mother. Dostoevsky, just like Andersen, provides a vision of a heavenly Christmas party. It too is described as sparkling, bright, blazing, even radiant. Ironically this illumination signifies the child's saintly death. In both the child excitedly addresses the parent and is reunited with the parent by God. In the devout Dostoevsky's case it is Christ. The Godhead, not a ghost, has been the ministering spirit in these great stories. In a sense God has been the literal *Deus ex machina*, rescuing the two children by an earthly death, and bringing them to a heavenly life. It is also convincing for the reader because it not only removes the event from pure fantasy, but gives it a final social bite, or theological uplift, whichever he or she wishes to perceive.

Dostoevsky, as Andersen, breaks this hallucinatory ascension into heaven with a final picture which realistically conveys the other side of the story. Compare Andersen's description with that of Dostoevsky:

> But in the corner by the houses, in the cold dawn, the little girl was still sitting, with red cheeks and a smile upon her lips—frozen to death on the last evening of the old year. The New Year's sun shone on the little body. The child sat up stiffly, holding her matches, of which a box had been burned. "She must have tried to warm herself," someone said. No one knew what beautiful

> things she had seen, or into what glory she had entered with her grandmother on that joyous New Year (155).

> And below the next morning, the yardman found the little corpselet of the boy who ran in and froze behind the firewood; they also sought out his mamma...That one had died even before him; both of them were reunited at the Lord God's in heaven (18).

The Danish version undeniably molded the Russian one.

The few divergences between Andersen and Dostoevsky are remarkable precisely because of their parallels. Compare: heroine to hero; shillings to kopeks; grandmother to mother; New Year's Eve to Christmas Eve; God to Christ. We might then look for a difference in the basic priorities of the two, between Andersen the romantic and Dostoevsky the realist. The Dane was writing a fairy tale for children primarily. Hence it was supposedly an entertainment. Yet so many of his stories, this one included, do contain an explicit teaching. "The Fir Tree," mentioned above, has an even more obvious message which would not likely pass unnoticed by the adult storyteller.

Dostoevsky's version was not intended as a light tale, particularly in view of its appearance in an adult publication with its Parts 1 and 3. Part 2, however, if taken alone, conceivably could be read to children as a bedtime story. Thus there is on the part of the writers, a surprising comparability of purpose in these two pieces: to entertain and to preach. Only a slight shift of emphasis appears to separate them. In addition both writers are similarly engaged or involved, albeit from a distance, in the story which they relate. The form of both, which is almost identical, demonstrates this.

Andersen's story is two and a half pages long, while Dostoevsky's is only four. This is amazingly succinct in view of the usual length of the Russian's works. In both the plot line moves straight to the climax. The paragraphs and sentences tend to be short, even staccato-like. Thus these stories are structurally direct and terse. This makes them most powerful. The language is highly charged with its vocabulary of fright and awe. Many exclamatory interjections color the texts. Diminutives are frequent, reflecting not only the size of the children but the sympathetic attitude of their creators. Little toes, feet, fingers, and hands literally sense the death agony. The latter then extend to become the metaphoric affectionate arms of the grandmother and Christ which carry the little ones to heaven. Appropriately such key words repeat. For instance Andersen's titular *little* (*lille*) recurs fourteen times. Dostoevsky's *suddenly* (*vdrug*) appears thirteen times within four paragraphs. These words reverberate along with the more significant repeating details of *money, cold,* and *light*. These linguistic repetitions, not only serve as emphases, but they also help maintain the stories' tempo and tension. Further in such reiteration there is a childlike quality, a simple excitement or naive suspense, which gives the effect, almost of a monologue, in the youngsters' consciousness. Moreover, this charged tone is punctuated by numerous exclamation and question marks. In sum the echoes of Andersen's story in that of Dostoevsky are strikingly loud and occur at many registers.

III

To conclude: it is curious that Dostoevsky, in view of his own highly developed craft, should have turned to the simple storyteller Andersen for his model. Clearly Dostoevsky was the greater artist. Nevertheless, I do not believe he improved on Andersen's crisp wonder tale. He did, however, provide an elegant, perhaps uncharacteristically fantastic, case study for the more philosophical, and therefore more Dostoevskian, first and third parts of his *Diary*'s Chapter Two. In this perspective the Andersenesque second part seems strangely novel and refreshing.

Finally, I will add that Dostoevsky, with a slight nudge from Dickens and a much stronger one from Andersen, firmly established the genre of the Christmas "carol" in Russian literature. These pieces are all unique because the central characters are poignant figurings of parents and children. Dostoevsky's stories were followed in the modern period by two other equally moving Russian stories. They were the Yule pieces "The Little Angel" (1899) of Leonid Andrea and "Christmas" (1925) of Vladimir Nabokov. The associations here are also very close, but unfortunately they must wait to be considered at another time and in another forum.

Source: Marina T. Naumann, "Dostoevsky's 'The Boy at Christ's Christmas-Tree Party': A Paraphrase of Andersen's 'The Little Match Girl,'" in *Revue de Littérature Comparée*, Didier Littératures, 1981, pp. 317–30.

Charles K. Trueblood

In the following review, Trueblood considers that Dostoevsky's An Honest Thief and Other Stories *illustrates the negative characteristics of Dostoevsky's method and mind.*

The eight stories and two novelettes in this volume show more than Dostoevsky's better known work the negative characteristics of his method and mind. There is not here the command and vision of sombre psychology, of the punished mind, the terrible adventures of the heart, described with peculiar effectiveness in *Crime and Punishment*. In the second longest story of the present series, "An Unpleasant Predicament," the wretched clerk Pseldonimov and his heroic mother, and Ivan Ilyitch, the official victimized by his own theories of good will among men, are in the particular mood characteristic of Dostoevsky; but "An Honest Thief," a single tone depiction of abjectness, is the only one among these somewhat miscellaneous tales really well within the range of qualities for which he is eminent. Between the two stories just mentioned and "Bobok," a ghoulish Poeistic irony, or the "Dream of a Ridiculous Man," a short study in asperity, there is considerable disagreement; and their contrast with "Uncle's Dream," the amplest tale in the volume, is even greater. Dostoevsky has, in the last named tale, in the character of Marya Alexandrovna, greatly elaborated on his customary rather broad and simple characterization. As the heroine of what is really a small novel, this spry and wily old desperado is copiously done, shown with an astonishing equipment for offence: piety, sentimentality, palaver, rhetoric, cant, sophistry, heroics; and how shrewdly she uses her weapons, with what a heartiness and daring, even in the middle of despair. Autocrat and flatterer in alternate breaths, she reduces her vacuous, stupid husband to shudders with a single aside, while enveloping in a din of amiability the old simpleton she proposes to stake down for her daughter. This simpleton, an archaic prize, is a nobleman, a prince temporarily deserted by the female Argus who is his guardian attaché; accordingly he enters the scene, the back county town of Mordasov, à la holiday, simpering and chirruping. On his appearance there is a concerted swoop by the spiteful and formidable gossips of the place, each of whom wants to snatch him away for her own purposes. Marya Alexandrovna fights them all off with the spirit of a Balkan chief, and in a great stroke gets the old simperer to propose marriage to her daughter. The ultimate defeat of this Napoleonic Mama is brought to pass by the rebuffed lover, villain of the piece, who gets the ear of the antiquity and instils into him the suggestion that the whole scene of the proposal is a dream had during the princely siesta; from this idea the old fellow, in a mush of befuddlement, cannot be shaken. It is done with high spirit and accomplishes more of the effect of insouciance, lightness, ease than the other longish story of the volume, "Another Man's Wife"; this latter, so evidently aimed at comedy, is little more than obscure wry farce.

Insouciance, self-possession of the absolute much prized French variety, the all-containing nonchalance, the iron-nerved sense of form, Dostoevsky apparently cannot claim. His close realism quite lacks easiness and is impersonal in a rough and elemental, not an accomplished way; he has no suggestion of the considered faint irony of Chekhov. From the present volume one comes to the opinion that the effects that are got by afterthought or forethought should not be looked for in Dostoevsky; he is not an artificer, not a pausing, self-possessed or contemplative man; as it is done once with him, so it is done always. His eminence is the eminence of endowment, not of training or consideration; he is the great artist of few accomplishments. The vitality of his many memorable persons, and their salience are due to the virility of his conception rather than to any accomplishment of his in the subtler sorts of picturing. Active and acute in observation as he is, he is yet not clever at intimacy, particularly intimacy with the ordinary, or knowing in the close-drawn distinctions of description and contrast in which many ordinary novelists now are fairly proficient. As a realist of the trivial, at least in the present volume, he is less successful than many persons of much inferior creative substance. He is, it is true, voluminous and detailed; but all his specificity, descriptive of these shallower realities, seems not to profit him much. He sees truly and deals accurately with the things of sense, but his assemblage and description of them is curiously naïve and mechanical. In spite of a rich sensibility, he is more or less neutral to the appeal of scene and appearance for their own sake or for the sake of picturesqueness. The detailed fulness of his description of ordinary, trivial, or farcical surfaces and events has something the effect of haste, of the unrewarded excess effort of stammering. He has not Chekhov's skill of irony or his meticulous sensitiveness. The habitual and natural going deep of his thought, the tremendousness which he can summon to the vision of states of suffering, his penetration into the secret places of consciousness are out of place where there is nothing but paltriness for consideration, nothing but shallows to fathom.

Source: Charles K. Trueblood, "Dostoevsky as Trivialist," in *Dial: a Semi-monthly Journal of Literary Criticism, Discussion, and Information* (1880–1929), June 1920, pp. 774–76.

SOURCES

Amoia, Alba, "Post-Siberian Short Stories," in *Feodor Dostoevsky*, Continuum, 1993, pp. 209–26.

Dostoevsky, Fyodor, and Constance Garnett, "The Heavenly Christmas Tree," in *"An Honest Thief" and Other Stories*, Wildside Press, 2008, pp. 151–55.

———, "The Boy at Christ's Christmas Party," in *A Writer's Diary: 1873–1876*, Vol. 1, translated by Kenneth Lantz, Northwestern University Press, 1994, pp. 310–14.

Freeborn, Richard, "The Nineteenth Century: The Age of Realism, 1855–80," in *The Cambridge History of Russian Literature*, edited by Charles A. Moser, Cambridge University Press, 1989, pp. 248–332.

Hayes, Carlton J. H., "The Russian Empire," in *A Political and Social History of Modern Europe*, Vol. 2, Macmillan, 1917, pp. 452–89.

Jackson, Robert Lewis, ed., Introduction in *Dostoevsky: New Perspectives*, Prentice-Hall, 1984, pp. 1–18.

Katasonov, Vladimir, "Integral Reason: Science and Religion in Russian Culture," in *Science & Spirit*, http://www.science-spirit.org/article_detail.php?article_id=178 (accessed October 14, 2009).

Keiji, Nishitani, "Nihilism in Russia," in *The Self-Overcoming of Nihilism*, translated by Graham Parkes, with Setsuko Aihara, State University of New York, 1990, pp. 127–56.

Kendall, Bridget, "Insight: Russia's Leading Men," in *BBC News*, September 15, 2009, http://news.bbc.co.uk/2/hi/europe/8257941.stm (accessed October 16, 2009).

Krag, Erik, "The Brothers Karamazov," in *Dostoevsky: The Literary Artist*, Humanities Press, 1962, pp. 247–91.

Lantz, Kenneth. A., "Nihilism" and "Socialism," in *The Dostoevsky Encyclopedia*, Greenwood Press, 2004, pp. 279–82, 402–406.

Leatherbarrow, W. J., ed., Introduction in *The Cambridge Companion to Dostoevskii*, Cambridge University Press, 2002, pp. 1–20.

Michell, T., ed., "Route 5—Moscow: The Foundling Hospital," in *Handbook for Travellers in Russia, Poland, and Finland*, John Murray, 1849; rev. ed., 1865, pp. 163–66.

Morson, Gary Saul, "Introductory Study," in *A Writer's Diary: 1873–1876*, Vol. 1, translated by Kenneth Lantz, Northwestern University Press, 1994, pp. 1–117.

Murav, Harriet, "Fedor Mikhailovich Dostoevsky," in *Dictionary of Literary Biography*, Vol. 238, *Russian Novelists in the Age of Tolstoy and Dostoevsky*, edited by J. Alexander Ogden and Judith E. Kalb, The Gale Group, 2001, pp. 42–70.

"Putin Grilled Over Press Freedom," in *BBC News*, June 5, 2006, http://news.bbc.co.uk/2/hi/europe/5049628.stm (accessed October 16, 2009).

"Russia," in *CIA World Factbook*, https://www.cia.gov/library/publications/the-world-factbook/geos/rs.html (accessed October 16, 2009).

Scanlan, James P., "The Russian Idea," in *Dostoevsky: The Thinker*, Cornell University Press, 2002, pp. 197–230.

Shishkoff, N., "Famine Relief in Samara," in *The Nineteenth Century: A Monthly Review*, Vol. 31, edited by James Knowles, January-June 1892, pp. 487–95.

FURTHER READING

Bellisustin, I. S., *Description of the Clergy in Rural Russia: The Memoir of a Nineteenth-Century Parish Priest*, edited and translated by Gregory Freeze, Cornell University Press, 1985.

Bellisustin wrote an account of the state of the clergy and religion in the Russian countryside in the 1850s. The memoir offers a firsthand perspective from a clergyman's point of view of nineteenth-century Russian religion and the challenges faced by rural parish priests.

Engel, Barbara Alpern, *Mothers and Daughters: Women of the Intelligentsia in Nineteenth-Century Russia*, Northwestern University Press, 2000.

Engel studies the roles Russian women played in radical, revolutionary movements during the nineteenth century, assessing the ways in which women operated differently than their male counterparts.

Frank, Joseph, *Dostoevsky: A Writer in His Time*, Princeton University Press, 2009.

In this acclaimed volume Frank offers an abridgement of his earlier, five-volume biographical and critical study of Dostoevsky and his works. The literary biography also explores the historical, cultural, and political atmosphere of nineteenth-century Russia.

Lindemann, Albert S., *A History of European Socialism*, Yale University Press, 1983.

Lindemann examines the origin, development, and spread of socialism and its related movements throughout Europe, discussing the transformations the original philosophy underwent in Russia and its evolution under Soviet governance.

Stacy, R. H., *Russian Literary Criticism: A Short History*, Syracuse University Press, 1974.

Stacy explores the ways in which Russian literary critics affected Russian culture and shaped literary values from the nineteenth century through the Soviet period of the twentieth century.

The Leap

LOUISE ERDRICH

1990

Originally published in the March 1990 issue of *Harper's* magazine and anthologized numerous times since, Louise Erdrich's short story "The Leap" was also included in the 2009 short-story collection *The Red Convertible: Selected and New Stories, 1978–2008*. As is true of all Erdrich's writing, this particular piece achieves momentum because of the author's rich characterization and descriptive pathos.

Although Erdrich dislikes the notion that she is a magical realist, or a writer who infuses the improbable into otherwise realistic stories, she does indeed seem to do just that. It is a technique that serves her well in "The Leap," a recalled memory of a mother by a daughter. Familiar Erdrich themes of familial love and the consequence of choice are covered here as the narrator recalls how her own life has been shaped and influenced by her elderly mother's choices.

Although "The Leap" has never been pointedly praised as outstanding or particularly influential, it is one of many short stories written by Erdrich that, when considered as a whole, provide an insightful, multicultural, and entertaining perspective on everyday life. Unlike most of her characters, those found in this story are not specifically identified as Native American, though they could be. The reader never learns the ethnicity of the narrator or her parents. In removing that label, Erdrich has made her story more universally appealing because it brings with it no cultural assumptions or inferences.

Louise Erdrich *(AP Images)*

AUTHOR BIOGRAPHY

Karen Louise Erdrich (pronounced AIR-drik), who writes as Louise Erdrich, was born on July 7, 1954, in Little Falls, Minnesota, the oldest of seven children. Her father, Ralph, was of German heritage, and her mother, Rita, was of Ojibwe descent. Both taught at a boarding school on one of the local Indian reservations.

Erdrich enrolled in Dartmouth College in New Hampshire in 1972. That same year, she met her future husband, Michael Dorris, chair of the newly created Native American Studies Department. Drawing on her rich and pervasive Ojibwe roots, Erdrich began writing poetry integrating Native American themes. Her efforts earned her the Academy of Poets Prize in 1975, one year before she graduated.

The years immediately following graduation were spent teaching poetry and writing at the State Arts Council of North Dakota. Thanks to a fellowship, Erdrich earned her master's degree in writing from the Johns Hopkins University in Baltimore, Maryland, in 1979.

During her graduate studies, Erdrich sent manuscripts to publishers but had no success in getting published. For a year after graduation, she worked as communications director and editor of *Circle*, a Boston Indian Council–sponsored newspaper. From there, she took a job writing textbooks for Charles Merrill Company.

Dorris and Erdrich crossed paths again in 1979 when she was invited back to Dartmouth to conduct a poetry reading. They married on October 10, 1981. That same year, Erdrich published her first collection of poetry.

Dorris brought to the marriage three adopted Native American children. Erdrich adopted her husband's children, and the couple eventually had three biological daughters.

In 1982, Erdrich was awarded the Nelsen Algren Fiction award for her short story "The World's Greatest Fisherman." The story eventually became the first chapter of her first novel, *Love Medicine*.

That novel was published in 1984, as was a volume of poetry titled *Jacklight*. The previous year, the author won the Pushcart Prize for one of her poems and the National Magazine Fiction Award for another short story. But it was *Love Medicine* that catapulted her to literary fame and won the National Book Critics Circle Award for best work of fiction, the Sue Kaufman Prize for Best First Novel, the Virginia McCormick Scully Award for best book of the year dealing with Indians or Chicanos, and many others.

Love Medicine was the first of four novels to feature four Ojibwe families living in North Dakota from 1912 into the 1980s. The book actually consists of interrelated short stories, and it won Erdrich the respect of readers of popular fiction and literary authors alike. But for her, the most important praise was that which came from her Native American readers. Erdrich received thousands of letters thanking her for giving them a voice, for bringing their lives into print, for portraying reservation life as it really was. Three more novels rounded out the series: *The Beet Queen* (1986), *Tracks* (1988), and *The Bingo Palace* (1994).

Erdrich's short stories have consistently appeared in literary periodicals throughout her writing career. "The Leap" was initially published in March 1990 in *Harper's Magazine*. Erdrich and Dorris co-wrote *The Crown of Columbus*, a novel praised for its humor and original voice, in 1991. Erdrich published *The Blue Jay's Dance* in 1995, a memoir of her pregnancy and first year with her newborn. She then wrote the first of several children's books as well as two more novels.

Personal and legal issues prompted Dorris to commit suicide in 1997, and in 1999, Erdrich moved her family to Minneapolis, where she and sister Heidi opened Birchbark Books, an independent bookstore, in 2000. The following year, Erdrich gave birth to another daughter, and in 2002, she published her first young-adult novel, *The Birchbark House*, which was a finalist for the National Book Award for Young People.

Erdrich continued writing throughout the first decade of the twenty-first century. By 2008, she had published five more novels. The last, titled *A Plague of Doves*, was a finalist for the Pulitzer Prize in 2009. That was the same year the author published *The Red Convertible*, a short-story collection spanning three decades of writing that includes "The Leap."

As of 2009, Erdrich was working on her next novel, *Shadow Tag: A Novel*, set to be published in 2010.

PLOT SUMMARY

"The Leap" begins with the narrator telling how her mother, Anna, is the surviving member of a blindfolded trapeze duo known as the Flying Avalons. Although now blind, Anna never stumbles or falls, never knocks over objects in the New Hampshire home she shares with the narrator, who has come back to her childhood home now that her father is dead and her mother cannot live alone.

Anna keeps no mementos of her former life in the circus. Everything the narrator knows about her mother's past under the big top has been gleaned from newspaper accounts. Acknowledging that "I owe her my existence three times," the narrator credits her mother's survival of a circus accident as the first time.

Harry and Anna were members of a traveling circus, and on this given day, weather conditions were just right for a wicked thunderstorm. The Flying Avalons were the fourth act to perform that day. Harry and Anna flirted with one another as they blindfolded each other and took their places on their trapezes, high above the crowd. No one watching knew that Anna was seven months pregnant at the time; her stomach muscles were so tight that she barely showed a bump.

Just as the pair were in mid-flight—Harry upside down, hanging by his knees, arms open wide to grab on to Anna, and Anna just having dived from her bar toward her husband—lightning struck the main tent pole and cruised down the wires. Harry dropped to his death, blindfold still in place. Anna, rather than following her husband to the grave, tore off her blindfold and twisted her body toward one of the wires. Although the metal singed all the skin from her hands, her life was spared.

While trying to pull her from the mess that lay on the ground, a rescuer broke Anna's arm and caused something to fall and knock her unconscious. She was rushed to the hospital, where she remained for a month and a half before giving birth to a stillborn baby girl.

Although Harry was buried in the circus cemetery, Anna's daughter was buried just around the corner from her New Hampshire home, the home in which the narrator grew up. The narrator mentions that she never really thought of the girl as anything but a less finalized version of herself, but that she often visited the grave as a child.

Anna met her second husband while recuperating in the hospital. Having spent time in the Air Force during the war—which war, the narrator never says—he became an expert at setting broken arms and legs. He stayed at Anna's bedside during her recovery, and she regaled him with stories of her life and travels. Always having wanted to travel himself, he considered these stories a gift. In return, he taught the illiterate Anna how to read and write.

Reading quickly became Anna's favorite pastime, and when her husband, the narrator's father, dies, the narrator comes home from her life in the West to care for and read to her mother. The house is an old farmhouse that the narrator's father inherited and is located in the same town in which the circus accident occurred. Although her husband never wanted to stay in such a small town, Anna loved the old house, and he loved her, so they made a life there. And that is the second time Anna was responsible for her daughter's existence, when she met and married her father.

The house caught fire when the narrator was just seven, although no one knew for sure how it started. Anna and her husband were gone, and the babysitter had fallen asleep. She was awakened by the smoke and used the phone to call for help. By the time the narrator's parents arrived, volunteers from the town were trying to put out the flames. They were getting ready to try to rescue the narrator, not realizing the only staircase to her bedroom was already destroyed.

The narrator woke up to find the house on fire, but she kept her wits about her and left the door closed, knowing what awaited her just beyond. She put on her robe and sat down on her bed to wait for rescue.

Anna, standing below her daughter's bedroom window, knew there would be no rescue unless she took it upon herself to make the attempt. When she asked her husband, who was about to rush to the other side of the house, to unzip her dress, he didn't understand. She explained what she planned to do, but he couldn't seem to make the zipper work. So Anna stripped right there in front of all the neighbors and the volunteers, climbed up a ladder to the top of a tree, and crawled along a skinny, brittle branch toward her daughter's window.

She stood, swaying on the fragile bough, and made a death-defying leap in the dark to an even smaller branch, one so skinny it was the size of Anna's wrist. As she grabbed hold of the branch, it cracked, and the crowd below was temporarily unable to see through the dark to locate where Anna had fallen. As it turned out, she was hanging by her heels from the rooftop gutter. And she was smiling. The narrator was not surprised to see her upside-down, smiling mother, for she knew that Anna lived "comfortably in extreme elements." Anna tentatively tapped on the window and gestured to her daughter to open and prop it up. Anna then swung down, caught the ledge, and crawled through the window. All the time, she was wearing nothing but her underwear. Her daughter was embarrassed by this, yet relieved at the rescue.

As the narrator held on to Anna, she realized that something her mother had told her years ago was true: there is time to do many things while falling through the air. While mother and daughter quickly fell through the darkness and into the safety of the fireman's tarp below, the narrator realized she was thinking, noticing the wind, the cold, wondering what might happen if they missed their target. But then she forgot to be afraid and instead felt only the safety of Anna's hands and body wrapped around her, felt her lips on her head, Anna's heartbeat in her ears as she pressed her head into the familiar comfort of her mother's body.

And that is the third time Anna ensured her daughter's existence.

CHARACTERS

Anna Avalon

Anna Avalon is the narrator's mother and the story's protagonist. At the time of the narrator's recollection, Anna is blind, though she was once able to see. Anna is the character who is most fully developed, the one whose history and emotions are explained and provide the meat of the story. Anna is also the character most directly related to the title of the story. A former trapeze artist, it is she who makes the leap that ultimately saves the narrator's life.

Although elderly and blind, Anna is still coordinated and graceful, making her way through a cluttered house without bumping into things or knocking things over. She has kept no mementos of her former life as a circus performer, yet her training has ingrained in her a certain physical precision.

Orphaned as a child, Anna was taken in by the circus and treated as family while being trained on the trapeze. Though illiterate, she had traveled extensively throughout Europe by the time she was a young woman.

Anna's first husband, Harry, was her performing partner as well, and at the time of the accident that killed him, she was seven months pregnant with their daughter. The trauma of the accident was too much for the fetus to withstand, and the baby was born dead and buried near the house in which Anna and the narrator currently live.

Anna eventually learned to read and write, and reading became a major part of her existence. Her inability to read once she went blind is, in fact, what brings the narrator back to her childhood home. Anna needs someone to read to her.

Harry Avalon

Harry (Harold) Avalon was Anna's first husband and performing partner. It was Harry who died in the trapeze accident.

Father

Anna's second husband is the narrator's father, and like the narrator, he remains nameless. He is not a major character in the story, though he is the doctor who took care of Anna after the trapeze accident left her injured and widowed. While she was recuperating, he taught her how to read and write, and the two fell in love and married. When he died, their daughter came home to live with Anna.

Narrator

The reader never learns the name of the narrator, but she is Anna's grown daughter by her second husband. The story is told from her perspective, and she focuses most intently on the background of her mother as well as on the influence her mother had on her.

The narrator has come home to live with Anna, who is now a blind widow and can no longer read on her own. But she does not mind leaving behind her life in the West, for it is a life she considers a failure.

The narrator feels indebted to her mother for ensuring her existence not once, but three times, and that gratitude is the basis for the entire story.

THEMES

Mother-Child Relationships

The entire story is a study of the mother-daughter relationship. The narrator credits her mother with her existence even beyond birth, and through recollection, makes clear the ties that bind them together.

Although she never directly says it, the way the narrator gives voice to her memory reflects an admiration for her mother. In contemplating the trapeze accident that took the life of her mother's first husband, the narrator clearly believes her mother's act of saving herself was the result of intelligent consideration even in the face of danger, rather than a chance event. "As he swept past her on the wrong side she could have grasped his ankle, or the toe-end of his tights, and gone down clutching him. Instead, she changed direction."

The reader sees this admiration again when the narrator discusses how her mother learned to read and write so as to ward off boredom while recuperating in the hospital. But nowhere is the daughter's admiration of her mother more obvious than in her recollection of the rescue. Anna, upon realizing there was no chance of rescue by the firefighters, put aside any embarrassment she might have felt and stripped down to her underwear so that she could climb the maple tree unencumbered.

After making what seems to be an astonishingly difficult leap from the tree to her daughter's window, Anna rescued her, and the duo jumped out the window to the safety of the firefighter's tarp. The narrator, securely wrapped in her mother's

TOPICS FOR FURTHER STUDY

- Write your own short story using imagery and magical realism (a literary genre in which elements that appear to be magic or not possible appear in otherwise realistic situations). Base the story on fact, but feel free to embellish the truth. Read your story to the class. Have your audience give you examples of imagery and magical realism from the story.
- Using a computer software program, draw or paint one of the following scenes from the story: the Flying Avalons' trapeze accident; Anna's rescue of her daughter from the burning house; Anna in the hospital, learning to read and write. Print your artwork and write a caption.
- Louise Erdrich considers herself a storyteller, and this attitude is reflected in her writing style. Research the history of Native American storytelling and write a report on your findings. Assume your readership knows nothing about your topic. Be sure to answer these questions: What, exactly, is Native American storytelling? Why is storytelling important to so many cultures? Is storytelling relevant in today's society? How is storytelling useful to the learner?
- Rewrite "The Leap" from Anna's point of view. Strive to communicate her emotions and feelings of the events.
- Read another short story written by young-adult author Erdrich. Create a T-chart or Venn diagram of the similarities and differences between that story and "The Leap." Remember to consider both style and content when developing your list.
- Read Gabriel Garcia Márquez's short story "A Very Old Man with Enormous Wings." How is this story similar to Erdrich's "The Leap"? What stylistic techniques do they share? Which story do you prefer and why? Discuss your findings with a group of peers.

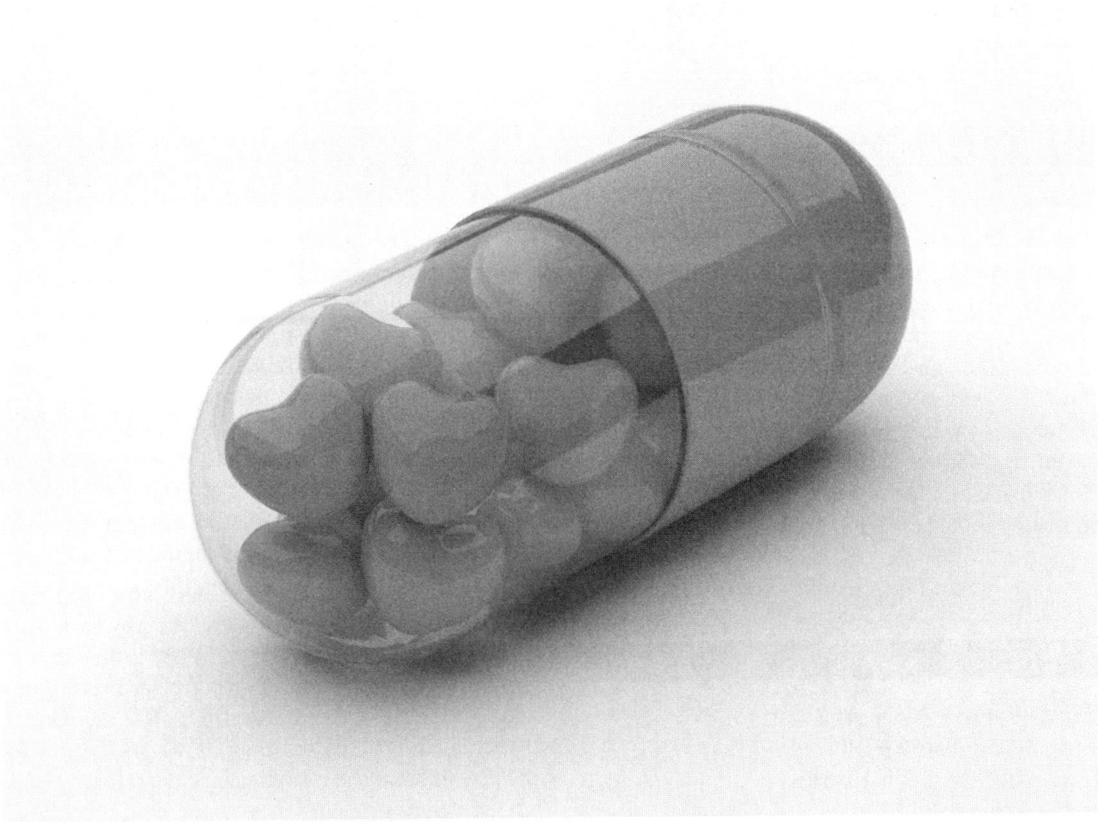

A major theme of Erdrich's works is "love medicine" (Image copyright Harper, 2009. Used under license from Shutterstock.com)

arms, forgot her fear and instead basked in the knowledge that she was out of harm's way.

Love

Aside from the love between the narrator and Anna, Erdrich explores the theme of love through Anna's relationship with Harry Avalon and then her second husband, the narrator's father.

There must be complete and unwavering trust between the Flying Avalons in order for them to perform their act on the flying trapeze. The narrator claims they made a "romantic pair," and although readers never know for certain, it is safe to assume that Anna had known Harry from a very young age, since she was taken in by the Avalons as a child orphan.

Anna and her second husband met as he doctored her after the accident. She regaled him with stories of her travels with the circus, and in return, he taught her to read and write. Having wanted to visit many of the places Anna had traveled, he rewarded her generosity of spirit by giving her a different sort of flying ability than the one he had honed in the Air Force: he gave her the gift of reading, and from that day on, she was never without a book. The two married and had one child, the narrator of the story.

Choice

Everyone must live with the consequences of the choices they make in a lifetime, and Erdrich examines that theme in "The Leap." The narrator has made a choice to leave behind her independent life in the West—admittedly, a failed life—to return home and care for her blind mother. Perhaps she sees this choice as the only logical one since she feels indebted to her mother for her very existence not once but three times.

Anna, if we are to understand how the accident under the circus tent unfolded that day, made the choice not to grab hold of Harry Avalon's foot and crash to her death but to instead turn away from him in the last second of his life so that she might save her own and that of her unborn child. That choice resulted in serious burns on her hands and also in a broken arm, which sent her to the hospital and into the care of a doctor who would eventually marry her.

The consequence of her choice to marry him resulted in the birth of the narrator, and like any parent, Anna spent the rest of her life making choices that affected her daughter. The day she chose to strip almost naked and make a dangerous climb to the window so that she might save her daughter was another choice that would carry consequences. In this case, the narrator's life was saved, and she eventually returns to her childhood home to care for the woman whose life directly and indirectly influenced and molded her own.

STYLE

First-Person Narrator

Erdrich considers herself a storyteller, and so it is fitting that she tells her stories in first person, that is, using the word "I," as if she is talking directly to the reader.

First person is a more personal way of telling a story; it is the technique used when friends talk to one another. In the case of "The Leap," the narrator is recalling a memory, something she experienced first-hand. The nature of any memory is one-sided; so it is with first-person narrative as well. Although the reader is told only one perspective of the memory (the narrator's), it is enough to understand the implications of the events that unfolded.

Had Erdrich chosen a different narrative perspective, the reader would feel as if he were on the outside looking in. With first person, the reader gets to actually walk through the memory and sequence of events with the narrator, allowing for a richer, more involved experience.

Magical Realism

Erdrich rejects the idea that she is a magical realist because she claims that all events in her stories have been documented in one way or another. Magical realism is a literary technique in which unusual or improbable events happen in an otherwise realistic story. There is no denying that "The Leap" includes some magical realism.

One example of this can be found in the second paragraph of the story, when the narrator tells how, when she is sewing in the rebuilt bedroom of her childhood, she hears the crackle and smells the smoke of the fire. "Suddenly, the room goes dark, the stitches burn beneath my fingers, and I am sewing with a needle of hot silver, a thread of fire." Realistically, this could never happen. Yet the narrator never says she feels as if this is what happens; she recounts it as an actual occurrence.

Another example of magical realism is the leap itself, that impossible feat that allowed Anna to save her daughter from certain death in the fire. The branches of that maple tree outside the narrator's bedroom window were covered in ice, making them brittle. And only one limb, its diameter no larger than Anna's wrist, touched the roof. The narrator concedes that even the weight of a squirrel would snap that branch. Yet Anna supposedly used that branch to hurl herself toward the roof, where she hung "by her heels on the new gutter."

By the time this event would have occurred, Anna would have been older, less physically fit. Despite her acrobatic training, there is no way she could have hung from a gutter by her heels, especially since ice covered everything. But the way in which Erdrich tells the tale allows the reader to believe in what she is saying. The narrator believes it, the neighbors *think* they saw it, so it must have happened.

Imagery

As she does in all her writing, Erdrich infuses this story with imagery to help the tale come alive for the reader. In her description of the Flying Avalons, she uses simile when she compares the couple to two sparkling birds as they drop gracefully from the sky in "their glittering, plumed helmets and high-collared capes."

Through imagery, the reader can actually see what causes Harry Avalon's tragic death. "It was while the two were in midair, their hands about to meet, that lightning struck the main pole and sizzled down the guy wires, filling the air with a blue radiance. . . . "

And again, it is eloquent use of imagery that allows the reader to imagine the narrator's sister's gravestone morphing into something it is not: "Somewhere the statue is growing more sharply etched as if, instead of weathering itself into a porous mass, it is hardening on the hillside with each snowfall, perfecting itself."

When used sparingly and in just the right places, imagery draws the reader in and gives a story life.

COMPARE & CONTRAST

- **1990s:** Circuses enjoy a resurgence in popularity as a youth pastime after experiencing a downward trend that began in the 1960s.

  Today: A new type of circus—one that features human skills over animal training and acts—has become the new norm in circus entertainment. It is more commonly known as Cirque du Soleil or Nouveau Cirque. Although this more modern type of circus was founded in the 1940s in Europe, it has only recently gained a following in the United States.

- **1990s:** By the end of the decade, adult children account for 44 percent of all primary family caregivers for a parent age 65 and older.

  Today: Approximately 41 percent of primary family caregivers for a parent age 65 and older are adult children.

- **1990s:** By 1995, 93.6 percent of all U.S. homes report having smoke alarms.

  Today: Approximately 96 percent of all U.S. homes have at least one smoke alarm installed, but just three-fourths of these homes have at least one smoke alarm that is in working condition.

HISTORICAL CONTEXT

Erdrich's Family

By 1990, Louise Erdrich had five children, three her husband had adopted prior to marriage and two biological daughters, both of whom were very young at the time "The Leap" was first published.

Given these circumstances, motherhood and writing were the two endeavors that required most of Erdrich's attention. It is quite possible that the mother-daughter relationship was on her mind often as she watched her young girls in those early, ever-evolving stages of development. Pregnancy itself and mothering a newborn were clearly topics of immediate interest in the early 1990s, as 1995 saw the publication of Erdrich's memoir, *The Blue Jay's Dance: A Birth Year*. This work of nonfiction combines the pregnancies of her three daughters and their early infancies and weaves together their stories so that they seem one cohesive tale. Erdrich analyzes her feelings and emotions along with those of her daughters from a philosophical standpoint, and the memoir reflects the intensity of Erdrich's pregnancy and birthing experiences.

Erdrich's life in the 1990s was all about balancing the role of mother with that of writer. Erdrich has praised her own mother for finding balance. In the 2003 interview with Jeannine Ouellette of *Secrets of the City*, Erdrich explains, "I was the oldest of seven children, and yet my mother made a tremendous effort to preserve a sense of childhood for me, to protect that space and freedom that is unique to childhood."

Erdrich feels a gratitude for her mother's choices, for her willingness to sacrifice her own comfort and desires so that Erdrich could have a childhood of her own without having to take on the burden of maternal duties. Her attitude toward her mother is directly reflected in the narrator's attitude toward Anna in "The Leap." Erdrich has the advantage of being able to write that particular story, at that particular time, from the perspective of a daughter and a mother.

In addition to living a life informed by the newly experienced (as a mother) and influential mother-daughter relationship, Erdrich was dealing with thoughts of death. In *The Blue Jay's Dance*, she does not avoid discussing her own depression and suicidal thoughts, yet it is her husband who eventually committed suicide, just two years after publication of the book. Erdrich has publicly stated that Dorris had suffered from depression since the second year of their marriage. If that is the case, she had been dealing with the theme of

Erdrich's roots help her explore new themes *(Image copyright Tom Antos, 2009. Used under license from Shutterstock.com)*

death in her personal life for nearly a decade by the time she wrote "The Leap."

Writers usually write what they know, and given the timing of the writing and publication of "The Leap," it would seem that the story was influenced more by the author's personal experiences in her life at the time than by any social, political, or cultural factors of the time.

Magical Realism

Although Erdrich's stories are praised for their realism, her novels and short stories also rely heavily on magical realism, a literary technique in which remarkable or extraordinary events occur in an otherwise realistic setting. This is not surprising, given that many Native American stories and myths rely upon magical realism. Erdrich rejects the label of magical realist, however, and claims that even the most unusual events she writes about are based on actual occurrences.

The term "magical realism" was first used by the German art critic Franz Roh in 1925 to describe a style of painting. Today, the term is used most often in relation to literature, and it is a technique used by many authors, particularly those whose native culture includes magical realism in its history and legends. Two of the most well-known writers who fall into this category are Isabel Allende and Gabriel Garcia Márquez, both of whom were born in Latin America.

Some writers and critics believe magical realism is just another term for fantasy fiction. There is a difference, however: In fantasy fiction, much, if not most of a story—plot, setting, characters—is far-fetched or improbable. Magical realism is the interjection of improbable or highly unusual events in an otherwise believable and plausible story.

CRITICAL OVERVIEW

Critical analysis of Erdrich's work since the publication of her first novel has focused almost exclusively on her novels, and primarily on her tetralogy (*Love Medicine*, *The Beet Queen*, *Tracks*, and *The Bingo Palace*). As indicated by Amy Leigh McNally and Piyali Nath Dalal in their Louise Erdrich presentation on the University of Minnesota's Web site *Voices From the Gaps*,

"Critics often make note of her narrative style, her cyclical portrayal of time, her technical writing ability, her use of tragic-comedy, and of the overall cultural significance of her novels."

Erdrich's writing style has been favorably compared to that of literary giant William Faulkner, the Nobel Prize–winning author of dozens of novels and short stories. Joanne Wilkinson of *Booklist* says of Erdrich's short stories in *The Red Convertible*, "Like Faulkner, Erdrich combines a supple, poetic style with a vividly realized setting and unforgettable characters often setting up complex, interlocking narratives."

Because most of her writing involves some aspect of Native American culture and/or characters, Erdrich has become an unintentional voice of the politics of that culture. And while many critics praise her representation for its accuracy, not all are in agreement on that. While Erdrich understands that she has become a political figure to some, she does not consider herself an expert in politics, nor does she use her writing to advance her own personal political viewpoints. In a 2002 interview in the *Progressive*, Erdrich explained to the journalist Mark Anthony Rolo why she writes on the topics and themes that find their way into her stories. "I just want to deepen my understanding of things I've only understood the surface of.... I've only understood anything I've ever written about on this surface level."

One thing all critics can agree upon, and that is that Erdrich is a storyteller above all else. Wilkinson writes of the stories in *The Red Convertible*, "Readers familiar with her novels will be stunned once again by the sheer virtuosity of her storytelling." Erdrich agrees that this is, indeed, her primary role. To Katie Bacon of the *Atlantic*, she explains, "Primarily, though, I am just a storyteller, and I take them [stories] where I find them."

CRITICISM

Rebecca Valentine

Valentine holds a B.A. in English, with an emphasis on literary analysis. In this essay, she argues that Anna, the protagonist of the short story "The Leap," is a quintessential feminist character.

Louise Erdrich is known for developing realistic, well-rounded characters whose emotional evolution is subtle yet unmistakable. Her female characters in particular are flawed yet embody a sense of strength, usually dormant until the character is forced to draw upon it for either emotional or physical survival. In the short story "The Leap," Anna is the quintessential feminist as she works within the confines of a patriarchal society and yet manages to exude a quiet, forceful strength that defines who she is and the quality of life she is willing to accept.

"IN THE SHORT STORY 'THE LEAP,' ANNA IS THE QUINTESSENTIAL FEMINIST AS SHE WORKS WITHIN THE CONFINES OF A PATRIARCHAL SOCIETY AND YET MANAGES TO EXUDE A QUIET, FORCEFUL STRENGTH THAT DEFINES WHO SHE IS AND THE QUALITY OF LIFE SHE IS WILLING TO ACCEPT."

Although Erdrich's story is set in an indeterminate time, she gives the reader hints of a general time frame. We know Anna is elderly at the beginning of the story and that she joined the circus in her early youth. We also know that the Flying Avalons and their circus traveled extensively through Europe before the war. The history of the traveling circus in America tells us that the circus reached its zenith in the years spanning the late nineteenth century through approximately the 1930s. By the time Anna meets her second husband, the narrator's father, she is living in New York, and that is where the circus tragedy takes place. In all likelihood, the war Erdrich mentions is World War II (1939–1945). Anna is still in her childbearing years when she meets her second husband. Another clue as to general time frame comes when the narrator describes Anna's underwear as "a tight bra of the heavy circular-stitched cotton women used to wear and step-in, lace-trimmed drawers." This type of underwear was popular in the 1950s and early 1960s.

If this general time frame is accepted as accurate, a glancing knowledge of circus history is in order to understand the world in which Anna grew up. In her book *The Circus Age: Culture and Society under the American Big Top*, Professor Janet Davis of the University of Texas explores the circus, once the most popular form of entertainment

WHAT DO I READ NEXT?

- *The Birchbark House* (2002) is Erdrich's first young-adult novel and was a finalist for the National Book Award for Young People. The story is told through the eyes of seven-year-old Omakayas, an Ojibwe girl who is the only survivor of a smallpox epidemic in 1847 and is rescued by another Native American family. The book follows Omakayas' life through a cycle of four seasons.
- Michael Dorris's coming-of-age novel *A Yellow Raft in Blue Water* was originally published in 1987 but was reissued as recently as 2003 by Picador. Set in Montana, the story is told in the first person by three generations of Native American women in the same family and explores themes of familial love, consequences of choices, and self-identity.
- Peter Beidler and Gay Barton have provided a valuable analytical tool for students in the revised, 2006 edition of *A Reader's Guide to the Novels of Louise Erdrich.* The book includes a dictionary of characters major and minor, a glossary of Ojibwe words, and discussions of interconnecting themes of all the novels through *The Painted Drum.*
- Larry Smith (of *SMITH* Magazine) and Rachel Fershleiser have compiled a book written exclusively by teens. *I Can't Keep My Own Secrets: Six-Word Memoirs by Teens Famous & Obscure* (2009) is a collection of six-word memoirs that reveal more than one could ever imagine.
- David Lewis Hammerstrom's *Fall of the Big Top: The Vanishing American Circus* (2008) traces the history of the circus from 1793 to the present day. The book includes photographs and in-depth interviews with performers and circus owners.
- Readers who appreciate memoirs may enjoy *Burned Alive: A Victim of the Law of Men* (2004). Palestinian Souad was set on fire at age eighteen because she was pregnant and single, a fact that brought shame on her parents. The honor killing failed, and twenty-five years later, Souad tells her story of life as a female in a remote Palestinian village where women do not count and are not wanted.
- Peter Canning's *Rescue 471: A Paramedic's Stories* (2000) is a memoir of the author's experiences as a medic. Alternately laugh-out-loud funny and wipe-your-tears emotional, Canning captures the daily experience of the life of a rescue worker.

---

in the nation. Davis's knowledge is featured in an article written by Kay Randall on the University of Texas Web site. According to "Under the Big Top," women in the circus in the early 1900s were presented as sex objects, dressed scantily and yet performing incredible feats of strength and agility, such as aerial gymnastics or twirling around on horseback. And yet the promotional materials were more concerned with social norms of the day and emphasized the performer's moral character. According to Davis, the advertisements stressed that "a young lady was traveling under the watchful eye of her father and liked nothing better than to stay home and bake cakes and knit in the evenings."

This near-schizophrenic portrayal of female circus performers would have demanded of them that they dress and behave in a repressed, ultra-feminine manner while at the same time perform with an agility and strength expected in men of that era. Anna lived in a man's world and was presented in a way that focused on sex appeal, yet her livelihood depended upon skill and razor-sharp accuracy. Even in her old age, her daughter describes her as possessing "catlike precision."

And so Anna spent her youth as a young woman trying to fit into a patriarchal mold, looking one way and performing in another. We are told she flirted with and kissed Harry as one half of a "romantic pair" whose lips were "never again to meet." And yet when disaster struck and she had a split second to determine her own fate, Anna had the intelligence and forethought as well as the physical strength to turn away from her ill-fated husband and save her own life. It was a literal as well as a figurative leap, and one that set her on the next leg of her life's journey, in which she would meet her future husband.

Anna's leap resulted in scarred hands and the death of her unborn child. Taken together—and combined with the sudden horrific death of her husband and professional partner—these occurrences must have caused intense physical and emotional trauma and pain, but Anna dealt with them with great inner strength and perseverance. She knew her life with the circus, the only life with the only family she had ever known, was over, and she was faced with the immediate confinement to bed for more than a month. Such forced inactivity would have been difficult for a woman accustomed to consistent thrill and physical activity, but Anna faced her situation with the determination not to let boredom or depression overtake her.

Her antidote to the confinement was to learn to read and write, and it was her future husband who taught her. As he opened up a new world, flightless in the literal sense but full of travel and flight in the figurative sense, Anna took another leap of faith and allowed him into her heart. Falling in love was that second major leap in Anna's life, and it was a risk that a weaker woman, one less sure of herself and her place in the world, would never have taken.

Anna's staunch if unrecognized feminism, already displayed in the saving of her own life and her commitment to bettering herself through literacy, allowed her to choose the setting for the next stage of her life. As an orphan, her life was basically chosen for her. This time, she exerted her own desire and "insisted upon" building a life in a small New Hampshire town, in the rundown farmhouse her husband had inherited. He had not wanted to stay within the confines presented by a rural life, but Anna's new husband loved her enough to agree to her demand, and the couple never left that house or that life.

In what the narrator considers the third time she owes her mother her existence, Anna's determination and ability to think on her feet in times of extreme chaos allowed her to save her daughter's life.

When it became clear to Anna that no fireman or volunteer was going to attempt to rescue her daughter, she instantly took matters into her own hands. When her husband's fumbling fingers could not assist her, she again took action, tearing off her dress to stand nearly naked in front of her neighbors, firefighters, and strangers.

Within seconds, Anna assessed the obstacles and challenges posed by the only possible path of rescue and went about ascending the frozen tree and its fragile branches. After making an impossible leap to the rooftop, Anna hung by her heels and tapped on her daughter's window, a plea to come inside. Despite the dire circumstances, Anna did not pound the windowpane. She did not rap on it. "She tapped on the window ... it was the friendliest tap, a bit tentative, as if she were afraid she had arrived too early at a friend's house." Anna was confident in her mission; she did not need to further frighten her young daughter or add to the drama of the moment. Her self-confidence in her ability to save the girl kept her clear-headed and focused.

As Anna and her daughter wrapped around each other and fell through the air, the narrator realized the truth in something her mother had once told her: you can do many things while falling. And in those few seconds, the narrator had an epiphany: no matter how frenzied or confusing one's life circumstances are at any given moment, fear is only what you make of it. It gets its power from you, and belief in yourself will kill that doubt faster than anything.

Anna started life alone and quite possibly timid. Her formative years were spent under the expectation that she would be strong and demure, appealing yet defiant, sexually inviting yet unavailable. It was a life of appearances and illusion, skill, and precision. In order for her to thrive in that world where others' desires came first, she had to develop an inner fortitude, fueled by courage and nurtured with a sense of self-assurance and confidence. In the face of immeasurable loss and tragedy, Anna's finely honed though subtle feminist attitude—the belief that she was strong and worthy and capable and in control of any situation—allowed her to flourish and thrive, and the last lines of the story indicate she has successfully passed down this idea to her daughter. "Then I forgot fear. I wrapped my hands around my mother's hands.... I heard the beat of her heart in my ears, loud as thunder, long as the roll of drums."

Source: Rebecca Valentine, Critical Essay on "The Leap," in *Short Stories for Students*, Gale, Cengage Learning, 2010.

Louise Erdrich

In the following preface, Erdrich explains her thought process when writing and publishing her stories.

Every time I write a short story, I am certain that I have come to the end. There is no more. I'm finished. But the stories are rarely finished with me. They gather force and weight and complexity. Set whirling, they exert some centrifugal influence. I never plan stories as novels, but it seems that the way I often (but not always) write novels is to begin with stories that I have to believe, every time, that I have finished.

Most of the stories in this volume are those germinal ones that would not let go of me. Some waited many years to make their way into books. Some were first published in magazines. Others stayed in my notebooks until I decided to finish them for this collection and are published here for the first time.

I own a bookstore, or rather, as the drink takes the habitual inebriate, the bookstore owns me. Over the years, the remarkable bookseller who manages the store, Brian Baxter, has insisted that I publish the short stories. When I answer that many of the stories are contained in the novels, he is not satisfied. I like stories as stories, too, so I decided to take his advice.

With the help of my admirable friend Lisa Record, who found and cataloged the stories as they were originally published, I have put together this collection. In almost every case I have not changed the stories from their first incarnations. I tried not to tinker around with them and have edited only when I could not help it, or when, as with "Naked Woman Playing Chopin," the story was cut for length.

As for the new and hitherto unpublished ones, I am certain, as always, they are finished and will remain stories.

I would like to thank the original magazine editors who took a chance on me; my editor, Terry Karten, for her omniscient work on this project; Trent Duffy, as ever and always; and, finally, my parents, Rita Gourneau Erdrich and Ralph Erdrich, who told me stories from the very beginning.

Source: Louise Erdrich, "Author's Preface to *The Red Convertible*," in *The Red Convertible: Selected and New Stories*, Harper Collins, 2009, pp. ix–x.

BEING INDIAN IS SOMETHING WE'RE TERRIBLY PROUD OF. ON THE OTHER HAND, I SUPPOSE THAT IN A GENERAL SENSE I WOULD RATHER THAT NATIVE AMERICAN WRITING BE SEEN AS AMERICAN WRITING, THAT ALL OF THE BEST WRITING OF ANY ETHNIC GROUP HERE WOULD BE INCLUDED IN AMERICAN WRITING."

Sharon White and Glenda Burnside

In the following interview, Erdrich and Dorris discuss the Native American experience and the details of their collaboration as writers.

The Bloomsbury Review: How did you set out to become writers?

Louise Erdrich: I think that we both have always written, really. We kept journals or diaries, wrote poems and that kind of thing, or at least I wrote a lot of poetry before writing fiction. I'm from a small town. I don't think either of us had fantastic educations, but in my family there was an eccentric collection of reading material around all the time—Shakespeare and *Marjorie Morningstar* and Classic Comics.

Michael Dorris: We had *Good Housekeeping* at mine. When I came home from college I used to read all the short stories in *Good Housekeeping* because they were all one bath's worth apiece. We didn't have a shower, so I'd get into the tub and read three short stories and be clean.

TBR: Did you have a traditional upbringing?

LE: It was a very mixed upbringing, an awareness of family on both sides. When I grew up, my mother and father worked for the Bureau of Indian Affairs, and we lived on campus in a small town. It was German and Norwegian, and quite a few people who had Indian backgrounds came down there to work at the school. It was the kind of background you take for granted until you look back and see that there was something really quite different about it.

MD: My background was slightly more schizophrenic. My father died when I was fairly young, and so I spent part of my time living with an extended family on his side and part of my time with my mother's side of the family, which is not Indian. They're from Kentucky. My parents met at a USO dance at Fort Knox during World War II. It was a jolt to go from one family to the other. They were in very different settings, but eventually you resolve such things. I mean, most mixed-blood people have experiences of this type. We're a kind of tribe in and of itself, almost.

TBR: Did you plan early on to go to college and to study writing?

LE: No. Michael didn't either.

MD: No, I didn't. Nobody on either side of my family had ever finished high school, so that was a great aspiration, to graduate. I thought I was going to be a rodeo star, like Rayona in *Yellow Raft*. She got thrown off the horse and won a hard-luck belt buckle, and she persisted in trying to make sense of her life. Me, I went off and took the SAT exam....

TBR: How do you affect each other's writing?

MD: It's hard to draw distinctions, even with such things as plotting, because there's so much give and take. I think Louise was a much more professional writer, more aware of herself as a writer than I was, even though I'd written a couple of books by the time we started working together. But now the process of everything that goes out, from book reviews to magazine articles to novels, is a give and take. I think we're so familiar with each other's critiques and pet peeves that even when the other person isn't actually in the room, he or she is kind of perched on the other's shoulder. I now know, for example, that I often have a tendency to overstate and overexplain, and Louise keeps me honest with that and reminds me that what I'm trying to get at is perfectly clear without beating people over the head with it....

TBR: Who would you say is the more critical of the two of you?

MD: I guess we both are.

LE: I think we're both pretty merciless.

TBR: In your own work, you don't end up kicking each other in the shins when the other one comes along and says, "This is terrible! This doesn't work"?

LE: I think it's harder to be the one who has to say those critical things. You know how hard it is to hear something critical.

MD: You don't want to bump into someone who's on a run, doing something they've finally been able to start, just because one word or sentence seems out of whack.

LE: Michael's very tactful.

TBR: Who—or what—influences your work?

MD: Well, Louise, primarily. I mean, I would not be writing if I were not working with her. Your previous work influences what you're doing. I read Barbara Pym for instruction, and for lots of different things. I don't think for me there's one particular source, except for the fact that I apprenticed with Louise.

TBR: Are the stories you write and the people you write about the ones you grew up with?

LE: No, we invent them out of our own heads. Every so often, though, there's something that comes from something that happened, or is suggested by something that happened.

MD: There are some writers who really do autobiography in the form of novels. We're not like that.

LE: It's not that we haven't tried. It was just so hard, and it turns into something else. That's one reason to admire, say, Philip Roth's novels. They seem to be autobiographical, but if you read what he writes as autobiography, you realize that these are so different and so constructed and invented that it's really a special art to make novels that play with real life.

TBR: So you didn't grow up, say, with people like the characters in Love Medicine.

LE: Not so that you'd recognize anyone. You know, you have to grow up with people who may say the kind of things those characters would say, or with some of those settings—especially the landscapes, which are as accurate as we could make them.

MD: Certainly we grew up in the contexts that we write about, but there is not someone particular who matches this character, someone who matches that character.

TBR: Are you breaking secrets?

MD: Well, we're making up the secrets. We would be violating only our own imaginations. None of our novels is based on real people. They are made of pure, dreamed-up characters and situations.

LE: But one of the oddest and most wonderful things that happens is that someone from a reservation we've never set foot in says, "How did you know that this was the way with my family?" or something like that. It may not be a particular incident, but the way in which the family interacts that reminds them.

MD: I think the greatest secret of all that we violate about Indians is that Indians don't have humor. The one thing that Indian people have said about our books, and the greatest relief to us, is that they find them very funny. Many literary reviewers read *Love Medicine* and saw it as a book about plight and despair and poverty and tragedy, all of which is there too. Many Indian readers saw the survival humor and the kind, odd, self-deprecating humor that Indians have.

LE: Indians have had mainly good responses to our books. Michael says that if people have bad responses, they've been kind enough not to say so.

TBR: How about the critics?

LE: We've been tremendously fortunate. There will always be some bad reviews that stick in your mind forever, but the response has far surpassed anything we could have hoped for.

MD: It's been a pleasant surprise, too, because you write a book in the privacy of your home and your thoughts and your shared feelings, and it all seems so very particular. It's such a surprise, because all of those books now have or soon will have lots of foreign editions, and the thought of people overseas reading them and finding things with which to identify in them is amazing and quite wonderful.

TBR: Do you think of yourselves as Native American writers, or as writers who happen to be Native American who happen to be writing about Native Americans?

LE: I don't know if we've made a decision about that. At least I haven't. Being Indian is something we're terribly proud of. On the other hand, I suppose that in a general sense I would rather that Native American writing be seen as American writing, that all of the best writing of any ethnic group here would be included in American writing. These are university-inspired divisions so that people can have courses and concentrate on certain areas.

MD: James Welch should not be taught only in Native American literature courses. He should be taught in contemporary American and World literature courses. To pigeonhole him is to deny access to him. To lump all Indians into one literary category just because their ancestors were here before the Europeans is hard to justify. . . .

TBR: One of your books is being filmed, isn't it?

MD: A Yellow Raft in Blue Water is optioned for the movies. It has not yet gone into production. The screenwriters wrote *American Graffiti* for George Lucas, as well as a number of other films, and Sidney Pollack optioned it for his production company. There's a long distance between optioning and writing the script and actual production. They have to find the cast and convince themselves that there's an audience for this kind of stuff.

TBR: And that it will make money.

MD: They've "costed it"—there's a whole new vocabulary one has to learn—and it would be a moderately priced film to make. It's just that they're not sure that people want to see movies about Indians in the United States. . . .

TBR: What aspects of your work would you especially like your readers to understand?

MD: Well, there's a political aspect to it that I think is kind of interesting and subtle. We got a wonderful note in a Christmas card from Vine Deloria in which he said that one of the functions of people like us is to remind each successive generation that Indians exist. And he said that it's unfortunate that we, as Indians, rarely get past that thing of just reminding people that we exist. You know, some day we're going to have to deal with this. We certainly don't write polemics; we write about communities of people who happen to be Indians, but in the current political climate—in the past two presidential terms, the amount of money for Indian health care, for welfare and legal expenses has declined dramatically. The number of Indians in college and graduate school has declined because the funding has evaporated. The problems of the one and half million Indians in this country have become abstract to the population at large. If people read what we have written and identify with the characters as people like themselves, people with needs and desires and wants, that's political. That's something that we're very grateful to be able to do.

Source: Sharon White and Glenda Burnside, "On Native Ground: An Interview with Louise Erdrich and Michael Dorris," in *Conversations with Louise Erdrich and Michael Dorris*, edited by Allan Chavkin and Nancy Feyl Chavkin, University Press of Mississippi, 1994, pp. 105–114.

Kay Bonetti

In the following interview with Bonetti, Erdrich explains her origins as a writer, her audience, and her responsibility to write from the Native American point of view.

... *INTERVIEWER: When did you start writing, Louise?*

ERDRICH: I was in college and had failed at everything else. I kept journals and diaries when I was a kid, and I started writing when I was nineteen or twenty. After college I decided that that's absolutely what I wanted to do.

Part of it was that I did not prepare myself for anything else in life. I had different kinds of jobs, here and there, and I kicked around until I finally got some extra money from writing a child's textbook, went to a writer's colony, and then to Dartmouth as a visiting writer. That's where I met Michael. I had known Michael before, but we just kind of faded out of each other's lives for a few years, and then when I came back, we Met. Capital *M*.

INTERVIEWER: You had been writing mostly poetry up to that point, is that right?

ERDRICH: At Johns Hopkins Writing Workshop, and I started writing fiction when I was there because I got encouragement, So I kept doing it, and then I started working on an urban Indian newspaper in Boston—this and that. I didn't really get anywhere until I went to Dartmouth as a visiting writer. Then Michael and I fell in love, married, and started working together. It was like overdrive, or something. I finally began to really get things together....

INTERVIEWER: Who do you see as your reader?

ERDRICH: I don't see one person. I see a real spectrum of people, and it's hard to say now what an ideal reader would be. We've been very lucky in that *Love Medicine* prompted many people to write. We got an enormous amount of mail from people who told stories on themselves, "This is what my life is like," you know. When I see our ideal readers I really see those people. We've had one letter that's pinned up on the wall because it's so beautiful; it's just a beautiful letter, but it wasn't signed. It said "You should be writing, and I'm not going to sign this, because you might take the time to write back."

DORRIS: And if that person is listening, thank you!

INTERVIEWER: Was this person a Native American?

ERDRICH: Are you asking whether our ideal reader is Native American?

INTERVIEWER: I am wondering about that. Do you see yourselves as Native American writers?

ERDRICH: Well, I think it's simply a fact, but I don't think it's right to put everything off in a separate category. All of the ethnic writing done in the United States is American writing, and should be called American writing.

INTERVIEWER: There is an impulse out of which some writers do write, which is to say, "I'm writing for a black audience, I'm writing for a Native American audience, I'm writing for a Chicano audience." I gather that in your case this really could not be true.

DORRIS: I think we are writing because the stories are interesting to us. We try and tell them as real as we can. We'd be terribly worried if Indians hated the books; it would tell us that we were doing something very wrong....

INTERVIEWER: In the New York Times *you mentioned that Native Americans have to write after the fact about the broken circle, the holocaust, the loss. I wonder how this applies here.*

ERDRICH: I think both of us feel, in writing from our background, that we're really spurred by this feeling that we have to tell the story. When both of us look backward we see not only the happiness of immigrants coming to this country, which is part of our background, but we see and are devoted to telling about the lines of people that we see stretching back, breaking, surviving, somehow, somehow, and incredibly, culminating in somebody who can tell a story. I think all Native Americans living today probably look back and think, "How, out of the millions and millions of people who were here in the beginning, the very few who survived into the 1920s, and the people who are alive today with some sense of their own tradition, how did it get to be me, and why?" And I think that quest and that impossibility really drives us in a lot of ways. It's central to the work, and so as we go about telling these stories, we feel compelled. We're, in a way, survivors of that tradition; there aren't a lot of people who are going to tell these stories, or who are going to look at the world in this particular way.

Source: Kay Bonetti, "Louise Erdrich and Michael Dorris: A Marriage of Minds", in *Conversations with American Novelists: The Best Interviews from the Missouri Review and the American Audio Press Library*, edited by Kay Bonetti, Greg Michaelson, Speer Morgan, Jo Sapp, and Sam Showers, University of Missouri Press, 1997, pp. 78–91.

SOURCES

"Adult Children: The Likelihood of Providing Care for an Older Parent," in *Georgetown University, Center for an Aging Society*, No. 2, May 2005, http://ihcrp.georgetown.edu/agingsociety/pdfs/CAREGIVERS2.pdf (accessed October 16, 2009).

Avery, Laura, ed., "Louise Erdrich," in *Newsmakers*, Thomson Gale, 2005.

Bacon, Katie, "An Emissary of the Between-World," in *Atlantic*, January 17, 2001, http://www.theatlantic.com/doc/200101u/int2001-01-17 (accessed October 18, 2009).

Davis, Janet, "Under the Big Top: History of Circus Is a Mirror of American Society," in *University of Texas*, 2003, http://www.utexas.edu/features/archive/2003/circus.html (accessed on October 18, 2009).

Erdrich, Louise, "The Leap," in *Harper's*, March 1990, pp. 65–68.

Erdrich, Louise, "The Leap," in *The Red Convertible: Selected and New Stories, 1978–2008*, HarperCollins, 2009, pp. 205–212.

"Fire Safety and Burn Injury Statistics," in *Children's Hospital, Boston*, http://www.childrenshospital.org/az/Site903/mainpageS903P0.html (accessed October 15, 2009).

McNally, Amy Leigh, and Piyali Nath Dalal, "Louise Erdrich: Biography and Criticism," in *University of Minnesota: Voices from the Gaps*, 1999, http://voices.cla.umn.edu/artistpages/erdrichLouise.php (accessed October 14, 2009).

Ouellette, Jeannine, "Louise Erdrich—The Rakish Interview," in *Secrets of the City*, February 21, 2003, http://archives.secretsofthecity.com/magazine/reporting/features/louise-erdrich-rakish-interview (accessed October 16, 2009).

Rolo, Mark Anthony, "Louise Erdrich—The Progressive Interview," in *Progressive*, April 1, 2002, http://www.accessmylibrary.com/coms2/summary_0286-25258514_ITM (accessed October 18, 2009).

"Selected Caregiver Statistics," in *Family Caregiver Alliance*, http://www.caregiver.org/caregiver/jsp/content_node.jsp?nodeid=439 (accessed October 16, 2009).

Wilkinson, Joanne, Review of *The Red Convertible: Selected and New Stories: 1978–2008*, in *Booklist*, Vol. 105, No. 6, November 15, 2008, p 5.

FURTHER READING

Alexie, Sherman, *War Dances*, Grove Press, 2009.

National Book Award winner Alexie's collection of tragicomic short stories provides an introspective into the balance of self-preservation and responsibility. His characters face mundane as well as life-changing choices as they grapple with death, hate, and love. Alexie is one of the twenty-first century's most highly praised Native American writers.

Chavkin, Allan, and Nancy Feyl Chavkin, *Conversations with Louise Erdrich and Michael Dorris*, University Press of Mississippi, 1994.

This volume contains twenty-five interviews with the two authors, conducted both separately and together. Published three years prior to Dorris's suicide, the book explores the collaborative writing process used by the duo, and readers are given a glimpse into how the professional influenced the personal aspect of their lives.

Erdrich, Louise, *Original Fire: Selected and New Poems*, HarperCollins, 2003.

Erdrich's poems often reflect the same themes and writing styles as her novels. This title is her third book of poetry and the first collection of her poetry to be published in fourteen years.

King, Thomas, *The Truth about Stories: A Native Narrative*, University of Minnesota Press, 2005.

English professor and novelist King explores the ways in which stories and their telling inform an individual's and a society's perception of people and how to interact with them. The narratives covered by King are largely Native American.

Kingsolver, Barbara, *Animal Dreams*, HarperCollins, 1990.

Fans of Erdrich often enjoy the novels of Barbara Kingsolver as well because of similar themes and the fact that both realistically address Native American culture. Kingsolver's characters are well developed, and this novel includes Native American legends as it weaves a tapestry of suspense, politics, love, and the quest for self-identity.

O'Nan, Stewart, *The Circus Fire: A True Story of an American Tragedy*, Doubleday, 2000.

On July 6, 1944, 167 people were killed when the big top of the Ringling Bros. circus caught fire during an afternoon performance in Hartford, Connecticut. Fifty years later, O'Nan moved to the town and found its residents still haunted by the tragic event. Painstaking research and photos make for a vivid, minute-by-minute account of the heartbreaking accident.

Love Must Not Be Forgotten

ZHANG JIE

1979

In Zhang Jie's "Love Must Not Be Forgotten," a woman discovers her deceased mother's diary and, along with it, a romantic secret from her mother's past. The narrator, who is debating whether or not to marry, learns that her mother had long been in love with a married man. As a child of divorced parents, the narrator is naturally concerned with making the right choice in terms of potential husbands. Her decision is complicated by the cultural atmosphere in communist China during the 1970s, when marriage is considered in terms of duty and tradition. It is a practical matter rather than something related to feelings of love or romance. The story is concerned primarily with the mother's relationship with the man she loves, as it is described in the mother's diary. The relationship between mother and daughter is explored more subtly. Through these bonds, Zhang explores themes of duty, integrity, and the nature of love. The work is often studied using feminist and political ideas, as Zhang advocates a woman's right to love whom she wants to love and the right to remain unwed despite the cultural and political pressures to marry. These pressures were suffocating during the time period when Zhang was writing, and modern Western readers should understand how strong they could be. Zhang was heavily criticized for undermining the moral values that her socialist government advocated through the exploration of love and marriage that she undertakes in "Love Must Not Be Forgotten."

In 1981 her novel *Leaden Wings* was published in China (translated into English in 1987). "Love Must Not Be Forgotten" was originally published in Chinese in 1979 in a collection of stories by the same name. The collection was translated by Gladys Yang and published in 1986 by China Books.

AUTHOR BIOGRAPHY

Zhang Jie was born in 1937. (In China, the family name or surname is listed first, followed by the given name. Zhang Jie's family would call her "Jie." When her work is discussed by critics, she is referred to her by her surname, Zhang.) Zhang's parents separated during China's anti-Japanese war (1931–1945). Zhang was subsequently raised by her mother, a school teacher, in a village in Liaoning province. The province was at the time known as Manchuria, and Zhang's mother was by birth Manchurian royalty. Her family, however, had been impoverished by the ongoing war with Japan and by China's own internal revolts. As a child, Zhang fled with her mother during the invasion of the Japanese Imperial Army, first seeking refuge in the mountains of the Shanxi province and then in Henan province in south-central China. When Zhang was eighteen years old, she entered the People's University in Beijing and was assigned to the study of economics. Zhang graduated in 1960. Zheng then began work as a statistician, a post to which she was assigned by the government, in the Ministry of Machine Building. Her mother joined her in Beijing. Zhang married a colleague from work, and the couple had a daughter in 1963. Mao Zedong, first the chairman of the Communist Party of China and then the chairman of the People's Republic of China, instituted the Socialist Education Movement in 1964, in an attempt to purify the theory and practice of socialism in China. Not long after, Chairman Mao instituted the Cultural Revolution in China, which lasted from 1966 through 1976. These years represented Mao's attempts to eliminate any threats to his vision of a classless communist China. Incorporated into Mao's Cultural Revolution was the idea that traditional Chinese and foreign art and culture must be eliminated due to the threat they posed to Mao's view of China. In pursuit of his goal, Mao authorized the death and imprisonment of countless individuals. It was during this time that Zhang was forced to work on a farm in the province of Jiangxi. For four years, Zhang was separated from her mother and daughter. She then was allowed to return to her work in Beijing. After Mao's death in 1976 and the rise to power of a leader who promised a more liberal approach to government (Deng Xiaoping), Zhang began writing. She published the volume *Love Must Not Be Forgotten* in 1979 in China; the English translation appeared in 1986. In the preface to the English translation of *Love Must Not Be Forgotten* and in subsequent reviews, critics cite Zhang's own divorce, although a date is not given, nor does Zhang provide one in interviews. Since the publication of this volume of short fiction, Zhang has continued to write award-winning novels. In 1992, the American Academy of Arts and Letters elected Zhang an honorary fellow. In 2006, she published the novel *The Painting of Z*.

Note: Communism and socialism are both referred to frequently in discussions concerning People's Republic of China. Both ideologies (systems of thought and sets of beliefs) are based on the notion of a society in which the classes are equal, a society in which there are no poor, middle, and wealthy classes. In such a society, everyone has equal access to things that the poor and the lower end of the middle class, sometimes called the working class, are often unable to obtain, such as a proper education, medical care, and necessities such as food and shelter. The difference between the two systems of thought lies in the notion of ownership. Under socialism, the government owns industries and administers various services to society, whereas under communism, the people themselves own and operate and distribute goods and services equally among members of society. Socialism is sometimes regarded as a stepping stone on the path to a true communist society, the ultimate goal of socialism.

PLOT SUMMARY

In Zhang's "Love Must Not Be Forgotten," the narrator is a thirty-year-old woman contemplating marriage. Shanshan, the narrator, describes her suitor Qiao Lin as handsome but quiet. Unable to discern whether his silence derives from a contemplative nature, which makes him reluctant to speak, or from the fact that he simply has nothing to say, Shanshan asks his opinion regarding various topics and in reply receives childlike, one-word answers. Qiao Lin similarly has a simplistic answer to Shanshan's question about why he loves her. Thinking a long while before responding, Qiao Lin tells Shanshan that he loves her because she is "good." Shanshan's reply is respectful, but her emotional response is a sense of loneliness and disappointment. She wishes for a bond stronger than the legal, moral one most people in her society accept as a typical marriage.

In contemplating her society's view of marriage, Shanshan thinks of her mother, wondering what her mother would have thought about Shanshan's ambivalence about marrying Qiao Lin. As Shanshan recalls, in the days before her death, Shanshan's mother advised her not to leap into marriage to a man she is uncertain about. In this remembered conversation, Shanshan expresses her fear that there is no "right man" for her. Shanshan's mother wants her daughter to be happily married but fears that Shanshan may never meet someone with whom she could be happy. Shanshan points out that her mother has done well enough without a husband. Mother and daughter then discuss how Shanshan's mother never loved Shanshan's father. Thinking of how her father left when she was quite small, Shanshan wishes her mother had remarried and wonders why she never did.

Shanshan's thoughts lead her to her mother's dying wish, that a set of prized books by Anton Chekhov and her diary, which she had titled *Love Must Not Be Forgotten*, be cremated with her after her death. Shanshan keeps the diary and begins to read it, discovering that for more than twenty years, her mother loved a man who was married to someone else. The diary reveals that Shanshan's mother, who is named Zhong Yu, and this man were colleagues and that the man used to do secret work for the Communist Party in Shanghai. When an older man died in order to keep the man's secret, Zhong Yu's lover married the older man's daughter out of his "sense of duty, of gratitude to the dead and deep class feeling."

Shanshan tries to remember whether she has ever met the man and recalls a spring night during her childhood when her mother and she attended a concert. A black limousine had stopped and an elderly gentleman got out and addressed her mother. In this memory, the young Shanshan feels the tension between the two adults; her mother's hand grows cold. The man's hand is freezing as well when he extends it to shake Shanshan's hand. Zhong Yu says little to the man. Instead, the man does most of the talking. He speaks with Shanshan, reminding her of a time when he saw her as a very young child. He then addresses Shanshan's mother, who is a writer, and mentions one of her stories in which Zhong Yu has "condemned the heroine." The man chastises Zhong Yu, telling her, "There is nothing wrong with falling in love, as long as you don't spoil someone else's life." Moments later, the man is asked by a police officer to have the limousine moved. After bidding Shanshan and her mother goodbye, the man departs to endure the lecture of the policeman.

Shanshan, once again in the present, begins to realize what this man meant to her mother. Shanshan sees that her mother was utterly devoted to loving the man, even though she could never have a relationship with him. Studying the diary, Shanshan determines that the man died several years after the incident with the limousine. Her mother's hair went all white that year. Shanshan guesses that the man's death was related to the Cultural Revolution, that the man probably had criticized government oppression, and that "because of the conditions then" her mother's diary became vague. As Shanshan reads on, she becomes amazed that her mother continued to love the man so long after his death. Several paragraphs from the diary are recounted, in which Zhong Yu speaks of her longing and of how their love for one another remained hidden, despite the anguish they both felt.

The story ends with Shanshan questioning her society's views on marriage. She states her opposition to the notion that by choosing not to marry, one's "behavior is considered a direct challenge" to "the old ideas handed down from the past." Shanshan longs for a society in which one may freely wait for the right person to marry, and she argues that making such a cultural shift would "be a sign of a step forward in culture, education and the quality of life."

CHARACTERS

Qiao Lin

Qiao Lin is the suitor (boyfriend) of Shanshan, the narrator of "Love Must Not Be Forgotten." He is described as extremely handsome. Shanshan has known him for about two years. Qiao Lin is quiet, so much so that Shanshan suspects he is either not particularly intelligent, a suspicion that remains after she attempts to ascertain Qiao Lin's opinions on various subjects. Contemplating married life with Qiao Lin, Shanshan wonders whether they will be able to consummate their marriage, considering that they lack a strong romantic connection. Despite his good looks and his earnest, innocent nature, which Shanshan reveals when she twice describes him as a child, Qiao Lin is not a man whom Shanshan is able to envision herself loving.

Shanshan

Shanshan is the main character of "Love Must Not Be Forgotten." She narrates the story and introduces its other characters. Shanshan, who is thirty and considering marriage to the handsome but otherwise uninteresting Qiao Lin, reveals her sarcastic nature in the opening lines of the story when she compares her age to that of the People's Republic of China, thirty. (At the end of a civil war in China, Mao Zedong and the Communist Party took over control of the government and declared that the nation was now the People's Republic of China. It is this 1949 establishment of the People's Republic to which Shanshan refers. The story, therefore, takes place in 1979, the year the Republic, and Shanshan, would be thirty years old.) Her wit comes into play when Shanshan observes that "for a republic thirty is still young. But a girl of thirty is virtually on the shelf." In Shanshan's culture, a thirty-year-old woman would not typically question whether or not to marry a handsome man she has known for two years, when there is no obstacle to the marriage. She is aware that people find her hesitancy about her possible marriage to Qiao Lin "preposterous." Her humorous nature is revealed once again when she describes her boyfriend's reticence and her application of a "small intelligence test" in order to determine the source of his apparent distaste for talking. As Shanshan describes Qiao Lin, he does not come off very well after these tests. Wondering, however, whether the problem really lies within herself, in her habit of persistently worrying about things that do not bother anyone else, Shanshan describes a typical Chinese marriage as "a form of barter or a business transaction in which love and marriage can be separated." She questions what it is within herself that refuses to accept such an arrangement. Indirectly answering her own question, Shanshan thinks of her mother and her mother's advice to not marry if she is uncertain about what she wants. The rest of the story is concerned with Shanshan's developing understanding of her mother, who is now deceased, after she reads her mother's diary. Shanshan's reluctance to marry Qiao Lin is put into a new perspective after Shanshan learns of her mother's love for a man she could never have. Having witnessed on paper, and then again, through memories that her mother's diary calls to mind, the love her mother felt for the man, Shanshan doubts that a man will ever love her in that way, "to the exclusion of anybody else." In the end, the diary brings Shanshan closer to knowing her mother in a new way, as a woman with her own secrets. Still, she claims that she does not wish to follow in her mother's path. Although she may desire to experience love as deeply as her mother did, the story confirms her belief that loveless marriages should be avoided, so that tragedies like that of her mother and her mother's lover can be prevented. Shanshan would rather "wait patiently" for the right person, and feels that being single indefinitely "is not such a fearful disaster."

Zhong Yu

Zhong Yu is Shanshan's mother. At the time the story takes place, Zhong Yu is dead. Through Shanshan's memories and Zhong Yu's diary, however, Zhong Yu operates in "Love Must Not Be Forgotten" as a significant and influential character. Shanshan recalls a time when she and her mother discussed the topic of marriage, a conversation in which Zhong Yu suggested it was better for Shanshan to be alone than to marry someone who was not right for her. In the course of this conversation, Zhong Yu stated that because of her ignorance about what she wanted in life, she married someone she did not love (Shanshan's father). Shanshan's other recollections reveal that Zhong Yu never married after she and Shanshan's father divorced, that she was a writer, and that she cherished a twenty-seven-volume set of stories by the Russian writer Anton Chekhov. Zhong Yu had asked Shanshan to cremate the diary and the Chekhov books with her when she died. As Shanshan reads these books, she begins to understand their importance to her mother. She realizes they must have been a gift from the man she loved. This, Shanshan begins to comprehend, is why her mother read something from the books every day, and why if Shanshan entered the room to find her mother staring at the books, Zhong Yu "either spilt her tea or blushed like a girl discovered with her lover."

Shanshan remembers that Zhong Yu could not even make eye contact with the man when he saw

Shanshan and Zhong Yu on the street. Shanshan recalls how upset her mother was when the policeman scolded the man who had approached them. The diary further reveals that the man died some years later. In her diary, Zhong Yu wrote about how she never forgot her lover; in fact, she addressed her writing to him as if he were still alive, describing how her love actually continued to grow. Zhong Yu's words further reveal her sense of torment at not being able to be with him, and she wonders whether anyone could possibly believe that with this depth of feeling and years of loving, she and the man "never once even clasped hands." Shanshan describes the last of Zhong Yu's diary entries, in which Zhong Yu states her wish that heaven existed and her belief that somehow the two of them (Zhong Yu and her lover) would "be together for eternity."

Zhong Yu's Lover

Zhong Yu's lover is not named directly. Shanshan suspects that her mother's lover is the man whom she remembers meeting when she and her mother went out one evening. Shanshan learns through the diary that the man felt compelled by duty and gratitude to marry someone else, the daughter of someone who had saved his life for the political cause for which he had fought and for which the dead man had sacrificed his life. Shanshan remembers that a limousine once pulled up near where Shanshan and her mother were walking. A white-haired, distinguished-looking man stepped out, and Shanshan felt her mother's hand tremble and grow cold. The man compared Shanshan favorably to her mother and spoke to her briefly about seeing her when she was little. Turning to Shanshan's mother, the man critiqued a story she had written. After insisting that she had judged the story's heroine too harshly, the man told her "the hero might have loved her too. Only for the sake of a third person's happiness, they had to renounce their love." Shanshan, looking back, knows it is for this strength, this ability to respect the other people involved, that her mother loved the man. Shanshan also understands that it was he who had given her mother the set of Chekhov novels she cherished. In the diary, Shanshan learns that the man died during the Cultural Revolution. Her mother reveals, through her writing about the man, that he held fast to his political beliefs even though they cost him his life.

THEMES

Marriage

According to Shanshan, marriage as it exists in the People's Republic of China in the 1970s is typically a simple business arrangement. Love rarely factors in, and marriage and procreation are necessary duties to be performed. Shanshan sums up the Chinese view of marriage by saying that it is focused on "law and morality." However, she craves a "stronger bond." She understands that she will be judged harshly by her society if she does not marry. She suspects that her reputation will be ruined and that people will make assumptions about her political beliefs. Before the death of her mother, Shanshan discussed her relationship with Qiao Lin with her mother. Shanshan's mother, herself divorced, advises Shanshan to wait until she knows what she wants to be happy, but she fears that Shanshan may not meet the right man. Shanshan thinks her mother sounds bitter about having married because she was talked into it before she knew what she wanted. In summarizing her own views on marriage, Zhong Yu states that she is a "wretched idealist." Zhong Yu does not elaborate on this point. Through the course of the story, though, Shanshan discovers what hasty marriages have done to Zhong Yu and her idealism. Having discovered what she believed to be true love, Zhong Yu figured out what she wanted—or rather whom she wanted—but it was too late. He was married to someone else, and she too had married, only to be divorced not long after. This is why she describes herself as both "wretched" and an "idealist"; she was an idealist because she believed in the notion of true love, but she felt wretched because hasty marriages to the wrong people had thwarted her chances of transforming the notion of love into the reality of a loving marriage. Shanshan speaks to this point at the story's end. If people had the freedom (from society's pressures) to wait until they met their ideal partners "instead of rushing into marriage, how many tragedies could be averted!" Shanshan exclaims.

Love

In "Love Must Not Be Forgotten," Zhang depicts a world in which love is often excluded from marriage. Shanshan's parents existed in such a marriage, at least on Zhong Yu's side. Shanshan speculates that in Chinese culture, marriage is

TOPICS FOR FURTHER STUDY

- Zhang has lived her life in a country shaped by communism. Communism in China, as both an ideology and a movement, was based on the ideas of the German philosopher Karl Marx. Marx, along with Friedrich Engels, wrote *The Communist Manifesto*, which was published in German in 1848. In practice, communism is often transformed greatly from the ideas Marx espoused. Using online and print sources, research Marx's original philosophy of communism. What were his aims in writing the manifesto? How did he hope to influence the socialist groups already in existence throughout Europe? What immediate impact did his work have on the politics of Europe? Present your findings in a format of your choosing, such as a written report, a Web page with links to sources and additional resources, or a PowerPoint presentation.
- Zhang's "Love Must Not Be Forgotten" is concerned with marriage and divorce in China in the late 1970s. Undertake a sociological look at such issues by comparing the attitudes of the Chinese toward marriage and divorce with those of Americans. Focus your study on either the time period in which the story was written (the late 1970s) or today. Look at statistics such as marriage and divorce rates. Search out reports in journals and newspapers, such as Seth Faison's August 22, 1995, article in the *New York Times*, "In China, Rapid Social Changes Bring a Surge in the Divorce Rate," in which Faison discusses Chinese and American divorce rates in the 1970s, or studies such as Weiyan Farmer's "Attitudes toward Marriage and Divorce in Modern China," which appears in *Between Generations: Family Models, Myths & Memories*, published in 2005 and edited by Daniel Bertaux and Paul Thompson. Compile your findings in a written report or a PowerPoint presentation. Be sure to cite all of your sources.
- Zhang's fiction was written during a time of the transformation of the Communist Party in China from a party of violence and oppression to one intended to be more open to progress. Ana Vecian-Suarez's young-adult novel *Flight to Freedom* has some similarities in structure and theme to Zhang's "Love Must Not Be Forgotten." Both stories are told by a first-person narrator, use the literary device of a diary, and are set against a backdrop of Communist oppression. Zhong Yu in Zhang's story endured much suffering, while the thirteen-year-old Yara Garcia and her family in Vecian-Suarez's novel are attempting to flee Communist Cuba. Read Vecian-Suarez's novel and compare it with Zhang's story. What other similarities do the stories possesses? What are the characters' attitudes toward communism in both stories? How do the authors portray their native countries? In a book group, discuss such issues and prepare a presentation to the class on your comparison of the two works.
- Zhang uses the literary device of the diary to explore Zhong Yu's experiences more fully than Shanshan's memories allow. Write your own short story in which you make use of a diary. Imagine that Shanshan has discovered not her mother's diary, but her boyfriend's diary or that of her mother's lover. Alternatively, put yourself in Shanshan's position and imagine that you have discovered the diary of one of your parents. In either case, you will be writing from the first-person perspective for two characters—the character telling the story and the character whose diary is discovered. Share your story by reading it aloud to the class, posting it on a Web page that your classmates can access, or playing an audio or video recording of yourself reading it aloud.

A young Asian couple in love *(Image copyright Grafica, 2009. Used under license from Shutterstock.com)*

about many things—business, duty, tradition—but seldom is it about love. Out of love for a man married to someone else, Zhong Yu never seeks a relationship again and instead clings to a love she cannot have. She treats objects such as the Chekhov books and her diary as stand-ins for her lover. She reenacts the "single stroll" she and her lover shared, and she admits that they never so much as held hands. The connection between Zhang Yu and her lover is depicted as an ideal form of love attained in the heart and mind but never allowed to blossom into a true relationship involving communication and contact. Rightly or wrongly, Shanshan assumes that having attained "undying love," her mother must have "obviously died happy." Shanshan's response to this notion of love is to regard it as a tragedy to be mourned but not emulated. She does not wish to follow down this path, and she seems prepared to embrace the idea of waiting alone rather than risk marrying the wrong man when there is still a possibility of meeting the right one. Shanshan appears to still long for the idealized notion of love that she perceives from her mother's diary. What she rejects is the idea of "an indifferent marriage" and the suffering it would inevitably entail.

Political Ideologies

An undercurrent of political tension runs through "Love Must Not Be Forgotten." Communism as an ideology serves as a backdrop for the action of the story. It is introduced in Shanshan's opening thoughts, when she compares her age to that of the People's Republic. Initially, Shanshan refers to marriage as a type of business transaction and believes that this the typical way of viewing marriage. At first, it is tied to tradition, not politics. Later, at the end of the story, Shanshan more vigorously unites her culture's view of marriage with politics. She states that not marrying is considered a "direct challenge" to traditional ideas and that if one does not marry, accusations of "having made political mistakes" will be made. One's reputation will be maligned by "endless vulgar and futile charges." Communism is referred to in relation to the man Shanshan's mother loves as well. Shanshan notes that during the 1930s, the man "was doing underground work for the Party in Shanghai." So entrenched was the man in his work with the Party that another man died to protect him. The man's marriage to his comrade's daughter (a comrade is a fellow believer in the communist or socialist ideology) is in part due to his sense of connection and loyalty to the deceased man as a fellow Communist. After Shanshan recalls meeting the man in the street when she was younger, in 1962, she realizes now how the man's "firm political convictions, his narrow escapes from death in the revolution" contributed to the way Shanshan's mother must have worshipped him. As Shanshan reads on, she finds that the man did die in the Cultural Revolution, probably in 1969. Shanshan believes, on the basis of her mother's account, that the man was killed for questioning the government's methods. However, the man kept his beliefs and, according to Shanshan's mother, clung to his Marxist ideals to the end.

STYLE

First-Person Narrator and Present Tense

A first-person narrative is one in which the person telling the story refers to himself or herself as *I*. In "Love Must Not Be Forgotten," the first-person narrator happens to be the main character in the story, Shanshan, although this is not always the case in stories narrated in the first person. Shanshan tells her story in the present tense, as if she is talking to the reader at the present moment. For example, at the beginning of the story, Shanshan announces, "I am thirty." If Shanshan told her story in the past tense, as if it were a recollection of what had already occurred, she might have said, "I was thirty years old at the time." "Love Must Not Be Forgotten" contains recollections of past time periods, and Shanshan, from her present perspective, describes these periods in the past tense. In the end, she returns to the present moment and her present thoughts. First-person narration is often chosen by authors because it allows them to fully explore and convey one character's thoughts and motivations. This type of narration does restrict the author's ability to depict the thoughts of other characters; everything must be presented from the first-person narrator's perspective, unless the author chooses to create an omniscient (all-knowing) first-person narrator who is not a participant in the story. In longer works of fiction, authors sometimes use the first-person narrative technique but alternate between various characters' perspectives. In "Love Must Not Be Forgotten," Zhang uses first-person narration and maintains a single point-of-view character (the character from whose perspective the story is being told). However, by allowing that character (Shanshan) access to a diary, Zhang enables another first-person perspective (that of Shanshan's mother) to be voiced.

Diary as Literary Device

A literary device is a tool the author uses to accomplish a narrative task. In "Love Must Not Be Forgotten," the author, Zhang, uses the diary of Shanshan's mother to provide Shanshan with access to information she would not otherwise have about her mother and her mother's lover. The diary also allows Shanshan's mother, Zhong Yu, to speak at length in her own voice. Within Zhang's otherwise first-person narrative, Zhong Yu is presented to the reader only through the filter of Shanshan's memory. The recurring use of the diary device offers the reader a direct view of Zhong Yu's thoughts and feelings. In this way, Zhang avoids the major limitation of utilizing first-person narration.

Some scholars, such as Judith Farquhar in her 2002 *Appetites: Food and Sex in Post-Socialist China*, have described Shanshan's personal story as a framing device for her mother's story as told in the diary. A frame narrative is one in which an introductory story provides the basis or introduction for another story. The inner story is told within the boundaries of the outer, or frame, story. In "Love Must Not Be Forgotten," the intermingling of Shanshan's own thoughts and memories with her reading of the diary creates a situation in which Shanshan's story and that of her mother are intertwined, so much so that one cannot truly be viewed as a frame for the other in the traditional sense.

HISTORICAL CONTEXT

Mao Zedong and the Cultural Revolution

Under the leadership of Mao Zedong, the Communist Party of the People's Republic of China in 1966 commenced a political campaign designed to protect and consolidate Mao's power and eliminate any threat posed by dissenters and enemies. Artists, academics, and intellectuals were accused of being elitists, and their works were destroyed and banned. Mao called for the destruction of the bourgeois (upper-middle-class) elements of society, and he focused his attention on young

COMPARE & CONTRAST

- **1970s:** In the aftermath of the Cultural Revolution (1966–1976), Chinese writing begins to focus on personal, private lives, a reaction against the Cultural Revolution's de-emphasizing of the individual in favor of the larger society. As the communist goals of the nation are reexamined by the country's leaders, writers are now free to explore their craft rather than glorify the party. Works in this more personal vein include fiction by Zhang Jie and Zhang Kangkang, which focus on love and marriage, and nonfiction autobiographical essays by, for example, Chinese doctors.

  Today: In 2009, China celebrates the sixtieth anniversary of the establishment of the Communist Party of the People's Republic of China. Modern Chinese fiction writers are free to embrace a variety of genres and themes. Short fiction is an increasingly popular form. Anthologized writers of short fiction include Chi Zijian, Liu Xinwu, and Yuan Yaqin.

- **1970s:** Deng Xiaoping becomes the chairman of the People's Republic of China in 1977. Under his rule, the Chinese government reverses some of the more oppressive regulations instituted under Mao Zedong during the Cultural Revolution. Nevertheless, restrictions involving the personal lives of Chinese citizens are still a part of daily life, as evidenced by the 1979 implementation of a policy that restricted families to only having one child.

  Today: China, ruled by President Hu Jintao and Premier Wen Jiabao, is still criticized for repressive policies. The one-child policy remains in place in China, having been renewed through at least 2010. Because of China's one-child policy, the administration of U.S. president Barack Obama is criticized for supporting the United Nations Population Fund, an organization representing more than 140 countries, including China. Critics claim that the Chinese government uses coercion to force citizens to comply with the policy.

- **1970s:** Marriage is regarded as a duty and is viewed within the context of upholding traditional Chinese values. Women who remain single are ostracized and criticized, and their political ideology is called into question. The divorce rate in the People's Republic of China is just under 4 percent in 1979, and divorce in general is something most people do not consider lightly.

  Today: Since 2003, when the Chinese government implemented a streamlined process for obtaining a divorce, the number of divorces has increased, according to a 2005 *New York Times* article. The divorce rate in 2005 is approximately 19 percent. Changing views of marriage make women more comfortable seeking a divorce. A 2009 article on Chinese society in *Global Times* indicates that younger couples who divorce typically do so after only one or two years of marriage, citing a hasty marriage or infidelity as the primary reason for the divorce.

---

people. He created the Red Guard. High school students who supported his extreme views and were encouraged to challenge teachers and government officials. Radical supporters of Mao tortured and abused those suspected of dissent. As the chaotic environment intensified, Mao ordered China's military, known as the People's Liberation Army, to help curtail the violence. In 1969, Mao introduced a new phase in the Cultural Revolution, one designed to purge society of class differences. Peasant youth attended urban schools and learned about Mao and his achievements. Individuals considered bourgeois were ordered to live and work among the peasants and were sentenced to hard labor, as were urban teenagers. Families were separated for years. As a government worker,

Zhang was directly affected by the Cultural Revolution in this way, and she was separated from her family for four years.

The Cultural Revolution ended with the death of Mao in 1976. In the years that followed, China's economy struggled to recover from the ruin it experienced during the Cultural Revolution. Peasant farmers, during the Cultural Revolution, could sell their products only to the government, and all reliance on foreign markets and aid had been halted. Aside from the rudimentary education offered to peasants, the educational system had all but collapsed as well. Mao's successor, Deng Xiaoping, instituted reforms designed to help support the economy and renew faith in the Communist Party of the People's Republic of China. Within the party, leaders struggled to reshape the ideals, to reframe the way the original Marxist tenets had been interpreted by Mao and were now in need of reevaluation.

Deng Xiaoping and the Aftermath of the Cultural Revolution

Deng Xiaoping became the new premier of the People's Republic of China in 1977. With Deng as chairman, the Communist Party pursued a new course, one that explored the economic benefits of market socialism. Under this system, the Marxist aim of an egalitarian, one-class society would be integrated with an economic policy that embraced a limited free market capitalist approach and would modernize China's economy. Deng also focused on revitalizing the educational system and allowed many exiled intellectuals and academicians to return to their families. He encouraged tourism and lifted restrictions on journalists and artists. At the same time, he attempted to retain some control over the Party's image. Some protestors were still sentenced to prison, and the more critical journals were banned. In 1979, the year Zhang published her collection of short stories *Love Must Not Be Forgotten*, China invaded Vietnam in a war over the Soviet presence in that region.

Also in 1979, the government instituted a policy that mandated that married couples could have only one child. The mandate was rooted in economic concerns about China's population. As Drs. Therese Hesketh, Li Lu, and Zhu Wei Xing explain in a 2005 *New England Journal of Medicine* article, "The government saw strict population containment as essential to economic reform and to an improvement in living standards." There are, however, some considerations and exceptions for families who live in underpopulated areas or in rural areas; these families are allowed, after a number of years, to have a second child. Deng is credited with refashioning China into a major political power in the world. (Deng retired in 1992 and died in 1997.)

Jie's writing captures a Chinese/feminist conflict
(Image copyright Szefei, 2009. Used under license from Shutterstock.com)

CRITICAL OVERVIEW

Zhang's "Love Must Not Be Forgotten" has been studied both as a political statement about the rights of women and as a work of short fiction. The story and the collection in which it appeared received critical attention in the English-speaking world after Gladys Yang's 1986 translation was published. In Yang's preface to the volume *Love Must Not Be Forgotten*, Yang observes that Zhang's story "Love Must Not Be Forgotten" was attacked by Chinese critics who believed that through this work of fiction, Zhang was "undermining social morality." According to Yang, the charge was leveled against Zhang because the story idealizes an extramarital love, because it implies that a marriage should be based on love to be considered moral, and because it advocates a woman remaining single if she chooses to do so. Zhang's story is surveyed by Delia Davin in the context of other Chinese literature about love, marriage, and divorce, in *New Frontiers in Women's Studies: Knowledge, Identity and Nationalism.* Davin comments on the controversial nature of the work and the way the criticism of it as threatening to the morality of the Chinese population could have resulted in permanent damage to Zhang's literary career. Not only did critics deride the work for its alleged immorality but they also, as Davin states, "claimed that it reflected [Zhang's] 'petty-bourgeois mentality.'" This is an attack on Zhang's commitment to a communist society. By associating Zhang with the bourgeoisie (the upper middle class, consisting of shop owners and other small property holders and professionals), critics suggest that Zhang did not subscribe wholeheartedly to the notion of a classless society. Critics such as Leo Ou-fan Lee comment on the political and feminist qualities of "Love Must Not Be Forgotten," but they also critique the work's literary elements. In a 1987 *New York Times Book Review* article, Lee observes that Zhang's fiction, collected in the volume *Love Must Not Be Forgotten*, concerns the freedom, or lack of freedom, that women in China possess. He states that even though "her feminism does not evince the expected militancy, she nevertheless shows a respect for genuine emotions, particularly those of women." Lee goes on to observe, however, that Zhang "is unable to exercise control over her narratives" and that she is prone to sentimentality and use of clichés. In a 1988 review for *China Quarterly*, Beth McKillop offers a similarly split assessment of *Love Must Not Be Forgotten.* Although she finds the stories in this collection to be "eloquent in their fury at the lot of women in China today," they contain characters that "are two-dimensional representations of ideas, not real people."

Taking another view of Zhang's collection of short stories, Kay Kendall, in a 1986 review of *Love Must Not Be Forgotten* for the *Christian Science Monitor*, praises Zhang as a "brave feminist" and goes on to describe the collection as "both imaginative and informative, well worth a second and even third reading." In a later analysis of the work, in Judith Farquhar's 2002 *Appetites: Food and Sex in Post-Socialist China*, "Love Must Not Be Forgotten" is assessed in terms of its structure and theme. Farquhar finds that while the work overtly treats "themes of self-realization and romantic love," it also studies the insistent devotion of a woman, Shanshan's mother, to her own "secret life of writing" during years of oppressive state control of the personal lives of individuals. In analyzing the story's structure, Farquhar contends that Shanshan's personal struggle with her views on marriage serve as "the framing device for Zhong Yu's story, which takes up more space and is the occasion for the text's most appealing writing."

CRITICISM

Catherine Dominic

Dominic is a novelist and a freelance writer and editor. In this essay, she asserts that the mother-daughter relationship, although often overlooked in critical assessments of "Love Must Not Be Forgotten," is nevertheless a major focus of Zhang's story. She maintains that the mother-daughter relationship in the story is characterized by the mother's emotional neglect and that the daughter's response to her deceased mother grows increasingly conflicted as she reads through her mother's diary.

In Zhang's "Love Must Not Be Forgotten," the narrator, Shanshan, discusses the discovery of her mother's love for a married man, and much of the story is devoted to the unfolding of the details of this secret attachment. Zhang uses Shanshan's memories, in conjunction with the diary, to allow the reader and Shanshan a glimpse into the emotional love affair to which Shanshan's mother, Zhong Yu, has devoted her life. Criticism of the story in China has been based on Shanshan's rejection of a marriage not based on love and on the extramarital love experienced by Zhong Yu and the married man for whom she has secretly longed. Following the story's English publication in 1986, critics explored Zhang's stylistic techniques and her political views. In addition, the mother's secret life and her relationship with her lover have been the subject of reviews, as has Shanshan's own journey of self-discovery. What is often overlooked, however, is the relationship between Shanshan and her mother. Zhang

WHAT DO I READ NEXT?

- Zhang's novella *The Ark* is featured in the collection *Love Must Not Be Forgotten*, published in English by China Books in 1986. Like the title story of the volume, *The Ark* explores themes of love, marriage, and divorce. It focuses on the lives of divorced professional women struggling to maintain their autonomy in lives dominated by powerful men, including their ex-husbands and the bureaucrats with whom they deal professionally.
- Zhang's novel *Heavy Wings* was originally published in Chinese in 1981, and an English translation by Gladys Yang was published by Virago in 1987. In it, Zhang explores the state of Chinese culture and industry in the aftermath of the Cultural Revolution.
- Chinese author Ha Jin, in *The Bridegroom: Stories*, writes about the same time period Zhang explores in her work, the aftermath of China's Cultural Revolution. Ha Jin's collection offers a male perspective on some of the same themes that Zhang explores, such as marriage and family. The collection was published by Vintage in 2001.
- *Anton Chekhov's Short Stories* is a collection selected and edited by Ralph E. Matlaw for a 1979 volume published by W. W. Norton. The work features thirty-four stories, which span Chekhov's career. Although Zhang's character Zhong Yu does not reveal the reasons for her love of Chekhov's work, it is significant for the student of Zhang's fiction to note that Chekhov wrote under an oppressive regime in czarist Russia—perhaps parallel to the situation in China—at a time when socialist movements were gaining power.
- Breena Clark's novel, *River Cross My Heart*, published by Bay Back Books in 1999, is concerned with a mother-daughter relationship in a culture filled with political and cultural tensions. Set in the 1920s, it concerns an African American family dealing with discrimination and segregation. Both mother and daughter are forced to stand up to legally sanctioned racial injustice, and Clark examines the impact of this stress on their relationship to one another, to their family as a whole, and to the larger community in which they live. The daughter is ten years old, and the work is regarded as a coming-of-age novel suitable for young-adult readers.
- Moying Li's *Snow Falling in Spring: Coming of Age in China During the Cultural Revolution*, published in 2008 by Farrar, Straus and Giroux, is a memoir aimed at a young-adult audience in which the author tells of growing up during the Cultural Revolution in China. The author focuses on her life from ages twelve to twenty-two.

explores not only Shanshan's childhood but also the evolution of her relationship with her mother and the changing of her perspective as she digests her mother's diary. Through the course of the story, Shanshan begins to comprehend the complexities of her mother's personality, as a woman and not simply as a mother. Zhang demonstrates that, as Shanshan's understanding of her mother deepens, Shanshan simultaneously begins to feel both more connected to and more isolated from her mother. That the mother-daughter relationship—particularly the relationship between a daughter and the single mother who raised her—is a primary feature of Zhang's story is unsurprising. This type of mother-daughter relationship mirrors Zhang's experience as both a daughter and a mother.

Early on in the story, Zhang introduces Shanshan's conflicted feelings about her mother. Shanshan recollects the persistent anxiety she felt as a child, discussing how she would wake

> "ZHANG DEMONSTRATES THAT, AS SHANSHAN'S UNDERSTANDING OF HER MOTHER DEEPENS, SHANSHAN SIMULTANEOUSLY BEGINS TO FEEL BOTH MORE CONNECTED TO AND MORE ISOLATED FROM HER MOTHER."

up crying and "disturbing the whole household." With the entire house aware of her distress, it is her nurse who attends to the young Shanshan in the middle of the night. Significantly, Shanshan's mother does not seek out her crying daughter and ease her fears during the night. Shanshan does not explain her mother's absence, nor does she make any judgments about her mother. However, the nurse, who is both "old" and "uneducated," simply tells Shanshan that an "ill wind had blown through [her] ear," and it is clear that Shanshan did not feel comforted.

Shanshan does think of her mother in the next paragraph, describing her as her "closest friend" and revealing how much she loved her. Shanshan goes on to recall that her mother was not the type who lectured. Rather, Zhong Yu (Shanshan's mother) discussed her own experiences in the hope that her daughter would learn from them. Shanshan perceives from these discussions that her mother's life was characterized by her many failures. In remembering the discussion shared with her mother on the topic of Shanshan's possible marriage to Qiao Lin, Shanshan observes that her mother admonished her to wait if she was uncertain, and she notes that, more than anything, her mother wanted her to be happy. Shanshan also discerns the bitterness in her mother's comments about her own experiences. Zhong Yu states that she had been talked into getting married before she knew what she really needed. She says that she has longed for "a fresh start." When Shanshan asks her mother why she does not consider remarrying, Zhong Yu is elusive, and Shanshan suspects that her mother is reluctant to tell her the truth regarding this matter. Shanshan thinks about her father and of how her parents divorced when she was very young. Shanshan remembers her mother's attitude about her father; Zhong Yu was ashamed of her decision to marry him, considering it a stupid mistake. In conveying these attitudes of shame and misjudgment to her daughter, Zhong Yu implies that if her marriage was a mistake, then so was Shanshan, the child of that marriage. Shanshan does not speak on this matter, but the logical progression of Zhong Yu's line of thinking is clear, and as a reader one must wonder whether Shanshan has considered it. At the very least, Shanshan observes the extent of her mother's sense of bitterness and regret where her past choices, particularly her marriage, are concerned.

The depth of Zhong Yu's regrets are made clear to Shanshan when, after her mother's death, Shanshan reads the diary her mother asked her to destroy. Shanshan sees her mother's love for a married man played out before her, in her mother's words, and realizes that the diary reflects her mother's torment at the fact that "for over twenty years one man occupied her heart, but he was not for her." One of the most telling lines in the story comes after Shanshan begins to understand that her mother's heart was "already full, to the exclusion of anybody else." Shanshan's words suggest her perception that her mother's love for the man operated in such a way as to not simply exclude other lovers but also, to some degree, Shanshan herself. In contemplating this exclusion, Shanshan thinks that the love between her mother and the man embodied a saying she recalls: "No lake can compare with the ocean, no cloud with those on Mount Wu." Connecting her mother's feelings for the man with those lines, Shanshan reflects, "No one would love me like this." Shanshan's comment implies that the "no one" includes her mother. Shanshan understands now all the evasions she witnessed during her mother's life and knows that her mother's love for the man she could not have shaped not only Zhong Yu's life but Shanshan's as well. Zhong Yu's love for the unnamed man took over her heart and became the focus of her life. This is not to say that Zhong Yu did not love her daughter, but, as Shanshan now knows, as a daughter she certainly did not experience the fullness of her mother's love. Zhong Yu's love for the man and her anguish at having never been able to pursue it held her back from embracing the life she did have, the life she shared with her daughter.

Shanshan's understanding of the extent to which she was excluded from her mother's heart is revealed to her when she reads her mother's words in the diary. Zhong Yu writes in the diary as if she is writing to the man she loves, and she reports feeling that something is perpetually missing, that "everything seems lacking, incomplete, and there is nothing to fill up the blank." Shanshan recalls not being allowed to meet her mother at the train station when she returned from a trip, as Zhong Yu preferred to be alone on the platform and imagine that the man was meeting her. After the man's death, Zhong Yu wears a black band around her arm in his honor. Shanshan asks if she, too, should wear one. Shanshan remembers the way her mother then patted her cheeks, as if she were still a young child. Years have passed, Shanshan recalls, since her mother had displayed her any such affection.

As the diary and her memories show Shanshan that her childhood was lacking in her mother's devotion, Shanshan considers this loss but focuses instead on the anguish her mother endured at never being able to be with the man she loved. Shanshan seems to pride herself on finally being able to understand her mother more fully. "I am the only one able to see into your locked heart," she says to the memory of her mother, fleshed out in the pages of the diary. While Shanshan recognizes the agony her mother endured, while she cries for her mother and finds the tragedy she experienced both "beautiful" and "moving," she also wonders at her mother's ability to continue to love the man so fully and passionately, even as she was dying. To Shanshan, "it seemed not love but a form of madness." Seeing such devotion as insanity and expressing her vehement desire to avoid following her mother's path, Shanshan in her way passes judgment on a mother virtually debilitated by "undying love."

As Shanshan's memories and thoughts reveal, her childhood suffered because her mother was distracted by her love for a man whose life she could not share. Zhong Yu was not a full participant in her daughter's life. She failed to comfort her or show her affection. Rather than devote herself to moving forward when it became clear that she and her lover could not be together, she devoted herself to loving him through her diary, through the brief moments when they saw each other at work, and through the set of Chekhov books he had given her. While Shanshan was unaware of the extent of her mother's emotional distraction as a child, she perceived absences in attention, quirks in her mother's behavior. She was told that her mother did not love her father, that the marriage had been a mistake, something Zhong Yu had been rushed into. As an adult considering marriage herself, Shanshan understands, through the diary, the reasons why her mother behaved the way she did, and now sees the full picture, the entirety of the secret her mother kept. Simultaneously hurt and sympathetic, Shanshan is compelled to take a stand against marriages that are not made for love. Whether or not Shanshan sees the possibility of the kind of love her mother possessed for the man she could not have, Shanshan is aware of the way that people rushed into "indifferent" marriages are tortured by such decisions. Shanshan regards her mother as both a figure of sympathy (because she endured such tragedy) and as someone to pity (because her love reduced her, Shanshan feels, to "madness"). Shanshan consequently takes what seems to her to be a safe position with regard to love and marriage when she advocates patient waiting.

Illustration of Chinese leader Mao Zedong. Jie wrote in the aftermath of the Chinese Cultural Revolution. (© The London Art Archive / Alamy)

Source: Catherine Dominic, Critical Essay on "Love Must Not Be Forgotten," in *Short Stories for Students*, Gale, Cengage Learning, 2010.

Robert E. Hegel

In the following review, Hegel notes Zhang's sentimental and engaging style.

Zhang Jie's (b. 1937) stories are widely read; some have won prizes in the national contests. This collection presents six, along with a novella and an autobiographical sketch. Their strength lies in the level of sympathy they invoke from the reader. Zhang regularly narrates the innermost thoughts of her protagonists, probing their motivations. Many of them here relive the "Hundred Flowers" and Cultural Revolution campaigns in their minds as ways to validate their identity, to excuse their past mistakes, and to find the strength to face the future. Tragedy abounds in such sentimental writing, and yet the engaging spirit of the author regularly appears in her female characters as she tackles the discrimination and abuses they face. Her novella, "The Ark," traces the constant struggles faced by women courageous enough to live as single divorcees: in addition to the unremitting discrimination faced by all Chinese women, these characters must cope with the widely held suspicion that a divorcee is, or might be, promiscuous. This self-congratulatory, traditional sense of morality serves to validate the meanness of all who take out political and sexual frustrations on them.

This volume is the first in a new collaborative publishing venture. It is well bound and physically attractive, putting it ahead of the Panda series from *Chinese Literature* in this regard. However, the translations here are mostly reprinted from that periodical. Hence little new is added beyond a more convenient format for undergraduate and general readers.

Source: Robert E. Hegel, Review of *Love Must Not Be Forgotten*, in *Chinese Literature: Essays, Articles, Reviews* (CLEAR), Vol. 9, No. 1/2, July 1987, p. 162.

May Wu

In the following interview, Wu talks with "China's first feminist novelist," Zhang Jie.

Zhang Jie, one of China's most popular authors, was born in 1937. As a child she had a passion for music and literature, but was persuaded to study economics instead. She worked in industry and in a film studio, but did not start to write until after the fall of the "Gang of Four" in 1976. From an initial focus on themes of love and youth, she has turned to write, often satirically, about social problems—male supremacy, hypocrisy, corruption, bureaucracy and nepotism.

Zhang Jie sees her responsibility as a writer to be the education of her readers, the stimulus to social change. She was a pioneer in exposing women's problems before the authorities recognized them: many of her stories were most controversial when they first appeared. "Love Must Not Be Forgotten," which implied that marriages must be based on love in order to be moral, was condemned for "undermining social morality"; "The Ark," about three women who are divorced or live apart from their husbands, was attacked for "distorting socialism." She has been called "China's first feminist novelist"; several of her books have been translated into other languages, and a collection of her short stories will be published for the first time in English translation this summer.

> "LIKE MOST WRITERS, I BEGIN NOT WITH A PERSON, PLACE, OR THING, BUT JUST A FEELING, A FEELING THAT INSTINCT TELLS ME IS INTERESTING. THEN I DIG DEEPER INTO THAT FEELING—LIKE BORING A WELL."

In May 1986, Zhang Jie spent three weeks visiting the United States as a member of an official delegation of writers, poets, critics and playwrights sent by the Chinese Writers' Association. I had first met her in 1982, when she first visited this country with a similar delegation. China Books, Zhang Jie's US publisher, arranged for me to interview her in New York with the help of two excellent interpreters, Hu Shiguang and Wang Hongjie.

I began by asking Zhang Jie when she first thought she might become a writer.

ZJ: To want to be a writer and to become a writer are two entirely different things. As a child, I had wanted to be a writer just as earlier I had wanted to be a pianist. As my family was very poor and couldn't afford a piano, that was not to be. In the fifties, I saw a Soviet film about a horse trainer which impressed me very much—one is easily impressed when one is young—and for a time I wanted to become a horse trainer, not the kind in a circus, but on a farm somewhere. But, as you know, I did not become a writer until fairly late in life. "The Child From the Forest" was the first story I ever wrote. Until it was published in 1978, when I was 40, I had no idea that I could be a writer. At the time, I was simply moved to write.

I thought to myself: This is a test. If I don't succeed, I will never write again. Since I was successful, I was encouraged to persevere. But I don't consider that story my best work. In fact, my early works are rather immature.

MW: How has your writing changed over time?

ZJ: I don't feel limited in my choice of subject-matter because the world is vast and life is infinitely rich. I don't think a writer should limit herself to only one theme or style. I like to write about major social phenomena, events in history—to give a panoramic view of the society—but I have also written what I call "pure fiction."

MW: In a number of your works, you write with passion and some bitterness about the difficulties women experience in a male-dominated society. Do you consider yourself—as others have hailed you—a "feminist writer?"

ZJ: I am a writer. I don't think the term "feminist writer" has any substantive meaning. When I write, I have in mind all the people in the world. Although I am not against feminism, I don't think it has any substantial meaning in contemporary life. Inequality, unequal treatment, exists universally. To treat inequality only as a problem between the sexes is to under-estimate the gravity of the problem.

In the final analysis, women's problems are social problems, and these problems can be solved only through the material and spiritual progress of the human race as a whole. The feminist movement may solve certain concrete aspects of the problem on a small scale, but it cannot solve the fundamental problem. I see the problem as one of social consciousness. For instance, I don't think appointing a woman to a high-level position will necessarily mean she gets respect or equal treatment. I think the feminist movement is rather extreme. After all, the world belongs to men as well as to women. If a man has integrity, courage, goodness and intelligence, he deserves my respect. As a writer, I feel responsible to all people, to inspire them to make life what they want it to be. . . .

MW: How much of your writing is based on real people, real incidents? How much is autobiographical?

ZJ: Like most writers, I begin not with a person, place, or thing, but just a feeling, a feeling that instinct tells me is interesting. Then I dig deeper into that feeling—like boring a well. As I dig deeper, the feeling connects with other feelings and experiences assimilated in the past.

Some people take it upon themselves to relate persons and events in my stories to my own life, but I think writing based on one's own life is not fiction, I don't know what to call it—reporting, maybe?—but it can't have much appeal for other people. My characters are composites of many people in real life, but they are still fictitious.

I will probably write an autobiographical novel in my old age, but not just yet; there are too many things I want to write about now. . . .

MW: Given the popularity of your works in China, have you been approached about adapting your stories for the screen?

ZJ: My stories cannot be made into films, at least not in China. Film directors, studio heads and television producers in China generally lack a solid literary education and have no appreciation of literature. They only want to make *kung fu* pictures or films with bizarre plots. They think my stories have no plot. And if they think a story has no commercial value, they won't touch it. After *Leaden Wings* won the Mao Dun Literary Prize in 1985, four studios did offer to buy the screen rights, but I adamantly refused. I wouldn't want one of my stories to be made into a film in China unless I could have a really good director. If a foreign studio were interested in making a film out of my story, that would be another matter. . . .

I went on to ask Zhang Jie about *Leaden Wings,* a novel originally published in 1981, which exposes corrupt practices and abuses of privilege.

MW: Tell me about what happened when Leaden Wings *first came out.*

ZJ: When the book was first published, the Peking correspondent of *The Christian Science Monitor* interviewed me for his paper. He said he thought it was a political work, supporting Chairman Deng Xiaoping's political line, and he asked me whether I expected any problems. I told him I did not, and that I was not afraid. I gave him my reasons. First, I believe that the new directions in foreign policy, economic policy, cultural matters and so forth will not change, and that those who opposed these policies would ultimately fail. Second, I believe that my work reflects the interests and the hopes of the Chinese people, and that my perspective is fundamentally correct. (All this was published in the *Monitor* on December 29, 1981.) My critics at the time were those people who held conventional views and could see themselves reflected in my writing. . . .

MW: As I understand, you did revise Leaden Wings *in light of the criticism and it was the revised version that was awarded the Mao Dun Literary Prize. Do you feel you have compromised your literary freedom?*

ZJ: Writers can always find ways to avoid offending people with conventional views and to get their works published without compromising their principles. That said, I must add that I did listen humbly and I did revise my book. There was one very good reason for revising it: I had written it in such a rush—in four months—that I had no time to read over the manuscript before it went to the publisher. It was full of errors of syntax and long, clumsy sentences. So I was glad to have a chance to clear up these problems. Under these conditions, there is no literary freedom or lack of literary freedom. . . .

MW: Has Western literature influenced your writing? Which Western writers do you admire?

ZJ: The Chinese of my generation have drawn a great deal of spiritual nourishment from the classical Western literature of the eighteenth and nineteenth centuries, especially from novels that explore the psychology of the characters. My own writings is in line with this tradition. Whereas Chinese fiction tranditionally emphasizes narrative and plot, I don't pay much attention to narrative or plot.

The Western writers whose works I admire include Victor Hugo, Romain Rolland, Charles Dickens, Emily Bronte, Virginia Woolf, Stefan Zweig, and, of course, Tolstoy and Chekhov—a mixed bunch. As for American writers, I like very much the work of Mark Twain and Jack London. I also like Kurt Vonnegut for his satire, Saul Bellow for his sensitive descriptions of the psychology of intellectuals, and Harrison Salisbury—especially his disposition. I think these are all writers who take literature seriously. For them, writing is not a game; it is their life.

MW: Do you read much contemporary Western fiction?

ZJ: I haven't read much because translation of foreign literature into Chinese has been rather slow in recent years.

MW: What are your impressions of current literary trends in the United States? Have your impressions changed since your first visit here in 1982?

ZJ: I can't say much about the changes because I haven't been here very long. However, I have met with many American writers both here and in China. I think that American writers, like some European writers I know, have gone through a period of experimenting with new devices and are now returning to a more serious style.

In China, this kind of experimenting in both theme and style is still going on. Some of our younger writers have departed in recent years from themes of social responsibility and write only about their feelings and trivial concerns of a personal nature I don't mean to say it's wrong to write about these things, but if writers only write about themselves and their own concerns they will disappoint their readers. So many people in the world cannot put pen to paper to express publicly their joys and sorrows, their life experiences. Only we writers can speak for them. If we ignore our responsibility as writers, we will let the people down. In terms of style, our younger writers are imitating fashionable devices, such as the "magical realism" of Gabriel Garcia Marquez. I happen to admire Marquez, but I think one Marquez in the world is enough. Imitation is not the way out, for no matter how faithfully and skillfully you imitate another writer you will only be an imitator. For young writers starting out, imitation is perhaps inevitable. The world is so complex, so vast. Young writers who have no idea how to tackle it need models.

MW: Are you working on a novel at the present time?

ZJ: Just before I left China to come here, I finished a novella and a short essay about my visit to four European countries last fall. The latter is about my impressions of the societies I visited and how they compare with Chinese society.

MW: What were some of your impressions of Europe?

ZJ: Actually, I can't say I saw very much! I was closeted most of the time with my publishers and the press. I went to Europe because the German editions of *Leaden Wings* and "The Ark" were very successful, especially in Austria and Switzerland. I was told the first printing of *Leaden Wings*—6,000 copies—sold out in three days, and has now gone into a fifth printing. The translator—a German—did an excellent job and won a prize for best translation of a foreign work. Virago Press in London is publishing the English-language edition, translated by Gladys Yang. "The Ark" was published in West Germany by a feminist press that was on the verge of bankruptcy. I am pleased that my book, which went into a third printing, helped to revive its fortunes. Now it is being translated into French. . . .

MW: Do you anticipate the same reception in the United States for your forthcoming collection, Love Must Not Be Forgotten? What aspect of your work do you think will appeal most to American readers?

ZJ: I think American readers will like three or four of the stories in the collection: the title story, "Love Must Not Be Forgotten,""Under the Hawthorn" and "The Ark." When Toni Morrison and Francine du Plessix Gray visited China, they told me they thought "Love Must Not Be Forgotten" was the most beautifully written story they have read in years.

MW: In what direction do you see your writing going in the future?

ZJ: I will continue to contribute everything I have toward the progress of all the people in the world. My writing always centers on this theme. It is immense, and will keep me busy for many, many years.

Source: May Wu, "China's Gadfly: May Wu Talks to Zhang Jie," in *Women's Review of Books*, Vol. 3, No. 10, July 1986, pp. 9–10.

SOURCES

"China," in *CIA: World Factbook*, https://www.cia.gov/library/publications/the-world-factbook/geos/ch.html (accessed October 27, 2009).

"Communist China Marks 60th Year," in *BBC News*, October 1, 2009, http://news.bbc.co.uk/2/hi/8284087.stm (accessed October 27, 2009).

"The Cultural Revolution," in *Oracle Think Quest*, http://library.thinkquest.org/26469/cultural-revolution/ (accessed November 13, 2009).

Davin, Delia, "The Political and the Personal: Women's Writing in China in the 1980s," in *New Frontiers in Women's Studies: Knowledge, Identity and Nationalism*, edited by Mary Maynard and June Purvis, Taylor & Francis, 1996, pp. 63–75.

Farquhar, Judith, "Introduction" and "Writing the Self: The Romance of the Personal," in *Appetites: Food and Sex in Post-Socialist China*, Duke University Press, 2002, pp. 1–36, 175–210.

Hesketh, Therese, Li Lu, and Zhu Wei Xing, "The Effect of China's One-Child Family Policy after 25 Years," in *New England Journal of Medicine*, Vol. 353, No. 11, September 15, 2005, pp. 1171–76.

Kendall, Kay, Review of *Love Must Not Be Forgotten*, in *Christian Science Monitor*, Vol. 78, October 27, 1986, p. 24.

Lee, Leo Ou-fan, "Under the Thumb of Men," in *New York Times Book Review*, Sec. 7, January 18, 1987, p. 36.

"The Life and Literature of Zhang Jie," in *Beijing Scene*, Vol. 7, No. 13, April 14–20, 2000, http://www.beijingscene.com/cissue/feature.html (accessed October 27, 2009).

McKillop, Beth, Review of *Love Must Not Be Forgotten*, in *China Quarterly*, Vol. 2, No. 114, June 1988, p. 308.

Meisner, Maurice J., "The Aftermath of the Cultural Revolution and the Close of the Maoist Era, 1969–1976," in *Mao's China and After: A History of the People's Republic*, 3rd ed., Free Press, 1999, pp. 376–412.

Purple, Matthew, "Flap over China's 1-Child Policy Stirs," in *Washington Times*, February 18, 2009, http://www.washingtontimes.com/news/2009/feb/18/revival-of-us-aid-stirs-unease-on-beijings-one-chi (accessed October 27, 2009).

Spence, Jonathan, "Deng Xiaoping: The Maoist Who Reinvented Himself, Transformed a Nation, and Changed the World," in *Time Asia: 60 years of Asian Heroes*, Vol. 168, No. 21, November 13, 2006, http://www.time.com/time/asia/2006/heroes/nb_deng.html (accessed October 27, 2009).

Xu Shengian, "Hasty Nuptials Lead to High Divorce Rates for Young," in *Global Times*, September 30, 2009, http://china.globaltimes.cn/society/2009-09/473431.html (accessed October 27, 2009).

Yang, Gladys, Preface to *Love Must Not Be Forgotten*, China Books, 1986, pp. ix–xiii.

Yardley, Jim, "Women in China Embrace Divorce as Stigma Eases," in *New York Times*, October 4, 2005, http://www.nytimes.com/2005/10/04/international/asia/04divorce.html (accessed October 27, 2009).

Zhang Jie, "Love Must Not Be Forgotten," in *Love Must Not Be Forgotten*, China Books, 1986, pp. 1–13.

FURTHER READING

Clark, Paul, *The Chinese Cultural Revolution*, Cambridge University Press, 2008.

Clark explores the state of culture itself, as it is understood in artistic terms, during the Cultural Revolution. He discusses developments in visual arts, performing arts, literature, and architecture that occurred during this time period.

Edwards, Loiuse, *Gender, Politics, and Democracy: Women's Suffrage in China*, Stanford University Press, 2007.

Edwards examines the various campaigns undertaken by female activists in modern Chinese history to gain equal access to political power.

Fong, Vanessa, *Only Hope: Coming of Age under China's One-Child Policy*, Stanford University Press, 2004.

Fong studies the long-term effects of China's one-child-per family mandate. Through statistical and anecdotal data, Fong analyzes the economic, educational, political, and societal effects of having so many urban children grow up as the only child in the household.

Mu, Aili, Julie Chiu, and Howard Goldblatt, eds. and trans., *Loud Sparrows: Contemporary Chinese Short-Shorts*, Columbia University Press, 2008.

The editors of this volume have collected an array of writings categorized as "short-shorts," or extremely short fiction, by modern Chinese writers. The works cover a variety of themes and reveal experiments with the form.

Shambaugh, David, *China's Communist Party: Atrophy and Adaptation*, University of California Press, 2009.

Shambaugh traces the recent modern history of the Chinese Communist Party, discussing its attempts, following the Cultural Revolution, to remain nimble in terms of ideology and administration.

Marriage Is a Private Affair

CHINUA ACHEBE

1952

"Marriage Is a Private Affair" is a short story by the renowned Nigerian writer Chinua Achebe. It was first published in 1952 under the title "The Old Order in Conflict with the New" in the *University Herald* of University College, Ibadan, Nigeria, where Achebe was a student. As "Beginning of the End," it was reprinted in Achebe's 1962 collection of short stories, *The Sacrificial Egg and Other Short Stories*. The title was changed yet again, this time to "Marriage Is a Private Affair," when the story was reprinted in 1972 in Achebe's short story collection *Girls at War, and Other Stories*.

"Marriage Is a Private Affair" is set in Lagos, the former capital of Nigeria, and in a rural village. It tells the story of Nnaemeka, a young man living in Lagos, whose choice of bride does not meet with his father's approval. When the son returns to his village, his father opposes the marriage because Nnaemeka's fiancée is not a member of the Igbo tribe, and it is not the custom for Igbos to marry outside their own ethnic group. (Achebe spells it *Ibo*, but the modern spelling is *Igbo*.) The story dramatizes the conflict been tradition and modernity in the Nigeria of the 1950s. Nnaemeka marries for love rather than in accordance with custom, triggering a generational conflict that is resolved only by the persistence and goodwill of the young couple. The story is one of Achebe's earliest published works. It is not a complex story in either structure or theme, but it does serve as an example of the kind of subject matter that Achebe would later develop in more depth in his novels.

Chinua Achebe (AP Images)

AUTHOR BIOGRAPHY

One of Africa's most renowned writers, the novelist, essayist, and poet Achebe was born on November 16, 1930, at Ogidi, east of Onitsha, Eastern Region of Nigeria. His parents were Christian evangelists, and Achebe's early education was at the school of the Church Missionary Society. He was initially taught in the Igbo language and first started to learn English when he was eight. In 1944, at the age of fourteen, he was one of the few students selected to attend Government College at Umuahia, which was known as one of the best schools in West Africa. In 1948, he entered University College, Ibadan, initially to study medicine, but he soon switched to English literature. University College was, at the time, affiliated with the University of London, and the curriculum Achebe studied was similar to that studied by British undergraduates. While he was an undergraduate, Achebe published four short stories in the university magazine, including "Marriage Is a Private Affair," which was originally titled "The Old Order in Conflict with the New" (1952). After graduating in 1953, Achebe became a journalist at the newly founded Nigerian Broadcasting Corporation in 1954. He remained there until 1966.

In 1958, Achebe published his first novel, *Things Fall Apart*, about the colonization of the Igbo people by the British in the 1890s. The novel was an immediate success and soon became known internationally, establishing Achebe's reputation. Today, *Things Fall Apart* remains Achebe's most famous novel. His second novel, *No Longer at Ease* (1960), continues the story of colonization. It was published in the same year Nigeria gained its independence from Britain.

In 1961, Achebe married Christie Chinwe Okoli. They would have two daughters and two sons. In 1962, he published a collection titled *The Sacrificial Egg and Other Short Stories*, which contained "Marriage Is a Private Affair," under the title "Beginning of the End." Achebe's third novel, *Arrow of God*, was published in 1964, followed by *A Man of the People* in 1966.

In 1967, Biafra, an Igbo-dominated state in southeastern Nigeria, seceded from Nigeria, leading to a three-year civil war. During the war, Achebe traveled as a spokesman for Biafra, bringing to the world's attention the suffering of the Igbo people. After the war, he published his first collection of poetry, *Beware, Soul Brother* (1971), which won the Commonwealth Poetry Prize. He also published another short story collection, *Girls at War, and Other Stories* (1972), which also contained "Marriage Is a Private Affair."

By that time, Achebe was an internationally renowned author, and from 1972 to 1976 he lived in the United States as a visiting professor of literature, first at the University of Massachusetts at Amherst and then at the University of Connecticut, Storrs. In 1976, he returned to Nigeria and became a professor of literature at the University of Nigeria, Nsukka. *The Trouble with Nigeria*, a collection of essays about social and political problems in Nigeria, was published in 1983. Four years later, Achebe published the novel *Anthills of the Savannah* (1987), which was short-listed for the Booker Prize.

In 1987, Achebe returned to the United States to teach successively at Dartmouth College, Stanford University, and Bard College, New York, where, in the fall of 1990, he became the Charles P. Stevenson Professor of Literature. In the same year, Achebe was involved in a car accident in Lagos, Nigeria, that left him paralyzed from the waist down.

In 1999, Achebe became a goodwill ambassador for the United Nations Population Fund. In

2007, he won the Man Booker International Prize for lifetime achievement.

As of 2009, Achebe is the David and Mariana Fisher University Professor and Professor of Africana Studies at Brown University. His most recent publication is a collection of autobiographical essays, *The Education of a British-Protected Child* (2009).

PLOT SUMMARY

"Marriage Is a Private Affair" is set in Nigeria, West Africa, in the early 1950s. The story begins in Lagos, the capital city. Nnaemeka, a young man, is visiting his girlfriend, Nene Atang, in her room. The couple has recently become engaged, and Nene asks her fiancé if he has written to his father to inform him of the engagement.

Nnaemeka says he would prefer to wait until he can see his father in person, when he goes home on leave in six weeks. He tells Nene he is not sure that his father will be pleased with the news. Nene is surprised to hear this, and Nnaemeka tells her that since she has lived in Lagos all her life, she knows nothing of the ways of people who live in distant rural areas. He says his father will object to the marriage because Nene is not from the Ibo tribe. Nene is astonished. She cannot believe that Nnaemeka's father would oppose the marriage for such a reason. She thought the Ibos were well disposed toward people from other tribes. Nnaemeka confirms that this is the case, but it is different when it comes to marriage. Nene says that his father will surely forgive him, but Nnaemeka insists that it would be better to wait until he can inform his father in person, rather than writing him a letter.

As Nnaemeka walks home that evening, he thinks of ways in which he might persuade his father to drop his certain opposition to the marriage. He is convinced that once his father meets Nene, he will be so charmed by her that he will change his mind. When he gets home, though, he finds a letter waiting for him from his father. In the letter, his father informs his son that he has found him a suitable wife. The young lady's name is Ugoye Nweke, and she is the eldest daughter of their neighbor. Like Nnaemeka's family, Ugoye is a Christian, and her father believes she will make a good wife. Nnaemeka's father concludes by saying that they will begin the negotiations for the marriage when Nnaemeka returns home in December.

Six weeks later, Nnaemeka returns home to his small village, and he and his father, whose name is Okeke, discuss the matter. Nnaemeka tells his father that it will be impossible for him to marry Ugoye, and he asks for his father's forgiveness. He says he does not love Ugoye. Okeke replies that love is not important; what matters is that she will make a good Christian wife. Nnaemeka then decides he must tell his father the whole truth. He explains that he is engaged to another girl, who is a good Christian and is a schoolteacher in Lagos.

Okeke replies that according to St. Paul in the Bible, women should remain silent; they should certainly not be teachers. When Nnaemeka further explains that Nene is not an Ibo, his father leaves the room without a word. He is annoyed and upset by what he sees as his son's foolishness.

The next day, Okeke tries, without success, to persuade his son to break off the engagement. Nnaemeka tells him that he will change his mind when he meets Nene, but his father says he will never agree to meet her. After their disagreement, father and son barely speak to each other. Nnaemeka hopes his father will reconsider, but when he returns to Lagos, they are still at odds with each other.

It turns out that never in the history of the Ibos has a man married a woman who did not speak his language. No one has ever heard of such a thing. Some of the men from the village come to Okeke and commiserate with him over his son's folly. One man quotes a scriptural passage that says sons will rise up against their fathers, while another, more practical man named Madubogwu suggests consulting an herbalist to prescribe medicine that will alter Nnaemeka's view of the situation, since the young man is obviously not in his right mind. Okeke refuses to consider that, however, citing a case involving a Mrs. Ochuba, who it seems, poisoned an herbalist with his own medicine.

Six months later, when Nnaemeka and Nene are married, Nnaemeka shows his wife a letter he has received from his father. Nnaemeka had sent him a wedding photo, but his father cut it in two, returning the portion containing Nene. He wants nothing to do with either of them.

Nnaemeka holds out hope that his father will relent, but eight years pass and nothing changes. During this time, Okeke writes to his son only three times. On one occasion he refuse to allow his son in his house.

Meanwhile, Nnaemeka and Nene are happily married in Lagos. At first, the Ibo people in the city are deferential to Nene, conscious that she is not of their tribe, but gradually her good nature wins them over and she is able to make friends. News of the couple's happiness reaches Nnaemeka's home village, but his father does not learn of it. He refuses to take part in any conversation in which his son is mentioned.

One day, Okeke receives a letter from Nene. She says that her two sons want to see their grandfather, and she asks his permission for Nnaemeka to bring them home for a visit. She promised to stay in Lagos.

Okeke tries to ignore her letter, but he feels the sting of conscience. After a fierce internal battle, he realizes that he cannot refuse to see his grandchildren. That night, he cannot sleep much because he feels remorse at having rejected his son and daughter-in-law for so long.

CHARACTERS

Nene Atang

Nene Atang is the young fiancée and later wife of Nnaemeka. She is a Christian, and she teaches at a girls' school in Lagos, a city she has lived in for her entire life. Nnaemeka tells his father she is from Calabar, which is a city in southeastern Nigeria. Perhaps he means that her family is originally from Calabar. Because she is a city girl born and bred, Nene knows nothing about the tribal life in rural areas of the country. She is therefore very surprised when she hears that Nnaemeka's father will object to her marriage because she is not an Ibo. She is modern in her views and cannot believe that such a distinction matters to people any more.

Nene is a charming young woman who is liked by everyone she meets. She appears to be the ideal wife. Nnaemeka is confident that she will win his father over if he will only agree to meet with her, and after she and Nnaemeka are married, the Ibos in Lagos soon overcome their prejudice toward her. They even admit that she is better at keeping house than they are. Finally, it is Nene who is instrumental in resolving the quarrel between her husband and his father. This happens when she writes to her father-in-law begging him to see his two grandchildren. She shows herself to be a woman who not only values keeping the family together but has the persuasive powers to make this happen under very difficult circumstances.

Madbogwu

Madbogwu is one of the men in the small village where Okeke lives. He is described as a practical man, and it is he who suggests that Okeke consult an herbalist about his son. Madbogwu is convinced that a dose of amalile will be effective. This is the medicine that is prescribed for women who want to win back the affection of their husbands.

Nnaemeka

Nnaemeka is a young man who originally came from a small village in the country but now lives in Lagos. His profession is not stated, but he appears to be an educated man, so he may be a member of the Nigerian civil service.

Nnaemeka appears to be a level-headed, courteous, considerate young man. He has chosen his bride well, as far as her personal qualities are concerned, but he also is under no illusions that his father will approve of his choice. No doubt since he started to live in Lagos, he has taken on the more modern ways of thinking. In a cosmopolitan city (that is, one with people from all over the world), people of all backgrounds tend to mix freely, but this is not so in the village he comes from. Nnaemeka does not want to upset his father, which is why he waits until he can see him in person before breaking the news of his engagement to a non-Ibo girl. Although he is courteous and respectful to his father, and the two men are fond of each other, Nnaemeka also shows that he has a strong will of his own. He is determined to marry Nene, and he tells his father the truth, even though he fears that his father will be angry about it. He also sticks to his guns, resisting all his father's efforts to convince him not to marry her. Nnaemeka is a man who knows his own mind and acts according to his affections and his convictions, rather than the customs of the past. The quarrel with his father upsets him, but he hopes, despite all indications to the contrary, that his father will eventually forgive him for marrying against his will.

Ugoye Nweke

Ugoye Nweke does not appear directly in the story, but she is the young woman who is selected by Okeke and his neighbor as a suitable wife for Nnaemeka. Ugoye has had enough schooling to make her a good wife, in Okeke's view, but not so much education that she might have opinions of her own.

Okeke

Okeke is Nnaemeka's father. He lives in a small village and thinks in a very traditional, conservative way. He believes that things should be done the way they have always been done; the old customs should be observed. This means that he cannot give his permission for his son to marry a non-Ibo girl, because this is something the Ibos in his village never do. They always marry amongst themselves. Okeke is a stubborn man, and he sticks to his position even though it means that he becomes estranged from his son, of whom he is very fond. However, Okeke is a devout Christian who believes that he has religion on his side. He does not approve of the fact that his son's fiancée is a schoolteacher. He believes that women should not teach, and he finds support for that position in the Bible. It is a subject he feels strongly about, and he leaves his son in no doubt about his views. He and the other men in the village do not think a girl's education is very important. She should acquire only the knowledge she will need to become a good wife. Okeke is set in his ways and cannot entertain new ways of thinking, even when his son is involved. He takes his objections to extreme lengths, refusing to talk to his son and rejecting his son's wife completely. Although he firmly believes that he is right, and Nnaemeka says his father is basically a good-natured man, his behavior seems unreasonable and cruel. Eventually, as a result of Nene's request to allow his grandsons to visit him, he softens his attitude and is filled with remorse over his past behavior.

THEMES

Tradition

The story centers around the clash between traditional values and a more modern way of conducting one's affairs. It also suggests the differences between life in the city and life in the country. The theme revolves around three characters: Okeke, who represents the traditional ways; Nene, who embodies the modernity of life in the city; and Nnaemeka, who is caught between the two.

In the small rural village where Okeke lives and where Nnaemeka must have grown up, traditional values are all-important. The Ibo tribe has a well-established way of doing things. They never marry outside their own tribe. No one has ever heard of anything like that happening in the entire history of their people. When news spreads in the village that Nnaemeka wants to marry a woman who is not an Ibo, it is regarded as a cataclysmic event. "It is the beginning of the end," says one man, who obviously fears that all the values by which the village people have lived, probably for countless generations, are about to be cast aside. In this Christian community, religion is used to explain what is happening. "Sons shall rise against their fathers," says another man, referring to a passage in the Bible. Nnaemeka's father believes his son has been tempted by Satan. These are people who live according to custom and religion. They cannot imagine anything different, and Nnaemeka's actions can be explained only by reference to theology or a belief that he must be sick.

In contrast, people who live in Lagos, the big city, have different values, as represented by Nene. She has been a city girl all her life, and when Nnaemeka first tells her that his father will not approve of their engagement, she does not take him seriously. In the city, old tribal allegiances are not so important. People mix freely with others from many different backgrounds. As the narrator points out about Nene, "In the cosmopolitan atmosphere of Lagos it had never occurred to her that a person's tribe could determine whom he married."

Another tradition in the village is that marriages are arranged by the families involved rather than the two people who are to be married. While Nnaemeka is in Lagos, his father selects a wife for him—Ugoye Nwake, the eldest daughter of a neighbor. It appears that Nnaemeka has never met this woman, but she is considered suitable by the two families involved, and the families expect to negotiate the details of the match (perhaps involving the payment of a dowry) when Nnaemeka returns in December.

In contrast, people in the city expect to choose their own partners rather than accept an arranged marriage. Nnaemeka and Nene are obviously in love, and they have freely chosen each other as their intended spouse. In the village, though, that does not count for much. In a wryly amusing moment, after Nnaemeka points out that he cannot marry Ugoye Nwake because he does not love her, his father replies, "Nobody said you did." He continues, "what one looks for in a wife are a good character and a Christian background."

Gender Roles

The society depicted in the village is strongly patriarchal; the men are in charge. Okeke tries

TOPICS FOR FURTHER STUDY

- Write a short story or sketch in which you update "Marriage Is a Private Affair" to a contemporary American setting. Try to create a believable scenario in which a young man or woman leaves the small town in which he or she grew up and moves to a big city. In the city, have the protagonist adopt new values that lead to conflict with his or her family.
- When "Marriage Is a Private Affair" was published in *The Sacrificial Egg and Other Short Stories*, it was accompanied by an illustration. Make your own drawing or painting showing Nnaemeka's confrontation with his father.
- Read Achebe's story, "Dead Man's Path," in *Girls at War, and Other Stories*. Create a presentation in which you compare and contrast it with "Marriage Is a Private Affair." In what ways do both stories illustrate the clash between traditional and modern values in Nigeria in the 1950s? What are the differences in how that theme is treated in the two stories? Use images, music, and words to illustrate the differences in a PowerPoint presentation.
- Watch the movie *Guess Who's Coming to Dinner* (1967), starring Spencer Tracy, Sidney Poitier, and Katharine Hepburn. Make a class presentation in which you briefly connect the theme of the movie to "Marriage Is a Private Affair." Then outline the social climate in the 1960s in the United States regarding questions of interracial marriage, which was illegal in many U.S. states at the time the film was made. How have attitudes changed since those times?
- Read Achebe's story written for young readers, *Chike and the River*, published by Cambridge University Press in 1966. The boy Chike, who is an Igbo, leaves his home village to live with his uncle in an urban environment. Chike notices many cultural differences between the town and the village. Write an essay in which you show how Achebe makes use of the each of the following in this story: food, songs, Igbo proverbs, and pidgin English (a form of English used in former British colonies).

---

to arrange with his neighbor for the man's daughter, Ugoye Nwake, to marry Nnaemeka. Ugoye appears to be given no say in the matter at all. The men assume they will just be able to tell her that she is to marry Nnaemeka, and that will be that.

The men in the village like to retain control by ensuring that the women do not receive too much education. Ugoye's father, for example, pulled her out of school when he thought she had learned enough to be able to fulfill her duties as a wife. That is all she will ever be required, or permitted, to do. Even her identity as an individual is overshadowed by her father. Nnaemeka refers to her not by her first name but as "Nwake's daughter."

Okeke holds similar views about the subservient place of women. When he hears that Nene is a schoolteacher, he is angry. The idea that women could be allowed to teach in schools is repellent to him. He justifies this attitude by referring to St. Paul's New Testament admonition to women, that they should keep silent in church.

Again, there is a contrast between attitudes in the village and in the city. In Lagos, Nene can be a schoolteacher and no one thinks it is remarkable. No doubt there are many female teachers in the city. The difference in attitude also hints at a contrast between two versions of Christianity, one that takes St. Paul's words literally, the other that has adopted a more liberal, progressive attitude.

STYLE

Nature Symbolism

When the conflict between father and son first erupts, it is December, and the weather is hot and

Traditional African wood carving symbolizing marriage *(Image copyright LiteChoices, 2009. Used under license from Shutterstock.com)*

dry, the sun "parching." Many years later, just before Okeke realizes the error of his ways, the weather is very different. There are black clouds, and soon the rain begins. This is the first rain of the year, and it soon develops into a thunderstorm that marks the change of the season. It also marks a change in the old man's heart. As the narrator says, "It was one of those rare occasions when even Nature takes a hand in a human fight." The harsh weather makes Okeke think of the grandchildren he has not yet met, and he imagines them shut out from his house in the rain. In that moment he knows that he must relent; he cannot reject his own grandchildren. The storm jolts him into repentance and forgiveness. It is as if a natural process has taken over that overcomes his stubborn resistance. The season is changing, and so must Okeke; the angry storm brings with it a message that finally he is able to hear. Notably, when the rain is coming down and he is trying not to think of his grandchildren, he attempts to hum the tune of a hymn, but "the pattering of large rain drops on the roof supplied a harsh accompaniment." The fact that the hymn tune is drowned out by the storm is symbolic. It shows that the stern religious ideology that Okeke has for so long used to justify his rigid position is being eclipsed by nature, which is always obliterating the past and making things new.

Language

In his mature work, Achebe is known for incorporating words and expressions from the Igbo language (Igbo is an alternative spelling of Ibo), as well as pidgin English (a simplified form of English spoken in many of the countries that were part of the British Empire). Achebe's purpose is to convey the flavor of the African cultural setting even though the language used is English. However, "Marriage Is a Private Affair" is an early work by Achebe, written when he was still an undergraduate, and he had not yet developed his mature style. It is noticeable that all the characters in the story speak in perfect British English. There are no Igbo expressions or pidgin English. From the way the characters speak, the reader would not be able to guess that the setting is in

COMPARE & CONTRAST

- **1950s:** Lagos, situated in the southwestern part of the country, is the capital of Nigeria. The majority of its inhabitants are from the Yoruba ethnic group, and Yoruba is the dominant language. However, because the ruling power is Britain, English is the language of education and government. The white European community in Lagos lives in the part of the city known as Ikoyi. During the 1950s, this area is opened for the first time to Africans who are senior members of the civil service.

  Today: Lagos is the largest city in Nigeria, but it is no longer the nation's capital. The capital was moved to Abuja, a city in central Nigeria, in 1991. Lagos remains Nigeria's chief port and is a center of business and industry. According to the 1996 census, the city has almost eight million inhabitants.

- **1950s:** According to the census of 1952–1953, the population of Nigeria is thirty-two million. Although still under British control, the country is being prepared for self-rule, and nationalist feelings run high.

  Today: The population of Nigeria is nearly 150 million, which makes it the ninth most populous country in the world. Nigeria is a democratic federal republic. In 2007, following the general election, there is a peaceful transfer of power from one civilian government to the next.

- **1950s:** The discovery of oil in 1956, at Olobiri in the Niger Delta, boosts the prospects for the Nigerian economy. Nigeria begins to export oil in 1958 from Port Harcourt.

  Today: Nigeria is one of the largest producers of oil in the world. The Nigerian economy depends heavily on oil exports, which account for over 95 percent of all exports and 85 percent of all government revenues. The recent discovery of more oil deposits allows the Nigerian government to increase its oil reserves.

Africa. Also, the language is rather literary throughout, reflecting a dignified, formal way of speaking associated with the English upper classes. For example, the narrator, after quoting one villager's comment, describes it as being "vouchsafed [by] a gentleman of quality who rarely argued with his neighbours because, he said, they were incapable of reasoning." When Nene asks Nnaemeka whether she can do anything to change his father's harsh attitude, he says, like an educated English gentleman of a certain class, "Not yet; my darling. . . . He is essentially good-natured and will one day look more kindly on our marriage." This use of language suggests that the African writer Achebe, at this very early stage in his career, before Nigerian independence, was content to write in the style of the literature of the colonial power rather than in a language adapted so that it would resonate with the specifically African experience.

HISTORICAL CONTEXT

Nigeria in the 1950s

In the 1950s, Nigeria was still under British rule. The British had controlled the country since the late nineteenth century, and it was the most important of British possessions in Africa during the height of the British Empire. The British brought with them Christian missionaries, and in Ogidi, Achebe's home village, Achebe's great-uncle had welcomed them. The British organized the Igbo territories in southeastern Nigeria into zones ruled by district commissioners. The commissioners would select willing Igbos to act as their local administrators. The hierarchical structure of government that resulted was at odds with the more democratic practices traditionally favored by the Igbos, who did not have chiefs or kings. Each village had a group of elders responsible for legal decisions and a variety of other groups that

Tribal culture in Africa (*Image copyright Urosr, 2009. Used under license from Shutterstock.com*)

decided issues that were relevant to them. Many Igbos resisted British rule, and the British responded with harsh measures designed to intimidate the local population. In 1914, the system of district commissioners was discontinued, and in 1930, the British attempted to reorganize the administration of eastern Nigeria to more closely reflect traditional Igbo practices.

After World War II ended in 1945, a new era gradually dawned in Africa. The European colonial powers accepted that the African territories they ruled must eventually be given their independence. In Nigeria, a nationalist movement grew up, demanding the extension of the franchise (the right to vote) and self-government. The British government accepted that Nigerian independence was inevitable and in the 1950s developed a series of constitutions designed to give the country greater autonomy. Nigeria was organized on a federal system, based on three regions, eastern, western, and northern, each with considerable autonomy. The reason given for this division was the need to minimize regional religious and tribal differences. The Igbos dominated in the east, the Yorubas in the west, and the Hausa and Fulani in the north. In 1954, a new constitution established two more regions, the Southern Cameroons and the federal territory of Lagos. In the late 1950s, the pace toward independence increased. A Constitutional Conference was held in London, England, in 1957, and then again in 1958. In 1959, a Nigerian Central Bank was created, and Nigerian currency was issued. Nigeria became independent on October 1, 1960. It was one of a number of African nations to gain independence from Britain during this period. Other such nations included Sudan (1956), Ghana (1957), Zambia (1960), Sierra Leone (1961), Uganda (1962), Kenya (1963), and Tanzania (1964). Several more African countries received their independence from other European colonial powers. Guinea (1958), Togo (1960), and Mali (1960) gained their independence from France and Congo from Belgium (1960).

The period leading up to and immediately after independence also produced a new literature in Nigeria, led by Achebe, whose influential novel *Things Fall Apart* was published in 1958. His work was soon followed by that of other Igbo writers, such as Nkem Nwanko, John Munonye, Chukwuemeka Ike, and Flora Nwapa, who took up Achebe's themes of the clash between the old and the new. One of Nigeria's great writers, the playwright Wole Soyinka, also began his work during this period.

CRITICAL OVERVIEW

As one of Achebe's earliest stories, published before he had reached his full powers as a writer, "Marriage Is a Private Affair" has not attracted as much attention from critics as his mature work. However, some critics have commented on it. In *Chinua Achebe: Novelist, Poet, Critic*, David Carroll points out the importance of the incident in which Nnaemeka's father refuses to consult an herbalist about his son:

> [It] suggests that what at first seems an added reluctance to influence his son is in fact a sign of what father and son have in common—a refusal to be controlled by ancient custom—which will eventually lead to a reconciliation.

C. L. Innes writes, in *Chinua Achebe*, that the theme of the story is "the conflict between traditional Igbo and European concepts of marriage, the one demanding obedience to family and community concerns, the other assuming the right to individual choice and marriage for love." Nahem Yousaf, in *Chinua Achebe*, points out that in the story, "Achebe explores the ways in which fundamentalist Christian belief is confining to women." Yousaf uses this example to argue that, contrary to some claims by feminist critics, Achebe did show some concern in his early works with the rights and status of women.

In *Achebe's World: The Historical and Cultural Context of the Novels of Chinua Achebe*, Robert M. Wren traces the theme of the story to Achebe's experience at University College, Ibadan, where he was a student when he wrote the story. Wren writes that the problem explored in the story was largely created by the college: "By bringing young people of both sexes together from variant language groups and then requiring them to work and speak in a common language, the university threatened all family and communal ties." Wren argues that, in the story, Achebe does not do justice to the father's point of view, presenting him as a reactionary who sees too much value in tradition and does not understand how things are changing for the better. Wren argues that although in the story Achebe clearly endorses the view that marriage is a "private" matter, "the whole thrust of Achebe's first two novels will say the opposite: that the clan is king, that nothing is private."

CRITICISM

Bryan Aubrey

Aubrey holds a Ph.D. in English. In this essay, he discusses "Marriage Is a Private Affair" in terms of some aspects of life in Nigeria in the 1950s and points out that the authorial voice in the story favors the young man's position over that of his father.

As any reader of "Marriage Is a Private Affair" will note, the Nigeria of the early 1950s was in a period of rapid change, some of it occurring too fast for those who adhere to traditional values to understand or accept. The story, one of Achebe's very earliest efforts, indirectly dramatizes some of the effects of the push toward independence that was sweeping through Nigeria at the time and changing the way people understood their social customs, including those affecting marriage and family.

Nnaemeka, the well-spoken young man who is determined to marry the woman he loves regardless of what his father and his village community think about the matter, might be thought of as a representative of the new rising class of men in Nigeria who were being trained by the British to take over the reins of the country. Finding himself in Lagos as a member of the civil service—his profession is not stated directly, but it seems likely that he holds a government position—he has been exposed to a more cosmopolitan world than his home village and appears to have assimilated some European values which make him insensitive to the traditions in which he was raised.

The small, unnamed village in the story likely has some resemblances to the village in which Achebe himself grew up. This was Ogidi, in southeastern Nigeria, where Achebe was born in 1930. Like the village in "Marriage Is a Private Affair," Ogidi was an Igbo community, and Achebe's parents, like many thousands of Igbos, were Christians. The British had first sent missionaries to Ogidi as early as 1892, and Achebe's father, Isaiah Okafor Achebe, had converted to Christianity sometime early in the twentieth century. He was trained as a catechist (an instructor in religious doctrine), and he founded St. Paul's Anglican church at Ikenga, Ogidi. Okafor married a Christian convert and raised his children in the faith. He rejected traditional Igbo religion in favor of the teachings of Christianity, although later in his life he softened his stance against what he had earlier condemned as heathen practices. Perhaps something of Achebe's father entered into the portrait

WHAT DO I READ NEXT?

- *Things Fall Apart*, first published in 1958, was Achebe's first novel. It has since become world-renowned as one of the foundational works of African literature in English. The novel begins in the late nineteenth century and shows daily life in an Igbo village before the British colonization. The second part of the book shows the encroachment of colonial administration and Christianity on that traditional way of life, and the last part shows the unsuccessful efforts by Okonkwo, the protagonist, to resist the destruction of his native culture. An edition of the novel was published by Anchor in 1994.
- *The Trials of Brother Jero* is a play by Nigerian writer Wole Soyinka. Soyinka, who won the Nobel Prize for Literature in 1986, attended University College, Ibadan, during the same period that Achebe was studying there. This play satirizes religious hypocrisy in the form of a charlatan who preaches to his followers on Bar Beach, in Lagos. It was first produced in Nigeria in 1960 and was published by Oxford University Press in 1964. It is currently available from Oxford University Press as one of the five plays in Soyinka's *Collected Plays 2*.
- *The Heinemann Book of Contemporary African Stories* (1992), edited by Achebe and Innes, contains twenty stories from five geographical regions in Africa. In all, fifteen African countries are represented, and the stories are written in a variety of styles. All the stories were first published after 1980. An introduction by Innes explains the criteria used to select the stories.
- *The Heart of the Matter* (1948), by British writer Graham Greene, is one of the best-known novels by one of the twentieth century's most renowned novelists. During World War II, Greene worked for British intelligence in Sierra Leone, in West Africa, and the novel is set in that place and time. It focuses on the unhappy life of Major Henry Scobie, a police inspector. It is likely that Achebe thought highly of the novel, since in his own novel *No Longer at Ease*, the protagonist, Obi Okonkwo, during a job interview, praises *The Heart of the Matter* as one of the finest novels he has read and certainly the best novel written by a European about West Africa. A Penguin edition of *The Heart of the Matter* was published in 1999 and remains in print.
- *Keesha's House* (2003), a young-adult book by Helen Frost, was named a 2004 Printz Honor Book by the American Library Association. The story is made up of dramatic monologues featuring the interlocking and troubled lives of seven teenagers. The monologues are written in traditional poetic forms, but they form a single story. The characters live in an inner-city neighborhood and struggle with various difficulties. For example, one girl is pregnant, but her boyfriend does not want her to have the baby. Other characters deal with addictions, absent parents, or other serious problems.
- *The Anchor Book of Modern African Stories* (2002), edited by Nadezda Obradovic, has a foreword by Chinua Achebe in which he provides a context for the short story genre in Africa. The diverse anthology contains thirty-four stories drawn from writers in many different African countries. Most of the stories have a contemporary setting and cover such topics as marriage, intergenerational family ties, race relations, AIDS, and capital punishment.

---

of Okeke, Nnaemeka's father in "Marriage Is a Private Affair." Okeke is a devout Christian, and although the story does not center on a conflict between Christianity and the traditional Igbo religion (this was a subject Achebe addressed in "Dead Man's Path," which appears in *The*

"AS THE STORY PITS AGE, CUSTOM, AND STUBBORNNESS AGAINST YOUTH, LOVE, AND FORGIVENESS, OKEKE IS RESCUED FROM HIS UNREASONABLENESS BY THE PATIENCE AND GOODWILL OF THE TWO YOUNG PEOPLE WHO HAVE BEEN MOST AFFECTED BY HIS BEHAVIOR."

Sacrificial Egg and Other Short Stories), a small incident in the story does hint at the underlying tension between the Christianity brought to the village by the British and the native healing practices and the beliefs associated with them. As the men of the village discuss the problem of Nnaemeka's choice of bride, one of the villagers suggests that Nnaemeka should consult an herbalist. This man is confident he knows just what medicine Nnaemeka needs, a herb called amalile, which, it appears, is used by women "with success to recapture their husbands' affection when it strays from them." However, Okeke will have none of it. He "was considerably ahead of his more superstitious neighbours" in that respect. In other words, Christianity, in his view, is the modern, progressive belief system, and the native practices are mere superstitions.

In other respects, though, especially regarding the customs surrounding marriage, Okeke is very traditional in his beliefs, especially the notions that Igbos should marry only within their own ethnic group and that marriages should be arranged only with family approval. This is where he and his son part company. Nnaemeka, who was raised in the village, knows very well that his father has these beliefs, as his comments to his fiancée early in the story indicate. Perhaps he once shared them himself, or just assumed that that was the way things were always done, but then he went to Lagos. One can imagine the kind of culture shock he must at first have encountered in Nigeria's largest, most cosmopolitan city. Indeed, Achebe depicted exactly this in his second novel, *No Longer at Ease* (1960), in which Obi Okonkwo, a young man from a rural area, goes to Lagos in the 1950s to being a career in the civil service. He quickly becomes acquainted with the extremes of luxury and poverty that abound in the great city, as well as the variety of languages spoken there. As Nnaemeka in "Marriage Is a Private Affair" probably felt when he first moved to Lagos, Obi feels a conflict between the lifestyle available in the city, with its entertainments and economic opportunities, and the traditional Igbo life back home in his village. No doubt Nnaemeka, being young and adaptable, soon became accustomed to life in the city, and perhaps he mingled with the Europeans in Ikoyi, the section of Lagos where the Europeans lived. Marrying for love, rather than as part of an arrangement made between families with the good of each family and the community in mind, had long been the way marriage was regarded in the West, even in the early 1950s. No doubt if Nnaemeka had made any British or European friends or acquaintances, they would have regarded an arranged marriage as a quaint throwback to a former era in their own societies. The belief that one should marry for love regardless of the ethnic background of one's partner seems to have penetrated deeply into the social fabric of Lagos in the 1950s, not only among those with European contacts, if the story is anything to go by. From the way that Nnaemeka's fiancée Nene is characterized, it seems that many, perhaps the majority, of young people in Lagos accepted without question that people should marry without regard to ethnic background. It seems that Nene has never encountered anyone with a belief to the contrary, which is why she reacts with such surprise when Nnaemeka informs her of what his father's attitude is likely to be. She is incredulous, as if she has been told about the way life is in some distant country.

When the story moves from Lagos to the village and the conflict between father and son, Nnaemeka does not for a moment consider another course of action than the one he has decided upon. Although he speaks respectfully to his father and asks him for forgiveness, he is convinced he is doing the right thing. To give up Nene for a woman he has not even met is unthinkable for him. At this point, the authorial voice is clearly in support of Nnaemeka's point of view, and it remains so throughout the story. The young author, Achebe, on the cusp of a period of great change in his country, sides with the young man, Nnaemeka, who embodies at least some of that spirit of change. To that purpose, Okeke, the father, is presented as unyielding and dogmatic. When his son first informs him of his plans to marry, Okeke thinks Satan must have got hold of him, and he looks at the situation in terms of rigid absolutes. "I owe it to you, my son, as a duty to show you what is right and what is wrong," he says, applying moral certainty in what most

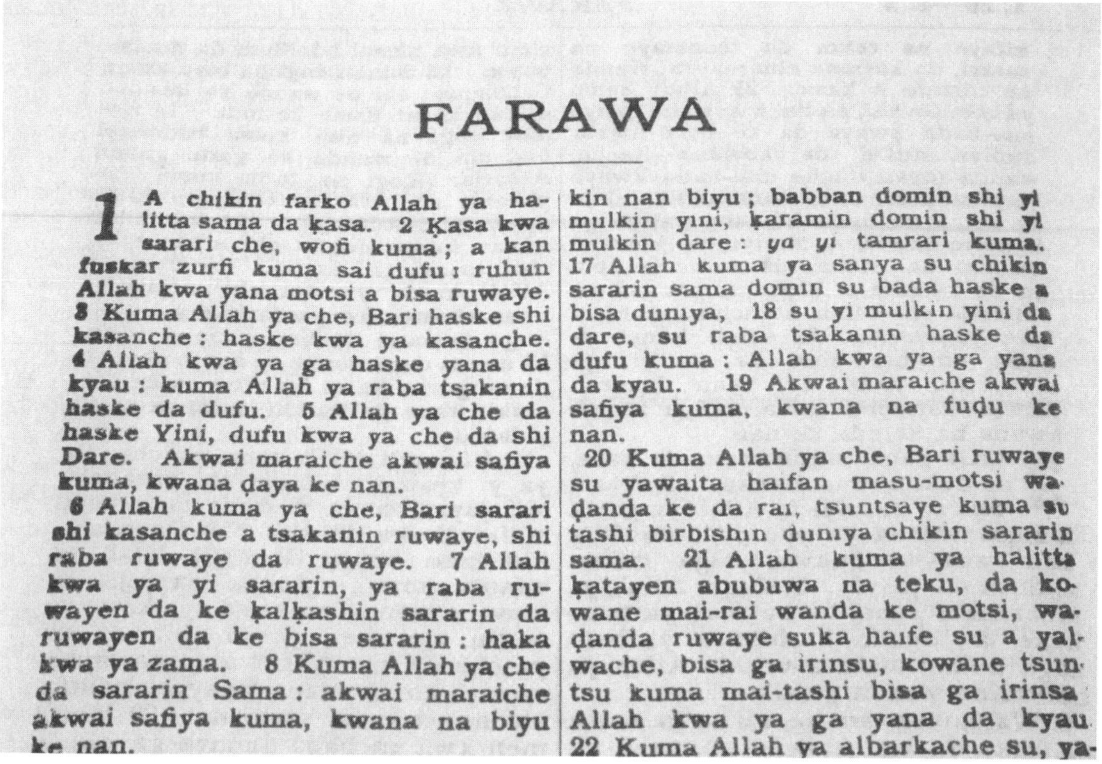

FARAWA

1 A chikin farko Allah ya halitta sama da ƙasa. 2 Ƙasa kwa
sarari che, wofi kuma; a kan
fuskar zurfi kuma sai dufu: ruhun
Allah kwa yana motsi a bisa ruwaye.
3 Kuma Allah ya che, Bari haske shi
kasanche: haske kwa ya kasanche.
4 Allah kwa ya ga haske yana da
kyau: kuma Allah ya raba tsakanin
haske da dufu. 5 Allah ya che da
haske Yini, dufu kwa ya che da shi
Dare. Akwai maraiche akwai safiya
kuma, kwana ɗaya ke nan.
6 Allah kuma ya che, Bari sarari
shi kasanche a tsakanin ruwaye, shi
raba ruwaye da ruwaye. 7 Allah
kwa ya yi sararin, ya raba ruwayen da ke ƙalƙashin sararin da
ruwayen da ke bisa sararin: haka
kwa ya zama. 8 Kuma Allah ya che
da sararin Sama: akwai maraiche
akwai safiya kuma, kwana na biyu
ke nan.

kin nan biyu; babban domin shi yi
mulkin yini, ƙaramin domin shi yi
mulkin dare: *ya yi* tamrari kuma.
17 Allah kuma ya sanya su chikin
sararin sama domin su bada haske a
bisa duniya, 18 su yi mulkin yini da
dare, su raba tsakanin haske da
dufu kuma: Allah kwa ya ga yana
da kyau. 19 Akwai maraiche akwai
safiya kuma, kwana na fuɗu ke
nan.
20 Kuma Allah ya che, Bari ruwaye
su yawaita haifan masu-motsi wa-
ɗanda ke da rai, tsuntsaye kuma su
tashi birbishin duniya chikin sararin
sama. 21 Allah kuma ya halitta
ƙatayen abubuwa na teku, da kowane mai-rai wanda ke motsi, wa-
ɗanda ruwaye suka haife su a yal-
wache, bisa ga irinsu, kowane tsun-
tsu kuma mai-tashi bisa ga irinsa:
Allah kwa ya ga yana da kyau.
22 Kuma Allah ya albarkache su, ya-

Genesis, the first book of the Christian Bible, translated into an African language (Image copyright Stephen Aaron Rees, 2009. Used under license from Shutterstock.com)

readers might regard as an inappropriate context. Were "Marriage Is a Private Affair" to be adapted into a one-act play, Okeke would clearly be in the role of the "blocking" figure, the stubborn, usually older character who tries to thwart the inevitable happy ending. He is certainly hard on his son, cutting off virtually all contact with him merely because of his choice of bride. The reader may ask, Is upholding a family and tribal tradition worth cutting oneself off from one's own son?

As the story pits age, custom, and stubbornness against youth, love, and forgiveness, Okeke is rescued from his unreasonableness by the patience and goodwill of the two young people who have been most affected by his behavior. Neither Nnaemeka nor Nene is prepared to condemn Okeke for his beliefs or his actions. Near the beginning of the story, Nene says she expects Okeke to forgive his son, and Nnaemeka, too, even when he has been cut off by his father, retains his kind view of him, expecting him eventually to soften his attitude toward them. It is the refusal on the part of the daughter-in-law to accept the finality of the estrangement, and her belief in the surpassing value of maintaining family connections, that eventually brings about a reconciliation. The father cannot resist the natural desire to become acquainted with his grandchildren. Youth comes to the rescue of age, and Okeke is left to regret his former stubbornness. He has come to realize that blood is thicker than custom and that family is more important than beliefs about how family should be chosen.

Source: Bryan Aubrey, Critical Essay on "Marriage Is a Private Affair," in *Short Stories for Students*, Gale, Cengage Learning, 2010.

SOURCES

Achebe, Chinua, "Beginning of the End" ("Marriage Is a Private Affair"), in *The Sacrificial Egg and Other Short Stories*, Etudo, 1962, pp. 21–26.

Booker, M. Keith, *The Chinua Achebe Encyclopedia*, Greenwood Press, 2003.

Burns, Sir Alan, *History of Nigeria*, George Allen and Unwin, 1964.

Carroll, David, *Chinua Achebe: Novelist, Poet, Critic*, Macmillan, 1990, pp. 146–47.

Innes, C. L., *Chinua Achebe*, Cambridge University Press, 1990, p. 11.

"Nigeria," in *CIA: World Factbook*, https://www.cia.gov/library/publications/the-world-factbook/geos/ni.html (accessed October 6, 2009).

"Nigeria," in *Energy Information Administration: Official Energy Statistics from the U.S. Government*, http://www.eia.doe.gov/cabs/Nigeria/Background.html (accessed October 7, 2009).

Wren, Robert M., *Achebe's World: The Historical and Cultural Context of the Novels of Chinua Achebe*, Northcote House, 2003, pp. 2–3.

Yousaf, Nahem, *Chinua Achebe*, Northcote House, 2003, p. 101.

FURTHER READING

Ezenwa-Ohaeto, *Chinua Achebe: A Biography*, Indiana University Press, 2008.

In this biography, Ezenwa-Ohaeto uses Achebe's life to shed light on his writing. The biography is also an exploration of the social, historical, and cultural forces that shaped Achebe's work. Achebe's huge contribution to and influence on African literature is fully conveyed.

Falola, Toyin, *Culture and Customs of Nigeria*, Greenwood Press, 2008.

A Nigerian historian provides an accessible and up-to-date account of all aspects of Nigerian culture and customs today. Topics include history, religion, literature, art, music, marriage and family, social customs, and lifestyle.

Lindfors, Bernth Olof, ed., *Conversations with Chinua Achebe*, University Press of Mississippi, 2000.

Achebe has given numerous interviews throughout his career. This book is a collection of twenty-one interviews he gave between 1962 and 1995. They give unparalleled insight into the man and his work.

Morrison, Jago, *The Fiction of Chinua Achebe*, Palgrave Macmillan, 2007.

This is a guide on how to read Achebe's work. Morrison explains different critical approaches, discussing the novels and the short stories.

No Witchcraft for Sale

DORIS LESSING

1964

Doris Lessing's short story "No Witchcraft for Sale" was published in her renowned 1964 collection *African Stories.* As the book's title implies, the story is set in Africa, and it portrays the cultural tensions and dissonance between blacks and whites in colonial Africa (a time when much of Africa was under European rule). Lessing's "No Witchcraft for Sale" embodies the characteristic themes and content for which the author became famous. Lessing was well acquainted with colonial Africa; her British family moved to Southern Rhodesia (now Zimbabwe) when she was only six, and Lessing was raised in the setting that she later used as the subject of her fiction.

"No Witchcraft for Sale" portrays the Farquar family and its beloved servant Gideon. When the Farquars' only son, Teddy, is at risk of losing his sight after a tree snake spits its venom into his eyes, Gideon retrieves a plant from the African bush (wilderness) country and uses it to effect a seemingly miraculous cure. This act, however, leads the Farquars and Gideon into conflict as they attempt to get him to disclose the whereabouts of the plant in order to make it available to others.

Because *African Stories* is one of the best-known collections by a preeminent twentieth-century feminist writer, it remained in print for several years after its initial release. As Lessing's output slowed on account of her advancing age, however, her work became more obscure, and

Doris Lessing (Getty Images)

the most recent edition of the collection was released by Simon and Schuster in 1981.

AUTHOR BIOGRAPHY

Lessing was born Doris May Tayler (some sources say Taylor) on October 22, 1919, in Kermanshah, Persia (now Iran). Her parents, Alfred Cook Tayler and Emily Maude McVeagh, were British citizens living abroad. The family moved to the British Colony in Southern Rhodesia (now Zimbabwe) in 1925, in the hopes of making its fortune farming corn there. They were, however, relatively unsuccessful in this endeavor. Lessing's childhood was spent joyfully exploring the wild with her brother Henry and miserably attending a rigid convent school. After being sent to attend high school in Salisbury (then capital of Southern Rhodesia), Lessing dropped out at age thirteen. However, she was a voracious reader and continued her education on her own.

Lessing's relationship with her mother was often tumultuous, and she left home at age fifteen to begin working as a nursemaid. In 1937, at age eighteen, Lessing moved to Salisbury, where she worked for a year as a telephone operator. The following year, she married Frank Wisdom. The couple had a son and a daughter, but by 1943, the marriage was dissolved. Lessing left both her husband and children, though she remained in Salisbury. She joined the Left Book Club, a communist reading group. There, she met Gottfried Lessing, whom she married in 1945. They had a son together, but again, Lessing left her husband within a few years. She moved to London, this time taking her son with her. Lessing's first novel, *The Grass Is Singing*, was published in 1950. The collection of short stories *This Was the Old Chief's Country* followed in 1951. Her next book, *Five: Short Novels*, was released in 1953.

During the early 1950s, Lessing grew apart from the Communist party and its ideals, and she severed her party affiliation in 1954. Two years later, as she continued to publicly critique the treatment of native Africans in colonial Africa, she was formally barred from entering Southern Rhodesia and South Africa. Despite this pressure, Lessing continued voicing her views. The 1950s and 1960s were two of her most prolific decades. One of her most famous novels, *The Golden Notebook*, was published in 1962. Although controversial, the book was ultimately hailed as a feminist masterpiece. The book also featured an experimental narrative structure, one reminiscent of the work of famed author Gertrude Stein. In 1964, Lessing's collection *African Stories*, including "No Witchcraft for Sale," was published.

Over the next two decades, Lessing's work became more experimental in form and more fantastical in content, an approach first established in *The Golden Notebook*. Such works from this period include *Briefing for a Descent into Hell* (1971) and *Memoirs of a Survivor* (1974). Later novels include *The Good Terrorist* (1985) and *The Fifth Child* (1989). Lessing has also written a graphic novel, plays, nonfiction, and two novels under the pseudonym Jane Somers. Her two-volume autobiography, *Under My Skin* and *Walking in the Shade*, was published in 1994 and 1997.

In 1995, Lessing traveled to South Africa. It was her first time back in the country since her 1956 banishment. There, she was hailed for the very work that initially led to her expulsion. In 2007, Lessing received further acknowledgment for her life's work when she was awarded the Nobel Prize in Literature. Lessing was the oldest living person to have received the honor. The following year, her novel *Alfred and Emily* was released, and Lessing declared that it would be her final work. As of 2009, she continued to live in London.

PLOT SUMMARY

After having been childless for some time, the Farquars finally have a son, Teddy. When he is born, all of their servants rejoice. They praise Mrs. Farquar and marvel over Teddy's blond hair and blue eyes. When Teddy is old enough to have his first haircut, the Farquars' cook, Gideon, is fascinated by Teddy's golden locks. He calls Teddy "Little Yellow Head." All the natives and servants call him that from then on. Gideon cares a great deal for Teddy. The two have a special bond, and when Gideon finishes his work, he plays with Teddy and makes toys for him. Mrs. Farquar likes Gideon because he clearly loves her son.

The Farquars do not have any other children, and Gideon tells Mrs. Farquar, "Little Yellow Head is the most good thing we have in our house." Mrs. Farquar is touched that Gideon has used the word "we," indicating that he thinks of himself as part of the family. She raises his pay at the end of the month. Gideon has worked for the Farquars for many years, and his own wife and children also live on the "compound." Unlike many other servants, Gideon does not require time off so he can travel to his distant home village in order to visit his family. This further binds and endears Gideon to his employers.

A native baby, born around the same time as Teddy, is in awe of the blond child. As Gideon watches the two boys, he states that one will be the master and one will be the servant. Mrs. Farquar observes that the same thought had crossed her mind. Gideon says that this "is God's will." Both he and Mrs. Farquar are religious, and this commonality bonds them yet more.

When Teddy is six, he is given a scooter, which he rides all over the compound. Gideon laughs at Teddy's youthful antics. His young son is in awe of the scooter, but Teddy teases the boy and scares him off by racing the scooter in ever-shrinking circles around the boy. Gideon admonishes Teddy for doing so, but Teddy haughtily remarks, "He's only a black boy." Gideon does not reply, but he turns his back on Teddy. The young master is upset that he has hurt Gideon. Teddy picks an orange and brings it to Gideon, but Teddy still cannot bring himself to say that he is sorry. Gideon accepts the orange "unwillingly." He says that Teddy will be sent away to school soon and when he returns he will be an adult, "and that is how our lives go." Gideon soon begins to distance himself from Teddy, not because he is angry but because he is preparing himself for "something inevitable." Gideon no longer plays with Teddy or gives him any physical affection. Teddy, in turn, begins to treat Gideon differently, speaking to him "in the way a white man uses towards a servant, expecting to be obeyed."

This formality evaporates, however, when Teddy falls victim to a tree snake. While out on his scooter, Teddy stops to rest by some plants. The snake has been sitting on a roof nearby, and it spits its venom directly into Teddy's eyes. Teddy rushes home in agony. He is in danger of permanently losing his sight; the Farquars know of many who have done so. Gideon calms Mrs. Farquar and promises to heal Teddy. He sets out into the bush in search of a cure.

Meanwhile, Teddy's eyes are swollen, and he is crying in both pain and fear. Mrs. Farquar is equally afraid. She washes Teddy's eyes out, but nothing seems to have an effect. She feels anxious and helpless. As far as she knows, there is no cure, so she can hardly understand how Gideon intends to help. Gideon returns quickly with a plant, from which he removes the leaves to reveal a white root. Gideon chews the root and holds Teddy down. He squeezes Teddy's eyes, and the boy cries out in pain. Gideon then pries open Teddy's swollen eyelids and spits the chewed-up root directly into his eyes. Gideon then declares that Teddy will retain his sight. Mrs. Farquar is shocked by the violent nature of Gideon's so-called cure, and she does not have any faith that it will work.

The remedy does indeed work, though, and both Mr. and Mrs. Farquar thank Gideon profusely,

MEDIA ADAPTATIONS

- The audiobook *Doris Lessing Reads: "No Witchcraft for Sale" and "The New Man"* was released by Spoken Arts in 1986. The recording was reissued in 1990.

feeling "helpless in their gratitude." They lavish Gideon and his family with gifts and give their cook a large raise. Mrs. Farquar says that Gideon is an "instrument" of God's "goodness." Gideon replies that God is indeed good.

News of the miraculous recovery travels throughout the compound and into the neighboring farms. Similar stories of extraordinary cures also abound. The white men and women in the area realize that the bush harbors many medicinal plants, but despite their best efforts, they are never able to get the natives to divulge their secrets. The tale of Teddy's cure is eventually heard by a doctor in the nearest town, who calls the story absurd. He has heard such rumors before, all of which have turned out to be false upon further investigation. Despite their skepticism, people from the laboratory in town travel to the Farquars' home to test the local plants.

The Farquars are "flustered and pleased and flattered" by the attention. They have lunch with the laboratory technicians and tell them their story. The head scientist and the technicians hope to discover a new drug that will help all humanity. The thought of contributing to such a noble endeavor pleases the Farquars. The head scientist also notes that the medicine could be highly profitable, but the Farquars are uncomfortable with this line of thought. They feel that Teddy's cure was a "miracle," and the thought of making money because of it is unappealing to them.

Nevertheless, the Farquars focus on the good that the proposed medicine might do. They call Gideon in and ask him to tell the scientists about the plant he used to cure Teddy. Gideon is flabbergasted and deeply hurt. He clearly feels betrayed. The Farquars explain that the medicine will help others, but Gideon only looks at the ground sullenly. The scientist then tells Gideon how the drug will be manufactured in an attempt to impress Gideon with modern technology. He then switches to bribery, telling Gideon that he would like to give him a gift.

Gideon still does not respond. When he does, he says flatly that he cannot remember which plant he used. He is clearly upset and lying. He looks coldly at his employers. Though the Farquars at first felt guilty about pressing Gideon for information, they become annoyed by Gideon's anger and his stubborn refusal to comply. Still, they sense that he will not relent and that his knowledge will remain a mystery to them. It will continue to be the inheritance of the descendants "of the old witch doctors whose ugly masks . . . and all the uncouth properties of magic were the outward signs of real power and wisdom." Still, despite their inward sense of defeat, they persist.

Gideon again says he cannot remember the plant he used, and then he says that no such plant exists, that his own spit cured Teddy. He gives all manner of excuses, many of which are directly conflicting. The Farquars begin to find him an "ignorant, perversely obstinate African" instead of "their gentle, lovable old servant." Finally, to everyone's surprise, Gideon agrees to show them the root, but he looks at his employers and the scientist with anger as he does so. Gideon, the scientist, the Farquars, and even Teddy head out into the bush. It is December, a summer month in Africa, and extremely hot outside.

The group walks for a suspiciously long time. When Gideon had rushed out to get the plant to heal Teddy, he was gone for only a little while. Every now and then, someone asks whether or not they are getting any closer to the plant. Gideon only replies that he is still looking. The Farquars grow increasingly angry, and the scientist, who thinks that that the story of the miracle cure is likely to be a scam, feels vindicated. As they walk, Gideon occasionally stops to run his hands through the plants as if he is searching for the right one, but it is clear he is merely putting on a show. After two hours have gone by, Gideon picks a plant with blue flowers on it and gives it to the scientist before storming away. The group has passed this exact plant many times over on the walk, so it seems that Gideon has led them on a wild goose chase.

Back at the house, the scientist politely thanks Gideon, but it is clear he thinks the whole episode is a ruse. Gideon remains in a bad mood for several days, speaking and acting rudely toward the Farquars, but over time, his naturally sunny disposition returns. The Farquars continue to ask the other servants for information on the actual cure, but no one will tell them anything. One servant tells them that Gideon is the son of a great medicine man and that he can cure anything. However, he quickly backpedals and says that Gideon is "not as good as the white man's doctor . . . but he's good for us."

As Gideon and the Farquars become friendly again, over time they come to laugh at the incident. The Farquars jokingly ask whether Gideon will ever show them the "snake-root." Gideon laughs and replies, "But I did show you missus, have you forgotten?" When Teddy is older and attending school, he also jokes with Gideon about the time they went searching for the "snake-root." He calls Gideon a "rascal" and says they walked so far that his father had to carry him. Gideon chuckles politely and calls Teddy "Little Yellow Head." He remarks that the boy has gotten older and that soon he will run his own farm.

CHARACTERS

Mr. Farquar

Mr. Farquar is Teddy's father and head of the Farquar household, but he is rarely a present figure in the narrative. He is referred to as an individual on only a handful of occasions and instead appears mainly as one portion of the Farquars. He and his wife are often described as a single unit that acts together. He is, however, mentioned as an individual when he learns of Gideon's role in saving Teddy's eyesight. However, his actions upon learning the news are again in concert with those of his wife: "They felt helpless in their gratitude: it seemed they could do nothing to express it."

Presumably, Mr. Farquar is away at work much of the time, as his wife is often portrayed as an individual during the day-to-day domestic activities. Both he and his wife are fairly provincial. When the laboratory technicians visit them from town, the couple is "flustered and pleased and flattered" by the attention. The Farquars are also religious and kind hearted. They see Teddy's cure as a "miracle" and are excited by the prospect of using the plant to help others. Given their pure intentions, they are made uncomfortable by the idea of producing the medicine for profit. Furthermore, they are not entirely insensitive to the uncomfortable situation they have placed Gideon in by asking him to show them the medicinal plant. However, they seem to feel that their good intentions justify the transgression. Although the Farquars are aware that they are overstepping a silently agreed upon boundary, they are nevertheless annoyed and angered by Gideon's irritation and noncompliance. This emotion likely stems from a felling of embarrassment; their servant openly defies them in front of the head scientist and the laboratory technicians.

Despite the Farquars' anger at Gideon's defiance, they ultimately come to laugh at the incident. However, they also persist (fruitlessly) in their quest to locate the plant. They ask all of their other servants but succeed only in learning that Gideon is the son of a great medicine man. He is described as an accomplished healer who can heal anything but who is nevertheless "not as good as the white man's doctor."

Mrs. Farquar

Mrs. Farquar is Teddy's mother, and she runs the Farquar household. It is she who works with the servants and decides their pay. She is also praised by the servants for bearing such a fine son. When no other children are forthcoming, Gideon comforts his mistress by implying that Teddy is so wonderful that no other children are needed.

Mrs. Farquar's actions are most often described in tandem with her husband. However, unlike her husband, Mrs. Farquar is also portrayed as acting independently on several occasions. Mrs. Farquar is fond of Gideon because he loves her son and because he thinks of himself as part of the family. She also likes him because he is agreeable, kind, and religious. When Gideon gazes at a black baby born around the same time as Teddy, he notes that one will become master and one servant and that this "is God's will." Mrs. Farquar replies that she has been thinking the same thing. In this instance, she shows that she is not insensitive to the imbalances of power that surround her.

Mrs. Farquar also acts independently when a snake spits its venom into Teddy's eyes. She is panicked, and she knows of many who have permanently lost their sight under the same circumstances. In fact, when Gideon promises to cure the boy and rushes out to the bush, she does not believe that anything will come of it. Instead, she uses everything she can think of to flush out Teddy's eyes.

Teddy Farquar

Teddy Farquar is the beloved only son of the Farquars. He lives in an undisclosed farming compound in Africa. The compound consists of Teddy, his family, and their servants. Teddy is beloved not only by his parents but also by all of the family's servants. He is blond and blue-eyed, and the black servants all marvel at these features. Teddy is given the affectionate nickname of "Little Yellow Head" by the family cook,

Gideon. Teddy and Gideon are particularly close, and the two play together often. However, as Teddy grows from an infant to a boy, he begins to act haughtily, and Gideon is increasingly sensitive to their different stations in life. Gideon's son is in awe of Teddy's scooter, but Teddy meanly races the scooter around the boy and frightens him away. When Gideon chastises Teddy for doing so, Teddy shows both his ignorance and his (arguably if unfortunately justified) sense of entitlement by responding: "He's only a black boy."

Teddy is aware that his insensitivity has upset Gideon, and he struggles to make amends. However, the young boy cannot bring himself to actually apologize. From then on, as Teddy ages, he begins to act more like Gideon's master than Gideon's friend. Despite the growing distance between them, Gideon finds a cure for Teddy when he is in danger of losing his eyesight. Later, when the scientist and laboratory technician come to investigate, Teddy is too young to truly understand the complex social pressures inherent in the situation. He sees the outing to locate the plant only as an adventure. As Teddy continues to age, he joins in his parents' gentle teasing about the "snakeroot" adventure.

Gideon

Gideon is the Farquars' beloved servant and cook. He has a wife and children who live in the Farquars' compound with him. Toward the end of the story, it is revealed that Gideon is also the son of a great medicine man and an accomplished healer himself. This identity is kept hidden from his employers, as Gideon dutifully plays the role of loyal servant. Despite this subterfuge, Gideon is genuinely kind and loyal. He adores young Teddy, with whom he has a special bond. It is he who lovingly nicknames the boy "Little Yellow Head."

Gideon is well aware, however, of the social restriction between black and white people in that time and place, and he comments on the different fates of two babies born at the same time. The white one (Teddy) will grow up to run a farm. The black one (who is unnamed) will become a servant. However, because this observation is made in front of Mrs. Farquar, Gideon is quick to add that this "is God's will." Whether this statement is sincere or not is unclear. Gideon's feelings become more clear, however, when he chastises Teddy for mistreating his own son. Teddy's response that Gideon's son is "only a black boy" profoundly offends the man, who turns his back on Teddy. The depth of this hurt is further demonstrated when he "unwillingly" accepts Teddy's peace offering. Following this incident, Gideon becomes increasingly aware of the widening gap between himself and Teddy. He grows increasingly distant from Teddy, and the boy in turn speaks to Gideon "in the way a white man uses towards a servant, expecting to be obeyed."

Despite this outward change, Gideon's love for Teddy remains constant, as is demonstrated when he rushes to save the boy's eyesight. In doing so, he begins to expose his hidden talents and the secrets of the bush (the only real power he possesses). His upset at being asked to divulge these secrets is understandable, and even the Farquars are aware that their request is a type of betrayal. In his anger, Gideon acts in a way that the Farquars have never before seen, and his persistent refusals incite them to anger and further determination. Gideon finally relents and takes the Farquars to find the plant, but he does so in a manner that leads them to conclude that he has lied to them. However, Gideon's enigmatic responses at the end of the story (in which he claims, "But I did show you missus, have you forgotten?") call this into question. It is possible that Gideon was truthful and only wished the Farquars and the head scientist to assume that he was lying. Regardless, Gideon's good nature again asserts itself when he forgives the Farquars for their transgression. Over time, both he and his employers are even able to laugh about the incident.

Head Scientist

The head scientist travels from town with some laboratory technicians in the hopes of finding the plant that was used to cure Teddy. The head scientist is somewhat skeptical of the Farquars' miraculous claims, and his skepticism is seemingly confirmed by the fact that Gideon apparently leads him and the Farquars on a wild goose chase. Nevertheless, the scientist earlier points out that the medicinal plant has the potential to help humanity and to generate revenue as well. In his arrogant attempts to persuade Gideon to divulge his secrets, the scientist first tries to impress Gideon with modern technology and then tries to bribe him.

THEMES

Racism

Because "No Witchcraft for Sale" is set in colonial Africa, racism is inherent in the basic social structure in which the story takes place. This is because the story accurately portrays a white upper class (which was historically British) ruling over a black (native) servant class. Although the Farquars are otherwise kind, loving, and God-fearing people, they see nothing wrong with the racism inherent in their way of life. Even Gideon seems to accept the status quo (the way things are). For instance, as he gazes at a native baby born around the same time as Teddy, he comments, apparently without criticism, that one will become servant and one master. The thought has also occurred to Mrs. Farquar.

As a child, Teddy innocently accepts the world around him, instantly understanding that as a white child, he is set above the black servants around him. This is made painfully evident when Teddy treats Gideon's son cruelly, racing his scooter around the boy until he is so frightened that he runs away. When Gideon chastises Teddy for his unkind behavior, the boy replies, "He's only a black boy." Furthermore, although Teddy is sad that he has upset Gideon and attempts to make peace by bringing the servant an orange, he finds himself unable to apologize or admit any wrongdoing on his part. That Gideon accepts Teddy's peace offering "unwillingly" is also a sign of the power of race. Gideon, as a native African, must bend to the will of a six-year-old white boy. Gideon understands that Teddy will one day run his own farm, "and that is how our lives go," he says. Gideon accepts the racism around him as "something inevitable." Still, the event is not without its consequences. Gideon and Teddy's close friendship has come to an end. Gideon treats Teddy with the same distant formality he would any white person. In exchange, young Teddy addresses Gideon "in the way a white man uses towards a servant, expecting to be obeyed."

Other instances of racism are apparent in the way the scientist speaks condescendingly toward Gideon and finds it hard to believe that Gideon should possess any knowledge of the medicinal plants of the region. Even Mr. and Mrs. Farquar, despite their apparent love for their servant, are dismayed by Gideon's resistance to their request to reveal the plant. Although they recognize that they are crossing a line by doing so, the basic fact of Gideon's disobedience is affront enough to make them persist. Class and race are inherently intertwined. It is the racism of colonial Africa that dictates its class structure.

Religion

Although the theme of religion in "No Witchcraft for Sale" is subtle, it speaks significantly

TOPICS FOR FURTHER STUDY

- Do you think that Gideon showed the Farquars and the scientists the actual plant and only fooled them into thinking that he did not? Why or why not? Explain your conclusions in a brief essay, using specific examples and quotations from the text.
- Use the Internet to research Southern Rhodesia in the 1960s. Look for information about the effects of colonialism on the country. Research the process by which they began to work toward independence. Be sure to print out any photographs or census information you can find. Use your printouts to create a timeline history of the country now known as Zimbabwe.
- Read Sheila Gordon's young-adult novel *Waiting for The Rain*, which portrays a young black boy and young white boy living in apartheid (segregated) South Africa. How does Gordon's portrayal of racial inequity compare to Lessing's in "No Witchcraft for Sale"? Use your notes on both stories to lead a class discussion addressing this question.
- Imagine Teddy as an adult running his own farm and write a short story portraying this scenario. Do you think Teddy would be a kind employer like his parents?
- Make a list of all of the medicinal herbs and plants that you know of. Feel free to ask parents, teachers, physicians, and peers for additional ideas. Afterward, use the Internet to research the origin and purpose of these plants and how they were discovered. Display your findings in a PowerPoint presentation.

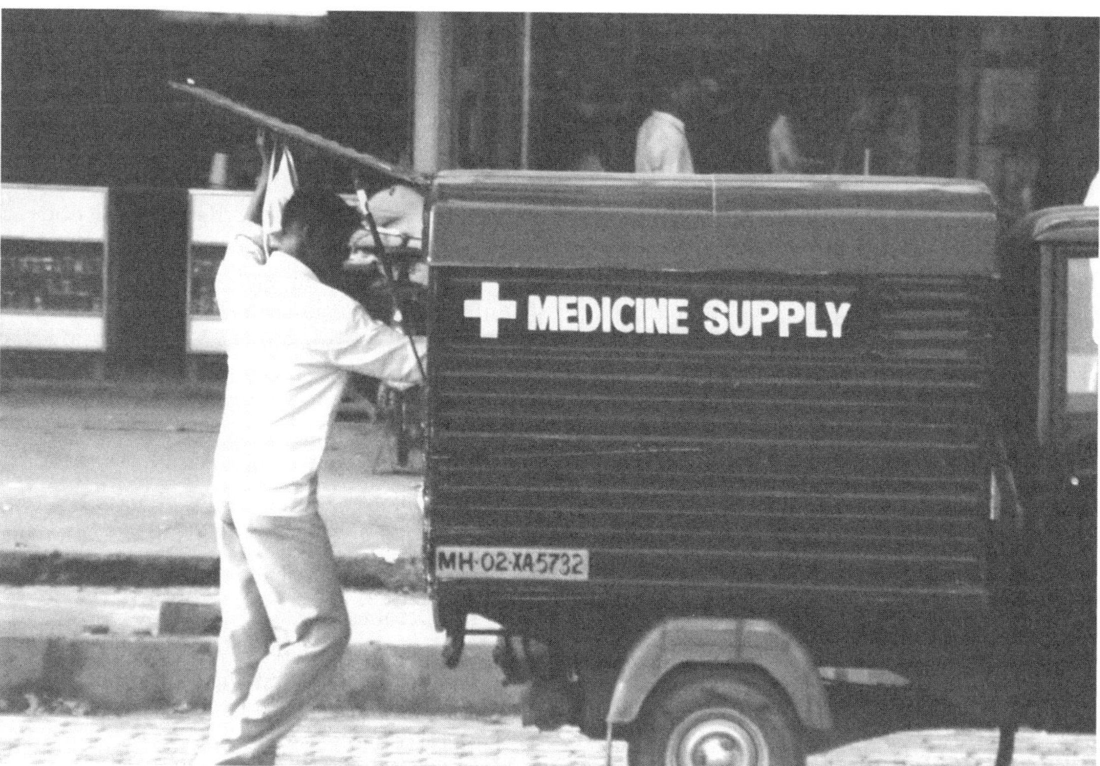

A medical house call (*Image copyright Kamil Fazrin Rauf, 2009. Used under license from Shutterstock.com*)

to the theme of racism. For instance, both Mrs. Farquar and Gideon are religious. For this reason (among others), the mistress of the house trusts Gideon. When both she and Gideon are meditating on the different fates of two boys born around the same time, fates dictated by the color of their skin, it is Gideon who is quick to add that this "is God's will." Whether or not Gideon is sincere is questionable. It is more than likely that he makes the hasty addendum to his observation in order to appear more agreeable and to avoid appearing as if he is challenging the status quo. This occurrence is echoed after Gideon saves Teddy's eyesight. Mrs. Farquar says that Gideon is an "instrument" of God's "goodness." Gideon replies that God is indeed good. Again, there is something rather flat in Gideon's tone, and it causes the reader to question Gideon's sincerity.

It is inarguably clear, though, that the Farquars are sincere in their faith. They believe that Teddy's cure was a "miracle." When the opportunity to share the plant with the world arises, it is the prospect of benefiting humanity that appeals to the couple. In fact, the suggestion that the endeavor could also be profitable is entirely distasteful to the Farquars. They feel that money sullies the pure nature of the miracle and their intent.

STYLE

Third-Person Omniscient Narrator

"No Witchcraft for Sale" is told by an unnamed narrator from the third-person omniscient point of view. A third-person narrator is one that refers to events and characters objectively (as, for example, "she" or "they") and does not participate directly in the story. The narrator is an unidentified and all-knowing being, one who can read the inner thoughts and feelings of more than one character in the story. In this story, the reader knows something about all of the characters' inner lives. This approach lends the reader maximum insight into the characters and their motivations. The interplay of conflicting motivations is also intriguing and entertaining, as is the case when the Farquars and the head scientist wish to learn which plant Gideon used to heal Teddy. The Farquars want to do good for humanity, and the scientist wants to turn a profit. On the other side of the divide, Gideon wants to do neither, as he feels betrayed by his employers and wishes to keep to himself this last part of his cultural heritage.

One drawback to this narrative approach is that it distances the reader from the action. The reader is never given an opportunity to identify closely with any one character (as would be the case in a story with a first-person narrator).

Dialect

Though the use of dialect in the story is subtle, its effect is not. Mr. and Mrs. Farquar and the head scientist, even six-year-old Teddy, all speak in grammatically correct English. Gideon and the other servants, however, speak broken and ungrammatical English. This difference underscores the gaps of wealth, privilege, and education that exist between employers and servants and between white and black.

Lack of Detail

Lessing's "No Witchcraft for Sale," while rich in plot, action, and the inner lives of its characters, is remarkably lacking in detail. For instance, the location of the Farquars' farm is not mentioned, nor is the name of the town nearby. That the tale is set in colonial Africa can be gathered only from the action that takes place in the story. The crops that the Farquars farm are never mentioned, nor is Mr. Farquar's general absence from the story (he appears only in relation to Teddy's near loss of eyesight and the resulting events). Neither Mr. nor Mrs. Farquar's first name is ever mentioned. The head scientist is never named, nor is Gideon's son or the host of servants who coo over Teddy. This lack of detail gives the story a universal quality, as if it could happen anywhere or among group of people. It also gives the tale the feeling of a parable, a generic story that exists mainly to communicate a moral or educational lesson.

HISTORICAL CONTEXT

Southern Rhodesia

Zimbabwe evolved from the Kingdom of Mapungubwe, a trade state that sold its goods to European and Portuguese explorers up to the twelfth century. The kingdom changed rulers and names several times over the next 600 years, but by the 1880s, the British entered the country via Cecil Rhodes's British South Africa Company. Rhodes was granted mining rights by the king of the Ndebele people there, and he also went on to earn additional land rights from other tribes in the area. Based on Rhodes's work to secure a British foothold in the region, the country was named Rhodesia in 1895. Southern Rhodesia and Northern Rhodesia were formed from this region. The former would ultimately become the Republic of Zimbabwe, and the latter would become Zambia. Native peoples unsuccessfully attempted to revolt against ensuing British rule during the 1890s. Later, under Rhodes's management, land was given to European settlers, and the native people were systematically displaced.

By October 1923, Southern Rhodesia was declared a self-governing British colony. Thirty years later, the United Kingdom joined Southern Rhodesia with another of its colonies, Nyasaland (now Malawi), forming the Federation of Rhodesia and Nyasaland. The federation lasted only ten years, crumbling in 1963 under protests and growing anticolonial sentiments. Two years later, in November 1965, the Rhodesian government, led by Ian Smith, made a Unilateral Declaration of Independence. Although the United Kingdom did not agree to the declaration, it also did not attempt to reassert control over the region through military force. However, the United Kingdom did request that the United Nations impose economic sanctions on Rhodesia, and the only country to recognize Rhodesia's legitimacy under Smith's leadership was South Africa. Later, in 1970, Southern Rhodesia renamed itself the Republic of Rhodesia, and the country fell into civil war, caught between two warring political factions, the Zimbabwe African People's Union (led by Joshua Nkomo) and the Zimbabwe African National Union (led by Robert Mugabe).

Beset by war, Smith signed a peace accord in March 1978 after extracting promises for the safety of Rhodesia's white residents. This accord, known as the Internal Settlement, led to the first native election in April 1979. The prevailing party in the election was the United African National Council (UANC). On June 1, 1979, Abel Muzorewa, the leader of UANC, became the country's prime minister. However, by February of 1980, Mugabe was elected head of state. He has held that

COMPARE & CONTRAST

- **1960s:** The political independence movements of the 1960s in Africa allow for the introduction of Western organizations such as the World Health Organization. Surprisingly, according to Kwasi Konadu in *African Studies Quarterly*, instead of conflict, there is cooperation of "indigenous healers with biomedicine in Africa."

  Today: In light of the HIV-AIDS epidemic in Africa, the African Academy of Sciences calls for the research and development of homegrown treatments based on herbal medicine. Scientists claim that the rich biodiversity of the African continent could contain the plants and herbs for new, effective drugs.

- **1960s:** The Rhodesian government declares its independence from the United Kingdom on November 11, 1965. However, the country soon becomes mired in civil war, and it does not achieve true independence until December 1, 1979.

  Today: Southern Rhodesia is now known as Zimbabwe, though its official name is the Republic of Zimbabwe. The country has been led by Robert Mugabe since 1980. He has served consecutively as prime minister and president but is essentially a dictator.

- **1960s:** In 1963, ten years after the British government consolidated Rhodesia with its neighboring colony Nyasaland (now Malawi), it disbands the union because of growing opposition and the rising tide of African nationalism.

  Today: Although Mugabe's plan to forcibly redistribute white-owned property to blacks has been ruled unconstitutional, the program persists.

---

post ever since, using various titles such as prime minister and president, while essentially becoming a dictator. Mugabe' rule has been so horrible that *Parade* magazine named him the world's worst dictator in 2009, citing as proof hyperinflation, 85-percent unemployment, crisis health conditions, and torture and beatings of nearly five thousand political opponents.

CRITICAL OVERVIEW

For the most part, Lessing's *African Stories*, the collection in which "No Witchcraft for Sale" appears, has been praised by critics. However, the stories have also been met with a great deal of controversy, and it is important to remember that the themes in "No Witchcraft for Sale" are highly political. Lessing was banished from the very countries she criticized in her stories. As Jane Hotchkiss writes in *Borders, Exiles, Diasporas*, Lessing's "sketches of Southern African societies were applauded for their realism, yet the urgent issues they raised were left lying . . . and the urgency was evaluated as a 'bitterness' that spoiled her 'art'"; her political critique was trivialized and dismissed.

Nation critic Mary Ellmann also comments on the political nature of the collection. Her 1966 review was written only a year after the Rhodesian government made its bid for independence from colonial rule. She finds that "it seems an ironic grace . . . that at the most inept moment of English relations with Southern Rhodesia, a writer who is English as well as Rhodesian should speak with so much talent to the point." Ellmann also finds that, "as political and social evidence, Doris Lessing's *African Stories* confirm in precise and painful detail, like stitches in a wound, the abuse of the native population of Southern Rhodesia by the white settlers of British descent."

Praising the literary merit of the collection, *Hudson Review* contributor William H. Pritchard

"Little Yellow Head" (Image copyright Vita Khorzhevska, 2009. Used under license from Shutterstock.com)

notes that the stories "are written in a direct, unadorned, intelligently observant prose to be admired." In a rare dissenting opinion, Fiona R. Barnes states in the *Dictionary of Literary Biography* that "the African characters in 'No Witchcraft for Sale' . . . are presented rather paternalistically by Lessing as naive moral touchstones who highlight the callousness of the whites." On the other hand, Barnes goes on to remark that "Lessing portrays the whites' disrespectful behavior as disgracefully uncivilized. . . . She also reveals that the whites are the losers in their determined struggle to dominate another culture."

CRITICISM

Leah Tieger

Tieger is a freelance writer and editor. In this essay, she presents a character examination of Gideon in "No Witchcraft for Sale."

At its heart, Lessing's "No Witchcraft for Sale," illustrates the rather incomplete nature of the subjugation (oppression) of one race by another. While the Farquars represent the stereotype of white colonial settlers, Gideon serves as the stereotype of the (seemingly) complacently compliant servant. It is clear that Gideon genuinely loves the infant son of his oppressors. The affection that the two have for one another is an instant and natural bond. If there is any question as to the sincerity of Gideon's love, it is erased when he rushes out into the night to retrieve the plant that will save Teddy's eyesight. This natural affection is also illustrated in other instances as well, as when Gideon dubs the boy "Little Yellow Head." However, when Gideon tells Mrs. Farquar, "Little Yellow Head is the most good thing we have in our house," his sincerity is questionable. It has the seemingly unintended effect of earning the cook a substantial pay raise. Not only is Mrs. Farquar flattered by Gideon's love for Tommy, but she is moved by his use of the word "we," which indicates that he thinks of himself as part of the family. Gideon's actual motivations in making this statement, however, remain a mystery. The statement may be heartfelt, but it may be a gesture meant to appease his employers and benefit Gideon.

WHAT DO I READ NEXT?

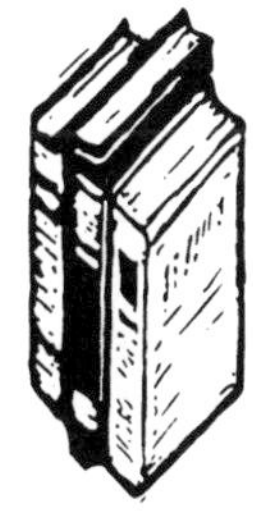

- Lessing's most famous book is the novel *The Golden Notebook*, which was published in 1962. Although it was initially received as controversial, the book was ultimately hailed as a feminist masterpiece. The novel features an experimental narrative structure, one that is reminiscent of the work of famed feminist author Gertrude Stein.
- Another Lessing novel worth reading is *Alfred and Emily*. The book was published in 2008, the year after Lessing won the Nobel Prize in Literature. It was released when Lessing was eighty-nine years old, and she announced that it would be her final work. The novel itself is an alternative history, one that imagines what the lives of Lessing's own parents (Alfred and Emily) would have been like if they had never married.
- Theodore Taylor's classic young-adult novel *The Cay* was initially published in 1969 and has since become a favorite in the American classroom. The story addresses themes of racism and prejudice as it portrays an unlikely pairing of two castaways in 1942. The first, an eleven-year-old white boy named Phillip Enright, is blinded when his ship sinks. The second castaway, Timothy, is a black man, and Philip must rely on him for survival. In doing so, Philip is forced to overcome his racist beliefs.
- A very different take on the perils of racism is given by the young-adult graphic novel *American Born Chinese* (2006). Written by Gene Luen Yang, the book won the 2007 Michael L. Printz Award. It portrays a Chinese American teen who learns to define himself amidst the racial stereotypes that he encounters.
- Timothy Keegan's 1997 volume *Colonial South Africa and the Origins of the Racial Order* provides an academic overview of the systemic racism in colonial Africa. The book particularly focuses on British rule in South Africa through the 1850s, a period that greatly influenced the social structure in Africa during much of the early twentieth century. Other topics discussed include the economics and industries of colonial Africa.
- The 2005 volume *Colonial and Postcolonial Literature*, by Elleke Boehmer, is both a historical and literary examination of the writing produced in colonized countries. The literature produced both during and after colonial times is unique in that it captures the blending (and clashing) of two cultures and the power struggles inherent in the colonial system. While this overview is not limited to Africa alone, it provides fascinating insight into the art of colonial and postcolonial literature.

That Gideon is a good-natured man is illustrated throughout the story. He cares for his young charge and saves his eyesight despite the consequences of doing so. Although the Farquars deeply offend Gideon by demanding that he reveal his sacred and secret knowledge of the bush, he ultimately forgives them. His sunny disposition reasserts itself, and he is later able to joke about the incident with Teddy and his employers. However, Gideon's behavior is also occasionally obsequious (flattering). This is perhaps most evident early on in the story when Gideon remarks upon the wildly different fates of two babies born around the same time. He notes that the black baby will be raised to become a servant and that Teddy will be raised to become the manager of his own farm. Mrs. Farquar observes that the same thought had crossed her mind, and Gideon is then quick to add that this "is God's will." By doing so, he ensures that his observation is not perceived as a challenge to the status quo.

Still, Gideon's true feelings as to the unjust nature of his situation are, at times, apparent.

The first such occurrence is when Teddy treats Gideon's son cruelly. When Gideon admonishes the Teddy for doing so, the child replies arrogantly, "He's only a black boy." This insensitive and deeply racist declaration cuts Gideon to the core, and he turns his back on Teddy. Gideon also shows his feelings, and the precarious nature of his position, when he "unwillingly" accepts Teddy's peace offering. Gideon has not truly forgiven the boy. (Teddy has not actually apologized, nor can he bring himself to do so.) However, Gideon must appear to be appeased so that his persistent upset does not reveal his true feelings about the injustice surrounding him. Of course, it seems to go without saying that if Gideon displeased the Farquars, he would put his income, his job, and the security of his family's home in jeopardy. Gideon, then, becomes complicit in his own subjugation—that is, he must play a part in his own oppression. He must participate in it not only willingly, but happily. Nevertheless, despite Gideon's surface acceptance of Teddy's peace offering, the relationship between boy and servant is forever changed. Gideon no longer plays with the boy and keeps his distance as he prepares himself for the "inevitable," that is, Teddy's future destiny as master of his own farm. Teddy's behavior changes as well, and he forever after addresses Gideon "in the way a white man uses towards a servant, expecting to be obeyed."

Gideon's suspect sincerity shows itself again when the Farquars request that he show them the plant he used to effect Teddy's miraculous cure. Here, even the Farquars seem aware that they are overstepping their bounds. However, their certainty that doing so will benefit humanity gives them to courage to proceed. Lessing's brilliant portrayal of the Farquars in this instance demonstrates their belief that the ends justify the means. Their religious faith also underscores this belief. It is the very set of beliefs that supposedly drove worldwide colonization in the first place; by subjugating native people, colonialists claimed they were introducing God and religion to a host of so-called heathen peoples whose souls would otherwise have remained unsaved. However, although the Farquars have justified their transgression to themselves, they quickly abandon their reservations when confronted by Gideon's anger. Gideon's sullen and belligerent reaction comes as an affront to their self-righteous faith in their own good intentions. This anger, then, incites the Farquars to persist and even creates a sense of entitlement in their endeavor to do so.

Gideon seems to sense this, and so he makes a great show of giving them exactly what they've asked for. First, he gives all manner of conflicting explanations regarding the existence (or nonexistence) and whereabouts of the plant itself. Next, he leads the head scientist, the Farquars, and Teddy on a two-hour-long wild goose chase through the swelteringly hot bush. As he does so, he puts on a show of inspecting the plants around him. Finally, he selects a blue-flowered plant without a second glance, a plant identical to those the group has passed several times throughout their two-hour trek. In this way, Gideon ensures that neither the head scientist nor the Farquars will take his selection seriously. However, the question of Gideon's possible sincerity arises when Teddy and the Farquars later tease Gideon about the incident. When Mrs. Farquar makes a joke of the misadventure, Gideon slyly replies, "But I did show you missus, have you forgotten?" This statement could lead the reader to consider the possibility that Gideon has been clever enough to lead his employers and the scientist to the actual medicinal plant while simultaneously guaranteeing that they will never use it.

These suppositions are also supported textually. For instance, Gideon, for all his apparent good nature, is essentially mysterious. He is mostly portrayed by the omniscient narrator through his actions. The Farquars, on the other hand, are not; rather, they are mostly portrayed through their thoughts and feelings. This subtle difference creates characters of varying dimensions. Where Gideon is all "show," the Farquars are all "tell." This interesting approach reflects the social and political moment in which the story is set. Gideon lives in a world where the greatest act of transgression is the act of revealing one's innermost thoughts.

Source: Leah Tieger, Critical Essay on "No Witchcraft for Sale," in *Short Stories for Students*, Gale, Cengage Learning, 2010.

Bella Bathurst

In the following interview, Bathurst chronicles an interview with Lessing, revealing the source of Lessing's inspiration.

Doris Lessing long ago joined that queenly group of female writers—Muriel Spark, Margaret Atwood, Toni Morrison, Maya Angelou—who

Lessing's major theme: difference in culture, class, and race (Image copyright Varina and Jay Patel, 2009. Used under license from Shutterstock.com)

have earned the right not to suffer fools. Lessing has little patience for those who have not done their research. If she is going to grant someone the favour of an interview, the least she can expect in return is that they have done their homework.

Lessing has written around 50 books. To date, I have read two of them. Twenty-four hours and one and a half books later, I am standing outside Lessing's door, wondering if it is true that she eats bad journalists for tea. Inside, things have taken an exciting new disorganisational twist.

The photographer—who was supposed to arrive after the interview—is waiting in Lessing's sitting room.

He looks about as apprehensive as I feel. Lessing herself is standing at the top of the stairs radiating politesse and disapproval at the same time.

"This is the third time this has happened," she says crossly. "These papers are very unfair." The photographer and I exchange nervous grins.

The house is almost exactly as one would expect: warm, homely, with a strong feline presence and a slipshod garden at the back crammed with fresh growth. Inside, the rooms ooze books: in piles, on shelves, seeping in a steady tide up the walls. Lessing sits neatly on the sofa, waiting. So does the photographer. A black and white cat stares accusingly at me. We start off with *Mara and Dann,* her latest book. Lessing remarks that I seem rather out of puff. I'm not out of puff, I'm terrified. Lessing, however, ploughs gallantly on. *Mara and Dann* follows the story of a brother and a sister who flee their homeland in Africa to join an immense human exodus to the north. It is, says Lessing, "a classic adventure story. And you have to have rules in adventure stories. You have to have people who start off very disadvantaged—poor, or in captivity or whatever—and they have to get themselves out of it one way or another, you have to have a very strong villain, and you have to have a lot of vicissitudes, and then they have to end up happily. But I wasn't following a formula. I started off, and I thought, my God, this is an adventure

"COURSING THROUGH HER WORK ARE THE EBB AND FLOW OF THREE MAJOR THEMES: THE AFRICA THAT SHE LEFT BEHIND WHEN SHE CAME TO LONDON IN 1949, HER BATTLES WITH POLITICS (BOTH PERSONAL AND COLLECTIVE) AND A FASCINATION FOR THE DARKER SIDES OF THE HUMAN MIND."

story that I'm writing, and I watched with fascination as it developed".

The book is set in the future, as are several of Lessing's works. When people think of her writing, they usually cite her first novel, *The Grass is Singing,* or her 1962 masterpiece, *The Golden Notebook*. But, much like Ian Banks, she interweaves "conventional" novels with what she calls "space fiction" books. What is it, I wonder, which interests her so much about the future? "This isn't the future, this is about the present," she corrects me. "Most space fiction is about the present. Space fiction is an interesting way of imagining a different society. It's very liberating; you're not bound down by realism, by what we're living in."

It's an interesting choice to make for an author who made her name as a realist. Born in 1919, Lessing was brought up first in Iran and then in what was then southern Rhodesia.

She married twice, first to a civil servant named Frank Wisdom with whom she had two children and then Gottfried Lessing, a communist "enemy alien." She left for London in 1949 taking with her only the manuscript of her first novel and the child of her second marriage, Peter.

Lessing has documented all of this herself in two recent volumes of autobiography, *Under my Skin* and *Walking in the Shade*. The books are striking not just for the amount of life Lessing has packed into her 80 years, but for their lucent objectivity both about herself and about others.

Coursing through her work are the ebb and flow of three major themes: the Africa that she left behind when she came to London in 1949, her battles with politics (both personal and collective) and a fascination for the darker sides of the human mind.

Some would also say that Lessing has been one of the great feminist writers of this century. Lessing herself is reluctant to be so pigeonholed. As she points out, she is fed up having her writing hijacked for other people's purposes; of being forced into a false position. "It has been my fate all my life," she wrote, "to be with people who assume I think as they do."

And she was certainly no feminist if feminism meant falsifying her own experience. *The Golden Notebook* portrayed women as neither martyrs nor victims, but as the gossipy, manipulative, generous, loving, resentful and complete human beings of reality. "Writers are a kind of Rorschach test," Lessing says now.

"People project on to us whatever their preoccupations are. *The Golden Notebook* got the most appalling reviews when it came out, really savage and angry. From women and from men. It's a myth that women accepted this book from the beginning. They didn't. The women's movement did, as a political thing, but at the beginning, these reviewers didn't like it. As a matter of fact it was mostly men who championed me, not women to begin with."

Lessing could, and did, seal her reputation with those two books alone. But, though the stage when she was under pressure from her publishers or from her bank to keep producing books has long gone, she still maintains a work rate that would shame Dickens. "The only pressure to write comes from me, not from anyone else," she says. "It's psychological. I describe it as the wolf snapping at your heels. I have to write. Very neurotic, no doubt, but if I don't write, I get very tetchy, I can tell you. I think all writers have it; I think it's a psychological balancing mechanism. All the time in writing, you are ordering experience one way or another." Does she, I ask, possess the splinter of ice which is supposed to exist in every writer's soul? "Oh yes," she says equably, "That's absolutely true, of course. Because you're always looking with a detached eye.

Even when you're perhaps dying of grief or madly happy, you're still observing yourself. You can't write if you're involved, you have to be watching." Age only helps the process. "When you get old, you become enormously remote from things. You see things much more clearly. I maintain that women between the ages of 14 and the menopause tend to be always at the mercy of emotions or hormones one way and another. And then after the menopause, you become free of it, detached. It's very nice."

I am fascinated, I say, by an experiment I had heard that she once conducted on herself. As an example of ruthless artistic objectivity, it could hardly be bettered. "It was during the Sixties, when everyone had these psychedelic ideas," she says. "It occurred to me that the accounts of prison camps, accounts of what African shamen do, accounts of schizophrenia—they're all very similar. The hallucinations, the sense of being very remote from yourself. Anyway, I had all these ideas and they coalesced, so I thought, right, well let's try. So I managed to get myself some time without being interrupted, and I deliberately didn't eat and didn't sleep, and in no time at all, I'd gone a bit crazy.

"So I thought, now this is really interesting because if I now went to a doctor with these symptoms, they'd lock me in the loony bin. It was difficult to find my way back and it took about a month before it all went.

"It wasn't difficult to start eating again but it was very difficult to lose the voice of what I call the self-hater, this very loud hammering voice of someone who dislikes you. If I knew what I know now I wouldn't have done it, but on the other hand I wouldn't have found out quite a lot of things. The thing is, you do learn a lot about yourself with these extreme experiences. But once is enough."

Sometimes, when she writes about her torn affair with the Communist Party, she describes it in similar tones of wonderment. That, too, was a form of madness, a madness exacerbated by the gulf between then and now. "What you're living through you take for granted and you can't see what's extraordinary about it. It was a very strong atmosphere, the Cold War, very nasty. It was after the war, don't forget, and everybody is mad in wartime, except they don't realise it. If you've lived through it, believe me, you know how people can be affected by mass emotions overnight. And switch sides; enemies become friends, friends become something else. Now, it's almost impossible to convey that."

Would she join any cause now? "No, God forbid. No. I've seen too many of them." Feminism? "I take it for granted that women are feminists. It's not that I'm not a feminist.

"But I dislike mass movements because they always turn into power elites. Certainly the women's movement did. All these little groups, fighting against each other and calling each other names." As she exclaims in *Walking in the Shade:* "Oh, I do loathe groups, clans, families, the human 'we'. How I do dread them, fear them—try to keep well away. Prides of lions or packs of wild dogs are kindly enemies by comparison."

Meanwhile, the photographer has been waiting patiently. Lessing poses obediently in the garden, tipping her head this way and that. I sit inside, grateful for Lessing's good manners and torn between wanting to talk all week and not say another word.

Artists or writers often complain that there's no point in being interviewed since all that they are, and all that they want to communicate, is already in their work. Lessing puts a better case than most. Fifty books, a good dozen of which have been autobiographical, countless previous interviews, two volumes of memoirs.

Whatever she wants to say about herself is already in print; all it would take is a little research. But I'm still here, burrowing inefficiently through old ground.

By the time she comes back in, I'm well on the way to talking myself out of a job. Lessing, however, is polite enough to complete the interview.

"How will you get back?" she asks at the end. I say I'll probably walk; it's a sunny afternoon. "I walked over the hill to the Royal Free last weekend," she says casually. Which, I calculate later, must be a good five miles there and back, most of it uphill. Some octogenarian, some writer. And, though she was kind enough not to eat me for tea, I got the point all the same. Go home and start reading.

Source: Bella Bathurst, "A Lessing Learned," in *Scotsman*, April 17, 1999, p. 3.

SOURCES

Barnes, Fiona R., "Doris Lessing," in *Dictionary of Literary Biography*, Vol. 139, *British Short-Fiction Writers, 1945-1980*, edited by Dean Baldwin, Gale Research, 1994, pp. 159–72.

"Biography," in *A Reader's Guide to The Golden Notebook & Under My Skin*, HarperPerennial, 1995; reprint, *Doris Lessing Home Page*, http://www.dorislessing.org/biography.html (accessed October 30, 2009).

Ellmann, Mary, "Stitches in a Wound," in *Nation*, January 17, 1966, Vol. 202, No. 3, pp. 78–80.

Freedman, Estelle, *No Turning Back: The History of Feminism and the Future of Women*, Ballantine, 2003.

Hotchkiss, Jane, "Coming of Age in Zambesia," in *Borders, Exiles, Diasporas*, edited by Elazar Barkan and Marie-Denise Shelton, Stanford University Press, 1998, pp. 81–91.

Konadu, Kwasi, "Medicine and Anthropology in Twentieth Century Africa: Akan Medicine and Encounters with (Medical) Anthropology," in *African Studies Quarterly*, Vol. 10, No. 2/3, Fall 2008, http://www.africa.ufl.edu/asq/v10/v10i2a3.htm (accessed November 4, 2009).

Lessing, Doris, "No Witchcraft for Sale," in *African Stories*, Simon and Schuster, 1965, pp. 67–74.

Meredith, Martin, *Mugabe: Power, Plunder, and the Struggle for Zimbabwe's Future*, PublicAffairs, 2007.

Mlambo, Alois, and Brian Raftopoulos, eds., *Becoming Zimbabwe: A History from the Pre-Colonial Period to 2008*, Weaver Press, 2009.

Njoroge, James, "Africa 'Must Better Exploit Herbal Medicines,'" in *Science and Development Network*, September 18, 2002, http://www.scidev.net/en/news/africa-must-better-exploit-herbal-medicines.html (accessed November 4, 2009).

Pritchard, William H., "Looking Back at Lessing," in *Hudson Review*, Summer 1995, Vol. 68, No. 2, pp. 317–24.

Smith, Ian, *Bitter Harvest: Zimbabwe and the Aftermath of Its Independence*, John Blake, 2008.

Wallechinsky, David, "The World's 10 Worst Dictators," in *Parade*, http://www.parade.com/dictators/2009/the-worlds-10-worst-dictators.html (accessed November 4, 2009).

FURTHER READING

Klein, Carole, *Doris Lessing: A Biography*, Carroll & Graf, 2000.

One of the few full-length biographies on Lessing, this book draws on interviews with the author and those her knew her to provide a view into the author's life beyond the one presented in Lessing's own autobiographies.

Miller, Frederic, Agnes F. Vandome, and John McBrewster, eds., *Rhodesia*, Alphascript, 2009.

This history of Lessing's childhood home (the place that inspired her *African Stories*) covers Rhodesia and Southern Rhodesia from colonial times to their modern incarnation as Zimbabwe.

Schneir, Miriam, *Feminism in Our Time: The Essential Writings, World War II to the Present*, Vintage, 1994.

This book of literary criticism discusses feminist writers and their work. Sixteen authors, including Lessing, are profiled.

Stein, Gertrude, *Selected Writings of Gertrude Stein*, Vintage, 1990.

Lessing's more experimental narratives have been compared to the work of her predecessor Gertrude Stein. This collection presents an overview of Stein's work, including the entirety of her best-known experimental work *The Autobiography of Alice B. Toklas*.

One Ordinary Day, with Peanuts

SHIRLEY JACKSON

1955

"One Ordinary Day, with Peanuts," by Shirley Jackson, is a typical Jackson story depicting everyday events in a normal setting that turn out to be a little strange and perhaps not so ordinary after all. "One Ordinary Day, with Peanuts" was published in January 1955 in the *Magazine of Fantasy & Science Fiction*, to which Jackson sold several of her stories. This short story was subsequently selected for inclusion in *Best American Short Stories: 1956*. It was also the inspiration for the title of a 1996 collection of her previously uncollected and unpublished work, *Just an Ordinary Day*, edited by two of her children, Laurence Jackson Hyman and Sarah Hyman Stewart.

"One Ordinary Day, with Peanuts" is a story about good and evil that appears straightforward, if a bit strange, on the surface yet contains a twist at the end. The main character, Mr. Johnson, spends his day wandering the city, committing random acts of kindness as he hands out money, advice, his time, candy, and peanuts to people and animals. His generosity seems to have no limit—or does it? "One Ordinary Day, with Peanuts" comments on life in the big city and the two-sided nature of good and evil.

AUTHOR BIOGRAPHY

Shirley Jackson was born on December 14, 1916, in San Francisco, California, to Leslie and

Shirley Jackson *(AP Images)*

Geraldine Jackson. Financially comfortable and socially aware, Jackson's parents—especially her mother—struggled with raising their headstrong but extremely talented daughter. One year before Shirley was to graduate from high school, the Jackson family relocated to the other side of the country, settling in Rochester, New York, where her father had found work.

Jackson was extremely intelligent but bored by school and left the University of Rochester with failing grades after three years. In the fall of 1937, she freed herself from her parents' yoke and enrolled at Syracuse University to study journalism. Jackson met her future husband, the critic Stanley Edgar Hyman, after he had read her first published story, "Janice," in a college publication and sought her out. They were married in 1940, shortly after graduating from Syracuse University, and lived in an apartment in New York City. In 1941, Jackson and Hyman moved to a rustic cabin in the backwoods of New Hampshire to spend a year writing. Jackson's first professional publication was the result. Her short story "My Life with R. H. Macy" was published by the *New Republic* at the end of 1941.

Jackson and Hyman returned to New York City shortly thereafter, immersing themselves in their respective careers and having their first child. Over the next ten years, they moved around New England in order for Hyman to pursue his work, eventually settling in North Bennington, Vermont, and Jackson regularly sold short stories to high-profile publications, including the *New Yorker* and *Harper's*. Her first novel, *The Road through the Wall*, was published in 1948. "One Ordinary Day, with Peanuts" first appeared in the *Magazine of Fantasy & Science Fiction* in 1955 and was later included in the 1956 edition of the *Best American Short Stories*.

Jackson experienced critical success during her lifetime. Her novel *The Haunting of Hill House* was nominated for a National Book Award in 1960. Another novel, *We Have Always Lived in the Castle*, was selected by *Time* magazine as one of the top ten novels of 1962. Over the course of her short life, Jackson published over fifty short stories, two collections, six novels, two memoirs, and four books for children. Two more collections of her work were published posthumously by her husband and by two of her children, respectively. Jackson suffered a fatal heart attack on August 8, 1965, in North Bennington, Vermont. She was only forty-eight years old.

PLOT SUMMARY

"One Ordinary Day, with Peanuts" opens with a cheerful Mr. John Philip Johnson, leaving home on a beautiful day wearing comfortable, newly soled shoes. Although he lives in a big city—probably New York, based on the street references in the story—he freely greets the people he passes, handing out candies, peanuts, and even the flower from his lapel. Many of the adults he encounters are initially wary, suspecting that his generosity is some sort of ruse, but most soon realize that he is just being friendly and smile back. The children in this story are perhaps more willing than the adults to trust and accept his gestures at face value.

Working his way uptown, Mr. Johnson wanders down a random side street, where he comes upon a mother and her son in the process of moving out of their apartment. The mother tries to keep an eye on her possessions, her child, and the movers simultaneously. Many strangers stand about watching, which only adds to her stress.

Mr. Johnson offers to sit on the front steps and entertain her son for a while. The mother is suspicious but has little choice, given her situation, and agrees. Mr. Johnson shares his peanuts with the little boy, who tells him they are moving to Vermont to live with his grandparents on a farm. Before leaving, Mr. Johnson gives the mother a card with the name of a friend who lives in the town to which she is moving. He tells her this friend will help her with anything she needs.

Mr. Johnson wanders farther uptown. When he stops to pet a kitten on a busy street, a young woman bumps into him. She is late for work and tries to brush past him, but Mr. Johnson insists on offering her money for her lost time. The young woman cannot fathom why a respectable-looking man would want to pay her to be late for work. Inexplicably, he asks her to wait for him while he wades into the crowd on the sidewalk and stops a harried young man. He is also late for work and is irritated with Mr. Johnson for stopping him. Mr. Johnson gives a day's pay to each of them and introduces the woman, whose name is Mildred Kent, to the man, Arthur Adams. He gives them each spending money and implores them to enjoy themselves rather than show up for work. They start to ask him questions, whereupon Mr. Johnson bids them good-bye and dashes off.

He continues his ramble, helping a woman put her packages into a taxi, feeding a peanut to a seagull, giving money and a peanut to a panhandler, and a peanut to a bus driver who has stuck his head out of the window to get some air. Mr. Johnson comes across a couple who remind him of Mildred and Arthur. They are looking for an apartment in the classifieds. He tells them about the apartment vacated this morning by the mother and little boy. Grateful, they rush off to check out his lead.

Mr. Johnson eats lunch alone, then gives money to a beggar panhandling outside the restaurant so he can order a similar meal. After lunch, he goes to a park to rest. There he watches over two children whose mother has fallen asleep, referees a few checker games, and feeds the rest of his peanuts to the pigeons. It is getting late, so he decides to head back home. He gives up the first several taxis to seemingly more desperate people. When he finally catches a taxi, the driver confesses that he didn't really want to stop—he had just been given ten dollars and a hot tip on a racehorse by his previous fare—but figured that Mr. Johnson was an omen not to place the bet. The horse's name is Vulcan and Mr. Johnson says that it would have been an unlucky bet and he was wise to keep the money. Mr. Johnson's reasoning is cryptic but firm: the name Vulcan indicates a fire sign, which isn't a good bet for a Wednesday. He tells the cab driver he can bet on Vulcan on a Monday or a Saturday or even a Sunday. The cab driver says the horse will not run on Sunday, so Mr. Johnson gives him another ten dollars and a new tip to wait until Thursday to bet on any horse with a name connected with grain. The cab driver comes up with a horse named Tall Corn and Mr. Johnson agrees that this is a good choice, whereupon the cab driver thanks him.

Back at home, Mr. Johnson greets his wife. He tells her he has had a decent day, having helped a few young people. She has also had a fine day, but her achievements are very different from his. Mrs. Johnson tells her husband that she accused a woman of shoplifting, sent some dogs to the pound, and quarreled with a bus driver, possibly costing him his job. Seeing how tired she looks, Mr. Johnson offers to switch with her the next day and she agrees. He asks what is for dinner and she tells him she made veal cutlets. Mr. Johnson informs her that he had the same for lunch, which can be interpreted as his slipping into the role of wicked person and telling his wife he does not want to eat the same thing for dinner.

CHARACTERS

Arthur Adams

Arthur Adams is a harried young man who finds himself late for work one ordinary Wednesday, when he is suddenly intercepted by Mr. Johnson and paid a day's wages to take the day off and do something enjoyable in the company of Mildred Kent, a young woman to whom he has just been introduced. Like Mildred, Arthur is suspicious of Mr. Johnson's motives but can find nothing amiss regarding the latter's generous offer other than the fact that it comes from out of the blue and from a stranger. Arthur is less willing than Mildred simply to accept the present situation, even going so far as to ask Mr. Johnson what would happen if he just took the cash and left Mildred behind. Mr. Johnson is not worried about the outcome, knowing that they will accept his offer and enjoy themselves. Nothing in the narrative indicates that Mr. Johnson has brought Arthur and Mildred together as a love match. He is simply asking two harried young people to give themselves over to fun and relaxation for a day.

Cab Driver

The cab driver picks up Mr. Johnson at the end of the day and takes him home. He is puzzling over a tip concerning a racehorse made by the person who was just in his cab. The cab driver decides that Mr. Johnson is an omen that he should not place the bet, an idea with which Mr. Johnson agrees. Given all the good deeds that Mr. Johnson has done that day, the reader is inclined to believe that the cab driver was indeed lucky to have picked up Mr. Johnson. It is even possible that the previous fare is intentionally stirring up trouble and ill will, like Mrs. Johnson. Mr. Johnson gives the cab driver a new tip concerning which horse to bet on plus another ten dollars on top of the ten dollars the cab driver was given earlier. The cab driver is thankful.

John Philip Johnson

Mr. Johnson is the main character of this story. He is described as being small in stature. Moreover, he is improbably cheerful in the midst of a bustling city where people do not always take the time to be friendly and are always worried about money. Mr. Johnson's main purpose is to wander the city doing good deeds. He helps people by giving them money, offering advice, and generally being a good neighbor. He treats animals with kindness and also offers them peanuts.

He seems to be the polar opposite of his wife yet offers to switch with her on Thursday— he will be hurtful and she will be helpful—suggesting that doing evil deeds is more exhausting. The Johnsons balance each other out, the husband offering cheer and displaying goodwill toward their neighbors, while the wife causes strife. These figures are meant to be understood as personifications of good and evil. When Mr. Johnson gives the single mother the name of his good friend in Vermont, and tells her that this man will be happy to help with anything—he also mentions that his friend has a wife—the author is suggesting that there may be other such pairings of opposites living elsewhere around the country.

Mrs. Johnson

Mrs. Johnson may be an unlikely personification of evil, but older women in mythology represent evil crones as often as fairy godmothers. As the evil half of this pair, she spends her day getting people into trouble and sending animals to their deaths. Sensitive to the toll this has exacted from his wife, Mr. Johnson offers to switch with her the next day, meaning that he will be the evil one on Thursday. She then tells her husband that she has made veal cutlets for dinner, which he immediately rejects, claiming he had the same for lunch earlier that day.

Mildred Kent

Mildred Kent meets Mr. Johnson when she accidentally bumps into him on the sidewalk after he stoops to pet a kitten. She is late for work and moving a bit too fast. Mr. Johnson notices that she has not taken the time to worry about her slightly disheveled appearance. At first her concerns are focused on money, time, and legal ramifications, but once she realizes that Mr. Johnson is sincere, she agrees to wait while he fetches Arthur Adams from the crowd on the sidewalk, a young man Mr. Johnson seems to choose with great care, presumably with her in mind. After Mr. Johnson leaves the two of them to determine how to spend the balance of the day, Mildred seems quite ready to do just as Mr. Johnson suggested, that is, to have fun.

Little Boy

The little boy is moving to Vermont with his mother, where they plan to live on his grandparents' farm. After asking the boy's mother for permission, Mr. Johnson sits with him and shares peanuts while they talk, allowing the mother to concentrate on the packing of their furniture. No mention is made of the father, leaving the reader uncertain as to whether the boy's parents are divorced or whether his father is dead. At the end of their impromptu chat, the little boy is much more cheerful and looks forward to moving to Vermont.

Mother

The mother of the little boy is torn between caring for her child, watching how the movers handle her furniture, and being observed by a circle of bystanders. Mr. Johnson sees how he can help and offers to sit with her boy so that she can focus on the furniture. She is naturally suspicious of Mr. Johnson, who is a total stranger, but allows him to sit with her child where she can keep an eye on both of them. The author does not explain whether she is a single parent because of divorce or the death of her husband. Mr. Johnson's final

TOPICS FOR FURTHER STUDY

- Good and evil are often personified in mythology by people or animals. Read some Native American myths (such as those in the young-adult collection *The Storytelling Stone: Traditional Native American Myths and Tales* by Susan Feldman) and prepare a multimedia presentation that describes the characters in these stories. Do you think they are good or evil? Are any of them similar to the characters in Jackson's short story "One Ordinary Day, with Peanuts"? Your presentation could take the form of a short film, a podcast, or a PowerPoint presentation.
- The generosity exhibited by Mr. Johnson is reminiscent of the "random acts of kindness" phenomenon that was popular during the 1990s in the United States. Perform at least one random act of kindness toward another person each day for a week. Keep a journal of your experience, writing down what you did, how it made you feel, and what effect it had on people around you, assuming you were present to evaluate the results. Using this field research, write a personal essay that addresses whether or not these random acts of kindness changed your life in any way. Share your essay with another student and discuss how your experiences were similar and/or different.
- Arthur Adams mentions communism in "One Ordinary Day, with Peanuts," which is set in the 1950s, the height of McCarthyism and the Red Scare. Under McCarthyism, people were encouraged to report friends, neighbors, and even family members to the government if they suspected them of being Communists or exhibiting unpatriotic behavior. This created a climate of fear and distrust throughout the United States, as illustrated by the wary people Mr. Johnson encounters during his wanderings. Using paint, collage, digital photography, or another visual medium, create an interpretation of and response to the subversive fear mongering of the 1950s that has come to be called McCarthyism.
- What if Mr. Johnson ran into someone he had helped before? Imagine it is one week following the events described in "One Ordinary Day, with Peanuts." Mr. and Mrs. Johnson have switched roles and Mr. Johnson runs into one of the other characters mentioned in the story. Write a one-act play depicting this scene and have the class read through everyone's plays. Discuss the different outcomes that have been imagined.

kindly gesture is to give her the name of a friend of his who lives in the same town she is moving to, suggesting that this friend will also provide a helping hand should she be in need.

THEMES

Good and Evil

"One Ordinary Day, with Peanuts" is primarily concerned with the presence of good and evil in everyday life, how they manifest themselves on a daily basis, and how arbitrary they can be. Mr. Johnson is the personification of good, wandering the streets of a big city with no other purpose than to find those in need of his help—or, as it has become known since the 1990s, to practice random acts of kindness. His good deeds extend to both people and animals, which is the first suggestion by the author that Mr. Johnson's behavior is arbitrary, that he is not performing good deeds out of a sense of charity but instead is just passing the time.

Good makes life pleasant. It is also defined by its opposite, namely, evil. Evil causes hardship in life and is often committed without

Mr. John Philip Johnson leaves his home with candy and peanuts. *(Image copyright Scott Bolster, 2009. Used under license from Shutterstock.com)*

concern for others. The absence of guilt following such a deed is what makes it evil rather than merely bad. Mrs. Johnson, who has a woman falsely arrested for shoplifting and tries to get a man fired from his job, personifies evil in this story. The interesting, Jacksonian twist is that Mr. and Mrs. Johnson decide to switch roles for a day and compare notes in the evening about what they have done to pass the time, emphasizing that good and evil are kept in balance. They are fully conscious of what they are doing. The moral of this story is that one never knows from one day to the next whether one is dealing with a Mr. Johnson or a Mrs. Johnson.

Urban Life

Life in a big city is one of the themes in Jackson's short story "One Ordinary Day, with Peanuts." It is the 1950s in an urban center that is probably New York City, which is a contemporary setting for the author, who lived there during the early 1940s. Mr. Johnson is extraordinarily cheerful and good-natured, but the people he encounters are wary and distrustful—a commentary by the author on city life at that time. In such a densely settled environment, people remain aloof in public, hurrying from one place to another. The presence of so many people means that there is also a greater likelihood of crime (evil), yet paradoxically there is also a greater opportunity to find and receive help. Mr. Johnson is persistent and everyone he encounters eventually realizes he is nothing if not well-intentioned, so they relax and smile back. Some, like Mildred Kent, are a little surprised to find someone so calm and congenial in the middle of a bustling city. The people who inhabit Jackson's city are concerned about money and holding on to their jobs, as illustrated by Mildred Kent, Arthur Adams, the cab driver, and even the bus driver Mrs. Johnson tries to get fired. These are the things Mr. Johnson often helps people with, the same things Mrs. Johnson preys upon when she seeks to hurt someone. The big city is also a place where a great diversity of people are brought together in a milieu that fosters the growth of new ideas. Amid this diversity is the odd couple, Mr. and Mrs. Johnson.

STYLE

Symbolism

Symbolism is a literary device an author uses to express complex ideas concisely by substituting simple objects to represent the complex ideas. In "One Ordinary Day, with Peanuts," the peanuts are an important symbol for generosity and goodness. Mr. Johnson fills his pockets with candy and peanuts before going out on the town, but it is the peanuts the author makes a point of mentioning repeatedly as he shares them with a little boy, a stray dog, a bus driver, a beggar, and a seagull. Peanuts even appear in the title of the story, underscoring the fact that this is not just any old ordinary day but rather Mr. Johnson's type of ordinary day— one filled with goodness. Peanuts are a healthy snack, providing a way to share food with others, a harmless ritual that brings people closer together.

Money symbolizes the struggle between good and evil in "One Ordinary Day, with Peanuts." Mr. Johnson spends much of his day handing out cash to people. He pays Mildred and Arthur to go out with each other so that they will have fun and forget about their jobs for a while. He gives a beggar money to purchase a fine meal. This struggle is especially clear in the scene with the cab driver. The cabbie has just been given ten dollars to bet on a certain horse. Mr. Johnson is certain that this is a bad deal and offers him a new tip plus more money to use for betting. Money sways people, and Mr. Johnson is on the side of good.

Personification

Personification involves the attribution of human characteristics to animals, ideas, or inanimate objects, and also the embodiment of abstract ideas as people. Mr. and Mrs. Johnson, an example of the latter, are personifications of good and evil. They take turns at being good or evil, going about the city as if they were normal citizens while harboring a secret agenda. They pick people at random to help and to hurt, seeming never to see the same people more than once. Whether or not there is something magical about the Johnsons is never explained, although something mystical is suggested by Mr. Johnson's odd musings about fire signs in his conversation with the cab driver over racehorses. In fact, they could be regarded as normal human beings who happen to share a strange hobby. Nevertheless, since they are a pair, good and evil remain in balance.

HISTORICAL CONTEXT

McCarthyism

On February 9, 1950, U.S. Senator Joseph McCarthy (R-WI) made a historic speech in which he declared that 205 Communists were working within the State Department. This speech is generally considered the beginning of the period known as McCarthyism, a term used to describe unsubstantiated accusations of political subversion and disloyalty. Communism, which first appeared on the international political stage during Russia's Bolshevik Revolution (1917), was regarded with deep suspicion by the mid-twentieth century. This was due, in part, to strained relations between the United States and the Soviet Union following World War II. The United States supported war against North Korea (who were supported by Communist China and the Soviet Union), believing that communism posed a threat to democracy. Despite the official government position against it, many Americans were intrigued by communism, including Jackson's husband, Stanley Hyman. However, as the cold war between the United States and the Soviet Union developed during the 1950s, communism became synonymous with a lack of patriotism. Espionage cases such as that of Julius and Ethel Rosenberg, who in 1951 were found guilty of leaking state secrets to the Soviet Union, supported the idea that communism was unpatriotic.

Senator McCarthy's accusations came at a time when people were already fearful of further war and, on a personal level, of losing their jobs for being unpatriotic. They were therefore ready to blacklist (refuse to allow access to employment), imprison, or exile anyone who might pose a threat to the safety of the nation. No one was exempt from scrutiny by the Federal Bureau of Investigation (FBI), which singled out members of the Hollywood film community because of the content of some films. Suspicion alone was sufficient to jeopardize one's livelihood; once a job was lost through blacklisting, it was difficult to find employment in the industry again. McCarthyism waned in the mid-1950s as public opinion turned against the senator and the courts began to rectify the damage done by false accusations fueled by McCarthyism. Senator McCarthy died in disgrace in 1957.

Korean War

For fifty years, the Korean peninsula was occupied by Japan, with Korean nationalists attempting to

COMPARE & CONTRAST

- **1950s:** The federal minimum wage in the United States is 75 cents in 1950 and one dollar in 1956. In Jackson's short story, Mildred Kent is earning \$1.20 per hour and Arthur Adams is earning \$1.50 per hour.

  Today: The U.S. federal minimum wage is raised to \$7.25 in 2009. Taking inflation into account, this wage is comparable to the minimum wage of 1956.

- **1950s:** Communism emerges as a significant political ideology following World War II, with the Soviet Union, China, and at least ten other nations adopting Communist forms of government by Middlebury. The U.S. government sees communism as a threat to democracy, kicking off a cold war between Communist nations and the United States that begins in the 1950s.

  Today: By the early twenty-first century, the Soviet Union and Eastern European nations have overthrown their Communist governments. The United States, now more concerned with acts of terrorism, maintains cool relations with Communist nations such as China and Cuba.

- **1950s:** In June 1950, war breaks out between North and South Korea. It ends with an armistice in July 1953. The United States aids South Korea in the hope of preserving democracy.

  Today: North Korea withdraws from the armistice in May 2009, leaving the future peace prospects of the two Koreas in question.

undermine Japanese rule. Upon the defeat of Japan in 1945, Korea was divided into two halves, with the Soviet Union claiming the northern half and the United States the southern half. In 1948, the United States returned control of South Korea to the Koreans after making sure the seated government for the Republic of Korea was pro-democracy. The Soviet Union established a Korean-run Communist government in North Korea. Initially, the intention was to unify the nation, but revolts, failed treaties, and the mounting cold war between the United States and the Soviet Union led to all-out war in June 1950. Both governments wanted a unified Korea, albeit with very different political ideologies. The Republic of Korea in the south was supported in the war by the United Nations and its member countries, including the United States. In Jackson's short story, Mrs. Johnson tells her husband about harassing a bus driver by asking him why he did not enlist in the army, which may be a veiled reference to the escalating presence of U.S. armed forces in South Korea.

After three years of war, in July 1953, a U.N.-sponsored armistice was signed by North Korea and the United States. Although the Republic of Korea refused to sign, a tenuous peace was established. In May 2009, amid worldwide concern that North Korea would begin to stockpile a nuclear weapons arsenal, North Korea withdrew from the fifty-six-year-old armistice leaving the area's future in jeopardy.

CRITICAL OVERVIEW

Jackson began publishing her short stories in magazines with a nationwide readership in 1941, but it was the 1948 publication in the *New Yorker* of her most famous story, "The Lottery," that attracted popular and critical attention. According to Judy Oppenheimer's account, published in the *New York Times Book Review* in 1988, a large number of readers of the *New Yorker* sent letters and made phone calls to the magazine complaining about Jackson's story and threatening to cancel their subscriptions unless the author apologized. Donald Barr, reviewing Jackson's short story collection *The Lottery* for the *New York Times* in 1949 acknowledges that although Jackson is adept in

New York City, the likely setting for the story
(Image copyright Javarman, 2009. Used under license from Shutterstock.com)

the short story form, "The Lottery," is "a good story, but there are far better [stories] in the book."

When Jackson died in 1965, book critic Eliot Fremont-Smith was quoted in the *New York Times* obituary that Jackson "was an important literary influence. She was a master of complexity of mood, an ironic explorer of the dark, conflicting inner tyrannies of the mind and soul." In 1996 two of her children, Lawrence Jackson Hyman and Sarah Hyman Stewart, compiled a volume of her short fiction, focusing on unpublished stories and pieces that had appeared only once in print. *Just an Ordinary Day* received little critical acclaim despite the fact that it signaled the revival of an old literary favorite. In her review for the *New York Times Book Review*, Joyce Carol Oates was critical of the editing and selection by her two children. She describes "One Ordinary Day, with Peanuts" as "one of Jackson's slighter fantasies," preferring that it as well as several other inferior stories remain out of print.

CRITICISM

Carol Ullmann

Ullmann is a freelance writer and editor. In this essay, she discusses the power of kindness as illustrated in Jackson's short story "One Ordinary Day, with Peanuts."

Shirley Jackson's short story "One Ordinary Day, with Peanuts" concerns a man who goes about his day dispensing kindness and generosity toward the people he encounters. For most of the story Mr. Johnson is seen as eccentric, harmless, and a force of good in a city where kindness seems to be in short supply, as evidenced by the wariness exhibited by the other characters. Kindness between people and even toward animals is important because it establishes relationships that, when woven together, create a community. Communities exist because people cannot live in isolation. Human beings rely upon each other for companionship and help.

"One Ordinary Day, with Peanuts" is set during the early 1950s, the postwar period. After World War II, many young couples settled down and started families. The nuclear family—which consists of a mother, a father, and children—became more dominant at this time. Traditional roles were emphasized, with the husband going to work and the mother devoted to housework and raising the children. This represented a significant change from life during the war, when so many men were abroad fighting that women had to take over jobs traditionally held by men.

Cities, which had been important centers of industry during the war, waned in popularity as people fled to the newly developing suburbs, a place that combined the best aspects of city and rural life. Levittowns, representing a new approach to home and community development, arose in the early 1950s as part of this cultural shift. Four Levittowns were established in the United States and Puerto Rico, setting the standard for suburban development. "One Ordinary Day, with Peanuts," which is set in a big city, depicts characters—especially mothers—who remain suspicious of strangers in order to protect their children from harm. Jackson illustrates how life in the big city can be full of fear and isolation.

The post-World War II period represented a time when, as a result of tense international relations between the United States and such countries as the Soviet Union, China, and North Korea, people were suspicious of communism. This fear came to be known as the Red Scare (red is a color typically associated with communism). Because he and others like him felt that communism posed a threat to the United States, Senator Joseph McCarthy used this nationwide unease

WHAT DO I READ NEXT?

- Arthur Miller's play *The Crucible* (1953) uses the historical setting of the Salem witch trials in late-seventeenth-century colonial America as a way of commenting on the evils and absurdities of McCarthyism. It won a Tony Award for Best Play in 1953.
- *Eight Days of Luke* (1975) is a young-adult novel by Diana Wynne Jones. It concerns an ordinary boy named David, who is spending a lonely summer at the home of his aunt and uncle's family. David becomes entangled with the Norse gods Odin and Thor, among others, who are attempting to find the mischievous Luke, also known as Loki, a Norwegian trickster god who has become David's only friend.
- *American Gods* (2001), by Neil Gaiman, is a fantasy novel about a twenty-first-century conflict between the old, traditional European "gods" of mythology and the new "gods" of modern America (modern things like credit cards, the Internet, freeways). It is a look at the clash of values in America. *American Gods* has won Hugo and Nebula awards for best novel, in addition to several other awards.
- *Everything That Rises Must Converge* is a collection of short stories by Flannery O'Connor published posthumously in 1965. A devout Catholic, O'Connor adds a grotesque, Southern twist to everyday situations while ostensibly exploring questions of morality. O'Connor and Jackson are similar in their use of the everyday in stories that end in unexpected ways.
- *The Haunting of Hill House* (1959), by Shirley Jackson, is a psychological thriller about a lonely woman who is drawn to a haunted mansion as a member of a group devoted to ascertaining the existence of ghosts. Once there, she finds herself unable to leave. One of the most celebrated horror novels of the twentieth century, it has been made into a play and two movies.
- Edith Hamilton's classic work *Mythology* (1942) collects Greek, Roman, and Norse myths that collectively provide an unparalleled introduction to the Western world's best-known tales. Hamilton's collection is valued for its readability, organization, insightfulness, and entertaining approach.
- *Year of Impossible Goodbyes* (1993), by Sook Nyul Choi, is a young-adult novel about a ten-year-old girl named Sookan who lives in North Korea at the end of World War II. Her homeland is first occupied by the oppressive Japanese and later by the equally oppressive Soviet Union. Sookan's family undertakes a perilous journey in order to resettle in South Korea.

to blacklist and even imprison people whom he suspected of harboring communist beliefs. His campaign of extreme scrutiny came to be known as McCarthyism. Although it lasted less than a decade, it destroyed lives. People reported each other out of fear rather than based upon hard evidence; careers were ruined, with mere accusations often leading to blacklisting. In the end, the mania surrounding the purported dangers of communism was generally believed to be of McCarthy's own devising.

Mr. Johnson's kindness is an antidote to all the fears that underlie this short story. His goodwill is relentless, and his supply of peanuts and money seems endless. He practices what came to be known in the United States forty years later as "random acts of kindness." As recounted in 1996 by Adair Lara in her *San Francisco Chronicle* column, the phrase "practice random kindness and senseless acts of beauty" was coined by Anne Herbert in the early 1980s and was subsequently popularized by journalists in national news outlets and periodicals. The phrase "random acts of kindness" was also the subject of books, was used in classrooms, and was even printed on coffee mugs and other novelty items. The idea of kindness being random and even anonymous is appealing because it gives one the feeling that the world is perhaps a better place than was previously thought. The phrase also imparts a sense of spontaneity, suggesting that acts of kindness emerge naturally on the part of people.

In her article, Lara notes that random kindness is not selfless but is, in fact, a method of personal gratification. She writes that "a random act of kindness, when performed correctly, is something one does for oneself." When Jackson's story is looked at in this light, the character of Mr. Johnson gains clarity. The end of the story reveals that he is not the paragon of goodness that he appears to be and that his daily routine on the streets is comparable to an actor's role. The interpretation of the story undergoes a transformation in the reader's mind, from wondering why Mr. Johnson is helping all these people so selflessly to determining why Mr. and Mrs. Johnson do what they do, the good and the evil.

What is the power of kindness in the lives of the people Mr. Johnson meets? Even while Mr. Johnson, in his role of do-gooder, ultimately holds himself above those he is helping, the power of his message does not fail to move those he has touched: the child who is moving to Vermont with his mother is happier, the cab driver is relieved, Mildred Kent and Arthur Adams are pleasantly surprised, both mothers in the story are glad to know their children are safe, the beggar is well fed, and many other people have been touched after having received Mr. Johnson's unexpected smile. Jackson ultimately chooses not to resolve the question of what comes next for the people who have been helped. Instead she unveils Mr. Johnson as a fraud: his generosity is part of a role he plays to perfection.

Is Mr. Johnson happy? His job, coupled with that of his wife, is to dispense goodwill and ill fortune, respectively, to the random people they meet in the city. Mr. Johnson appears to be content with his lot, strange as it appears, so it does not require a great leap on the part of the reader to believe that he is happy. Yet his happiness, arising as it does from such an odd occupation, makes the reader wonder what life must be like within the Johnson household. Do they practice their jobs upon each other? The last three lines of the story seem to suggest this.

Themes of community and good and evil appear frequently in Jackson's short stories. "One Ordinary Day, with Peanuts" dwells specifically upon the good (kindness) within a famous story, "The Lottery," which is about a lottery no one wants to win, presents a different perspective in chilling fashion, revealing the evil that exists within a community.

Ultimately what Jackson imparts to her readers in "One Ordinary Day, with Peanuts" is the assurance that kindness—which, given the Johnsons' strange approach to good and evil, may or may not be inborn—is required for the smooth functioning of communities and that good and evil have a way of balancing each other out. Irrespective of his intentions or degree of sincerity, Mr. Johnson brings people together at a time when fear and isolation threaten to tear them apart. Isolated by the nuclear family structure, fearful of international politics, and weary of big-city life, the people in Jackson's world would otherwise be easy pickings for the likes of Mrs. Johnson.

Source: Carol Ullmann, Critical Essay on "One Ordinary Day, with Peanuts," in *Short Stories for Students*, Gale, Cengage Learning, 2010.

Laurence Jackson Hyman and Sarah Hyman Stewart

In the following essays, Hyman and Stewart explain how they chose the stories in the collection Just an Ordinary Day.

Several years ago, a carton of cobwebbed files discovered in a Vermont barn more than a quarter century after our mother's death, arrived without notice in the mail. Within it were the original manuscript of *The Haunting of Hill House,* together with Shirley Jackson's handwritten notes on character and scene development for the novel, as well as half a dozen unpublished short stories—the yellow bond carbons she kept for her files. The stories were mostly unknown to us, and we began to consider publishing a new collection of our mother's work.

Soon we located other stories, some never published anywhere, and some published only once, decades ago, in periodicals, many long defunct. Shirley's brother and sister-in-law, Barry and Marylou Jackson, supplied more stories in well-preserved copies of magazines; other pieces our sister, Jai Holly, and brother, Barry Hyman, had filed away over the years. Many more were found in the archives at the San Francisco Public Library. A windfall came when we learned that the Library of Congress held

Jackson's main theme is good versus evil *(Image copyright Christy Thompson, 2009. Used under license from Shutterstock.com)*

twenty-six cartons of our mother's papers—journals, poetry, plays, parts of unfinished novels, and stories, lots of stories. After a week spent there photocopying, we began to feel we had the makings of a book, the first new work by Shirley Jackson since *The Magic of Shirley Jackson* and *Come Along With Me,* both published shortly after her death in 1965 at the age of forty-eight. We hoped Shirley Jackson's work could now be discovered by a whole new generation of readers.

We uncovered a wealth of early writing from the late thirties and early forties, but very little from her precollege years. She claimed to have burned all her writings just before she left home to go to the University of Rochester, in 1934, and she may have done so, although some of her high school journals are among her preserved papers at the Library of Congress. While we could place them in a general time frame, none of the new stories we discovered had dates on them or any indication of when they were first written. Rather than be inaccurate we have left the stories in Part One undated.

Later visits to the Library of Congress enabled us to find missing parts of incomplete stories or versions that we liked better. Soon we had assembled more than 130 stories, and of these we agreed on the fifty-four presented here, those that we feel are finished and up to Shirley Jackson's finely tuned standards. When we approached Bantam we were met with considerable enthusiasm for the project, and the book began to take shape as a significant collection of Jackson's short fiction. Of the stories included in this collection, thirty-one have never been published before. The remaining stories had been previously published in magazines, but never before included in a collection of Jackson's short fiction; and of these, only two or three have appeared in book form at all, mostly anthologies. One of those anthologized (and very hard to find) is "One Ordinary Day, with Peanuts."

Many of the stories we found untitled or with working titles, since she often waited until publication to name them. In these instances we have created titles in the best muted Jackson style we could manage. In other instances we decided to change repetitive character names, often arbitrarily assigned by Jackson and intended to be changed before publication. We decided not to alter the archaic money references in these stories, however dated they may be, feeling that the integrity and understanding of the stories ought not be compromised.

We include a full range of Jackson's many types of short fiction, from lighthearted romantic pieces to the macabre to the truly frightening. We also include a few of the humorous pieces she wrote about our family, since those, too, were what Shirley Jackson pioneered with as a writer, as well as her shocking and twisted explorations of the supernatural and the psyche. We want this collection to represent the great diversity of her work, and to show the writer's craft evolving through a variety of forms and styles.

Our mother lived and wrote in a time—the thirties through the sixties—when smoking and drinking were both widespread and fashionable. Her characters grimly and gleefully chain-smoke and throw down drink after drink, in between boiling their coffee and spanking their children. But underneath these literary folkways of her time the universal themes glitter.

The stories we include here are not all charismatic heart-stoppers on the level of "The

Lottery." Most of her short fiction was written for publication in the popular magazines of her day (*Charm, Look, Harper's, Ladies' Home Companion, Mademoiselle, Cosmopolitan, The Magazine of Fantasy and Science Fiction, Reader's Digest, The New Yorker, Playboy, Good Housekeeping, Woman's Home Companion,* etc.). She actually wrote very few horror stories, and not many stories of fantasy or the supernatural, probably preferring to develop those themes more thoroughly in her novels. She had the courage to deal with unfashionable topics and to twist popular icons. Some of the stories gathered here are so unusual in style or point of view that they resemble almost none of the rest of her work.

We discovered that some stories tried to get themselves written over and over throughout Jackson's life. "The Honeymoon of Mrs. Smith" is shockingly different in attitude, theme, and climax from the version it precedes here, "The Mystery of the Murdered Bride." They are the same story, told years apart and from almost opposing viewpoints. This is the only instance—but a fascinating one for students of short fiction—in which we have chosen to include two versions of the same story. We have also included a few "feel-good" stories beloved by readers of the (mostly women's) magazines of the fifties and sixties. They are tucked between tales of murder and trickery, among ghostly rambles and poetic fables, between hugely funny family chronicles and dark tales of perfect, unexpected justice.

Our mother tried to write every day, and treated writing in every way as her professional livelihood. She would typically work all morning, after all the children went off to school, and usually again well into the evening and night. There was always the sound of typing. And our house was more often than not filled with luminaries in literature and the arts. There were legendary parties and poker games with visiting painters, sculptors, musicians, composers, poets, teachers, and writers of every leaning. But always there was the sound of her typewriter, pounding away into the night.

This collection of short fiction, taken as a whole, adds significantly to the body of Shirley Jackson's published work. These stories range from those she wrote in college and as a budding writer living in Greenwich Village in the early forties, to those she churned out steadily during the 1950s, to those nearly perfect, terrifying pieces crafted toward the end of her life in the mid-sixties. This collection demonstrates her lifelong commitment to writing, her development as an artist, and her courage to explore universal themes of evil, madness, cruelty, and the humorous ironies of child-raising. She took the craft of writing every bit as seriously as the subject matter she chose (the *Minneapolis Tribune* once said: "Miss Jackson seemingly cannot write a poor sentence") and in the work presented here the reader will find the wit and delight in storytelling that were her trademarks.

Source: Laurence Jackson Hyman and Sarah Hyman Stewart, "Introduction to *Just an Ordinary Day*," in *Just an Ordinary Day*, edited by Laurence Jackson Hyman and Sarah Hyman Stewart, Bantam Books, 1997, pp. vii–xii.

Brad Hopper

In the following review, Hopper notes that Just an Ordinary Day *exemplifies Jackson's stylistic growth.*

The late author of "The Lottery," a short story found in nearly every anthology and never to be forgotten once read, left behind several published novels and story collections. She also left many unpublished story manuscripts as well as several stories that were published in magazines but never gathered in book form; now her children have selected 54 of these stories for inclusion in this posthumous collection, all of which they believe are "up to Shirley Jackson's finely tuned standards." Artistic development is obvious as we read through her career's worth of writing, from her salad days in college (when she was already demonstrating considerable talent) to the flowering of her mastery of the short story form in the 1960s, the last decade of her life. Not all of them are dark in the fashion of "The Lottery," some are light and funny. One of the most delightful is one of the unpublished pieces, "Maybe It Was the Car," about a woman—writer, wife, and mother—who one day walks out on frying the supper hamburgers in a moment of self-assertion. An important addition to fiction collections.

Source: Brad Hopper, Review of *Just an Ordinary Day*, in *Booklist*, Vol. 93, No. 3, October 1, 1996, p. 291.

Publishers Weekly

In the following review, Jackson is praised for her humor and narrative point of view.

From the hilarious first story in this treat of a collection, in which a college girl tricks the devil (horns, hoofs and all) into selling her his soul, we know we are in Jackson territory—the Jackson of the classic short story "The Lottery" and the novel *The Haunting of Hill House*. For Jackson devotees, as well as first-time readers, this is a feast: more than half of the 54 short stories collected here have never been published before. The circumstances that inspired the volume are appropriately bizarre. According to Jackson's children, "a carton of cobwebbed files discovered in a Vermont barn" arrived in the mail one day without notice; along with the original manuscript, of her novel, the box contained six unpublished stories. Other pieces, culled from family collections, and from archives and papers at the San Francisco Public Library and the Library of Congress, appeared in print only once, in various magazines. The stories are diverse: there are tales that pillory smug, self-satisfied, small-town ladies; chilling and murderous chronicles of marriage; witty romantic comedies; and tales that reveal an eerie juxtaposition of good and evil. The devil, who can't seem to get an even break, makes several appearances. Each of Jackson's ghost stories—often centered around a child, missing or dead—is beautifully anchored in and thoroughly shaped by a particular point of view. A few pieces that qualify as humorous takes on the predicaments of modern life add a relaxed, biographical element to a virtuoso collection. (Dec.)

FYI: Jackson, who died in 1965 at age 48, is poised for a literary revival: the BBC is releasing a biography in the fall, and a new film version of *The Haunting of Hill House* is currently in production.

Source: Review of *Just an Ordinary Day*, in *Publisher's Weekly*, Vol. 243, No. 42, October 14, 1996, p. 63.

Lenemaja Friedman

In the following excerpt, Friedman explores the idea of the feminine evil within many of Jackson's short stories, including the humorous "One Ordinary Day, with Peanuts."

Miss Jackson, who first acquired fame through her short stories, quickly became known as a talented and prolific writer. At the end of her career, even after several successful novels, she was still best known as the author of the short stories and of "The Lottery" in particular. Before dealing with the characteristics of her style—her straightforward manner of presentation, her use of symbolism; her irony; and her treatment of ambiguity, mystery, and suspense—one should examine the variety of themes that are the subject of her tales.

> "BUT MISS JACKSON'S CHARACTERS ARE NOT 'HEAVIES'; SHE TREATS THEM LIGHTLY SO THAT THE REVELATION, DESPITE ITS SERIOUSNESS, BECOMES FUNNY. AGAIN, ONE SEES EVIDENCE OF MISS JACKSON THE ENTERTAINER."

I: THEMES

One easily thinks of Miss Jackson's creations as "tales" since, even in the serious works, one suspects that her primary purpose is to entertain. The fact that she is, as will be seen, a master storyteller does not deny the truth and validity of her message. Her insights and observations about man and society are disturbing; and in the case of "The Lottery," they are shocking. The themes themselves are not new: evil cloaked in seeming good; prejudice and hypocrisy; loneliness and frustration; psychological studies of minds that have slipped the bonds of reality; studies of persons subjected to suspense and terror; and the humorous helplessness of parents in the inevitable crises of family living. As indicated, these themes may not be new, but her treatment of them often is. She creates microcosms, private worlds set apart from the larger universe of crowds and cities, pushing-and-shoving functional people; away from the problems of ecology and population growth and urban housing renewal. Even in the tales of family life, the experiences are almost entirely confined within the limits of the house, and they center on the mother who is, of course, Shirley Jackson herself. Neither is "The Lottery," a story of community social evil, exempt from presentation as an isolated world; for, as typical of other communities as this particular village is meant to be, it is pictured as almost isolated from the rest of mankind, which is also basically unenlightened, narrow, and evil.

The isolation, the loneliness, and the frustrations that plague Miss Jackson's characters have many causes; but one of the major sources, and one of her favorite topics, is mental illness—a subject that she knew well, for she had suffered from bouts of depression and anxiety for years. However, she had always been fascinated with the shadowy world of the mind, with the powers the mind controls, and with the confusion that results from disturbed thoughts and repressed anxieties. She sees the psychotic and emotionally disturbed as victims of some demonic spirit whose capricious nature feeds on loneliness and unhappiness. And, though man manufactures many of his own problems, evils exist over which he has little control; among these are his own fears. His anxieties trap him. As a result, her people—those whose vision of reality is no longer clear-cut—are very much alone.

In the psychological stories (the critics term them "thrillers"), Miss Jackson's protagonists suffer varying degrees of anxiety. In the more advanced stages, they are unaware of what is happening to them until one day nothing in the real world is significant or meaningful; and they find themselves powerless in a tangle of dreams and shadows. Occasionally, the reader is allowed to share the author's secret, to witness the disintegration of a troubled mind; more often the reader is startled into the discovery that all is not well, and the heroine's flight into fantasy comes as something of a surprise, but Miss Jackson's workmanship is such that a review of past events reveals that the signs have been there all along. Suspense is created by the unpredictability of the character's behavior.

In the story "The Beautiful Stranger" (1946), the reader is warned at the outset to expect the unusual: "What might be called the first intimation of strangeness occurred at the railroad station. She had come with her children, Smalljohn and her baby girl, to meet her husband when he returned from a business trip to Boston." Through the anxious eyes of Margaret, a young housewife, the reader explores the unusual situation in which she finds herself. One learns that not only has the young couple quarreled before John left for Boston, but also that theirs has been a home of tension and—on Margaret's part, at least—ill will. While John's thoughts are never revealed, Margaret's show her to be tense and afraid. At the station, her odd sensations increase; and the homecoming is marred also by Smalljohn's unruly behavior and by the baby's screaming rejection of her father.

Later, at home, Margaret is suddenly struck with the idea that this man is not her husband but a beautiful stranger who, for some unknown but perfectly logical reason, has come to take John's place. Since the thought is exciting to her, she willingly entertains the man, convinced that he is aware of her discovery and is—at the same time—enjoying the deception as much as she is. She tests him with a few questions; and, while the reader sees that the answers are inconclusive, Margaret is happily convinced that the man is not John. He doesn't look quite like John, she decides; his hair is a little darker; his hands, a bit stronger. Suspense increases, for the reader knows that something is amiss; but, at this point, he cannot assess the situation or judge the direction of future events, as the laws of logic and probability seem to be inoperative.

Margaret's obsession persists, and she is happy for the first time in many months. The following day (home from the office), John remarks, "Someone told me today . . . that he had heard I was back from Boston, and I distinctly thought he said that he heard I was dead in Boston." She replies, "At any rate, . . . *you* were not dead in Boston, and nothing else matters" (p. 71). But the reader is perplexed. Is this an element of fantasy; has a dead husband returned? The uncertainty the reader experiences at this point is characteristic of the reaction to events in many of the stories.

Shirley Jackson keeps her audience guessing. Increasingly pleased with her stranger, Margaret is sad when it is time for him to leave for the office. On the afternoon of the second day, instead of taking the children to the park as usual, she calls a baby-sitter, takes a taxi into town to shop for a gift for him, and enjoys wandering about the strange shops "choosing small lovely things." Since it is almost dark when she returns, she indicates to the driver what she believes to be her home; but, when the taxi leaves and she walks toward the house, nothing is familiar. She hesitates: ". . . surely she had come too far? This is not possible, she thought, this cannot be; surely our house was white? The evening was very dark, and she could see only the houses going in rows, with more rows beyond them and more beyond that, and somewhere a house which was hers, with the beautiful stranger inside, and she lost out here." Thus the story ends with Margaret in a state of confusion. One realizes then that her previous anxiety has caused her mind to play trick on her, as it has in the past two days; now she can no longer control its behavior or focus her wandering attention. Familiar objects are no longer meaningful; and, since she has lost touch with reality, she is, indeed, lost.

In the story "Island," one is told immediately that Mrs. Montague has "lost her mind." The opening lines read: "Mrs. Montague's son had been very good to her, with the kind affection and attention to her well-being that is seldom found toward mothers in sons with busy wives and growing families of their own; when Mrs. Montague lost her mind, her son came into his natural role of guardian. There had always been a great deal of warm feeling between Mrs. Montague and her son, and although they lived nearly a thousand miles apart by now. Henry Paul Montague was careful to see that his mother was well taken care of;..."

From the point of view of society, wealthy Mrs. Montague is an invalid; this condition relegates her to confinement in her handsome apartment with a constant nurse-companion. While Henry Paul is described as a devoted son—for he is careful to supply money for all her needs, to pay the bills promptly, and to send weekly tender letters in longhand inquiring about her health—he comes to visit his mother only on rare trips to New York. Her physical needs, therefore, receive considerable attention while her emotional ones do not. Separated from the one person she loves, she has had, instead, for six years, Polly Oakes, a firm, rigid, insignificant individual who occupies herself by reading magazines, knitting, and studying the daily menu. Miss Oakes is kind to Mrs. Montague, but she becomes understandably exasperated when the elderly lady spills oatmeal on her beautiful dresses, refuses to eat, or tries to run away during the spells of restlessness that overcome her every year in late spring.

Except for one glimpse into the liberated spirit and dreams of Mrs. Montague, one sees events and objects as they appear to Miss Oakes, who is impressed with the thick, luxurious carpet; the silken curtains; the lovely clothes sent by the exclusive dress shop for Mrs. Montague's selection (her own clothes are garish reds and yellows, since the white uniforms seem to upset the old lady). She admires Mrs. Montague's shiny dark mink, the rich appointments of the apartment hotel, and especially the gourmet restaurant below from which she orders their meals. Eating has become the major preoccupation, a daily ritual that begins with careful devotion to an elaborate menu and ends with the offering up of the repast by hotel personnel and the religious consumption marred only by Mrs. Montague's mishaps. While Miss Oakes partakes of exotic foods, Mrs. Montague's fare is always oatmeal with pudding for dessert and sometimes, if she is good, ice cream.

One soon begins to pity the old woman, for she seems to yearn for color and beauty and for a wild outdoor freedom. In the apartment, she spends much time with crayons and a simple coloring book. Blue is her favorite; she loves the blue sky, blue water, a softly curved blue bowl she had seen in a shop window; and she paints everything blue. "Why look at you," Miss Oakes says. "You've gone and made the whole thing blue, you silly child." Mrs. Montague violently covers the picture. "Mine," she says. "Get away, this is mine." Later she says to her companion, "You don't know what things *are,* really." The materialistic Polly lacks the sensitivity to understand the loneliness and the hidden yearnings of the older woman. Every day on their walks Mrs. Montague pauses at the same shop windows, sometimes to admire the blue bowl, or some tea cakes, or a red and yellow plastic bird dipping its beak mechanically into a glass of water. "Pretty," she whispers, "pretty, pretty."

Without warning, the viewpoint changes, and the reader discovers the old lady's dreams. She is on an island: "She opened her eyes suddenly and was aware that she saw. The sky was unbelievably, steadily blue, and the sand beneath her feet was hot; she could see the water, colored more deeply than the sky, but faintly greener. Far off was the line where the sky and water met, and it was infinitely pure." In her world of fantasy, following an impulse, she discards and then buries her clothing: fur coat, hat, shoes—all. Then, exulting in her freedom, she runs wildly across the sand; in a grove of nearby trees, she hears a parrot calling her. "Eat, eat," it shrieks, "eat, eat." For a moment the unpleasant idea of food comes to her, and she runs on; but later among the trees she sees and again hears the parrot, a "saw-toothed voice and a flash of ugly red and yellow." When she sits down a moment later in the cool grass by a little brook to eat, she has by her side "a shimmering glass... of dark red wine, a blue plate of soft chocolate cakes filled with cream"; and there are pomegranates, cheese, and "small sharp-flavored candies"—all of the delicacies she yearns for, but never receives in the prison of her sheltered, prosaic life.

Somewhere overhead, the parrot continues to scream; and she puts out a bit of cake for him.

He hesitantly comes to feed, nibbling cautiously, lifting his beak, then lowering his head and lifting it again. The movement—which she has observed in the shop window—seems familiar to her, but she does not know why. The parrot, one realizes, is the insistent Miss Oakes, who, afraid of the host sand and the water, stays always in the trees "near the food." The dream sequence ends as abruptly as it began; in Miss Jackson's fiction, there is often no clear-cut distinction between the dream world and the real world, and the disturbed personality slips easily between the two. The reader has rather more difficulty; and, if for this reason alone, one must read the stories carefully and thoughtfully, and examine the subtleties of character, plot, and symbolism.

As the dream ends and one no longer shares Mrs. Montague's thoughts, the two ladies turn the corner and are almost home; back in their apartment, Miss Oakes orders their food, beginning with a martini for herself, prune juice for the old lady, and her usual oatmeal. And, while the younger woman busies herself with the ritual of the dinner menu, Mrs. Montague bends over her coloring book, busily at work on a farmyard scene—hens, a barn, trees, which she colors blue. With sudden inspiration she places a red and yellow blob in one of her blue trees, an outward sign of rebellion perhaps, but also one of inner satisfaction as she quietly puts Polly Oakes in her place.

As the blue suggests to her the freedom of the sky and the sea, the island of her dreams is a haven, far from the repressions she does not understand, where she can behave as her spirit pleases. Mrs. Montague is another of the confused, lonely persons that one finds in the fiction of Miss Jackson and for whom she shows sympathy. The Polly Oakeses, lacking sensitivity and therefore unresponsive to the needs of others, are the villains.

Loss of direction nevertheless may stem from many sources. An overdose of pain-deadening drugs is responsible for Clara Spencer's mental confusion in the story "The Tooth" (1950). One assumes her condition to be temporary, although the story ends with Clara's having forgotten her identity and with her running barefooted through the streets of New York, hand in hand with an imaginary man. Both Clara Spencer and Mrs. Montague ("The Island") yield to an urge to recover the natural freedom of youth....

V: EVIL BENEATH A MILD EXTERIOR

What evil lurks within the hearts of men—and old women? In addition to those mentioned previously in "The Little House," there are three notable examples of grandmotherly types who differ from the popular image of goodness, grace, and charm. Each of the older ladies in "Trial by Combat,""Whistler's Grandmother," and "Possibility of Evil" is intent on mischief. The least harmful, yet a rather sinister character—because she seems to have no conscience —is Mrs. Archer in "Trial by Combat," a respectable old lady who unashamedly steals from the other inhabitants of her rooming house.

The "sweet" old grandmother in "Whistler's Grandmother" (1945) is on her way to New York City to warn her returning soldier-grandson that his city wife has been receiving strange letters from men. She loves her grandson but cannot tolerate his pretty wife; therefore, she is about to expose her for nonexistent crimes. Obviously irony is an important ingredient in each of these stories, for the reader sees these old women in quite a different way from that in which they see themselves and from which society views them. Whistler's Grandmother, a hypocrite, is intent on injuring an innocent human being. The story's title emphasizes the contrast between the outward show of goodness and gentleness and the ugliness within.

In 1965, Miss Jackson was still pursuing the wicked old lady theme; and perhaps the most malicious of her characters of this type is Miss Adela Strangeworth in "The Possibility of Evil," her last short story which appeared in the December 18, 1965, issue of *The Saturday Evening Post,* four months after Miss Jackson's death. Seventy-one-year-old Miss Strangeworth, the last of a well-known and respected family, decides that there is too much evil in the world, especially in "her" town. To correct this situation and to warn others of evil, she, ironically becomes evil. She writes short, cryptic —poison-pen—notes in penciled block letters to various people in town, and secretly mails them at night. "Miss Strangeworth never concerned herself with facts; her letters all dealt with the more negotiable stuff of suspicion." Completely hypocritical, she is outwardly friendly to the same people she secretly attacks. To the young couple, concerned with the seemingly slow progress of their six-month-old baby, she writes: "DIDN'T YOU EVER SEE AN IDIOT CHILD BEFORE? SOME PEOPLE JUST SHOULDN'T HAVE CHILDREN,

SHOULD THEY?" To Mrs. Harper, to whom she has written previously and who, she decides, looks rather shaky, she writes: "HAVE YOU FOUND OUT YET WHAT THEY WERE ALL LAUGHING ABOUT AFTER YOU LEFT THE BRIDGE CLUB ON THURSDAY? OR IS THE WIFE REALLY ALWAYS THE LAST ONE TO KNOW?"

In contrast, the poor, hard-working people surrounding Miss Strangeworth seem harried and guiltless; but she insidiously destroys their peace of mind until she accidentally drops a letter one night. Again, with a stroke of irony, one of the past victims sees her; but, unknowingly and out of kindness, the finder delivers the dropped letter to the intended victim. Miss Strangeworth awakens the next morning with "a feeling of intense happiness" at the thought of the letters sent the night before until, among the mail on the hall floor, she finds and opens a poison-pen letter addressed to her. She has been discovered. She begins to cry silently for "the wickedness of the world" as she reads: "LOOK OUT AT WHAT USED TO BE YOUR ROSES." Her beautiful roses have always been her most prized possession, a fact Miss Jackson has carefully developed. And they have now been destroyed in retaliation for her wickedness, but it is characteristic of these ladies not to recognize their own evil. It is not they who are at fault, but the rest of the world—the final irony.

But not all of the perpetrators of evil are female; some males, who are also not what they seem, have a polite, smiling exterior that hides their ugliness within. Sometimes Miss Jackson uses this revelation as the special twist at the end of the story. In one of the earlier *New Yorker* stories, "On the House" (1943), a blind man and his supposed bride come into a liquor store to buy supplies to celebrate their wedding. Artie, at the counter, offers to give them either scotch (which the man wants) or brandy (which she favors) at a discount as a wedding present. After they choose the brandy, the better buy, the blind man produces four bills since the price is four dollars; however, he presents a five and three singles. Not wishing to embarrass the man, Artie quietly calls this to the wife's attention. She states proudly that her husband knows one bill from another, and then silently takes the change as Artie gives it to her.

A few minutes later, the blind man returns with his wife and loudly proclaims that he has been cheated. He says that he realizes now that he had handed Artie a five and three singles. Artie, acknowledging this, says he gave the change to the wife. The wife denies it and threatens to call the police. Artie, who knows when he has been taken, produces four more dollars, which the man pockets, and then, putting the brandy under his arm, he and she leave. Through this cunning ruse, they have acquired a $4.97 bottle of brandy for nothing. The irony lies in the reversal of expectation: the blind man has used his affliction and the resulting sympathy to defraud an unsuspecting, and, momentarily, kindhearted individual.

Another unusual story with the same theme and with a twist is "One Ordinary Day With Peanuts"—selected for *Best American Short Stories, 1956* and first published in *Fantasy and Science Fiction Magazine*. In this story, Mr. John Philip Johnson leaves his house in the morning armed with candy and peanuts. Throughout the day, he seeks opportunities to perform kind acts and, in the process, gives away not only peanuts but money. At the end of the day, coinciding with the end of the story, he comes home to his wife, who has spent the day performing evil deeds: accusing an innocent lady of shoplifting; sending three dogs to the pound, etc. Mr. Johnson applauds her fine efforts and then suggests that they *trade* tomorrow, implying that he will then be the wicked one and she the distributor of good. The reader suddenly realizes that this standard exchange is the way in which Mr. and Mrs. Johnson get their enjoyment: by taking turns at playing God and Satan. For the reader, the ultimate horror of the situation lies in the lack of conscience of the two and in their utter disregard for right and wrong as they interfere with the lives of others for sport. But Miss Jackson's characrters are not "heavies"; she treats them lightly so that the revelation, despite its seriousness, becomes funny. Again, one sees evidence of Miss Jackson the entertainer.

There are other stories in which young people are the victims of either thoughtlessness or malicious intent: for instance, one has the ill treatment of a young girl whose parents have been killed in an accident, and who has been taken in by a hypocritical neighbor, in the story "All She Said Was Yes" (1962); and the injury to the teen-age boy by the man he aided in "Seven Types of Ambiguity" (1948). But such cruelty also extends into the animal world; and the most pleasant, harmless-looking people can expose the ugliness of their natures in their treatment of less fortunate creatures.

In the story "The Renegade" (1948), for example, the victim is a dog belonging to the Walpoles who have recently moved from the city to a country community. Lady Walpole, a gentle and lovable family pet, has suddenly killed, but not eaten, three of the neighbor's chickens; and everyone asks Mrs. Walpole what they are going to do about the dog. Once a chicken-killer, they say, always a chicken-killer. Kindhearted Mrs. Walpole is shaken by the "cures" suggested. Through the use of the outsider and her reactions to the advice given, Miss Jackson gives the reader a horrifying glimpse of man's innate cruelty. The more humane persons advise chaining or shooting the dog. Old Mr. White proposes that they tie a dead chicken around the dog's neck until it rots and falls off by itself. The grocer then recalls his father's cure for an egg-eating dog:

> So he took an egg once, set it on the back of the stove for two, three days, till the egg got good and ripe, good and hot through and that egg smelled pretty bad. Then—I was there, boy twelve, thirteen years old—he called the dog one day, and the dog come running. So I held the dog, and my daddy opened the dog's mouth and put the egg, red-hot and smelling to heaven, and then he held the dog's mouth closed so's the dog couldn't get rid of the egg any way except to swallow.

To the grocer's comment that thereafter the dog would run when he saw an egg, Mrs. Walpole asks, "But how did he feel about you?... Did he ever come near *you* again?" The grocer seems surprised, as though the question were irrelevant, but then he says, "No,... I don't believe you could say's he ever did. Not much of a dog, though."

Another man says she should take her dog "and put him in a pen with a mother hen's got chicks to protect." When asked what would happen, he replies, "Scratch his eyes out... He wouldn't ever be able to *see* another chicken." Understandably upset, Mrs. Walpole leaves the store. Even at home, when the children arrive from school, she discovers that they, too, can discuss the possible tortures without visible emotion. A Mr. Shepherd, a genial man who gives the children nickels and takes the boys fishing, had told them that they could get a collar for the dog in which they were to hammer spikes, attach it to a long rope, and pull the rope when the dog chases a chicken. "And," says her son Jack, "the spikes cut her head off." As the children laugh, Mrs. Walpole stares at them in amazement, and retreats then to the out-of-doors to get a breath of fresh air, to be reassured by the peaceful landscape: the sunny sky and the gentle line of the hills.

The children, perhaps, are not aware of the significance of their chatter; moreover, the hypothetical situation is not real to them, although they are delighted with its possibilities. They love their dog; but Mrs. Walpole realizes, nevertheless, as Miss Jackson obviously does, that children are not immune to the latent cruelties that sprout in adults. They, too, contain their share of the evil that is the lot of mankind. Miss Jackson, one presumes, believes that man has a choice; he need not be evil, and it behooves him to fight these tendencies toward evil, not only in himself, but in others. None of the stories—except the comic ones—has a happy ending. The dilemmas remain unresolved, as does the problem with Lady Walpole in this story. The situation is presented; and the lesson, if any, comes from the reader's exposure to the evil and from the insights he gains therefrom....

Source: Lenemaja Friedman,"The Short Stories," in *Shirley Jackson*, Twayne Publishers, 1975, p. 44–61.

SOURCES

Barr, Donald, Review of *The Lottery*, in *New York Times Book Review*, April 17, 1949, p. 4.

"Federal Minimum Wage Rates, 1955–2009," in *InfoPlease*, http://www.infoplease.com/ipa/A0774473.html (accessed October 19, 2009).

Friedman, Lenemaja, *Shirley Jackson*, Twayne Publishers, 1975.

Haywood, John, *Atlas of World History*, Barnes & Noble, 1997, pp. 109, 121.

"History of Federal Minimum Wage Rates Under the Fair Labor Standards Act, 1938–2009," in *U.S. Department of Labor*, http://www.dol.gov/esa/minwage/chart.htm (accessed October 19, 2009).

Jackson, Shirley, "One Ordinary Day, with Peanuts," in *Just an Ordinary Day*, edited by Laurence Jackson Hyman and Sarah Hyman Stewart, Bantam Books, 1998, pp. 329–38.

Lara, Adair, "The Day Has Come for Random Kindness," in *San Francisco Chronicle*, February 15, 1996, p. D10.

Oates, Joyce Carol, Review of *Just an Ordinary Day*, in *New York Times Book Review*, December 29, 1996.

Oppenheimer, Judy, "The Haunting of Shirley Jackson," in *New York Times Book Review*, July 3, 1988.

Oppenheimer, Judy, *Private Demons: The Life of Shirley Jackson*, G. P. Putnam's Sons, 1988.

"Shirley Jackson, Author of Horror Classic, Dies," in *New York Times*, August 10, 1965, p. 29.

FURTHER READING

Bernays, Anne Kaplan, and Justin Kaplan, *Back Then: Two Literary Lives in 1950s New York*, Harper Perennial, 2003.

This memoir recounts in two distinct threads how Bernays and Kaplan each came of age in New York City during the 1950s and went on to pursue literary careers.

Ferrer, Margaret Lundrigan, and Tova Navarra, *Levittown: The First 50 Years*, Arcadia Publishing, 1997.

This book is a photographic record of Levittown, New York, the suburban model town built between 1947 and 1951. Communities like Levittown were thought to be a better place to raise a family than in a big city.

Jackson, Shirley, *"The Lottery" and Other Stories*, Farrar, Straus, 1968.

This is Jackson's first published collection of short stories and provides a good introduction to her unique and powerful style.

Oppenheimer, Judy, *Private Demons: The Life of Shirley Jackson*, G. P. Putnam's Sons, 1988.

This exhaustive biography about Jackson is considered one of the most thorough studies of her life. It includes black and white photographs.

The Prisoner Who Wore Glasses

BESSIE HEAD

1973

Although "The Prisoner Who Wore Glasses" is the author Bessie Head's most widely anthologized short story, it is unusual in her overall body of work. Head is best known as the author of novels, most of them set in Botswana and featuring female protagonists, but this short story set in South Africa has no important female characters. The story is about Brille, a black political prisoner in South Africa under apartheid, and Hannetjie, the white man who is assigned as the prison section's new warder. The political prisoners assigned to Span One have become accustomed to stealing and eating cabbages and other food from the prison farm, smoking contraband tobacco, and whispering in secret conversations. When Hannetjie is transferred to Span One, however, he uncovers and shuts down all of these activities. Through the course of the action, Brille, who appears small and inconsequential, engages in a psychological battle with the physically powerful guard, eventually persuading him to behave less harshly toward the prisoners.

"The Prisoner Who Wore Glasses" was first published in 1973 in *London* magazine; after the author's death, it was published in book form as part of the 1989 collection *Tales of Tenderness and Power*. Head's collection is no longer in print, but the story may be found in the anthology *Under African Skies: Modern African Stories* (1997), edited by Charles Larson.

Bessie Head (Reproduced by the kind permission of the Estate of Bessie Head)

AUTHOR BIOGRAPHY

Bessie Amelia Emery was born July 6, 1937, in a mental institution in Pietermaritzburg, South Africa. Her mother, a white woman also named Bessie Amelia Emery, had been institutionalized by her family when they discovered she was pregnant but not by her husband; they did not know until the birth that the child's father—never identified—was black. The child was placed in foster care with the Heathcotes, a mixed-race family, and her mother died in the institution in 1943. Although they helped pay for her education, her mother's family did not contact Bessie after her mother died, and Bessie was raised to believe that Mrs. Heathcote was her real mother. Bessie's foster family was barely able to feed itself, and at twelve Bessie was transferred to St. Monica's Anglican mission school for coloured girls, where she became a voracious reader. Two years later, she learned that the Heathcotes were not her birth family—that she was alone in the world.

Bessie trained to become a teacher, and when she was twenty, she moved to Durban to teach at an elementary school for coloured children. Away from the sheltered environment of school, she encountered for the first time the indignities of South Africa's state-sponsored system of racial segregation called apartheid. After a year, she moved to Cape Town and became the only woman journalist for a weekly newspaper with a black readership. She enjoyed the work but did not earn much money from it, and her poverty and always-fragile mental condition made life difficult. Moving to Johannesburg in 1959, she became involved in anti-apartheid politics. In 1960, she married fellow journalist Harold Head and changed her name to Bessie Head; two years later her son Howard was born. The marriage was stormy and did not last long, in part because of Bessie Head's deteriorating mental health. Unable to support herself as a writer and disgusted with apartheid, politics, and religion, Head moved in March 1964 to the village of Serowe, in what would become Botswana. Because she was granted an exit permit, not a passport, she was never able to return to South Africa.

Head worked as a teacher and a typist while trying to sell her short stories and essays. In 1966, she was asked by the New York publisher Simon and Schuster to write a novel about the newly independent Botswana; the result was her first and best-known novel, *When Rain Clouds Gather* (1969). She spent periods in a mental institution over the next five years, but she also managed to publish two more novels, a collection of short stories, and an oral history of Serowe. In 1973, Head published "The Prisoner Who Wore Glasses" in *London* magazine. By the 1980s, she was a Botswana citizen and a world-renowned author, traveling throughout Africa, Europe, and the United States as a writer and lecturer. But she began to have difficulty completing projects and to drink heavily. She died of hepatitis on April 17, 1986, at the age of forty-eight. Four of her books were published after her death.

PLOT SUMMARY

As "The Prisoner Who Wore Glasses" opens, the narrator describes rows of cabbages, white clouds, and a blue sky on a still day. Not until the third sentence does the reader learn that this is not an idyllic farm but a prison; the cabbages are grown by prisoners who work long days and are not allowed to eat what they grow. One of the prisoners is a thin man with glasses—the title character, whose real name is never given. He is called "Brille" by the others, because in Afrikaans, a language spoken in the western part of South Africa, that is the word for someone who wears glasses. Brille is standing up to look at the clouds passing overhead, and imagining that they might carry a message to his children, when he is reprimanded by the new prison warder, Jacobus Stephanus Hannetjie.

Hannetjie, the prisoners understand, is going to treat them more harshly than the warders they have had in the past. These prisoners are part of a unit known as Span One, a group of ten black political prisoners imprisoned for their resistance to South Africa's legal segregation system known as apartheid. Because they are imprisoned together and kept apart from the more ordinary criminals, and because they always have a white warder guarding them, the prisoners of Span One have managed over the years to outsmart and manipulate their warders. Because they believe they have committed no crimes, they feel no guilt, but feel instead that they are entitled to whatever they can manage to obtain. For years, they have lied, cheated, stolen cabbages, smoked forbidden tobacco, and covered up for each other while they quietly disobeyed the prison's rules. Clearly, life with Hannetjie will be different.

One day, Brille is caught with a stolen cabbage that he has been eating. Although Hannetjie knows that Brille is the thief, he punishes the entire group by ordering that they will go without the next three meals. He orders Brille to call him "Baas," but Brille refuses, and Hannetjie beats him with a knobkerrie, an African club with a large knob on one end. Brille promises the others he will steal something for them to eat. Thinking about his injuries that night, Brille thinks back to his former life as a schoolteacher with a wife and twelve children. His children, he remembers, were a violent lot, always fighting among themselves. It was their violence as much as anything, he remembers, that led him to become involved with the resistance movement—a well-organized movement that frequently called him away from his chaotic home—and the work that led to his arrest.

The day after his beating, Brille is caught by Hannetjie stealing grapes from a shed, and Brille is given a week in isolation. Hannetjie, it appears, is more observant than previous warders have been, and the men are no longer able to obtain stolen cabbages or tobacco, or to have private conversations. But after two weeks of this suffering, Brille appears with a packet of tobacco and tells his fellow prisoners an amazing story: he has gotten the tobacco from Hannetjie himself. The warder was caught by Brille stealing bags of fertilizer for use on his own farm, and Brille accepted the tobacco as a bribe for his silence. However, although he has promised to keep quiet, Brille reports Hannetjie's theft to the authorities, and the warder is publicly reprimanded and fined. From that day on, Brille has the upper hand, and the prisoners resume their former habits.

For a while, Hannetjie tests the new relationship. He orders Brille to pick up his jacket and carry it for him, but Brille refuses. He orders the prisoner to call him "Baas," but Brille refuses, declaring that one day the blacks will rule South Africa and the whites will be the servants. Ultimately, Brille tells a commander that the tobacco he is smoking came from Hannetjie, and the warder is again reprimanded by his superiors. Finally, Hannetjie asks Brille what he can do to stop the psychological abuse. "We want you on our side," Brille says. Accepting his fate, Hannetjie makes life easier for the prisoners, helping them with their physical labor and bringing them better food and cigarettes. For their part, Span One becomes the hardest-working span in the entire prison, and the prisoners help Hannetjie steal fertilizer and other goods for his own farm.

CHARACTERS

Brille

"Brille" is the nickname given to the story's protagonist by his fellow prisoners; his real name is never stated. Brille is a black political prisoner being held in South Africa because of his activities in resistance to apartheid. He is a small man, described as "a thin little fellow with a hollowed-out chest and comic knobbly knees." He is also "short-sighted," or what would be called "near-sighted" in the United States, and his nickname comes from the Afrikaans-language word for a person who wears glasses. He seems to be the informal leader of the group of political prisoners in his work unit, called Span One, in part because he is older than the rest of them.

When the new prison warder, Hannetjie, comes to the prison, it is Brille who first challenges his authority. Pausing one day in his work on the prison cabbage farm, he gazes at the passing clouds and thinks about his children back home;

when Hannetjie reprimands him for being idle, he meets the warder's eyes and instantly judges him to be "not human." He and his fellow prisoners have engaged in psychological battles with their previous guards, but Brille can tell that this one will be more difficult to handle. Still, his initial acts of rebellion are innocent enough: he looks at the clouds for a moment, and he steals a cabbage to eat—a crime to which he confesses as soon as Hannetjie discovers the half-eaten head. When the warder decides to punish the entire group for Brille's theft, Brille refuses to exhibit the deference he is expected to show. Instead, he protests directly and calmly, confusing and infuriating Hannetjie, who hits Brille in the head with his club. Even the physical injuries do not make Brille humble and subjective, Hannetjie finds. From that point on, the two men are determined to overpower each other psychologically.

Although he is a prisoner, Brille is remarkably dignified and detached. He will not call the warder "Baas," as he is expected to, because he is older than the warder; he rejects outright the notion that his position in the prison is a reason to show respect for the other man. Brille's passivity, it turns out, has more to do with his former home life than his political and social situation as an oppressed black South African living under apartheid. For sixteen years, he lived with his wife in a small house in the Eastern Cape region, and their family grew to include twelve children whom he tried to support on a teacher's wages. Home life was very chaotic; the children were uncontrollable and violent. Brille became active in politics in large part because he was looking for reasons to be away from home. Now, after years in prison, he has a structured life that he has made more endurable by lying and stealing and by forcing or persuading the warders to overlook his and the other political prisoners' transgressions. Brille waits for his chance, and when he catches Hannetjie stealing fertilizer for his own farm, he knows he can cow this warder as he has all the others. With care and patience he toys with Hannetjie as a cat with a mouse, reporting him for small offenses, refusing to call him "Baas," and encouraging Hannetjie to trust him, only to betray him again.

When he has finally broken Hannetjie's spirit, he reveals all that he wants from the warder: "We want you on our side." Brille knows that no matter what else he might accomplish, he will not gain his freedom. He is not greedy or ambitious, and in the end he does know his place; he is only trying to make what will surely be a long imprisonment a little easier.

Jacobus Stephanus Hannetjie

Hannetjie is the new warder, or prison guard, for Span One, a group of ten black political prisoners in a large prison complex that also holds ordinary criminals. His name identifies him as an Afrikaner, one of the white Afrikaans-speaking people of South Africa whose ancestors were Dutch or German. He has eyes "the colour of the sky," and from their first encounter Brille can see that he has a "simple, primitive, brutal soul." Hannetjie is smarter and more observant than the previous warders for Span One. It takes him only days to discover how the prisoners are stealing cabbages and hiding tobacco, and he manages to stop their secret conversations and plotting. He demands the respect that goes along with his authority over the prisoners, insisting they call him "Baas" while freely calling Brille a "kaffir," an offensive term used against black people in South Africa. But demanding respect is not the same thing as receiving it, and Brille, who is twenty years older than Hannetjie, refuses to submit.

Hannetjie does what he can to force Brille and the other prisoners to obey him. He capriciously punishes the entire group for Brille's minor theft of a cabbage; he strikes Brille on the head with a club, becoming the first warder of Span One to hit a prisoner; he sends Brille to a week of solitary confinement for stealing grapes. But when Brille catches him stealing fertilizer for his own farm and then reports him to the authorities, Hannetjie's confidence is shaken. He bribes Brille with tobacco, but Brille tells the authorities who has given him the forbidden treat. For all his bluster, the warder is not as strong willed as the older prisoner, and gradually Brille breaks down his nerve. Hannetjie asks for a truce, and Brille agrees to stop tormenting him if he will leave the men alone. Hannetjie begins to treat the men more humanely, occasionally helping them with their farm work and smuggling extra food to them. In return, the men work especially hard, and they help Hannetjie steal supplies for his farm.

Martha

Martha is Brille's wife. Before her husband was imprisoned, she gave birth to twelve children in sixteen years, and she was continually overwhelmed by her responsibilities as a mother. Eventually, she gave up disciplining the children entirely, and they became rowdy and violent, ceasing their chaotic behavior only when Brille would come home from work.

THEMES

Apartheid

"The Prisoner Who Wore Glasses" is set in South Africa during the years of apartheid, the state-sponsored system of laws that officially divided all residents into four racial classifications and reserved power and wealth for the white minority. The ten black men in Span One are all political prisoners, arrested for being part of the internal resistance that organized violent and nonviolent protests and demonstrations against apartheid. The narrator observes that these prisoners "felt no guilt nor were they outcasts of society," because they have not been charged with crimes like robbery or murder; instead, they seem to feel that their imprisonment is part of a noble journey as well as a marker of an obviously unjust judicial system, so they are bolder and less shamed than most prisoners. Under apartheid, members of the black and "coloured" racial groups could obtain certain low- or middle-level jobs, and so there are black warders in the prison. However, the whites in charge worry that a black warder of Span One might be persuaded by the prisoners to join their revolution, so only whites like Jacobus Stephanus Hannetjie are allowed to guard Span One.

Naturally, in any prison, the guards have power over the prisoners. In this instance, however, the warder's power is enhanced simply by his being white and the prisoners' being black. Hannetjie expects the prisoners to call him "Baas," a word used mainly by nonwhite South Africans to speak of whites who have authority, and he confidently uses the racist term "kaffir," knowing that he cannot be challenged. Under apartheid, a younger white man would expect deference from an older black man, whether in a prison or not. In "The Prisoner Who Wore Glasses," apartheid is the driving force behind everything: it is the reason for the balance of power between Brille and Hannetjie, and the reason the warder, afraid to be seen as aiding or sympathizing with the black men under his control, is willing to make a secret deal with them. It is the reason the previous warders had no experience dealing with "assertive black men." And it is the reason a schoolteacher has become a prisoner, and the reason he has further become a liar and a thief.

Cooperation

The broad arc of the plot of "The Prisoner Who Wore Glasses" is a movement from conflict to cooperation. Although it is set in a divided society, everything good that happens in the story is the result of cooperation. The prisoners of Span One have become masters of "group concealment," and the narrator reports that they "moved, thought and acted as one." By banding together instead of competing for scarce resources like cabbages and tobacco, they have made the imprisonment endurable. This is why they do not resent Brille when his theft of a cabbage leads to them all being punished—why they say, "What happens to one of us, happens to all."

Brille wishes he could be home to teach his unruly children the lessons he has learned; he wishes he could tell them, "Be good comrades, my children. Co-operate, then life will run smoothly." Instead, he teaches the lesson to Hannetjie the warder. At first, he and Hannetjie are at odds, each punishing and betraying the other. Brille punishes and betrays Hannetjie intentionally and with purpose, but the warder behaves out of instinctive brutality: he simply does not know any other way to treat black prisoners. By the end of the story, however, he has learned the value of cooperation. Brille stops tormenting him, and the prisoners work hard on the prison farm while stealing supplies for the warder's private farm; Hannetjie sometimes helps with the labor and provides "unheard of luxuries like boiled eggs" for the men. Through cooperation, it is possible that both warder and prisoners will "be able to manage the long stretch ahead."

Psychology

In the world of "The Prisoner Who Wore Glasses"—a prison under apartheid—the threat of brute force is always just under the surface. A theme explored in the story, however, is the power of psychological strength and its ability to determine a person's fate even if he is not physically strong. Brille, the glasses-wearing prisoner, is unusually small, he is nearsighted, and he is older than the others. After years in prison, he is still capable of tender thoughts about his children. Yet, he overpowers Hannetjie, the younger white warder who carries a club, by using psychology. Hannetjie is not the first warder to be treated this way; the narrator reports that previous warders have lasted only a week or less with Span One, and that "the battle was entirely psychological."

Hannetjie tries physical violence first, hitting Brille on the head with his knobkerrie, or club—something no previous warder has ever done. Brille does not respond to the beating, but later, when Hannetjie simply removes privileges and contraband (a psychological rather than a physical punishment), the men live in "acute misery."

TOPICS FOR FURTHER STUDY

- Visit the Web site of the Robben Island Museum at www.robben-island.org.za and examine how the site treats the island's history as a maximum security prison for political prisoners. Based on what you find, particularly in the "virtual tour," "exhibitions," and "history" sections, write a paper in which you analyze the site's treatment of political prisoners. Does the site devote enough attention to this dark part of the island's history? How do the descriptions of the individual prisoners and their activities demonstrate new beliefs or attitudes about the anti-apartheid movement?
- A common story in American movies is about the group of prisoners who outsmart their captors. Examples include *Chicken Run* (2000), *The Shawshank Redemption* (1994), *Escape from Alcatraz* (1979), *Cool Hand Luke* (1967), and *The Great Escape* (1963). Watch one of these movies and write a paper in which you compare the conflict between prisoners and guards in the film with the conflict in "The Prisoner Who Wore Glasses."
- Research the history of the Afrikaner people in South Africa. Prepare a PowerPoint presentation for your class, explaining why Afrikaners in the twentieth century might have felt entitled to the land they occupied.
- Research the history of the Hawaiian Islands and how they became part of the United States. You may wish to watch the History Channel documentary *Conquest of Hawaii* (2003) for an overview of the story. Write a dialogue between a black South African and a native Hawaiian in which they tell each other what happened to their people's homeland and share information about possible next steps.
- Read Maya Angelou's poem "Caged Bird," Pablo Armando Fernandez's "To a Young Freedom Fighter in Prison," or another poem your instructor may suggest. Write a poem in the voice of Brille, a political prisoner, or of Hannetjie, a prison warder, reflecting on imprisonment and freedom.
- Read the young-adult novel *Monster* (1999), by Walter Dean Myers, about a sixteen-year-old boy in prison for a murder he says he did not commit. The novel is written as though it were the boy's journal, as well as notes he is making for a screenplay he is writing about his own life. Retell the story of "The Prisoner Who Wore Glasses" from Brille's point of view, writing in the form of Brille's journal entries.

Now the battle is on. Brille refuses to follow orders or to show respect, and he betrays Hannetjie's trust; gradually, he gets to the point where the warder's "nerve broke completely." Without being able to use physical force, Brille has driven the warder to the brink of suicide, to "desperation," through the power of psychology.

STYLE

Antihero

Many stories from cultures the world over feature a hero, typically a large, handsome, physically strong man who defeats his enemies and gains wealth and glory through a combination of physical combat, virtue, and shrewdness. In "The Prisoner Who Wore Glasses," on the other hand, the protagonist, Brille, might be better labeled an "antihero." In literature, the antihero demonstrates qualities opposite of those expected of the hero. Brille, for example, is not large and powerful but rather a small, thin, older man with glasses. He is not particularly virtuous; rather, he is one of the best liars and thieves in the prison who begins his defeat of Hannetjie by breaking a promise. He is not seeking wealth, or even his freedom; he knows he is going to be in

A symbolic representation of apartheid *(Image copyright Kevin Renes, 2009. Used under license from Shutterstock.com)*

prison for a long time, and he only wants the time to be endurable. The only quality he shares with the traditional hero is his shrewdness; he sees that the way to defeat his enemy is with psychology, and he patiently waits for the best moments to torment the warder.

Conflict

Conflict, or the setting of two people or groups or forces in opposition to each other, is at the heart of "The Prisoner Who Wore Glasses." The plot focuses on the conflict between the prisoner Brille and the warder Hannetjie, each struggling to overcome the other in a psychological battle. Hannetjie, of course, has more than psychology among his weapons: as a prison warder, he is also free to use physical violence against Brille. In the prison, all of the warders are in conflict with all of the prisoners, but the prisoners are united, they are "comrades," they "moved, thought and acted as one." The prison authorities are not united in this way, and Brille is able to gain an advantage over Hannetjie by exploiting the fact that the warders are hierarchical rather than equals.

The setting of the story is South Africa under apartheid. On a national level, the country is also defined largely by its internal conflict between the whites who hold most of the power and wealth, and the other racial groups (black, Indian, coloured) seeking self-determination. It is the broader conflict established by apartheid that is the reason Brille and the others are in prison, and the reason Span One never has a black warder. Thus, the conflict between Brille and Hannetjie is brought about by the larger racial and political conflict and can be seen as a tiny, hopeful reenactment of how the larger conflict might play out.

Flashback

About halfway through the story, after Brille has been beaten by Hannetjie, the narrator presents a flashback; that is to say, the narrator disrupts the orderly chronology to tell about events that occurred before the story began. In his cell, thinking about his head wounds, Brille thinks about his home, the sixteen years he spent with his wife, Martha, and their growing family in a small house in the Eastern Cape region of South Africa. His memories are focused on his children and how

COMPARE & CONTRAST

- **1973:** Thousands of black political prisoners are held in South Africa because of their activities in opposition to apartheid.

  Today: The anti-apartheid political prisoners have been out of prison for well over a decade, and the most infamous prison, on Robben Island, is now a museum dedicated to preserving the history of apartheid.

- **1973:** Afrikaners control the nation of South Africa through the Afrikaner National Party and through the president, Afrikaner Jacobus Johannes Fouché.

  Today: Many Afrikaners, along with English-speaking whites, have joined the liberal Democratic Alliance, the official opposition party to the African National Congress (ANC). The Democratic Alliance broadly calls for equal opportunity for all.

- **1973:** Large families are common in South Africa. According to a government report by Tom A. Moultrie and Ian M. Timaeus, the average fertility rate in the early 1970s is 5.5 children per woman.

  Today: The fertility rate in South Africa has declined dramatically. The 2009 fertility rate is estimated by the U.S. Central Intelligence Agency to be 2.4 children per woman.

chaotic and violent his home life was. It was his wish to escape the chaos, more than any strong desire for justice, which drove him to join the anti-apartheid struggle, with its meetings and conferences far away from home. The story never again refers to Brille's family, and Brille does not seem to change in any way after this memory, this flashback. Placed in the center of the story, this flashback serves the characterization, not the plot, and gives the reader a clearer sense of Brille as an ordinary man.

HISTORICAL CONTEXT

When Head published "The Prisoner Who Wore Glasses" in 1973, South Africa was about halfway through the era of apartheid, which lasted from 1948 to 1994. Although Head herself was living in Botswana when she wrote this story, many of her friends and acquaintances were, like the men of Span One, in prison as a result of their political activities in opposition to apartheid, the state-sponsored series of segregation laws that kept the white minority of the country in power. Activists were imprisoned for various actions against apartheid: for refusing to carry their pass books, the government identity cards that indicated the bearer's race; for joining the African National Congress (ANC), the Pan Africanist Congress, or other anti-apartheid groups; for participating in peaceful demonstrations and boycotts; or for committing violent acts, including sabotage of government facilities. Head herself spent a short time in jail in 1960, part of a large group of resisters who refused to carry their passes. The poet Dennis Brutus, an activist friend of Head's, had served eighteen months in the dreaded Robben Island prison beginning in 1963, and Nelson Mandela, leader of the armed wing of the ANC, was in 1973 only nine years into what would be twenty-seven years as a political prisoner.

The era of apartheid began officially in 1948, when the conservative Afrikaner National Party won power in a national election. Afrikaners were people like Jacobus Stephanus Hannetjie, white South Africans whose ancestors arrived from Germany and the Netherlands in the seventeenth century. Although whites in South Africa made up only about 10 percent of the population by the twentieth century, they controlled most of the wealth, owned most of the factories and large businesses, and controlled the military. Still, they feared that they would

Cape Town, South Africa, a source of Head's inspiration (Image copyright Sculpies, 2009. Used under license from Shutterstock.com)

gradually lose their control, so the government began creating laws to protect their power. Residents of South Africa were now assigned to one of four racial groups—white, black, Asian or Indian, and coloured—and were required to carry pass books that identified their assigned racial group. Mixed-race people like Head were given the label "coloured." Although the races in South Africa tended to live separately already, interracial marriage was officially outlawed in1949, and libraries and universities were closed to blacks a decade later. Blacks and "coloureds" were not allowed to vote, and they were restricted to living, shopping, and even swimming in areas set aside for them. In 1970, blacks were officially declared to no longer be South African citizens.

Resistance to apartheid was steady, and sometimes violent. As early as 1912, the ANC was formed to counter oppression of blacks. In 1949, the group, led by Mandela, organized strikes, boycotts, and other acts of civil disobedience. It was after sixty-nine people were shot by police during a protest in the town of Sharpeville in March 1960 that Head briefly joined active political resistance. But she had little faith in political solutions, and even less faith that a male-centered movement would produce benefits for women. Joyce Johnson, author of *Bessie Head: The Road of Peace of Mind*, believes that Head's lack of faith in political activism, and her desire to create literature with a viewpoint in opposition to the movement's, led her to leave South Africa for a place where she would feel freer to write what she wished. When Head finally decided to leave South Africa in 1964, she was denied a passport because of her past involvement with the resistance. Instead, she was given only an exit permit, which allowed her to leave, but made it impossible for her to ever return. Head, who died in 1986, did not live to see the end of apartheid, which came in 1994. She did not live to see Mandela released from prison in 1990 or elected president in 1994.

CRITICAL OVERVIEW

Although "The Prisoner Who Wore Glasses" is Head's most frequently anthologized story, there is little critical analysis of it. There are several reasons for this: Head was chiefly known as a novelist during her lifetime, and most criticism of her work has focused on the novels; she is thought of primarily as a writer about Botswana, and her work set in South Africa was little known until after her death; she is recognized as an important feminist figure, and much attention has been drawn to her works exploring the roles of women. Those who have written about the story, however, have found it to be important and powerful. Charles Larson, reviewing *Tales of Tenderness and Power* in the February 17, 1991, issue of the *Washington Post Book World*, observes that "The Prisoner Who Wore Glasses" is a rare example of Head treating apartheid directly, and comments that "no other story that Head wrote equals the vision of unity depicted" in the story. Gillian Stead Eilersen, in her biography *Bessie Head: Thunder Behind Her Ears*, reports that the story is based on the experiences of a former political prisoner Head met in Botswana, and finds in the story "an unusual blend of traditional story-telling techniques and sharp social commentary." And Craig MacKenzie, author of the 1999 Twayne's "World Author" series volume on *Bessie Head*, describes the story as "a tale about resilience, compassion, humanity, and brotherly feeling."

In 1981, the South African critic Lewis Nkosi famously observed in *Tasks and Masks: Themes and Styles of African Literature* that Head's fiction was concerned with morality, but not with politics. Critics since then have argued with Nkosi, either overtly or indirectly. Virginia Uzoma Ola, in her 1994 *The Life and Works of Bessie Head*, agrees with Nkosi, but finds Head's stance a strength. She comments that her characters' "totality as human beings transcends politics, and is fully realised in spite of it." Annie Gagiano, in *Achebe, Head, Marechera: On Power and Change in Africa* (2000), notes that "Head's particular origins . . . brought political and social structures heavily to bear on her," and that in her writing "Politics and personal experience intertwined and mirrored each other." In a 2009 analysis of Head's most political novel, *A Question of Power*, in *Twelve Best Books by African Women: Critical Readings*, Chikwenye Okonjo Ogunyemi calls Head's life "a political statement, interrogating the arrogant power displayed in the scramble for Africa."

CRITICISM

Cynthia A. Bily

Bily is a freelance writer and editor, and an instructor of writing. In this essay, she considers Head's attitudes toward political solutions to evil in the world in "The Prisoner Who Wore Glasses."

Set in a prison in South Africa during the time of apartheid, "The Prisoner Who Wore Glasses" presents many of the elements one might expect from a "typical" political story about oppression, or about prison. The prisoners are black, occupying the lowest rung on the racial and racist ladder established by the state-sponsored system of segregation and oppression. Hannetjie, their warder or prison guard, is a casually racist white man, an Afrikaner who addresses the black men with the racist term "kaffir" and demands that they call him "Baas." The prisoners, "assertive black men," are intelligent, patient, and unified; Brille, the protagonist, is even well-educated enough to have been a teacher. The warder, on the other hand, is said to have a "simple, primitive, brutal soul." The prisoners in Span One are all political prisoners, charged not with ordinary crimes but with actions against apartheid and the government that supports it. And near the end of the story, in a fit of anger, Brille tells Hannetjie, "One of these days we are going to run the country. You are going to clean my car."

It might be tempting to read this as a story about apartheid and the struggle to overthrow it. One can read the story as a small example of the battles waged across South Africa between 1948 and 1994, and Brille's psychological victory over Hannetjie and his warning that "one of these days we are going to run the country" as a beacon of hope, a promise of what the future holds. Certainly Head, the mixed-race or "coloured" author, who herself left South Africa to find more personal and artistic freedom, had all of this in mind as she created the story. Head biographer Gillian Stead Eilersen reports in *Bessie Head: Thunder Behind Her Ears* (1995) that Head got the idea for the story from a man she met in Francistown, one of the large cities in Botswana. Eilersen writes, "He had been a political prisoner in South Africa and he told the story of how he had humanised a brute of a white warder." The author "embroidered it slightly, adding 'certain tendernesses.'" Head lived under apartheid until she was twenty-seven; she knew activists and political prisoners, including her friend the poet Dennis Brutus, who was arrested as a political prisoner in 1963 and was

WHAT DO I READ NEXT?

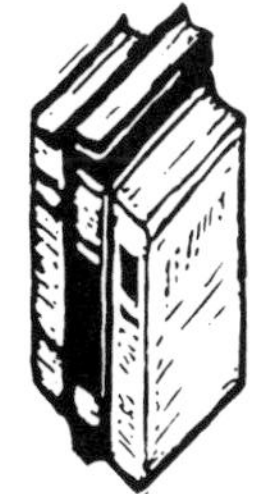

- Head's *When Rain Clouds Gather* (1969) is a novel about Makhaya, a young man who leaves oppression of his native South Africa to find a new home in a poverty-stricken village in Botswana before independence from Great Britain. There he helps the villagers adapt to modern life, while he learns to overcome the burden of the hatred he carries within.
- *Hungry Flames and other Black South African Short Stories* (1986), edited by Mbulelo Vizikhungo Mzamane, is a collection of fifteen stories exploring the lives of black South Africans under apartheid. In addition to "The Prisoner Who Wore Glasses," the collection includes works by well-known authors, including Peter Abrahams, Alex La Guma, and Njabulo Ndebele, as well as less famous writers.
- Nelson Mandela's *The Struggle Is My Life* (1986) is a collection of speeches and essays, as well as historical documents, that describe—and argue for the release of—political prisoners in South Africa. The book appeared four years before Mandela was released after serving twenty-seven years as a political prisoner, many of them in dreary isolation in a prison on Robben Island.
- Lyn Miller-Lachmann's award-winning young-adult novel *Gringolandia* (2009) is a historical novel set in the 1980s during the struggle to overthrow the brutal Chilean dictator Augusto Pinochet. The protagonist is Daniel, whose family has fled to Wisconsin after his father's arrest. After five years of torture as a political prisoner, Daniel's father rejoins the family and tries to reconnect with his son.
- *The Surrender Tree* (2008), by Margarita Engle, is a powerful collection of poems about Cuba's fight for independence from Spain between 1850 and 1899. It is written as a series of free-verse poems spoken by four characters: a nurse, her husband, an escapee from a prison camp, and a Spanish lieutenant.
- American Indian Movement activist Leonard Peltier is considered by his supporters to be a political prisoner held by the U.S. government. In *Prison Writings: My Life Is My Sundance* (1999), he describes his work in the movement, his actions on the day in 1973 when two FBI agents were killed, and his life behind bars since 1977, and he argues for fair and compassionate treatment for Native Americans.
- The title character of Herman Melville's classic short story "Bartleby, the Scrivener" (1853) engages in a psychological battle with his employer, a lawyer who has hired him to copy and proofread documents. Bartleby's reply to every request from his employer is, "I would prefer not to."
- In Brian Azzarrello's *Hellblazer: Hard Time* (2000), part of the graphic novel series featuring the magician John Constantine, the protagonist finds himself in a maximum-security prison, sentenced for murder. Here, he discovers that the skills that helped him survive on the streets are not the ones that will help him succeed in prison. The art is by Richard Corben and Tim Bradstreet.
- Most books about prisons and prisoners focus on male characters, but Anita Diamant's *Day after Night: A Novel* (2009) is the story of four young women held in the British-run Atlit internment camp in Palestine after World War II. Each has fled the Nazis under dramatic circumstances and entered Palestine illegally, surviving the Holocaust only to face new challenges.

"THE DISMISSIVE WAY IN WHICH THE NARRATOR SIMPLIFIES THE CALL FOR THE END OF RACIAL OPPRESSION AS 'JUST A FEW BASIC SLOGANS' IS BREATHTAKING."

still in the notorious Robben Island prison when Head left South Africa; and Eilersen reports that when the founder of the Pan Africanist Congress, newspaper editor Robert Sobukwe, was arrested and brought to trial in 1960, Head was there. Reading the story as a microcosm of apartheid, then, is certainly reasonable.

But Head takes steps to ensure that although apartheid is the setting of her story, it is not the focus. A peculiar thing happens midway through the story, after Hannetjie has become the first warder to strike a prisoner in Span One. Brille thinks about his head injuries and reflects that "it was the first time an act of violence had been perpetrated against him but he had long been a witness of extreme, almost unbelievable human brutality." Given the setting, given the author, given the time, the reader expects this line to be followed with a scene of racial violence, perhaps police brutality in breaking up a demonstration. But after leading her readers to this point, Head goes off in an unexpected direction: she shifts the focus away from politics entirely, to Brille's memories of his home and family, which he thinks of as "sixteen years of bedlam."

The details in the long paragraph that follows are small and domestic, and none of them have anything to do with race or apartheid. Before being arrested, Brille was a schoolteacher who constantly struggled to feed his family on a teacher's pay. He lived in "a small drab little three-bedroomed house in a small drab little street in the Eastern Cape" with his wife Martha and their twelve children. Brille and his wife had access to contraceptives, but never could use them successfully. The twelve children, home all day with an overwhelmed mother, became more and more unruly until it was not uncommon for them to "get hold of each other's heads and give them a good bashing against the wall." Martha gave up trying to discipline them, resorting instead to that familiar line spoken by 1950s situation-comedy mothers, "Wait 'til your father gets home." Brille, like overworked weary breadwinners everywhere, found after a time that he could not face the chaos at the end of a long day at work, and he looked for more and more reasons to stay away from home.

It would have been easy for Head to make Brille's memory less universal, to add details that would point to apartheid as the reason for his small salary, for the location of his home, for the violent attitudes absorbed by his children. And these details could easily have been used to explain Brille's turning to politics—a hard-working husband and father risking imprisonment to ensure that his children would live in a country free of oppression. But Head makes it clear that these are not the reasons for Brille's activism. He got involved in politics because it gives him a respectable reason to be away from his chaotic family. "At one stage," he remembers, "before things became very bad, there were conferences to attend, all very far away from home." He is not passionate about the cause or the theories behind it. Instead, he remembers that the anti-apartheid movement presented "an ordered beautiful world with just a few basic slogans to learn along with the rights of mankind."

The dismissive way in which the narrator simplifies the call for the end of racial oppression as "just a few basic slogans" is breathtaking. According to some critics, this dismissiveness reflects Head's own attitude toward politics through most of her life. South African essayist Lewis Nkosi, who, like Head, left South Africa in the 1960s, famously wrote in 1981, "Bessie Head is not a political novelist in any sense we can recognise; indeed, there is ample evidence that she is generally hostile to politics." For nearly thirty years, critics have argued with Nkosi about this remark, trying to pin down the extent and the nature of Head's political passions. Whatever their conclusions about her work overall, it is clear that the author of "The Prisoner Who Wore Glasses," by showing Brille's turn to politics in such an unflattering light, shifts the reader's gaze from the underlying social and political *reason* for Brille's imprisonment to the simple *fact* of it. Brille is not a heroic figure like Nelson Mandela, true believer and leader of a great cause, and he is not a murderer or robber like the prisoners in other sections of the prison. He is simply a small old man in prison, for a reason that scarcely matters.

At the end of his reverie, Brille realizes, "I'm only learning right now what it means to be a politician. All this while I've been running away from Martha and the kids." But what has he learned? What *does* it mean to be a politician? The line occurs nearly exactly at the center of the story, and it seems fraught with significance, but what really changes after Brille thinks it? In fact, not much changes on the surface. Brille and his comrades had been thieves and liars before, and they continue to be. They have won an "entirely psychological" battle with every warder in the past, and Brille defeats Hannetjie in the same kind of contest. Perhaps what Brille has learned about politics is this: It needs to be undertaken seriously, not simply as a way to get out of the house, and one's focus needs to be on results, not on slogans. And there might be danger. Apparently, the prisoners of Span One have won every psychological battle with the previous warders: "Up until the arrival of Warder Hannetjie, no warder had dared beat any member of Span One and no warder had lasted more than a week with them." Hannetjie begins the shift that is at the heart of the story by overturning the first half of that description—he beats Brille with a knobkerrie, or club, leading Brille to examine his past. But it is Brille, understanding now "what it means to be a politician," who changes the nature of the battle with Hannetjie. Rather than simply trying to win, to defeat and humiliate him, to send him away, Brille realizes that the best result he can obtain is to break Hannetjie only enough to win his cooperation.

While she is de-emphasizing apartheid as the focus of the conflict, Head finds small ways to underline the ways in which Brille and Hannetjie are alike. Both are observant and intelligent; Brille and his comrades are excellent at sneaking and stealing, but Hannetjie is the first warder they have had who uncovers their tricks. The narrator mentions Brille's glasses repeatedly—they are his most important physical characteristic—but when Hannetjie is introduced the only physical description is of his eyes, which "were the colour of the sky." To explain why Hannetjie is so good at uncovering their deceptions, the narrator uses the familiar metaphor that he had "eyes at the back of his head." And after Brille has been referred to several times as the "father of many children," Hannetjie, nearly at the breaking point, begs him, "This thing between you and me must end. You may not know it but I have a wife and children."

In the 1979 essay "Social and Political Pressures that Shape Literature in Southern Africa," Head commented on racialism in South Africa:

> Exploitation and evil is dependent on a lack of communication between the oppressor and the people he oppresses. It would horrify an oppressor to know that his victim has the same longings, feelings, and sensitivities as he has.

Of course, when she wrote that, she was thinking primarily about racial oppression in South Africa, of white people like Hannetjie imprisoning and brutalizing black men like Brille. But she was also concerned with the nature of evil and the nature of oppression, and in "The Prisoner Who Wore Glasses," Brille takes on in some ways the role of oppressor. And he responds exactly as Head predicted he might. As soon as Hannetjie mentions his wife and children and tries to bribe Brille with tobacco, Brille is "struck with pity, and guilt. He wondered if he had carried the whole business too far."

In the end, the prisoners and the warders reach an agreement that benefits everyone. The prisoners will have more luxuries and more help with their work, Hannetjie will have stolen goods for his farm, and everyone will be "able to manage the long stretch ahead." Head does not ignore apartheid in "The Prisoner Who Wore Glasses," but by refusing to make Brille an anti-apartheid hero and by emphasizing the commonalities between Brille and Hannetjie, she seems to be saying that political solutions cannot address underlying evil. Brille learns "what it means to be a politician" and he achieves a compromise with Hannetjie. But apartheid is not ended, racism still thrives, Martha is still stuck at home with twelve children and no breadwinner, and Brille is still in prison.

Source: Cynthia A. Bily, Critical Essay on "The Prisoner Who Wore Glasses," in *Short Stories for Students*, Gale, Cengage Learning, 2010.

Coreen Brown

In the following essay, Brown explains how Head created a new identity for South African woman writers.

...POLITICAL AND FEMINIST READINGS

Although critics are conscious of the danger of drawing too closely upon an author's life in order to interpret his or her work, it is nonetheless to the autobiographical *A Question of Power* that critics turn to establish the "political" impetus of Head's writing. Elizabeth is the absolute victim.

A female African dancer. Head has strong ties to her African community and culture. (Image copyright Anke van Wyk, 2009. Used under license from Shutterstock.com)

As Margaret Tucker observes, as "stranger, exile, bastard, and woman, she is the Other, the dispossessed" (1988, 170). So, critics have not failed to point out that the context of Head's/Elizabeth's experience is one ideally suited to provide a critique of postcolonialism and patriarchy—the voice of a black woman "talking back," or subverting a racially prescribed and gendered identity. Huma Ibrahim, in her book *Bessie Head: Subversive Identities in Exile,* begins her critique of Head's work by taking issue with "Western feminists" who see Head as their "icon—a Third World woman writer who is interested in women's issues" (1996, 3). Ibrahim herself wishes to "relocate that assumption" by reasserting the context of postcoloniality. She argues that:

> Each woman character in Head's narratives resists being dismissed or misused just "because she became" a woman or because there was no place for her in the phallogocentric economy. These women claim a space within the equivocal boundaries of neocolonialism. Resistance becomes part of the dialectics of women's identities in exile, which become subject places "negotiated as strategies." They not only claim a place for themselves in the postcolonial economy but they have to define themselves within that sphere. (1996, 10)

"THE POISE AND ASSURED EASE OF THESE SHORT PIECES SUGGESTS THAT THE WRITER ENJOYS HERE A LESS COMPULSIVE AND MORE DETACHED REGARD FOR THE DILEMMAS SHE IS RECOUNTING."

One of the challenges that arise when confronting this kind of argument is to try and decide how helpful it is towards an understanding of Head's writing. Other than Elizabeth, it is difficult to find evidence that exile places such a burden of identity on Head's characters. In *When Rain Clouds Gather,* Head creates females, who by virtue of their status as newcomers to the village, are more likely to accept innovations, which are also introduced from outside. Head emphasizes not only how these changes increase prosperity for the village, but how they are instrumental in making the village more of a community, and this is what is of paramount importance. Time and place are immaterial to the kind of utopia of Head's vision. That Head creates this utopia also allows her to define the terms by which men and women will begin to live together, terms that open the way towards increased equality between male and female, but are nonetheless dictated largely by the male. The consciousness that defines most of Head's female characters is one preoccupied by their overriding concern to find husbands and establish homes. In order to secure these goals, "resistance" is not offered because it is not needed, for Head also creates the "new" men to negotiate these improved relationships.

Elizabeth does offer resistance. Elizabeth in order to survive has to resist the "inferno" of her hallucinations in order to believe in the possibility that goodness exists. Doubtless "postcolonialism," "neocolonialism," and "phallogocentric economy" are all structures of the power apparatus included within the "question of power" that Elizabeth has to interrogate and resist. But the whole focus of

Head's examination in *A Question of Power* is that it goes beyond the particular conspiracies of social and historical nomenclatures to the universal soul of man. Head is searching for first causes, the first reason why one should want power over another; thus her solution is also universal. Elizabeth may be socially and temporally placed, but her quest and its solution are most certainly not. Thus, issues of identity caused by postcolonialism or exile are only marginal in Head's concerns.

The critic Arun Mukherjee, writing from a political milieu similar to Ibrahim's, voices her unease at the supposition that she, as a postcolonial subject, will write from only one perspective—one that maintains an antagonistic or parodic relationship with the metropolis. Mukherjee condemns Rushdie's claim that postcolonial writers do not write out of their needs but rather out of their "obsession with an absent other," because, she argues, this theorizing leaves the writer with "only one modality, one discursive position" (1990, 6). In order to widen the scope of a writer's choice Mukherjee suggests that critics "should stop making and accepting homogenizing theories that create a 'unitary' field out of such disparate realities" (7).

Mukherjee is expressing her concern with the way in which the application of "external" critical schemata may lead readers to ignore all that is not relevant to their theoretical claims. Such an approach, she feels, encourages a limited perspective; or, as Rooney suggests, the literature under scrutiny becomes "one whose own creative originality is critically appropriated" (1991, 101). Head herself always refused to be labeled and voiced her suspicions of those tempted to label her: "If people wish to place one into certain categories they do so for their own purposes" (Adler et al. 1989, 7).

The very complexity of *A Question of Power* has, however, made it susceptible to a variety of readings. Head, in retrospect, was able to accept that the "uncertainty" of this novel was "an open invitation to the reader to move in and re-write and reinterpret the novel in his/her own way," that it "is a book that is all things to all men and women" (Appendix 18). Some critics, for instance, see the condensed and complex imagery that describes Elizabeth's breakdown as a highly structured literary convention symbolizing paradigms of oppression operating in an "insane" society. Thus, Kirsten Holst Petersen claims that "madness is an obvious metaphor for the kind of social organisation prevailing in South Africa, and the most striking use of this metaphor is made by the coloured writer Bessie Head" (1991, 131). Hence, madness in this interpretation is not literal but literary, a reading that endorses the primacy of the political, and in so doing suppresses the significance of the personal.

A similar kind of prescriptive reading occurs when some feminist critiques are applied to the symbols and imagery of Elizabeth's breakdown. Within the narrative, Head presents Elizabeth as forcibly compelled to observe Medusa's display of explicit sexuality and Dan's parade of his sexual conquests. They convince Elizabeth of her own inadequacy; she experiences intense distress and total despair. However, in order to identify Elizabeth as a radical feminist, Ibrahim interprets Elizabeth's response to Medusa, and to Dan's use and abuse of his "nice-time" girls as one of defiance. She argues that Head's writing illustrates Hélène Cixous's contention that women "write through their bodies." Elizabeth feels "an exile's urgent need . . . to reclaim her body through language in order to seek her lost, primary fundamental 'home'" (1996, 130). But the text contradicts this reading. Elizabeth prefers to believe in the idea of romantic, ideal male/female relationships that prioritize spiritual union and thus deny the importance of sexuality. It is a resolution that has evolved from Head's own particular experience and her self-perception of her lack of physical attraction—"I am so ugly to look at that I don't think too much about these things" (Appendix 2). Elizabeth is, initially, far too vulnerable "to reclaim her body." She is tormented by the contrast implied between herself and the succession of women Dan parades before her eyes.

Although Head, especially in her short stories, offers a critique of the domination women often suffer, she never suggests that emancipation for women can be achieved by their remaining single, free, or otherwise liberated. In a personal letter she expresses the specific nature of her own anxiety: "There is a horror somewhere in my mind Jean, a long story about a long string of gentlemen who always belonged to someone else, so my subconscious produces all kinds of people in advance whom I don't know" (Appendix 2). For Head, "man/woman relationships are like some kind of turning point in our age and time" (Appendix 8). Thus, whereas feminist critics choose to parallel the oppressive colonial regime with the structures of power implicit within patriarchal institutions, and thus seek autonomy and empowerment for their female protagonists,

Head's portrayal is much more multilayered, negotiating as it does the political and gender implications of her social context with more urgent, personal preoccupations. Significantly, especially in Head's earlier work, these urgent personal preoccupations are resolved, for her heroines, by the creation of successful relationships with powerful male figures.

Head was always acutely aware that the urgency of political solutions for apartheid-torn South Africa did create a particular form of "protest" literature, a writing that dealt directly with committed revolutionary participation. Many critics noted the sheer inevitability of this development. The South African situation became what Ezekiel Mphahlele, in *Down Second Avenue,* defined as "a terrible cliché as literary material" (1959, 210). Writing thirty years later, critics were still claiming that it was impossible to write in Southern Africa in an unpolitical way. "Political" meant "marching shoulder to shoulder with others or breathing in and out the stink of prison cells" (Sepamla 1988, 190). For women, solidarity with the cause for liberation was also a priority. Feminist issues were not foregrounded, and although Ellen Kuzwayo contends that every black woman, particularly in Africa, has "an extra burden, as a black and as a woman" (James 1990, 55), these problems became peripheral in Third World writing, where matters relating to national politics, religion, and economics were prioritized over sexism, real or imagined.

Because it was expected that writing out of South Africa would closely reflect urgent social and political concerns, Head often felt compelled to defend her own literary position. She was conscious of the need for South African writing to be "functional" but recognized her own inability to "cope with the liberatory struggle—a world of hot, bickering hate, jealousy, betrayal and murder" (WDIW, 1). Head's interpretation of the struggle within South Africa totally negates the idealism of comradeship expressed by the poet Lindiwe Mabuza. His lines "We would love less / You and I / If we loved not freedom more" (1988, 197) expresses the idea of solidarity in the face of acute oppression that is a central theme of much South African writing. The poet addresses his reader as "comrade"; his desire for freedom intimates both a freedom from the oppression of the apartheid regime and a freedom to share with another the camaraderie of cultural identity. It is this shared cultural cohesion that Head lacks, her feeling of nonbelonging. She had remarked on the significance of the absence of any known relatives. She had not even "a sense of having inherited a temperament, a certain emotional instability or the shape of a fingernail from a grandmother or great-grandmother." As she always insisted, "I have always been just me, with no frame of reference to anything beyond myself" (*AWA,* 3).

Head's biographer Eilersen has commented that although this "aloneness" often distressed Head, it also gave her the freedom to create as an individual. As Head stated in a letter, "My writing is not on anybody's bandwagon. It is on the sidelines where I can more or less think things out with a clear head" (Appendix 12). It is this feeling that underlies her refusal to be labeled, her avowed antifeminism, her dislike of the title "African writer." As she said emphatically in a letter to Randolph Vigne:

> What is an African writer? Too bad. B. Head is just B. Head now. See how grim you can get? Fighting like mad for your own integrity however worthless this may be to others. (Vigne 1991, 19)

She continued to defend her right to be "international," to create her own "highly original" portrayal of the "African personality" in order to avoid the "dark dungeon called the 'proper' and recognisable African" (WDIW, 3). Nevertheless, her writing originated from an impulse to "answer some of the questions" aroused by her South African experience, and the "human suffering" of people—"black people, white people, loomed large" on her horizon (*AWA,* 67). It was clearly her solutions to these problems, the way her characters ignore political participation as irrelevant to their philosophy that made "the black student," according to Head, a "hostile audience" for her work (WDIW, 2). In *When Rain Clouds Gather,* Makhaya renounces all political affiliation and chooses to work towards creating his own idea of community. Head's creative output is properly seen as the aesthetic realization of Makhaya's dream. But for some, Makhaya is "a traitor to the African cause" (*WRCG,* 81), for his ideal community will not be a paean to African nationalism. Head stressed that her "sense of belonging" was "not to the country" but to "the human race" (*AWA,* 10). Because of Head's determination not to see new societies emerging from cohesive revolutionary action but rather from the intuitive desires of individual heroes, this choice of emphasis, for some of her audience, implied too close an identification with "western civilisation" (WDIW, 3).

This response echoes the trend in the past few decades to make a clear distinction between the socially orientated and committed art of the colonized world and the more personal, autonomous "art for art's sake" of the Western world. As an isolated individual the Western artist is cast as a representative of the current malaise in Western philosophy, that leads to the questioning of the existence of "absolutes" such as Reality, Truth, Self, or even Author. Authors and characters reflect an existential angst, such as the nihilism of Jean-Paul Sartre's Roquentin. Another kind of alienated Western artist is represented by James Joyce's Stephen Dedalus in *A Portrait of the Artist as a Young Man.* Exiled from his society, Dedalus encounters the "reality of experience" in order to "forge in the smithy of [his] soul the uncreated conscience of [his] race" (Joyce, 1916, 253). Both Sartre and Joyce move from the individual, the particular, to the general, their protagonists' specific form of alienation suggestive of a contemporary and "universal" preoccupation.

However, this "universalism" is, to some Third World critics, an unwelcome Western import, and Ibrahim comments that the "theme of 'univarsalism'" is an "aspect of [Head's] writing that has come under considerable attack" (1996, 19). Many Third World critics and writers view the idea of universalism with some misgivings, because they fear that it might eclipse "important social and cultural determinants" of their own national writing (Nasta 1991, xxvi). Other critics and writers view the term "universalist" with more suspicion, feeling that when this label is applied to their writing it is a form of Eurocentric appropriation. Onwuchekwa Jemie Chinweizu, one of the most extreme advocates of this view, argues that universalism is "a cloak for the hegemonic thrust of Anglo-Saxon cultural nationalism" (1983, 150). This critical perspective implies that there is a particular African experience that ought to be the priority of its writers, and indeed a particular experience that should be the priority of women writers. Thus Ibrahim, even after she has conceded Head's universalism, and accepts the implications of Elizabeth's "soul-searching" for "all individuals in all societies" (1996, 19) still finds it difficult to prioritize the breadth of Head's perspective, and interprets Elizabeth's healing as the securing of "her own salvation, as well as the salvation of all of womankind" (19). But Elizabeth has achieved more than this; she has "fallen into the warm embrace of the brotherhood of man" (*QP,* 206). Nothing could state more clearly than this the nature of Head's cause and the enduring passion of her protagonists.

Craig MacKenzie, in *Bessie Head: An Introduction,* points to the way in which Head's heroes and heroines have similar preoccupations and an identical goal shaped as they are by the desires of their creator:

> The central characters in the three novels, Makhaya, Margaret and Elizabeth, all share some aspects of the author herself and move sequentially closer to her own experience. This progression has a direct bearing on the shape each novel takes. (1989a, 19)

The writing that portrays the experience and concerns of her main protagonists in Head's earliest writing bears a greater affinity to what Northrop Frye defines as "literature of process," than to "literature of product" (1990, 66). It records a process of becoming rather than a product of being. There is, within each of the longer narratives, a discursive element that examines the developing thoughts, the desires and the evolution of the philosophy of her main characters. This discursive element is, as Frye explains, a literary convention in which "a state of identification" (67) occurs between the reader, the literary work, and the writer. During this process "the external relation between author and reader becomes more prominent, and when it does, the emotions of pity and terror are involved or contained rather than purged" (66). It is at this level that the reader engages sympathetically with the line of inquiry that the protagonist is following. The discourse, the fact and argument control the portrayal of the social situation out of which her protagonists emerge, their confrontation with the racism and oppressions with which they are familiar. It is this area of the narrative that portrays the author's own social context, her critique of society. The authorial voice is never absent. The resolution never depends on the historical or social contingencies of political change (and this makes her writing very different from other South African writing of the sixties), but on the creation of asocial and ahistorical utopias.

In many of Head's short stories she employs a different authorial stance, developing a clearer aesthetic distance. Christopher Heywood's comment that Head's novels "have the consistency and mathematical balance of ballads" (1976, xiv), applies more obviously to the style of her short stories. The poise and assured ease of these short pieces suggests that the writer enjoys here a less compulsive and more detached regard for the dilemmas she is recounting. After reading "Witchcraft" the reader does not feel that the author has personally been intimidated by the superstitions of her adopted country, even though they exist as a frightening reality for the character she is portraying. The irony and humor that Head employs to emphasize the inevitability of the human folly she describes in her short stories are not at her disposal when it comes to the portrayal of her own subjectivity in her earlier writing.

The discursive style of Head's longer pieces and the more aesthetic coherence and control of her short stories both describe the social, political, and temporal contexts within which her characters live. The reality she describes is often a grim world of experience. The antithesis to this, usually the province of the artists, dreamers, or unreal heroes of her longer narratives, is an imagined world defined by the writer's perception of what should be. Although some of the short stories, in their concentration on individual dilemmas, are more "real," thus denying the protagonists the expectation of romantic fulfillment, the role of the story teller is dramatized and universalized; it becomes her responsibility to find "gold amidst the ash" (*CT,* 91). This reflects Head's view of art, her role as a writer, to discover within the heroes she creates the power to dream of other realities. With the portrayal of Elizabeth and Maru, the idea of dreaming has an added significance, with which the author is also implicated. Head's resolution becomes an act of writing that no longer depends upon the discursive, the fact or the argument, and is, as Frye contends, an act of "creation, whether of God, man, or nature," that "seems to be an activity whose only intention is to abolish intention, to eliminate final dependence on or relation to something else, to destroy the shadow that falls between itself and its conception" (1990, 89). Frye's contention helps to explain the origin of Maru. . . .

Source: Coreen Brown, "The Literary Context of Head's Writing," in *The Creative Vision of Bessie Head,* Fairleigh Dickinson University Press, 2003, pp. 23–31.

Craig MacKenzie

In the following essay, MacKenzie notes the themes of resilience, compassion, humanity, and brotherly feeling within "The Prisoner Wore Glasses."

Two posthumous volumes of Head's uncollected writings have appeared. *Tales of Tenderness and Power* (1989) is a collection of short writings, some published, others previously unpublished but which, editor Gillian Eilersen notes, Head was in the process of assembling into a volume. A useful introduction precedes this miscellany of short pieces, giving a brief outline of Head's short and unhappy life. The pieces themselves defy neat categorization: some closely approximate the received notion of "fiction"; others are manifestly autobiographical. All of them, Eilersen claims, are closely rooted in actual events. This is not surprising, since Head's imagination was sparked by incidents she encountered in Botswanan village life and by stories other villagers told her.

The Serowe village milieu provides the backdrop for some of the pieces in *Tales of Tenderness,* although others originate from South Africa of the 1950s and 1960s. Two stories stand out, because of both their intrinsic merit and their South African setting: "The Prisoner Who Wore Glasses," which first appeared in 1973 and was subsequently reprinted in a dozen later anthologies, and "The Coming of the Christ-Child" (1981).

"The Prisoner Who Wore Glasses" is a tale about resilience, compassion, humanity, and brotherly feeling. A group of long-term political prisoners headed by their thin, myopic leader, called, appropriately, "Brille" ("Glasses"), comes into conflict with their new Afrikaans warder, Hannetjie. The group, called Span One, are no ordinary prisoners: "As political prisoners they were unlike the other prisoners in the sense that they felt no guilt nor were they outcasts of society. All guilty men instinctively cower, which was why it was the kind of prison where men got knocked out cold with a blow at the back of the head from an iron bar. Up until the arrival of Warder Hannetjie, no warder had dared beat any member of Span One and no warder had lasted more than a week with them. The battle was entirely psychological."

Hannetjie is determined to subdue Span One. He catches Brille stealing grapes from the farm shed and has him confined to isolation for a week. He also discovers how Span One manage to conceal and eat half of the cabbages they are required to dig up on the prison farm, and they are punished. Then there is a dramatic turn of fortune: Warder Hannetjie is discovered by Brille in the act of stealing fertilizer and bribes him to keep quiet. Brille decides nonetheless to expose Hannetjie, and the warder is fined heavily. The psychological war continues until Hannetjie breaks down and pleads: "Brille . . . [t]his thing between you and me must end. You may not know it but I have a wife and children and you're driving me to suicide." They enter into a pact: the prisoners are treated more humanely, and in return they steal certain commodities that Hannetjie needs for his farm. The message that Brille conveys to his children becomes the theme of the story: "'Be good comrades, my children. Co-operate, then life will run smoothly.'"

"The Coming of the Christ-Child" is a tribute to Robert Sobukwe—leader of the Pan Africanist Congress when it broke away from the African National Congress in the 1950s. It is a fictionalized account of the passive resistance campaigns of the 1950s and 1960s, the rise of the ANC and the PAC, and their movement toward militancy. At the center of all this activity Head describes the life of a man who is born into a long line of mission-educated men whose family tradition is to become priests. The latest in this long tradition rejects this course: he is driven from a nonviolent stance to espouse increasingly militant ideas. He is ultimately detained in the general suppression of opposition movements in the 1960s, after becoming a highly vocal opponent of the National Party regime. He is sentenced to life imprisonment, then released after nine years but served with several banning orders.

The story ends on a premonitory note: nonviolent opposition to the state is no longer possible, and the freedom struggle is now going to be conducted along military lines:

> The crack-down on all political opposition was so severe that hundreds quailed and fled before the monstrous machine. It was the end of the long legend of non-violent protest. But a miracle people had not expected was that from 1957 onwards the white man was being systematically expelled from Africa, as a political force, as a governing power. Only the southern lands lay in bondage. Since people had been silenced on such a massive scale, the course and direction of events was no longer theirs. It had slipped from their grasp some time ago into the hands of the men who were training for revolution.

The concluding sentence of the story is more characteristic of Head. It illustrates her sense that the writer's role "is to make life magical and to communicate a sense of wonder" (*Woman Alone*, 67): "When all was said and done and revolutions had been fought and won perhaps only dreamers longed for a voice like that of the man who was as beautiful as the coming of the Christ-Child" ("Christ-Child," 140).

These two stories provide a rare insight into the kind of writer Bessie Head might have been had she remained as preoccupied with South African themes and issues as were most of her contemporaries. Significantly, however, many of the other pieces in *Tales of Tenderness* caution against the corrupting influence of political power, a feature that is far more characteristic of her work, and others evoke for the reader the by now familiar texture of village life in Botswana. All bear the distinctive mark of their idiosyncratic author: they contain a rare power and freshness and, in the end, an elusive significance.

Many of the pieces included in *A Woman Alone* have been quoted extensively and commented on elsewhere in this study; the purpose of this section; then, is to provide an overview of the collection as a whole.

Like *Tales of Tenderness, A Woman Alone: Autobiographical Writings* (1990) collects pieces Head wrote in both South Africa and Botswana. The pieces are arranged roughly chronologically—from 1962 to 1985 (the years during which they were written)—and are divided into three periods, each of which is introduced by an autobiographical passage in which the author sets the scene for the period that follows. These introductory passages provide a narrative thread that links the three major periods of her life: her early life in South Africa (1937–1964), her period of exile in Botswana (1964–1979) and finally her life as a Botswanan citizen (1979–1986).

The focus of *A Woman Alone* is not principally on the writer Bessie Head's oeuvre but on the life of a South African-born woman who happened to become an internationally recognized author. The writings that make up this collection, in other words, present a piecemeal portrait of this life, a mosaic of sketches, essays, and personal notes, making the work a primarily biographical study.

There is a small but significant overlap between the two posthumous collections that attests interestingly to Head's defiance of the boundaries that traditionally exist between literary genres. The generic classification of the pieces in *A Woman Alone* poses a special challenge to the literary critic. The pieces span a number of overlapping genres: letters, journalism, autobiography, fictional sketches, essays, forewords, explanatory notes on novels. These genetic markers do not denote discrete and insular categories, however. "Snowball: A Story," for example, should on the strength of its title be classified as a fictional sketch, but three-quarters of the piece is devoted to the author's reflections on her day-to-day life in District Six.

Another example is "An African Story": its title promises fictional narrative, and indeed it begins like a story but then quickly becomes autobiographical, even anecdotal, and ends with a philosophical reflection on the future of South Africa. This indeterminacy characterizes almost every piece in the volume.

The majority of the pieces assembled in *A Woman Alone* defy classification. At their two extremes they represent autobiography and (very nearly) pure fiction. Most of them are, however, strung somewhere between these two extremes, and (with a few exceptions) each represents an amalgam of self-reflection, semifictional narrative, journalistic reportage, and cultural comment. The significance of each piece is that it reveals something about the extraordinary life of the author Bessie Head.

Source: Craig MacKenzie, "Posthumously Published Works: *Tales of Tenderness and Power* and *A Woman Alone*," in *Bessie Head*, Twayne's World Authors Series, No. 882, Twayne Publishers, 1999, pp. 112–15.

SOURCES

Beck, Roger B., *The History of South Africa*, Greenwood, 2000.

Buntman, Fran Lisa, *Robben Island and Prisoner Resistance to Apartheid*, Cambridge University Press, 2003.

Eilersen, Gillian Stead, *Bessie Head: Thunder Behind Her Ears*, David Philip Publishers, 1995, pp. 46–49, 160.

Gagiano, Annie, *Achebe, Head, Marechera: On Power and Change in Africa*, Lynne Rienner Publishers, 2000, pp. 123, 125.

Head, Bessie, "Social and Political Pressures that Shape Literature in Southern Africa," in *World Literature Written in English*, Vol. 18, No. 1, April 1979, pp. 20–26.

———, *Tales of Tenderness and Power*, Heinemann, 1990, pp. 125–30.

Johnson, Joyce, *Bessie Head: The Road of Peace of Mind: A Critical Appreciation*, University of Delaware Press, 2008, p. 25.

Larson, Charles, "Bessie Head, Storyteller in Exile," in *Washington Post Book World*, February 17, 1991, p. 4.

MacKenzie, Craig, "Chronology," "Chapter One: Early Life," and "Chapter Eleven: Posthumously Published Works," in *Bessie Head*, Twayne's World Authors Series, No. 882, Twayne Publishers, 1999, pp. xiii–xvi, 1–14, 112–15.

Moultrie, Tom A., and Ian M. Timaeus, *Trends in South African Fertility Between 1970 and 1998*, MRC South Africa, 2002, p. 2.

Nkosi, Lewis, *Tasks and Masks: Themes and Styles of African Literature*, Longman, 1981, p. 102.

Ogunyemi, Chikwenye Okonjo, "Mapping a Female Mind: Bessie Head's *A Question of Power* and the Unscrambling of Africa," in *Twelve Best Books by African Women: Critical Readings*, edited by Chikwenye Okonjo Ogunyemi and Tuzyline Jita Allan, Ohio University Press, 2009, p. 137, 141.

Ola, Virginia Uzoma, *The Life and Works of Bessie Head*, Edwin Mellen Press, 1994, p. 4.

"South Africa," in *CIA: World Factbook 2009*, https://www.cia.gov/library/publications/the-world-factbook/geos/sf.html (accessed October 9, 2009).

FURTHER READING

Clark, Nancy L., and William H. Worger, *South Africa: The Rise and Fall of Apartheid*, Longman, 2004.

This volume is an excellent overview of the era of apartheid in South Africa, from 1948 through the 1990s, when it was officially dismantled, to the twenty-first century, when its effects are still felt. The book includes primary documents from supporters of apartheid and from opposition groups, such as those to which the prisoners of Span One would have belonged.

Head, Bessie, *A Woman Alone: Autobiographical Writings*, edited by Craig MacKenzie, Heinemann, 1990.

MacKenzie put together this collection of Head's nonfiction writings after her death. The volume includes memoir; important early pieces written about South Africa; and social, political, and critical essays covering Head's entire adult life.

Ibrahim, Huma, ed., *Emerging Perspectives on Bessie Head*, Africa World Press, 2004.

Although this volume's thirteen essays concentrate on Head's novels and on her feminist writings, they present a solid view of the author's uses of biography and autobiography in her work, and the essays examine Head's placement—or misplacement—in the canon.

Sample, Maxine, ed., *Critical Essays on Bessie Head*, Praeger, 2003.

Volume 205 in Praeger's Contributions in Afro-American and African Studies series, this book focuses on Head's novels. However, among its eight essays is Sample's "Bessie Head: A Bibliographic Essay," which provides an excellent narrative overview of scholarship relating to the author.

The Son from America

ISAAC BASHEVIS SINGER

1973

"The Son from America" is a short story by Jewish American writer Isaac Bashevis Singer. It was first published in the *New Yorker* on February 17, 1973, and was reprinted later in the same year in Singer's collection of stories *A Crown of Feathers and Other Stories*. Singer was born in Poland but immigrated to the United States in 1935. He continued to write in his first language, Yiddish, and this story has been translated from the Yiddish by author Dorothea Straus. Like many of Singer's stories, it is set in a Jewish community in Poland like the one Singer knew in his youth. It takes place somewhere around the beginning of the twentieth century in Lentshin, a tiny Jewish village. Berl and Berlcha, an old couple, are astonished one day when their son Samuel, who immigrated to America forty years ago, comes to visit them. He has prospered in his new country and wants to help his parents and the village financially, but he soon learns that the people in Lentshin are happy with what they have; they need nothing from him. Singer is considered one of the finest of twentieth-century American short story writers, and "The Son from America," with its clearly drawn characters, interesting plot, and economical style, is an excellent introduction to his work.

AUTHOR BIOGRAPHY

Isaac Bashevis Singer was born in Leoncin, Poland, on November 21, 1904. His father was

Isaac Bashevis Singer (© Alex Gotfryd / Corbis)

a Hasidic rabbi, and his mother was the daughter of a rabbi. Singer had two brothers and one sister. When Singer was four, the family moved to Warsaw. During World War I, the Germans occupied Warsaw, and the family experienced hardship. In 1917, Singer and his mother and younger brother moved to Bilgoray, where Singer studied the Talmud and the Jewish mystical writings of the kabbalah. He also learned and taught modern Hebrew.

In 1923, Singer returned to Warsaw, where he worked as a proofreader for a journal, *Literarisshe bleter*. He also wrote reviews and translated novels into Yiddish. His first published fiction was a short story written in Yiddish that won a literary prize from *Literarisshe bleter* in 1925. Singer continued to publish short fiction during the 1920s and 1930s. His first novel, *Satan in Goray*, was serialized in *Globus* magazine in 1933 and published in book form in 1935 in Warsaw. This was also the year that Singer, believing that Adolf Hitler's Germany would soon invade Poland, emigrated to the United States. He lived in New York City and worked as a journalist for the *Jewish Daily Forward*.

In 1940, Singer married Alma Wasserman, a German immigrant, and in 1943, he became a U.S. citizen. After eight years in which he wrote only nonfiction essays, he returned to fiction. In 1944, a story that was to become one of his best known, "The Spinoza of Market Street," was published in Yiddish. Translated into English, it would become the title story of a short story collection by Singer in 1961. In 1950, Singer's novel *The Family Muskat* became the first of his novels to be published in English. Three years later came Singer's major breakthrough. This was the publication in the *Partisan Review* of his short story "Gimpel the Fool," translated by Saul Bellow. Following this, Singer had no difficulty finding publishers for his work. *Gimpel the Fool and Other Stories*, his first short story collection, was published in 1957.

For the next thirty years, Singer published his work regularly. His major works of the 1960s and 1970s include the novels *The Slave* (1962); *The Manor* (1967); *A Day of Pleasure* (1970), which won the National Book Award; and *Enemies, a Love Story* (1972). His short story collections included *Short Friday and Other Stories* (1964); *The Seance and Other Stories* (1968); *A Friend of Kafka and Other Stories* (1970); *A Crown of Feathers and Other Stories* (1973), which contained "The Son from America" and won Singer his second National Book Award; and *Passions and Other Stories* (1975). He also published the memoir of his childhood *In My Father's Court* (1966) and a number of books for children, including *Zlateh the Goat and Other Stories* (1966) and *When Shlemiel Went to Warsaw and Other Stories* (1968), which won the Newbery Award.

In 1978, Singer won the Nobel Prize in Literature, and in 1988, he was awarded the Gold Medal by the American Academy and Institute of Arts and Letters. During the 1980s, he published the short fiction collections *The Image and Other Stories* (1985) and *The Death of Methuselah and Other Stories* (1988), as well as the novel *The King of the Fields* (1988). His last novel was *Scum*, published in 1991.

Singer died in Surfside, Florida, on July 24, 1991, following a series of strokes.

PLOT SUMMARY

"The Son from America" is set in Lentshin, a small Jewish village in Poland in the late nineteenth or early twentieth century. In Lentshin live old Berl, a man in his eighties, and his wife, Berlcha. Berl was driven from Russia by the persecution of Jews there, and he and his wife settled in Poland. They live in a one-room hut and keep a goat, a cow, and chickens, and they have a field of half an acre. They also have a son called Samuel, who emigrated to the United States forty years ago. It is said that he became prosperous there, and every week he sends a money order to his parents. Every four months, Berl and Berlcha drive to a larger town, Zakroczym, and cash the money orders, but they never use the money, since their wants are few, and they have all they need. No one knows or cares where they put the money, since there are no thieves in the village.

Berl and his wife are happy with what they have and the simple life they lead. They do not envy the more prosperous villagers who have kerosene lamps, since they do not trust such new devices.

Berl keeps in touch with world events at the synagogue. He tells his wife that there is unrest in Warsaw, Poland's capital city, where striking workers are calling for the abdication of the czar. A man named Dr. Herzl is promoting his idea that the Jews should return and settle in Palestine. This is a reference to Theodore Herzl (1860–1904), founder of the Zionist movement, which sought the establishment of a Jewish state in Palestine. Berl's wife expresses astonishment at what goes on in cities nowadays. In the tiny village of Lentshin, nothing out of the ordinary ever happens. There are few young people there. The young seek their fortunes elsewhere, in the big cities and sometimes even in the United States.

Samuel sends Berl and Berlcha photographs of his children and grandchildren, but they have gentile names that Berl and Berlcha cannot remember. They know nothing of life in the distant land of America.

One winter morning, when Berlcha is preparing bread for the Sabbath the following day, a tall man she believes to be a nobleman appears at the door. A coachman carries his bags. The nobleman pays the coachman and then turns to Berlcha and tells her that he is Samuel, her son. Berlcha is astonished. Then Berl enters and is equally astonished when the stranger announces that he is Berl's son. Berl does not recognize Samuel because he was only fifteen years old when he left home. Samuel asks whether they received his cable telling them that he was coming, but Berl does not even know what a cable is.

Berlcha begins to cry and says she must knead the dough in preparation for the Sabbath. She must make a bigger meal now that her son is here. Samuel offers to help, but she refuses to let him, but Samuel removes his coat and rolls up his sleeves, saying that for many years he was a baker in New York. Berlcha is overcome with joy and collapses on the bed, while Berl goes to the shed to get some wood.

The neighbors hear the news and come to meet Samuel. The women help Berlcha prepare for the Sabbath, and everyone asks Samuel questions about what life is like in America, especially for the Jews.

Berl and Samuel go to the synagogue together. When they come out, snow covers the village. Samuel remarks that the village is the same as he remembers it.

Over the evening meal, Samuel talks a lot, but his parents do not understand everything he says because, although he speaks in Yiddish, the language of the Eastern European Jews, he adds foreign words to it. Samuel asks his father what he did with all the money that was sent. It transpires that Berl stored the money in a boot placed under the bed. When Samuel asks him why he never spent any of it, Berl replies that there is nothing to spend it on, since they have everything they need. They have no desire to travel. When Samuel asks what will happen to the money, Berl suggests that Samuel should take it back. Samuel suggests that perhaps they need a larger synagogue, but Berl replies that the synagogue is big enough. He also says, in response to another idea of Samuel's, that the village does not need an old people's home.

The next day, while Berl and Berlcha take a nap, Samuel goes for a walk. He enters the synagogue, where he finds an old man reciting scriptures. He asks the man whether he makes a living, but the old man does not understand the question. He says that he goes on living as long as God gives him health.

Samuel returns home at dusk. Berl goes to the synagogue, and Samuel remains at home with his mother. Berlcha recites a prayer, which includes a petition for wealth. Samuel says she does not need to pray for wealth because she is wealthy already. He thinks back over the plans for the village he has brought with him. He wanted to give the village gifts. There is even a Lentshin Society in New York that has collected money for the cause, but now Samuel realizes that the village needs nothing.

The story ends with the sounds of the crickets outside, the chanting from the synagogue, and Berlcha still reciting her prayers.

CHARACTERS

Berl

Berl is a man in his eighties, married to Berlcha. Berl is Jewish, and he used to live in Russia but was driven from that country by persecution. He settled with his wife in a small village in Poland, where they keep a goat, a cow, and chickens and a small field. Berl walks with a shuffle, and his eyesight is fading, but he is the kind of man who is content with what he has and makes no complaint. He cannot conceive of a kind of life other than the one he lives. He and his wife have a son, Samuel, who lives in America and regularly sends them money, but Berl has no use for it. He cashes the money orders and puts the money in an old boot that he keeps under his bed. He and his wife live simply in their one-room hut. They have all the necessities of life and have no aspirations for anything more. Berl simply has no material desires. He keeps in touch with what is happening in the world through his visits to the village synagogue, but his own horizons are very narrow. He has no desire to travel and see the world, and he rejects all of his son's suggestions about how the village might be improved. Berl is also a very pious man. When he realizes that the stranger who is visiting them is in fact his own son, his reaction is to "recite holy words that he had read in the Yiddish Bible." He refuses to touch money on the Sabbath, because it is forbidden. Berl follows the precepts of his religion without question, and this is enough for him.

Berlcha

Berlcha is Berl's wife. She is also old, and her appearance is described as follows: "Her face was yellowish and wrinkled like a cabbage leaf. There were bluish sacks under her eyes." Berlcha has been married to Berl for well over fifty years. She is half deaf, and as with Berl, her eyesight is failing, but also like her husband, she makes no complaint about her life, which follows a simple routine of performing household chores and cooking meals. She also sells chickens and eggs so there is enough money to buy flour for bread. On winter evenings, she spins flax at her spinning wheel. This is probably the routine she has followed almost all her life, and like her husband, she cannot envision things being any different. She does not take much interest in current affairs. When Berl reports what he has heard at the synagogue about life in the wider world, she simply wonders at the strange events that go on in the cities. She has no idea what life is like in America, where her son Samuel lives.

In the story, Berlcha's main activity is to prepare the Sabbath meal, and she is very emotional when her son, absent for forty years, returns home. She is also touched when Berl calls her Pescha, which is her first name. Normally he does not use it. Like her husband, Berlcha has a simple religious faith. She observes the rituals and prayers of her Jewish religion as she has known them all her life and as has been the practice for generations before her. She prays for divine protection. It seems that for Berlcha, prayer is as natural as breathing.

Samuel

Samuel is the son of Berl and Berlcha. He left the family home when he was fifteen to go to America. He has been successful there, settling in New York City and marrying and raising a family. He worked many years as a baker. He is well dressed and prosperous, and when his mother sees him for the first time in forty years, she thinks he is a nobleman.

It appears that Samuel has at least partially assimilated into mainstream American life, since his children have gentile names, but when he returns to visit his parents after a long absence, it is clear that he still identifies himself to some extent as a Jew. He still speaks Yiddish, although his parents do not understand it well because it is different from the Yiddish they speak and contains foreign words.

All the years he has been in America, Samuel has sent money back to his parents. He has also been active in the Lentshin Society in New York, which raises funds to help the impoverished village where his parents live. Samuel is therefore the dutiful son, and he is full of plans to inject funds into the village. Living so long in a materialist society, he thinks that everyone must need money. He cannot understand why his parents did not make use of what he sent them, but he also notices that the village has not changed in forty years, and eventually he realizes that it does not need the gifts he has brought.

The Old Man

When Samuel goes alone to the synagogue at night, he finds an old man there who is reciting psalms. Samuel questions him and discovers from the man's simple answers the gulf that separates the ideas he has brought with him from America and the traditional, pious life led by the villagers.

THEMES

Materialism

From a modern perspective, Berl and Berlcha do not possess much. They have enough to eat, and they have a roof over their heads, but that is about all. They are poor. They have no luxuries. The only extras they make sure they have are the candles needed for the Sabbath, but they regard those as essentials. These are people for whom religious faith is all important. They live by the precepts of the Torah (the Jewish holy book of scriptures and laws) handed down from generation to generation. It is a spiritual way of living that accepts with composure what the Lord gives or does not give. Berl and Berlcha trust that God will provide for their needs, and they are not disappointed. Their prayers are heard, and their lives seem to them full rather than empty or deprived. Secure in the unchanging rhythm of their days, Berl and Berlcha do not believe in progress. They do not care for "newfangled gadgets" such as kerosene lamps. They live in a static world where change is neither sought nor desired. This is what Samuel notices when he returns after a forty-year absence. "Nothing has changed here," he says. The world of Lentshin is defined by simple, everyday tasks and religious faith, ritual, and worship. There is no need for anything to change, at least as far as Berl and Berlcha are concerned. All things, they believe, come from God. There is no need for people to try to take the lead and alter what God gives, although Berl and Berlcha do pray for divine support and protection in their lives, but that is up to the will of God; it is not for Berl and Berlcha to decide what is best for them.

In contrast, Samuel has for forty years lived in a society that values material things and is always in the vanguard of progress, understood in terms of improving the material lot of people. The materialism that prevails in a city such as New York is completely at odds with the spirituality that permeates the simple village of Lentshin. One worldview defines the value of life in terms of how many possessions and material comforts people have; people who do not have much by definition must be in want of more. In contrast, in the religious view of life that dominates with the villagers of Lentshin, fullness and plenty are spiritual terms. Plenty is provided not by the ingenuity and inventions of humans on the material plane of existence but by the "God of Abraham, Isaac, and Jacob," who always gives enough.

Samuel is a bridge between these two worlds. He grew up in the village but made the United States his adopted home. He obviously values the material aspects of life and has much that others might envy. This is obvious from the first description of him, in which he is dressed in a cloak with a fur border and carries leather suitcases with brass locks on them. He also wears a solid-gold watch chain. He overpays the coachman but will not allow the man to give him any change. He is clearly a representative of that prosperous world across the ocean of which Berl and Berlcha know nothing. At first, Samuel, who has been away so long, cannot understand the way his parents think about such matters as human need. Surely they and the other villagers are in need of the money and other gifts that he brings? Slowly he comes to remember what life in this village is all about. By the end of the story, he realizes that the village needs nothing from him. He tells his mother, "You are wealthy already," thus showing his understanding that wealth can mean different things to different people. He may have a certain kind of wealth that is honored in New York City, but his parents have another form of wealth that flows from the spirit and is not counted in gold coins.

Assimilation

Lentshin is a thoroughly Jewish village; all of its inhabitants share the same culture and religion, but it is a different matter for Samuel. He grew up in Lentshin but departed for America when he was fifteen. Like thousands of other Jews who immigrated to the United States in the second half of the nineteenth century, he has been subject to the process of assimilation into the mainstream of American life. He appears to have married a non-Jew, since his children do not have Jewish names. The extent to which he has

TOPICS FOR FURTHER STUDY

- Watch the movie *Fiddler on the Roof* (1971), which is based on a Broadway musical that in turn is based on a story by Yiddish writer Sholem Aleichem. The film is set in a *shtetl* (small town) in Russia in 1905. Based on the film, what characteristics does the *shtetl* have? Write an essay in which you describe similarities you see between the film and the setting of "The Son from America."
- Kiryas Joel is a village within the town of Monroe, Orange County, New York. The majority of residents are Hasidic Jews who speak Yiddish and strictly observe the traditions of their faith. Using the Internet, research Kiryas Joel and create a PowerPoint presentation about it, using images as well as text to describe the village. When was it first established, and why? Describe the characteristics of the people who live there and the lifestyle they follow. What might be the advantages and disadvantages of living in such a village?
- Singer also wrote stories for young-adult audiences. Read two of the eight stories in *Naftali the Storyteller and His Horse, Sus: And Other Stories* (1987). Like "The Son from America," they are all set in a Jewish community in pre-World War II Poland. Write a brief essay in which you explain the theme of each one. Note any similarity in these stories to the themes and setting of "The Son from America."
- Think about the issue of conflict between immigrant children and their parents in the United States. Immigrants often feel strongly about maintaining their own culture and traditions, but their children, especially those born in the United States, may be less attached to their parents' culture and identify more with being Americans. Write a short story or a single scene in which a young protagonist tries to explain to his or her parents why he or she wants to do something or why he or she believes something of which the parents disapprove.
- Use the Internet or library resource materials to look up information about U.S. immigration statistics in the late 1800s and early 1900s. Create a graphic presentation (charts and graphs) to illustrate the diversity of that immigration. Create charts to show where the immigrants came from, where they settled, what religions they practiced, and other categories of information that you can uncover in your research. Complete the assignment by writing five generalizations about immigration to the United States during the time period.

---

remained a Jew is a subject of concern for his parents. They ask him how Jews fare in America: "Do they remain Jews?" Samuel's reply is a little ambiguous. He replies not with a positive statement that he is still a Jew but with the negation, "I am not a Gentile," which suggests perhaps that he is not as strict in his observance of Jewish laws, customs, and rituals as the people of Lentshin are, but he has not altogether abandoned the Jewish culture or religion. He is perhaps, like many immigrants, caught between two worlds.

Another indication of the extent of assimilation is language. In Lentshin, the inhabitants speak Yiddish, but when the young people leave the village, which most of them do, they write back to their families in Yiddish intermixed with words from the languages of the countries in which they now live, which their families cannot understand. Berl and Berlcha cannot understand Samuel's letters because he uses English words along with the Yiddish.

STYLE

Nature Symbolism

Berl and Berlcha live simply, guided by their religious faith. They also live close to nature and in

The Statue of Liberty and Ellis Island *(Image copyright Mike Liu, 2009. Used under license from Shutterstock.com)*

harmony with it. Human and natural worlds interpenetrate, almost like paradise described in the book of Genesis in the Bible, before the fall of man. In the winter, the chickens and the goat live inside Berl and Berlcha's hut for protection from the cold. There is a kind of primordial oneness about the old people and their environment, with no rupture between the human, animal, and spiritual realms. In summer, the two old people rise with the sun and retire "with the chickens." When Samuel arrives, the goat follows him into the house like a member of the family. She sits near the oven, gazing at the newly arrived stranger with as much surprise as Berl and Berlcha display. As Samuel listens to the sounds of the village at the end of the story, the spiritual and the natural mingle together, suggesting that at all levels of life in this quiet village, harmony prevails: "This village in the hinterland needed nothing. From the synagogue one could hear hoarse chanting. The cricket, silent all day, started again its chirping." The alliteration (repetition of initial consonants) in the words "chanting" and "chirping" reinforces this effect of harmony.

Religious Symbolism

The action of the story takes place on the day before the Sabbath and on the Sabbath itself. It also centers around the rituals that are performed on the Sabbath. This is a very effective way of presenting the contrast between the religious and secular worlds (the latter represented at least in part by Samuel) and suggesting that for these villagers, every action they perform is in some way connected to an understanding of the divine and the responsibilities of being human.

The Sabbath (also written *Shabbat*) is a weekly day of rest observed by Jews. The Sabbath begins at sunset on Friday and continues until Saturday night when three stars are visible in the sky. Jews are not permitted to work on the Sabbath, which is a time for getting together with family and friends. Also, religious services are held at the synagogue on the Sabbath. The Sabbath begins with the lighting of candles (in the story, Berlcha always buys three candles for the Sabbath) and includes three festive meals.

The piety of the Jews is therefore at the heart of the story, which mentions several aspects of Jewish faith and practice. The Jews in the village are likely Hasidic Jews. Singer himself was born into a Hasidic family, and Hasidism, founded by Rabbi Israel Baal Shem Tov, was an important movement in eighteenth- and nineteenth-century Eastern European Jewry.

Another reference to Jewish religious life in the story is to *Kaddish*. Kaddish is a prayer about the greatness of God that is recited at every prayer service. It is also a mourning prayer. For much of Jewish history, only men were permitted to say Kaddish. Among Eastern European Jews, it was considered a blessing for parents to have a son rather than a daughter in part because a son would be able to recite Kaddish after their deaths. This is what Berlcha refers to when she says excitedly that Samuel is her son who will say Kaddish for her.

HISTORICAL CONTEXT

East European Jewry

During the nineteenth century, the number of Jews relative to the non-Jewish population in Poland rose steadily, from 8.7 percent in 1816 to 13.5 percent in 1865 and 14 percent in 1897. This growth was in spite of extensive Jewish emigration and was due to a lower death rate among Jews compared with that among non-Jews. In Warsaw, the Polish capital, one resident in three was Jewish. This was also true of the second largest city, Lodz, and in that city, by 1910, Jews accounted for nearly 41 percent of the population. This represented a marked trend toward urbanization for Polish Jews. In 1865, 91.5 percent of Polish Jews lived in cities. (This suggests that a village like Lentshin in "The Son from America" was representative of only a small proportion of Jews in Poland at the time. As the story mentions, most of the town's young people move to bigger towns or emigrate.) Many of the urban Jews in Poland were wealthy through trade and the ownership of banks, although most were shopkeepers without much financial capital.

Throughout the nineteenth century, legal efforts aimed at reducing the separatism of the Jews and assimilating them into Polish life had little influence on the majority of Jews. Some Jewish intellectuals, however, did hope for assimilation. They were sympathetic to Poland's aspirations to independence, believing that the establishment of a Polish state free of Russian domination would lead to a reduction in anti-Semitism.

Anti-Semitism in Poland, however, was not as severe as it was in Russia. In "The Son from America," Berl fled from Russia to Poland at some unspecified time in the past. Russia was particularly notorious for its anti-Semitism during the reign of Czar Alexander III, from 1891 to 1894. Alexander's nationalistic policies favored Orthodox Christianity at the expense of other groups, and burdensome restrictions were placed on Jews, who were not permitted to be members of local governments and also suffered from educational and property restrictions. From 1881 to 1883, there were also pogroms in Russia, in which mobs attacked and killed Jews.

Jewish Immigration to the United States

There is a long tradition of Jewish immigration to the United States, especially from Eastern Europe. In "The Son from America," Samuel immigrated at the age of fifteen, which might place his arrival in the United States at around 1860. This would have coincided with a large increase in the number of Jews in the country. In 1860, there were an estimated 150,000 Jews in the United States, 40,000 of whom lived in New York City. By 1880, the overall figure had jumped to 280,000. Most of the increase was due to immigration from Germany and the areas of Poland under Prussian control. Most Jews in the United States during this period were occupied in commerce and in skilled crafts rather than the professions such as medicine or law. They had full equality under the law and did not in general face discrimination or prejudice, certainly not as much as that faced by Roman Catholic Irish immigrants. It is not surprising, then, that in the story Samuel is able to prosper, reputedly becoming a millionaire. However, it was noticeable that in the 1870s and beyond, there was a tendency in the cities for Jews to be excluded from elite social circles. Many of the upper-class social clubs refused membership to Jews.

COMPARE & CONTRAST

- **Early 1900s:** Poland is under Russian rule. Poland has a large Jewish community and is a center for Jewish culture.

  1970s: Poland is an independent nation ruled by a communist government. It forms part of the Eastern bloc that is dominated by the Soviet Union. Following the Holocaust that took place during World War II, in which 90 percent of Polish Jews died (about three million), the Jewish population is small. Anti-Semitism still exists in Poland, and many Jews leave the country.

  Today: Poland is a democratic country and, since 1999, a member of the Western alliance NATO (North Atlantic Treaty Organization). It is also a member of the European Union. The Polish Jewish community is very small, numbering about twenty thousand people. Most live in Warsaw, the capital city of Krakow, and Bielsko-Biala.

- **Early 1900s:** The Zionist movement grows, calling for Jews to establish their own state in Palestine, their historic homeland. Theodore Herzl, who founded the Zionist movement in France in the 1890s, dies in 1904. The British propose a home for the Jews in Uganda, in east Africa, which is under British control. The proposal does not win enough support and is rejected. Jews move to Palestine on a small scale. From 1902 to 1914, twenty-nine Jewish settlements are established, with support from the Zionist Organization.

  1970s: Israel, established as a state in 1948, fights its fourth war against its Arab neighbors in October 1973, when Egypt and Syria launch a surprise attack on Israel and the Yom Kippur War begins. The conflict lasts for nearly three weeks before a cease-fire is brokered by the United States.

  Today: Although Arab nations, including Egypt and Jordan, have made peace with Israel, the violent conflict between the Israelis and the Palestinians continues. The goal of an independent state for the Palestinians has yet to be realized.

- **Early 1900s:** Continuing a process that was established in the second half of the nineteenth century, there is large-scale immigration of Eastern European Jews to the United States. At the beginning of the twentieth century, there are about one million Jews in the United States, giving that country the third-largest Jewish population in the world. About half of American Jews live in New York City.

  1970s: Outside the state of Israel, the Jewish community in the United States is the largest, wealthiest, and most influential in the world. Jews remain numerous in New York, but the population has also spread out to cities such as Los Angeles and Miami and to the suburbs. Many American Jews strongly support Israel in its wars against the Arab nations and also lend support to Jews who are persecuted in the Soviet Union.

  Today: Based on U.S. census figures from 2000 and estimates as of 2007, Jews constitute about 2 percent of the population. The states with the largest Jewish populations include New York (1,618,000 or 8.4 percent of the population) California (1,194,000 or 3.3 percent), New Jersey (479,000 or 5.5 percent), and Florida (655,000 or 3.6 percent). Some Jewish leaders are concerned about the long-term effects on the Jewish community of intermarriage. More than 50 percent of American Jews marry non-Jews, which in many cases indicates they and perhaps their children are less likely to identify strongly with their Jewish heritage.

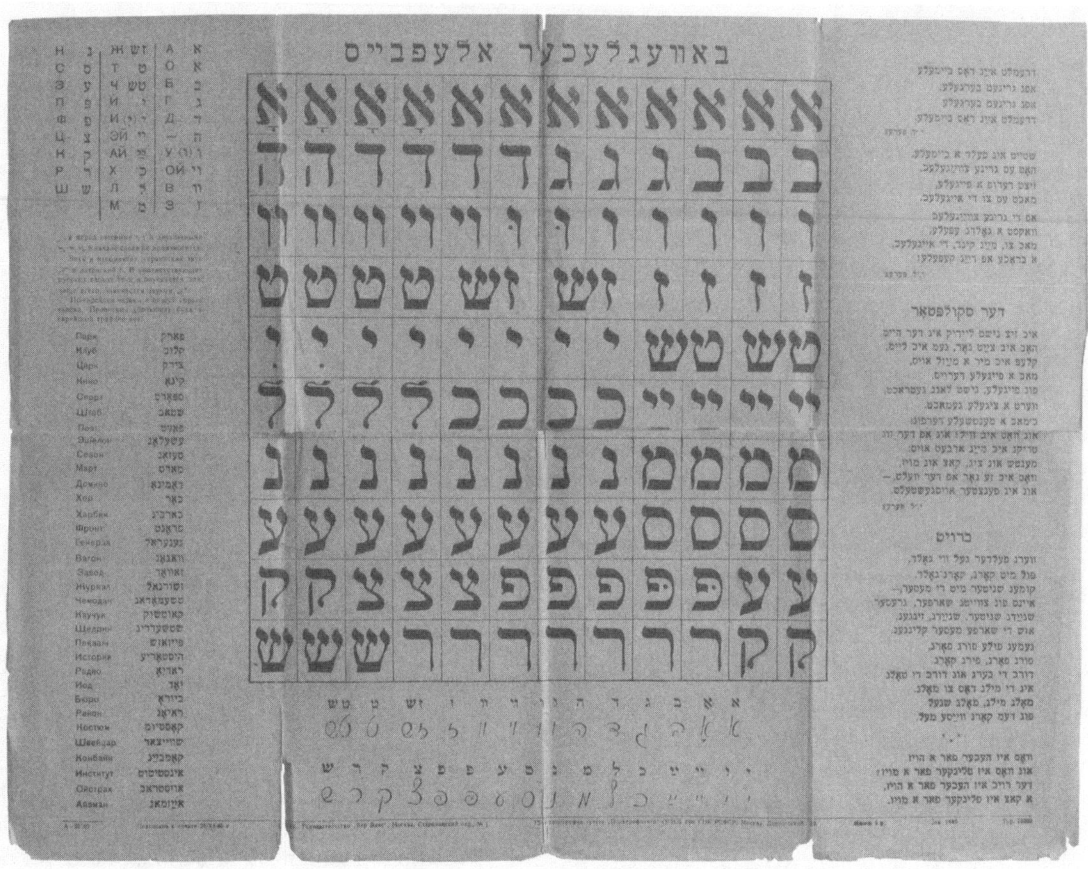

Yiddish alphabet *(Image copyright Feliks Gurevich, 2009. Used under license from Shutterstock.com)*

From 1880 to the mid-1920s, there was another wave of Jewish immigration to the United States. This is during the time period of "The Son from America," when so many of the young people of the village are leaving, some bound for the United States. Between 1880 and 1925, when restrictions were placed on immigration, approximately 2,378,000 Jews, the vast majority from Eastern Europe, immigrated to the United States. The rise in Jewish immigration was partly due to anti-Semitism in Russia but also to the fourfold increase in the number of Jews in the Russian empire, Austrian-controlled Poland, Hungary, and Romania over the course of the nineteenth century. The level of economic development in these countries could not provide Jews with an acceptable standard of living, and they immigrated in large numbers in search of a better life. In some cities such as New York, the Jewish immigrants clustered together in areas that became almost entirely Jewish. One such area was New York City's Lower East Side. In 1915, 350,000 Jews lived there in crowded conditions, in an area covering less than two square miles. Many thousands of these and other Jewish immigrants were employed in the clothing industry, where they would labor in unhygienic sweatshops for up to sixteen hours a day for low pay. Conditions such as these inspired the growth of the Jewish labor movement in the 1880s.

CRITICAL OVERVIEW

Singer was a prolific author of short stories, and many critics regard his short stories rather than his novels as his chief contribution to American literature. *A Crown of Feathers and Other Stories*, in which "The Son from America" appeared, was Singer's sixth short story collection. Few reviewers picked out "The Son from America" for comment, but one exception was the reviewer for the London *Times Literary Supplement*, who argues that "The Son from America" is "one of the best of the twenty-four" stories. After noting that "a simple Polish village is accorded a kind of pastoral naivety, its peasant farmers yoked to the time-honoured observances," the reviewer concludes that "few other writers could make this sort of Arcadian fable work so convincingly."

In a glowing review of the collection in the *New York Times Book Review*, Alfred Kazin points out that "East European Jews have produced many stories, narratives, legends, but until our day, very little fiction." Offering the view that Singer is "interested in truth," Kazin writes that he "is an extraordinary writer. And this new collection of stories ... represents the most delicate imaginative splendor, wit, mischief and, not least, the now unbelievable life that Jews once lived in Poland."

In a comment that might well be applied to "The Son from America," P. S. Prescott writes in *Newsweek*, "Singer, in his short and humorous tales drawn from an old tradition, celebrates the dignity, mystery and unexpected joy of living with more art and fervor than any other writer alive."

CRITICISM

Bryan Aubrey

Aubrey holds a Ph.D. in English. In this essay, he discusses "The Son from America" in terms of the contrast between the materialism of the Americanized Jew Samuel and the traditional religion of his parents.

Singer plays a unique role in Jewish American literature. He immigrated to the United States from Poland in 1935, when he was in his early thirties, and continued to write in Yiddish, his native tongue. Although he would become an American citizen and live in the United States for the remainder of his long life, much of his work continued to look back and memorialize a vanished world, that of the *shtetl* (small town), which was characteristic of the lives of so many Eastern European Jews in the early part of the twentieth century and before. That world was to disappear forever as a result of historical events such as wars, revolution, and industrialization as well as the Holocaust during World War II, in which millions of Jews from Eastern Europe

ONE WORLD RELIES ON AN ETERNAL BIRTHRIGHT MEDIATED THROUGH TRADITION AND FAITH; THE OTHER IS LIVED IN TERMS OF MATERIAL ACQUISITION AND THE RESTLESS DESIRE ALWAYS TO IMPROVE, TO ENLARGE, TO MAKE THINGS BETTER IN A MATERIAL SENSE."

died. Singer's other main concern as a writer was to portray the lives of Eastern European Jewish immigrants in the United States. In "The Son from America," Singer manages to bring these two worlds together, drawing in just a few deft pages the sharp contrast between the prosperous, Americanized Jew Samuel and the traditional simple piety of his parents in the shtetl. The village is probably based on Singer's memories of his childhood and youth, especially the period from 1917 to 1921 when he lived in his grandfather's village, the shtetl Bilgoray. This was the period when he studied Hasidic culture and its timeless ways. In an interview with Joel Blocker and Richard Elman in 1963, Singer acknowledged the influence of these years in Bilgoray, calling it a "very old-fashioned" town:

> Not much had changed there in many generations. In this town the traditions of hundreds of years ago still lived. There was no railroad nearby. It was stuck in the forest and it was pretty much the same as it must have been during the time of Chmielnicki. [Chmielnicki was a Cossack who was responsible for the deaths of many Jews in mid-seventeenth-century pogroms in Poland.]

In this simple, brief exchange is the entire difference between two cultures and two ways of seeing the world. To this old man, Samuel might as well be speaking a foreign language.

In his book, *God, Jew, Satan in the Works of Isaac Bashevis-Singer*, Israel Ch. Biletzky quotes a passage written by Singer's brother, I. J. Singer, that identifies Lentshin (the name of the village in "The Son from America") as the small town of Singer's birth, which is usually called Leoncin. I. J. Singer describes it as follows:

> The houses were small and low. The roofs were not made of straw, like the houses in villages all

WHAT DO I READ NEXT?

- Singer's short story "Gimpel the Fool," first published in 1953, was the story that first brought him widespread attention in the United States. It is considered one of his masterpieces. Gimpel is a simple man, a baker, who is ridiculed by the other folk in his village, but he also has a self-awareness that shows he is far less of a fool than others take him for. The story is witty, imaginative, and completely convincing. It is available in *Gimpel the Fool: And Other Stories* (2006).
- *Walk in the Light and Twenty-three Tales* (2003) is a collection by the great nineteenth-century Russian writer Leo Tolstoy. This volume includes Tolstoy's short didactic tales that in their simplicity, clarity, and moral force resemble Singer's "The Son from America." Notable stories include "What Men Live By," "How Much Land Does a Man Need," "God Sees the Truth, But Waits," and "The Story of Ivan the Fool." The last-named story should be compared with Singer's "Gimpel the Fool."
- In *Resistance: The Warsaw Ghetto Uprising* (1998), Israel Gutman, who took part in the battle, tells the story of the Warsaw Ghetto uprising in 1943. In the 1930s, Warsaw had a flourishing Jewish community, but after the Nazis invaded Poland in 1939, the Jews were herded into a ghetto in the city. Suffering all manner of deprivation, they finally rose up against their oppressors. Gutman uses diaries, letters, survivors' accounts, and other documents to present a vivid account of the courageous fight by the Jews and its tragic outcome.
- *The Oxford Book of Jewish Stories* (1998), edited by Ilian Stavens, is a collection of fifty-two short stories by Jewish writers from the nineteenth century to the present. The stories were originally written in twelve different languages. Writers represented include Singer, Sholem Aleichem, Elie Wiesel, Franz Kafka, Isaac Babel, Grace Paley, Cynthia Ozick, Philip Roth, Bernard Malamud, Saul Bellow, Francine Prose, Jonathan Rosen, and many others. Stavens's introduction surveys Jewish literature from around the world and gives a chronology for the period 1767–1997.
- *Jewish Love Stories for Kids* (2002) is the fourth book in a popular series for young adults. It contains five love stories with Jewish themes by authors including Leslie Cohen and Devorah Grossman. Each story is a substantial one of thirty to forty pages.
- *The Chosen*, by Chaim Potok, was first published in 1967 and has become a classic. Set in Brooklyn during the 1940s, it tells the story of two Jewish boys, Reuven Malther and Danny Saunders. Reuven is an Orthodox Jew and Danny is a Hasid, but despite their differences, they become lasting friends. The story also explores their stormy relationships with their fathers, all against a background of current events: World War II, the Holocaust, and the establishment of the state of Israel. The novel is available in an edition published by Ballantine in 1996.

> around, but of up-ended tiles. Many bird nests chirped inside the tiled roofs. Only one house possessed a parapet. The roads were not tarred but were not muddy as the soil was sandy. . . . The little shops sported many various drawings over their doors: drawings of cloths, perfumes, sugar-cones, pots, candles, horseshoes and scythes. Near these little shops there were workshops belonging to tailors, shoemakers and bakers.

Biletzky comments that this passage accurately describes many of the villages in Poland in which poor Jews managed to live "a full Jewish life."

When Singer comes to write about such a village in "The Son from America" he idealizes the shtetl almost to the point of myth or fable. It becomes a kind of pastoral paradise in which, despite poverty, there is no such thing as want or suffering, and spiritual and natural life flow smoothly together in a serene, timeless rhythm. Whether there was ever a Jewish village (or a non-Jewish one, come to that) that actually embodied all these qualities is beside the point. Singer makes it a reality in this imaginative story because he wants the best possible contrast with another kind of life that certainly did exist—that of the Jewish immigrant to America who prospered and developed a different set of values than he had grown up with in the shtetl. The story thus revolves around the collision of cultures in one suddenly reunited family.

Singer is known as a masterful writer who can create whole characters and worlds in short stories of only a few pages, and this is what he does in "The Son from America," telling the story with great economy but opening up worlds of thought and behavior in a few key phrases. A good example of this is the paragraph in which the narrator describes how remote the land of America is to Berl and Berlcha and how a Talmud teacher who once came to Lentshin explained that "Americans walked with their heads down and their feet up." (The Talmud is the collection of ancient writings that interpret the laws and traditions of Judaism.) What the teacher meant by walking with one's feet up is obscure, but walking with one's head down is surely intended as a metaphor for a kind of individualism, a certain way of life in which people are preoccupied with their own pursuits, confined in their own private worlds, oblivious to wider community concerns. The phrase certainly creates an evocative picture of people in America walking around looking downward, unaware of others and their needs—or so it might seem. America in such a view is the land of individualism, where fortunes can be made by those who pursue their own interests with sufficient zeal, like Samuel, the immigrant boy who made it good and is now reputedly a millionaire (and a millionaire one hundred years ago, when a dollar could buy a lot more than it can today, was certainly very rich).

Berl and Berlcha do not have a clue as to what the Talmud teacher means—they think he is speaking literally—but they conclude, "But since the teacher said so it must be true." This captures in a phrase an entire way of thinking in this tradition-bound rural environment. It would never occur to anyone in this village to question the word of a religious teacher, who is a trusted interpreter of the scriptures and a wise man in all other respects. For the residents of Lentshin, those who interpret the divine laws set out in the Torah and the Talmud have an absolute authority, and these villagers would no more question or doubt them than they would ask the sun if it was rising at the correct time in the morning. Things that cannot be understood must just be accepted, as the sympathetic narrator wryly notes in a paradox: "From too much thinking—God forbid—one may lose one's wits." This is a community that lives by faith, not rational human understanding. As one character says in "The Recluse," another Singer story in *A Crown of Feathers and Other Stories* that is set in Eastern Europe a long time ago, "The Torah was not given to us to exercise the brain, but to serve the Almighty."

Another example of Singer's ability to say a great deal in a short space occurs in the incident in which Samuel goes for a walk alone after the Sabbath meal. Wanting to find someone to talk to, he enters the synagogue, where he finds an old man reciting psalms. Samuel asks him if he is praying, and the old man replies, "What else is there to do when one gets old?" Samuel responds with a question: "Do you make a living?" But the old man does not understand the question. He simply replies, "If God gives health, one keeps on living." In this simple, brief exchange is the entire difference between two cultures and two ways of seeing the world. To this old man, Samuel might as well be speaking a foreign language. Samuel's question has relevance only in a world in which people must participate in an economic system in order to prosper, to "make a living." But the old man, who can speak only from what he knows, does not regard living as something a person can "make." Life comes from God, who may extend it or withdraw it as he pleases; it is not something that a person can create for himself. Once again the reader is made aware that in this village, everything the people do is a kind of prayer: a thought, word, or action that is connected to something larger—to the Torah, to God. If it is not, Berl and Berlcha might say, why would one do it? Samuel, however, has for forty years been busy making a living—as he understands the phrase—in the huge metropolis that is New York. He has made it his business to store up wealth, some of which—to his credit—he intends to use for what he thinks is a noble purpose, but Samuel finds that he and the

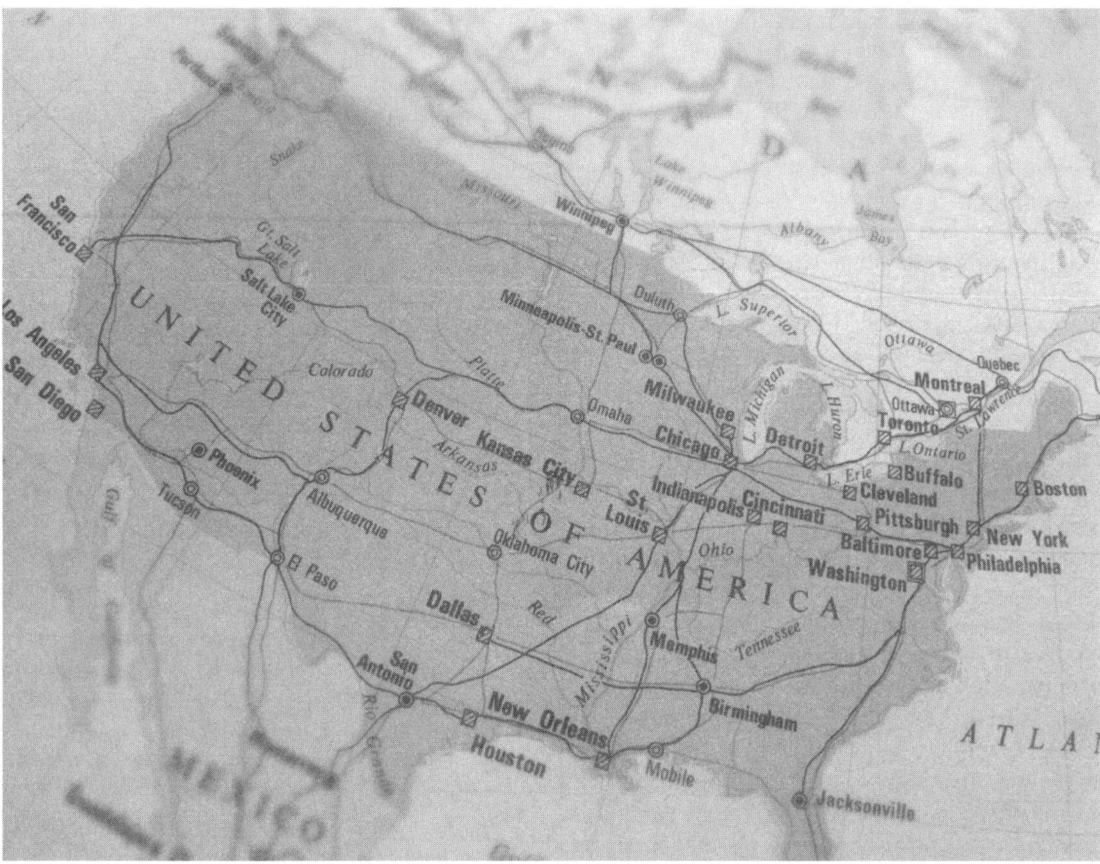

Singer's travels to America greatly influenced his work. *(Image copyright Sean Gladwell, 2009. Used under license from Shutterstock.com)*

people in the village live in distinct cultural worlds that barely intersect. One world is upheld by faith; it looks beyond itself to a God who protects his people through their observance of prescribed rituals and practices. On the other hand is a world lodged in the here and now that carries with it the imperative to acquire and accumulate the things of this world. One world relies on an eternal birthright mediated through tradition and faith; the other is lived in terms of material acquisition and the restless desire always to improve, to enlarge, to make things better in a material sense.

The wealthy Samuel therefore gets a huge shock when by the end of the story he has realized that the village needs none of his gifts or the development projects he had in mind. Singer gives little clue as to how Samuel feels at this moment or the thoughts that are going through his mind. The author prefers to let his themes reveal themselves through his characters' words and actions. In this case, the image with which the story ends is extremely powerful. Samuel stands silently in his parents' home, touching in his pocket his checkbook and letters of credit, while his mother, seemingly oblivious to his presence, sways and recites a prayer that she "inherited from mothers and grandmothers." The prosperous New Yorker, steeped in his commercial world of getting and spending, is suddenly being reminded that all good does not necessarily flow from a checkbook.

Source: Bryan Aubrey, Critical Essay on "The Son from America," in *Short Stories for Students*, Gale, Cengage Learning, 2010.

Jill P. May

In the following excerpt, May explains Singer's travels to America as an immigrant and how his desire for an idealized world affected his writing.

"SINGER'S SENSE OF INJUSTICE WOULD NOT ALLOW HIM TO CREATE AN IDEALIZED WORLD. ALL OF HIS WRITING, EVEN THAT WRITTEN SPECIFICALLY FOR CHILDREN, CONTAINS LINKS BETWEEN LOCAL CUSTOMS AND PROVINCIAL ATTITUDES WITHIN THE EVERYDAY LIVES OF SIMPLE PEASANTS AND THE CABALISTIC SPIRITUAL WORLD."

. . . I.

Isaac Singer won the Nobel Peace prize for his writing in 1978. By then he had received the Newbery Honors for *Zlateh the Goat and Other Stories,The Fearsome Inn* and *When Shlemiel Went to Warsaw* and was awarded the National Book Award in Children's Literature for *A Day of Pleasure*. Singer never won the coveted Newbery Award, and his Nobel Prize was not given to him because he was a children's author. As an author of adult literature prior to turning to children's literature, Singer won his Nobel Prize for "his impassioned narrative art which, with its roots in Polish-Jewish cultural tradition, brings universal human conditions to life" (Noble 162).

When asked what caused him to write about Poland, he reasoned: "the lost world is the world of my childhood, of my younger days. . . . We are bound to write about the things of our younger days and to remember them better than the things that happened yesterday or the day before. . . . I write about people from Poland—Yiddish-speaking Poles, Jews—I do this to be sure that I write about people I know best" (Teicholz 219–220). Singer left Poland when the country was on the ebb of war; it was not yet a country with the political practice of Jewish termination. He was a young man who had fathered a son and divorced his wife. Singer and his older brother Joseph, also a writer, chose to immigrate in the mid-thirties, and they settled in New York City.

Once in America, Isaac Singer did not immediately feel comfortable. His memories of a vibrant Jewish community with a rich heritage led him to have certain language and cultural expectations. Singer later explained: "When I came to this country I lived through a terrible disappointment. I felt then—more than I do now—that Yiddish had no future in this country. In Poland, Yiddish was still very much alive" (Blocker and Elman 14). Although he chose to emigrate to America over going to Israel or Russia, Singer remained an exiled Jew for the major part of his life. After visiting Singer in 1967, Melvin Naddocks observed:

> What a strange amalgam Singer is! Hunched over a 32-year-old Yiddish typewriter in New York City, in 1967, he writes of the Polish past—of dybbuks he does not believe in and of shetls (East European Jewish villages) long disappeared. By his own admission he writes "as if none of the terrible things that happened to the Jewish people during the last two decades really did occur." (33)

Singer is thus depicted as an alienated Jew who lives in his past, in a time prior to World War II, and who refuses to acknowledge that the people he left behind are truly dead.

Singer's fiction was first published in the *Jewish Daily Forward,* New York's Yiddish-language newspaper; throughout his career, Singer wrote in Yiddish. He once quipped: "Yiddish is a sick language because the young people don't speak it. And many consider it a dead language. But in our history between being sick and dying is a long way" (Anderson 101). Singer admitted in *A Little Boy in Search of God* that he was aware of injustice throughout his life:

> I had heard about the cruelties perpetrated by Chmielnicki's Cossacks. I had read about the Inquisition. I knew about the pogroms on Jews in Russia and Spain. I lived in a world of cruelty. I was tormented not only by the sufferings of men but by the sufferings of beasts, birds, and insects as well. Hungry wolves attacked lambs. Lions, tigers, and leopards had to devour other creatures or die from hunger. The squires wandered through forests and shot deer, hares, and pheasants for pleasure. I bore resentment against not only man but against God, too. . . . It was He who had made man a blood thirsty creature ready to do violence at every step. I was a child, but I had the same view of the world that I have today—one huge slaughterhouse, one enormous hell. (49)

Born in Radzymin, Poland, on July 14, 1904, Isaac Singer grew up hearing two kinds of stories. From his father, Rabbi Pinchos Menachem, he heard stories with a moral, stories about religious beliefs and practices. From his mother he heard tales "so pointless that you really could learn nothing from them" (*Children's Literature* 9). Although the expectations for their listeners were different, both parents would be considered to be excellent storytellers throughout Singer's life. Oral storytelling and community traditions became significant elements to Singer in his own storymaking. Often, during interviews, Singer would talk of his family's conversations about religion and of his parents' fear that he and his older brother were becoming too cosmopolitan. Both boys read secular novels and European philosophy that had been translated into Hebrew and Yiddish. When asked once if his parents approved of his writing fiction, Singer replied: "They considered all the secular writers to be heretics, all unbelievers.... Everybody who read such books sooner or later became a worldly man and forsook the traditions. In my family, of course, my brother had gone first, and I went after him. For my parents, this was a tragedy" (Blocker and Elman 13).

When Isaac Singer left Poland he chose to break with his rabbinical heritage, but he did not lose his belief in the Jewish traditions he grew up in or his need to be thought of as an Eastern European Jewish writer. At one point he explained the significant difference between western literature and Yiddish literature as one of characterization, noting that the western hero "is the Superman, the Prometheus character" while the Yiddish hero is "the little man. He's poor but proud, always struggling against his personal, financial, and political odds to maintain his dignity and status" (Flender 42–43). Singer never suggested that his stories were simple adaptations of the stories he learned as a child, but there are obvious strands of his childhood reading and his Jewish upbringing in his writing for children. Shlemiel is a prominent character in his stories, as are witches and spirits; many of the stories also take place in Chelm where the wise men live. Concerning those elements found in all of Singer's writing, Howard Scwartz commented:

> Singer was born into a rabbinic family in Leoncin, a village in Poland, in 1904 and grew up in Warsau, where he began his writing career in 1925. It is important to emphasize the crucial role played by his older brother ... in the career of his younger brother.
>
> Singer's emigration to the United States in 1935 and the subsequent destruction of the Polish Jewish communities by the Nazis in World War II created a situation in which he had to turn, of necessity, to his memory and imagination for subject matter. So great was his success that for many readers Singer's descriptions of life in prewar Poland form the basis for their conception of this period. To his detractors, Singer's character portraits . . . are overworked and exaggerated. But Singer has always emphasized the primary role of the imagination in his stories and novels. (184)

Singer liked to talk about his need to write beyond orthodoxy. In one interview he attested: "The truth is that the Yiddishists don't consider me a writer who writes in their tradition. Neither do I consider myself a writer in their tradition. I consider myself a writer in the Jewish tradition but not exactly the Yiddish tradition" (Howe 126). Singer maintained that stories are not universal creations, that each person's rendition is his own, and this gave his writing personal impetus: "After all, these folktales were invented by someone; the people did not tell them all.... I say to myself, 'I am a part of the folk myself. Why can't I invent stories?' ... Sometimes I hear a little story, a spark of a story, and then I make from the spark a fire" (*Children's Literature* 11). Efraim Sicher explains Singer's need for a personal sense of creativity within a Jewish folklore tradition as his haunting by a legendary dybbuk, "a wandering spirit of a deceased person who returns to fulfill some uncompleted task or undo a wrong" (56). As a folkloric figure, the dybbuk seeks *tikkum*. Sicher feels that *tikkum* forced Singer to "grapple with the past, with the unprecedented revelation of evil in the Holocaust." Thus, he reasons, Singer's creative freedom caused him to consider that "the demonic existed in the lost East European community of belief" and allowed him to "exorcise" his past through his writing, admitting his "schizophrenia" between his desire for spiritual perfection and acknowledgment of human defilement (57).

Singer hoped to keep his Jewish heritage intact. Once, in an interview, he argued: "If we reach a time when Yiddish and Yiddish customs and folklore are forgotten, Hitler will have succeeded not only physically but also spiritually.... I wish Yiddish could be as alive today as when I was a child and that there were many young talents writing in Yiddish" (Lottman 123). Because he lost those who remained behind in Poland, Singer was forced to recreate that other time and place, to resolve the loss of a spiritual and intellectual community.

Throughout his life, Singer tied reading and religion together. At one point he argued that one need not worry about the particular social system where one lived as much as why God "created the world the way it is," adding, "It's He who has caused all these troubles, and I often rebel against Him. But the fact that I rebel against Him shows that I believe in Him and I really do" (Anderson 106). Grace Farrell Lee observes,

> . . . while Singer fills his fiction with a wide variety of folk figures—comic angels and imps, maliciously demonic narrators, dream phantoms and apparitions—the significance of the demonic in his fiction is always related, not to traditional notions of sin and retribution, but to his major theme of exile and the problem of meaning. (32)

Singer's sense of injustice would not allow him to create an idealized world. All of his writing, even that written specifically for children, contains links between local customs and provincial attitudes within the everyday lives of simple peasants and the cabalistic spiritual world. Singer's children's literature falls into two categories: that built around the mundane events of a Yiddish Polish village and that inhabited by spirits. The mundane stories depict the Jewish peasants in the small village where as a teen he lived with his mother. This community is isolated and seems oblivious to the dangers without. Humor is often found in Singer's village. Yet, it is barbed humor, usually pointing out the foibles of blind trust and the worries of persecution from those who live just beyond the village, while relating the humorous escapades of a likable anti-hero.

In *Zlateh the Goat,* Singer writes: "Literature helps us remember the past with its many moods. To the storyteller yesterday is still here as are the years and the decades gone by.... For the writer and his readers all creatures go on living forever" (xi). Within this collection, logic is often misconstrued as simple faith in what one is told. Thus, in "Fool's Paradise," the lazy young hero determines he is dead because he hears of paradise, a place where one need not work or study. Singer explains:

> Since his old nurse had told Atzel that the only way to get to paradise was to die, he made up his mind to do just that as quickly as possible. He thought and brooded about it so much that soon he began to imagine that he was dead.... The family did everything possible to try to convince Atzel he was alive, but he refused to believe them. He would say, "Why don't you bury me? You see that I am dead. Because of you I cannot get to paradise." (6)

A great specialist is brought in, and he places Atzel in a chamber called "paradise" where Atzel is continually fed the same diet and not allowed to do a thing. Finally, Atzel asks when his family and his beloved will come. His servant replies that his father will come in five years. Then he observes that his sweetheart will not come for 50 years, adding, " . . . you know, my lord, that one cannot mourn forever. Sooner or later she will forget you, meet another young man, and marry. That's how it is with the living" (12). The young man resolves to return to earth, marries his sweetheart and later tells their children how a great doctor had cured him when he had lived in "fool's paradise" and how he returned to marry their mother. Singer ends: "But, of course, what paradise is really like, no one can tell" (16).

There are seven stories in this first collection; a wide range of main characters sit side-by-side within the small compilation. The foolish young man who believes himself dead represents all the village fools with impractical solutions to their obstacles, beloved because they helped those around them see the need for work or for traditions. The wise men of Chelm are later depicted discerning how to travel about the town without making tracks in the newly fallen snow, and they are representative of a collective logic that accepts solutions others would consider nonsensical. This is one of three stories from the book first published with Sendak's illustrations in *Commentary*. Later, Singer writes a tale of the devil and his wife tormenting young David, "a poor boy with a pale face and black eyes . . . alone with his baby brother on the first night of Hanukkah" (71), and he places the cosmic world of demonic spirits inside the ordinary peasant's "one-room hut, with a low ceiling and soot-covered walls" (71), later allowing the youngster to meet with them and trick them into returning his parents as he wanders outside, in the raging snowstorm. Interspersed throughout the collection is Singer's introduction of Shlemiel, a Hanukkah miracle story with a talking goat and a simpleton bridegroom, who learns from the Elder that his lengthy betrothal to a young woman in another town is hazardous: "The road between East Chelm and Chelm is fraught with all kinds of dangers, and that is why such misfortune occurs. The best thing to do is to have a quick marriage" (49).

In her book-length study of Singer's children's fiction, Alida Allison calls *Zlateh the Goat*

Singer's "standard" children's work, adding, "In it he demarcated and transmitted his lively world in full dimension, establishing from the first page ... the complexity and originality of his use of his native material" (31). When discussing his writing for children, Singer once commented: "In real life many of the people that I describe no longer exist, but to me they remain alive ... with their wisdom, their strange beliefs, and sometimes their foolishness" (Toothaker 532). While he was alive, Singer's writings were defined by Leo W. Schwarz as stories tied to "a pre-modern culture" and he concluded: "Singer has come to terms with himself; he is committed to the hallowing of man and life" (12)....

Source: Jill P. May, "Envisioning the Jewish Community in Children's Literature: Maurice Sendak and Isaac Singer," in *Journal of the Midwest Modern Language Association*, Vol. 33, No. 3, Autumn-Winter 2000, pp. 137–42.

Isaac Bashevis Singer

In the following interview, Singer explains his main source for writing: traditional folk tales.

Emanuel Goldsmith, author of *Architects of Yiddishism at the Beginning of the Twentieth Century,* has described Isaac Bashevis Singer as "one of the most remarkable authors who has ever lived ... wiry, inescapable style, an intensely personal, inimitable vision, a Machiavellian wit, but above all else, it is the bracing, revivifying character of his insights that makes him important."

Mr. Singer is a born story teller beloved both by children and adults because of the warm humor and wisdom of heart embodied in his writing.

Question (Q). Most folktales and fairytales were originally intended for adults. Through the years they have been abandoned to the children. What kinds of behavior do these tales try to teach and what is the effect of these teachings on children?

I. B. Singer (A). I don't believe that most of the fairytales and stories were created to teach people anything, and this is a good thing, because once a story is made to teach, one can foresee what it is going to say. Fairytales I admire most. You read a story and then when the story is ended you ask yourself what does it teach? What is it saying? You are bewildered by their pointlessness, but they are beautiful anyhow and I think that children love these kinds of stories.

"ONLY IF I SEE THAT THIS STORY HAS MY 'SEAL,' IT IS SORT OF, SAY, MY STORY, I WILL TELL IT. AND THIS IS THE REASON I WILL NOT JUST WRITE STORIES ABOUT ABSTRACT THINGS WHICH ANY OTHER WRITER MIGHT BE ABLE TO DO."

For example, my father used to tell me stories—religious kinds of stories—about a man who was a good man on this earth and then he died and went to Paradise. These kinds of stories used to bore me, because I knew already that the good people go to Paradise and the bad people are roasted in Hell. But sometimes my mother told me stories which were so pointless that you really could learn nothing from them. Let's say that a bear swallows three children or something like this and then they cut open his belly and the children go free. A story like this had no meaning, but it had beauty. In children's literature the writers of course can tell a story with a moral, but they should be careful not to be too much on the didactic side. The stories should have beauty in themselves. The great works of literature actually teach us nothing. What does *Madame Bovary* teach us? That a woman that was unfaithful to her husband commits suicide? We know that not all women who betray their husbands commit suicide or are killed. Many of them live to an old age. When Tolstoy wrote *Anna Karenina,* the story was the same. Anna also betrayed her husband and she also committed suicide. We learn actually from *Anna Karenina* nothing, for whatever we had to learn we could already have learned from *Madame Bovary*. But the story is beautiful anyhow. I think it is a great tragedy that modern writers have become so interested in messages that they forget that there are stories which are wonderful without a message; that the message isn't everything. I once said that if all the messages would disappear and only the Ten Commandments would be left, you would have enough messages for the next 10,000 years. It is not the message which is so important but the story itself. But many writers live today in a kind of amnesia. They forget that a story has an independent life. It can exist without a message, although a message is sometimes good for it, but only sometimes.

Q. Were you a writer or storyteller as a child? Who told stories to you when you were a child?

A. Well, first of all my father and mother were both excellent storytellers. They told us stories. I heard stories all the time. In addition I used to read what they used to call storybooks in Yiddish. These were little books which cost a penny apiece. I used to buy them. I said once that if I would have a million rubles—I would buy all these storybooks. Actually there were not enough storybooks to buy them for a million rubles; there were only maybe a few score. I read the stories of the famous Rabbi Nakhman of Bratzlav, a famous rabbi who was not only a great saint and a great Jewish scholar, but also a great poet, one of the most puzzling personalities who has ever lived. And he told stories which his disciple wrote down and these stories influenced me immensely. I would say that although he was a rabbi and a saint there was no message in his stories. His disciple said that those who know the Cabala will find out what the message is. Since I was not a great Cabalist then and I am not yet today, I love the stories by themselves. I never found any message in them, but they are most fantastic and wonderful. I am astonished that these stories are not yet made as literature for children. I intend, if it's possible, to write a kind of digest of them. I still love stories and readers always call me up, since my telephone is listed in the telephone book, and if they tell me they have a story to tell me, I say immediately, "Come up! I want to hear it." I still think that the story is the very essence of literature. When writers forget the art of storytelling, they forget literature. It's a great tragedy that writers have forgotten their main aim, that they have to tell stories.

Q. Will you please explain the origin of Yiddish folktales and do you take all your children's stories from Yiddish folktales?

A. I don't take all my stories from Yiddish folktales because I invent stories myself. After all, these folktales were invented by someone; the people did not tell them all. There was always a man who talked out the story and then it became a part of folklore. I would say I use both methods. If I find some that are beautiful folktales, especially those which were told to me by my mother and father, I would use them. And if not, I say to myself, "I am a part of the folk myself. Why can't I invent stories?" And, of course, I have invented a number of stories. Sometimes I hear a little story, a spark of a story, and then I make from the spark a fire. At least this is what I try to do. My mind is full of stories and to me the human history is actually an aggregation of millions of little stories. If a day passes in my life without a story, I am disappointed. But thank God, one way or another, the Almighty is always sending stories to me. As far as the origin of the stories, their origin is the human imagination. What else?

Q. In your lecture here a year ago, you stated that "Symbolism is not good for children because although by nature a child is a mystic, he is also by nature a realist." In what ways is a child a mystic and a realist, and how conscious are you of simplifying the symbolism for children for the sake of clarity as you put it?

A. As a rule every good story is symbolic and if it doesn't have a symbol, you can try to find a symbol or invent a symbol. Children have a great feeling for mysticism. They believe in the supernatural; they believe in God; they believe in angels; they believe in devils. They don't question you if you tell them a story which is connected with the supernatural. But children don't like nonsense. There are some writers who think that if they write a story which doesn't make any sense, just because it makes no sense it is full of symbols. Symbolism is often a wall behind which unable writers hide in order to make themselves important. I have seen many writers who think that a child can take nonsense, and it isn't true. A child will believe in the supernatural, but even in a supernatural story, the child wants logic and consistency. I once read a story where a man said that three little stones fell into a kettle and out came three little monkeys. The child just does not believe in these things. Although I am very much against Russia, I think that they are right about one thing: that writing nonsense and telling children things that are completely unbelievable is not good for the child's mind. Because although the child has less experience than the adult, the child has already a sense of logic and knows what makes sense and what doesn't make sense. Distortion of reality is not really symbolism. Distortion of reality is bad writing. Many of these little books which make no sense at all are doing damage to children's literature. First of all, a lot of people set out to write, because if you are not bound by any logic and by any consistency, everybody can be a writer. The child, good and independent reader that he is, is also a severe critic. The wonderful thing about children is that you cannot hypnotize a child to read a story because the author was a great man. You can tell him it was written by Shakespeare or by the Almighty himself, but the child does not care about authority. If the child doesn't like a story, the child will reject it immediately. The same thing is true about reviews. No child will read a story because it got good reviews. Children, thank God, don't read reviews. Of course, children don't care at all about advertising. If the story was advertised on the whole page of *The New York Times* it will not change the child's mind about the story. I wish that our adult readers would be as independent in this respect as the children are. And because they are great readers and independent readers and because they are not hypnotized by all this mish-mash, one should be very careful with them. One should never give them nonsense and say that this is symbolic. The great symbols don't come from nonsense but from sense. The stories from the Bible and the Book of Genesis are full of sense and at the same time highly symbolic.

Q. When asked why your stories for children always have happy endings you have been quoted as saying, "if I have to torture someone, I would rather torture an adult than a child." In what other specific ways do you alter your writing for children?

A. I try to give a happy ending to a story for a child because I know how sensitive a child is. If you tell a child that a murderer or a thief was never punished and never caught, the child feels that there is no justice in the world altogether. And I don't like children to come to this conclusion, at least not too soon.

Q. Many of your children's stories include traditional folk material from Jewish culture. Would you call yourself more of a storyteller or a story creator?

A. First of all the reason why they all come from Jewish tradition is that I believe literature must have an address. You cannot write a story just about people. When you tell a story to a child, "There was somewhere a king," the child would like to know where the king was. In Ireland, in Babylonia? The same thing is true about adult literature. Literature, more than any other art, must have an address. The more the story is connected with a group, the more specific it is, the better it is. Let's say we write a letter to Russia. First, you say it's to Russia. Then you have to say, what city? What part of Russia? What is the number of the house and so on and so on until you come to the specific person, and when you mail it, it will come right there to the intended person. The same thing in a way is true about literature. The more specific it is the more influence it has on a reader.

Q. Critic Marilyn Jurich argues that the nature of Yiddish folk humor is to urge acceptance. She says, "Change for the poor, oppressed, cannot be realized, not by the ordinary man. To urge change is to meet despair or destruction. Only deliverance is from God and the only joy is in experiencing God's presence in whatever peace is attainable." Do you feel this urging of acceptance is a characteristic of your writing for children?

A. I would say that all generalizations, especially about literature, are false. Of course, there may be such stories also, but to say that all Jewish stories are of this kind is false to me. By the way, I don't really understand exactly what she means by "accept." Of course, if we write a story we want it to be accepted. What is the meaning of the word "acceptance"? She wants the poor people to be accepted by the rich? You explain it to me; do you know what this critic is saying?

Q. Well, I think that she is saying by acceptance to accept that which is given to you, if it is suffering, to accept suffering. If it be fortune, to accept fortune.

A. I don't really try to teach my readers that they should accept all the troubles in the world. In other words, if there was a Hitler, they should accept Hitler. Actually the Jew has not accepted the badness of the world. It is a Christian idea that we should accept everything. I would say that a Jew, although he believes that everything is sent by God, he is also a man of great protest. Of rebellion. Fighting evil. And because of this to say that the Jewish story is of acceptance is kind of a generalization, which does not really jibe with our reality. We have never accepted neither Hitler nor Haman, none of the enemies of humanity. The opposite. We fought them. It is true that in the Hitler holocaust, the Jew who fought Hitler, was like a fly fighting a lion. But just the same it is not in our nature to be passive when the evil powers come out.

Q. What do you think about the study and criticism of children's literature in the universities?

A. I know that the universities teach writers who want to write for children and it's a wonderful thing; and I am very happy to see so many people here interested in this. But I really don't know enough about the universities to come to any generalization. I would say that wherever I go, people are interested. Children's literature is not anymore a stepchild of literature. It's becoming a very legal kind of literature. Of course, children's literature is still very young. One hundred years ago it almost did not exist. It did not exist among the Jewish people in my time. We didn't have such a thing as literature for children. I think that children's literature has a great future because it is still telling a story. In this respect it has never become ultra-modern.

Q. Some children's book experts believe in a prescribed vocabulary for children at various age levels. Your stories, even for the very young, contain much vocabulary that some might call too advanced for young children. How conscious are you of your vocabulary when writing for children?

A. I would say that if you don't remember all the time that a child is a child and you treat him as an adult, there is a good chance that the child will act like an adult; if not one hundred percent at least fifty percent or sixty percent. Because of this I am not very careful about using words which people think that the child will not understand. Of course, since I write in Yiddish sometimes these words in Yiddish may be more simple than they come out in English but I will say a child will not throw away a book because there are a few words that he does not understand. The opposite—the child will be intrigued and will look into a dictionary or it will ask the mother or the teacher what the word means. A child will throw away a book only if there is no story, if it doesn't make sense and is boring. Amongst the adults there is lately a theory that a good book has to be boring; that the greater a bore, the better writer he is; some writers even boast about it—how boring they are. The great masters tried their best to be easy and to be understood. Any child can read *Anna Karenina* or even *Madame Bovary* if it has a feeling for love and sex. So I am not afraid of difficult words.

Let's not forget about one hundred years ago, eighty years ago or even fifty years ago, whole generations were brought up on poetry. They were brought up on Pushkin and Byron. A book of poetry was in every house. Many young women and young men learned poetry by heart. But what happened to poetry now-a-days? It has become so erudite, so confused and so obscure, that people just stopped enjoying it. So now the biggest publishing company publishes a book of poetry in 800 copies and 500 are given away to reviewers and other poets. The poet of today began to speak to other poets. He speaks to nobody else. There is a great danger that this may happen to adult literature altogether. It will become so profound and so erudite that it will be like a crossword puzzle, only for pedantic minds who like to do these puzzles. I am often afraid that this may happen to children's literature. I know that it cannot happen, because the child will say, "No," in a big voice.

Q. In your discussion last year of the conditions necessary for you to write, you spoke of three things. You must have a plot, you must have a passion to write, and you must feel that you are the only one that can write that particular story. What special thing do you think that you have that you share with children?

A. I would say that I see to it that the stories which I tell the children no other writer would have told them. This does not mean that they are better than other stories. When you read a story by Andersen, you will know that this is not a Grimm story. It is an Andersen story. When you read a story by Chekov, you say this is not a Maupassant story, but a Chekov story. The real writer manages to put his seal on his work. He tells you a story which others cannot tell. Only if I see that this story has my "seal," it is sort of, say, my story, I will tell it. And this is the reason I will not just write stories about abstract things which any other writer might be able to do. A Russian story must be Russian and a French story must be French. You may be an internationalist, you may be cosmopolitan, you may think that all the nations are clannish and we should unite. But when it comes to literature, you cannot really move away from the group and its culture.

When I write a story, whether it's adult or for children, I have to say, "This is my story."

Source: Issac Bashevis Singer, "Isaac Bashevis Singer on Writing for Children," in *Children's Literature*, Vol. 6, 1977, pp. 9–16.

SOURCES

"Alien Presences," in *Times Literary Supplement* (London, England), September 20, 1974, p. 993.

Biletzky, Israel Ch., *God, Jew, Satan in the Works of Isaac Bashevis-Singer*, University Press of America, 1995, pp. 6–7.

Blocker, Joel, and Richard Elman, "An Interview with Isaac Bashevis Singer," in *Isaac Bashevis Singer: Conversations*, edited by Grace Farrell, University Press of Mississippi, 1992, p. 13; originally published in *Commentary*, November 1963, pp. 364–72.

Farrell, Grace, "Chronology," in *Isaac Bashevis Singer: Conversations*, edited by Grace Farrell, University Press of Mississippi, 1992, pp. xix–xxx.

"Jewish Population in the United States, 2007," in *Mandell L. Berman Institute North American Jewish Data Bank*, http://www.jewishdatabank.org/ajyb.asp (accessed October 20, 2009).

Kazin, Alfred, "The Atheist Who Hears God's Voice," in *New York Times Book Review*, November 4, 1973, p. 1.

Margolis, Max L., and Alexander Marx, *A History of the Jewish People*, Temple, 1975.

Michnik, Adam, "Poles and the Jews: How Deep the Guilt," in *New York Times*, March 17, 2001, http://www.nytimes.com/2001/03/17/arts/poles-and-the-jews-how-deep-the-guilt.html?n=Top/Reference/Times%20Topics/People/W/Walesa,%20Lech (accessed October 20, 2009).

"Poland," in *CIA: World Factbook*, https://www.cia.gov/library/publications/the-world-factbook/geos/pl.html (accessed October 20, 2009).

"Poland," in *Encyclopaedia Judaica*, Vol. 13, Keter, 1972, pp. 736–37.

Prescott, P. S., Review of *A Crown of Feathers and Other Stories*, in *Newsweek*, November 12, 1973, p. 113.

Sarna, Jonathan D., and Jonathan Golden, "The American Jewish Experience in the Twentieth Century: Antisemitism and Assimilation," in *National Humanities Center*, http://nationalhumanitiescenter.org/tserve/twenty/tkeyinfo/jewishexp.htm (accessed October 20, 2009).

Singer, Isaac Bashevis, "The Recluse," in *A Crown of Feathers and Other Stories*, Farrar, Straus, and Giroux, 1973, p. 228.

———, "The Son from America," in *A Crown of Feathers and Other Stories*, Farrar, Straus, and Giroux, 1973, pp. 102–109.

Slutsky, Carolyn, "Poland Selects New Chief Rabbi," in *Jewish Times*, January 8, 2005, http://www.polish-jewish-heritage.org/eng/05-01_Polan_Selects_New_Chief_Rabbi.htm (accessed October 18, 2009).

Telushkin, Joseph, "Kaddish, a Memorial Prayer in Praise of God," in *My Jewish Learning*, http://www.myjewishlearning.com/life/Life_Events/Death_and_Mourning/Burial_and_Mourning/Kaddish.shtml (accessed October 21, 2009).

"United States of America," in *Encyclopaedia Judaica*, Vol. 15, Keter, 1972, pp. 1595–1616.

FURTHER READING

Farrell, Grace, ed., *Critical Essays on Isaac Bashevis Singer*, G. K. Hall, 1996.

This is a collection of six reviews and thirteen essays about all aspects of Singer's work. It includes an introduction by Farrell in which she reviews the critical reception of Singer's work.

Hadda, Janet, *Isaac Bashevis Singer: A Life*, Oxford University Press, 1997.

Hadda is a psychoanalyst and Yiddish scholar. In this detailed although not especially flattering portrait of Singer, she explores his life and work and some of the contradictions and complexities of his personality.

Howe, Irving, *World of Our Fathers: The Journey of the East European Jews to America and the Life They Found and Made*, rev. ed., Shocken, 1990.

Howe was a distinguished literary critic and left-wing intellectual who also played a role in introducing Yiddish literature to America. In this book he tells the story of the more than two million Jewish immigrants who came from Eastern Europe to the United States during the period from the 1880s to the 1920s. He explains what conditions they lived in when they arrived and how they tried to preserve their Jewish culture while adapting to life in their new country.

Malin, Irving, *Isaac Bashevis Singer*, Frederick Ungar, 1972.

This is a very useful, concise guide to Singer's work up until 1970. It includes a chapter on the short stories. Malin argues that Singer's short stories are superior to his novels and provides analyses of several of the major stories.

Sorry, Right Number

STEPHEN KING

1987

"Sorry, Right Number" has the distinction of being one of the few stories by Stephen King to be published in the form of a script. It was originally written for *Amazing Stories*, a television series created and produced by Steven Spielberg, and was eventually produced by George Romero and Richard Rubenstein to be broadcast on November 22, 1987, as an episode of their series *Tales from the Darkside*. King published it along with twenty-four other stories in his 1993 story collection *Nightmares and Dreamscapes*.

The story, in typical King fashion, postulates happens to ordinary people who find themselves beset by unexplainable circumstances. Katie Weiderman, the wife of a successful horror novelist, receives a phone call one evening from a woman who is nearly hysterical with fear and unable to talk. When the line goes dead, Katie is left with only one certainty: that the voice on the phone belonged to someone related to her. Throughout the rest of the story, she and her husband try to contact all of her female relatives before the tragedy that inevitably strikes. The story is told with humor and yet is fraught with suspense, weaving in elements that readers have come to expect from one of the most popular authors of all time.

AUTHOR BIOGRAPHY

King was born on September 21, 1947, in Portland, Maine. He began writing at a young age, creating

Stephen King (*AP Images*)

his first character, Mr. Rabbit Trick, around the age of six. When he was nine, he wrote for *Dave's Rag*, a newspaper published by his older brother. King attended Lisbon High School from 1962 to 1966. While there, he published his first short story, "I Was a Teenage Grave Robber," in *Comics Review*. He started college at the University of Maine in 1966 and graduated from there with a bachelor of arts degree in English in 1970. In 1967, he was paid for his fiction for the first time, selling his story "The Glass Floor" to *Startling Mystery Stories* for thirty-five dollars. He also wrote a regular column, "King's Garbage Truck," for the college newspaper.

The year after he graduated from college, King married Tabitha Spruce. Their first child was born later that year. King took a job teaching English at Hampden Academy in Hampden, Maine, where he worked for two years. In 1973, he sold his first novel, *Carrie*, for twenty-five hundred dollars. Later that year, New American Library bought the paperback rights to *Carrie* for four hundred thousand dollars, and he quit teaching to become a full-time writer.

Since then, King has published a novel a year, on average, with unprecedented commercial success, often writing under the pseudonym Richard Bachman. He was the author of seven of the twenty-five books that *Publishers Weekly* listed as the best selling books of the 1980s. Estimates of how many books he has sold run in the range of 350 to 400 million. He has won several Bram Stoker Awards from the Horror Writers Association, and in 1996, he won the O. Henry Award for Short Fiction for "The Man in the Black Suit." In 2003, he was recognized for his contributions to genre fiction and to fiction writing in general with a Lifetime Achievement Award from the Horror Writers Association and a National Book Foundation Medal for Distinguished Contribution to American Letters.

On the afternoon of June 19, 1999, King nearly died when, walking along a country road while reading a book, he was struck by a van. He suffered multiple broken bones and a collapsed lung. After weeks in the hospital and five operations, he returned home, but his injuries left him unable to sit up and write. In 2002, he announced his retirement from writing, claiming frustration with his impaired condition and a dwindling imagination. He was back in 2008, however, with a collection of short stories, *Just after Sunset*, and a new novel, *Duma Key*. In recent years, he has also written for graphic novels and published poems. His son, Joe Hill, is also a novelist in the horror genre.

PLOT SUMMARY

Act 1

The first act of "Sorry, Right Number" begins in the Weiderman house. Katie Weiderman, the family's mother, is on the telephone in the kitchen, talking with her sister Lois. In the living room, the three children are watching the television. An argument ensues among the children. Thirteen-year-old Dennis and ten-year-old Connie plan to watch the same situation comedies they watch every week, but their younger brother, Jeff, wants to watch the movie *Ghost Kiss*, which is based on the first book published by their father, now a famous author. Jeff suggests that they can videotape the movie, but his siblings are planning to use the videocassette recorder (VCR) to tape the news for their mother. Jeff is deeply bothered, and the others taunt him for it, joking that he might commit suicide in his duress. The conversation ends when Dennis suggests that Jeff can

MEDIA ADAPTATIONS

- This story, along with others from King's collection *Nightmares and Dreamscapes*, is read on the compact disc collection *Sorry, Right Number and Other Stories*, a 2009 Simon and Schuster audiobook featuring Stephen King, Joe Montegna, and Joe Morton.
- This story was originally produced on the *Tales from the Dark Side* television series as part of the show's fourth season. It was directed by John Harrison. The episode aired in 1987, with Deborah Harmon in the starring role as Katie Weiderman. That production is available on videotape and DVD on *Tales from the Dark Side, Volume 4*, from Worldvision Home Video.
- A film of this script was made by director and writer Brian Berkowitz, with Darrin Stevens, Karla Droege, and Barbara Weetman in the key roles. *Sorry, Right Number* appeared in theaters in 2005. It is not available on video, but it can be viewed online at http://www.spike.com/video/sorry-right-number/2731005.

probably tape the movie on the television in their father's study, down in the basement. He leaves, passing by his mother just as she calls for the children to be quiet. Jeff tells her that they will be quiet now.

In the basement office, Bill Weiderman is sitting at his word processor. He is trying to write but is blocked, and the screen is blank. Jeff sneaks up and jumps at him to surprise him, but Bill shrugs it off; he is in the business of writing scary things, he explains, and so does not scare easily. Jeff asks him to tape *Ghost Kiss*, but Bill does not think a child of Jeff's age should be watching such violent material. Still, he takes Jeff up to the kitchen to ask Katie where they might find a blank videotape.

As they enter, the second phone line rings. Katie puts Lois on hold to answer that line. On the other end is a woman who sobs, "Take … please take. … " The woman is crying too hard to speak clearly, and after a few more disjointed words the line goes dead.

Katie is certain the caller was her sixteen-year-old daughter Polly, who has recently gone away to school. She rummages around to find Polly's telephone number, blaming Bill for sending the girl away to school when she is too young. The number is in a book Bill carries with him, so Katie dials it. The phone is answered in Polly's dormitory by another girl, who goes looking for Polly, leaving the line dead for a moment while Katie becomes increasingly frantic. When Polly comes on the line, though, she assures her mother that she is having a good time: She is doing well in her classes, and a popular boy asked her to an upcoming dance. She is happy.

Katie is still worried, feeling sure that the caller was someone in her family. She dials her mother, who tries to engage her in small talk before Katie hurriedly says she is ill and hangs up. The only other family member it could be is her sister Dawn, but Dawn's phone number is busy. Bill calls the operator, to ask her to cut into Dawn's phone conversation, but the operator recognizes his name and wants to talk about his novels instead. When Bill does get her to focus and try Dawn's line, the operator tells him that there is no conversation, that the phone is off the hook.

Bill and Katie decide to drive out to the country house where Dawn lives. She has a newborn daughter, but her husband is out of town on business. Act 1 ends with a close-up of the telephone in the Weidermans' kitchen, "looking like a snake ready to strike."

Act 2

As the second act begins, the Weidermans' car approaches Dawn's farmhouse. When Bill takes out a pistol, Katie is surprised; he kept it a secret, Bill explains, because he did not want to frighten her or the children, but he is in fact licensed to carry it. The suspense builds when they reach the front door and find scratches on the lock, indicating that someone has tampered with it. The door is unlocked, and the television is loud.

Bill enters first, leading with his gun, but relaxes when he sees Dawn sleeping on the couch with her son Justin on her lap. She does not notice them because she is listening to a portable stereo and wearing headphones. When Bill wakes her, she explains that the damage to the door was done by her husband Jerry, who had locked himself out the previous week. She did not phone Katie earlier that evening, having been completely exhausted by the baby. Katie phones the children to let them know that their aunt is fine. On the way home, she apologizes for being so needlessly worried, but Bill admits that he had been worried too, despite what he had told Jeff earlier about his job making him immune to fright.

Bill tucks Jeff into bed, promising to tape the rest of *Ghost Kiss* for him. He returns to his study to watch the rest of the movie, even though Katie tries to persuade him to go to bed. Before she goes to bed herself, she repeats her certainty that the voice on the phone was someone from her family. Katie wakes in the middle of the night to find that Bill has not come to bed yet. She goes down to the study to find him in his chair, dead.

After Bill's funeral, the gravedigger who tamps dirt onto his grave reflects that his wife was sorry to hear that Bill had died of a heart attack, though the gravedigger himself did not care for his type of writing.

A title card identifies the next scene as taking place five years later. The family stands outside a church. The wedding march plays; Polly is the bride. Katie is accompanied by her new husband, Hank. Polly apologizes to her stepfather for unspecified behavior problems that she displayed over the previous years.

Later, at home, Katie sits in the study, which has been redecorated; Bill's framed book jackets have been removed and replaced with pictures of buildings Hank designed. When Hank comes in to call her to bed, Katie explains that Polly's wedding was five years to the day since Bill's death. When he leaves, she turns on the television, only to find that a station is broadcasting *Ghost Kiss* that night.

Moved by the coincidence, Katie cries uncontrollably. She bumps the side table and knocks the telephone to the floor, she hears Bill's voice, asking who she would call if it were not too late. Katie dials the phone. Her old self answers, and she speaks the disjointed dialog that she heard five years earlier. Just as the line goes dead, she blurts out that Bill needs to go to the hospital because he is on the verge of a heart attack, but she says it too late.

She tries to recall the old telephone number, and the scene cuts to Bill, in the kitchen, telling the number of the Weiderman house to the operator who is going to cut into Dawn's line. When Katie finishes dialing, a recorded message tells her that the number is no longer in service. Katie throws the telephone across the room in frustration, and stage directions indicate that the camera inches up to the phone, making it look ominous. The screen fades to black.

CHARACTERS

Dawn

Katie Weiderman's younger sister Dawn has an infant son, Justin. Dawn lives in an isolated farmhouse with her husband Jerry, who is out of town on business at the time of the story. Bill and Katie are worried when Dawn does not answer her phone, and they are even more worried to find that the lock of her house has been damaged and the door is unlocked, but Dawn has explanations for all of these oddities. The phone was knocked off of its receiver by the toddler, and Dawn, exhausted by playing with her son all day, did not hear the Weidermans approach because she fell asleep with earphones. She is apologetic about the trouble they went through but remains dazed when they wake her, unable to concentrate on the situation because her child has worn her down.

Frieda

Frieda is a girl who lives at Hartshorn Hall with Polly Weiderman. She answers the communal phone with a racy joke and is embarrassed to hear that it is Katie, the mother of one of her dorm mates, calling.

Hank

Hank is Katie Weiderman's new husband, having married her at some unspecified time in the five years since Bill's death. He is much like Bill in his work habits, putting up pictures of buildings he designed where Bill had framed book covers and using the same study for his work. While Bill was suffering from writer's block, however, Hank thinks he might be kept awake while new ideas race through his mind.

The story hints that there has been trouble between Hank and the Weidermans' oldest daughter, Polly. By the time of Polly's wedding, though, the trouble is past. Polly apologizes, and Hank dismisses her apology because he does not take whatever she said to him or about him personally. He understands that he was viewed as a person coming in to take her father's place, and he does not blame her for her anger.

The Operator

The operator is a Bill Weiderman fan who Bill happens to reach while trying to contact Dawn. Katie is worried because her sister Dawn's line is busy, so Bill thinks to call the telephone company to break into Dawn's line. The operator who he gets on the line recognizes his name. While the

Weidermans are anxious about Dawn's well-being, the operator wastes time trying to engage Bill in a conversation about his works, until he just ends up hanging up on her in midsentence.

Bill Weiderman

Bill Weiderman is a forty-four-year-old horror writer, the author of popular books with titles such as *Ghost Kiss*, *Spider Doom*, and *Night of the Beast*. At the time of this story, however, he is struggling to come up with another idea for a new book, sitting in front of a blank computer screen until he can think up something to write. He is self-conscious about being a hack writer, using the banal expression "through a veil of shimmering tears" twice while drawing attention to it as something a hack writer would say.

Because he writes about scary subjects, Bill is not easily frightened, as he explains when his young son jumps out at him unexpectedly. When his wife Katie explains the frantic phone call she received, Bill stays calm, although throughout the story he becomes increasingly concerned. The fact that he has secretly bought a pistol and brings it to Dawn's house shows that he has always had the capacity to be fearful and that the current situation scares him. Later on the night of the phone call, he is found dead in his chair, having succumbed to a heart attack.

Connie Weiderman

Connie is ten years old at the start of this story. She joins with her brother Dennis in tormenting their younger brother, Jeff. Connie does not seem to take pleasure in picking on Jeff until he corrects her, telling him that he does not like being called "Jeffie"; then, she repeats the name over and over to antagonize him. Tormenting Jeff does not interest her, though, and she drifts away from arguing with him to stare at the television show, losing interest in Jeff's concerns.

Dennis Weiderman

Thirteen-year-old Dennis is the oldest Weiderman child living at home. He bullies his eight-year-old brother, Jeff, who he feels is being a bother when he wants to watch television. From their conversation and from King's stage directions, readers can tell that Dennis would not be shy about hitting his brother just to establish his own superiority.

Jeff Weiderman

Jeff, the youngest Weiderman, is eight years old. His siblings take advantage of his age and treat him poorly. When he wants to watch a movie based on one of his father's books, they will not let him use the television. His aunt questions whether he is old enough to watch such a gory movie, but his parents assure her that the television network will remove the more violent images before broadcasting it.

Jeff shares with his father an interest in the macabre. He is the only one in the house interested in watching the movie of Bill's novel. When he approaches Bill in his study, Jeff tries to startle him, in keeping with the spirit of Bill's horror writing. He has a good relationship with his parents and goes to them when his brother and sister pick on him.

Katie Weiderman

Katie Weiderman is the protagonist of this story. She is happily married to a prominent writer of horror stories, and she feels confident that he will be able to overcome the writer's block that is troubling him. Katie is focused on her husband and four children, as well as the extended family of her mother and two sisters. She is on the phone with her sister Lois at the start of "Sorry, Right Number." She is convinced that the mysterious phone call is from someone related to her, so she calls her daughter, her mother, and her younger sister. She has to look up the phone numbers for Polly and Dawn (she does not know them by heart), but they have both recently moved.

Katie's anxiety about the mysterious phone call is intensified by her anxiety about seeming foolish to her husband. She does not know what he would do in a difficult and potentially dangerous situation such as an invader terrorizing her sister, and she is surprised to find that Bill has bought and registered a gun, which he kept a secret so as not to worry her. When they find out that Dawn is all right, Bill tries to convince Katie that the voice she heard only seemed to be that of a family member, but she remains firm in her conviction; despite all evidence, and having eliminated any possible family members, she is certain that her feeling about the voice is true.

After Bill's death, Katie marries Hank in a fairly short span of time. The story indicates that she was already with him while Polly was working out her feelings about losing her father. Katie stays in the house she shared with Bill, replacing Bill's things in the study with Hank's things, although the chair that Bill died in is still there. None of the other characters notices that the day of Polly's marriage is the day of Bill's death, and Katie, who is acutely aware of it, does not tell them. In the end, she is so emotional that given a chance to talk to the past and avert Bill's heart attack, she is too choked up to spit out her warning until the line is dead.

Polly Weiderman

Polly is the Weidermans' sixteen-year-old daughter who has recently been sent away to Bolton, a prep school. She has two important scenes in this story. When Katie, her mother, is certain that someone in her family has phoned her in distress, her call to Polly's dormitory is delayed when another girl answers the phone and goes to find Polly, increasing the tension. Polly turns out to be fine, though. She is doing well in her classes and a boy she likes has asked her out to the Harvest Ball. "I'm so all right that if one more good thing happens to me today, I'll probably blow up like the *Hindenburg*," Polly tells her mother.

Five years after her father's death, at her wedding, Polly apologizes to her mother's new husband. King implies that she acted out against her mother dating and remarrying. Whatever bothered Polly about Hank is forgotten, though, implying that her bad feelings toward him arose from the situation they were in, not from anything that he did. Polly's apology shows that she has grown up enough to see him now for who he is and not just as a substitute for her father.

THEMES

Fear

"Sorry, Right Number" is at heart a suspense story, and as such it relies on elevating the reader's feelings of anxiety. The mysterious call Katie Weiderman receives at the beginning of the story is not just strange, it is terrifying. The sound of a woman crying would be disconcerting to anyone, and King makes it even more terrifying by making the voice that is crying familiar to Katie, but not familiar enough for her to know whose voice it is. Katie's uncertainty fuels the reader's fear, and the suspense builds as the story progresses.

King uses the comfortable domestic setting to amplify Katie's fear. As soon as she hangs up from hearing a person in panic, Katie is faced with her children. They are oblivious to her experience, and Katie does what she can to keep them from knowing about her fear. She struggles to project a sense of calmness, though they can sense that something is the matter. She later apologizes to Bill for being "a hysterical idiot," and Bill, who previously told Jeff that his job as a horror writer made him immune to fear, admits that he was scared for Dawn's safety as well.

The story's worst tragedies occur when characters are no longer afraid. Bill dies in the night, alone, sitting comfortably in an easy chair. Katie makes the frantic phone call to the past in a reflective moment after Polly's wedding, when she is alone. In both cases, the movie of Bill's story *Ghost Kiss* is on the television, showing a distinction between scary fiction stories and the fear that comes from real-life vulnerability. In this story, as in King's other works, bad things do not happen to fearful people, they happen to the people who least expect them.

Supernatural

There are two major supernatural elements in this story. One is Katie Weiderman's absolute certainty that the voice she has heard on the other end of the phone is someone related to her. Bill feels that this hunch of hers can be explained as a naturally occurring event, likening it to an ordinary case of mistaken identity. "There are sound-alikes as well as look-alikes," he tells her, trying to convince her that the feeling she has, while unusual, is not really all that strange. Katie is resolute, however. She cannot explain why she thinks it is someone related to her, but she is absolutely convinced that she is just somehow capable of knowing that it is.

The other supernatural element is the driving force for the entire story, its reason for existing: the phone call that the present receives from the future. King does not have any character explain this link out loud. He does not offer viewers of a television or film version any reason for what has happened, but he does have the stage notes explain this impossible occurrence to people reading "Sorry, Right Number" as a printed text. "On some level," he says, Katie "understands that the depth of her grief has allowed a kind of telephonic time-travel." King does not explain how grief could cause this; he leaves it as an unexplained, supernatural event, which readers must accept if they are going to accept the story.

Psychological Realism

One element that critics often mention about King's writing is his ability to maintain psychological realism in his stories, even when they are based on fantastic, other-worldly premises. In

TOPICS FOR FURTHER STUDY

- Suppose you could reach out to the past with a text message or Tweet. Prepare the briefest message you can think of with instructions that you would give yourself of five years ago. Make sure to include the single most important piece of information you would like your former self to know.
- Find a picture of the kind of telephone King describes in this story. Draw or paint your interpretation of it, making it look ominous. Explain to your class what artistic techniques you used to achieve the sinister effect.
- Read Edgar Allan Poe's classic short story "Ligeia," about a man who mourns the loss of his true love and how he compares her to his new wife. Write a comparison essay between that story and "Sorry, Right Number," pointing out ways in which King can be considered a literary descendant of Poe.
- Rewrite this story, with Katie from the future contacting one of the other characters on the phone, instead of herself. Track how that character would respond, what steps he or she would take to find out who had called, and whether or not that character's actions would prevent Bill's death.
- Read four or five traditional stories from other cultures, such African or Native American tribes, that concern dead people communicating from beyond the grave. After comparing the ways these stories have their ghosts present themselves, write a paper in which you explain why King did not just have Bill's ghost appear to Katie directly, or at least why Bill did not call her himself on the telephone that can transcend time.
- Choose another of Stephen King's short stories. Using "Sorry, Right Number" and your other choice write a short essay that describes the reasons you think Stephen King has been so popular with readers of all ages. Be specific in your discussion of theme, style, and character development.

Carrie, for instance, a high school introvert develops telekinetic powers; in *The Stand*, almost all of civilization has been destroyed; in *It*, an unidentified entity murders children; in the award-winning short story "The Man in the Black Suit," a boy meets a man who turns out to be the devil incarnate. Despite the stretches of reality in these basic premises, King's characters always respond to the situations in realistic ways. The strangeness of events in his stories does not affect the reality of his characters' emotions.

This realism can be seen frequently in "Sorry, Right Number." One example is Katie's embarrassment about calling attention to what she feels without a doubt to be true. She honestly believes that the voice on the other end of the phone is someone she is related to, someone who is in danger, but she alternates between panic and self-doubt. Bill has the same kind of ambivalence. He proves to have been worried about his family's safety long before the start of this story, when he bought and licensed his pistol, but the current dilemma forces him to face his doubts. King also implies an interesting psychological conflict between Polly and her stepfather, Hank, but he does not explore it in the story. Readers learn about the tension between them only after it has been settled, when Polly tells Hank, at her wedding, "I'm sorry I was a creep for so long." The tension between a girl whose father has died and the man who arrives to replace him is so common that King has no reason to explore it further than this one line, since readers are likely to recognize the situation.

Creative Process

"Sorry, Right Number" does not give a specific cause for Bill Weiderman's heart attack, but it

A phone call makes the story. *(Image copyright Benjamin Mercer, 2009. Used under license from Shutterstock.com)*

does show him to be carrying a burden that goes beyond the events of the story. He is a creative writer who cannot create anything new. In the story's first line of dialog, Katie makes light of this while on the phone with her sister Lois, telling her that Bill is going through an ordinary cycle in his writing process, a phase that includes being overly worried about his own health. His inability to create is confirmed later, when Jeff goes to see Bill in his study and finds him staring at a blank computer screen. The fact that the film adaptation of his first novel, *Ghost Kiss*, plays on television on this night only serves to remind Bill of the promise he once had, making his inability to write more bitter.

On the night of his heart attack, Bill does not go to bed along with Katie because he wants to remain in his study, in case an idea might come to him. One of the last things she says to him is how tired he looks. By the time she finds out that anything is wrong with him, he is already dead. King implies that the inability to write could be a cause of his heart attack, as much as the stress of racing to Dawn's house, thinking she was in danger.

King highlights Bill's inability to write by contrasting it with Hank's productivity. Hank has taken Bill's place in the family and in the basement office, replacing Bill's personal effects with his own. Hank is still productive and vital, in contrast to Bill, who died while he was experiencing writer's block.2

STYLE

Script

The fact that King intends "Sorry, Right Number" to be read as a story is clear from the author's note that precedes it, explaining the conventions that script writers use to a general audience that he assumes would be unfamiliar with such techniques. The abbreviations that he describes are not so complex that his reader could not translate them with just a little thought, as King points out by saying, "Probably most of you knew all that stuff to begin with, right?" By addressing the reader directly, King uses the author's note to bridge the gap between script and story.

Being presented in script form creates several distinct effects for "Sorry, Right Number." For one thing, there is very little visual description, since most decisions about how this story should look would be relegated to the hands of costume designers, set designers, and lighting experts. When King does give descriptions in the stage notes, they are for aspects that are necessary for developing the character's inner personality. His stage notes also provide clues to the character's feelings, with notes such as "Her face is filled with an agonizing mixture of hope and fear. If only she can have one more chance to pass the vital message on, it says." In a conventional short story, it would be the author's responsibility to describe just how such feelings manifest themselves on a face, but writing in script format allows King to leave that to the discretion of the actor who would be playing Katie.

Anthropomorphism

Anthropomorphism is the literary technique of giving inanimate objects qualities that are normally associated with humans. Near the end of this story, King directs the camera to move in toward the telephone in an extreme close-up, until it seems that the camera view is going right inside the holes in the phone's earpiece. For the very last camera shot of the story, King's direction repeats the extreme close-up, describing the phone as looking "somewhat ominous." The story does not say that the phone is alive or that it holds malicious intentions, or how it could be so, but these camera angles imply that it is capable of human intentions.

Predestination Paradox

A predestination paradox is created when a fictional character has foreknowledge of an event or outcome and tries to avoid it, but to no avail. A paradox is an impossible or contradictory situation, and trying to avoid a fated, or predestined, situation is impossible. It is a technique that goes back to the dramas written by the ancient Greeks, who often used oracles to warn characters about the fates that lay in store for them. A well-known example is the prophesy that Oedipus would kill his father and marry his mother, which, despite actions to prevent it, is exactly what he ends up doing.

In "Sorry, Right Number," Bill and Katie Weiderman know that someone is in trouble, and they do what they can to stop it. They are hindered by the fact that it is an incomplete prophesy: although Katie is sure that the person in trouble is a family member, they do not know who the caller is or the nature of the problem she faces. They do not even know that the mysterious call is a prophesy of the future until Katie pieces together what has happened in the last scene. Still, the story is driven by the fact that readers know the call will have some serious impact on the characters, even when its relevance is not clear.

HISTORICAL CONTEXT

Gothic Roots

By the time this story was published, King was well on his way to becoming the best-selling horror fiction writer of all time. Horror, as a genre, has had a long history, and like other popular genres, it has often been considered inferior writing. Its roots are usually traced back to British author Horace Walpole's 1764 Gothic novel *The Castle of Otranto*, which set in place many conventions that were to be associated with Gothic writing in the years to come, including castles with hidden chambers, ancestral curses, heroines in distress, and a not-always-faint hint of sexual cruelty. The British Gothic was brought to America in 1789 in *Wieland or, The Transformation: An American Tale*, by Charles Brockden Brown. Brown's novel, about a man driven to madness by a ventriloquist, started a strain of psychological realism that came to be associated with American horror writing. This tradition was carried on through Edgar Alan Poe in the early nineteenth century and by minor works of the American romantic writers, such as Herman Melville and Nathaniel Hawthorne, while the British romantics who dabbled in Gothicism—Keats, Shelley, Byron, and especially Mary Wollstonecraft Shelley, who published *Frankenstein* in 1818—generally focused on the external reality of the horror story.

In the twentieth century, literary Gothic writing continued in America, particularly in Southern literature, with writers such as William Faulkner, Flannery O'Connor, and Carson McCullers using exaggerated settings, extreme character traits, and physical abnormalities to explore ideas about the human condition. Horror writing developed a separate strain of popular fiction. In the late nineteenth and early twentieth centuries, there developed several popular genres, such as horror, science fiction, crime or detective writing, romance, and fantasy. These categories of genre fiction are marked by their distinctly nonliterary character. They were written and published because they sold well, and they sold well because their readers could dive into formulaic, unchallenging stories. Readers were familiar with the conventions that writers used and certain that they could be engrossed in gripping tales without being asked to question their own values. Pulp horror magazines of the 1920s and 1930s, such as the still existing and still influential *Weird Tales*, published content by hundreds of writers, many of them forgotten today. Some of these writers went on to establish names for themselves in other genres, as Robert Bloch did in the field of mystery or suspense and Ray Bradbury did in science fiction.

Horror Fiction in the Electronic Media Era

With the popularity of television in the 1950s, horror writing became more specialized and complex. The audience that had read works for simple amusement was satisfied with watching whatever was on, and some people lost interest in reading entirely. At the same time, though, television provided a training ground for writers such as Rod Serling, Richard Matheson, and Charles Beaumont, who earned their pay from writing scripts

COMPARE & CONTRAST

- **1987:** A home with a business in it might install a two-line telephone, so that personal calls can be answered at the same time that business is being transacted.

  Today: Cell phones are so common that many homes do without a house telephone line, instead opting for a separate phone for each member of the family.

- **1987:** A girl like Polly, away from her family for the first time, has to wait until the communal telephone in her dorm is available until she can tell them good news about her grades or dating prospects.

  Today: Polly could use e-mail, text, Twitter, Facebook, or several other methods to send messages to her family.

- **1987:** Most households watch broadcast television, which is censored to remove graphic content.

  Today: Most American households receive cable or satellite television. Movies shown on premium channels are run in their original theatrical form, without editing.

- **1987:** To capture a television broadcast on tape, Bill Weiderman must use his VCR, which is not reliable. Programming the start and stop times is difficult, and the tape often runs out.

  Today: Digital video recorders that are built into cable boxes take their programming directly from the cable guide, and they have the capacity to record hundreds of hours of broadcasts.

- **1987:** A movie such as Bill Weiderman's *Ghost Kiss* shows on television only once in a while. People interested in seeing it have to wait until it is broadcast or go to the store to rent a tape of it.

  Today: DVDs of movies can be rented or purchased and delivered to one's door the next day. Movies are also available on the Internet as streaming video or for download.

---

and then used the storytelling skills they developed in their own fiction. Serling's *The Twilight Zone* and the similar *The Outer Limits*, as well as *Alfred Hitchcock Presents*, hosted by the legendary film director, were just a few of the anthology series that presented new teleplays each week, combining horror, science fiction, and suspense.

In the late 1960s and early 1970s, horror fiction broke into the mainstream, with novels such as William Peter Blatty's *The Exorcist*, *The Other* by Thomas Tyron, and *Rosemary's Baby* by Ira Levine rising to the tops of the best-seller list. It is in this climate that King rose to prominence when his first novel, *Carrie*, was adapted as a popular movie, establishing a link between King's writing and theatrical adaptations that make his name familiar to nonreaders around the world.

As the twentieth century drew to a close, the popularity of mainstream horror novels dimmed. They were enjoyed by a much wider fan base than literary fiction, but other types of entertainment captured their audiences. Role-playing games became popular, and graphic novels, such as Will Eisner's *A Contract With God and Other Tenement Stories* and Art Spiegelman's *Maus*, gained mainstream acceptance as a literary art form. King has had great success crossing over to this genre, with a popular series released by Marvel publishers adapting his *Dark Tower* series, which he began writing in 1970, and his recent *Cycle of the Werewolf* series, illustrated by Bernie Wrightson.

In recent years, a newer movement toward horror and supernatural literature, targeted at young adults, has arisen in the wake of the phenomenal success of Stephanie Meyers's *Twilight* saga, which has raised the profile of the entire "dark fantasy" genre.

King's recommendation to other authors: read, read, read (*Image copyright Tatiana Mrozova, 2009. Used under license from Shutterstock.com*)

CRITICAL OVERVIEW

There is no question about King's popularity. With close to four hundred million books sold, he is one of the best-selling authors of all time. Audiences have been fascinated with his works since the publication of his first novel, *Carrie*, in 1974. *Nightmares and Dreamscapes*, the collection that included "Sorry, Right Number," was number six on the best-seller charts, with 1.5 million copies sold, in the week *before* the first copy had been shipped to bookstores.

Critics have not always been as enthusiastic about King's works as popular audiences have been. Often, his works were just ignored by literary critics, while reviewers for mainstream media, such as newspapers, expressed amazement that his writing is actually quite good, often positing themselves as being among the few who could achieve a clear view of King's writing. An example of this is Albert Pyle's review of *Nightmares and Dreamscapes* in the *Chicago Tribune*, which cites the locations of several universities known for producing literary writers when it notes, "Unpretentious, untenured, unwelcome in Iowa City, Chapel Hill and Berkeley, Stephen King has sentenced himself to a life in unfashionable exurbia." The review praises King while implying that literary snobs would not understand what makes his works so good. As Don Herron put it in the 1980s in an essay called "Stephen King: The Good, the Bad, and the Academic," "As far as I know, none of the major critics—whoever has inherited the mantles of T. S. Eliot or Ezra Pound or Edmund Wilson—has yet done anything more than perhaps mention King's name in passing, in much the same way a serious American historian might mention a popular figure such as Davy Crockett." His article predicts that critical studies will come, noting, "I saw it coming, you see. I have never read fiction as readymade for critical explication as King's."

Herron's expectations came to pass. In 1996, King won the prestigious O. Henry Award for his short story "The Man in the Black Suit." The 1999 car accident that severely curtailed his writing output made several critics look back on his career with appreciation. Sometime around the 2000 publication of King's book about his literary theory, *On Writing: A Memoir of the Craft*, the literary establishment lost any remaining reluctance to give King due recognition for the literary value of his work. In 2004, he was awarded a lifetime achievement award, the Medal of Distinguished Contribution to American Letters, by the prestigious National Book Foundation. At King's induction speech, novelist Walter Mosley said,

> Mr. King's novels are inhabited by people with everyday jobs and average bodies, people who have to try to find extraordinary strength when they've never been anything but ordinary.... He takes our daily lives and makes them into something heroic. He takes our world, validates our distrust of it and then helps us to see that there's a chance to transcend the muck.

For his part, King noted in his acceptance speech that the foundation had taken a great risk in presenting the award to someone who was looked down upon by the literary establishment. In 2007, J. Madison Davis, considering the controversy over the lifetime National Book Award and King's recognition, at the same time, as a "Grandmaster" by the Mystery Writers Guild of America, pointed out that

> quibbling about whether he is a 'serious' writer or whether he deserves a mystery writer's award is meaningless. And it isn't about the money he carts away or the movies that appear like clockwork or his awkward role as a celebrity, either.... We know, though we try to laugh it off, that he is telling us the truth. That is the essence of literature.

CRITICISM

David Kelly

Kelly is a writer who teaches creative writing and literature. In this essay, he examines the question of motivation in "Sorry, Right Number," and whether it is necessary to know why the events of this horror story take place.

King's 1987 teleplay "Sorry, Right Number," as published in his 1993 collection *Nightmares and Dreamscapes*, suffers from a malady common to supernatural stories in general and King's stories in particular: that of questionable motivation.

"IT WOULD BE ONE THING IF KATIE HAD SPENT THE ENSUING YEARS PLANNING THE EXACT MESSAGE SHE WOULD TELL HER YOUNGER SELF, WHEN THE TIME TO SPEAK THROUGH TIME CAME, BUT AS IT IS, THERE IS NO REAL IRONY, JUST AN UNPLEASANT SURPRISE."

Readers can be amazed at the events that take place in the story, but their amazement does not mean much if, in the end, all they are left with is a sense that something occurred in a work of fiction that they have never seen happen in real life.

The story concerns King's image of an ordinary family. The children bicker over control of the living room television set, the wife gossips with her sister about a mutual acquaintance, and the husband struggles with writer's block on the night that the film of his first novel, presumably having worked its way through theaters and video, is being broadcast on commercial television. Every good story has a complication. In this one, the wife, Katie, answers a phone call on the second line. She does not know who the terrified, unintelligible caller is, but she is certain that it is someone in her family. This conviction kicks off a frantic search for female members of her family who might be vulnerable on this particular night, but it eventually turns out that they all are secure. The payoff of the story is that five years after her husband Bill's fatal heart attack, Katie dials the telephone in a hypnotic trance, and her voice reaches back through the years to that fateful night, though she is able to get out only a few terrified, unintelligible words before being cut off. She sobs then, realizing that the voice she heard on the phone that night was in fact her own, trying to warn her former self about Bill's imminent attack.

The motivations that drive the characters in this story are clear enough. Katie, horrified by the crying that comes to her over the phone line, is driven to find the source of the panic. Bill is not initially upset, but as he spends time helping Katie contact family members, her fear rubs off on him, until he finally admits to her that this bit of reality has gotten beneath his skin. The youngest son,

WHAT DO I READ NEXT?

- King's 1999 book *Storm of the Century* is like "Sorry, Right Number" in that it was published in screenplay form, an unusual format for King. The story, involving a ghastly murder, a mysterious stranger, and a once-in-a-lifetime climate event, was adapted as a miniseries on network television soon after the book was published.
- A direct, contemporary biography of King and his writing career is *Dark Dreams: The Story of Stephen King*, written by Nancy Whitelaw and published by Morgan Reynolds in 2006. It follows King's life from his childhood through his announced retirement after his car accident.
- R. L. Stine has often been referred to as the Stephen King for young adults, not only for his imaginative horror stories but also for the lack of respect his million-selling books earned him. One that is, like "Sorry, Wrong Number," concerned with the fluctuations of time is *Cuckoo Clock of Doom*, about a young man who encounters an enchanted clock and afterward wakes up a few years younger each morning. It is part of Stine's vaunted *Goosebumps* series, published by Scholastic in 1995.
- Native American writer Sherman Alexie wrote *Flight*, the story of a troubled boy named Zits who has been moved from one foster home to another. Zits becomes involved with a violent gang, is shot, and ends up traveling from one body to another and from one time period to the next. Written for a teen audience, it is frank in its depictions of racism and violence. *Flight* was published in 2007 by Grove Press.
- King laid out his theories about what made him a writer and what it is to create gripping stories in his 2002 mix of memoir and analysis called *On Writing*. The book helped cement his reputation as a serious writer and teacher.
- King has said he was strongly influenced by H. P. Lovecraft, often considered the greatest writer of horror, fantasy, and weird fiction of all time. The best sampling of Lovecraft's fantastically complex vision can be found in the sixteen stories collected in *The Best of H. P. Lovecraft: Bloodcurdling Tales of Horror and the Macabre*, published by Del Rey in 1987.

Jeff, wants to experience the thrill and pride of watching his father's horror story brought alive in a movie, the oldest brother wants to experience the power of denying Jeff that pleasure, and the daughter in the living room just wants to lose herself in television watching. The daughter who is away at school wants decent grades and a date to the dance, and Katie's sister Dawn wants to rest after a day with her active toddler. Nobody seems to have the sort of psychological drive that would normally trigger a supernatural event.

Before giving up and saying that what happens is just something that the author has tossed in without cause, it would be worth considering other controlling factors. King's script points a finger at a supernatural, potentially conscious, being—the telephone. His first stage directions call for a close-up on Katie's mouth, inches from the receiver, and soon the phone itself is examined. Attention is drawn to its "one not-quite-ordinary thing," the buttons it has allowing for two lines. There is nothing particularly suspicious about the phone in this first scene. Still, the emphasis on any such irregularity in the phone system in a story called "Sorry, Right Number" is a point to be watched.

At the end of the story, the telephone reveals its true sinister nature. The final image is of the phone, again. King indicates that this shot should be an extreme close-up that makes the phone look ominous. Indeed, the telephone does seem culpable in the Weiderman family tragedy. When Katie tries to warn her former self to beware of Bill's hidden heart condition, the line goes dead before she can get to the words needed to explain herself; then, when realizes that she can change history and calls back, the magic connection to the past is no longer available to her. It even makes sense to say that this telephone that looks ominous in the last scene is responsible for taking Bill's life, since it is only because of the first call from the future that he spends a tense evening driving through the night and creeping through the door of a young mother's home, gun in hand. The night's activities are certainly contributing factors, if not the main causes, for Bill's heart giving out.

Accepting that the phone could come alive and make a conscious choice to attack the Weiderman family is still a far cry from understanding why it would. King's fiction is full of inanimate objects coming to life, as in the 1993 novel *Christine*, about a car that comes to life and kills. The field of science fiction is rife with stories about machines, often computers or their human-like counterparts, such as androids or robots, making sentient decisions. In *The Science of Stephen King: From "Carrie" to "Cell," the Terrifying Truth behind the Horror Master's Fiction*, Lois H. Gresh and Robert Weinberg examine the 1978 story "Trucks," which, like *Christine*, concerns killer vehicles. Taking the premise seriously, they conclude, "There is no believable explanation why trucks gifted with artificial intelligence would want to kill their builders. This leads us to conclude that the machines in "Trucks" are not the product of artificial intelligence but instead are the victims of possession." Such speculation is fine, but a theory involving demonic possession only throws the question of motivation aside, rather than answering it. Inanimate objects kill, it says, because they are evil, and killing is what evil does.

Motivation is an important question for determining whether "Sorry, Right Number" is an effective story or merely a series of coincidences imposed by the author. There may be people who feel it would be fine to leave this question alone, but these are often people who fear that any curiosity about a work constitutes over-thinking. A good story cannot be damaged by asking questions about it, and if there is any one question it would be fair to ask of a story, it is why the events take place.

There is a simple answer to why the telephone would cause Bill's death. It lacks complexity, but then, horror fiction does not necessarily need depth, just basic plausibility. The only "not-quite-ordinary" thing in the Weiderman household, as mentioned before, is the fact that the phone has a second line. Whether King intended it so or not, the phone represents some sort of duality, a division in the Weiderman family. The family's squabbling may be no worse than that in other families, and the father's obsession with the macabre might even give him a healthy connection to the concerns and fantasies of children, but in the end, that unusual telephone configuration represents some kind of aberration. It might represent Bill introducing his business into the family dynamic, or it might represent a family that is splintering, so that several members need to reach out to people beyond the household at once. Either interpretation can help make sense of what has happened. If Bill has done something to deserve the wrath of the universe, then the malicious telephone is simply the instrument the universe uses to punish him. It tricks Katie into phoning her former self and thereby being instrumental in Bill's heart attack.

Although this explanation helps explain most of the events in the story, the ending of the story invalidates it. In the last scene, Bill's voice comes out of the phone, speaking from beyond the grave. He nudges Katie toward learning a lesson from these events, asking, "Who *would* you call, if it weren't too late?" He is in on the scheme. Whatever it was that allowed Katie's voice to travel back in time, its intent was not to punish Bill; Bill's death seems to just be one part of a larger plan designed to teach Katie a lesson.

The message for Katie, based on what Bill says through the magical telephone, is that she should stop and think about life, looking deeper for what she feels is really important. However, what is most important to Katie at the start of this story is Bill, her "big guy," and he dies in the process of bringing that message to her. Maybe Bill's message was meant to tell her that she should seize the day, give up on mourning for the husband who died five years ago and get on with living her life, but then, what was act 1 for? Katie was not looking toward the past until supernatural forces began the process of teaching her the folly of doing what she was not doing already. If her own voice had not traveled through time to drag Katie and Bill out into the night, it is possible that he might have died anyway, but if that is the case, then the supernatural intervention is spectacularly irrelevant.

The ability to speak from the future seems intended to run Bill into the ground or drive Katie crazy. It cuts her off before she can communicate a coherent message, and then, five years later, the phone brings advice from Bill, telling her to think about who she would like to call just moments after she was unable to save his life. It would be one thing if Katie had spent the ensuing years planning the exact message she would tell her younger self, when the time to speak through time came, but as it is, there is no real irony, just an unpleasant surprise.

Using the screenplay format for this story allows King to remain at arm's length from the action. He does not have to say that it is Katie who thinks the phone looks ominous in the last scene, or why: instead, the phone just looks evil in general. King implies that this evil telephone has given Katie limited ability to talk to the past, but the story does not work if readers are not given any reason why it would do that. There are many possibilities: The power behind the call could intend to punish Bill for bringing his work into his family life, or it may be teaching Katie a *carpe diem* lesson. It could just be that a malicious universe decided, this one night, to break all known rules of physics in order to play a weird prank on an unsuspecting, undeserving family. However, if uncaused, disjointed events were acceptable, then anything any writer might choose to put on paper would be good. All writers, even Stephen King, have to account for what they say.

Source: David Kelly, Critical Essay on "Sorry, Right Number," in *Short Stories for Students*, Gale, Cengage Learning, 2010.

Lisa Rogak

In the following introduction, Rogak talks about King's method of overcoming fear—writing about it.

> I'M AFRAID OF EVERYTHING. —STEPHEN KING

It's probably no surprise that his fears rule every second of Stephen King's existence. He's surrounded by them, and anyone who's read even one of his novels knows that the most innocent item can be a harbinger of terror.

At various times through the years, King has rattled off a veritable laundry list of his fears: the dark, snakes, rats, spiders, squishy things, psychotherapy, deformity, closed-in spaces, death, being unable to write, flying—fill in the blank, the list is long. He's described himself as having a permanent address in "the People's Republic of Paranoia."

"IN SHORT, STEPHEN KING HAS NEVER GOTTEN OVER FEELING LIKE AN ABANDONED CHILD AND HE NEVER STOPPED BEING A CHILD PERMANENTLY HAUNTED BY HIS FATHER'S ABSENCE."

His treatises on his fear of the number thirteen—triskaidekaphobia—are particularly revealing. "The number 13 never fails to trace that old icy finger up and down my spine," he wrote. "When I'm writing, I'll never stop work if the page number 13 or a multiple of 13; I'll just keep on typing till I get to a safe number.

"I always take the last two steps on my back stairs as one, making thirteen into twelve. There were after all, thirteen steps on the English gallows up until 1900 or so. When I'm reading, I won't stop on page 94, 193, 382, since the sums of these numbers add up to thirteen."

You get the picture. King—he prefers to be called Steve—draws upon his fears quite liberally in his writing, yet at the same time, part of the reason that he writes is to attempt to drown them out, to suffocate them and put them out of their misery once and for all so he'll never be tormented by them again.

Yeah, right. He doesn't believe it either.

The only way he can block them out is when he's writing. Once he gets rolling and is carried along by a story about a particular fear, it's gone, at least temporarily. He writes as fast and furiously as he can because if there's one thing Stephen King knows after spending decades writing, it's this: the moment the pen stops moving or the computer switches off, the fear will rush right back, ready for another round.

Despite his fear of therapists, he once went to see one. When he began cataloging his fears, the therapist interrupted him, telling him to visualize his fear as a ball he could close up in his fist. It was all he could do not to run for the door. "Lady, you don't know how much fear I've got," he replied. "I can maybe get it down to the size of a soccer ball, but fear is my living and I can only get it so small."

In an exchange with Dennis Miller on his former TV talk show, Steve was thrilled to discover that he had found a kindred spirit in the Land of Fear. The men were discussing their shared dread of flying when King offered his theory about how the collective fear of people on a plane helps prevent a crash.

"Right," said Miller with a knowing nod. "The degree of rigidity in our body keeps the wings up."

Not quite, as Steve went on to explain. "It's a psychic thing, and anybody with half a brain knows that it shouldn't work. You have three or four people who are terrified right out of their minds. We hold it up. The flight you have to be afraid of is the flight where there's nobody on who's afraid of flying. Those are the flights that crash. Trust me on this."

A few nervous laughs came from the audience. Both men blinked past the glare of the lights and then looked at each other. They think we're *kidding?*

Without fear where would Stephen King be? It's almost as if he's hooked on his anxiety, just one more thing for him to mainline, like the booze and drugs he was hooked on for decades. In fact, he's made no secret of his lifelong struggle with substances.

"All those addictive substances are part of the bad side of what we do," he said. "I think it's part of that obsessive deal that makes you a writer in the first place, that makes you want to write it all down. Writing is an addictive for me. Even when the writing is not going well, if I don't do it, the fact that I'm not doing it nags at me."

One of the amazing aspects of Stephen King's life is that his copious drug and alcohol abuse didn't interfere with either the quantity or the quality of his prodigious output. However, while he would later acknowledge his surprise that his work didn't suffer—especially when the haze was thickest—he's also spoken with regret that he couldn't remember writing certain books, such as *Cujo*. This clearly bothered him, for he always fondly looked back on each of his novels and stories, revisiting them as if they were old friends, rerunning the memories of the nuances and the idea of a world and people that he just happened to have pulled out of his head.

Writing horror and telling stories had become so ingrained in him over the years that cranking out thousands of words every day of the year was second nature to him, despite a daily input of booze and drugs that would easily have killed a college kid on a weekend binge. Indeed, some of the tall tales and denial extended to what he told interviewers. For years, he told them that he wrote every day, taking a break from writing only on the Fourth of July, his birthday, and Christmas. That was patently untrue. He later said that he couldn't *not* write every day of the year, but he thought telling fans that he allowed himself a whole three days away from writing made him seem more personable. He hadn't yet realized that admitting his addictions to his fans would make him appear even more human.

While he's long been an unapologetic admirer of everything mainstream—he's referred to himself as the Big Mac of authors—he isn't always comfortable on the pedestal. Steve's iconic position in popular fiction was cemented early on, only a few years after his first novel, *Carrie,* was published. And yet, he isn't above—or below—using his fame when it suits him.

King claims to hate being famous—his wife Tabby detests it even more, calling life with a celebrity spouse like being in "a goddamn fishbowl"—but even after three decades in the public spotlight, he still talks to journalists from media large and small, gives public talks, attends Red Sox games, and conducts book signings. After all, with more than thirty years in the business, his ability to sell books has little to do with whether he gives a bunch of interviews. Though he claims to be shy, he's still as open and self-deprecating as he was when he first started out.

Then, of course, there's the flip side: "When you get into this business, they don't tell you you'll get cat bones in the mail, or letters from crazy people, or that the people on the tour bus will be gathered at your fence snapping pictures."

Because he lives a life that is so out and about, pick a random New Englander and chances are he'll have a story about a Stephen King sighting.

A New Hampshire man who regularly visited Fenway Park knew that Steve had season tickets to the Red Sox games. For several years, he kept an eye out for Steve, but he never spotted him. One day at the stadium, he saw King walking toward him and he froze. He couldn't think of anything to say. Finally, all he could come out with was "Boo!" as they came eye to eye. Steve said "Boo!" back and headed for his seat.

"He's just a competitive guy who wants to be the best at what he does," says Warren Silver, a friend from Bangor.

This, after sixty-three books published in thirty-five years, including collaborations, short-story collections—and having *The Green Mile* count as six separate books. Since the publication of *Carrie* in 1974, none of his books has been out of print, an accomplishment that can be matched by few bestselling authors. Proof still that his fears loom large.

Does he write for a particular person? While he admits that he writes to vanquish his fear, and writing for an audience of one—himself—he has occasionally provided a glimpse of the real man behind the curtain, a man whom Steve has no real recollection of: his father, who walked out of the family home one evening for a pack of cigarettes and kept on going, leaving his wife and two sons—David, age four, and Steve, two—to fend for themselves throughout a childhood of wrenching poverty and great uncertainty.

"I really think I write for myself, but there does seem to be a target that this stuff pours out toward," he said. "I am always interested in this idea that a lot of fiction writers write for their fathers because their fathers are gone."

Steve coped with a difficult childhood by turning first to books and then to writing his own stories. And as he put it, it's a world that he has never really left.

"You have to be a little nuts to be a writer because you have to imagine worlds that aren't there," he said. "You're hearing voices, you're making believe, you're doing all of the things that we're told as children not to do. Or else we're told to distinguish between reality and those things. Adults will say, 'You have an invisible friend, that's nice, you'll outgrow that.' Writers don't outgrow it."

So who is Stephen King, really? The standard assumption of casual fans and detractors is that he must be a creepy man who loves to blow things up in his backyard. Loyal fans usually go a bit deeper, knowing him to be a loyal family man and a benefactor to countless charities, many around his Bangor, Maine, home.

His friends, however, present a different, more complex picture.

"He's a brilliant, funny, generous, compassionate man whose character is made up of layer upon layer," says longtime friend and coauthor Peter Straub. "What you see is not only not what you get, it isn't even what you see. Steve is a mansion containing many rooms, and all of this makes him wonderful company."

According to Bev Vincent, a friend whom Steve helped out with Vincent's book *The Road to the Dark Tower,* a reference guide to King's seven-volume magnum opus, his self-image is somewhat surprising: "Steve still sees himself as a small-town guy who has done a few interesting things but doesn't think that his personal life would interest anyone."

And he doesn't understand why anyone would want to read an entire book about him—let alone write one. On the other hand, he has no problem if people want to discuss his work, either face-to-face or in a book.

But we all know he's wrong. Stephen King has led an endlessly fascinating life, and because we love, admire, and are scared out of our minds by his books, stories, and movies, of course we want to know more about the man who's spawned it all. Who wouldn't?

This is a biography, a story of his life. Of course his works play into it, they are unavoidable, but they are not the featured attraction here. Stephen King is.

Through the years, Steve's fans have been legendary for taking him to task whenever he's gotten the facts wrong in his stories. For instance, in *The Stand,* Harold Lauder's favorite candy bar was a PayDay bar. At one point in the story, Harold left behind a chocolate fingerprint in a diary at a time when the candy contained no chocolate. In the first few months after the book was published, Steve received mailbags full of letters from readers to inform him of his mistake, which was remedied in later editions of the book. And then of course, the candy company began to make PayDays with chocolate. Though some might claim Steve was prescient, you can't blame the man; after all, this is a guy who isn't exactly fond of doing research when he's deep into the writing of a novel. "I do the research [after I write]," he said. "Because when I'm writing a book, my attitude is, don't confuse me with facts. You know, let me go ahead and get on with the work."

On the other hand, his lack of concern with the facts of both his fictional and real lives has proved to be more than a bit frustrating to me and other writers. In researching this biography, I've attempted to check and double-check the facts of his life, but whether it's the natural deterioration of memory that comes with age or two solid decades of abusing alcohol, cocaine, and other drugs in various combinations, the guy can't be faulted for fudging a few dates here and there.

For example, in *On Writing,* he wrote that his mother died in February 1974, two months before *Carrie* was first published. However, I have not only a copy of his mother's obituary but her death certificate, both of which show that she most definitely died on December 18, 1973, in Mexico, Maine, at the home of Steve's brother, Dave.

Once I knew I was going to be writing about King's life, I got busy. I dug up old interviews in obscure publications that only published one issue back in 1975, read numerous books, and watched almost all of the movies based on his stories and novels—good and bad, and, boy, the bad ones can be a hoot. I also plunged into the many books that have been written about him and his work since the early eighties. As with the films, there are some good ones and some that are not so good.

The thing that struck me was not the blood and guts and special effects; the gory scenes in his books and movies weren't as bad as I'd imagined they would be. And it wasn't his ability to draw and develop characters; I already knew that was one of his particular talents.

What really got me was how funny the man is. I mean, really funny. Yes, his use of pop-culture references and brand names can be amusing when placed side by side with a guy who has a cleaver sticking out of his neck, or as with a corpse in an office setting with an Eberhard pencil stuck in each eye, but his sense of humor just knocked me over. I fell off the couch when the ice cream truck in *Maximum Overdrive* started playing "King of the Road," and again in *Graveyard Shift* when rats are trying to stay on top of broken planks coursing down a fast-moving stream in the middle of a mill's floor and the music playing is "Surfin' Safari" by the Beach Boys. King did not write the screenplay for the latter, but you just know his long arm of influence made it into the film.

Steve has gone on the record countless times to say that the one question he hates most is "Where do you get your ideas?" To me as a biographer, all you have to do is ask, "Is it authorized?" to make my face screw up like King's after an awestruck fan has asked him the idea question.

No, this biography is *not* authorized. The running joke among biographers is that if it is authorized, the book makes a good cure for insomnia. King does know about this book and told his friends that they could talk with me if they desired. I visited Bangor over several gray, bleak November days in the fall of 2007 to check out all of the key Stephen King haunts. In other words, all the highlights on the local Stephen King tours. It was sheer serendipity that one morning I found myself sitting in his office in the former National Guard barracks out near the airport, with his longtime assistant Marsha DeFillipo grilling me about my aim for this book.

For most of that half-hour interrogation, the man himself hovered just outside the doorway, listening in on our conversation but never once stepping inside.

In the end, perhaps the most surprising thing about Stephen King is that he is a die-hard romantic, which is evident in all of his stories. And to the surprise of his millions of fans, he would be the first to admit it, though to hear him explain it, maybe it's not really much of a revelation.

"Yes, I am a romantic," he said back in 1988. "I believe all those sappy, romantic things, that children are good, good wins out over evil, it is better to have loved and lost than never to have loved at all. I really believe all that shit. I can't help it. I see a lot of it at work."

However, the most romantic hearts are often the most haunted. I chose *Haunted Heart* as the title of this biography because it's clear that Stephen King's childhood indelibly shaped him for both good and not so good.

In an interview with the BBC, when Steve talked about his father and growing up without him, he began with a bit of an edge, a defiance as if to say, "Why are we talking about this? I'm *so* over it and have been for decades." Once he got going, however, things got painfully intimate, revealing the hurt, petulant boy that still exists close to the surface beneath Stephen King's skin. During his childhood, the other kids had fathers and he didn't, he explained. Male relatives were around, to be sure, but it wasn't the real thing. It would *never* be the real thing.

"At least the father in *The Shining* was there, even though he was bad," he said. "For me, there was a vacuum that was neither good or bad, just an empty place." At that point, his face crumpled a little, he distractedly ran a hand through his hair, and he looked away from the camera, which remained focused on him for a second or two before abruptly cutting away.

In short, Stephen King has never gotten over feeling like an abandoned child and he never stopped being a child permanently haunted by his father's absence. That's something that will never change. It has affected his entire life, from his childhood and his marriage to his books. *Especially* his books.

Keep this in mind as you read both this book and Steve's novels, and you'll find that it will go a long way toward a deeper understanding of the man and the worlds he's created.

Source: Lisa Rogak, "Introduction," in *Haunted Heart: The Life and Times of Stephen King*, Thomas Dunne Books, 2008, pp. 1–7.

Stephen King

In the following excerpt, King elaborates on why reading short stories as a child has influenced his later writings and continues to stimulate his imagination.

. . . All I started to say . . . was that the act of faith which turns a moment of belief into a real object—i.e., a short story that people will actually want to read—has been a little harder for me to come by in the last few years.

"Well then, don't write them," someone might say (only it's usually a voice I hear inside my own head, like the ones Jessie Burlingame hears in *Gerald's Game*). "After all, you don't need the money they bring in the way you once did."

That's true enough. The days when a check for some four-thousand-word wonder would buy penicillin for one of the kids' ear infections or help meet the rent are long gone. But the logic is more than spurious; it's dangerous. I don't exactly need the money the *novels* bring in, either, you see. If it was just the money, I could hang up my jock and hit the showers . . . or spend the rest of my life on some Caribbean island, catching the rays and seeing how long I could grow my fingernails.

But it *isn't* about the money, no matter what the glossy tabloids may say, and it's not about selling out, as the more arrogant critics really seem to believe. The fundamental things still apply as time goes by, and for me the object hasn't changed—the job is still getting to *you,* Constant Reader, getting you by the short hairs and, hopefully, scaring you so badly you won't be able to go to sleep without leaving the bathroom light on. It's still about first seeing the impossible . . . and then saying it. It's still about making you believe what I believe, at least for a little while.

I don't talk about this much, because it embarrasses me and it sounds pompous, but I still see stories as a great thing, something which not only enhances lives but actually saves them. Nor am I speaking metaphorically. Good writing—good *stories*—are the imagination's firing pin, and the purpose of the imagination, I believe, is to offer us solace and shelter from situations and life-passages which would otherwise prove unendurable. I can only speak from my own experience, of course, but for me, the imagination which so often kept me awake and in terror as a child has seen me through some terrible bouts of stark raving reality as an adult. If the stories which have resulted from that imagination have done the same for some of the people who've read them, then I am perfectly happy and perfectly satisfied—feelings which cannot, so far as I know, be purchased with rich movie deals or multi-million-dollar book contracts.

Still, the short story is a difficult and challenging literary form, and that's why I was so delighted—and so surprised—to find I had enough of them to issue a third collection. It has come at a propitious time, as well, because one of those facts of which I was so sure as a kid (I probably picked it up in *Ripley's Believe It or Not!,* too) was that people completely renew themselves every seven years: every tissue, every organ, every muscle replaced by entirely new cells. I am drawing *Nightmares and Dreamscapes* together in the summer of 1992, seven years after the publication of *Skeleton Crew,* my last collection of short stories, and *Skeleton Crew* was published seven years after *Night Shift,* my first collection. The greatest thing is knowing that, although the leap of faith necessary to translate an idea into reality has become harder (the jumping muscles get a little older every day, you know), it's still perfectly possible. The next greatest thing is knowing that someone still wants to read them—that's you, Constant Reader, should you wonder. . . .

What I've tried hardest to do is to steer clear of the old chestnuts, the trunk stories, and the bottom-of-the-drawer stuff. Since 1980 or so, some critics have been saying I could publish my laundry list and sell a million copies or so, but these are for the most part critics who think that's what I've been doing all along. The people who read my work for pleasure obviously feel differently, and I have made this book with those readers, not the critics, in the forefront of my mind. The result, I think, is an uneven Aladdin's cave of a book, one which completes a trilogy of which *Night Shift* and *Skeleton Crew* are the first two volumes. All the good short stories have now been collected; all the bad ones have been swept as far under the rug as I could get them, and there they will stay. If there is to be another collection, it will consist entirely of stories which have not as yet been written or even considered (stories which have not yet been *believed,* if you will), and I'd guess it will show up in a year which begins with a 2.

Meantime, there are these twenty-odd (and some, I should warn you, are *very* odd). Each contains something I believed for awhile, and I know that some of these things—the finger poking out of the drain, the man-eating toads, the hungry teeth—are a little frightening, but I think we'll be all right if we go together....

Source: Stephen King, "Myth, Belief, Faith, and Ripley's Believe It or Not!" in *Nightmares & Dreamscapes: Stories from the Darkest Places*, New American Library, 1993, pp. 5–9.

SOURCES

Davis, J. Madison, "Thoughts on a New Grandmaster," in *World Literature Today*, Volume 81, No. 3, May-June 2007, p. 20.

Gresh, Lois H., and Robert Weinberg, *The Science of Stephen King: From "Carrie" to "Cell," the Terrifying Truth behind the Horror Master's Fiction*, John Wiley & Sons, 2007, p. 77.

Herron, Don, "Stephen King: The Good, the Bad, and the Academic," in *Fear Itself: The Horror Fiction of Stephen King*, edited by Chuck Miller and Tim Underwood, Miller-Underwood, reprinted in *Stephen King*, updated ed., "Bloom's Modern Critical Views" series, edited by Harold Bloom, Chelsea House, 2007, p. 21.

Jodhi, S. T., "Introduction," in *The Modern Weird Tale*, McFarland, pp. 1–11.

Magistrale, Tony, and Michael A. Morrison, *A Dark Night's Dreaming: Contemporary American Horror Fiction*, University of South Carolina Press, 1996.

Mosley, Walter, "Introduction of Stephen King, Recipient of the National Book Foundation's Medal for the Distinguished Contribution to American Letters, 2003," *National Book Awards Acceptance Speeches*, http://www.nationalbook.org/nbaacceptspeech_sking_intro.html (accessed October 19, 2009).

Pyle, Albert, "Stephen King Stories, Scary and Real," in *Chicago Tribune*, November 7, 1993, Books Section, p. 9.

Weiner, Stephen, *Faster than a Speeding Bullet: The Rise of the Graphic Novel*, Nantier Beall Minoustchine Publishing, 2003.

FURTHER READING

Carroll, Noel, *The Philosophy of Horror: Or, Paradoxes of the Heart*, Routledge Publishers, 1990.

This book represents one of the most serious scholarly examinations ever done about the narrative traditions and styles of horror writing, weaving in an encyclopedic quantity of references from across the ages.

Indick, Ben P., "King and the Literary Tradition of Horror and the Supernatural," in *Stephen King*, updated ed., "Bloom's Modern Critical Views" series, edited by Harold Bloom, Chelsea House, 2007, pp. 5–16.

This essay, first published in 1982, looks at the argument about literary value that has shadowed King's entire publishing career.

King, Stephen, *Danse Macabre*, Berkley Press, 1981.

In this nonfiction book, King, through stories and anecdotes from his own life, relates the history of the science fiction and horror field. The book is based on his notes from a class he taught in horror writing.

Rolls, Albert, *Stephen King: A Biography*, Greenwood Press, 2009.

This volume is a densely sourced, comprehensive biography that covers King's life from birth to the present day. The last four chapters are about King's continuing attempts at retirement.

Russell, Sharon A., "Genre," in *Revisiting Stephen King*, Greenwood Press, 2002, pp. 19–34.

Russell's chapter about genre considers what the horror genre is; what it means to Stephen King to be categorized in that genre; and the other genres, such as science fiction, thriller, suspense, and fantasy, that overlap in his fiction.

Winter, Douglas E., *Stephen King: The Art of Darkness*, Signet, 1986.

Winter's book, published before "Sorry, Right Number," was one of the first critical collections to examine and praise King's style. In it, he shows appreciation for the power of sturdy storytelling that has always been King's driving force.

Sweet Potato Pie

EUGENIA COLLIER

C. 1972

Eugenia Collier's short story "Sweet Potato Pie" is about Buddy, a professor who was raised in poverty. The simple tale is told in the first person, by Buddy, and is largely composed of recollections of his childhood and rise from destitution. Buddy's memories of his siblings also feature significantly in the plot, particularly his love and respect for Charley, the older brother who effectively raised him. The only action in the story that takes place in the present is Buddy's surprise visit to Charley and Charley's family. This heartwarming story of the love between two brothers is not only touching and sincere but also a subtle exploration of the cost of poverty and the schisms it can cause. For instance, although Buddy has become a professor, thanks to the sacrifices his family made to provide him with an education, Charley works as a cab driver and lives in Harlem (a poor but culturally rich black neighborhood in New York City). The story also addresses the nature of class and race through Buddy and Charley's upbringing as the sons of near-destitute sharecroppers.

Although original publication information for "Sweet Potato Pie" is unknown, its earliest known copyright date is 1972. The story can be found in the 2000 anthology *Glencoe Literature: Course 4*.

AUTHOR BIOGRAPHY

Short story author, essayist, and poet Collier (occasionally referred to as Eugenia W. Collier)

was born Eugenia Maceo on April 6, 1928, in Baltimore, Maryland. Her mother, Eugenia Williams, was a teacher, and her father, Harry Maceo, was a doctor. Collier earned her bachelor of arts degree from Howard University in 1948. Following her graduation, she married Charles S. Collier on July 23, 1948. The couple had three sons before divorcing. In 1950, Collier received her master's degree from Columbia University. Collier then began her career as a caseworker for the Baltimore Department of Public Welfare, a post she held from 1950 to 1955. She then worked as an assistant instructor at Morgan State University. Collier was ultimately promoted to the position of professor before leaving the university in 1966. The same year, Collier went to work as an assistant professor at the Community College of Baltimore (now Baltimore City Community College). She was again promoted to the position of professor, leaving the institution in 1974. While working as an associate professor at the University of Maryland, she earned a doctorate degree in 1976.

Collier's writing began to appear around 1969. That year, she earned her first major recognition with the Gwendolyn Brooks Award for Fiction for her short story "Marigolds." Her first credited work, *Impressions in Asphalt: Images of Urban America*, written with Ruthe T. Sheffey, was published in 1969. The following year, she wrote *A Bridge to Saying It Well* with Joel I. Glasser and others. Also in 1970, her work was featured in the anthology *Brothers and Sisters*. In 1972, Collier contributed to two anthologies, *Accent* and *Oral and Written Composition: A Unit-Lesson Approach*. Her short story "Sweet Potato Pie" was also copyrighted in 1972. One of her better-known works, the two-volume *Afro-American Writing: An Anthology of Prose and Poetry*, was edited with Richard A. Long and released in 1972. In 1976, Collier adapted her short story "Ricky" into a one-act play of the same title. Her first full-length collections, *Spread My Wings* and *Breeder and Other Stories*, were published in 1992 and 1993, respectively.

In addition to her writing, Collier has maintained her academic career, working as a professor at such institutions as Coppin State University and Morgan State University. She has also served as a visiting professor at Southern Illinois University and Atlanta University. Though Collier's output has not been prolific, her impact has been great. Her stories remain widely studied in schools throughout the country. As of 2009, she still lives in Baltimore.

PLOT SUMMARY

"Sweet Potato Pie" is set in both the present and the past, telling the story of the narrator's day while he simultaneously recalls his childhood. The exact time in which the story is set is unclear, though it is likely the time in which it was written, that is, the 1960s or early 1970s. This estimate is further bolstered when one considers that sharecropping (a system in which tenants farm the land they live on and pay their rent with a share of the harvest) in the United States largely died out in the 1940s. Since the narrator, now an adult, grew up in a sharecropping family, it is fair to assume that he was a child sometime during the 1920s or 1930s.

The narrator, whose name is first revealed as Buddy halfway through the story, states that he is on the fourteenth floor, looking down at his brother Charley on the sidewalk. From that height, Charley looks small to Buddy, "an insect scurrying among other insects." It appears that Charley senses that he is being watched because he looks up at the building, but he does not see Buddy. Instead, he walks down Fifth Avenue, headed toward his run-down taxi. It becomes clear that the story is set in New York City. The narrator remarks that Charley will be headed uptown any minute.

Buddy moves away from the window and plops down on the bed, still wearing his shoes. He hints that something out of the ordinary has happened and says that he rarely sees Charley. In a poetic turn of phrase, Buddy says of his brother, "My thoughts hover over him like hummingbirds."

The room that Buddy is in is neat and impersonal, sterile, a strong contrast to Charley's apartment in Harlem (a historically poor black neighborhood in New York City). The room also presents a stark contrast to the shack in which they grew up. Buddy can see Charley now, as he was as a child, and he thinks of his Charley with love and thankfulness. Charley is the eldest and did not have much of a childhood because he was always caring for his younger siblings. Their parents were sharecroppers. Buddy was the youngest child, and he rarely saw his parents since they were always out working in the field. He mentions his other siblings as well: Lil, Alberta, and Jamie.

Buddy remembers that one of the few times he saw his parents was the day when the sharecroppers were paid. Each year, they would sell the harvest, and the family would gather quietly as Mama counted out the proceeds. They normally ran out of supplies toward the end of the year and needed the money to restock. Mama would divide the money into piles for each expense. When she deemed it enough, everyone would relax, secure in the knowledge that they would be able to survive for at least another year.

Buddy also recalls spending time with his parents on Sundays, when they would go to the Baptist church. He thinks of how small he was and how his parents looked like "mountains" as he sat between them. His father's face was still, like a "mask"; his mother's face was serene, but it would grow more and more animated as the power of the religious service affected her. These are the only occasions Buddy can recall when his parents were not in the field. Mostly, he was raised by Charley and Lil, the eldest daughter in the family. He thinks of how each acted as father and mother to him. Buddy had a stutter as a child, and Charley was determined to cure it. Charley heard of a remedy consisting of hitting a stutterer across the mouth with a wet rag when they stuttered. He employed the technique with Buddy. Although it did not work, Buddy did eventually grow out of his speech impediment.

The family was poor and uneducated, but the children tried to go to school as often as they could. However, the demands of the farm and the family, of ensuring their basic survival, kept most of them from having any chance at a real education. Buddy, as the youngest, was the only child in the family who had any real opportunity to attend school. His father recognized Buddy's intelligence and intended him to make use of it. Charley also wanted Buddy to make something of himself, to "break the chain of poverty." In the narrative, this is where Buddy's name is first revealed, as Charley admonishes him to succeed.

Buddy loved going to school, appreciating it all the more for the sacrifices his family made to ensure that he could complete his education. He took pride in outshining his other classmates, the same ones who teased him for the holes in his clothing. Over time, the family's burden began to ease. Alberta left home at age sixteen to look for work and Jamie died at age twelve. Because the family had fewer members to support, Buddy was able to enter high school. His family was exceedingly proud of him when he graduated as valedictorian. His siblings and parents gave him the coins and dollars they had saved and told him to buy a new suit, the first suit Buddy owned that was not a hand-me-down.

Even now, years after Mama's death, Buddy pictures her as she was on the night of his graduation. He states, "I realized in that moment that I wasn't necessarily the smartest—only the youngest. And the luckiest."

Buddy comments that the war started, though it is not clear which war Buddy is referring to. Given the estimated time frame, it could have been the Korean War or the Vietnam War. Buddy joined for the G.I. Bill, an act that ensured former soldiers a college education at government expense. He says that since then, the years have passed in a blur. His childhood home is vacant and his siblings have gone their separate ways. In one sentence, Buddy relates that he has gotten married, gone to graduate school, had kids, and secured work as a professor. He is fatter and older and balder. The story now returns to the present. Buddy is looking at Charley, who is "still gentle-eyed, still my greatest fan."

Buddy is in town for a conference, and he surprised his brother with a visit earlier that day. He was afraid to tell Charley and Charley's wife, Bea, that he was coming, because he knew they would have spent days cleaning and fussing in preparation for his arrival. Buddy was in town for a few days, staying at a fancy hotel, before he was able to break away from the conference and head to see Charley in Harlem. To Buddy, the neighborhood feels like home; it has an "epic" quality to it. It is "as if all black people began and ended there . . . as if in Harlem the very heart of Blackness pulsed its beautiful, tortured rhythms."

Buddy describes the people on the street and the general hustle and bustle. Some stores are still boarded up from the riots. Buddy can still feel "a terrible tension in the air." He then goes on to describe Charley's building, which is run down, like all the buildings in the neighborhood. He remarks upon the graffiti. Buddy then comments on surprising Charley and Bea and their joyful welcome of him. They call for Mary and Lucy, Buddy's nieces. They are bashful at first, and Buddy hugs them.

The group sits merrily at the table while Bea cooks for them. Buddy comments, "It felt good there. Beautiful odors mingled in the air." He tells the family about his conference, at which he gave a speech earlier that day. Charley and Bea are proud of him. They talk about Bea's job at the school cafeteria. Buddy mentions his wife, Jess. Charley says the family is too scattered; they never get to see one another, especially since Mama and Pa have died. Charley comments that it has been years since he has seen Alberta. Bea points out that everyone is too busy to visit because they are all just trying to get by.

Charley mentions Buddy's sending money to Lil's family last Christmas after her husband, Jake, lost his job. Buddy tells Charley that he owes Lil and Charley far more than that. Charley then tells Buddy that he ran into one of his students, but he did not tell the student that he was Buddy's brother. Buddy is a "*somebody*," and Charley sees himself as just a taxi driver. It seems clear that Charley is afraid his lowly status would sully the student's perceptions of Buddy. Buddy then calls Charley crazy. He wants to tell Charley that he would be no one if not for Charley's support, but he refrains because he knows it will embarrass his brother.

When the family has finished dinner, Bea serves Buddy a giant slice of her homemade sweet potato pie, Buddy's favorite. Afterward, Buddy is sad to take his leave, and Bea insists that he take the rest of the pie with him. Buddy enthusiastically agrees. He comments, "I'd eaten all I could hold, but my *spirit* was still hungry for sweet potato pie." Bea wraps the pie in a brown paper bag, and they all say goodbye. The love between them is evident. Charley drives Buddy back to his hotel in his cab.

Outside the hotel, Charley stops Buddy and tells him that he cannot bring a brown bag into the lobby. He explains that carrying a brown bag into a fancy hotel is not proper, that it is beneath Buddy's status as a "*somebody*." Buddy tries to argue and says he has "nothing to prove," but he eventually gives in, marveling at his brother's crazy notions. The two men say their goodbyes, and Buddy enters the hotel. In the lobby, everyone is carrying expensive suitcases; no one is carrying anything close to a brown bag. Buddy notes, "I suppose we all operate according to the symbols that are meaningful to us, and to Charley a brown paper bag symbolizes the humble life he thought I had left."

As Buddy is thinking this, he looks behind him. What he sees inspires "tears of laughter." It is Charley, "proudly carrying" the brown paper bag for his brother.

CHARACTERS

Alberta

Alberta is one of Buddy's older sisters. She is a middle child in the family, as Lil is the eldest daughter. Alberta leaves home at the age of sixteen and moves north in search of work. This was a fairly common phenomenon for poor African Americans living in the South, as the industrial centers in the North offered far better opportunity for employment. Alberta's leave taking also lessens the family's burden; she is one less dependent to worry about and care for. Buddy's graduation is so important that she travels back home to witness the event. Still, she is described as being "different," set apart from the family to which she was once so close. Alberta's physical distance from the family eventually becomes an emotional distance. As Charley points out, in the last few years, he has not so much as received a Christmas card from her.

Bea

Bea is Charley's wife and the mother of Mary and Lucy. She works in a school cafeteria and lives in Harlem. These traits indicate her lower socioeconomic class. She holds a menial job and lives in a run-down neighborhood. Despite this, she is happy. The love in her home is evident as she cooks for her family. Bea points out, however, that the distance between Charley and his siblings is the result of their economic status. Everyone is too busy to visit because they spend all of their time just trying to get by. Notably, Bea's homemade sweet potato pie is one of Buddy's favorite foods. She shows her generosity by giving Buddy a huge slice to eat and then sending him home with the remainder.

Buddy

Buddy is the story's narrator and main character. He can also be seen as the hero, though this role is arguably held by Charley. Certainly Buddy believes this to be the case. Buddy is a professor and the only person in his family to receive an education. He was raised in near destitution as the child of sharecroppers, and his family worked day in and day out just to survive, with barely enough to make it from one harvest to the next. Still, Buddy's family is determined to allow him the opportunity to escape this lifestyle, and they work hard to ensure that he can go to school. Buddy is well aware of this fact, and at his high school graduation, he acknowledges that he was chosen to go to school not because he was the smartest child but because he was "the youngest. And the luckiest."

Because his parents were always out working in the field, Buddy was predominantly raised by his eldest siblings Charley and Lil. He loves both of them, especially Charley, who always wanted the best for his little brother. Buddy is well aware of the debt that he owes them. He loves both Lil and Charley and feels nothing but gratitude toward them. Buddy thinks of Charley's potential, lost because he had no education and no childhood. He is also proud of Charley, even though Charley is ashamed to associate himself in public with his brother on account of his lower socioeconomic status. Buddy refrains from warning Charley of his visit to prevent him from fussing over unnecessary preparations for his arrival. Buddy's success has led him to live apart from his brother and from his own roots. Charley will not claim to be Buddy's brother in public because of Buddy's success; he will not even allow Buddy to carry the pie he so dearly loves into the expensive hotel.

Charley

Charley is Buddy's eldest brother and the man responsible for raising Buddy and ensuring his success. Charley is described as loving and caring even when Buddy relates the episode of him hitting Buddy across the mouth with a wet rag. Even this violent act comes from a place of love, as Charley was attempting to cure Buddy's stutter. Charley sacrificed his childhood to care for his younger siblings, particularly Buddy. As a young man, he gave up his own potential and chance at a better life in order to ensure the very same for his youngest brother. As an adult, Charley works a menial job and lives in a poor neighborhood. It is clear, though, that he is happy. He is married and has two daughters, and his home is filled with love and warmth. Charley never bemoans his circumstances or the sacrifices he has made, nor does he resent Buddy's success or even demand thanks for his part in it. In fact, Buddy would like to thank Charley for this very thing; he wants to tell Charley that he would be no one if not for his brother. However, Buddy refrains from doing so because he knows it would embarrass Charley.

Charley's only foible is that he feels that he is a nobody while Buddy is a "*somebody*." This belief forces a social distance between the two men. Charley even refrains from mentioning that he his Buddy's brother, lest his own lower status reflect poorly on Buddy. Charley also feels that Buddy must comport himself according to his status, and therefore he will not allow Buddy to take the pie, wrapped in a brown paper bag, into the expensive hotel. Still, Charley understands Buddy's desire for the pie, so he takes it upon himself to carry the brown bag in his brother's stead. Once again, Charley debases himself for his brother's sake.

Jake

Jake is Lil's husband. It is mentioned that Buddy sent money to Lil and Jake's children last Christmas when Jake was unemployed. Jake's circumstances indicate how the legacy of poverty in Buddy's family continues.

Jamie

Jamie is one of the middle siblings in Buddy's family. It is not clear whether Jamie is a boy or a girl. Jamie dies at age twelve, but Buddy does not say why or how. The fact is related simply, in one sentence, with no further comment. This is rather striking, but it indicates how commonplace death was in the world in which Buddy was raised.

Jess

Jess is Buddy's wife and the mother of his children, who are never named in the story. When Buddy first mentions that he got married, he does not indicate his wife's name or provide any information about her. Jess's name is later mentioned in passing.

Lil

Lil is Buddy's eldest sister, and she acted as a mother to him. Lil and Charley are the only two characters in the story whom Buddy devotes a great deal of description to, signifying their importance to him. He says of Lil that she was the loudest of the siblings, the one who cooked for them and cleaned them. She sent them all to school when they could go, and she administered both discipline and love. She captivated everyone with her singing and her infectious laughter. Buddy is aware of how indebted he is to Lil. He sends her family money when they are struggling, but he acknowledges that he owes her far more than money.

Lucy

Lucy is one of Charley and Bea's daughters. Her age is unknown, as is her birth order. Lucy, like her sister, is bashful around her uncle Buddy at first. She and her sister highlight the warm family atmosphere in Charley's run-down apartment. She seems to have a better childhood than the one her uncle and father shared.

Mama

Mama is dead during the present action of the story, but Buddy recalls her counting out the money from the harvest and declaring the family's financial solvency for another year. Buddy also recalls Mama at church, how she would be calm and serene and then become more animated as the spirit of the service affected her. He also recalls how happy and bright she looked at his high school graduation. These events, Buddy says, seem like the pinnacle of her life. Aside from these moments, Buddy had little interaction with his mother; she was always out working in the field.

Mary

Mary is one of Charley and Bea's daughters. It is not clear how old she is or whether she is the eldest or youngest child. All that is said of her is that she is shy around her uncle at first but then warms up. Her presence largely serves to underscore the happy family tableau as Buddy visits with his brother. Her circumstances also seem much improved from those of her father and uncle's childhood.

Pa

Pa is an even more elusive character than Mama. He, too, is always out in the field. Buddy recalls his face at church being like a "mask." Buddy says that his father and mother seemed like "mountains" as he sat beside them. Aside from these memories, Buddy recalls Pa putting the harvest proceeds on the table for Mama to count out. He also notes his father's insistence that Buddy get an education.

THEMES

Poverty

Buddy was raised in poverty. His eldest siblings acted as his parents because his actual parents were working in the fields. Buddy is able to go to school and complete his education not because he is the smartest in the family but because he is the youngest. His older siblings shoulder the burden of maintaining the family. Charley is determined that Buddy "break the chain of poverty," and he sacrifices his own childhood to allow this to happen. Here, the trappings of poverty are clear. Buddy lives in hand-me-down clothing that often has holes in it. He derives pride from outperforming the other students who are better off than he is.

Buddy's poverty also leads him to join the army. Taking advantage of the G.I. Bill is the only way he can secure the funds for a college education. This decision costs him a few years of life, and he literally risks his life for the opportunity. The lasting legacy of poverty can also be seen in the basic odds of Buddy's transcendence of it. Of five siblings, he is the only one to complete his education and enjoy financial success in adulthood. Lil's family struggles when her husband is out of work. Alberta is rarely heard from. Charley drives a cab and lives with his family in a run-down apartment in a poor neighborhood.

African American History

Race is a considerable factor in the characters' poverty. Buddy's family is African American and living in the South during the early twentieth century. They are only a few generations removed from the abolition of slavery, and they live in a segregated society that has yet to be affected by the civil rights movement. Race and its role in the family's reduced circumstances and opportunities are not overtly addressed in the story, but they are hinted at. One such hint is Charley's residence in Harlem, a poor neighborhood that is predominantly black.

Social Class

One of the main themes in "Sweet Potato Pie" is that of social class and the contrasts and gaps that divide members of different classes. This separation is largely illustrated through the figure of Buddy, the only character to bridge the divide. As a person who straddles these lines, he brings them into focus. This is especially true in Charley's treatment of his brother. Charley would have made a big fuss over his successful brother's impending visit if he had known in advance, so Buddy decides to surprise Charley. Charley frequently mentions that his brother is a "*somebody*," implying by contrast that he is a

TOPICS FOR FURTHER STUDY

- Use the Internet to research the experiences of sharecroppers. What are their common experiences? Were there any positive aspects to their lifestyles? Did sharecroppers' lives vary according to the different states they lived in? Compile your findings in a detailed PowerPoint presentation.
- Write a short story by reimagining "Sweet Potato Pie" from Charley's point of view. In doing so, keep the following questions in mind: What was his childhood like? How did he feel about Buddy? How was his life different from his younger brothers? Does he ever think about this difference, as Buddy does?
- In the story, Buddy mentions the Harlem riots, noting that some of the stores in the neighborhood are still closed because of them. What are the riots to which Buddy refers? Find out everything you can about riots in Harlem and present your findings to the class in an audio-visual format.
- Read Mildred D. Taylor's classic young-adult novel *Roll of Thunder, Hear My Cry* (1976). The book portrays a black family in 1930s Mississippi growing up in much the same manner as Buddy's family. In an essay, compare and contrast the two stories and each fictional family's respective experiences.
- The tone of Collier's story is one of brotherly love and gratitude. Buddy is grateful to his brother and his family for the sacrifices they made to ensure a better life for him. In an essay, discuss the nature of gratitude as it is portrayed in "Sweet Potato Pie." What subtle and not-so-subtle instances in the story indicate the depth of Buddy's feelings? Be sure to cite examples from the text.
- Harlem is an example of an urban ethnic enclave. What examples of ethnic neighborhoods can you find in your city, town, or state? What historical and economic factors led to their existence? Give an oral presentation in which you address these questions. Be sure to use visual aids or invite a guest speaker to talk to your class.

nobody. Charley's belief that he is a nobody is illustrated when he refrains from introducing himself as Buddy's brother. He feels that his lowly status as a taxi driver will reflect negatively on Buddy. It is Charley, also, who insists that Buddy leave behind his humble roots, which are symbolized by the sweet potato pie wrapped in a brown paper bag. For Buddy to carry such an unimpressive package strikes Charley as inappropriate, not befitting Buddy's improved circumstances. To some degree, Charley is correct, as no one else in the fancy hotel is carrying anything so modest.

Family

The importance of family in the story is clear. Though Buddy's childhood is marked by poverty, he is happy. Lil and Charley are loving and competent surrogate parents. Even Buddy's parents, who are always working, clearly love their family. It is Buddy's father who decides that Buddy should have an education. Buddy's mother is prouder and happier than she has ever been when she attends her youngest child's graduation. All of the members of Buddy's family make sacrifices to ensure his success and the family's day-to-day survival. Despite these hardships, though, the family is always portrayed as happy, loving, and without resentment. Buddy never looks down on his less-educated family members; he feels nothing but gratitude toward them. When Buddy visits Charley as an adult, he finds another happy family. Charley and Bea and their daughters welcome Buddy into their apartment and cook for him. To Buddy, "it felt good there."

Sweet potato pie (Image copyright Barbara Ayrapetyan, 2009. Used under license from Shutterstock.com)

STYLE

First-Person Narrator

"Sweet Potato Pie" is told by Buddy, the first-person narrator. The reader is privy to all of Buddy's thoughts and feelings. On the other hand, the other characters can only be seen though Buddy's perceptions of them. The events in the story, past and present, can only be seen this way as well. The reader feels close to Buddy for these reasons, but it is often harder to understand the other characters objectively (since they can only be seen through the narrator's subjective point of view). Because Buddy feels so close to his family, this detriment is less apparent in the story. Still, the reader is left with some questions, as when Buddy mentions Jamie's death in passing. The lack of details and dismissive nature are striking. Other examples of this lack of information include Buddy's mention of the war and being injured as a soldier and of his marriage and children. All of these seemingly important life events are mentioned only briefly and without explanation. In this manner, what the narrator does and does not discuss at length indicates what is and is not important to him. This reveals more about Buddy's character than it does about the subjects under discussion. It would seem that Buddy's wife and children are less important to him than Charley is.

Dialect

Although Buddy's speech and narration are in standard English, all of the other characters speak in dialect, a typically non-standard type of speech that often features the heavy use of slang and contractions. Charley, as both a child and an adult, speaks in dialect. He uses words such as "ain't" and "git" (for "get"). In one instance, when telling Buddy not to bring the brown bag into the hotel, Charley says, "You can't neither." Charley speaks in dialect because he is uneducated. Bea also speaks in this manner, indicating that she had little access to education as a child as well. Dialect indicates not only the level of education of the speaker but often also his or her socioeconomic class. It was Charley's childhood poverty that prevented him from receiving an education in the first place, and this is likely the case for Bea as well. That Buddy does not speak in dialect is a further indication of the social divide that exists between Buddy and his family, despite his evident love for them and theirs for him.

HISTORICAL CONTEXT

Sharecropping

The practice of sharecropping consists of tenant farmers who pay the landowner with a portion, or share, of the crops they harvest on their rented land. The system became common in the South during the Reconstruction era (the period following the end of the Civil War and the abolition of slavery). It was a practical solution that provided freed slaves with the means to make a living, while allowing former plantation owners to maintain their land and holdings. However, although the practice of sharecropping is not necessarily oppressive in itself, landowners took advantage of the system to maintain their power. (Although there were white sharecroppers, most were black, and those who were white were usually treated more fairly.) It was common practice for tenant farmers to buy their necessities and supplies from a company store that was owned by the landowner. Often, supplies were sold at an exorbitant markup, one designed to keep tenant farmers from ever turning a profit from their labors. In this manner, sharecroppers were essentially slaves working for little more than their basic survival, with no opportunity to improve their lot. As Trudier Harris notes in *The Oxford Companion to Women's Writing in the United States*, "Sharecropping reflected the power and ownership whites wielded over black people in spite of the Emancipation Proclamation."

COMPARE & CONTRAST

- **1970s:** The success of the civil rights movement can be felt in continued advances toward racial equality. African Americans have begun to secure positions of power, as is the case with Buddy.

  Today: Although racial equality has not been completely established, its continued advancements are inarguable. In 2009, Barack Obama takes office as the first African American president of the United States.

- **1970s:** African American voices in literature are prevalent, and Collier is writing among such renowned peers as Toni Morrison, Maya Angelou, and Alice Walker. It is the first time that African American literature enters the mainstream.

  Today: Popular multicultural literature is produced predominantly by Indian writers, such as Jhumpa Lahiri, and Caribbean writers, such as Edwidge Danticat.

- **1970s:** The poverty rate for families headed by an African American in 1969 is 36.7 percent but falls to 28.1 percent by 1979, according to data from the Integrated Public Use Microdata Series (2003).

  Today: By 1999, the poverty rate for families headed by an African American falls to 21.2 percent, still over three times the rate for families headed by whites.

Because of the lack of opportunity for blacks in the South (a region where the economy was based mainly on farming), many moved north beginning in the early 1900s in search of work in the factories located there. This is true of Alberta in "Sweet Potato Pie." This steady migration served to undermine the labor base required to support the sharecropping system. In addition, agriculture was hard hit by the Great Depression in the 1930s, and yet more tenant farmers moved North. Illegal and unfair practices on the part of landowners also continued with impunity, leading to the establishment of the Southern Tenant Farmers' Union in 1934. These developments, coupled with the advent of more mechanized agricultural practices, signaled the end of sharecropping as a viable economic system.

Harlem

A neighborhood located in the northern part of New York City, Harlem was initially founded in 1658 as a Dutch settlement (as was much of the city). The area is named after Haarlem, a town located in the Netherlands. Black tenements began appearing in Harlem around 1880, but the neighborhood did not become predominantly African American until 1904. At this time, the Great Migration of blacks from the segregated South began, and the neighborhood's black population expanded. Building developers at the time took advantage of this trend to entice blacks from other neighborhoods in New York City to move there as well. This strategy was largely spearheaded by Philip Payton, head of the Afro-American Realty Company. The Great Migration continued in World War I, as black laborers were in demand on account of the draft, which sent the white men who would have normally filled those jobs to war. The collapse of the economy during the Great Depression sent yet more waves of Southern blacks to Harlem in search of work. The expansion at this time was exponential, with Harlem's African American population growing from 32 percent in 1920 to 70 percent in 1930.

The migratory explosion led to a high population density and competition for housing, replete with price gouging and poor housing conditions, over the next thirty years. By 1960, only half of the housing in Harlem was deemed

Sweet potatoes in a basket *(Image copyright Creatista, 2009. Used under license from Shutterstock.com)*

habitable. This is reflected in the run-down appearance of the buildings that Buddy remarks upon as he goes to visit Charley.

CRITICAL OVERVIEW

Because Collier is predominantly an essayist and academic, there is little available discussion of her fiction. However, while no specific criticism for "Sweet Potato Pie" has been published, some of the general discussion of her work certainly applies. For the most part, critics and biographers have noted Collier's attempt to portray the African American experience and to chart the hardships and the triumphs therein. In a biographical profile of Collier in the *Encyclopedia of African American Women Writers*, T. Jasmine Dawson finds that "she writes passionately about language in her stories and addresses issues and concerns of poorer blacks, particularly urban blacks." Offering further praise, Dawson remarks that "Collier always sought authenticity and honesty" in her work.

Discussing *Breeder and Other Stories*, Collier's best-known collection, in *Black Issues in Higher Education*, Opal J. Moore writes that "Collier elaborates on the destructiveness of American slavery upon African people and their families and, predictably, draws connections between past and present conditions." Certainly, this is the case in "Sweet Potato Pie." In addition, Moore notes that, "far from indulging in self-pity, these stories should engage our understanding and questioning of our revulsion of the past, as well as our self-protective embracing of it." Her stories, Moore observes, "in their best moments, take us to the feeling parts of the history of slavery that we simultaneously clutch to us and revile." They also map "a condition of profound loss—not the loss of love itself, its pulse or impulse, but of its embrace." Though Buddy does not seem to know it, his success causes him to live with a similar loss.

CRITICISM

Leah Tieger

Tieger is a freelance writer and editor. In this essay, she explores the relationship between Buddy and Charley in "Sweet Potato Pie" and the sacrifices that each must make to maintain their respective roles.

Collier's "Sweet Potato Pie" is a delightfully subtle, but optimistic, story that portrays the love between two brothers. At its heart, however, it shows the legacy of poverty that hangs over one African American family, even over the one member who has ostensibly escaped that legacy. The structure of the story is also quite remarkable. It begins with Buddy in his hotel room, watching Charley below on the street. This image already hints at the difference in the brothers' respective statuses. From this final moment, Buddy recalls his childhood and the series of circumstances that have led him to that hotel room. Buddy's thoughts "hover over" his brother "like hummingbirds," and these poetic words lead Buddy to think of Charley as a child. As Buddy recounts the paternal role that Charley played then (and that, as the story later shows, he still plays), it is clear that Buddy loves Charley as a father.

This love for Charley can be seen both in Buddy's adult behavior and in his childhood recollections. Buddy says that Charley was so tall that he seemed taller than God. Buddy literally and figuratively looks up to his older brother. He also thinks of Charley's propensity to whittle, the toys he would fashion from scraps of wood, and the illustrations he would make with charcoal. Buddy also remembers the fabulous ghost stories Charley would tell to entertain his siblings. These memories make it clear that

WHAT DO I READ NEXT?

- In the 1981 young-adult novel *Let the Circle Be Unbroken*, Mildred D. Taylor revisits the Logan family, which first appeared in *Roll of Thunder, Hear My Cry*. In this novel, protagonist Cassie talks of the Great Depression of the 1930s and its devastating effects on the sharecroppers in her community. Racial discrimination is also addressed, as Cassie helps the disenfranchised blacks in her community fight for their right to vote.
- Collier's best-known collection of short stories is the 1993 volume *Breeder and Other Stories*. The book predominantly portrays African American women and their struggles. Other recurring themes include drug abuse, poverty, and dysfunctional families. "Rachel's Children," another story in the collection, explores how those in academia become isolated from the world around them. This echoes a secondary theme in "Sweet Potato Pie," as the distance caused by Buddy's success as a professor inadvertently separates him from the rest of his family.
- *The Origins of Southern Sharecropping*, by Edward Royce, was published in 1993. The book is an academic and historical exploration of sharecropping practices. The volume features first-person narratives and also looks at how sharecropping arose as the predominant labor option in the South following the abolition of slavery. In essence, Royce explains that sharecropping was a superficial solution to plantation owners' attempts to maintain their power.
- At the height of the population boom in Harlem during the 1920s, black artists, poets, and writers in the neighborhood formed a distinct movement known as the Harlem Renaissance. For better insight into this phenomenon, read *The Portable Harlem Renaissance Reader*, edited by David Lewis. Published in 1995, the anthology features poems and essays produced during the Harlem Renaissance. Many of the pieces were originally printed in African American periodicals of the day, such as *Fire!*, *Opportunity*, and *Crisis*.
- Lloyd A. Williams's *Forever Harlem: Celebrating America's Most Diverse Community*, edited by Voza W. Rivers, was released in 2006. The volume is a cultural history of Harlem, and it includes original newspaper articles printed throughout the nineteenth and twentieth centuries. The book tracks Harlem through its transformation from an enclave of European immigrants to a center for African American culture.
- For a different look at race relations and subsistence farming in the South during the first half of the twentieth century, read Hillary Jordan's 2008 novel, *Mudbound*. The book earned a 2009 Alex Award, honoring adult books that are recommended for young adults. Notably, the novel addresses the racial tensions of the day, but it does so through the experiences of a white family.
- Jhumpa Lahiri's *The Namesake* (2003), set in the 1960s, explores the themes of social class and family relationships within a family that immigrates from India to the United States.

Charley is a talented and creative individual, but those talents are lost as he plays father to his siblings. They remain lost as he is forced to make his way in the world, working as a cab driver to support his family. Buddy is well aware of this loss. As he graduates from high school, he sees the potential in all of his family members, and he acknowledges that Charley has "the hands of an artist." These observations lead Buddy to the epiphany that he is not smarter or better than any of them, "only the youngest. And the luckiest."

Although it was Buddy's father, the elusive man with a face like a "mask," who first decided that Buddy should be the child to attend school, it is Charley who ensures that it is possible. He is the one who is "determined" to see Buddy "break the chain of poverty." It is Charley who insisted that Buddy become "*somebody*" and who continuously marvels at this fact when that goal is achieved. However, Charley's joy at Buddy's success does not counter his own lack of self-esteem. He feels himself to be nobody in comparison to his brother. This is both the spoken and unspoken aspect of Charley's constant declarations pertaining to Buddy's status. Charley says that he is "nothing but a cab driver." He feels that his lowly status will reflect poorly on Buddy, and he does not tell Buddy's acquaintances that they are brothers.

Here, Charley reveals his belief that being "*somebody*" is about more than simple accomplishment; it is about divorcing oneself from all that is connected to poverty. Buddy does not feel this way; he is proud of his brother, so much so that the only reason he does not acknowledge Charley's role in his success is because he does not wish to embarrass his brother. Charley never acknowledges the part he played in Buddy's accomplishments, not even, it seems, to himself. Later, when Charley refuses to allow Buddy to carry the modest brown paper bag into the expensive hotel, he again asserts his belief that Buddy should act according to his success. In doing so, Charley underscores how hyperaware he is of status and of the proper and improper behaviors associated with it. This is largely because he has no status himself. By contrast, because Buddy is secure in his milieu, he tells Charley he has "nothing to prove."

Nevertheless, it is Charley who is correct in this instance. When Buddy enters the hotel lobby, dejected and without his beloved pie, he is surrounded by people with fancy suitcases and packages from the high-end shops nearby. Charley, however, is a man who has nothing to lose by appearing in the lobby with a brown paper bag, and he does so in a supreme act of love that is both paternal and brotherly. Charley once more puts Buddy's needs ahead of his own. Buddy, though, is the one who ultimately must sacrifice himself, on a daily basis, to maintain his role as a "*somebody*." Buddy never has the opportunity to eat the modest foods of his childhood, such as the sweet potato pie Bea makes for him. The statement "I'd eaten all I could hold, but my *spirit* was still hungry for sweet potato pie" calls to mind the term *soul food*, often used to describe such dishes. This is the food that Buddy, in his success, lacks.

Buddy loves his family, but he is separated from them physically in order to pursue his career. In fact, he never mentions where he lives, only that Harlem feels like home to him. To Buddy, the neighborhood has an "epic" quality to it. It is "as if all black people began and ended there . . . as if in Harlem the very heart of Blackness pulsed its beautiful, tortured rhythms." If one considers the old adage that home is where the heart is, it is clear that Buddy's hear is in Harlem and with Charley. There is no indication that he experiences that sense in his own town. Buddy neglects to mention so much as the names of his own children, and he recalls little more than this of his wife. Buddy, then, lives in constant exile. The distance between him and Charley is also undeniable; no matter the love they have for one another, even their speech is at odds. Charley and Bea speak in dialect while Buddy speaks as the educated man that he is. This, then, is also the legacy of poverty. Of his five siblings, Buddy is the only one to escape poverty, but that escape is not without its own costs.

Source: Leah Tieger, Critical Essay on "Sweet Potato Pie," in *Short Stories for Students*, Gale, Cengage Learning, 2010.

Eugenia Collier

In the following essay, Collier describes the influence of her professor on her writing and life.

"Achilles, of course," the professor continued, "wasn't right bright."

And suddenly the world—my world—was less intimidating, less large, more manageable. Everything intimidated me in those days, more than fifty years ago: the university, the mountain of studies confronting me, the dreadful reality of being away from home for the first time—everything. But here was the brilliant professor snatching away the shroud of mystery from classical literary figures, making them accessible to the likes of me, making them breathe.

That was Sterling's way. He would cut right through the outer layer and touch the core of the matter, the core here being the living humanity of mythical characters.

My initial acquaintance with Professor Sterling Brown was brief: After a week or so, the

Sharecroppers in the south pick cotton. (© Ivy Close Images / Alamy)

class was turned over to a most unremarkable graduate student, whose name, face, and subject matter I have forgotten. But Sterling Brown had impressed me indelibly. A handsome, vigorous man in his mid-forties, he was warm and informal with students, even lowly freshmen like me (and upperclassmen who were repeating the course), in the manner of one who is at home in his world. I have since learned that teachers/scholars sometimes envy their students' youth or exploit it, resent time spent in the classroom away from their research, or harbor frustrations which they ventilate on students. Sterling was never like that. His warmth and informality, through which one could sense his keen intellect and scholarly capacity, seemed—to me at least—an invitation into the realm of the mind. He was the link between ourselves and the ancient world of the *Iliad*. He broke the bonds that held us to the here and now; he showed us vistas of limitless possibilities.

I had heard that Sterling Brown was a distinguished poet. I had never read any of his poems; in the segregated schools of Baltimore, we were taught precious little about our black heritage except during Negro History Week. For five days we learned about Phillis Wheatley, Booker T. Washington, Paul Laurence Dunbar, George Washington Carver, and Langston Hughes. Nobody actually read Wheatley's work or understood what Washington had said or Carver had done. Somebody always recited Dunbar's "In the Morning" or "When Malindy Sings" and Hughes' "I, Too, Sing America." The thrust of our discussion was always the contributions which the Negro had made to America and our abiding hope that someday white people would accept us as equals—an equality that, sadly, many of us did not, in our heart of hearts, believe. Certainly little that we read or said reflected the tragic reality of our historical experience or even the reality of our everyday lives. We never read slave narratives, Du Bois, Harper, McKay, Walker, Hurston, Wright—or Sterling Brown.

Howard University—the Capstone of Negro Education, it was called—was no better. There was a course in Negro literature, but it was seldom offered, and no black authors were included in American literature or humanities courses.

"I BELIEVE THAT A WRITER MUST SPEAK TO THE GENERATIONS. A WRITER MUST HAVE A VISION OF A WORLD BEYOND THE PHYSICAL; HE/SHE MUST HAVE A SENSE OF THE TIMELESSNESS OF HUMAN EXPERIENCE AND THE LIMITLESS POTENTIAL OF THE HUMAN SELF."

Prodded by curiosity about Professor Brown's poetry, I began to read on my own. I had never ever read such poems! They had nothing to do with trees and sunsets, lost loves and melancholy. There was no obscure symbolism to crack, no obsolescent vocabulary, no elusive theme to discover. I did not have to enter another world to experience these poems. They spoke to me in language I had heard all my life without realizing its beauty, in the voices of people I knew and respected, even loved. Sister Lou was my grandma. Slim Greer did odd jobs in our neighborhood. And sitting out on the front steps on a Saturday, I often watched Sportin' Beasley steppin' it till the sun went down. But now I saw the people and their lives in a new dimension which broadened and deepened my insights into my world and my essential self.

The years have given me this realization. I was too young, too callow then to know that I had turned a corner into the true direction of my life. Epiphany is usually a lightning bolt, but it can also be so subtle that you don't know until years later that this was the moment of enlightenment. First the poems, then *The Negro Cavalcade* were the gateway. They set the direction of my career and my absorbing interest. They launched in me a lifetime commitment which still flowers, and ever will.

After graduation from Howard, when I found myself in the white, impersonal milieu of Columbia University, working on a Master's degree in American Literature, I turned eagerly—desperately, perhaps—to the warmth of African-American literature. I decided to do my thesis on Sterling Brown.

It was then that I began to know him as a poet, mentor, friend. He was the one who really directed my thesis, since my advisor at Columbia, a seasoned scholar in American literature, was innocent of any knowledge of African-American writing. Sterling made himself available for conferences with me from the outset. He not only guided me gently through his works and theories but also fanned the fires of my interest in black culture. He was patient and encouraging; he made me feel as if we were kinfolk. That was Sterling's way.

I could see how Slim Greer and Big Boy Davis and all the grassroots people would accept him as their own. He was, in a sense, a liaison between themselves and the unreachable world of artists and scholars. He belonged to them, and he belonged to the rest of us, and he was one of the few who drew us all together and reminded us that we are one.

The endless finally ended: I finished my thesis, got my degree, and eventually began my life's work as a college teacher. As the years passed, I saw Sterling seldom, but he remained a vital influence in my life. I say "in my life" rather than "in my career" because to a black person whose discipline is some aspect of black culture, career and life merge. The career yields insights that have profoundly personal meaning, because they reveal the truth behind the distortions of our image, and each revelation is a personal as well as a professional triumph. So as each of Sterling's works—cornerstones in the body of our poetry and scholarship—helped me to grow in my knowledge and interpretive skills, each also had impact upon my concept of who I am/we are. When I finally got around to writing a doctoral dissertation, I wrote on African-American criticism, and Sterling Brown was, of course, important in my study. Reading his reviews of books and plays, as well as his more enduring works from the 1920s on, I experienced the wisdom, perception, and humor which were ever a part of him.

With the passing years, both Sterling and I continued to grow in our respective directions. Although those directions often overlapped, they were not the same. For example, whereas we were both angry, as any sensible African American must be, his anger seemed more contained, more humane than mine. He published other poems and essays. In time he became our wise elder, the father figure of African-American literature. A number of artists and thinkers from succeeding generations gathered about him and made him a part of their own careers. Roy Lewis the photographer, for example, further immortalized Sterling in sensitive, skillfully wrought photographs. Bibliophile James Lucas collected and cataloged all his books. When Richard Long and I published our anthology of African-American writing, we dedicated it to Sterling and to Arna Bontemps. Poet Michael Harper selected and facilitated a collection of Sterling's poems. I was particularly jubilant when my former student and later daughter/sister/friend Joanne Veal Gabbin wrote her dissertation on Sterling, directed by another gifted scholar and friend, Chicago University professor and critic George Kent. The dissertation later was expanded into a brilliant critical analysis. Each of these artists and scholars not only recognized Sterling's genius and his place in African-American literature, but they also loved him.

One cannot separate a man's self from his works. I cannot revere our slave-holding American "heroes"—Washington, Jefferson, and the hordes of others. What kind of philosopher, for example, can declare that "all men are created equal" while holding other human beings, including, it is said, his own children, in slavery? I cannot find wisdom and beauty in the works of authors with racist assumptions. An evil tree produces evil fruit, no matter how luscious it might appear.

Sterling Brown's essential goodness and humanity shone not only in his works but in his relationships with people. Academics and the completely unlettered, honored poets and tellers of folk tales in barber shops and pool halls—he accepted us all on the bottom line of our common humanity. He met us on our respective levels and spoke to us in our languages, whatever they were. His perceptions and therefore his works were not bound by the temporal; they plunged into the universal sea of myth. It was this deep humanity that we all sensed in him, this that led not only to assessments of his work but also to our love and appreciation on a deeply human level.

He was not, however, a god to be worshipped. He was human, like the rest of us, and that humanity meant that, like the rest of us, he had troubles. Sterling Brown was a man touched by tragedy. He was devoted to Howard University—he used to say that he was born on Howard's campus, in a house located in an area later acquired by the university as the campus expanded. He spent virtually all of his teaching career at Howard. Yet it was rumored that he could not get promotions because he had no Ph.D., having spent his time creating rather than engaging in sterile research. Certainly during his productive years, the Capstone had the reputation for valuing things white far above things black. In any case, Sterling made no secret of his bitter disappointment with Howard.

But far more important than that, he was haunted by mental/emotional illness. Sometimes, especially after the death of his beloved Daisy, he had widely divergent emotional peaks and valleys. I can't say much about that, having no documented facts and not being a doctor. But I would hear, every now and then, that Sterling was back in the hospital. The last time I talked with him on the phone, he called me to invite me to join a grandiose project to reissue *The Negro Caravan,* a project which would involve a great horde of scholars, white as well as black. He talked long and fast, sometimes rambling. He did hold a meeting at his Kearney Street home, but nothing definitive was discussed, and the meeting became purely social. The project never came to fruition. The last time I actually saw him was at a social gathering at Julian Mayfield's apartment (Julian being another writer of staggering importance whom Howard undervalued because he had no Ph.D.), at which Sterling took center stage as usual, entertaining us all with his tales and repartee.

I treasure my memories of Sterling Brown. Now, as I write this essay, I savor them one by one, like photographs in an old album. I see him patiently guiding my thesis; reading his poems at the Library of Congress; holding admirers rapt at a gathering after a conference by telling folk tales while we sat at his feet and listened with our whole selves. Sterling was a great raconteur, using all the gestures and changing voice tones which marked the best storytellers from our African beginnings. Raconteurs call these stories "lies." Sterling used to brag that he was the best liar on Howard's campus. I handle each memory-photograph lovingly, then return it gently to the album.

I believe that a writer must speak to the generations. A writer must have a vision of a world beyond the physical; he/she must have a sense of the timelessness of human experience and the limitless potential of the human self. I am not speaking of conventional dogma or

> "EACH OF THE STORIES IN 'BREEDER' DESCRIBES A CONDITION OF PROFOUND LOSS—NOT THE LOSS OF LOVE ITSELF, ITS PULSE OR IMPULSE, BUT OF ITS EMBRACE. THEY TELL OF A LOSS OF ORDERLINESS, OF ANY OF THE TRADITIONAL ILLUSIONS OF SAFETY, OF THE PURE LUXURY OF EXPECTANCY."

organized religion—or of religion at all. I speak of an awareness, conscious or not, defined or not, that this temporal world of blood and bones is not all, that what counts is the spirit, invisible but real as the wind. Without reflecting this awareness, fiction is merely a skillful narration of events, and poetry is a pretty bauble from Woolworth.

Sterling Brown had this vision, this sense, this awareness. It infused his works. It was apparent in his love for the grassroots people and his admiration for their ability to endure and to triumph. It showed in his impact upon students, artists, audiences, and scholars, and in the warmth of his greeting even to strangers. I felt it as a freshman when he told us that Achilles, like my cousin Leroy, was big and strong but not right bright.

That was Sterling's way.

Source: Eugenia Collier, "Sterling's Way," in *Callaloo*, Vol. 21, No. 4, 1998, pp. 884–87.

Opal J. Moore

In the following review, Moore explains that Collier's stories are written from a woman-centered point of view and strive to describe the psychological and emotional losses of black women and the resultant damage to their children.

Dr. Eugenia Collier has recently retired as chair of the English department at Morgan State University in Baltimore, ending a distinguished and dedicated career as professor of African American literature. She is now contributing to that body of literature.

In *Breeder and Other Stories,* a collection of seven tales, Eugenia Collier elaborates on the destructiveness of American slavery upon African peoples and their families and, predictably, draws connections between past and present conditions. With the exception of the final tale, "Dead Man Running," the stories are rendered from a female or woman-centered point of view and strive to describe the psychological and emotional losses of Black women and the resultant damage to their children. "Dead Man Running," told in the voice of an anonymous omniscient narrator, closes the book with the story of the teenager, Jazzy, caught up in a drug deal that ends in murder. As a concluding story, it appears to represent the culmination or our pageant of slavery—missing fathers, grieving mothers, and death.

Much recent fiction by Black women has focused upon telling the largely unrecorded stories of the lives of enslaved Black women. Contrary to some critical commentary, the purpose of the best of these works has not been to present the Black woman as martyr or as an icon to redemptive suffering, but rather, to address Toni Morrison's observation that despite the factual accounts of slavery and the lives of its former inmates, "there was no mention of their interior life."

So much contemporary writing about slavery and the men and women caught in that web of economics, power, and pain suggests the need to understand more about the interior lives of our forebearers—more than the much rehearsed tales of whippings and humiliations. There may be a need to understand and accept the feeling parts hidden by veils of polite or politic speech, especially the neat language of the law so carefully crafted to obscure the human aspects of the confrontations between life and jurisprudence. These realities, so long hidden, omitted or obscured through renaming (as when rape becomes property damage) can soon be denied and forgotten. Even when the facts of official records are revived and reviewed, where is the story of the interior life to be found? How is it to be revived and (re)viewed?

The stories offered in Eugenia Collier's collection, in their best moments, take us to the feeling parts of the history of slavery that we simultaneously clutch to us and revile.

The lives of the women that she chooses to explore remind us of Melton McLaurin's history, *Celia, A Slave* (1991), which described the passion and striving of Celia, a slave who was hanged in

Missouri on December 21, 1855, for murdering her master who'd kept her in forced concubinage since she was fourteen years old. What elevates McLaurin's rendition of a tragic story is his acute attention to the absence of information regarding Celia herself, despite the official record of her own testimony, according to which she killed her master when he refused to quit his sexual use of her, and incinerated his body in the large cooking fireplace. What did Celia, or other women like her, feel? What did they believe in? Where does feeling begin and end?

In stories like "Rachel's Children," and "Journey Through the Woods," and the title work, "Breeder," Collier confronts us with the moral nightmares of her female characters who are able to kill in order to keep for themselves some shred of personal integrity.

The collection opens with "Marigolds," written in the style of memoir. In the episode, as it is recounted from memory, the youthful Lizabeth is in transition, between girlhood and womanhood. The narrator tells us that even now the marigolds remind her of, " ... the chaotic emotions of adolescence, elusive as smoke, yet as real as the potted geranium before me now.... I recall the devastating moment when I was suddenly more woman than child, years ago in Miss Lottie's yard."

Miss Lottie is an old woman, poor, isolated, living with her son who is what people once called 'simple.' Miss Lottie possesses nothing valuable except the beauty in her impulse to cultivate a bright patch of marigolds every summer. One night, Lizabeth overhears her father weeping because he has no employment and must depend upon his wife's income as the total family support: "My Mother, who was small and soft, was now the strength of the family; my father, who was the rock on which the family had been built, was sobbing like the tiniest child. Everything was suddenly out of tune. . . ."

The girl, Lizabeth, asks, "Where did I fit into this crazy picture?" Having no answer, she climbs out of bed and carries her rage to Miss Lottie's yard to stamp, rip, and uproot the marigolds.

"Marigolds" sets the tone for the entire collection, a world where everything is out of tune, and women repeatedly ask, "Where do I fit into this crazy picture?" Sometimes, having no answers, they turn their hands to destruction. Sometimes, like Miss Lottie, they raise marigolds, obscenely beautiful, and seemingly pointless, in the midst of death and dust. And sometimes, they give up. When Lizabeth destroys the marigolds, Miss Lottie never replants her garden.

The second story, "Ricky," elaborates on the themes of "Marigolds" and predicts the closing story, "Dead Man Running." Ricky is Vi's young nephew, left orphaned and homeless by the disappearance of his father and the mental deterioration of his mother. Against the advice of family and friends, the elderly Vi who has been abandoned by her husband, takes in the eleven-year-old and tries to undo all of the damage done by poor parenting and incompetent functionaries of social institutions—including the courts, the schools and the child welfare agencies.

Vi discovers that though Ricky has considerable charm, he also has secret demons. He is a seemingly incurable bed wetter and harbors violent tendencies that he acts out upon other children and helpless animals. In other words, Ricky is beautiful and scary. Realizing this, Vi reneges on her rescue mission. Feeling tired and overwhelmed, she puts Ricky out of her home and remands him to the failing systems of the state. But she is haunted by his absence, and she has forgotten to retrieve from him the key to her front door.

In nearly every story, we encounter the women who face the impossibility of motherhood, both in and beyond literal slavery. In "Breeder," Collier creates the voice of old Aunt Peggy, which conjures a memory of the days of kitchen talk, of the unique moment when an old mother would turn from the potato salad preparations with the sudden unrehearsed resolve to tell a story she never could tell if she were not near death. The story that Aunt Peggy tells is not meant to be original. It is a dramatization of the frequently referenced breeding slave woman, a story not detailed in any of the celebrated narratives of Frederick Douglass, Harriet Jacobs, William Wells Brown, or well-known others.

We are told that, having barely come into her womanhood, Peggy was one day ordered out of the fields and into a shed where she was expected to couple with a male slave brought over from another plantation. Peggy bears two daughters in succession who are sold to the slave trade. When she bears a son, she decides she will keep this one, and chops off his foot with an axe to ruin him for the trade.

Other stories explore a similar desperation. In "Rachel's Children," a lonely college professor confronts the ghost of a slave mother seeking beyond the grave for her children. In "Journey," Azuree takes her own child's life as a protective measure.

These stories of women and their children fail if they can do no more than excite a knee-jerk pity or outrage, or worse, weariness of the past. They succeed if they can bear us up and into the feeling life of people who have lived and died before us. What must a woman feel when she is called out of the fields one day and sent into a shed to be initiated into her first sexual experience through the authorized and routinized rape of the slave breeding industry? What would such a woman feel about the birth of the child bred for sale? How does she know this child? How does she know herself? At what point did Black mothers turn from the fierceness of Celia, who killed her master for the love of a Black man, to killing and maiming our own children for the same love of them? When Aunt Peggy severs the foot of her infant son to make him unfit for sale, is she a hero or a co-conspirator in the madness of slavery? When Vi turns her nephew out into the streets to be dealt with by the system, is she a character in a story, or is she us? Are we, in America, destined, as these women seem to be, to remain trapped in an immoral machine, madly inventing our own moralities of death and mutilations? Far from indulging in self-pity, these stories should engage our understanding and questioning of our revulsion of the past, as well as our self-protective embracing of it.

Each of the stories in "Breeder" describes a condition of profound loss—not the loss of love itself, its pulse or impulse, but of its embrace. They tell of a loss of orderliness, of any of the traditional illusions of safety, of the pure luxury of expectancy. If such stories sound too gloomy or pessimistic, readers should remember that stories do not predict the future. Only our individual and collective answer to Lizabeth's question—Where do we fit in this crazy picture?—can deliver hope or justify despair.

Source: Opal J. Moore, "A Bill of Wrongs: Stories for the Children," in *Black Issues in Higher Education*, Vol. 14, No. 2, March 20, 1997.

SOURCES

Arana, Marie, "We Are a Nation of Many Voices," in *Multicultural Literature in the United States Today*, February 5, 2009, http://www.america.gov/st/diversity-english/2009/February/20090210140048mlenuhret0.4137842.html (accessed October 6, 2009).

Byres, T. J., *Sharecropping and Sharecroppers*, Routledge, 1983.

Collier, Eugenia, "Sweet Potato Pie," in *Multicultural Perspectives*, edited by David W. Foote and others, McDougal, Littell, 1993, pp.67–74.

Dawson, T. Jasmine, "Eugenia Collier," in *Encyclopedia of African American Women Writers*, Vol. 1, edited by Yolanda Williams Page, Greenwood Press, 2007, pp. 103–104.

"Eugenia W. Collier, Dr.," in *Who's Who among African Americans*, 23rd ed., Gale, Cengage Learning, 2009.

Farley, Reynolds, and John Haaga, eds., *The American People, Census 2000*, Russell Sage Foundation, 2005, p. 58.

Harris, Trudier, "Sharecropping," in *Modern American Poetry Review*, http://www.english.illinois.edu/maps/poets/a_f/brown/sharecropping.htm (accessed October 7, 2009); originally published in *The Oxford Companion to Women's Writing in the United States*, Oxford University Press, 1995.

Lewis, David Levering, *When Harlem Was in Vogue*, Penguin, 1997.

Moore, Opal J., "A Bill of Wrongs: Stories for the Children," in *Black Issues in Higher Education*, Vol. 14, No. 2, March 20, 1997.

Murray, Williamson, and Robert H. Scales, Jr., *The Iraq War: A Military History*, Belknap Press/Harvard University Press, 2005.

Osofsky, Gilbert, *Harlem: The Making of a Ghetto; Negro New York, 1890–1930*, Ivan R. Dee, 1996.

Williams, Juan, *Eyes on the Prize: America's Civil Rights Years, 1954–1965*, Penguin, 1988.

FURTHER READING

Adams, Michael Henry, *Harlem: Lost and Found*, photographs by Paul Rocheleau, Monacelli, 2001.

This unique book about Harlem tracks the neighborhood's boom and bust cycles through its architecture, forming a work of both art history and social history.

Angelou, Maya, *I Know Why the Caged Bird Sings*, Random House, 1970.

This classic memoir by a contemporary of Collier's tracks Angelou's experiences as an African American growing up in Arkansas.

Jaynes, Gerald David, *Branches without Roots: Genesis of the Black Working Class in the American South, 1862–1882*, Oxford University Press, 1986.

This highly academic exploration addresses the transition period during Reconstruction. It traces the ways in which the South's agrarian economic structure changed from one that was plantation based to one that relied on sharecropping.

Morrison, Toni, *Beloved*, Knopf, 1987.

Morrison's famed novel tells the story of Sethe, an emancipated slave who is haunted by the death of her infant daughter, Beloved. This story presents another African American perspective, as Morrison is a another contemporary of Collier's.

The Thrill of the Grass

W. P. KINSELLA

1984

"The Thrill of the Grass," by W. P. Kinsella was published in a short story collection of the same name in 1984. It is Kinsella's seventh book and the third about baseball, following his best-selling *Shoeless Joe*. Narrated by a nameless, first-person narrator, "The Thrill of the Grass" takes place during the hiatus in play caused by the 1981 baseball strike. In a semi-magical fashion, the narrator discovers a secret door into the ballpark and leads a dreamlike project in which men appear at the door every night, bearing gifts of real grass with which to replace the hated artificial turf in the stadium. Like most of Kinsella's baseball stories, it portrays baseball as a romantic pastime and followers of the game as fellow believers in a secular religion.

Although Kinsella is Canadian, he fell in love with baseball when attending and then teaching at the University of Iowa, and many of his baseball stories are set in small midwestern cities. While not as well-known as *Shoeless Joe*, which was later adapted into the movie *Field of Dreams*, the short stories in *The Thrill of the Grass* have been widely anthologized.

AUTHOR BIOGRAPHY

William Patrick (W. P.) Kinsella was born in Alberta, Canada, on May 25, 1935, to John Matthew and Olive Mary (Elliot) Kinsella. For the

W.P. Kinsella (AP Images)

first ten years of his life, he lived in a log cabin sixty miles from Edmonton, Canada. Because of the isolation, his parents home schooled him. When he was ten, the family moved to Edmonton and Kinsella described the transition to public school as deeply disorienting. Kinsella's father fell ill and died of stomach cancer during his last year of high school. For the next few years, Kinsella worked and in 1957 he married Myrna Sails. Their daughters, Shannon and Erin, were born in 1958 and 1961 respectively. In 1963, he and Myrna divorced and Kinsella was a single parent until he married Mickey Heming in 1965. In 1967 the Kinsellas moved to Victoria, British Columbia, where Kinsella ran a pizza parlor for several years. In 1970 he started taking classes at the University of Victoria from which he graduated in 1974 with a degree in creative writing. He was thirty-five years old. He had sold his pizza parlor in 1972 and, while driving a cab to make ends meet, decided to devote a year to writing. He applied to the University of Iowa graduate writing program and was accepted in 1976, just as his first collection of stories, *Dance Me Outside*, was accepted for publication.

In 1978, Kinsella received his MFA from the University of Iowa and took a teaching position at the University of Calgary. In 1976, he and Mickey Heming were divorced and he married Ann Knight in 1978. Kinsella taught at the University of Calgary until the success of his first novel, *Shoeless Joe*, published in 1982, afforded him the financial freedom to quit teaching and to write full time. In 1989, *Shoeless Joe* was adapted into the movie *Field of Dreams*. The short story collection *The Thrill of the Grass* was published in 1984. Since leaving Calgary, Kinsella has split his time between British Columbia and Iowa City, Iowa. In 1993, he was divorced from Ann Knight and, in 1999, he married Barbara Turner.

Kinsella published twenty-four books before suffering a head injury in 1997. He recovered fully from his injury, but lost all desire to write, and has not published a book since. He has, however, become a dedicated tournament Scrabble player, and is a member of the National Scrabble Association. Kinsella was awarded the Houghton Mifflin Literary Fellowship in 1982, the Books in Canada First Novel Award in 1983, and the Writers Guild of Alberta's Howard O'Hagan Award for Short Fiction in 1984. In 1993, he was made an Officer of the Order of Canada; in 2005, he was awarded the Order of British Columbia; and in 2009, he was awarded the George Woodcock Lifetime Achievement Award.

PLOT SUMMARY

The story opens in 1981, about a month into the baseball strike that truncated the season. The first-person narrator, who remains unnamed, finds the absence of baseball "a disruption to the psyche." The narrator is an older man who considers himself a "failed shortstop" and who once had aspirations of playing professionally. On his way home from work one evening, he drives by the deserted stadium and parks in his usual spot at the far corner of the lot. He notices small weeds coming up through the empty parking lot, before discovering a strange door cut into the green boards of the stadium wall. The door seems to be somehow magical, "more the promise of a door than the real thing," and it inspires him for the first time in his forty-year career as a locksmith to break the law. He uses his locksmith tools to pick the lock, and enters the empty stadium.

Inside the ballpark, the narrator is spellbound by the magic of the ball field, but is

MEDIA ADAPTATIONS

- *The Thrill of the Grass*, Kinsella's collection of short stories, has been adapted as a stage play. It first opened at the New Play Centre in Vancouver in April 1988. Stephen Godfrey, in the *Globe and Mail*, said that with the adaptation Kinsella "expands his territory a little, making his theatrical debut with his awe of baseball magic intact."
- *Shoeless Joe* was adapted by Kinsella and Phil Alden Robinson into the classic baseball film *Field of Dreams*. Originally released by Universal Studios in 1989, it was directed by Robinson and starred Kevin Costner, Timothy Busfield, and James Earl Jones. It is available in multiple DVD editions.

disturbed by the artificial turf. Taking off his shoes, he finds "it is like walking on a row of toothbrushes." He muses that "it was an evil day when they stripped the sod from this ballpark," even as he notices a lone weed growing out of the pitcher's mound.

Over the following days, the narrator nurtures an idea, an idea so marvelous that it feels "like knowing a new, wonderful joke." But he has no one to share this idea with until he remembers that there is a rich and powerful man who has season tickets in a box near his. This man is a true fan, one who stays to the end of even lost or rained-out games because he truly loves "the beauty and mystery of the game." Also, like our narrator, this wealthy man sits in the stands on the first-base side of the park. The narrator believes that the positions from which fans choose to watch the game are a powerful sign of the way they see the universe, and that those who choose to watch the game from the same position are like members of a secret club. The narrator introduces himself to the rich man's secretary as a fellow fan, and then waits all afternoon for an interview. Finally he is ushered into the office, where he is recognized from the ballpark. The narrator tells the rich man that he has an idea, and a key to the ballpark, and tells the rich man that he seems like "a man who dreams." The narrator invites the rich man to meet him at the ballpark, and they agree to meet at one o'clock the next morning.

The narrator meets the rich man at the door in the wall with a pizza box in his hands. They walk to the left field corner, where the narrator unveils a perfect, green, square foot of real grass. The rich man touches it reverently. "Oh, I see," he says. The narrator pulls a knife from his pocket, and cuts a hole in the artificial turf, into which he places the grass. The two men have a cryptic conversation in which the rich man indicates that he understands what the narrator has in mind, and asks if he can come back the next evening, with friends. The narrator suggests that perhaps those friends have friends as well, and the rich man says he imagines they must.

Thus begins the nocturnal procession of older men bearing squares of grass. They come every night, slowly replacing the artificial turf with squares of grass. Then they bring tools, hoses and sprinklers and rakes and bags of soil to build up the infield. Little by little they rebuild the ball field.

As he watches this process, the narrator thinks about his daughters, the one who lives in Japan, and sits behind first base, and the one who lives in his town, and sits behind third base with her husband. He feels this as a sort of betrayal, and decides that because she has gone over to the people of the third base, he cannot trust her or her husband with the secret of the nighttime visits to the ball field. The narrator also does not tell his wife where he goes at night, although he loves her deeply, and realizes he is disturbing her sleep by creeping out at night. The other old men share this problem, imagining their wives think they are out with young girls, imagining that the wives have hired private detectives to discover their secrets. This gives them great pleasure, because their secret is so innocent.

Night after night the men meet at the ball field, and the narrator watches as "row by row," the artificial turf is replaced with real grass. The narrator imagines how it will be when the strike ends, and they all return to the ballpark, each carrying the secret of these nights. The narrator looks forward most to the surprise, wondering what the ball players will think when they return to the stadium and find "the miracle we have created." The story ends with the narrator, alone in the stadium, putting his face to the wet grass, "which, wonder of wonders, already has the ephemeral odours of baseball about it."

CHARACTERS

Maggie

Maggie is the narrator's wife, and the mother of his daughters. They have been together for so long that Maggie "knew me when I still dreamed of playing professionally." Although they have a warm and affectionate marriage, the narrator does not tell his wife where he goes at night because, although she loves him, she does not seem to be a "true believer."

The Narrator

The story is narrated in the first person and we never learn the narrator's proper name. He remains "I" throughout the story. He is an older man, a locksmith by trade, who has been married for "over half a lifetime" to his wife, Maggie. He has two daughters and a granddaughter. He has season tickets on the first-base side of the park, and he often takes his granddaughter to games. He spearheads the mysterious nighttime effort to replace the artificial turf with real grass during the baseball strike of 1981.

The Narrator's First Daughter

The narrator's first daughter is grown up now, and lives in Japan, where she has season tickets for the Yokahama team, and she sits on the first-base side. She sends him box scores from the Japanese newspapers and Japanese baseball magazines.

The Narrator's Granddaughter

The narrator's granddaughter is the child of his second daughter, and lives in the same town that he does. He takes her to games with him, and although she often falls asleep in his lap in the late innings, she is learning how to calculate the earned runs average, even though she is only in second grade. The narrator would trust his granddaughter with the secret of the night visits but, because she is so young, he feels it would be unfair to ask her to keep a secret from her parents. So he does not confide in her.

The Narrator's Second Daughter

The narrator's second daughter lives in the same town where he lives. She married a man who has season tickets on the third-base side of the park, and the narrator feels that this is a sort of betrayal, like "marrying outside the faith." She is the mother of his granddaughter, whom he often takes to games with him. Despite his love for his daughter, because she has gone over to the third-base side, he does not feel he can trust her with the secret of the night visits to the park.

The Rich Man

The rich man is never named in the story. He is a man of substance who has appeared in the financial pages of the newspaper. He is also a fan who has season tickets close to the narrator's box. The narrator goes to him with his idea, and it is the rich man who first signs on, promising to bring his father and friends with him to help with the project of replacing the artificial turf.

THEMES

Family

The characters in this story are, for the most part, older people for whom family takes a place of central importance in their lives. The narrator not only loves his wife but his love of baseball is closely tied to his relationships with his daughters and granddaughter. One daughter, who lives in Japan, is physically far away, but because she has remained a fan who sits on the first-base side of the park, he feels close to her. His other daughter, who lives in the same town, he feels less close to, since she has gone over to the third-base side of the park. And his granddaughter travels between the two, sitting on his lap when she goes to games with him, and sitting with her parents on the other side of the park when she attends games with them. That the narrator sits with his granddaughter is one of the first things the rich man mentions when he meets with the narrator, and he laments that his own grandchildren "live over a thousand miles away." Baseball is often described as a family sport, one that families attend together and that has rituals, like how to fill out a score card, that are passed down from generation to generation. Part of the nostalgia both the narrator and the rich man feel for a golden age of baseball stems from their love of their children, and the pleasure they derived from taking them to games and teaching them the culture of baseball.

TOPICS FOR FURTHER STUDY

- The narrator's daughter follows baseball from her home in Yokahama, Japan. He notes that she sends him "Japanese baseball magazines with pictures of superstars politely bowing to one another." Using the Internet, research Japanese baseball customs and culture. How are Japanese fans similar to or different from fans in the United States? What is a typical experience of attending a game in Japan? What kinds of food do they serve in the ballpark? Are there still Japanese baseball magazines, and if so, how are their portraits of stars similar to or different from the way stars are portrayed in the United States. Prepare a presentation for your class that includes visual aids to illustrate your points.
- Baseball has a long oral history that is often passed down from one family member to another. Interview older members of your family and find out what their memories of baseball are. What were their favorite teams and favorite players? Did they attend games? Did they play baseball? Did they collect baseball cards? Write a history of how baseball has been experienced in your family. Include photographs if possible.
- Baseball is a sport in which statistics play a vital part. Create a visual presentation for your classmates that explains how to read a box score. Include a list of definitions for all the abbreviations on the box score. Include mathematical explanations about how to calculate the following vital baseball statistics for batters: BA, HR, RBI, and SLG; and for pitchers: CG, ERA, G, GS, IP, K, SHO, SV, and W.
- Although most people are familiar with the classic baseball song "Take Me Out To The Ballgame," many do not realize that there is a long history of baseball in song. Research how music has been used in live games, and prepare a presentation tracing the history of music in baseball. Learn at least one baseball song and perform it, with instrumental accompaniment if you play an instrument.
- Read the young-adult novel *Shakespeare Bats Cleanup* by Ron Koertge (2003) about a teen, Kevin Boland, who writes about his love of baseball to relieve the stress of his life. In an essay, compare how Kevin feels baseball affects him with how the men in "The Thrill of the Grass" are affected by baseball.

Nature

The restoration of nature to its rightful place is the driving force behind the nighttime project to replace the artificial turf with real grass. Baseball is a game that these characters feel "is meant to be played . . . on grass just cut by a horse-drawn mower," not on "plastic grass." Throughout the story, nature is a force that refuses to be defeated by the efforts of human beings. When the narrator first pulls up to the empty ball field, he notices that weeds are popping up through the gravel of the parking lot "surprised at their own ease." When the narrator enters the park, despite the carpet of artificial turf, he notices that there is a single weed near the pitcher's mound, "perhaps two inches high . . . defiant in the rain-pocked dirt." And after the narrator and the rich man place their first square foot of real grass, they contemplate sending the cut pieces of artificial turf to the baseball executives who need reminding "not to tamper with Nature." Both the narrator and the rich man, as well as the parade of elderly men who come bearing grass and the tools to care for that grass, all seem to share a sense that baseball itself is a sort of natural activity. It's a game that takes place outdoors, on gentle summer evenings, and they all bring to it memories of playing as

Baseball is traditionally played on natural grass. *(Image copyright Sandra Cunningham, 2009. Used under license from Shutterstock.com)*

children, on dirt and grass, and the restoration of the park is seen by them all as a restoration of the game to its true nature.

Nostalgia

Nostalgia is a longing for the conditions of the past. It is usually a sentimental condition, however, sometimes, as in "The Thrill of the Grass," nostalgia can be a powerful motivating force. The narrator starts events in motion because of his nostalgia for a time when the baseball season was not interrupted by strikes between the players and managers, for a time when baseball was played on proper natural grass, and for a time when he was young, and still filled with the hope that he could have a career as a shortstop. While the narrator and the other old men know they cannot turn back the clock, their goal is not simply to replace the hated artificial turf with real grass but to rekindle their memories of why they loved the game so much in the first place. The narrator invites the men to care once again, and to demonstrate their care, as they once did when "delivering a valentine to a sweetheart's door," by bringing gifts to the park. In replacing the artificial surface of the park, they both look to the past, when they feel that baseball was a more pure game, and prepare for the future, when the strike will end, and baseball will move once more into the present.

Transcendence

Because baseball is the only major-league sport that is not timed and games can take as much time as they need to play out, it transcends, or rises above, the time constraints that rule most other pastimes. This appeals to true fans, because they feel that games can play out as they should, without the artificial constraints of timed periods. However, because baseball games play out in their own time, some impatient people find baseball boring. Baseball is also considered transcendental because of the nearly religious beliefs its fans bring to it. In "The Thrill of the Grass," the narrator refers to the sides of the park from which fans choose to watch the game as being like religious denominations. The narrator is drawn to the rich man not only because he sits near him in the park, but because he can tell that the rich man is drawn to "the beauty and mystery of the game." There are any number of images in this story that underscore the transcendent nature of the narrator's quest. He tells us that he "often remain[s] high in the stadium, looking down on the men moving over the earth," as though he is a godlike figure. He looks forward to the surprise when the grass is revealed because he feels "like a magician," and he refers to the restoration of the grass as "the miracle we have created." These older men take on this secret task in order to transcend the ordinary realities of their lives, and to restore some of the sense of magic they felt about not only baseball but life when they were younger.

STYLE

Magical Realism

Magical realism is a term used to describe those fictions in which the fantastic becomes part of a story in which events are otherwise narrated using the objective tone that characterizes realistic fiction in general. It is often associated with Latin American writers like Jorge Luis Borges or Gabriel García Márquez, although it is not exclusive to them, and it is a fictional technique that W. P. Kinsella has used in a number of his works. In "The Thrill of the Grass," the magical intrudes upon a realistic story when the narrator discovers the door in the wall of the stadium. The door is initially described not as a door but as a "door-shape," and the narrator has to check twice to make sure that it is real, and even then it remains "more the promise of a door than the real thing." It is, however, the appearance of the "golden circle" of a lock that marks this door as belonging to the realm of the magical. It is a lock that seems at once ominous and promising, that glows in such an alluring manner that the narrator, for the first time in his forty-year career as a locksmith, breaks the law and picks a lock. The door in the wall is like something from a fairy tale, and by breaching it, the narrator opens the realm of possibility to other magical events, like the replacement of the artificial turf with real grass, like the parade of old men in the middle of the night. "The Thrill of the Grass" portrays these fantastical events as though they are real, which is what marks it as a story that uses the technique of magical realism.

Verisimilitude

Verisimilitude is a term that is used to describe how a work of art imitates and represents the known world. Written works that rely on verisimilitude accurately describe a knowable external world that seems familiar to the reader. A verisimilar text is one in which the author has successfully created an illusion of truthfulness: the story told is very similar to the truth. Even works of fantasy (or magical realism) or fable require verisimilitude in order to create the illusion of a coherent world in which the reader can believe. In "The Thrill of the Grass," the narrator seems to be an ordinary older man living in a small city in America. He has a job and a family and a life we can recognize, and even when he stumbles upon the magical door in the wall of the stadium, his experience of the ball field is portrayed as a realistic experience. The ball field is described as realistically empty, it smells of "rancid popcorn and wilted cardboard," and the artificial turf feels "like walking on a row of toothbrushes" against the narrator's bare feet. These are realistic sensory descriptions that encourage a reader to think of the events of the story as plausible in the ordinary world in which we live. Magical realism depends upon this sort of verisimilitude in order to create the illusion that the magic could actually happen, and it is from this illusion of realism that the magic in the story gains its power.

First-Person Narrator

Point of view is the perspective from which the events of a story are observed and narrated to the reader. A first-person narrative is one in which the central character speaks in his or her own voice as though addressing the reader directly. The hallmark of a first-person narrative is that the narrator refers to him- or herself as "I." Sometimes, as in "The Thrill of the Grass," the narrator remains unnamed, known simply by the pronoun "I," a choice that can lend a story a tone of intimacy, as though it is being told to the reader by someone he or she knows well. Use of a first-person narrator necessarily limits the story in that the reader only knows what the character knows. While this limited knowledge is sometimes used to ironic effect, as when a first-person narrator is unreliable, this is not the case in "The Thrill of the Grass." While some of the events of the story are, on the surface, fantastical, the narrative voice maintains a realistic and reliable tone. This has the effect of heightening the transcendental nature of the magical events of the story.

HISTORICAL CONTEXT

Baseball Strike and Free Agency

The 1981 baseball strike was largely fought over the issue of free agency. Baseball owners had become accustomed to thinking of players as property—assets to be traded at will. However, during the decade leading up to the strike, players had been lobbying to obtain the rights of more modern employees, including the right to collective bargaining and the right to become free agents. Since the inception of baseball, team owners had relied on the "reserve clause" to assure that players would be tied to a single team. This clause stated that owners reserved the right to renew a player's contract at the end of the year. Owners interpreted this to mean that they could automatically renew a player's contract every year. In 1975, two pitchers, Dave McNally and Andy Messersmith, refused to sign their contracts for the year. While the reserve clause bound them for the 1975 season, there was no way to invoke it for the 1976 season. An arbitrator held up their decision, and free agency was established. However, owners were upset that after bringing a player along in the early years of his career, he could just leave the team and they would not be compensated. Things came to a head in 1981, and the players went out on strike. Players maintained that compensating teams would undermine the free agency system, since players would not be free to fully negotiate their own contracts. The strike resulted in the cancellation of 712 games and lasted until August of that year. A compromise was eventually reached in which teams that lost a valuable player could not demand monetary compensation but could choose a replacement player from a pool of "unprotected" players drawn from multiple teams. The strike was bitterly fought, and was so hostile that when it ended, the chief negotiator for the Major League Baseball Players Association, Marvin Miller, refused to have his photo taken with Ray Grebey, the chief negotiator for the owners' association. This agreement held until the 1994–1995 season when the free-agency issue once again led to a walkout, this time one that caused the World Series to be cancelled.

Artificial Turf

Artificial turf came into favor when teams started building domed stadiums and discovered that grass would not grow inside them. Domed stadiums like the Houston Astrodome, which opened in the mid-1960s, were seen as state-of-the-art, shining examples of a new "modern" approach to professional sports in which the players and spectators would no longer be at the mercy of the weather. Houston was famously hot and plagued with mosquitoes, and when the Astrodome opened, it had Lucite panels on the dome to let the light in. These interfered with the players' ability to field fly balls, however, so the panels were made opaque, which caused the grass to die. The owner contacted Monsanto and worked with them to develop a short-pile artificial turf. It was installed in the Astrodome in 1966 and throughout the 1960s and early 1970s. Artificial turf advocates praised its ease of maintenance and better drainage, and claimed that it reduced injuries. Artificial turf also gained footing because many of the stadiums being built during this time were multipurpose, used for both football and baseball. Football teams in particular liked artificial turf because they did not have to worry about tearing up the surface during practice and therefore avoided having to maintain practice fields. The late 1960s and early 1970s saw teams like the Chicago White Sox, the San Francisco Giants, and the St. Louis Cardinals replacing the natural grass in their outdoor stadiums with artificial turf; however, by the mid-1970s artificial turf was coming to represent all that had gone awry with baseball. Since baseball is traditionally a summertime game, it does not inflict the same damage to natural grass as does football, which is often played hard in inclement weather. Baseball fans began to clamor for a return to the traditions of the game, outdoor stadiums, natural grass, and, starting once more with the Chicago White Sox, teams began replacing artificial turf with natural grass.

Iranian Hostage Crisis and American "Malaise"

On November 4, 1979, a mob of Iranian revolutionaries overran the American Embassy in Tehran, took fifty-three Americans hostages, and held them for 444 days. In October of 1979, the U.S. government had allowed the ailing shah, Mohammed Reza Pahlavi, to seek treatment at the Mayo Clinic. Despite denials by the U.S. government that this did not constitute asylum, but was a humanitarian gesture only, the revolutionaries who were seeking to form an Islamist state were enraged. In retaliation, a group of

COMPARE & CONTRAST

- **1980s:** On June 11, 1981, talks between ball players and owners over contract rules, and free agency in particular, come to a head. The players walk out. The owners expect a strike and have insured the season against fifty million dollars in losses. Seven weeks and 712 cancelled games later, the strike ends and the players return to play.

  Today: On August 9, 2009, Sonia Sotomayor is sworn in as the first Hispanic justice on the Supreme Court of the United States. In 1995, as a U.S. district court judge, Sotomayor issued an injunction ending the nearly eight-month strike that caused the World Series to be cancelled that year. When Sotomayor ruled that the owners must reinstate salary arbitration, competitive bidding for free agents, and the anti-collusion provision of the free agency rules, the *New York Times* reported that her ruling noted that "This strike has placed the entire concept of collective bargaining on trial." The *New York Times* also reported that President Barack Obama, when announcing her nomination for the Supreme Court, said that she is widely credited with "saving baseball."

- **1980s:** The 1980s was the zenith of artificial turf in ballparks. When the enclosed roof in the Houston Astrodome, home field of the Houston Astros, kills the natural grass, the owner works with Monsanto to develop a green plastic grass they rename "Astroturf." All ten of the new baseball stadiums built between 1970 and 1990 have artificial surfaces. While artificial surfaces are originally considered superior to grass because they require less maintenance and provide a faster surface for play, the tide is turning once again toward natural surfaces by the end of the 1980s.

  Today: There are just three ballparks left that use artificial turf, all of them domed. They are located in Toronto, Canada (Blue Jays), St. Petersburg, Florida (Tampa Bay Rays), and Minneapolis, Minnesota (Minnesota Twins). The Minneapolis Metrodome stadium is being replaced, and the new stadium, slated to open in 2010, will not be domed and will have natural grass. Artificial turf has almost completely fallen out of favor for baseball, although a number of professional and college football teams still use it.

- **1980s:** Pete Rose is coming to the end of a twenty-three-year career during which he leads the Major League in hits, outs, and at-bats. In 1984, he is traded back to the Reds, where he becomes a player-manager and where, in 1985, he breaks Ty Cobb's career hits record. He retires from baseball in 1989, the same year that evidence surfaces that he has bet on games both as a player and while managing the Reds. In exchange for an agreement that Major League Baseball will not prosecute him for gambling, he accepts a place on the list of players who are permanently ineligible for induction into the Baseball Hall of Fame. Rose's record-breaking career ends in disgrace.

  Today: In 2009, there is some discussion about lifting the ban against Pete Rose and allowing a vote among members as to whether he should be allowed into the Baseball Hall of Fame. Hank Aaron, in an interview in which he states that he would like to see asterisks next to the hitting statistics of players who used steroids, also mentions that he thinks it is time to reconsider the ban on Pete Rose.

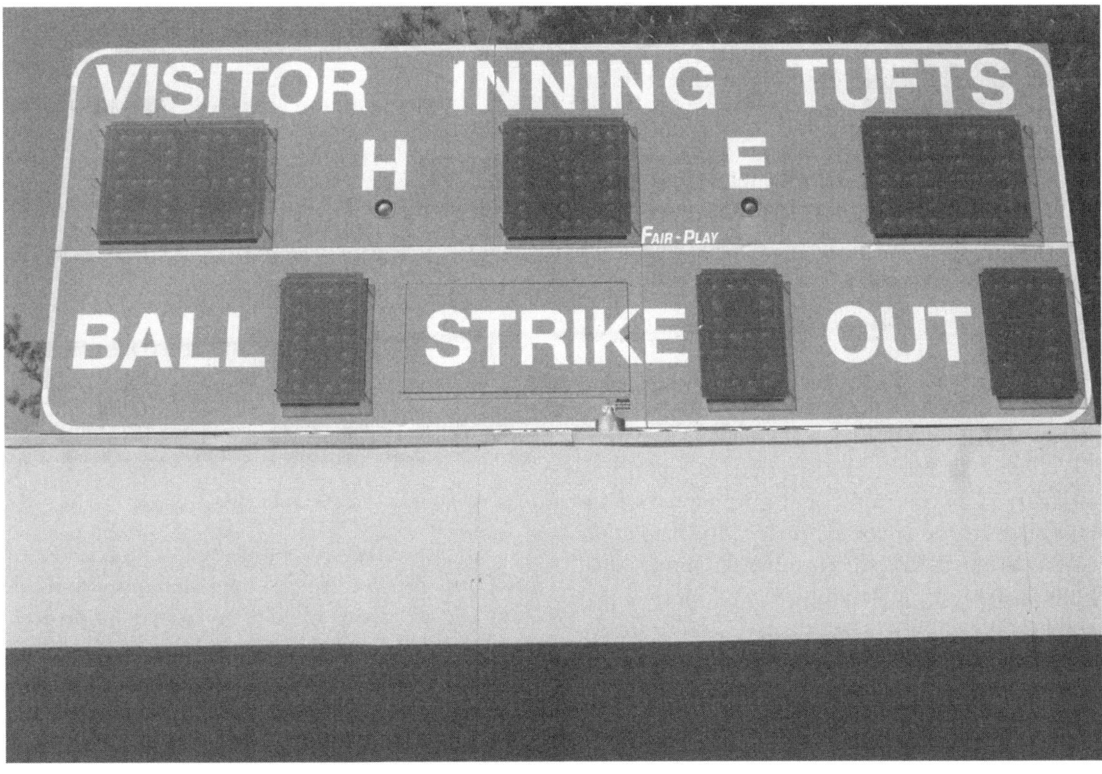

The 1981 baseball strike silenced scoreboards across America. (© Seamus Ditmeyer / Alamy)

students stormed the embassy, took the hostages, and demanded that the shah return to face charges. They also demanded that the United States apologize for interfering in internal Iranian affairs during the shah's regime. President Jimmy Carter took the hostage crisis extremely personally, and it was in part because the internal state of affairs was so volatile in Iran, as well as his fears that hostages would be killed if he attempted military action, that the crisis dragged on for so long. Although President Carter gave what has come to be known as the "Malaise Speech" during the summer of 1979, two years before the summer of the baseball strike during which "The Thrill of the Grass" takes place, the sense that something was fundamentally wrong lingered throughout the rest of his presidency. President Carter said in that speech that America was beset by a "crisis of confidence. It is a crisis that strikes at the very heart and soul and spirit of our national will. We can see this crisis in the growing doubt about the meaning of our own lives and in the loss of a unity of purpose for our nation." By the summer of 1981, this sense of malaise had been exacerbated by events like the hostage crisis and the baseball strike, and is mirrored in the narrator's sense at the beginning of the story that he suffers from a "disruption of the psyche." This was a pervasive mood in the national psyche during the summer of 1981.

CRITICAL OVERVIEW

"The Thrill of the Grass," was published in 1984 as part of the Penguin Short Fiction series in a volume of the same name. It is W. P. Kinsella's third book of baseball fiction, and it has remained consistently in print, although it was not a bestseller like its predecessor, *Shoeless Joe*, and it was received with mixed reviews. For example, Antanas Sileika of the Canadian *Globe and Mail* writes about the collection:

> In his introduction to this new collection of short stories, W. P. Kinsella says that he might be a wizard. This particular wizard wants us to be taken in by his illusions, and in *The Thrill of the Grass*, he succeeds about half the time. When the illusion flops, it is forgettable, but when it works, it sticks in your

memory and you keep wondering just what was so good about the story.

However, Charles Davies, writing for the *Financial Post Magazine*, also of Canada, finds the collection "magical and moving."

Critical reception to Kinsella's work seems to be divided between those who find his use of magical realism and his romantic view of the game compelling and those, such as critic John Richardson (quoted in Neil Randall's article "Shoeless Joe" in *Modern Fiction Studies*), who find this approach "mawkish and sentimental." As Valerie Sayers writes in her *New York Times* review of Kinsella's collection *Shoeless Joe Jackson Comes to Iowa*, "Either that sort of thing strikes you as charming or it doesn't." As Kinsella states in the introduction to *The Thrill of the Grass*, "I like to keep attempting the impossible. I like to do audacious things. I like to weave fact and fantasy. I like to alter history." In the stories collected in *The Thrill of the Grass* he has done just that.

CRITICISM

Charlotte Freeman

Freeman is a freelance writer and editor who holds a Ph.D. in English. In this essay, she examines how Kinsella uses elements of both fantasy and realism in "The Thrill of the Grass" to convey the transcendent nature that baseball plays in the lives of his characters.

"The Thrill of the Grass" is not an entirely realistic story, nor is it a work of pure fantasy. Like much of Kinsella's fiction, it falls somewhere in between, portraying not the world as it is, but rather, the world as Kinsella imagines it might be. Kinsella writes in his introduction to "The Thrill of the Grass" that the storyteller has an obligation to "be anything other than boring," and his means for achieving this is to "keep attempting the impossible. I like to do audacious things. I like to weave fact and fantasy. I like to alter history." While Kinsella uses some of the techniques of magical realism, he is not a magical realist in the mold of South American writers like Jorge Luis Borges or Gabriel García Márquez. While Kinsella's goal, as stated in his introduction to the collection, is to be an old-fashioned "storyteller," holding his audience spellbound with tall tales of what might have been, he uses his own form of magical realism to accomplish this.

"THE STORY DEPENDS ON THIS MIXTURE OF REALISM AND FANTASY, THAT THERE MIGHT BE A MYSTERIOUS DOOR IN THE BALLPARK THROUGH WHICH A STREAM OF REAL OLD MEN WOULD ENTER AND CREATE, WITH REALISTIC, PROSAIC RAKES AND SHOVELS AND SPRINKLERS, A MARVELOUS SURPRISE FOR THE TEAM AND THE FANS."

In an interview published in an issue of *Modern Fiction Studies* devoted to baseball, Kinsella dismisses realism as an artistic project, stating that "Fiction writers work with the imagination. *Anyone* with basic skills can write documentary realism. Sport realism is boring; the good authors of sport literature realize that and rise above it, often way above it." While one could argue the merits of this statement as a general rule about fiction, it is clear from the events portrayed in "The Thrill of the Grass" that it accurately summarizes Kinsella's project. He is interested in portraying a world where extraordinary events occur, and he uses baseball as his medium for this because he believes baseball to be a particularly open-ended and somewhat magical sport.

In "The Thrill of the Grass," Kinsella establishes that we are in the world as we know it by starting with a real event, the long hiatus that the baseball strike of 1981 forced on the game. The narrator of the story takes to haunting the empty park, and one evening, as he is circling the walls of the locked stadium, he discovers a door. But while it turns out to be a real door, it is not a *realistic* door. It is first described as a "door-shape" and then as "more the promise of a door than the real thing, the kind of door, as children, we cut in the sides of cardboard boxes with our mother's paring knives." While it is a real door that opens and closes, by making the comparison to childhood make-believe, Kinsella links the door to the realm of fairy tales. Underscoring the link to fable, the door contains a lock, which confronts the narrator with the sort of challenge that is typical of heroes in fairy tales. Will he violate the integrity of his profession and

WHAT DO I READ NEXT?

- W. P. Kinsella's most famous baseball story is *Shoeless Joe* (1982). It is the story of an Iowa farmer and baseball fan, named Ray Kinsella, who hears a voice telling him to build a ball field in the middle of his corn crop. When he does, it becomes a portal through which his baseball heroes, the "Black Sox" (disgraced members of the 1919 Chicago White Sox team), come back. The team plays night games under a strand of lights, while Kinsella, his wife, and his daughter watch, enraptured. The second half of the novel concerns Kinsella's quest to drive to New Hampshire and rescue the reclusive novelist J. D. Salinger "from his pain." This novel was ultimately made into the popular movie *Field of Dreams* in 1989.
- Bernard Malamud's 1952 novel *The Natural* is considered a classic of baseball literature. The story is about Roy Hobbs, a man whose early "natural" talent is wasted when, in a moment of youthful indiscretion, he entertains an unbalanced woman who shoots him. As an aging player, he makes one last shot at a comeback, only to find himself confronted with off-field enemies he has never anticipated encountering, including the team owner, the fixers, and a beautiful woman whose temptations he cannot seem to resist. This classic tale of talent and temptation takes on the American need for heroes, and our simultaneous wish to see them fail. It was also made into a movie in 1984 starring Robert Redford as Roy Hobbs.
- *The Samurai Way of Baseball: The Impact of Ichiro and the New Wave from Japan* (2004) by Robert Whiting provides a look at the success of Japanese baseball players who have transitioned to the American game. Whiting earlier wrote *You Gotta Have Wa* (1989) to look at the experiences of American players who played professional baseball in Japan. The two combine to make a great comparative study.
- *Baseball without Borders: The International Pastime* (2006) by George Gmelch is a collection of essays by baseball authorities from fourteen nations describing what "America's pastime" has come to mean in their countries. The book is organized by region, and covers topics ranging from high school baseball in Japan and Little League in Taiwan to fan behavior in Cuba and the politics of baseball in China and Korea.
- John H. Ritter has written a number of books about baseball and other sports for younger readers. *Over the Wall* (2002) is the story of Tyler Waltern, who desperately wants to hit a ball over the outfield wall. Tyler is a talented ball player, but he struggles to contain his temper, as well as to negotiate the tricky emotional terrain of his family life.
- Mike Lupica is best known as a sportswriter for the *New York Daily News* and as a commentator for ESPN. He has also written several novels for young adults, among them, *Heat* (2006). Based on the story of the Danny Almonte scandal in the South Bronx Little League, *Heat* is the story of Michael Arroyo, a 13-year old Cuban American living near Yankee Stadium. Michael is a talented player whose dream is to lead his team to the Little League World Series when he is sidelined by accusations from a rival team that he is older than he claims. He must somehow get a copy of his birth certificate from Cuba, without alerting Child Protective Services to the fact that he and his brother have been living on their own since their father died. Lupica combines all his talent as a sportswriter with a vivid ear for dialogue in this novel.

to use his locksmith's tools to pick the lock? Will he take up the challenge the story offers him? Like a hero in a fairy tale, the narrator takes the challenge, picks the lock, and thereby gains entrance to and control over the door that is at once both magical, and very real. Kinsella uses the tropes of a fairy tale when setting up his story, and yet the narrator is such a prosaic character that the veil of realism is not broken. To offer a fairy tale challenge to an older man, a father, an upstanding member of the community instead of to a young man trying to prove himself underscores one of Kinsella's themes: the renewal of vitality in the twilight of life.

For nostalgia is a driving force in this story, and by the nature of its longing for an idealized past, nostalgia is rarely a realistic impulse. No one longs for the past as it actually was, fraught with the uncertainties that it presented at the time, but rather nostalgia is a longing for a better version of the past than the one actually experienced. Kinsella uses the nostalgic impulses of the narrator and the rich man to establish another layer of nonrealism in the story. Nostalgia functions as a sort of magic in this story. Once inside the ballpark, confronted with the artificial turf that feels like "walking on a row of toothbrushes," the narrator finds himself longing for the "ballfields of my childhood, the outfields full of soft hummocks and brown-eyed gopher holes." Much of his relationship to baseball is tinged with this longing for the past, for a past when the field was made from real grass, when the players and owners did not squabble over salaries and benefits, and where his daughters neither moved to foreign countries nor married men who watch the game from the wrong side of the ballpark. It is by appealing to nostalgia that the narrator brings the rich man on board the project, a man who believes that "Baseball is meant to be played on summer evenings and Sunday afternoons, on grass just cut by a horse-drawn mower." The men who are drawn to the park, who bear gifts of sod, are also driven by nostalgia for they are, as the narrator notes "mostly men my age or older, for we are the ones who remember the grass." Even the nature of the surprise is couched in the language of nostalgia. Imagining the surprise of the reveal when the strike ends, the narrator compares it to the thrill of "delivering a valentine to a sweetheart's door in that blue-steel span of morning just before dawn." Even in 1981 the memories of ballparks mowed by horses and men leaving valentines on doorsteps were antique, but such is the power of nostalgia in the history of baseball that Kinsella harnesses it as a realistic source of motivation for all these old men to secretly, square by square, replace the artificial turf with green grass.

Baseball itself is a source of mystery and magic for Kinsella, and the game itself, with its storied past, provides a site of nonrealistic magic for the author. Baseball is also the only one of the major-league sports that is not timed, and for Kinsella this is a source of much of its magic. "The other sports," he says in the interview published in *Modern Fiction Studies*, "are twice enclosed, first by time and second by rigid playing fields. There is no time limit on a baseball game. On the true baseball field the foul lines diverge forever.... This openness makes for larger than life characters, for mythology." To Kinsella, baseball itself carries a sort of romantic transcendence: it is a game one attends because of the "beauty and mystery of the game" (as his narrator in "The Thrill of the Grass" describes it), not just to see who wins. The game's connection to the natural world is part of this beauty and mystery, and although the baseball strike had nothing to do with artificial turf, in "The Thrill of the Grass," it is that turf that comes to symbolize all that has gone wrong with the game. The old men have a pastoral vision of baseball in their heads. Their baseball is a game characterized by the smell of fresh-cut grass, by the sunshine of summer, and the warmth of midsummer dusk. This is not a realistic vision since by 1981 most baseball was played in big stadiums, often under lights, and often on artificial turf. Indeed, the narrator experiences the summer without baseball as a "disruption to the psyche," almost as a disruption of nature itself. It is as though by replacing the turf with natural grass that the old men hope somehow to restore the sport itself to a more natural balance.

In many ways, Kinsella's true subject in "The Thrill of the Grass" is transcendence. Kinsella is not interested in creating a realistic portrait of how fans survived the baseball strike of 1981, but rather in transcending that mundane reality with a vision of what might have been. Just as his characters seek to transcend the ordinary reality of their lives through their nighttime project of replacing the artificial turf, Kinsella wants to transcend the mundanity of realistic fiction by adding a magical element of imagination to his stories. We can see this in the image with which Kinsella closes the story, lowering himself to the wet grass, the narrator is symbolically baptized in the water that nurtures it: "My palms are sodden. Water touches the skin between my spread fingers. I lower my face to the silvered grass, which, wonder of wonders, already has the ephemeral odours of baseball about it." The narrator, an old man, is symbolically reborn at the end, watered like the grass the others have borne to the ballpark, revitalized along with it. He and the other old men might have accessed the ballpark in a semi-magical way, but there is a realism to their project, by working together, by collectively believing in the dream of a real grass field, they have not only created a marvelous surprise, but have renewed their own senses of hope and joy. The story depends on this mixture of realism and fantasy, that there might be a mysterious door in the ballpark through which a stream of real old men would enter and create, with realistic, prosaic rakes and shovels and sprinklers, a marvelous surprise for the team and the fans.

In his interviews and writings Kinsella decries realistic fiction as "boring." Just as his characters turn to baseball as a medium by which to transcend their ordinary lives, and turn to the restoration of the ball field to natural grass as a symbolic restoration of their own waning vitalities, so Kinsella embeds the tropes of magic and fairy tale in "The Thrill of the Grass" in order to transcend the mundane nature of realistic fiction.

Source: Charlotte M. Freeman, Critical Essay on "The Thrill of the Grass," in *Short Stories for Students*, Gale, Cengage Learning, 2010.

Brooke K. Horvath and William J. Palmer

In the following interview, Kinsella and two other baseball fiction writers discuss the literature of sports.

We thought it only fair to give a few novelists the opportunity to respond to what Michael Hirschorn in *The New Republic* once described as the "swamp of cliches and rhetorical overkill" with which "would-be egghead populists" confront sport and, one presumes, the literature of sport. Because we thought the chance to compare answers would add to the interest of these brief interviews, we decided to ask our questions of three authors of some of the best recent baseball fiction: David Carkeet (*The Greatest Slump of All Time*), Mark Harris (*The Southpaw,Bang the Drum Slowly,Ticket for a Seamstitch,* and *It Looked Like Forever*), and W. P. Kinsella (*Shoeless Joe,The Thrill of the Grass,* and *The Iowa Baseball Confederacy*).

ANYONE **WITH BASIC SKILLS CAN WRITE DOCUMENTARY REALISM. SPORT REALISM IS BORING; THE GOOD AUTHORS OF SPORT LITERATURE REALIZE THAT AND RISE ABOVE IT, OFTEN WAY ABOVE IT."**

We have run the questions and responses to simulate a roundtable discussion, but the format was otherwise. Each author responded separately, David Carkeet and W. P. Kinsella choosing to reply in writing, Mark Harris agreeing to be interviewed by phone, which permitted a dialog to grow, part of which has been retained. Scissors and tape eventually created the text presented here.

We are at best only partially sympathetic to the sort of attitudes expressed by Mr. Hirschorn and others. We did, however, find refreshing the common sense and craftsman's concern for materials and their proper uses with which these three novelists responded to two would-be egghead populists. We hope readers are similarly refreshed.

MFS: What is your sports background?

CARKEET: As a boy I was an active athlete, but my performance fell far short of the excellence I imagined for myself. I still play ball (slow-pitch), and I still think I'm better than I am. In this I am not quite as arrogant as other fans, however; according to one survey I've read, nearly half the people in the stands seriously think, on occasion, that with training they could play baseball as well as the pros they are watching.

HARRIS: Well, I played ball as a kid. I never was a professional or anything like that, but I played all the sports kids play—baseball, basketball, football, team games. Baseball was the one I enjoyed most. I never got much into individual games; in fact, once I was very hurt when the gym teacher in junior high school told me I ought to take up golf. I thought that might be something I'd like to do later, but it was of no interest to me then.

KINSELLA: Limited. I was raised in isolation on a homestead in rural Alberta, didn't see a baseball game until I was eleven years old, didn't see a major league game until I was about thirty. I never played baseball; I was a mediocre outfielder in a softball league for a year or two, hit for average but not for power. I was an excellent table tennis player, might have had some future as a golf pro if anyone had encouraged me to take the game seriously, but rural Albertans didn't dream of being golf pros in the 1950s.

MFS: Are these experiences what brought you to the writing of sports fiction?

HARRIS: No, not that directly. Sports were something that were in my head as an experience of the past; they were material to write about: as I looked back into my life for things to write about, there sport was.

CARKEET: If I hadn't played the game, I never would have written a baseball novel.

KINSELLA: One of my first short stories, written in 1948 at age thirteen was called "Diamond Doom" and concerned a murder in a baseball park. Other than that I didn't write any baseball fiction until 1978; I was living in Iowa City, Iowa, and for some reason recalled my dad telling me stories of Shoeless Joe Jackson; I went to the library and reread *Eight Men Out,* then said "What would happen if Shoeless Joe Jackson came to Iowa in this time scene" and the story that would later be expanded into *Shoeless Joe* was born.

MFS: What special knowledge or type of knowledge did you find necessary to acquire in order to write your sports fiction?

HARRIS: It's kind of the other way around for me. I didn't need to acquire any special knowledge, but when I thought back to what in my life I could write about, sports were there; I already had that knowledge for the most part. I did do a little bit of research, but nothing you could call starting from the ground up, you know? I am really a writer first and everything else after that. Research and subject matter follow rather than come first for me.

CARKEET: I did a lot of reading for *The Greatest Slump of All Time,* and for inside, technical material, I found the books by and about umpires the most helpful. Their judicial stance makes them a good source for a novelist. It makes them unconscious ironists. But to *feel* the game, one needs to have played it—at some level, at least—and one needs to have seen it again and again. The spectator's imagination is constantly at work during a baseball game. The more ignorant the spectator, the less active the imagination and so the duller the game. But the informed fan is working all the time. I found much of this work spilling over onto the pages of my novel very easily. Years of watching the game had created a reservoir of images I was unaware of until I began to write about it.

KINSELLA: I acquired a copy of *The Baseball Encyclopedia.* That was about it. I still don't read a lot of sports nonfiction. I am a fiction writer; I work from imagination. Just as a writer doesn't have to commit suicide in order to write about it, I don't have to have a phenomenal knowledge of baseball to write baseball fiction. I've proven in some 100 stories that I don't need to be a social worker or an American Indian to write convincingly about the Indian community in North America.

MFS: How do you feel about being tagged a "baseball novelist"?

KINSELLA: I'm delighted. I do other work, but the words "Baseball Novelist" open doors and attract the attention that is vital if a writer wants to be successful.

HARRIS: I think I am a novelist; in fact, most of my writing has not been about baseball—I have eleven or twelve novels that aren't baseball novels, so I would resist being tagged strictly by that phrase. I have written some novels that have baseball as their setting: I'd prefer to put it that way.

CARKEET: All baseball novelists I know of have written other kinds of fiction. It's an incomplete label for everybody.

MFS: Then none of you considers yourself "a baseball writer"; baseball is simply something you write about? We are thinking of that notion one often hears expressed to the effect that the best sports literature isn't really about sports—a notion captured, for instance, in the epigraph to Bang the Drum Slowly.

KINSELLA: I am someone who writes peripherally about baseball. I agree that the best sports literature isn't really about sports. I, for instance, write love stories that have baseball as a background.

HARRIS: As soon as that epigraph comes up, I realize that at the time I chose that epigraph, I was much more in need, as were many other people, of dissociating myself from baseball; that is, I was going to be earning my living at a university, the way many modern critics who are writing about books are, and I felt that I somehow had to earn my image—the image of someone who was serious. Therefore, I tried to say about *Bang the Drum Slowly,* "Oh, it isn't really about baseball; it's really about something else." I wouldn't do that anymore. I would now say that if one writes a book that has baseball as its setting, then it's about baseball! Whatever you write about, that's what it's about. Other people may see symbolic extensions to the work, but the fact is, it's about baseball. *Huckleberry Finn* is about two people on a raft—and some other things. So I wouldn't use that epigraph if I had it to do over; I would get away from the idea of the book's not being about baseball.

CARKEET: Baseball is a highly structured framework with a built-in social group of rich diversity, chances for success and failure, and—given the pressure to win—opportunities for good and evil. It's a great context, and any novel "about baseball" will be about something else as well. The only book that is about baseball and nothing else is the rule book.

MFS: George Grella, writing on the subject of "Baseball and the American Dream" (a perennial subject—see Donald Honig's Baseball America *and Joseph Durso's recent* Baseball and the American Dream*), says "anyone who does not understand the game cannot hope to understand the country." Is this true, do you think; true for you?*

KINSELLA: True.

CARKEET: I'm not tremendously interested in the symbolic richness of the game itself, and if I'm typical of other novelists, we may differ from sports sociologists and essayists and the like in this regard. I love the game of baseball on its own terms. I also think, as I've said, that it's a great context for fiction. But my impulse to become literary about it ends there.

HARRIS: Well, such statements seem to me like saying that *Bang the Drum* is not about baseball. I mean, such statements are again excuses for liking baseball, attempts to make baseball intellectually acceptable. I don't feel a need to do that anymore, and I don't think that it's true that you have to understand baseball to understand this country. Insofar as anybody can understand the country, lots of other things can lead you to an idea about the United States besides baseball. See what I mean?

HORVATH: Yes, and I think a lot of people are getting tired of such notions—Dan Jenkins, for example, who agrees with what you've just said: that such talk is an attempt to gain respectability for something you might otherwise be ashamed of liking.

HARRIS: Right. They have to get over this idea that people are criticizing them for engaging in kid stuff.

MFS: A related question: why has baseball (in contrast to other major American sports: football, basketball, boxing) generated such a large body of quality fiction?

HARRIS: I have never understood that, and people often ask why they haven't read as much about other sports. Well, for one thing, I think people are going increasingly to write about other sports. Somehow, baseball was truly the national game, but it probably is not so much anymore. I mean, as many people now watch other sports, and even traditionally unpopular sports like tennis and golf are becoming national games—partly because of television. So I never have known the answer to that question or even understood it really except in simple terms like the fact that baseball was always available to poorer people, whereas football for many years was just for college people. And certainly tennis and golf were not the common man's games. Golf clubs and tennis clubs by their own rules excluded anybody but white males, etc.

CARKEET: For the average American boy, baseball is the means by which well-meaning adults introduce him to the world of organized play. It is his first glimpse of that awful game called manhood, and it scares the hell out him. Any fiction about this national early trauma is bound to be emotionally resonant. Reading baseball novels is a repetition compulsion.

KINSELLA: The other sports, football, basketball, hockey, are twice enclosed, first by time and second by rigid playing fields. There is no time limit on a baseball game. On the true baseball field the foul lines diverge forever, the field eventually encompassing a goodly portion of the world, and there is theoretically no distance that a great hitter couldn't hit the ball or a great fielder couldn't run to retrieve it. In *The Iowa Baseball Confederacy* I have a fielder run from Iowa to New Mexico after a fly ball. This openness makes for larger than life characters, for mythology. In, say, hockey, the feats of even the greatest player are so enclosed that they can be likened to a magician doing card tricks on television, interesting but not condusive to quality fiction.

MFS: Are there inherent limitations to sports fiction as a genre?

CARKEET: (1) What about women? Or, if you write about a women's team, what about men? A fictional world where an entire sex must be second banana is limited. (2) When I read baseball fiction, it is never like the real thing. It falls short of verisimilitude to a degree that no other kind of fiction does. I believe this is because real games are visual experiences. A baseball game could take place in complete silence and be fairly normal. In a novel, though, what you've got is language working like the devil trying to do the same thing. So it's always a little forced, a little strained.

HARRIS: No, I think the novel, writing fiction, has limitations. There are different problems, but sea fiction, fiction about the woods, about office life: there would be limitations there, too. The kinds of people who are involved in baseball and who enter into a book about baseball present a cross-section of life, just as does almost any field.

KINSELLA: There are no limitations, at least to baseball fiction.

MFS: How, in dealing with a subject already so overlaid with values and meanings (baseball as myth, as religion; baseball as a tie uniting the generations; baseball's presumed political and sociological significances; and so on), do you restrain the reader from bringing to your fiction all these almost automatic associations? Do you try to restrain him or her, or is the ready exploitation of this wealth of associations part of the reason baseball has that large body of quality fiction?

KINSELLA: The exploitation of and endless permutations and combinations of these associations is one reason why there is a body of quality fiction about baseball.

CARKEET: This question did not occur to me at any point in my writing.

HARRIS: Some combination. First of all, you can't avoid it. You know that people will bring these associations to the book. In many cases, you just can't prevent it, and that's true for baseball or anything else: people read what they know into things. That's what gives rise to jokes that turn on someone's assuming the doctor is a man, you know? So the novelist has to deal with people's assumptions. But then, as you say, the fact that associations are so numerous is a way or reason for inviting people in. If you go back to what we were talking about earlier, about special knowledge, well, a great deal of my knowledge of baseball did come from fiction rather than from a direct acquaintance with the game, at least at the professional level, although I certainly knew about it as a school player and as a reader of magazines, books, newspapers. So it was all literary in a way—off the page rather than from life.

HORVATH: The more I think of it, the sillier my question seems: obviously everyone has ideas about things before they come upon those things in a novel. However, consider how often, for instance, one hears football talked about as metaphoric warfare. Now, if one were to write a football novel, how could that notion be avoided? You could, as Don DeLillo did, dismiss the idea even as you exploited it so as to clear some imaginative space.

HARRIS: I wouldn't dismiss it because it is a legitimate discussion. In my own work, though, I am in a much different mode. I do think I write about baseball realistically, and then if readers make these interpretations and give it symbolic breadth, well, then they do, but there is nothing I can do about that in advance. Once in a while when writing—baseball or other writing—I get to a moment when I feel that such-and-such a phrase or sentence or idea belongs to the book but will be distracting to the symbol-searching reader. I tread very carefully at that point. But I know people do have automatic associations, and I try to work around them sometimes, saying, "well, I can't do anything about that." These associations are there, they're a part of our lore: put George Washington into a novel somewhere, and right away you've got people who have their own cluster of associations.

MFS: Shoeless Joe is as much about J. D. Salinger as about Joe Jackson. Henry Wiggen is an author, and the characters in The Greatest Slump of All Time *seem clearly asking to be read as uniformed Camuses and Sartres and Dostoevskys. How are the artist and the ballplayer alike?*

HARRIS: I don't know. *The* artist and *the* ballplayer. I have sometimes thought that, yes, Henry Wiggen is not only an author literally, but he very much reflects my own troubles as a writer. I feel the artist, like the player, is subject to criticism from everybody else, and only he knows, if he knows, what he (or she) is doing. So in that respect, the artist and the ballplayer are alike. But the more I think about it, I feel artists and ballplayers are just like everyone else; they just have different problems: the ballplayer is and is not like the artist, and the artist is and is not like his neighbor; they are not that much alike, nor are they special. Artists vary from one to the other—it is very difficult to generalize.

KINSELLA: A baseball player is only as good as his last fifty at-bats, an author is only as good as his last book. The work each does is mercilessly scrutinized by critics and the public. In both professions only the wily, the ruthlessly ambitious, and those with an eye for the absurd have long careers.

MFS: Why do baseball novels emphasize fantasy so strongly rather than documentary realism?

CARKEET: Baseball is pretty inflexible in real life. Minor departures become big news. A few years back, Cardinal shortstop Ozzie Smith ended an inning by flipping the ball to the second-baseman for a force out *behind his back*. His momentum was carrying him toward first base, and it was the natural thing for an athlete to do. But St. Louis buzzed about it for months afterward. That very rigidity invites violation. My own book is a peculiar case with regard to this question. Because my ballplayers are so bizarre mentally, it was important to me to maintain a rigid naturalism in the on-the-field action. But I recall feeling a pull toward fantasy as I narrated the games, and I had to revise some fantasy out of it. It didn't fit. But the fact that the pull was there proves the rightness of your question. There are those who would say that my players behave fantastically, but once you get beyond my premise (the nine star players are all clinically depressed), and also keeping in mind that I exaggerate for comic effect, I think my novel is very realistic psychologically.

HARRIS: I would put my novels in the area of realism, and this is related to what we were talking about earlier: the desire to say (true also of scholars and critics) that we're not talking about sports really but about something else. I think many novelists have been anxious to say that, to disclaim the baseball aspect of their work. *The Natural* came out right about the time *The Southpaw* did, and I remember being very disappointed with *The Natural* because it was so symbolic, indulging so much in myth and so forth. I tend to enjoy not books like that but those that are realistic. For example, I feel that *The Greatest Slump of All Time* is rather realistic, whereas *The Natural* and Coover's *The Universal Baseball Association* are too symbolic for me.

KINSELLA: Fiction writers work with the imagination. *Anyone* with basic skills can write documentary realism. Sport realism is boring; the good authors of sport literature realize that and rise above it, often way above it.

MFS: How do you determine the quality of voice—the stance, perspective, tone, attitude—of your baseball fiction? Where does that voice come from? Why does baseball seem most often to elicit a comic voice?

KINSELLA: The process of actually establishing a voice is a mystery. I keep retelling the opening pages until I have a voice I'm certain will sustain itself for 300+ pages. The world is absurd, therefore everything in it is absurd; ninety percent of people in positions of power are incompetent and probably corrupt as well. To those of us who *see*, everything therefore *must* be comic.

CARKEET: There were many stories to tell in *The Greatest Slump of All Time*, so there are many voices—the star players all get their say, as does an ironic, sometimes malevolent narrator, whose purpose is to fortify the central theme that life is cruel. The omniscient point of view automatically struck me as the right one for this book. With a different emphasis, a limited point of view—like Henry Wiggen's or Ray Kinsella's—would be better. I don't see any rules unique to sports fiction here. As for the comic voice, like fantasy it is a consequence of the deadly earnestness of the game. Look at the ump. What a great figure he is. A comic writer just has to go after him. He cries out for it. He turns his stony face on you and says, "Take me. I'm yours. I'm putty in your hands."

HARRIS: Partly, baseball may elicit the comic voice for the same reason it invites myth: the people who write it or who are critics of it feel self-conscious about baseball's being unserious, not really literary. In my autobiography I tell about this: fellow students in creative writing who said, "You shouldn't be writing about that; that's not serious." And so you say, okay, I recognize that—I'll call it comedy. And then comedy is natural to me—which is perhaps why

I didn't go toward the symbolic or mythic—something that came from reading *Huckleberry Finn* and other things. I feel comedy is my mode. But I'm not sure: can you really write comedy about people dying?

HORVATH: You did. *Bang the Drum* is a sad story, but it's also very funny.

HARRIS: Those things do get mingled, but I think the key problem for me is, as you say, how to determine the quality of voice; well, it seems to me that voice evolves as I work—it isn't something I decide ahead of time or even something I can explain exactly afterward except I do know as I look back over a manuscript in various stages that I can see how it developed, how at one point I decided, "well, I started out to do this, but it's really not the voice called for here," so I drifted into the voice the work was beginning to dictate. Not all writers would work that way.

MFS: Let us return to something Mr. Carkeet said earlier concerning the fan's imagination. John Hildebidle, in an essay entitled "The Intellectual Game: Baseball and the Life of the Mind," observed that the best baseball writing, in his opinion, came "not from an effort to understand the game itself so much as an effort to capture and record what occurs in the minds of the onlookers, because it is there that imagination is at work." How do you determine the narrative perspective for the presentation of a sports story, that is, whether to focus on the participant or the fan? A view from or of the field, or a view that looks off the field—at the surrounding action and at the players in their nonplaying moments?

HARRIS: There again, to use the word I used before, it's not something that's determined; it's something discovered. Sometimes I can't remember exactly where or why I began a work. I was just glad to be able to get started, which caused a narrative to suggest itself. Once things start, I'm glad enough and follow that narrative line. I have always focused on the participant, which addresses your earlier question about whether Henry is an artist: I guess with Henry I was deeply interested in his translating the relationship of a writer to that baseball scene. So I guess that is what dictated that—it was really my own concern that took over, so to speak, so that, since I was interested in myself as writer, Henry became the center rather than, say, the spectators and so forth, just as in writing I think more about the writer than I think about the spectators, the readers.

CARKEET: My novel is mainly about the players, but the fans' perspective is important to some of the comedy in it. My ballplayers are crazy with depression, but they look absolutely normal to the fans—a comment on the inaccessibility of other minds. The fans aren't treated a lot in the novel, but the reader knows they're ignorant, and this is a source of some of the humor.

KINSELLA: I've no idea. Every story concept calls for a different interpretation. How I know when I have the right one is equivalent to birds migrating; I just know.

MFS: Do you think the scholarly attention sports fiction is now getting is good or bad? Are academics spoiling it?

CARKEET: Nah.

KINSELLA: Most of what academics say is silly, because most lack a sense of humor. But their musings will eventually sell a few books for those of us who are studied, and *that's* important. The whole Lit Crit Industry needs to be looked at closely; the idea that several thousand people in North America make a living dreaming up patently ludicrous interpretations of novels and stories is so absurd as to defy description.

HARRIS: I don't think people are spoiling it. You probably know the journal *Arete* at San Diego—I think that is quite good. No, I think the more things we talk about and think about, the better. If you say, is the attention good, well: good for what? The whole idea of academic life is to illuminate things—though not everyone engaged in it is illuminating. After all, people who are fundamentally, temperamentally academic people, in a good sense, and who also have an interest in sports: well, they can't talk about sports only in terms of who won last night, so they mingle their interest in sports with their larger views of psychology and history and many aspects of life the participant may be unaware of, just as they would see the political side of other things we are concerned with. Academics see it and try to interpret it in some larger terms, and I think that is good. I mean, think what a terrible thing it would be if we were taking everything just at face value, in the simplest, everyday terms of the evening news: who's ahead? what are the standings? what's going to happen tomorrow? who's going to pitch? who's going to run for office? That kind of stuff. That's not interesting to a person with a larger mind: that's just what is happening today, and is in one sense important—one follows it, gets swept up in it. But one also (and this is the academic function) puts things into larger settings.

MFS: Have you exhausted baseball as a topic in your fiction? Or do you plan to pursue it further?

HARRIS: Well, you know, I would if something presented itself to me, if I could see Henry as a character. I might put him in another setting. I don't have any thoughts or plans now. I sort of doubt that I will because *It Looked Like Forever* had been on my mind for quite some years—Henry's retiring—and something made it click. But there is nothing now that has been bouncing around in my mind that I think would make a good story, so I don't foresee one. Yet I mean what I said before about exploring a manuscript until I find out where the border line is going to be, what the narrative is going to be, and this could happen: I could be trying to work on something else and not succeeding, and then say, "Henry Wiggen could tell this story!" At the moment, no plans, but I certainly wouldn't want to say never to anything. I still have an interest in baseball, watched the playoffs and Series rather closely.

HORVATH: Maybe someday we'll find out what happened between Henry's first and fourth years.

HARRIS: Go way back? Yes, sure. I hadn't thought of that, but maybe what you say is the first idea.

CARKEET: Never again. I can't stand reviewers' use of baseball metaphors to describe the book: "A home run!" "An ignominious third strike bunted foul!" It's awful.

KINSELLA: I have a collection of baseball stories sitting with a publisher. I have two novels in progress, one about an exbaseball player who has become an investigative reporter and is sucked in by an extraterrestrial story he believes to be true. He finds himself unemployed and unemployable, and on the run with his sister-in-law and a stolen baby. The other will make my previous novels of magic realism look as staid as Louis Auchincloss; it is set in a Dominican Republic-like country where there is a factory that turns out iron-armed shortstops. Being accepted as a baseball novelist is like striking a vein of gold; when one strikes a vein of gold, one does not abandon it until every last nugget is mined.

Source: Brooke K. Horvath and William J. Palmer, "Three On: An Interview with David Carkeet, Mark Harris, and W. P. Kinsella," in *Modern Fiction Studies*, Vol. 33, No. 1, Spring 1987, pp. 183–94.

Lesley Choyce

In the following review of The Thrill of the Grass, *Choyce notes Kinsella's ability to let the fantasy take over the facts.*

W. P. Kinsella's *Shoeless Joe* performed one of the rarest accomplishments in my reading history: it successfully sucked me into one man's private modern vision of ecstasy, and that vision wrapped itself like soft calf leather around the sport of baseball. *The Thrill of the Grass* promised to do it all over again, this time with 11 short stories, each knitting a revised vision of the universe as potential but never fully realized no-hitter.

Penguin wisely allowed three of these four writers to provide their own introductions (S. J. Duncan not being around for the revival of her work), and Kinsella's pitch is this:

> Someone once said, "Those who never attempt the absurd never achieve the impossible." I like to keep attempting the impossible. I like to do audacious things. I like to weave fact and fantasy. I like to alter history.

Kinsella is at his best when he lets the fantasy overtake the facts. In "The Last Pennant Before Armageddon," for example, Chicago Cubs manager Al Tiller has been informed from on high that his team will finally win a pennant but that when it wins (according to some inexplicable holy design) it will signal the end of the world by nuclear war. For Tiller, it's a conflict of interests. For the reader, this unlikely plot works like pure magic.

TV baseball always bores me stiff, yet here's this West Coast Canadian writer, former Edmontonian, ex-life insurance salesman, and retired pizza parlour manager successfully selling me his personal euphoria over baseball. Even in the title story, I genuinely *care* about the absurd conspiracy to plant patches of real grass, tuft by tuft, back into a big-time ballpark, replacing the synthetic turf and thereby making a stand against the creeping artificiality in contemporary life.

Behind the ecstasy and the magic, however, lies an undercurrent of sadness whenever the real world takes a big enough chunk out of "the game." "The Baseball Spur," "Barefoot and Pregnant in Des Moines," and "Nursie" exhibit the melancholy of professional (public) players trying to live out private lives with minimal success. "Driving Toward the Moon," the only story actually set in Canada, does a masterful job of conveying the *angst* of a rookie leaguer willing to sacrifice the game for a woman he falls in love with. These are the sort of trade-offs Kinsella worries about when he keeps his fiction down to earth.

Kinsella's baseball world is populated by few genuine winners, and he makes little use of any Howard Cosell play-by-play narrative. He admits in his introduction that stories about athletic heroics bore him. "Ultimately, a fiction writer can be anything except boring," he states, and since *The Thrill of the Grass* packs many surprises, it is freighted with no boredom. . . .

Source: Lesley Choyce, "Three Hits and a Miss," in *Books in Canada*, Vol. 13, No. 9, November 1984, p. 23.

SOURCES

Armour, Mark, "The Rise and Fall of Artificial Turf," in *The Baseball Analysts*, http://baseballanalysts.com/archives/2006/04/the_rise_and_fa_2.php (accessed October 19, 2009).

Baldick, Chris, "First-person Narrative," "Magical Realism," and "Verisimilitude," in *The Oxford Dictionary of Literary Terms*, Oxford University Press, 2009, pp. 131, 194, 349.

Besner, Neil, "Kinsella, William Patrick," in *The Canadian Encyclopedia*, http://www.thecanadianencyclopedia.com/index.cfm?PgNm=TCE&Params=A1ARTA0004326 (accessed September 28, 2009).

Davies, Charles, "The Books of Spring," in *Financial Post*, March 1, 1991, p. 64.

Godfrey, Stephen, "*The Thrill of the Grass*: Kinsella Almost Pulls Off Triple Play," in *Globe and Mail*, April 14, 1988.

Hegerfeldt, Anne, "Magic Realism, Magical Realism (1960)," in *The Literary Encyclopedia*, http://www.litencyc.com/php/stopics.php?rec=true&UID=682 (accessed October 19, 2009).

Horvath, Brooke K., and William J. Palmer, "Three On: An Interview with David Carkeet, Mark Harris, and W. P. Kinsella," in *Modern Fiction Studies*, Vol. 33, No. 1, Spring 1987, pp.183–94.

Kinsella, W. P., "Introduction," and "The Thrill of the Grass," in *The Thrill of the Grass*, Penguin Group, 1984, pp. ix–xii, pp.187–96.

Mattson, Kevin, "Examining Carter's 'Malaise Speech,' Thirty Years Later," excerpted in *National Public Radio Weekend Edition Sunday*, http://www.npr.org/templates/story/story.php?storyId=106508243 (accessed October 16, 2009).

McKinley, James C., "Baseball: Woman in the News; Strike-Zone Arbitrator—Sonia Sotomayor," in *New York Times*, April 1, 1995, http://www.nytimes.com/1995/04/01/us/baseball-woman-in-the-news-strike-zone-arbitrator-sonia-sotomayor.html (accessed October 13, 2009).

Randall, Neil, "*Shoeless Joe*: Fantasy and the Humour of Fellow-Feeling," in *Modern Fiction Studies*, Vol. 33, No. 1, Spring 1987, pp. 173–82.

Sayers, Valerie, "If He Wrote It, They Will Read," in *New York Times*, December 19, 1993, http://www.nytimes.com/1993/12/19/books/if-he-wrote-it-they-will-read.html# (accessed October 13, 2009).

Sileika, Antanas, "The Timeless Metaphors of Baseball: *The Thrill of the Grass*," in *Globe and Mail*, November 17, 1984.

"Text: Obama's Remarks on the Nomination of Sonia Sotomayor to the Supreme Court of the United States," in *New York Times*, May 26, 2009, http://www.nytimes.com/2009/05/26/us/politics/26obama.sotomayor.text.html?ref=politics&pagewanted=all (accessed October 13, 2009).

Ward, Geoffrey C., and Ken Burns, "Home: The Modern Era," in *Baseball: An Illustrated History*, Knopf, 1994, pp. 434–53.

FURTHER READING

Bronson, Eric, ed., *Baseball and Philosophy: Thinking Outside the Batter's Box*, Open Court, 2004.

This collection of twenty-four essays covers a wide range of philosophical, aesthetic, moral, and ethical issues as they relate to the game of baseball. Organized by innings as though the book itself were a baseball game, the collection offers an interesting departure point for those looking to address the larger meaning of the game.

Lewis, Michael, *Moneyball: The Art of Winning an Unfair Game*, W. W. Norton, 2004.

Lewis, a business writer, spent the 2002 season following Billy Beane, the general manager of the beleaguered Oakland A's. Conventional wisdom had it that teams with tiny budgets, like the A's, could not field championship teams, but Beane's attention to an often-overlooked set of statistics helped him put together a great team. Lewis was granted total access, and delivers a tense, exciting, inside view of the business of baseball.

Kinsella, W. P., *The Thrill of the Grass*, Penguin Group, 1984.

This is the short-story collection in which the story "The Thrill of the Grass" appears, along with ten other short stories about baseball. This collection includes one of Kinsella's most acclaimed baseball stories, "The Last Pennant Before Armageddon," about a manager for the Chicago Cubs who is visited in his dreams by an archangel, who warns him that should the Cubs win the division title, the world will come to an end.

Kinsella, W. P., *Shoeless Joe*, Mariner Books, 1999.
This is Kinsella's most famous baseball book, and the one from which the movie *Field of Dreams* was made.

Veeck, Bill, with Ed Linn, *Veeck—As In Wreck: The Autobiography of Bill Veeck*, University of Chicago Press, 2001.
Bill Veeck was a baseball visionary who is most remembered for his showmanship and gimmickry. But he also integrated the American League, bringing in the first black player in 1947, and his ideas about revenue sharing are still considered radical. He was also very funny, and this book contains many hilarious anecdotes about his long career.

Glossary of Literary Terms

A

Aestheticism: A literary and artistic movement of the nineteenth century. Followers of the movement believed that art should not be mixed with social, political, or moral teaching. The statement "art for art's sake" is a good summary of aestheticism. The movement had its roots in France, but it gained widespread importance in England in the last half of the nineteenth century, where it helped change the Victorian practice of including moral lessons in literature. Oscar Wilde and Edgar Allan Poe are two of the best-known "aesthetes" of the late nineteenth century.

Allegory: A narrative technique in which characters representing things or abstract ideas are used to convey a message or teach a lesson. Allegory is typically used to teach moral, ethical, or religious lessons but is sometimes used for satiric or political purposes. Many fairy tales are allegories.

Allusion: A reference to a familiar literary or historical person or event, used to make an idea more easily understood. Joyce Carol Oates's story "Where Are You Going, Where Have You Been?" exhibits several allusions to popular music.

Analogy: A comparison of two things made to explain something unfamiliar through its similarities to something familiar, or to prove one point based on the acceptance of another. Similes and metaphors are types of analogies.

Antagonist: The major character in a narrative or drama who works against the hero or protagonist. The Misfit in Flannery O'Connor's story "A Good Man Is Hard to Find" serves as the antagonist for the Grandmother.

Anthology: A collection of similar works of literature, art, or music. Zora Neale Hurston's "The Eatonville Anthology" is a collection of stories that take place in the same town.

Anthropomorphism: The presentation of animals or objects in human shape or with human characteristics. The term is derived from the Greek word for "human form." The fur necklet in Katherine Mansfield's story "Miss Brill" has anthropomorphic characteristics.

Anti-hero: A central character in a work of literature who lacks traditional heroic qualities such as courage, physical prowess, and fortitude. Anti-heroes typically distrust conventional values and are unable to commit themselves to any ideals. They generally feel helpless in a world over which they have no control. Anti-heroes usually accept, and often celebrate, their positions as social outcasts. A well-known anti-hero is Walter Mitty in James Thurber's story "The Secret Life of Walter Mitty."

Archetype: The word archetype is commonly used to describe an original pattern or model from which all other things of the same kind are made. Archetypes are the literary images that grow out of the "collective unconscious," a theory proposed by psychologist Carl Jung. They appear in literature as incidents and plots that repeat basic patterns of life. They may also appear as stereotyped characters. The "schlemiel" of Yiddish literature is an archetype.

Autobiography: A narrative in which an individual tells his or her life story. Examples include Benjamin Franklin's *Autobiography* and Amy Hempel's story "In the Cemetery Where Al Jolson Is Buried," which has autobiographical characteristics even though it is a work of fiction.

Avant-garde: A literary term that describes new writing that rejects traditional approaches to literature in favor of innovations in style or content. Twentieth-century examples of the literary avant-garde include the modernists and the minimalists.

B

Belles-lettres: A French term meaning "fine letters" or "beautiful writing." It is often used as a synonym for literature, typically referring to imaginative and artistic rather than scientific or expository writing. Current usage sometimes restricts the meaning to light or humorous writing and appreciative essays about literature. Lewis Carroll's *Alice in Wonderland* epitomizes the realm of belles-lettres.

Bildungsroman: A German word meaning "novel of development." The *bildungsroman* is a study of the maturation of a youthful character, typically brought about through a series of social or sexual encounters that lead to self-awareness. J. D. Salinger's *Catcher in the Rye* is a *bildungsroman*, and Doris Lessing's story "Through the Tunnel" exhibits characteristics of a *bildungsroman* as well.

Black Aesthetic Movement: A period of artistic and literary development among African Americans in the 1960s and early 1970s. This was the first major African-American artistic movement since the Harlem Renaissance and was closely paralleled by the civil rights and black power movements. The black aesthetic writers attempted to produce works of art that would be meaningful to the black masses. Key figures in black aesthetics included one of its founders, poet and playwright Amiri Baraka, formerly known as Le Roi Jones; poet and essayist Haki R. Madhubuti, formerly Don L. Lee; poet and playwright Sonia Sanchez; and dramatist Ed Bullins. Works representative of the Black Aesthetic Movement include Amiri Baraka's play *Dutchman,* a 1964 Obie award-winner.

Black Humor: Writing that places grotesque elements side by side with humorous ones in an attempt to shock the reader, forcing him or her to laugh at the horrifying reality of a disordered world. "Lamb to the Slaughter," by Roald Dahl, in which a placid housewife murders her husband and serves the murder weapon to the investigating policemen, is an example of black humor.

C

Catharsis: The release or purging of unwanted emotions—specifically fear and pity—brought about by exposure to art. The term was first used by the Greek philosopher Aristotle in his *Poetics* to refer to the desired effect of tragedy on spectators.

Character: Broadly speaking, a person in a literary work. The actions of characters are what constitute the plot of a story, novel, or poem. There are numerous types of characters, ranging from simple, stereotypical figures to intricate, multifaceted ones. "Characterization" is the process by which an author creates vivid, believable characters in a work of art. This may be done in a variety of ways, including (1) direct description of the character by the narrator; (2) the direct presentation of the speech, thoughts, or actions of the character; and (3) the responses of other characters to the character. The term "character" also refers to a form originated by the ancient Greek writer Theophrastus that later became popular in the seventeenth and eighteenth centuries. It is a short essay or sketch of a person who prominently displays a specific attribute or quality, such as miserliness or ambition. "Miss Brill," a story by Katherine Mansfield, is an example of a character sketch.

Classical: In its strictest definition in literary criticism, classicism refers to works of ancient Greek or Roman literature. The term may also be used to describe a literary work of recognized importance (a "classic") from any time period or literature that exhibits the traits of classicism. Examples of later works and authors now described as classical include French literature of the seventeenth century, Western novels of the nineteenth century, and American fiction of the mid-nineteenth century such as that written by James Fenimore Cooper and Mark Twain.

Climax: The turning point in a narrative, the moment when the conflict is at its most intense. Typically, the structure of stories, novels, and plays is one of rising action, in which tension builds to the climax, followed by falling action, in which tension lessens as the story moves to its conclusion.

Comedy: One of two major types of drama, the other being tragedy. Its aim is to amuse, and it typically ends happily. Comedy assumes many forms, such as farce and burlesque, and uses a variety of techniques, from parody to satire. In a restricted sense the term comedy refers only to dramatic presentations, but in general usage it is commonly applied to nondramatic works as well.

Comic Relief: The use of humor to lighten the mood of a serious or tragic story, especially in plays. The technique is very common in Elizabethan works, and can be an integral part of the plot or simply a brief event designed to break the tension of the scene.

Conflict: The conflict in a work of fiction is the issue to be resolved in the story. It usually occurs between two characters, the protagonist and the antagonist, or between the protagonist and society or the protagonist and himself or herself. The conflict in Washington Irving's story "The Devil and Tom Walker" is that the Devil wants Tom Walker's soul but Tom does not want to go to hell.

Criticism: The systematic study and evaluation of literary works, usually based on a specific method or set of principles. An important part of literary studies since ancient times, the practice of criticism has given rise to numerous theories, methods, and "schools," sometimes producing conflicting, even contradictory, interpretations of literature in general as well as of individual works. Even such basic issues as what constitutes a poem or a novel have been the subject of much criticism over the centuries. Seminal texts of literary criticism include Plato's *Republic,* Aristotle's *Poetics,* Sir Philip Sidney's *The Defence of Poesie,* and John Dryden's *Of Dramatic Poesie.* Contemporary schools of criticism include deconstruction, feminist, psychoanalytic, poststructuralist, new historicist, postcolonialist, and reader-response.

D

Deconstruction: A method of literary criticism characterized by multiple conflicting interpretations of a given work. Deconstructionists consider the impact of the language of a work and suggest that the true meaning of the work is not necessarily the meaning that the author intended.

Deduction: The process of reaching a conclusion through reasoning from general premises to a specific premise. Arthur Conan Doyle's character Sherlock Holmes often used deductive reasoning to solve mysteries.

Denotation: The definition of a word, apart from the impressions or feelings it creates in the reader. The word "apartheid" denotes a political and economic policy of segregation by race, but its connotations—oppression, slavery, inequality—are numerous.

Denouement: A French word meaning "the unknotting." In literature, it denotes the resolution of conflict in fiction or drama. The *denouement* follows the climax and provides an outcome to the primary plot situation as well as an explanation of secondary plot complications. A well-known example of *denouement* is the last scene of the play *As You Like It* by William Shakespeare, in which couples are married, an evildoer repents, the identities of two disguised characters are revealed, and a ruler is restored to power. Also known as "falling action."

Detective Story: A narrative about the solution of a mystery or the identification of a criminal. The conventions of the detective story include the detective's scrupulous use of logic in solving the mystery; incompetent or ineffectual police; a suspect who appears guilty at first but is later proved innocent; and the detective's friend or confidant—often the narrator—whose slowness in interpreting clues emphasizes by contrast the detective's brilliance. Edgar Allan Poe's "Murders in the Rue Morgue" is commonly regarded as the earliest example of this type of story. Other practitioners are Arthur Conan Doyle, Dashiell Hammett, and Agatha Christie.

Dialogue: Dialogue is conversation between people in a literary work. In its most restricted sense, it refers specifically to the speech of characters in a drama. As a specific literary genre, a "dialogue" is a composition in which characters debate an issue or idea.

Didactic: A term used to describe works of literature that aim to teach a moral, religious, political, or practical lesson. Although didactic elements are often found inartistically pleasing works, the term "didactic" usually refers to literature in which the message is more important than the form. The term may also be used to criticize a work that the critic finds "overly didactic," that is, heavy-handed in its delivery of a lesson. An example of didactic literature is John Bunyan's *Pilgrim's Progress.*

Dramatic Irony: Occurs when the reader of a work of literature knows something that a character in the work itself does not know. The irony is in the contrast between the intended meaning of the statements or actions of a character and the additional information understood by the audience.

Dystopia: An imaginary place in a work of fiction where the characters lead dehumanized, fearful lives. George Orwell's *Nineteen Eighty-four,* and Margaret Atwood's *Handmaid's Tale* portray versions of dystopia.

E

Edwardian: Describes cultural conventions identified with the period of the reign of Edward VII of England (1901–1910). Writers of the Edwardian Age typically displayed a strong reaction against the propriety and conservatism of the Victorian Age. Their work often exhibits distrust of authority in religion, politics, and art and expresses strong doubts about the soundness of conventional values. Writers of this era include E. M. Forster, H. G. Wells, and Joseph Conrad.

Empathy: A sense of shared experience, including emotional and physical feelings, with someone or something other than oneself. Empathy is often used to describe the response of a reader to a literary character.

Epilogue: A concluding statement or section of a literary work. In dramas, particularly those of the seventeenth and eighteenth centuries, the epilogue is a closing speech, often in verse, delivered by an actor at the end of a play and spoken directly to the audience.

Epiphany: A sudden revelation of truth inspired by a seemingly trivial incident. The term was widely used by James Joyce in his critical writings, and the stories in Joyce's *Dubliners* are commonly called "epiphanies."

Epistolary Novel: A novel in the form of letters. The form was particularly popular in the eighteenth century. The form can also be applied to short stories, as in Edwidge Danticat's "Children of the Sea."

Epithet: A word or phrase, often disparaging or abusive, that expresses a character trait of someone or something. "The Napoleon of crime" is an epithet applied to Professor Moriarty, arch-rival of Sherlock Holmes in Arthur Conan Doyle's series of detective stories.

Existentialism: A predominantly twentieth-century philosophy concerned with the nature and perception of human existence. There are two major strains of existentialist thought: atheistic and Christian. Followers of atheistic existentialism believe that the individual is alone in a godless universe and that the basic human condition is one of suffering and loneliness. Nevertheless, because there are no fixed values, individuals can create their own characters—indeed, they can shape themselves—through the exercise of free will. The atheistic strain culminates in and is popularly associated with the works of Jean-Paul Sartre. The Christian existentialists, on the other hand, believe that only in God may people find freedom from life's anguish. The two strains hold certain beliefs in common: that existence cannot be fully understood or described through empirical effort; that anguish is a universal element of life; that individuals must bear responsibility for their actions; and that there is no common standard of behavior or perception for religious and ethical matters. Existentialist thought figures prominently in the works of such authors as Franz Kafka, Fyodor Dostoyevsky, and Albert Camus.

Expatriatism: The practice of leaving one's country to live for an extended period in another country. Literary expatriates include Irish author James Joyce who moved to Italy and France, American writers James Baldwin, Ernest Hemingway, Gertrude Stein, and F. Scott Fitzgerald who lived and wrote in

Paris, and Polish novelist Joseph Conrad in England.

Exposition: Writing intended to explain the nature of an idea, thing, or theme. Expository writing is often combined with description, narration, or argument.

Expressionism: An indistinct literary term, originally used to describe an early twentieth-century school of German painting. The term applies to almost any mode of unconventional, highly subjective writing that distorts reality in some way. Advocates of Expressionism include Federico Garcia Lorca, Eugene O'Neill, Franz Kafka, and James Joyce.

F

Fable: A prose or verse narrative intended to convey amoral. Animals or inanimate objects with human characteristics often serve as characters in fables. A famous fable is Aesop's "The Tortoise and the Hare."

Fantasy: A literary form related to mythology and folklore. Fantasy literature is typically set in non-existent realms and features supernatural beings. Notable examples of literature with elements of fantasy are Gabriel Gárcia Márquez's story "The Handsomest Drowned Man in the World" and Ursula K. Le Guin's "The Ones Who Walk Away from Omelas."

Farce: A type of comedy characterized by broad humor, outlandish incidents, and often vulgar subject matter. Much of the comedy in film and television could more accurately be described as farce.

Fiction: Any story that is the product of imagination rather than a documentation of fact. Characters and events in such narratives may be based in real life but their ultimate form and configuration is a creation of the author.

Figurative Language: A technique in which an author uses figures of speech such as hyperbole, irony, metaphor, or simile for a particular effect. Figurative language is the opposite of literal language, in which every word is truthful, accurate, and free of exaggeration or embellishment.

Flashback: A device used in literature to present action that occurred before the beginning of the story. Flashbacks are often introduced as the dreams or recollections of one or more characters.

Foil: A character in a work of literature whose physical or psychological qualities contrast strongly with, and therefore highlight, the corresponding qualities of another character. In his Sherlock Holmes stories, Arthur Conan Doyle portrayed Dr. Watson as a man of normal habits and intelligence, making him a foil for the eccentric and unusually perceptive Sherlock Holmes.

Folklore: Traditions and myths preserved in a culture or group of people. Typically, these are passed on by word of mouth in various forms—such as legends, songs, and proverbs—or preserved in customs and ceremonies. Washington Irving, in "The Devil and Tom Walker" and many of his other stories, incorporates many elements of the folklore of New England and Germany.

Folktale: A story originating in oral tradition. Folk tales fall into a variety of categories, including legends, ghost stories, fairy tales, fables, and anecdotes based on historical figures and events.

Foreshadowing: A device used in literature to create expectation or to set up an explanation of later developments. Edgar Allan Poe uses foreshadowing to create suspense in "The Fall of the House of Usher" when the narrator comments on the crumbling state of disrepair in which he finds the house.

G

Genre: A category of literary work. Genre may refer to both the content of a given work—tragedy, comedy, horror, science fiction—and to its form, such as poetry, novel, or drama.

Gilded Age: A period in American history during the 1870s and after characterized by political corruption and materialism. A number of important novels of social and political criticism were written during this time. Henry James and Kate Chopin are two writers who were prominent during the Gilded Age.

Gothicism: In literature, works characterized by a taste for medieval or morbid characters and situations. A gothic novel prominently features elements of horror, the supernatural, gloom, and violence: clanking chains, terror, ghosts, medieval castles, and unexplained phenomena. The term "gothic novel" is also applied to novels that lack elements of the traditional Gothic setting but that create a similar atmosphere of terror or dread. The term can also be applied to stories, plays, and poems. Mary Shelley's *Frankenstein* and Joyce Carol Oates's *Bellefleur* are both gothic novels.

Grotesque: In literature, a work that is characterized by exaggeration, deformity, freakishness, and disorder. The grotesque often includes an element of comic absurdity. Examples of the grotesque can be found in the works of Edgar Allan Poe, Flannery O'Connor, Joseph Heller, and Shirley Jackson.

H

Harlem Renaissance: The Harlem Renaissance of the 1920s is generally considered the first significant movement of black writers and artists in the United States. During this period, new and established black writers, many of whom lived in the region of New York City known as Harlem, published more fiction and poetry than ever before, the first influential black literary journals were established, and black authors and artists received their first widespread recognition and serious critical appraisal. Among the major writers associated with this period are Countee Cullen, Langston Hughes, Arna Bontemps, and Zora Neale Hurston.

Hero/Heroine: The principal sympathetic character in a literary work. Heroes and heroines typically exhibit admirable traits: idealism, courage, and integrity, for example. Famous heroes and heroines of literature include Charles Dickens's Oliver Twist, Margaret Mitchell's Scarlett O'Hara, and the anonymous narrator in Ralph Ellison's *Invisible Man.*

Hyperbole: Deliberate exaggeration used to achieve an effect. In William Shakespeare's *Macbeth,* Lady Macbeth hyperbolizes when she says, "All the perfumes of Arabia could not sweeten this little hand."

I

Image: A concrete representation of an object or sensory experience. Typically, such a representation helps evoke the feelings associated with the object or experience itself. Images are either "literal" or "figurative." Literal images are especially concrete and involve little or no extension of the obvious meaning of the words used to express them. Figurative images do not follow the literal meaning of the words exactly. Images in literature are usually visual, but the term "image" can also refer to the representation of any sensory experience.

Imagery: The array of images in a literary work. Also used to convey the author's overall use of figurative language in a work.

In medias res: A Latin term meaning "in the middle of things." It refers to the technique of beginning a story at its midpoint and then using various flashback devices to reveal previous action. This technique originated in such epics as Virgil's *Aeneid.*

Interior Monologue: A narrative technique in which characters' thoughts are revealed in a way that appears to be uncontrolled by the author. The interior monologue typically aims to reveal the inner self of a character. It portrays emotional experiences as they occur at both a conscious and unconscious level. One of the best-known interior monologues in English is the Molly Bloom section at the close of James Joyce's *Ulysses.* Katherine Anne Porter's "The Jilting of Granny Weatherall" is also told in the form of an interior monologue.

Irony: In literary criticism, the effect of language in which the intended meaning is the opposite of what is stated. The title of Jonathan Swift's "A Modest Proposal" is ironic because what Swift proposes in this essay is cannibalism—hardly "modest."

J

Jargon: Language that is used or understood only by a select group of people. Jargon may refer to terminology used in a certain profession, such as computer jargon, or it may refer to any nonsensical language that is not understood by most people. Anthony Burgess's *A Clockwork Orange* and James Thurber's "The Secret Life of Walter Mitty" both use jargon.

K

Knickerbocker Group: An indistinct group of New York writers of the first half of the nineteenth century. Members of the group were linked only by location and a common theme: New York life. Two famous members of the Knickerbocker Group were Washington Irving and William Cullen

Bryant. The group's name derives from Irving's *Knickerbocker's History of New York.*

L

Literal Language: An author uses literal language when he or she writes without exaggerating or embellishing the subject matter and without any tools of figurative language. To say "He ran very quickly down the street" is to use literal language, whereas to say "He ran like a hare down the street" would be using figurative language.

Literature: Literature is broadly defined as any written or spoken material, but the term most often refers to creative works. Literature includes poetry, drama, fiction, and many kinds of nonfiction writing, as well as oral, dramatic, and broadcast compositions not necessarily preserved in a written format, such as films and television programs.

Lost Generation: A term first used by Gertrude Stein to describe the post-World War I generation of American writers: men and women haunted by a sense of betrayal and emptiness brought about by the destructiveness of the war. The term is commonly applied to Hart Crane, Ernest Hemingway, F. Scott Fitzgerald, and others.

M

Magic Realism: A form of literature that incorporates fantasy elements or supernatural occurrences into the narrative and accepts them as truth. Gabriel Gárcia Márquez and Laura Esquivel are two writers known for their works of magic realism.

Metaphor: A figure of speech that expresses an idea through the image of another object. Metaphors suggest the essence of the first object by identifying it with certain qualities of the second object. An example is "But soft, what light through yonder window breaks? / It is the east, and Juliet is the sun" in William Shakespeare's *Romeo and Juliet*. Here, Juliet, the first object, is identified with qualities of the second object, the sun.

Minimalism: A literary style characterized by spare, simple prose with few elaborations. In minimalism, the main theme of the work is often never discussed directly. Amy Hempel and Ernest Hemingway are two writers known for their works of minimalism.

Modernism: Modern literary practices. Also, the principles of a literary school that lasted from roughly the beginning of the twentieth century until the end of World War II. Modernism is defined by its rejection of the literary conventions of the nineteenth century and by its opposition to conventional morality, taste, traditions, and economic values. Many writers are associated with the concepts of modernism, including Albert Camus, D. H. Lawrence, Ernest Hemingway, William Faulkner, Eugene O'Neill, and James Joyce.

Monologue: A composition, written or oral, by a single individual. More specifically, a speech given by a single individual in a drama or other public entertainment. It has no set length, although it is usually several or more lines long. "I Stand Here Ironing" by Tillie Olsen is an example of a story written in the form of a monologue.

Mood: The prevailing emotions of a work or of the author in his or her creation of the work. The mood of a work is not always what might be expected based on its subject matter.

Motif: A theme, character type, image, metaphor, or other verbal element that recurs throughout a single work of literature or occurs in a number of different works over a period of time. For example, the color white in Herman Melville's *Moby Dick* is a "specific" motif, while the trials of star-crossed lovers is a "conventional" motif from the literature of all periods.

N

Narration: The telling of a series of events, real or invented. A narration may be either a simple narrative, in which the events are recounted chronologically, or a narrative with a plot, in which the account is given in a style reflecting the author's artistic concept of the story. Narration is sometimes used as a synonym for "storyline."

Narrative: A verse or prose accounting of an event or sequence of events, real or invented. The term is also used as an adjective in the sense "method of narration." For example, in literary criticism, the expression "narrative technique" usually refers to the way the author structures and presents his or her story. Different narrative forms include diaries, travelogues, novels, ballads, epics, short stories, and other fictional forms.

Narrator: The teller of a story. The narrator may be the author or a character in the story through whom the author speaks. Huckleberry Finn is the narrator of Mark Twain's *The Adventures of Huckleberry Finn.*

Novella: An Italian term meaning "story." This term has been especially used to describe fourteenth-century Italian tales, but it also refers to modern short novels. Modern novellas include Leo Tolstoy's *The Death of Ivan Ilich,* Fyodor Dostoyevsky's *Notes from the Underground,* and Joseph Conrad's *Heart of Darkness.*

O

Oedipus Complex: A son's romantic obsession with his mother. The phrase is derived from the story of the ancient Theban hero Oedipus, who unknowingly killed his father and married his mother, and was popularized by Sigmund Freud's theory of psychoanalysis. Literary occurrences of the Oedipus complex include Sophocles' *Oedipus Rex* and D. H. Lawrence's "The Rocking-Horse Winner."

Onomatopoeia: The use of words whose sounds express or suggest their meaning. In its simplest sense, onomatopoeia may be represented by words that mimic the sounds they denote such as "hiss" or "meow." At a more subtle level, the pattern and rhythm of sounds and rhymes of a line or poem may be onomatopoeic.

Oral Tradition: A process by which songs, ballads, folklore, and other material are transmitted by word of mouth. The tradition of oral transmission predates the written record systems of literate society. Oral transmission preserves material sometimes over generations, although often with variations. Memory plays a large part in the recitation and preservation of orally transmitted material. Native American myths and legends, and African folktales told by plantation slaves are examples of orally transmitted literature.

P

Parable: A story intended to teach a moral lesson or answer an ethical question. Examples of parables are the stories told by Jesus Christ in the New Testament, notably "The Prodigal Son," but parables also are used in Sufism, rabbinic literature, Hasidism, and Zen Buddhism. Isaac Bashevis Singer's story "Gimpel the Fool" exhibits characteristics of a parable.

Paradox: A statement that appears illogical or contradictory at first, but may actually point to an underlying truth. A literary example of a paradox is George Orwell's statement "All animals are equal, but some animals are more equal than others" in *Animal Farm.*

Parody: In literature, this term refers to an imitation of a serious literary work or the signature style of a particular author in a ridiculous manner. Atypical parody adopts the style of the original and applies it to an inappropriate subject for humorous effect. Parody is a form of satire and could be considered the literary equivalent of a caricature or cartoon. Henry Fielding's *Shamela* is a parody of Samuel Richardson's *Pamela.*

Persona: A Latin term meaning "mask." Personae are the characters in a fictional work of literature. The persona generally functions as a mask through which the author tells a story in a voice other than his or her own. A persona is usually either a character in a story who acts as a narrator or an "implied author," a voice created by the author to act as the narrator for himself or herself. The persona in Charlotte Perkins Gilman's story "The Yellow Wallpaper" is the unnamed young mother experiencing a mental breakdown.

Personification: A figure of speech that gives human qualities to abstract ideas, animals, and inanimate objects. To say that "the sun is smiling" is to personify the sun.

Plot: The pattern of events in a narrative or drama. In its simplest sense, the plot guides the author in composing the work and helps the reader follow the work. Typically, plots exhibit causality and unity and have a beginning, a middle, and an end. Sometimes, however, a plot may consist of a series of disconnected events, in which case it is known as an "episodic plot."

Poetic Justice: An outcome in a literary work, not necessarily a poem, in which the good are rewarded and the evil are punished, especially in ways that particularly fit their virtues or crimes. For example, a murderer may himself be murdered, or a thief will find himself penniless.

Poetic License: Distortions of fact and literary convention made by a writer—not always a poet—for the sake of the effect gained. Poetic license is closely related to the concept of "artistic freedom." An author exercises poetic license by saying that a pile of money "reaches as high as a mountain" when the pile is actually only a foot or two high.

Point of View: The narrative perspective from which a literary work is presented to the reader. There are four traditional points of view. The "third person omniscient" gives the reader a "godlike" perspective, unrestricted by time or place, from which to see actions and look into the minds of characters. This allows the author to comment openly on characters and events in the work. The "third person" point of view presents the events of the story from outside of any single character's perception, much like the omniscient point of view, but the reader must understand the action as it takes place and without any special insight into characters' minds or motivations. The "first person" or "personal" point of view relates events as they are perceived by a single character. The main character "tells" the story and may offer opinions about the action and characters which differ from those of the author. Much less common than omniscient, third person, and first person is the "second person" point of view, wherein the author tells the story as if it is happening to the reader. James Thurber employs the omniscient point of view in his short story "The Secret Life of Walter Mitty." Ernest Hemingway's "A Clean, Well-Lighted Place" is a short story told from the third person point of view. Mark Twain's novel *Huckleberry Finn* is presented from the first person viewpoint. Jay McInerney's *Bright Lights, Big City* is an example of a novel which uses the second person point of view.

Pornography: Writing intended to provoke feelings of lust in the reader. Such works are often condemned by critics and teachers, but those which can be shown to have literary value are viewed less harshly. Literary works that have been described as pornographic include D. H. Lawrence's *Lady Chatterley's Lover* and James Joyce's *Ulysses*.

Post-Aesthetic Movement: An artistic response made by African Americans to the black aesthetic movement of the 1960s and early 1970s. Writers since that time have adopted a somewhat different tone in their work, with less emphasis placed on the disparity between black and white in the United States. In the words of post-aesthetic authors such as Toni Morrison, John Edgar Wideman, and Kristin Hunter, African Americans are portrayed as looking inward for answers to their own questions, rather than always looking to the outside world. Two well-known examples of works produced as part of the post-aesthetic movement are the Pulitzer Prize–winning novels *The Color Purple* by Alice Walker and *Beloved* by Toni Morrison.

Postmodernism: Writing from the 1960s forward characterized by experimentation and application of modernist elements, which include existentialism and alienation. Postmodernists have gone a step further in the rejection of tradition begun with the modernists by also rejecting traditional forms, preferring the anti-novel over the novel and the anti-hero over the hero. Postmodern writers include Thomas Pynchon, Margaret Drabble, and Gabriel Gárcia Márquez.

Prologue: An introductory section of a literary work. It often contains information establishing the situation of the characters or presents information about the setting, time period, or action. In drama, the prologue is spoken by a chorus or by one of the principal characters.

Prose: A literary medium that attempts to mirror the language of everyday speech. It is distinguished from poetry by its use of unmetered, unrhymed language consisting of logically related sentences. Prose is usually grouped into paragraphs that form a cohesive whole such as an essay or a novel. The term is sometimes used to mean an author's general writing.

Protagonist: The central character of a story who serves as a focus for its themes and incidents and as the principal rationale for its development. The protagonist is sometimes referred to in discussions of modern literature as the hero or anti-hero. Well-known protagonists are Hamlet in William Shakespeare's *Hamlet* and Jay Gatsby in F. Scott Fitzgerald's *The Great Gatsby*.

R

Realism: A nineteenth-century European literary movement that sought to portray familiar characters, situations, and settings in a realistic manner. This was done primarily by using an objective narrative point of view and through the buildup of accurate detail. The standard for success of any realistic work depends on how faithfully it transfers common experience into fictional forms. The realistic method may be altered or extended, as in stream of consciousness writing, to record highly subjective experience. Contemporary authors who often write in a realistic way include Nadine Gordimer and Grace Paley.

Resolution: The portion of a story following the climax, in which the conflict is resolved. The resolution of Jane Austen's *Northanger Abbey* is neatly summed up in the following sentence: "Henry and Catherine were married, the bells rang and every body smiled."

Rising Action: The part of a drama where the plot becomes increasingly complicated. Rising action leads up to the climax, or turning point, of a drama. The final "chase scene" of an action film is generally the rising action which culminates in the film's climax.

Roman a clef: A French phrase meaning "novel with a key." It refers to a narrative in which real persons are portrayed under fictitious names. Jack Kerouac, for example, portrayed various friends under fictitious names in the novel *On the Road.* D. H. Lawrence based "The Rocking-Horse Winner" on a family he knew.

Romanticism: This term has two widely accepted meanings. In historical criticism, it refers to a European intellectual and artistic movement of the late eighteenth and early nineteenth centuries that sought greater freedom of personal expression than that allowed by the strict rules of literary form and logic of the eighteenth-century neoclassicists. The Romantics preferred emotional and imaginative expression to rational analysis. They considered the individual to be at the center of all experience and so placed him or her at the center of their art. The Romantics believed that the creative imagination reveals nobler truths—unique feelings and attitudes—than those that could be discovered by logic or by scientific examination. "Romanticism" is also used as a general term to refer to a type of sensibility found in all periods of literary history and usually considered to be in opposition to the principles of classicism. In this sense, Romanticism signifies any work or philosophy in which the exotic or dreamlike figure strongly, or that is devoted to individualistic expression, self-analysis, or a pursuit of a higher realm of knowledge than can be discovered by human reason. Prominent Romantics include Jean-Jacques Rousseau, William Wordsworth, John Keats, Lord Byron, and Johann Wolfgang von Goethe.

S

Satire: A work that uses ridicule, humor, and wit to criticize and provoke change in human nature and institutions. Voltaire's novella *Candide* and Jonathan Swift's essay "A Modest Proposal" are both satires. Flannery O'Connor's portrayal of the family in "A Good Man Is Hard to Find" is a satire of a modern, Southern, American family.

Science Fiction: A type of narrative based upon real or imagined scientific theories and technology. Science fiction is often peopled with alien creatures and set on other planets or in different dimensions. Popular writers of science fiction are Isaac Asimov, Karel Capek, Ray Bradbury, and Ursula K. Le Guin.

Setting: The time, place, and culture in which the action of a narrative takes place. The elements of setting may include geographic location, characters's physical and mental environments, prevailing cultural attitudes, or the historical time in which the action takes place.

Short Story: A fictional prose narrative shorter and more focused than a novella. The short story usually deals with a single episode and often a single character. The "tone," the author's attitude toward his or her subject and audience, is uniform throughout. The short story frequently also lacks *denouement*, ending instead at its climax.

Signifying Monkey: A popular trickster figure in black folklore, with hundreds of tales about this character documented since the 19th century. Henry Louis Gates Jr. examines the history of the signifying monkey in *The Signifying Monkey: Towards a Theory of Afro-American Literary Criticism,* published in 1988.

Simile: A comparison, usually using "like" or "as," of two essentially dissimilar things, as in "coffee as cold as ice" or "He sounded like a broken record." The title of Ernest Hemingway's "Hills Like White Elephants" contains a simile.

Socialist Realism: The Socialist Realism school of literary theory was proposed by Maxim Gorky and established as a dogma by the first Soviet Congress of Writers. It demanded adherence to a communist worldview in works of literature. Its doctrines required an objective viewpoint comprehensible to the working classes and themes of social struggle featuring strong proletarian heroes. Gabriel Gárcia Márquez's stories exhibit some characteristics of Socialist Realism.

Stereotype: A stereotype was originally the name for a duplication made during the printing process; this led to its modern definition as a person or thing that is (or is assumed to be) the same as all others of its type. Common stereotypical characters include the absent-minded professor, the nagging wife, the troublemaking teenager, and the kindhearted grandmother.

Stream of Consciousness: A narrative technique for rendering the inward experience of a character. This technique is designed to give the impression of an ever-changing series of thoughts, emotions, images, and memories in the spontaneous and seemingly illogical order that they occur in life. The textbook example of stream of consciousness is the last section of James Joyce's *Ulysses.*

Structure: The form taken by a piece of literature. The structure may be made obvious for ease of understanding, as in nonfiction works, or may obscured for artistic purposes, as in some poetry or seemingly "unstructured" prose.

Style: A writer's distinctive manner of arranging words to suit his or her ideas and purpose in writing. The unique imprint of the author's personality upon his or her writing, style is the product of an author's way of arranging ideas and his or her use of diction, different sentence structures, rhythm, figures of speech, rhetorical principles, and other elements of composition.

Suspense: A literary device in which the author maintains the audience's attention through the buildup of events, the outcome of which will soon be revealed. Suspense in William Shakespeare's *Hamlet* is sustained throughout by the question of whether or not the Prince will achieve what he has been instructed to do and of what he intends to do.

Symbol: Something that suggests or stands for something else without losing its original identity. In literature, symbols combine their literal meaning with the suggestion of an abstract concept. Literary symbols are of two types: those that carry complex associations of meaning no matter what their contexts, and those that derive their suggestive meaning from their functions in specific literary works. Examples of symbols are sunshine suggesting happiness, rain suggesting sorrow, and storm clouds suggesting despair.

T

Tale: A story told by a narrator with a simple plot and little character development. Tales are usually relatively short and often carry a simple message. Examples of tales can be found in the works of Saki, Anton Chekhov, Guy de Maupassant, and O. Henry.

Tall Tale: A humorous tale told in a straightforward, credible tone but relating absolutely impossible events or feats of the characters. Such tales were commonly told of frontier adventures during the settlement of the west in the United States. Literary use of tall tales can be found in Washington Irving's *History of New York,* Mark Twain's *Life on the Mississippi,* and in the German R. F. Raspe's *Baron Munchausen's Narratives of His Marvellous Travels and Campaigns in Russia.*

Theme: The main point of a work of literature. The term is used interchangeably with thesis. Many works have multiple themes. One of the themes of Nathaniel Hawthorne's "Young Goodman Brown" is loss of faith.

Tone: The author's attitude toward his or her audience maybe deduced from the tone of the work. A formal tone may create distance or convey politeness, while an informal tone may encourage a friendly, intimate, or intrusive feeling in the reader. The author's attitude toward his or her subject matter may also be deduced from the tone of the words he or she uses in discussing it. The tone of John F. Kennedy's speech which included the appeal to "ask not what your country can do for you" was intended to instill feelings of camaraderie and national pride in listeners.

Tragedy: A drama in prose or poetry about a noble, courageous hero of excellent character who, because of some tragic character flaw, brings ruin upon him- or herself. Tragedy treats its subjects in a dignified and serious manner, using poetic language to help evoke pity and fear and bring about catharsis, a purging of these emotions. The tragic form was practiced extensively by the ancient Greeks. The classical form of tragedy was revived in the sixteenth century; it flourished especially on the Elizabethan stage. In modern times, dramatists have attempted to adapt the form to the needs of modern society by drawing their heroes from the ranks of ordinary men and women and defining the nobility of these heroes in terms of spirit rather than exalted social standing. Some contemporary works that are thought of as tragedies include *The Great Gatsby* by F. Scott Fitzgerald, and *The Sound and the Fury* by William Faulkner.

Tragic Flaw: In a tragedy, the quality within the hero or heroine which leads to his or her downfall. Examples of the tragic flaw include Othello's jealousy and Hamlet's indecisiveness, although most great tragedies defy such simple interpretation.

U

Utopia: A fictional perfect place, such as "paradise" or "heaven." An early literary utopia was described in Plato's *Republic,* and in modern literature, Ursula K. Le Guin depicts a utopia in "The Ones Who Walk Away from Omelas."

V

Victorian: Refers broadly to the reign of Queen Victoria of England (1837-1901) and to anything with qualities typical of that era. For example, the qualities of smug narrow-mindedness, bourgeois materialism, faith in social progress, and priggish morality are often considered Victorian. In literature, the Victorian Period was the great age of the English novel, and the latter part of the era saw the rise of movements such as decadence and symbolism.

Cumulative Author/Title Index

C

N

O

T

U

V

W

Cumulative Nationality/Ethnicity Index

Antiguan

Argentinian

Asian American

Australian

Austrian

Bosnian

Canadian

Chilean

Chinese

Colombian

Indian

Irish

Israeli

Italian

Japanese

Jewish

Kenyan

Mexican

Native American

Nepalese

New Zealander

Nigerian

Subject/Theme Index

R

S

T

U

V